MW01247315

Handbook of Research on the Role of Human Factors in IT Project Management

Sanjay Misra
Covenant University, Nigeria

Adewole Adewumi
Covenant University, Nigeria

A volume in the Advances in IT Personnel and
Project Management (AITPPM) Book Series

Published in the United States of America by
  IGI Global
  Business Science Reference (an imprint of IGI Global)
  701 E. Chocolate Avenue
  Hershey PA, USA 17033
  Tel: 717-533-8845
  Fax: 717-533-8661
  E-mail: cust@igi-global.com
  Web site: http://www.igi-global.com

                    Library of Congress Cataloging-in-Publication Data

Names: Misra, Sanjay, editor. | Adewumi, Adewole, 1987- editor.
Title: Handbook of research on the role of human factors in IT project
  management / Sanjay Misra and Adewole Adewumi, editors.
Description: Hershey, PA : Business Science Reference, 2019. | Includes
  bibliographical references and index. | Summary: ""This book examines
  the role of human factors in the design and development of new
  technology"--Provided by publisher"-- Provided by publisher.
Identifiers: LCCN 2019026572 (print) | LCCN 2019026573 (ebook) | ISBN
  9781799812791 (hardcover) | ISBN 9781799812807 (ebook)
Subjects: LCSH: Information technology--Management. | Human-computer
  interaction. | Project management.
Classification: LCC HD30.2 .H36437 2019 (print) | LCC HD30.2 (ebook) |
  DDC 004.068/4--dc23
LC record available at https://lccn.loc.gov/2019026572
LC ebook record available at https://lccn.loc.gov/2019026573

This book is published in the IGI Global book series Advances in IT Personnel and Project Management (AITPPM) (ISSN:
2331-768X; eISSN: 2331-7698)

British Cataloguing in Publication Data
A Cataloguing in Publication record for this book is available from the British Library.

The views expressed in this book are those of the authors, but not necessarily of the publisher.

For electronic access to this publication, please contact: eresources@igi-global.com.

Advances in IT Personnel and Project Management (AITPPM) Book Series

Sanjay Misra
Covenant University, OTA, Nigeria
Ricardo Colomo-Palacios
Østfold University College, Norway

ISSN:2331-768X
EISSN:2331-7698

MISSION

Technology has become an integral part of organizations in every sector, contributing to the way in which large enterprises, small businesses, government agencies, and non-profit organizations operate. In the midst of this revolution, it is essential that these organizations have a thorough knowledge of how to implement and manage IT projects as well as an understanding of how to attract and supervise the employees associated with these projects.

The **Advances in IT Personnel and Project Management (AITPPM)** book series aims to provide current research on all facets of IT Project Management including factors to consider when managing and working with IT personnel. Books within the AITPPM book series will provide managers, IT professionals, business leaders, and upper-level students with the latest trends, applications, methodologies, and literature available in this field.

COVERAGE

- IT Career Development
- IT Strategy
- IT Entrepreneurship
- Communication between Managers and IT Personnel
- Project Sponsorship
- Requirements Management
- IT Personnel Management
- Cost-Effective Methods for Project Management
- Agile Project Management
- Project Planning

IGI Global is currently accepting manuscripts for publication within this series. To submit a proposal for a volume in this series, please contact our Acquisition Editors at Acquisitions@igi-global.com or visit: http://www.igi-global.com/publish/.

Titles in this Series

For a list of additional titles in this series, please visit:
https://www.igi-global.com/book-series/advances-personnel-project-management/77666

Knowledge Management Techniques for Risk Management in IT Projects Emerging Research and Opportunities
Muhammad Noman Riaz (National University of Sciences and Technology, Pakistan)
Information Science Reference • © 2019 • 117pp • H/C (ISBN: 9781522583899) • US $135.00 (our price)

Project Portfolio Management Strategies for Effective Organizational Operations
Luca Romano (PMI Central Italy Chapter - CUOA Business School, Italy)
Business Science Reference • © 2017 • 388pp • H/C (ISBN: 9781522521518) • US $200.00 (our price)

Handbook of Research on Leveraging Risk and Uncertainties for Effective Project Management
Yuri Raydugin (Risk Services & Solutions Inc., Canada)
Business Science Reference • © 2017 • 504pp • H/C (ISBN: 9781522517900) • US $275.00 (our price)

Managing Project Risks for Competitive Advantage in Changing Business Environments
Constanta-Nicoleta Bodea (Bucharest University of Economic Studies, Centre for Industrial and Services Economics, Romania) Augustin Purnus (Technical University of Civil Engineering Bucharest, Romania) Martina Huemann (WU-Vienna University of Economics & Business, Austria) and Miklós Hajdu (Budapest University of Technology and Economics, Hungary)
Business Science Reference • © 2016 • 348pp • H/C (ISBN: 9781522503354) • US $210.00 (our price)

Strategic Integration of Social Media into Project Management Practice
Gilbert Silvius (LOI University of Applied Sciences, The Netherlands & University of Johannesburg, South Africa)
Business Science Reference • © 2016 • 343pp • H/C (ISBN: 9781466698673) • US $210.00 (our price)

Strategic Management and Leadership for Systems Development in Virtual Spaces
Christian Graham (University of Maine, USA)
Business Science Reference • © 2016 • 389pp • H/C (ISBN: 9781466696884) • US $210.00 (our price)

Modern Techniques for Successful IT Project Management
Shang Gao (Zhongnan University of Economics and Law, China) and Lazar Rusu (Stockholm University, Sweden)
Business Science Reference • © 2015 • 374pp • H/C (ISBN: 9781466674738) • US $225.00 (our price)

Handbook of Research on Effective Project Management through the Integration of Knowledge and Innovation
George Leal Jamil (Informações em Rede, Brazil) Sérgio Maravilhas Lopes (CETAC.MEDIA - Porto and Aveiro Universities, Portugal) Armando Malheiro da Silva (Porto University, Portugal) and Fernanda Ribeiro (University of Porto, Portugal)

701 East Chocolate Avenue, Hershey, PA 17033, USA
Tel: 717-533-8845 x100 • Fax: 717-533-8661
E-Mail: cust@igi-global.com • www.igi-global.com

List of Contributors

Table of Contents

Detailed Table of Contents

    Chika Yinka-Banjo, University of Lagos, Nigeria
    Gafar Lekan Raji, University of Lagos, Nigeria
    Ifeanyi Precious Ohalete, Alex-Ekwueme Federal University of Ndufu-Alike, Ikwo, Nigeria

The threat posed by cyberbullying to the mental health in our society cannot be overemphasized. Victims of this menace are reported to have suffered poor academic performance, depression, and suicidal thoughts. There is need to find an efficient and effective solution to this problem within the academic environment. In this research, one of the popular deep learning models—long short-term memory (LSTM)—known for its optimized performance in training sequential data was combined with Word2Vec embedding technique to create a model trained for classifying the content of social media post as containing cyberbullying content or otherwise. The result was observed to have shown improvements in its performance with respect to accuracy in the classification task with over 80% of the test dataset correctly classified as against the existing model with about 74.9% accuracy.

    Ikedinachi Ayodele Power Wogu, Rhema University Nigeria, Aba, Nigeria
    Morris Edogiawere, Igbenigiong University, Okada, Nigeria
    Jesse Oluwafemi Katende, Covenant University, Ota, Nigeria
    Edith Awogu-Maduagwu, Covenant University, Ota, Nigeria
    Charles Nathaniel Chukwuedo, Federal College of Education Technology Asaba, Asaba,
        Nigeria
    Sanjay Misra, Covenant University, Ota, Nigeria

Recent research on the application of artificial intelligence (AI) technology in the education industry for teaching and learning has stirred up a revolution via the use of platforms like the massive open online courses (MOOC) the likes of which the world have never seen before. Millions through this platform can now enroll online to get one form of education or the other. Many scholars, however, doubt the quality of education transmitted and acquired via these platforms; hence, some scholars describe the education gotten through this medium as artificial education. A situation that has resulted in a kind of revolution in the education industry described as education tsunami. The Marxian theory of alienation offers an appropriate theoretical platform for the analysis conducted in the paper. The ex-post factor method of analysis and Deidra's critical analytic method was adopted for attaining the objectives of the paper. The dilemmas eroding the quality of education were identified. Blended learning approaches, as against present methods, were recommended.

Chapter 3

Quality education is arguably the instrument par excellence for national development. Psychological assessment (PA) is an authentic means of monitoring progress and attainment of set goals. Virtually all over the world, teachers and students tend to dance to the tune of psychological assessment. PA tools are therefore potential devices for catalyzing quality education and development. The core objective of this study is to explore the potential of the development-oriented psychological assessment (DOPA) model in catalyzing quality education in IT project management training, thus enhancing the quality of human factor driving it. Documentary analysis design was adopted. The overriding inference drawn from the exploration is that consistent application of the DOPA model holds the potential of enhancing human factors that drive pragmatic IT project management and by extension national development.

Chapter 4

Information technology (IT) is a vital source of economic growth across developed and developing countries. Skill gaps are significant barriers to technology adoption by many industries; therefore, this chapter reviews research studies sampling IT professionals to identify a whole gamut of IT professionals' skills and competencies. This systematic literature review comprises of exhaustive search for articles through Scopus database with empirical evidence or theoretical models meant for working IT professionals. Critical analysis of prominent papers is done to bring forth existing research categories (typology) and furnish generic as well as specific skills and competencies. This study attempts to become a resource for integration of IT professional capability research and a comprehensive report for researchers, practitioners, educators, and institutions. Tables containing list of publishing journals, country- and industry-wise article distribution, and prominent paper methodology are provided.

    Ambrose Agbon Azeta, Covenant University, Nigeria
    Raymond Ativie, Covenant University, Nigeria
    Sanjay Misra, Covenant University, Ota, Nigeria
    Angela E. Azeta, FIIRO, Nigeria
    Felix Chidozie Chidozie, Covenant University, Nigeria
    Olufunmilola Amosu, FIIRO, Nigeria

The social media network is one of the trending platforms engaged for communication by students. Regrettably, this system has been used by persons to plan and commit cyber fraud and public vices. Some of the tertiary institutions including secondary and university in Nigeria have been turned to cultist environments resulting in killings and disorder amongst students in the school and environs. This is a situation that has continued to struggle with solutions in most higher institutions in the country, particularly in the government owned institutions. This obviously is a human factor issue that needs to be addressed. The objective of this study is to provide social media-based system that is integrated with anti-cultism component services towards combating cultism on campus. The platform will support interaction and learning on and off campus while at the same time helping to curtail cultism among students through filtering of keywords communicated on social media that are crime-based or cultism-related. In carrying out this study, appropriate research methods and implementation techniques such as modeling, design, server-side programming, database were deployed. The platform provides a dual platform that will enable active students to participate in learning, and also cultism control in the school system.

    Franklin Johnson, Universidad de Playa Ancha, Chile
    Broderick Crawford, Pontificia Universidad Católica de Valparaíso, Chile
    Ricardo Soto, Pontificia Universidad Católica de Valparaíso, Chile
    Sanjay Misra, Covenant University, Ota, Nigeria

Currently, there are multiple factors that affect the projects management. These factors may have different origins, but the human factor is still one of the main elements that affect decisions when managing a project. Another important factor is the use of software that supports these decisions and reduce the human factors. Given the complexity of current management problems, powerful software is needed to solve these problems. Constraint solvers are a kind of software that are based on a constraint approach. Currently there are different constraint solvers. Some are intricate software, and others are libraries for a programming language. This chapter presents a framework that allow to compare a constraint system based on the usability attributes of the solvers in order to reduce the human factors for the selection of the constraint solver. The authors show that it is possible to establish a comparison according to usability attributes, allowing to reduce the risks of decision making by the experts when working with a constrain solver in a project.

Luis Fernández Sanz, University of Alcalá, Spain
Vera Pospelova, Universidad de Alcalá, Spain
Ana Castillo, Universidad de Alcalá, Spain
María Teresa Villalba, Universidad Europea de Madrid, Spain
Manuel de Buenaga, Universidad de Alcalá, Spain
Marián Fernández de Sevilla, Universidad de Alcalá, Spain

IT project management requires qualified staff capable of facing the rapidly changing conditions and even terminology of technology while managing large teams of people where main costs come from human work. A key factor for managing human side of IT is the understanding of the essential feature of people performance: skills. Capability to cope with this highly demanding field should firstly rely on clear and standardized frameworks for skills, not only the technical or hard ones but also the soft or behavioral ones, considered by employers as essential for employees' productivity. This chapter shows how the recent development of frameworks and standards in European Union (e.g. EN16234 or ESCO classification) is enabling the powerful exploitation of open big data from existing skills analysis systems for a more precise and solid determination of recommended skills for IT project management. The analysis will especially focus on the behavioral skills.

Thais Andrea Baldissera, FCT, NOVA University of Lisbon, Portugal
Luis M. Camarinha-Matos, FCT, NOVA University of Lisbon, Portugal
Cristiano De Faveri, FCT, NOVA University of Lisbon, Portugal

This chapter provides a brief overview of the demographic evolution and aging process, introducing a collaborative framework to assist senior citizens. The importance of supporting the age-related care needs, and the potential technologies for aging support are highlighted. A conceptual model for an elderly care ecosystem (ECE) and methods for care service personalization and evolution based on a collaborative environment are presented. To facilitate the consideration of human factors in the early design stage of ECE, a care need goals taxonomy and human-centered design principles are introduced. Customer, service, and service provider template profiles to design the elderly care ecosystem are proposed. Experimental results and feedback from lead users are presented and discussed. The goal of the ECE framework is to provide assistance in service recommendation (and adaptation) for the elderly care domain taking into account human factors.

Jitao Yang, Beijing Language and Culture University, China

Genomics has been used to more accurately support the realization of scientific research, personalized healthcare, and precision medicine. Professional knowledge and expertise are required to process the genomics project and laboratory workflows which include project enrollment, project and sample tracking, sample warehousing, nucleic acid extraction, library construction, concentration and peak map detection, pooling, sequencing, etc. Therefore, the digitizing management of projects and laboratory workflows is very important to support the handling of tens of thousands of samples in parallel. This chapter implements the human knowledge and expertise to a project and laboratory management platform, which can integrated manage the complex genomics projects, the laboratory workflows, the sequencing instruments, the analysis pipelines, and the genetic interpretation service. The platform can automate routine tasks, facilitate communication, optimize business procedures and workflows, process tens of thousands of samples parallelly, and increase the business efficiency.

Chapter 10

  Emmanuel Oluwatobi Asani, Landmark University, Nigeria
  Olumide Babatope Longe, American University of Nigeria, Nigeria
  Anthony Jatau Balla, Landmark University, Nigeria
  Roseline Oluwaseun Ogundokun, Landmark University, Nigeria
  Emmanuel Abidemi Adeniyi, Landmark University, Nigeria

In this chapter, CAPTCHA was presented as a measure for secure human-computer interaction. A multi-factor CAPTCHA scheme that integrates facial recognition and real-time functionality as a secure verification mechanism to check the activities of bots that try to assume human status was designed, developed, and tested. The real-time functionality is premised on the human user's ability to complete trivial tasks which though simple for human is difficult to break by bots. This was motivated by the need to combat attackers' tendencies to beat existing CAPTCHA schemes through optical character recognition, image annotation, tag classifier, etc. Literature on a number of existing schemes was reviewed with a view to identifying gaps and establishing the research agenda. The system design and analysis were done using scalable design techniques. Implementation was done using Javascript and a set of APIs. The scheme was tested on an intel core i7 3GHz computer and further evaluated. Preliminary results and findings show a promising effectiveness and efficiency of the developed system.

Chapter 11

  Adekanmi Adeyinka Adegun, Landmark University, Nigeria
  Roseline Oluwaseun Ogundokun, Landmark University, Nigeria
  Marion Olubunmi Adebiyi, Landmark University, Nigeria & Covenant University, Nigeria
  Emmanuel Oluwatobi Asani, Landmark University, Nigeria

Machine learning techniques such as deep learning methods have produced promising results in medical images analysis. This work proposes a user-friendly system that utilizes deep learning techniques for detecting and diagnosing diseases using medical images. This includes the design of CAD-based project that can reduce human factor-related errors while performing manual screening of medical images. The system accepts medical images as input and performs segmentation of the images. Segmentation process analyzes and identifies the region of interest (ROI) of diseases from medical images. Analyzing and segmentation of medical images has assisted in the diagnosis and monitoring of some diseases. Diseases such as skin cancer, age-related fovea degeneration, diabetic retinopathy, glaucoma, hypertension, arteriosclerosis, and choroidal neovascularization can be effectively managed by the analysis of skin lesion and retinal vessels images. The proposed system was evaluated on diseases such as diabetic retinopathy from retina images and skin cancer from dermoscopic images.

Solomon Adelowo Adepoju, Department of Computer Science, Federal University of
Technology Minna, Nigeria
Ishaq Oyebisi Oyefolahan, Department of Information and Media Technology, Federal
University of Technology Minna, Nigeria
Muhammad Bashir Abdullahi, Department of Computer Science, Federal University of
Technology Minna, Nigeria
Adamu Alhaji Mohammed, Department of Mathematics, Federal University of Technology
Minna, Nigeria
Motunrayo O. Ibiyo, Department of Computer Science, Federal University of Technology
Minna, Nigeria

One of the ways universities ensure constant touch with the human populace is through their websites. Therefore, websites must be engaging, interactive, easy-to-use, and provide users with the necessary information needed. Unfortunately, most universities have found this objective quite difficult to achieve. This chapter presents an evaluation the usability of six Nigerian university websites using a model which is based on seven usability criteria of speed, ease of use, navigation, content, aesthetic, accessibility, and security. The best six university websites based on webometric ranking were selected for the study with 233 participants via an online questionnaire using Google Docs. The overall results of the evaluation indicate that the usability of Nigerian university websites performed fairly well in ease of use, navigation, and aesthetic, averagely on speed and content, while the ratings based on accessibility and security are not very satisfactory.

Hector Florez, Universidad Distrital Francisco Jose de Caldas, Colombia

Enterprise models are created for communicating and documenting the current state of the enterprise. However, these models can also be used for supporting analysis processes and are fundamental assets in project management. But, analysis is a process made by humans, and due to enterprise models that are complex and have a large amount of elements, analysis is usually a tough process. Then modeling tools might provide support for analysis. It is possible to offer this support through the use of automated analysis methods, which are algorithms for providing specific calculations based on the elements included in the model. The results of said automated analysis methods support decision-making processes. It is also possible to execute a sequence of analysis methods by the configuration of analysis chains. This chapter presents a proposal and strategy for analyzing enterprise models by the execution of automated analysis methods and automated analysis chains. This strategy is presented using enterprise models that conform to ArchiMate as modeling language.

    Ikedinachi Ayodele Power Wogu, Rhema University, Nigeria
    Jesse Oluwafemi Katende, Covenant University, Ota, Nigeria
    Ayotunde Elegbeleye, Covenant University, Ota, Nigeria
    Comfort Olushola Roland-Otaru, Independent Researcher, Nigeria
    Hosea Abalaka Apeh, University of Abuja, Nigeria
    Nkechi J. Ifeanyi-Reuben, Rhema University, Nigeria
    Sanjay Misra, Covenant University, Ota, Nigeria

While the majority of scientists agree that artificial intelligence (AI) technology have provided excellent platforms for inventing tools beneficial for enhancing man's quality of life on earth, there are a host of others who have identified existential and ontological hazards associated with the proliferation of super-intelligent machines (SIM), now utilized for virtually every human endeavor. The Marxian alienation theory was adopted for the study while Creswell's qualitative and Marilyn's ex-post facto research design approaches were adopted as viable methodologies for the study. Justifiable grounds by which existentialist scholars continue to promote the 'extinction risk threat' and the impending job annihilation theory were identified. Scientists and existentialist scholars are therefore enjoined to urgently identify pathways for aligning the goals of SIM with those of mankind.

    Ikedinachi Ayodele Power Wogu, Rhema University, Nigeria
    Ayotunde Elegbeleye, Covenant University, Ota, Nigeria
    Kalu Uche Uwaoma, Rhema University, Nigeria
    Charles Nathaniel Chukwuedo, Federal College of Education Technology, Asaba, Nigeria
    Morris Edogiawere, Igbenigiong University, Okada, Nigeria
    Chidiebere Aguziendu, Covenant University, Ota, Nigeria
    Sanjay Misra, Covenant University, Ota, Nigeria

Studies on domestic violence against women (DVAW) reveals that the patriarchal and socio-cultural mindset of Nigerians, which tend to dignify the roles of men over women, thus encumbering the full implementation of the laws designed to protect the dignity of womanhood, is at the crux of factors militating against women. With the culture violence theory as theoretical framework for the study, Marilyn's ex-post-facto research method was adopted since the chapter utilized data gathered from previously analyzed studies on the subject of DVAW. Socio-cultural and the lackadaisical behavior of politicians were identified as pertinent factors influencing the rising cases of DVAW recorded, despite the presence of the Violence Against Persons Prohibition Act (VAPPA) laws that prohibit violence against persons in states, a factor impeding most women from attaining their full potential and dignity in African societies. The need to strengthen and increase sensitization about the essence of VAPPA laws and what women and girls stand to achieve by its enforcement were emphasized.

Chapter 16

In this chapter, a linear process model is proposed for outcome-based education. Then an agile-based approach is presented that aims to integrate the Instruction design and student assessment to improve the quality of design and delivery. An agile process model suitable for virtual learning environments is proposed. The agile project management artifacts that include a content story, test plan, etc. are being used in the education domain. There is a need for human interaction in the teaching and learning process to improve the outcomes. The feedback generated after the student assessment process will help in improving the process of content designing and delivery in subsequent increments. The proposed agile model for the virtual learning environment is adapted for a graduate course offering. Based on the continuous assessments and feedbacks, various instructional methods are used for the delivery of the course. The results show that there is an improvement in student's grades, learning outcomes, and there is a considerable reduction in failures and dropout rates.

Chapter 17

In the current scenario, social media play a key role for the customers because the content generated by users through social media has a great influence on their purchase intention. The objective of this study is to examine the impact of social media factors that influence the student's purchase intention through social media. Three factors, namely trust, perceived usefulness, and social commerce construct, were tested and examined the impact on purchase intention of the students. Data were gathered from 240 undergraduate and postgraduate students. Structural equation modelling was used to get the results from the data. The outcomes of the data analysis show that majorly prevailing factor that influences the purchase intention of young consumers was consumer trust via social media interface. Further, that is followed by social commerce construct and perceived usefulness. Furthermore, it has also been found that all the constructs are positively associated with purchase intention. In the end, practical implications, limitations, and future research scope of this study were discussed.

Chapter 18

Emerging human resource management (HRM) practices are focusing on background checks, training and development, employer-employee relations, responsibility and accountability, and monitoring of information systems security resources. Information systems security ensures that appropriate resources and adequate skills exist in the organization to effectively manage information security projects. This chapter examined the role of HRM in enhancing organizational information systems security. Using importance-performance map analysis, the study found training, background checks, and monitoring as crucial HRM practices that could enhance organizational information systems security. Moreover, four indicators, consisting of training on mobile devices security; malware management; background checks; and monitoring of potential, current, and former employees recorded high importance but with rather low performance. Consequently, these indicators should be improved. On the contrary, the organizations placed excessive focus on responsibility, accountability, and employee relations.

Chapter 19

The HSD&E activities are supported by a central decision-making system (DMS) (in which a HR subsystem is included), knowledge management system (KMS), and an enterprise architecture project (EAP). The chapter's proof of concept (PoC) is based on a business case from the insurance domain where the central point is the capacity of the selected manager skillset to successfully start and finalize a BTP or an EAP (or simply a project). The PoC shows the selection process of a manager's skillset to transform the traditional insurance enterprise into an agile and automated enterprise. Projects are managed by managers, who are (or should be) supported by a methodology and a framework that can estimate the risks of failure of a project; at the same time, they should be capable of managing the implementation project processes.

Although Latin America has exhibited lately the largest growth in terms of ERP adoption rate worldwide, there is a gap in the literature focused in examining the success and underlying causes of such adoptions. After an extensive literature review, the authors found little evidence of studies oriented to the study of human factors in ERP projects in higher education institutions (HEIs) in the region, which is the aim of this study. It is known that the success of these projects is limited, and that the failure rate is high (between 60% and 90%). Therefore, it is worth identifying the human factors that may serve as reference for the HEIs that are planning to implement these systems. This work compiles the experiences of experts who have participated in projects at universities in Latin American countries, establishing a set of unique features and the specific factors to lead successful ERP projects.

This chapter examines virtual collaboration tools from the perspective of project managers of EU-funded projects. The chapter overviews virtual collaboration tool types, users types, and their motivation to use the chosen tool alongside the human factors. The authors have observed 40 EU project managers, who have managed 244 EU projects. Despite of the abundance of modern, web-based, and mobile tools, project managers are still not familiar with the advantages of cloud-based document systems and communication tools. Factors such as un-friendliness, security concerns, and lack of IT skills prevent more wide usage of virtual collaboration tools. Live meetings are still perceived as the most efficient channel for distributing and receiving project tasks, but they are closely followed by virtual meetings using the communication software. The authors propose a standardized process of including virtual collaboration tools to distributed project teams. Their experiences show that strong leadership and defined process increase the usage of IT tools and consequently the success of EU-funded projects.

Chapter 22

Leon J. M. Rothkrantz, Czech Technical University in Prague, Czech Republic
Siska Fitrianie, Delft University of Technology, The Netherlands

In this chapter, the authors present a massive open online course (MOOC) on a flooding disaster in the city of Prague. The goal of the MOOC is to increase awareness of citizens of Prague about flooding disasters and to provide a training facility for first responders and the crisis management team of the city. The MOOC is modeled and organized as an IT project. A dedicated didactical model has been designed for distant-learning. To complete a MOOC successfully, three human factors have to be considered: physical ergonomics, cognitive ergonomics, and organizational ergonomics. As an example of interactive learning materials, the authors describe a game-based assignment, where students have to take a role in the virtual crisis management team and to save citizens, properties, and infrastructure as much as possible. This assignment is organized as IT projects, where the human factors play again an important role. The chapter will also discuss educational experiments.

Chapter 23

Jitendra Singh Tomar, Amity University, India

Rise in economy and higher global standards are making Indian organizations to develop employee-centric HR policies for optimal use of workforce. Organizations, operating in global environment, are more sophisticated, have better HR policies, leading to increased productivity through better engagements. A better engaged workforce has improved the bottom lines of these companies significantly. This study explores employee engagement factors by recording perception of 500 employees serving 10 prime business sectors in India and compares the engagement antecedents in these sectors. Thematic analysis is done on identified themes: insightful work, pragmatic management, positive work environment, growth opportunity, and engaging leadership. These significant factors are visualized specifically for IT sector. By resolving the engagement issues raised in this study, it is anticipated that the employers can address overall efficiency of their workforce and improve the employer-employee relationship.

Chapter 24

Organizations have to manage human resources effectively, as these are fundamental to their success. Indeed, it is widely recognized that human resources have a direct influence in the performance of organizations. Therefore, organizational success is highly dependent on an adequate management of human resources. In this context, the performance assessment of people is crucial, as it is an important process for implementing efficient and effective motivational and rewarding systems. However, in the case of information systems projects, there is not much research work focused on human resources performance evaluation. This chapter aims to contribute to fill this gap by reviewing several approaches and methods for performance assessment, which can be applied to information systems projects. The presented approaches and methods are focused on personality, behaviors, comparison, and outcomes/ results.

Chapter 25

The effect of digitalization and its transformative power in all aspects of corporate strategies and organizations are visible everywhere. As leaders try to make sense of the "digital tornado" and prepare, try out, and set courses in new business directions, the authors propose to take a step back and focus on what is still at the core of corporate change – the people of your organization. In this chapter, the authors reflect on the forces and challenges that employees are facing in times of rapid and digitally driven change. They also mirror this, considering structural, sociological, and demographic change in the workforce, especially with regards to younger employees. They provide a set of fundamental metrics that can quantify the human resource strategy of an organization to derive measures which can be controlled via a DMAIC cycle. This contribution is an extended version of and includes an enhanced set of metrics to address challenges of digitalization and agile work environments. Further, approaches to possible solutions and first steps for an implementation in companies are presented.

Chapter 26

This chapter aims to explore the human attitude towards the use of IT in education, especially teacher attitudes towards the use of social media in teaching practice. The study is based on a survey questionnaire, which aims to investigate to what extent and for what purposes teachers from different countries from all over the world use social networking in their teaching practice. The chapter presents the method (an exploratory survey using questionnaire for data collection), organization of the study, and thorough analyses of the results in accordance with the study objectives. Finally, summarized results of the survey are presented, depending on the continent where the countries of the participants are located. The analysis of the survey results is presented on the basis of valid responses of 19,987 teachers from 75 countries around the world who participated in the survey.

Preface

Managing information technology (IT) projects is no trivial task. The outcome of such projects—positive or negative—can stem from a number of factors. The most crucial factor though is the human factor. Human Factors is an evolving body of knowledge focusing on human abilities, human limitations, and other human characteristics that are relevant to the IT project management domain. It can be divided into three areas: physical ergonomics, cognitive ergonomics and organizational ergonomics. Physical ergonomics is mainly concerned with human anatomical, physiological and biomechanical characteristics as they relate to physical activity. Cognitive ergonomics focuses on perception, memory, information processing and reasoning relevant to, e.g. task analysis, human-machine interactions (HMI), workload, and alarm philosophies. Organizational ergonomics address issues relevant to organizational structures, policies, processes and operational philosophies. This book comprises of studies that cover the three areas.

As regards physical ergonomics, a conceptual model for an elderly care ecosystem along with methods for care service personalization in a collaborative environment was presented. Another study introduced enhanced set of metrics to address challenges of digitalization and agile work environments. With the advent of artificial intelligence (AI) machines and the fear among many of impending job annihilation, a study has stressed the need for scientists and existential scholars to identify ways of aligning the goals of AI machines with those of their human counterparts so as to foster a seamless workforce.

As regards cognitive ergonomics, the introduction of constraint solvers to aid human decision making during IT projects has been proposed. In another study, the implementation of a digital platform to support the management of genomics project was discussed. The platform automates routine tasks, reduces workload thereby increasing business efficiency. In order to reduce human factor related errors while performing manual screening of medical images, a deep learning system was proposed to detect and diagnose diseases using medical images. Similarly, a deep learning model – Long Short-Term Memory (LSTM) was combined with Word2Vec embedding technique to realize a model that recognizes cyberbullying content in social media which is known to have adverse effects on students' academic performance. Furthermore, in the learning domain, an agile process model was introduced to improve learning outcomes and reduce dropout rates in a virtual learning environment. In another study, a dedicated didactical model was designed for distance learning. An exploration of human attitude towards the utilization of IT in education was also considered. In addition, a study opined that consistent application of development-oriented psychological assessment (DOPA) model can enhance human factors which in turn drive pragmatic IT project management.

As regards organizational ergonomics, the need to define clear and standardized frameworks for determining behavioral skills to be possessed by employees managing IT projects has been stressed. In this regard, a systematic review was conducted to identify skills and competencies of different IT professionals. Another study explored various approaches and methods that can be adopted for individual performance assessment in IT projects. In order to secure projects during incubation, a multi-factor CAPTCHA scheme that integrates facial recognition and real-time functionality was presented. It helps to check the activities of bots that may try to assume human status and gain access to sensitive project information. In addition, the role human resource management (HRM) staff in ensuring organizational information systems security was emphasized. Aside security concerns, one of the studies identified a need for learning organizations to improve on the accessibility of their sites to various users. Also, a proposal was made for analyzing enterprise models by the execution of automated analysis models as a way of supporting individuals involved in managing IT projects. The need for political leaders to enforce laws that prevent violence and discrimination against the female gender was emphasized in one of the studies. Another study found that organizations can leverage social media in influencing consumer behavior by building trust among the consumers through the social media interface. In one study, the unique features and specific factors that result in successful ERP projects were identified. A standardized process of including virtual collaboration tools in distributed project teams was proposed as a means of fostering the success of IT projects. Insightful work, pragmatic management, positive work environment, growth opportunity and engaging leadership were also identified as factors that increase employee engagement which impact on project success.

This book is targeted at professionals and researchers working in the field of information and knowledge management in various disciplines, e.g. library, information and communication sciences, administrative sciences and management, education, adult education, sociology, computer science, and information technology. Moreover, the book provides insight and support to executives concerned with the management of expertise, knowledge, information and organizational development in different types of work communities and environments.

Sanjay Misra
Covenant University, Nigeria

Adewole Adewumi
Covenant University, Nigeria

Chapter 1

Auto-Detection of Human Factor Contents on Social Media Posts Using Word2vec and Long Short-Term Memory (LSTM)

Chika Yinka-Banjo

(iD) https://orcid.org/0000-0002-0712-7413

University of Lagos, Nigeria

Gafar Lekan Raji

University of Lagos, Nigeria

Ifeanyi Precious Ohalete

Alex-Ekwueme Federal University of Ndufu-Alike, Ikwo, Nigeria

ABSTRACT

The threat posed by cyberbullying to the mental health in our society cannot be overemphasized. Victims of this menace are reported to have suffered poor academic performance, depression, and suicidal thoughts. There is need to find an efficient and effective solution to this problem within the academic environment. In this research, one of the popular deep learning models—long short-term memory (LSTM)—known for its optimized performance in training sequential data was combined with Word2Vec embedding technique to create a model trained for classifying the content of social media post as containing cyber-bullying content or otherwise. The result was observed to have shown improvements in its performance with respect to accuracy in the classification task with over 80% of the test dataset correctly classified as against the existing model with about 74.9% accuracy.

DOI: 10.4018/978-1-7998-1279-1.ch001

INTRODUCTION

Cyberbullying (also referred to as cyber-victimization) is a term used to describe the action of individuals (The Bully) targeted at other individuals (The Bullied) to threaten, blackmail, embarrass, annoy or hurt the victim with the use of digital media or cyber-technology. Cyberbullying could also be defined as a deliberate use of some form of electronic technology to repeatedly pass out some bullying behavior. The advantage of social media has been well documented and most people have leverage the social media to their benefits. However, social media is often taken advantage of by some individuals (mostly young adults) to commit cybercrimes such as swindling other people, cyberbullying, and so on.

In order to curb the menace of cyberbullying, traditional mechanisms such as blacklisting some words and appointing individuals to cross-examine the content of posts were deployed to checkmate people's behavior and how they engage others on social media. However, these mechanisms have not been effective on social networking sites due to the dynamic nature of the contents generated on the said social media.

(Chatzakou et al., 2017) opined that effectiveness of a cyberbullying detection system can be broken down into the following stages

1. Filtering and Detecting bullying contents from messages within a tweet.
2. Determining the severity of the bullying incident
3. Identification of every individual involved
4. Assignment of roles to each of the individual involved.
5. Prediction of resulting event as a result of the cyberbullying incident

The effectiveness of such system is largely dependent on how effective it is able to filter and classify the contents of the tweets. This research proposes the use of long short term memory (LSTM) to effectively classify the contents of tweets as containing cyberbullying contents or otherwise.

We proposed to tackle the menace of cyberbullying especially on Twitter by casting it as a sentiment analysis problem which is a subset of natural language processing (NLP). In an effort to make our model all inclusive, we are working with a diverse corpus of tweets. Our dataset contains one million, six hundred thousand (1,600,000) tweets which depict various social interest such as business, travel, sports, racism, sexism, and so on. We adopted the use of Word2Vec for our word embedding technique.

AIM AND OBJECTIVES

The aim of this research is to develop a model that can filter and effectively identify tweets containing cyberbullying contents.

The objectives are:

1. To develop a model that would be able to check the presence of cyberbully content in messages before it gets posted
2. To build a model that learns the dataset and effectively classify the content of new inputs as containing cyberbully content or otherwise, using Long Short Term Memory (LSTM)

RELATED WORKS

Twitter has been said to have a telling impact on its users, especially teenagers and young adults. This is culminated in the number of cyberbully cases reported daily from this platform. The number of affected individuals is said to have been on the increase, thus drawing attention to its negative impact (Dani, Li, & Liu, 2017). Detection of online bullying and subsequent preventive measure is the main course of action to combat it.

Cyberbullying detection is getting a lot of research attention in the recent past due in part to the proliferation of social media and its detrimental effect on the mental health of young people. A recent study by (Agrawal & Awekar, 2018) revealed that between 10% - 40% of internet users have been victim of cyberbullying at one time or another.

The existing cyberbullying detection scheme can be categorized into 4 main classes namely; Supervised Learning, Lexicon-Based, Rule-Based and Mixed-Initiative approaches. Each of the stated approaches deals with cyberbullying detection tasks differently. The supervised learning approaches developed and used predictive models using traditional classifiers such as SVM and Naïve Bayes for the task of cyberbullying detection. An example of such approach is (Bienstein & Werner, 2018). Lexicon based systems are designed to check a statement against a specified word lists and use the presence of such words within the lists to detect cyberbullying. An example of such system is (Hon & Varathan, 2015). In the Rules-based approach the texts are matched with a predefined set of rules, once it conforms with such pattern, cyberbullying presence is established. An example of such could be found in the works of: (Luker & Curchack, 2017). Some other researchers have combined two or the three of the approaches described above in the detection of cyberbullying content. Such approach is referred to as mixed-initiatives approach and it is said to have been more efficient than any single method. An example of such is (Dinakar, Picard, & Lieberman, 2015).

(Luker & Curchack, 2017) investigated perceptions of cyberbullying within higher education among 1,587 professionals from Australia, Canada, the United Kingdom, and the United States. They observed that the country or professional role the victim does not matter. The victims suffered the consequence alike. A group-serving bias was replicated; cyberbullying was perceived as more problematic at some institutions than others. The authors then call for evidence-based, systematic policy development and implementation, including how to train those who see cyberbullying as a positive phenomenon.

(Faryadi, 2011) in his research investigates the emotional and physiological effects of cyber bullying on the university students. He intends to investigate and identify the victims of cyber bullying by critically analysing their emotional state and frame of mind in order to provide them with a workable and feasible intervention in fighting cyber bullying. The author adopted triangulation method (quantitative, qualitative and descriptive) in the investigation process and the study was conducted among 365 students. It was recorded that that a significant number of the students 35 (13%) had suffered emotionally due to cyber bullying, majority of the students 255 (70%) agreed that cyber bullying adversely affects students' academic performance. It is interesting to note that majority of the students 75 (20.8%) signify that they have heard bullying taking place inside the university.

(Li, 2006) in their study, investigates the nature and the extent of adolescences' experience of cyberbullying. A survey study of 264 students from three junior high schools was conducted. The results show that close to 25% of the students were bully victims at one time or the other. Over 50% of the students reported that they knew someone being cyberbullied. Almost 50% of the cyberbullies used electronic means to harass others more than three times. The majority of the cyber-bully victims and bystanders did not report the incidents to adults. When gender was considered, significant differences were identified in terms of bullying and cyberbullying. Males were more likely to be bullies and cyberbullies than their female counterparts. In addition, female cyberbully victims were more likely to inform adults than their male counterparts.

(Hinduja & Patchin, 2010) conducted empirical studies to demonstrate a link between suicidal ideation and experiences with bullying. The authors were able to establish some high-profile link between suicidal ideation and experiences with bullying victimization or offending. Their findings provide evidence that adolescent peer aggression must be taken seriously both at school and at home, and suggest that a suicide prevention and intervention component is essential within comprehensive bullying response programs implemented in schools.

(Dinakar et al., 2015) presented an approach for cyberbullying detection based on natural language processing and a common sense knowledge base, which permits recognition over a broad spectrum of topics in everyday life. The authors analyse a row range of particular subject matter associated with bullying (e.g. appearance, intelligence, racial and ethnic slurs, social acceptance, and rejection), and construct BullySpace, a common sense knowledge base that encodes particular knowledge about bullying situations. The authors then perform joint reasoning with common sense knowledge about a wide range of everyday life topics. Messages were analysed using AnalogySpace common sense reasoning technique.

While reviewing related literature for this research, we observed that the challenges faced by most of the researchers includes lack of quality, all-inclusive and labelled datasets on the one hand and the subjective nature of the problem on the other. These two challenges have limited the scope of the research done so far to partial consideration of what makes up cyberbullying and how to detect same from messages posted on the internet.

In an effort to provide properly annotated dataset for use by researchers interested in cyberbullying research, (Van Hee et al., 2018) provided a list of criteria founded in critical race theory, and use them to annotate a publicly available corpus of more than sixteen thousand tweets. The authors analyse the impact of various extra-linguistic features in conjunction with character n-grams for hate-speech detection. They also present a dictionary based on the most indicative words in their data. This is particularly useful as (Salawu, He, & Lumsden, 2017) observed that lack of quality representative labelled datasets and non-holistic consideration of cyberbullying by researchers when developing detection systems are two key challenges facing cyberbullying detection research.

Waseem & Hovy, (2016) established the fact that perpetrators of cyberbullying take advantage of anonymity to perpetrate the act. The authors further seek to introduce a penalty for such users that could be identified as a cyberbully by withdrawing the anonymity such users enjoy on the social media platform. The prevalence of cyberbullying is on one hand, a function of the conceptualization used in describing the problem amongst the affected people, and on the other hand, research variables considered while conceptualizing it amongst the researchers trying to provide scientific solutions to the problem. Such variables include age range and the location of those involved. cyberbully.org is a non-governmental organization that dedicate their services to helping people that have suffered from the effect of cyberbullying. They reported that self-reported effects of cyberbullying include negative effects on school grades and feelings of sadness, anger, fear, and depression. In extreme cases, cyberbullying could even lead to self-harm and suicidal thoughts.

Dinakar *et al.*, (2015) presented an approach for cyberbullying detection based on natural language processing and a common sense knowledge base, which permits recognition over a broad spectrum of topics in everyday life. The authors analysed a narrow range of particular subject matter associated with bullying (e.g. appearance, intelligence, racial and ethnic slurs, social acceptance, and rejection), and constructed BullySpace, a common sense knowledge base that encodes particular knowledge about bullying situations. The authors then perform joint reasoning with common sense knowledge about a wide range of everyday life topics. Messages were analysed using AnalogySpace common sense reasoning technique. The authors also consider social network analysis and other factors

Some other researchers such as Go, Bhayani, & Huang, (2007), Nahar, Unankard, Li, & Pang, (2012), Dani *et al.*, (2017) and more recently Agrawal & Awekar (2018) have proposed various frameworks for auto-detection of cyberbullying. The challenges that has always been left opened for research are

1. Improving the accuracy of the model that was used to identify cyberbullying content in a post on social media.
2. A model that can address more than one topic of cyberbullying e.g. racism, sexism etc.
3. The proposed models until now rely on manual data annotation.
4. Some of the models adopted frequency based embedding such as count vector, TF-IDF vector and so on for the word embedding in their model.

Some of the attention cyberbullying has received in the research community since it came to bare can be attributed to the massive effect it has on the social community. Nahar *et al.*, (2012) in an effort to effectively detect cyberbully online proposed a statistical detection approach for identifying hidden bullying features. The authors proposed a graph model to detect the user-relationship between various users. The authors used the well-known "Bag of Words" approach for its word embedding. Meanwhile, "Bag of words" failings have been documented for its failure to put context into consideration while representing words.

In an effort to provide properly annotated dataset for use by researchers interested in cyberbullying research, Waseem & Hovy, (2016) provided a list of criteria in critical race theory, and use them to annotate a publicly available corpus of more than sixteen thousand tweets. The authors analyze the impact of various extra-linguistic features in conjunction with character n-grams for hate-speech detection. They also present a dictionary based on the most indicative words in their data. This is particularly useful as Salawu, He, & Lumsden, (2017) observed that lack of quality representative labelled datasets and non-holistic consideration of cyberbullying by researchers when developing detection systems as two key challenges facing cyberbullying detection research. The authors proposed that a tweet should be considered offensive if any of the following condition is met

- If it contains racial slur or a sexist statement
- If it was intended to attack a targeted minority or seeks to silence them.
- If it was used to criticize minority without a well-founded argument.
- If it promotes hate speech or violent crime.
- If it misrepresents truth
- If it shows support of problematic hash tags. e.g. "#BanIslam", "#whitegenocide"
- If it negatively stereotypes a minority and/or contains a screen name that is offensive

The accuracy of machine learning models depends directly on the supplied data. The features used for cyberbullying detection by the existing models could be considered based on the following criteria:

- Content-Based features
- Sentiment-Based features
- User-Based features
- Network-Based features.

Bienstein & Werner, (2018) define content-based features as the extractable lexical items of a document such as keywords, profanity, pronouns and punctuations. Emotion-based features are said to be features that are indicative of emotive content; they are generally keywords, phrases and symbols (e.g. emoticons) that can be used to determine the sentiments expressed in a document. User-based features are those characteristics of a user's profile that can be used to make a judgement on the role played by the user in an electronic exchange and include age, gender and sexual orientation and finally, they define Network-based features as usage metrics that can be extracted from the online social network and include items such as number of friends, number of followers, frequency of posting, and so on.

Huang, Inkpen, Zhang, & Van Bruwaene, (2018) stated that the detection of cyberbullying and online harassment is often formulated as a classification problem. Techniques typically used for document classification, topic detection, and sentiment analysis can be used to detect electronic bullying using characteristics of messages, senders, and the recipients.

This research aims to improve the existing cyberbullying detection model by leveraging Long Short Term Memory (LSTM) – a deep learning architecture – with its capacity to process a very large dataset while adding memory capability to learn the semantic relationship among the text in the corpus.

METHODOLOGY

In this research, we propose to tackle the menace of cyberbullying on Twitter by using Long Short Term Memory (LSTM) – a deep learning model – to identify tweets with cyberbully content. LSTM is a type of recurrent neural network that is structured in such a way that it can learn the order of dependence between items in a sequence. LSTM is a special neuron for memorizing long-term dependencies. LSTM is characterized by internal states variable, modified by some "Operation Gates" and is passed from one cell to the other. This special neuron is used for memorizing long-term dependencies. LSTMs were introduced by (Hochreiter & Schmidhuber, 1997). Since its introduction, LSTM have recorded a huge success in a variety of large problems, and are now widely used in academic research.

The LSTM does have the ability to remove or add information to its cell state, carefully regulated by structures called gates. Gates are a way to optionally let information through. They are composed out of a sigmoid neural net layer and a pointwise multiplication operation. In this research, LSTM is adopted for the classification task. It is considered to be most appropriate model for this research because of its ability to correct the problem of vanishing gradients associated with the earlier variation of RNNs. This implies that LSTM can remember the contextual meaning of words long after the model have learnt the words.

Figure 1. Proposed model for auto-detection of cyberbully contents (© 2019)

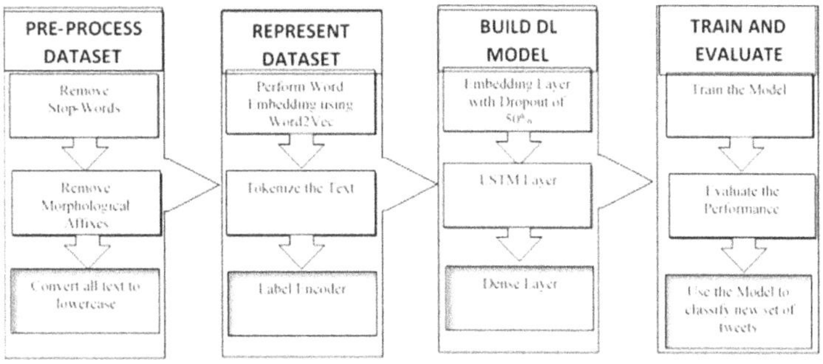

Dataset

The dataset used for this project is available as an open resource for researchers interested in sentiment analysis and opinion mining. The dataset is tagged as "*sentiment140*" and available for download on Stanford University server. The dataset contains one million six hundred thousand tweets. In this research, eighty percent (80%) of the tweets were used as the training set while the remaining twenty percent (20%) were used as the test set.

ANNOTATION OF DATASET

The dataset was annotated using the approach suggested by (Read, 2005) was used to label the dataset. In his approach, tweets that has:) emoticon are considered not to have cyberbully content while those with): emoticon are considered to likely contain cyberbully. The emoticons serve as noisy labels. The tweets were annotated to have equal distribution of tweets containing cyberbully content and those without cyberbully content.

WORD EMBEDDING

Word embedding allows us to consider both semantic and syntactic relationship of words while representing them internally for computer use. Attributes and contextual underlying in human language can be captured using word embedding. A subjective interpretation of words can also be captured using word embedding. One such word embedding technique is Word2Vec which was invented by (Mikolov, Corrado, Chen, & Dean, 2013). The idea was based on the assumption that the semantic meaning of a word can be gotten by considering other words around it. Since the proposition of word2vec, its usage in natural language related tasks has resulted in improved performance from the NLP models and it is considered a breakthrough in natural language representation.

Word2vec was adopted in this research so as to leverage the advantage of semantic understanding it is characterized with. The technique comprises of dense vector representations of words, with consideration for semantic meanings of the words. The output vector of the Word2vec is passed to the long short term memory (LSTM) as input which is in turn used as the classifier

RESULT AND EVALUATION

The entire dataset was used to train the word2vec neural network so as to learn the semantic relationship among the text in the dataset. There are 30369 unique sentence in the corpus. The sentence was tokenized and the relationship between the corpus was then investigated. This returns a total of 290419 unique set of vectors for the words within that corpus.

Social media posts generally contains noise and ambiguity. People have coined out some words to replace longer words, for example people use "luv" in place of "love", while some others use words such as "hahahaha" to express emotions such as laughing. It is pertinent to investigate the effect those "words coinage" has on the model as it will generally affect the prediction accuracy of the model. Hence, the similarity of the words that made up the corpus was investigated and the result of some of the words similarity are shown in Figure 2 and Figure 3.

HYPER-PARAMETER

The hyper-parameters used for training the model is summarized in the Table 1. The word embedding passed to the LSTM model for training was evaluated. The size of the input was computed as 290419 x 300 (with 300 being the word2vec size set as part of the hyper-parameters). This gives a total of 87,286, 201 parameters.

The summary of the model used is given in Figure 4.

Figure 2. Similarity test for the word "love" within the corpus (© 2019)

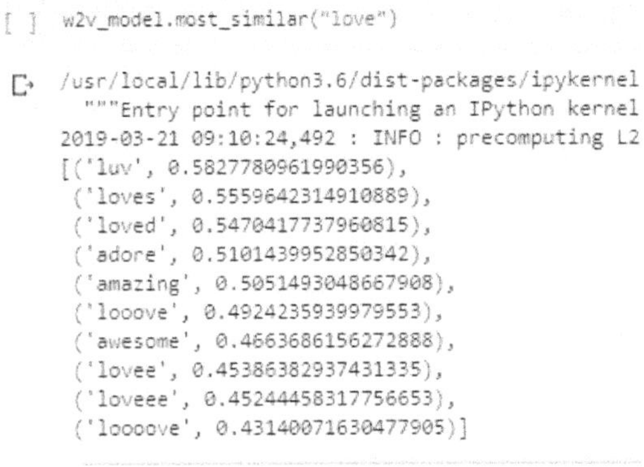

```
[ ]  w2v_model.most_similar("love")

[→  /usr/local/lib/python3.6/dist-packages/ipykernel
    """Entry point for launching an IPython kernel
    2019-03-21 09:10:24,492 : INFO : precomputing L2
    [('luv', 0.5827780961990356),
     ('loves', 0.5559642314910889),
     ('loved', 0.5470417737960815),
     ('adore', 0.5101439952850342),
     ('amazing', 0.5051493048667908),
     ('looove', 0.4924235939979553),
     ('awesome', 0.4663686156272888),
     ('lovee', 0.45386382937431335),
     ('loveee', 0.45244458317756653),
     ('loooove', 0.43140071630477905)]
```

Figure 3. Similarity test for the "bully" within the corpus (© 2019)

```
[ ]  w2v_model.most_similar("bully")

[➤  /usr/local/lib/python3.6/dist-packages/ipykernel_1
       """Entry point for launching an IPython kernel.
     [('offended', 0.27338963747024536),
      ('hahahah', 0.2727299928665161),
      ('vile', 0.265267014503479),
      ('loner', 0.2629106044769287),
      ('shaped', 0.25152140855789185),
      ('comma', 0.25054970383644104),
      ('anorexic', 0.24924525618553162),
      ('ollie', 0.24735796451568604),
      ('poisonous', 0.24681591987609863),
      ('theyll', 0.24674417078495026)]
```

Table 1. Hyper-parameters used for training the model

Hyper-parameter	Value
Size of Training Dataset	1,280,000 tweets (80% of the datasets)
Size of Test Dataset	320,000 tweets (20% of the datasets)
Word2Vec Window size	7
Word2Vec size	300
Batch Size	1024
Loss	Binary cross entropy
Optimizer	Adam optimizer
Metrics	Accuracy
LSTM Layers	100
Dropout percent	50%

Figure 4. Model Summary (© 2019)

```
Layer (type)                 Output Shape              Param #
=================================================================
embedding_1 (Embedding)      (None, 300, 300)          87125700
_____
dropout_1 (Dropout)          (None, 300, 300)          0
_____
lstm_1 (LSTM)                (None, 100)               160400
_____
dense_1 (Dense)              (None, 1)                 101
=================================================================
Total params: 87,286,201
Trainable params: 160,501
Non-trainable params: 87,125,700
```

Figure 5. Training and Validation Accuracy (© 2019)

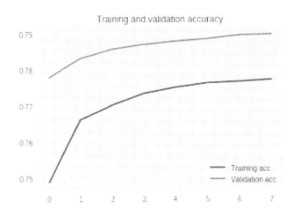

Figure 6. Training and Validation Loss (© 2019)

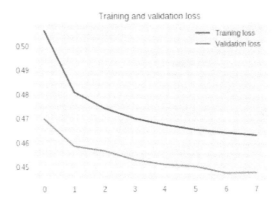

TRAINING AND VALIDATION LOSS AND ACCURACY

It was observed that the training loss decreases from 0.590 to 0.4630 and the validation loss decreases from 0.470 to 0.4470 as the training progresses. The training accuracy was also observed to increase from 74.8% to 77.8% while the Validation accuracy increases from 77.4% to 79.6%. These metrics represent a significant improvement to the currently obtainable as reported by (Bienstein & Werner, 2018).

CONFUSION MATRIX

A normalized confusion matrix for the model was plotted so as to investigate the performance of the model with respect to accuracy. It was observed that 88% of the tweets were correctly classified as either containing cyberbully content or otherwise. The correctly classified tweets are represented as the "True

Table 2. Confusion matrix

True Positive	81%
True Negative	7%
False Positive	8%
False Negative	4%

Positive" and "True Negative" scores on the confusion matrix, with the remaining 12% wrongly classified. This represents a significant improvement against the existing model by (Bienstein & Werner, 2018) which was reported to have around 79% classification accuracy. The confusion matrix is given Table 2.

CONCLUSION AND RECOMMENDATION

This research was aimed at developing and implementing a model that is capable of auto-detecting cyberbullying content within tweets and effectively classify them as containing same or otherwise. The model was developed with consideration for improved accuracy over existing model and an optimized performance.

We combined Word2Vec and Long-Short Term Memory (LSTM). Word2Vec was used as the embedding technique in order to have improved performance compared to the one-hot encoding that has been used in the previous research. The embedded words were then fed into LSTM for classification.

We achieved improved accuracy in the performance of the model when compared with the existing model. Our model, when subjected to the test dataset, was observed to have correctly classify 88% of the tweets in the test dataset as having cyberbullying content or not while the existing model as reported by Bienstein & Werner, (2018) was reported to have about 79% accuracy.

However, this model could still be improved, so as to get better accuracy in its classification task. The model does its classification based on an ongoing discussion. It could not account for conversation history between two friends. Friends could sometimes address each other in such a way that could be identified as bullying, meanwhile, in their context, it is just a regular conversation. Future research could explore social network graph in order to understand the relationship between two people, and what are the acceptable norms amongst them before classifying their conversation as containing cyberbully content or not.

Also, the perpetrators of cyberbullying seem to be going one step further with use of images and videos to harass their victims. This should also be given research attention in the future. Multi-modal algorithms could be developed and used to detect social media contents with offensive images or videos. This could then be integrated with this proposed model that detect text with cyberbully content.

Finally, integration of these models as a background app on every social media apps and sites should be prioritized. This will go a long way in ensuring the social media is safe for all and sundry.

REFERENCES

Agrawal, S., & Awekar, A. (2018). Deep learning for detecting cyberbullying across multiple social media platforms. Lecture Notes in Computer Science, 10772, 141–153. doi:10.1007/978-3-319-76941-7_11

Bienstein, P., & Werner, N. (2018). *Using Machine Learning to Detect Cyberbullying.* Psychische Gesundheit Bei Intellektueller Entwicklungsstörung. doi:10.1109/ICMLA.2011.152

Chatzakou, D., Kourtellis, N., Blackburn, J., De Cristofaro, E., Stringhini, G., & Vakali, A. (2017). *Mean Birds: Detecting Aggression and Bullying on Twitter.* Academic Press. doi:10.1145/3091478.3091487

Dani, H., Li, J., & Liu, H. (2017). Sentiment Informed Cyberbullying Detection in Social Media. Lecture Notes in Computer Science, 10534, 52–67. doi:10.1007/978-3-319-71249-9_4

Dinakar, K., Picard, R., & Lieberman, H. (2015). Common sense reasoning for detection, prevention, and mitigation of cyberbullying. *International Joint Conference on Artificial Intelligence,* (3), 4168–4172. 10.1145/2362394.2362400

Faryadi, Q. (2011). Cyber bullying and academic performance. *International Journal Of Computational Engineering Research, 1*(1), 23–30.

Go, A., Bhayani, R., & Huang, L. (2007). Twitter Sentiment Classification using Distant Supervision. *Sedimentary Geology, 195*(1–2), 75–90. doi:10.1016/j.sedgeo.2006.07.004

Hinduja, S., & Patchin, J. W. (2010). Bullying, cyberbullying, and suicide. *Archives of Suicide Research, 14*(3), 206–221. doi:10.1080/13811118.2010.494133 PMID:20658375

Hochreiter, S., & Schmidhuber, J. (1997). Long Short-Term Memory. *Neural Computation, 9*(8), 1–32. PMID:9377276

Hon, L. C., & Varathan, K. D. (2015). Cyberbullying Detection System on Twitter. *International Journal of Information Systems and Engineering, 1*(1), 1–11. doi:10.24924/ijise/2015.11/v3.iss1/36.47

Huang, Q., Inkpen, D., Zhang, J., & Van Bruwaene, D. (2018). Cyberbullying Intervention Based on Convolutional Neural Networks. *Proceedings of the First Workshop on Trolling, Aggression and Cyberbullying (TRAC-2018)*, 61–70. Retrieved from http://aclweb.org/anthology/W18-44%0A700

Li, Q. (2006). Cyberbullying in schools: A research of gender differences. *School Psychology International, 27*(2), 157–170. doi:10.1177/0143034306064547

Luker, J. M., & Curchack, B. C. (2017). International Perceptions of Cyberbullying Within Higher Education. *Adult Learning, 28*(4), 144–156. doi:10.1177/1045159517719337

Mikolov, T., Corrado, G., Chen, K., & Dean, J. (2013). Efficient Estimation of Word Representations in Vector Space. *Sciencejournal.Withgoogle*, 1–12.

Nahar, V., Unankard, S., Li, X., & Pang, C. (2012). Sentiment analysis for effective detection of cyber bullying. Lecture Notes in Computer Science, 7235, 767–774. doi:10.1007/978-3-642-29253-8_75

Read, J. (2005). *Using Emoticons to reduce Dependency in Machine Learning Techniques for Sentiment Classification.* Department of Informatics, University of Sussex United Kingdom.

Salawu, S., He, Y., & Lumsden, J. (2017). Approaches to Automated Detection of Cyberbullying: A Survey. *IEEE Transactions on Affective Computing, 3045*(c), 1–20. doi:10.1109/TAFFC.2017.2761757

Van Hee, C., Jacobs, G., Emmery, C., Desmet, B., Lefever, E., & Verhoeven, B. (2018). Automatic Detection of Cyberbullying in Social Media Text. Academic Press. doi:10.1371/journal.pone.0203794

Waseem, Z., & Hovy, D. (2016). Hateful Symbols or Hateful People? Predictive Features for Hate Speech Detection on Twitter. *Proceedings of the NAACL Student Research Workshop*, 88–93. 10.18653/v1/N16-2013

14

Chapter 2
MOOCs, Artificial Intelligence Systems, and the Dilemma of Tertiary Education in the 21st Century:
A Theoretical Appraisal of the Human Factors

Ikedinachi Ayodele Power Wogu
Rhema University Nigeria, Aba, Nigeria

Edith Awogu-Maduagwu
Covenant University, Ota, Nigeria

Morris Edogiawere
Igbenigiong University, Okada, Nigeria

Charles Nathaniel Chukwuedo
Federal College of Education Technology Asaba, Asaba, Nigeria

Jesse Oluwafemi Katende
Covenant University, Ota, Nigeria

Sanjay Misra
https://orcid.org/0000-0002-3556-9331
Covenant University, Ota, Nigeria

ABSTRACT

Recent research on the application of artificial intelligence (AI) technology in the education industry for teaching and learning has stirred up a revolution via the use of platforms like the massive open online courses (MOOC) the likes of which the world have never seen before. Millions through this platform can now enroll online to get one form of education or the other. Many scholars, however, doubt the quality of education transmitted and acquired via these platforms; hence, some scholars describe the education gotten through this medium as artificial education. A situation that has resulted in a kind of revolution in the education industry described as education tsunami. The Marxian theory of alienation offers an appropriate theoretical platform for the analysis conducted in the paper. The ex-post factor method of analysis and Deidra's critical analytic method was adopted for attaining the objectives of the paper. The dilemmas eroding the quality of education were identified. Blended learning approaches, as against present methods, were recommended.

DOI: 10.4018/978-1-7998-1279-1.ch002

Copyright © 2020, IGI Global. Copying or distributing in print or electronic forms without written permission of IGI Global is prohibited.

INTRODUCTION

Background

The quest to attain the highest global education rate in the nearest future, continues to be the desire and objective of all concerned bodies and organizations in the world. The 2ⁿᵈ agenda of the just elapsed Millennium Development Goals (MDG's) and the 4ᵗʰ agenda of the Sustainable Development Goals (SDG's) both seeks to promote and achieve a universal primary education for all in the nearest future (UNSDG Knowledge, 2015 and UNOD, 2016). These goals notwithstanding, accessing higher education by all who require it in this dispensation has not been an easy task, seeing that those who desire these form of education have been on a geometric increase: For instance, the demand for higher education globally is predicted would have doubled by 2025, to 200 million number of persons seeking such education per year. This number would come mostly from emerging economies (NAFSA 2010).

The quest to provide adequately for the rising demand for education at all levels in the 21ˢᵗ century - researchers like (Wogu, 2016; Wogu, 2018; Wogu, 2019) believe - is responsible for jump-starting the great revolution in global online education which has hit the education industry like a *tsunami* (Brooks and Collins, 2012). The thought about the gains associated with the advent of online global education excites the ordinary man since this new trend is believed, would further liberate the ordinary man from poverty and increase the individual's chances of getting better and new jobs and long over-due promotions from ones place of work. To this end, contemporary researchers tend to argue that of all other factors, education seems to be that one factor with the most potential to unlock billions of brains for solving the world's biggest problems in the 21ˢᵗ Century (Friedman, 2013; Kolla and Ng, 2013; Scagnoli, 2014; Richter, 2014 and Siemen, 2014). The platform believed would be instrumental in delivering the mandate of making education available to all, is the platform of 'Massive Open Online Course, also known as MOOC. Studies however reveal that this platform is currently undergoing further development at the instance of great institutions like Massachusetts Institute of Technology (MIT) and Stanford University. Other companies like Udacity, Coursera, Wiz IQ, edX, UPEx, iversity, Stanford Online and Etcetera, are also actively engaged in the use of this MOOC platforms (Friedman, 2013).

As profound as the goal of making affordable /free education available to the less privilege and all desiring such education via the platform of MOOC is, there are an increasing number of researchers who believe that the move to make education affordable and available to all desiring it, is beginning to have an untold damage on the whole essence of the goal of education and on the original values of the institution on which the whole idea of teaching and learning was founded upon. This paper therefore critically investigates the roles which AI powered MOOCs have played in fostering the goals of education in the 21ˢᵗ century.

The Problem of the Research

The concept of education among other things, is perceived as the major drive for any kind of professed empowerment; as in political power, financial power and intellectual power. This is why education is perceived as the right knowledge you have in your head which gives you the capacity to display wisdom (Friedman, 2013 and Wogu, 2016). The etymological meaning of education arise from a Latin word *Educatum* which when translated refers to the act of training or teaching. Another Latin derivative of the term education *Educare*, refers to the art of 'bringing up' or the art of 'rising up'. From the above explanations, it can be deduced that the word education strives to nurture the worthy qualities in individuals with a view to drawing out the best from them. Similarly, education largely strives to spark off inherent capacities in man that would enhance his chances to better his life on earth. Any acclaimed art of education that fails to achieve these set goals, cannot be perceived as the rightful meaning of education.

This paper identifies serious conceptual problems which the notion of education espoused by operators of AI powered MOOC platform like Etcetera, Udacity, Coursera, Wiz IQ, edX, UPEx, iversity, Stanford Online, Massachusetts Institute of Technology (MIT) and Stanford University. This is because recent studies reveal that many who enroll to learn and acquire one form of education or the other, via these MOOC platforms, tend to feel their finger burnt out when they fail to get expected outcomes from the online platform they looked up to for education. Sabastian Thruns' lamentation on this matter, which was captured on November, 2013 – perhaps - paints a more appropriate picture of the problem inferred here: "We were on the front pages of newspapers and magazines, and at the same time, I was realizing, we don't educate people as others wished, or as I wished. We have a lousy product… It was a painful moment." (Holton, 2013). Others who view the craze for AI technology driven MOOC's as inimical and hazardous to mankind and the goal of education generally include: (Holton, 2013; Brooks and Collins, 2012; Vardi, 2013; Basu, 2013; Rivard, 2013 and Brooks, 2013).

The study among other things, infers the presence of dehumanizing ethical dilemmas which affects many who enroll on these MOOC platforms for one form of education or the other. Studies also reveal that the learners, teachers/educators who are directly or indirectly involved with the teaching and learning processes on the MOOC's platform, are also not left out in this dilemma.

Objectives of the Paper

In the light of the above stated challenges associated with AI powered MOOC platforms, the paper seeks to attain the following objectives:

1. To critically assess the quality of education provided by AI driven MOOC's in the education industry
2. The paper seeks to identify and evaluate the pros and cons for AI driven MOOC platforms for education in the 21st century.
3. The paper evaluates the consequences of the dilemma that operators and users of AI powered MOOC's for education, suffer from every now and then.
4. To suggest ways of sustaining the goals of education amidst innovations in AI for the Education industry.

Theoretical and Methodological Considerations

Karl Marx's *Alienation theory* which essentially highlights the various kinds of estrangement which individuals experience from aspects of their essence, is adopted for the study. (Mészáros, 1970; Ollman, 1976 and Cox, 1998). The theory was chosen because it offers to the researcher, the basic foundation and justifications for conducting investigations on the subject areas of the paper. The kind of investigation which focuses on understanding the class of Alienations which exists between users and operators of AI powered MOOC's and the quality of education the platform offers mankind generally. (Cox. 1998; Cohen, Manion, & Morison, 2000 and Wogu, 2017). The *ex-post facto* research method (Cohen, Manion, & Morison, 2000 and Marilyn, 2013) was adopted as the methodology appropriate for this study since the paper largely relies on previous analysis of data critically evaluated on the subject of this paper. Deriders' deconstructive and critical reconstructive analytic method of enquiry in philosophy (Derrida, 1976; Balkin, 1987 and Derrida, 1992) was also adopted for the study.

ARTIFICIAL INTELLIGENCE, MOOCs AND THE EDUCATION INDUSTRY

"Everything we love about civilization is a product of intelligence, so amplifying our human intelligence with artificial intelligence has the potential of helping civilization flourish like never before – as long as we manage to keep the technology beneficial" (Max Tegmark, President of the Future of Life Institute 2017).

About Artificial Intelligence

The notion of Artificial Intelligence used for this paper conceives AI as an area of study in computer science which lays emphasis on the need to create and design machines which will possess and in most cases, acquire variant degrees of the feature of human intelligence, with the view to be able to carry out and solve human like activities and problems such as: Processing knowledge, Reasoning, Learning, Speech and image/facial recognition, Planning and manipulation of objects and ideas (Wogu, 2011 and Technopidia, 2017).

AI today is perhaps, best conceived from the narrow (or weak AI) perspective which is designed to perform narrow tasks such as internet search or facial recognition. Researchers are currently more interested in creating general AI (AGI also known as strong artificial intelligence which will in the nearest future, likely outperform man in virtually all tasks as has been so far displayed in the game of chess and other cognitive tasks. A clear example of where AI has excelled in complex cognitive tasks can be seen in IBM's "Watson" which to the surprise of many, defeated two champions of the game of *Jeopardy* 'Ken Jennings and Brad Rutter' (Gustin, 2011). In more recent times, sophisticated systems like Watson have now been deployed into other sensitive and fundamental human endeavours. Today's researchers have concluded research on how computers via the platform of AI technology, could now become what (BOSS Magazine, 2016) called Artificial Teaching Assistant (ATA).

A Georgia Tech Professor has just finished teaching a course where an Artificial Teaching Assistant (ATA) based on IBM's Watson-powered services, more than held its own against actual graduate students. As MOOC providers seek to deliver higher-quality education to students all over the world, some are suggesting that artificial intelligence could quickly fill a significant gap (BOSS Magazine, 2016).

This ATA will thus be able to help very large number of students understand the basic requirements of their various courses, unlike the single man behind the systems of an MOOCs environment who needs to grapple with hundreds or thousands of students' projects and assignments online.

The ATA study by a Professor in Georgia Tech, Ashek Goel, revealed that ATA held its grounds effectively when it attended to over 300 students needing various kind of attention, alongside eight other humans who were also overseeing the activities of over 300 students.

AI Powered MOOCs and Education in the 21ˢᵗ Century

Recent studies on the meaning of Massive Open Online Courses (MOOC) conceives it as an effort to provide one form of learning and educations via an online platform, from a University base, to a group of persons who normally wouldn't have been able to access or afford the kind or quality of education that is being made available by the vendors, at little or no cost whatsoever to the student (Konnikova, 2014; Wogu, Atayero, Olu-Owolabu, Sholarin, Ogbuehi, Akoleowo and Ubogu, 2016; Yu, Miao, Leung, and White, 2017). This move to provide accessible quality educations via the platform of MOOCs - many argue - constitute 'a disruptive technology challenging traditional education models' (Yu *etal,* 2017). The question of whether this platform has been advantageous to the learners and educators making use of this AI powered MOOC platform, remains a subject of heated debate among certain scholars (Konnikova, 2014; The Economist, 2016, Wogu, 2016).

This notwithstanding, one of the main factor behind the proliferation of MOOCs platforms for educational purposes in the 21ˢᵗ century, is captured in an address by Geoffrey Crowther, which was presented to major stake holders of the future of education, in an inaugural meeting of the members of Open University in Britain, on July 23ʳᵈ, 1969. In his words:

The first, and most urgent task before us is to cater for the many thousands of people, fully capable of a higher education, who, for one reason or another, do not get it, or do not get as much of it as they can turn to advantage, or as they discover, sometimes too late, that they need," he told his audience. "Men and women drop out through failures in the system…, "through disadvantages of their environment, through mistakes of their own judgment, through sheer bad luck. These are our primary material."… Open University wanted the tired, the poor, and the huddled masses. To them, most of all, it opened its doors (Konnikova, 2014).

Corroborating this view, Nathan Heller noted in a magazine that 'considering the essence and need to disseminate quality education to all those who need it the most', he argued that 'the quality of education by all standards, should not be a luxury good. Thus, MOOC's should be flexible, and where possible, free (Konnikova, 2014).

Records indicate that radical MOOC's began largely in 2011 with Sabastian Thrun, a Professor at Stanford University, when he offered to make public his foundation and introductory notes on AI free of any kind of charges, via online platforms. The three months that followed after his first announcement, saw a record of over a hundred and sixty thousand students participating. This mode of disseminating knowledge was what encouraged him to found the platform today known as *Udacity,* suggested to be the biggest MOOC platforms in the world today. Since the setting up of Udacity, other platforms such as edX, a platform developed by the collaboration of two great institutions: Harvard University and MIT emerged. Another platform, Coursera, established by Sabastian Thrun's friends from Khan and Stanford also emerged with the objectives of providing flexible, qualitative and free education to all desiring them. Today, records indicate that 'there are four hundred and ninety-five MOOCS listed as in-progress on the MOOC aggregator Class Central, a number perceived to be five times as many as they were, a year ago' (.Konnikova, 2014). The fact of rising acceptance of these MOOC platforms as viable avenues for achieving the objectives and goals of education for all desiring it in the nearest future, notwithstanding, there are those who still worry about the quality of teaching and learning undertaken via these MOOC platforms. One of such individual is Sabastian Thrun. In his words: 'We were on the front pages of newspapers and magazines, and at the same time, I was realizing, we don't educate people as others wished, or as I wished"… *"We have a lousy product"* (Holton, 2013).

Despite these misgivings, this chapter observes that MOOC's by all standards, have granted millions of subscribers all over the world, with free or at very low prices, access to educational resources of all kinds. The number of people who continue to enroll for one course or the other continue to rise each year, even though the rate of those who actually complete the programmes they enrolled for continue to dwindle. A study conducted in 2013 for instance revealed that only about 5% of students who enrolled in about seventeen Coursera classes which took place in the University of Pennsylvania, actually completed the program. Another not too interesting news about results arising from MOOC's platforms is that, not all the 5% of subscribers who completed the program really passed the course. Maria Konnikova tried to provide an explanation for this supposed negative report about MOOC platforms when she observed that:

The problem with MOOCs begins with the fact that, as their name says, they're 'Massive' and 'Open', which means that it can be easy to get lost in them. There are tens or even hundreds of thousands of students in some classes. Often, the students receive no personal acknowledgment or contact to hold them to account. Thus, they can generally drop out the second they're unhappy, frustrated, or overwhelmed (Konnikova, 2014).

This feeling of Alienations espoused by the Marxian theory of alienation is thus established here as one of the fundamental problem which subscribers and indeed, established vendors like Sabastian Thrun, suffer from whenever they find themselves falling short of either attaining the goals and aspirations for subscribing or establishing these MOOCs platforms or failing to attain desired results and knowledge from the platform, in the first instance.

Gains of AI Technology in the Education Industry

It has become a clear fact for all to see that technology has become an essential part of the human progress (Tiles, 2017), irrespective of the form it comes in, be it in the form of sticks, stones or even in the form of smart phones as we have them today. It is no longer a strong issue of controversy that technology has allowed us to conquer our environment. The fact that educational platforms like Udacity, Coursera and edX, were all birthed from projects carried out in artificial intelligent laboratories, adds credence to the conviction that AI technology has been embraced as the tool for the much needed overhaul anticipated in the education industry. (The Economist, 2016). It is therefore established that AI technology has the potential to influence the education industry more than ever before. For example: features like "Adaptive learning' (The Economist, 2016), a software feature that fashions individual courses to the capacity of each student. By this, the student in question is presented with concepts in the order he will find most suitable and easy to comprehend, thus allowing him to work at his own pace, a pace quite different from those of other students with different capacities. This method of learning has before now, being a dream educators wondered how they will achieve, but the introduction of AI's and machines leaning capabilities and techniques have delivered on this vision in today's MOOC's platform.

Other clear gains or avenues thorough which AI technology offers the traditional class room or the online MOOC's platforms, outstanding benefits are discussed below:

Personalized Learning (PL): This is a scenario that give more attention to what students learn at each point in time. The use of AI software's and platforms in this instance, gives the teacher or educator a vivid understanding and perspective of how the student is learning, thereby allowing the teacher to customize his curriculum, as and when necessary for the sake of the student.

Intelligent Tutoring Systems (ITS): This method is also known in other parlance as the Artificial Teaching Assistant (ATA). This used to be some far off vision which has today come to a reality. These systems are thus able to function in the absence of the teacher while effectively supporting the learner in different and efficient ways.

Adaptive Group Formation (AGF): The system in this respect is able to analyze personal data and the information on each learner with the view to helping the teacher to generate groups and categories of learners where certain students will be placed so as to enhance their learning speed and thus balance any weakness that may exist with the strength of other persons in the group or other groups.

Intelligent Moderation (IM): This system/software largely makes use of machine learning systems. Such systems makes it possible for the human tutors, teachers and moderators to be able to analyze very large data produced by groups. Information arising from the analysis of data further increases the efficiency of the educator in the class room or online.

Essay Grading Software (EGS): This software perhaps, marks one of the immense achievements of AI technology in the education sector. The software is able to grade all manner of student's essays and projects. Every new graded project adds to a central database to which future essays are compared (Tiles, 2017).

ARTIFICIAL INTELLIGENCE OR ARTIFICIAL EDUCATION?

As novel as AI technology has become in the 21st century, it among other things, have been identified by scholars as one of those tools designed to aid in the achievement of all those goals and aspirations which educators and learners of the 21st century look forward to achieving. This high optimism notwithstanding, the adoption of AI technology in the education industry have been identified as responsible for some drawbacks which have been reported to be responsible for making a mess of the initial goals its vendors set out to achieve. This section is dedicated to discussing a few of these draw backs and challenges arising from the adoption and implementation of AI technology in the education industry via MOOC platforms.

The Dilemma of AI Technology in the Education Industry

Technology Addiction

One of the foremost problem which AI technology poses to the education industry is the *Problem of technology addiction.* As more reliance is placed on AI technology to run the affairs of education - on account of the set goals which educators today hope to achieve via this platform - vendors and educators/ governments, often run the risks of causing technology addiction among learners and educators as well. When and where this scenario sets in amongst learners and educators, a derogatory feeling of alienation sets in on all concerned and affected. The kinds of alienations inferred to exist here is the kind discussed in the Marxian Alienation theory which manifests itself in four varying classes (Gouldner 1984 and DOP, 1984). Where this class of alienation sets in on man, they are known not to easily recover from it (Ollman, 1976 and Cox, 1998).

The Lack of Personal Connections

The lack of personal connection is another example of the class of Alienations which affects both the learner and the educator at the same time. Instances where so much reliance have been placed on the use of smart machines because doing so tends to improve the educational experience of both the learner and the educator comes to play here. Studies however reveal that both learners and educators, more than ever before, now rely on these machines for everything, thereby causing the kind of situation which (Brooks and Collins, 2012) described as the campus tsunami, a scenario that describes the arrival of a storm (a *Tsunami)* that distorts the status quo of things in the education industry. The kind of distortion referred to here is likened to the distortion which the introduction of IT in the communication industry, has had on the newspaper and magazine business/industry, where people now easily read the information they need online without the need for buying papers or the magazines from the respective vendors. In the words of Brooks and Collings: "…What happened to the Newspaper and Magazine business is about to happen to higher education".

The lack of personal connections between the educator and the learner, as described in (Basu, 2013; Rivard, 2013; Vardi, 2013 and Wogu, 2016), are clear indications of the kind of dilemma the learner and the educators are facing as a result of total reliance on smart machines. Relying on machines to grade or teach the students may also lead to what is referred to as *Educational oversight*, a situation that causes both emotional and psychological harm to the learner, more than it was initially set to be beneficial to them (Tiles, 2017). The situation discussed in the above context falls into various classes of alienation as proposed in the Marxian Alienation theory.

Unemployment

The mass reliance on machines to do virtually every individual tasks in the academia, now creates less and less demands for educators. Thus, with the emergence and need for MOOC platforms for educational purposes, there will be a decrease in the demand for educators, teaching aids and teaching assistants (Vardi, 2013).

High Failure Rates Recorded on the MOOC Platform

Studies reveal that while one of the goals of MOOCs was to make or bring the quality of education closer to those who need it the most, at little or no cost to the learner, results from recent studies (Konnikova, 2014 and BOSS Magazine, 2016) reveals that majority of persons who enroll and eventually complete the courses and programs on the MOOC platforms, are not the less privileged individuals, nor are they among those who really need the education they applied for. Rather, studies (Konnikova, 2014; Tiles, 2017) reveals that majority of persons who enrolled for courses on the MOOC's platforms were already first degree holders, etc, persons desiring to improve on the quality of their degrees and certificates. This realization notwithstanding, this same study revealed that higher failure rates were recorded from the percentage of students who eventually completed the program. The failure rates were discovered to be more pronounced and higher in courses taken via online MOOC platforms, compared to results of courses taken in traditional class room settings (Konnikova, 2014). Consequent on these findings, most scholars like Di Xu, resolved that: MOOCs were the least effective at serving the students who needed educational resources the most' (Konnikova, 2014).

Are They Cheating or Learning?

In view of the goals and aspirations which justified the radical adoption of MOOC platforms as viable and relatively free avenues though which quality education could be disseminated to all those in dear need of one form of higher education or the other, contemporary scholars have questioned the degree to which these MOOC platforms have lived up to the original goals and aspirations that justified its wide adoption as the platform, and the solution to the problem of education in the 21st century. Scholars in this category include: (Vardi, 2013; Kolowich, 2013; Rivard, 2013 and Jaschik, 2013). The concerns of some of these scholars and authors have produced books with titles like: *A future with only 10 Universities…* by Audrey Watter; *MOOC's, Not There yet…* by Mark Guzdial. *MOOC's a fundamental Misrepresentation of how teaching Works… by* Mark Guzdial. *What's Right and What's Wrong about Coursera style MOOC's, MIT and Magic…* both by Toni Bates.

The Problem of Learning With MOOCs

For most students who are transcending from the typical and traditional learning environment of everyday classroom to the kind of learning undertaken online and on platforms organized by the likes of Coursera and edX, studies indicates, are usually not able to cope with the realities associated with online platforms. This fact most research agree, results to a kind of dilemma for the learner and the educator who is forced to contend with these realities. A study conducted on communication research and Philosophy (Diderot, 1993 and Ginsberg, 1994) highlights what scientist refer to as the *distancing effect*. A kind of problem that affect students and their educators who are separated from the time and place of their study, as a result of using mediums such as MOOC's . This separation, studies (Greene, 1974 and Rubin, 1996) reveals, often have adverse effects which cause issues like: A reduced understanding of the wellbeing of the individual, among other serious issues.

To corroborate this fact, another researcher (Russell, 2004) who had conducted extensive research on the psychological implications of the use of MOOCs for online studies argued that when all forms of electronic devises are used in lieu of the conventional teaching methods for learning (Mediating human experiences), the consequence of this transformation and approach to learning, Russell believes, tend to produce related tendencies such as: 'Psychological propinquity, Media richness, Psychological distancing and Moral distancing (Russell, 2004), to mention but a few. Another scholar similarly noted that: '…technology increases the propensity for unethical conduct by creating a moral distance between an act and the moral responsibility for it. The situation referred to as 'the *Moral Distancing Hypothesis*, draws on earlier pre-internet theories' (Rubin, 1996). It is from the above premise that Palmer M. T. concluded that: 'Face to face communication would appear to remain the idealized form of interpersonal communication, embodying all the features which humans developed to facilitate the rapid, explicit, and implicit negotiation of relational information' (Palmer, 1995).

The Problem of Cheating With MOOC's

The quality and kind of education disseminated on the platform of AI powered MOOC is one of the main focus of scholars like (Vardi, 2013; Kolowich, 2013; Rivard, 2013; Jaschik, 2013; Yang, 2013 and Skapinker, 2013). While some vendors of distant learning platforms are known to be none profit and solely humanitarian in their dispositions, there are a host of other outfits who are for profit organizations, who for the purpose of making profit and maximizing the share-holders profits margin, compromised certain standards in other to retain customers and to keep subscription levels on their platforms high at all times. The quest to remain the most subscribed platform with perhaps, the highest success/pass rate of students by most vendors, studies (Marcuse, 1998) indicate, are responsible for the high level of compromise which most of these for-profit AI powered MOOC's platforms, encounter from time to time.

A high number of cases of plagiarized papers are now observed to be the order of the day for majority of learners who conduct projects and assignments via online platforms. Studies (Anders, 2012 and Wogu, 2016) reveals that some students, in an effort to make the highest grades in assignments, initially register courses with fictitious names after which they re-register with their real names when they would have gotten acquainted with the tests and examination questions raised for the course. This criminal behaviour gives the student the chance of making the best grades in such courses. This problem and more perhaps, were among the issues that troubled Sabastian Thrun, founder of *Udacity,* when he lamented that 'their MOOC platform was yet to device convenient ways of affirming that the assignments and project submitted online by students were true representations of the students' capabilities. Consequent on this position, he concludes: Providers of MOOC's who desire to offer full credentials to graduates, must first come to terms with the kind of strategies they will need to put in place to verify student's submission online. Anything outside this state of affairs, this papers considered as being tantamount to artificial education as against the qualitative education these AI powered MOOC platforms propose to provide.

CONCLUSION

Summary of Findings

The paper so far had made conscious efforts to address the objectives it set out to achieve in the introductory pages of this chapter. The first objective which sort to assess the quality of education provided by AI powered MOOC's in the education industry, discovered that, while MOOCs platforms emerged from artificial intelligent laboratories projects - projects embarked upon by star Professors in major ivy league Universities around the world, with the view to catering for the teaming population of those who for one reason or the other, are not able to assess qualitative education from the best Professors and world class Universities of their choice - around the world - to their satisfaction. The vision to provide free education to all who desired it, seemed to have been largely achieved in 2013 - hat is - going by the records of individuals who were noted to have attempted and participated in one online course or the other. This seeming laudable achievement notwithstanding, key scholars like Sabastian Thrun, one of the founder of the AI powered MOOC's project, found ample reasons to condemn the platform as one that was not so viable for achieving the initial goals for which the platform was designed to achieve.

The second objective which sort to identify the pros and cons for AI driven MOOC platforms for education in the 21st century, identified and discussed more than 6 clear cut advantages which AI power

MOOC's brings to the education sector. These advantages notwithstanding, the paper identified and discussed at least six crucial hazards which AI powered MOOC's platforms are presently causing to humanity. Hazards the paper identified as dilemmas which have put a lot of strain on learners, educators and vendors of MOOC platforms. These strains, the chapter identified, were responsible for the lamentation and outburst expressed by the likes of Sabastian Thrun who lamented about the dilemma which AI powered MOOCs have caused both the vendors, learners and educators on the MOOC's platforms (Holton, 2013 and Konnikova, 2014).

The third objective of the paper investigated the consequences of the dilemma which educators, learners and vendors of MOOC platforms suffered from. The paper discussed over 5 points on the subject matter from where it found justifications for making the recommendations it made at the end of the paper. The forth objective focused on identifying ways of sustaining the initial goals of the UN and other major stake holders of the education sector, amidst the various AI innovations currently being introduced into the education sector. Findings from this objective were also highlighted in the recommendations proposed for the paper.

CONCLUSION

The paper set out to provide a critical appraisal of the role of AI technologies on Massive Open Online Courses and how it impacts on academic activities in tertiary institutions of learning all over the world. The critical evaluations conducted in the study revealed that, while online education via AI powered MOOC's platforms are identified as platforms with high potentials for revolutionizing the education industry, the vendors and promoters of this platforms have not yet devised precise plans for using the potentials inherent in this technology to realize the goals and aspirations which the promoters of this MOOC platforms have for the education industry, in the nearest future.

RECOMMENDATIONS

1. More research and experiments grounded in psychology, would need to be re-conducted on the efficient use AI powered MOOCs as viable platforms for conducting the sensitive business of education in the 21st century.
2. Promoters of MOOC platforms need to diligently consider old methods, from the era when education was not as open, not as massive nor was it online.
3. The need to promote the art of learning to re-learn is espoused since learning is better conceived as a lifelong process and not necessarily what you can acquire from any platform over a specific duration of time. A continuous learning exercise is thus emphasized.
4. The flipped classroom model is recommended as a method which institutions and educators need to embrace since it offers a win-win situation for both students and facilitators.

REFERENCES

Anders, C. (2012, August). Are they learning or cheating? Online teaching's dilemma. *Forbes*, 16.

Balkin, J. M. (1987). Deconstructive practice and legal theory. *Yale L.J., 96*.

Basu, K. (2013). Faculty groups consider how to respond to MOOCs. *Inside Higher Ed*. Retrieved from https://ipfs.io/ipfs/QmXoypizjW3WknFiJnKLwHCnL72vedxjQkDDP1mXWo6uco/wiki/Massive_open_online_course.html

Brooks, D., & Collins, G. (2012). The campus tsunami. *New York Times*.

Cohen, L., Manion, L., & Morison, K. (2000). *Research methods in education*. London: Routledge Falmer.

Cox, J. (1998). An introduction to Marx's theory of Alienation. *International Socialism: Quarterly Journal of the Socialist Workers Party, 79*(5).

Derrida, J. (1976). *Of Grammatology*. Baltimore, MD: Johns Hopkins University Press.

Derrida, J. (1992). *Force of law: Deconstruction*. Academic Press.

Dictionary of Philosophy. (1984). Alienation. In The Dictionary of Philosophy (2nd ed.). Academic Press.

Diderot, D. (1993). Conversation of a father with his children (P. N. Furbank, Trans.). In Furbank P. N. (Ed.), *This is not a story and other stories* (pp. 126–159). Oxford, UK: Oxford University Press.

Farrakhan, I. (2012). *The true meaning of education*. FCN Publishing. Retrieved from http://www.finalcall.com/artman/publish/Minister_Loui s_Farrakhan_9/article_8731.shtml

Friedman, L. T. (2013). Revolution hits the Universities. *New York Times*.

Gais, H. (2014). Is the developing world "MOOC'd out"? *Al Jazeera*. Retrieved from http://america.aljazeera.com/opinions/2014/7/mooc-education-

Ginsberg, C. (1994). Killing a Chinese Mandarin: The moral implications of distance. *Critical Inquiry*, *21*(Autumn), 46–60. doi:10.1086/448740

Gouldner, A. W. (1984). *The two Maxims*. New York: Oxford University Press.

Greene, G. (1974). The third man. In G. Greene (Ed.), *The third man and the fallen idol* (pp. 3–148). London: Heinemann.

Gustin, S. (2011). IBM Watson Super Computer Wins Practice Jeopardy Round. *Wired Business Online publication*. Retrieved from https://www.wired.com/2011/01/ibm- watson-jeopardy/

Holton, D. (2013). *The spectrum of opinion about MOOCs*. Centre for Teaching and Learning Excellence. Embry-Riddle Aeronautical University.

Jaschik, S. (2013). Feminist Anti-MOOC. *Inside Higher Ed*. Available: http://www.insidehighered.com/news/2013/08/19/feminist-professors-create-alternative-moocs

Koller, D., Ng, A., Do, C., & Chen, Z. (2013). Retention and Intention in Massive Open Online Courses. *EDUCAUSE Review Online*. Retrieved from https://er.educause.edu/articles/2013/6/retention-and-intention-in-massive-open-online-courses-in-depth

Kolowich, S. (2013). An open letter to Professor Micheal Sandel from the Philosophy Department at San Jose State University. *Chronicles of Higher Education*. Retrieved from http://chronicle.com/article/TheDocument-Open-Letter-From/138937/

Konnikova, M. (2014). Will MOOCs be flukes? *The New Yorker Online publication*. Retrieved from https://www.newyorker.com/science/maria-konnikova/moocs-failure-solutions

Marcuse, H. (1998). Some social implications of modern technology. In D. Kellner (Ed.), *Technology, War and Fascism - Collected Papers of Herbert Marcuse* (Vol. 1, pp. 41–65). London: Routledge.

Marilyn, K. (2013). *Ex-post facto research: Dissertation and scholarly research, Recipes for success*. Seattle, WA: Dissertation Success LLC. Retrieved from http://www.dissertationrecipes.com/wp-content/uploads/2011/04/Ex-Post-Facto- research.pdf

NAFSA. (2010). *The changing landscape of global higher education*. Washington, DC: Association of International Educators.

Ollman, B. (1976). *Alienation: Marx's conception of man in capitalist society*. Retrieved from http:www.alienationtheory.com/

Palmer, M. T. (1995). Interpersonal communication and virtual reality: Mediating interpersonal relationships. In F. Biocca & M. R. Levy (Eds.), *Communication in the age of virtual reality* (p. 277-299). Hillside, NJ: Lawrence Erlbaum.

Richter. (2014). Do MOOCS need a special instructional design? *Proceeding of EDULEARN14*.

Rivard, R. (2013). EdX Rejected. *Inside Higher Education*. Available at: http//www.insidehighered.com/news/2013/04/19/despite-courtship-amherst-decides-shy-away-star-mooc-provider

Rubin, R. (1988). Moral distancing and the use of information technologies: The seven temptations. In J. M. Kizza (Ed.), *Social and ethical effects of the computer revolution* (pp. 124–125). Jefferson: McFarland and Company.

Russell, G. (2004). *The distancing dilemma in distance education*. Retrieved from Monash University: http://www.itdl.org/journal/feb_04/article03.htm

Scagnoli. (2014). How to design an MOOC. *Proceeding of EDULEARN14*.

Siemens, G. (2012). MOOCs are really a platform [Web Log Post]. Retrieved December 05, 2013, from http://www.elearnspace.org/blog/2012/07/25/ moocs-are-really-a-platform/

Skapinker, M. (2013). Open web courses are massively overhyped. *Financial Times*. Retrieved 5 April 2013. https://ipfs.io/ipfs/QmXoypizjW3WknFiJnKLwHCnL72vedxjQkDDP1mXWo6uco/wiki/Massive_open_online_course.html

Technopidia. (2017). *Artificial Intelligence Definition*. Retrieved from https://www.techopedia.com/definition/190/artificial-intelligence-ai

The Economist. (2016). *Re-educating Rita. A Special Report on Education and Policy*. Retrieved from https://www.economist.com/news/special-report/21700760-artificial-intelligence-will-have-implications-policymakers-education-welfare-and

Tiles, L. (2017). *15 Pros and 6 Cons of Artificial Intelligence in the classroom*. Retrieved from https://blogs.technet.com/b/nzedu/archive/2013/01/07/collaboration-and-the-role-of-technology-in-the-21st-century-classroom.aspx

UNSKP. (2015). *United Nations – Sustainable Development knowledge platform*. UNSKP.

Vardi, M. Y. (2012). Will MOOCs destroy academia? *Communications of the ACM, 55*(11), 5. doi:10.1145/2366316.2366317

Wogu, I. A. P. (2011). *Problems in mind: A new approach to age long problems and questions in philosophy and the cognitive science of human development*. Pumack Nigeria Limited Education Publishers.

Wogu, I. A. P., Atayero, A. A. A., Olu-Owolabu, F. E., Sholarin, M. A., Ogbuehi, U. K., Akoleowo, O., & Ubogu, P. C. (2016). *The changing face of education and the dilemma of Massive Open Online Courses (MOOCS) in Nigeria's tertiary institutions: Implications for development*. Paper delivered at the 3rd International Conference on African Development Issues (CU-ICADI2016). Retrieved from https://scholar.google.com/citations?user=J5h7gSwAAAAJ&hl=en

Wogu, I. A. P., Misra, S., Assibong, P. A., Olu-Owolabi, E. F., Maskeliunas, R., & Damasevicius, R. (2019). Artificial Intelligence, Smart Classrooms and Online Education in the 21st Century: Implications for Human Development. *Journal of Case on Information Technology, 21*(3). Retrieved from https://www.igi-global.com/article/artificial-intelligence-smart-classrooms-and-online-education-in-21st-century/227679?camid=4v1

Wogu, I. A. P., Misra, S., Olu-Owolabi, F. E., Assibong, P. A., & Oluwakemi, D. (2018). Artificial Intelligence, Artificial Teachers and the Fate of Learners in the 21st Century Education Sector: Implications for Theory and Practice. *International Journal of Pure and Applied Mathematics, 119*(16), 2245-2259. Retrieved from https://acadpubl.eu/hub/2018-119-16/issue16b.html https://acadpubl.eu/hub/2018-119-16/2/232.pdf

Wogu, I. A. P., Olu-Owolabi, F. E., Assibong, P. A., Apeh, H. A., Agoha, B. C., Sholarin, M. A., . . . Igbokwe, D. (2017). Artificial Intelligence, Alienation and Ontological Problems of Other Minds: A Critical Investigation into the Future of Man and Machines. *Proceedings of the IEEE International Conference on Computing, Networking and Informatics (ICCNI 2017)*. DOI:10.1109/ICCNI.2017.8123792

Yang, D. (2013). *Are We MOOC'd Out? Huffington Post*.

Yu, H., Miao, C., Leung, C., & White, T. J. (2017). Towards AI-powered personalization in MOOC learning. *Science of Learning, Nature Partner Journals, 2*(15). doi:10.103841539-017-0016-3

Chapter 3
The DOPA Model:
Facilitating the Development of Human Factors in IT Project Management

Jonathan Adedayo Odukoya
Covenant University, Nigeria

ABSTRACT

Quality education is arguably the instrument par excellence for national development. Psychological assessment (PA) is an authentic means of monitoring progress and attainment of set goals. Virtually all over the world, teachers and students tend to dance to the tune of psychological assessment. PA tools are therefore potential devices for catalyzing quality education and development. The core objective of this study is to explore the potential of the development-oriented psychological assessment (DOPA) model in catalyzing quality education in IT project management training, thus enhancing the quality of human factor driving it. Documentary analysis design was adopted. The overriding inference drawn from the exploration is that consistent application of the DOPA model holds the potential of enhancing human factors that drive pragmatic IT project management and by extension national development.

INTRODUCTION

The quality of education often determines the quality of development in all spheres of life. Information technology [IT] project management is integral to quality education because of the spate of current global digitalization. IT project management entails the integration of information technology resources of a firm to maximize the attainment of its needs and priorities. The resources often include computer hardware, software, data, networks and data centre facilities, and the staff. This further entails basic management functions like budgeting, organizing, controlling, staffing, as well as software design, network planning and rendering technical support (McNurlin, 2019). Apparently, the human factor is vital in rendering effective IT project management. For instance, a chunk of IT project management requires knowledge of programming and networking. This is a product of quality education cum high intellectual capability. These are vital human factors that ultimately determine the spate of development

DOI: 10.4018/978-1-7998-1279-1.ch003

worldwide. The development of these vital human factors could hardly be complete without pragmatic psychological assessment. The central thesis of this study is that psychological assessment tools can be used to catalyze development. It is this hypothesis that inspired the Development-Oriented Psychological Assessment [DOPA] model.

PSYCHOLOGICAL ASSESSMENT

The American Psychological Association [APA] described psychological assessment as the process of testing that uses a combination of techniques to arrive at some hypothesis about a person's behavior, personality and capabilities. It is the administration of a battery of assessment tools on a person (APA, 2018). The Author posits that psychological assessment constitutes all empirically validated means of collecting psychological data or information to allow for evaluation and deduction of inferences on the trait being measured. Some popular psychological assessment tools are: psychological tests like achievement and aptitude tests, questionnaire, checklist, anecdotal record, interview guideline, focused group discussion guide and observation guide. These are vital tools needed in enhancing quality education that evolve astute IT project managers.

THE DOPA MODEL

What possible model of testing can be adopted by Examining Boards to enhance quality education that could develop the human factors in fields like IT project management?

The DOPA model in Figure 1 seems the most plausible solution.

In the case of IT-PM, the first critical step in the implementation of the DOPA model is the astute assessment of the IT project management curricula in the light of the prevailing company and national needs. The needs will inform what should be reviewed in the curricula. Thereafter, the reviewed curricula

Figure 1.
Source: Odukoya, 2015

is given wide circulation while a special task force is set up to enforce its implementation given that all necessary infrastructure is in place for the implementation of the curriculum. While the first three steps are being implemented, Psychometricians, in conjunction with IT-PM subject experts, shall concurrently commence work on the development and validation of the digital DOPA questions and tools. Concerted and consistent administration of the DOPA tools shall be made without compromise. With time, it is expected that the Trainers and IT-PM Students will naturally align to operating more at the higher levels of cognitive abilities which is apt to birth witty invention, productivity and national development.

Empirical Evidence in Support of DOPA Model

In a critical review of the past examination papers of the West African Examination Council [WAEC] and the University of Cambridge Local Examinations Syndicate (UCLES) for development-oriented questions, Odukoya et al (2014) found that the percentage of recall questions featured by WAEC were consistently higher than comprehension and other higher domain of reasoning, except in 2011. However, Cambridge featured more application questions, many of which were related to real life issues [e.g. 12% to 0% in 12% to 0% in 2013 and 2012 in Physics Objective paper respectively for UCLES and WAEC]. The same trend was observed in Chemistry. Cambridge fielded more questions in the higher domains of reasoning than WAEC [e.g. 100% to 18% in 2013 practical Chemistry; and 34% to 2% in 2013 Chemistry theory paper for UCLES and WAEC respectively].

It was the same pattern in Biology. Cambridge again featured more application questions than WAEC [e.g. 52%, 17% and 20% as against 0%, 0% and 5% in 2013 Practical, Theory and Objective Biology papers respectively]. Except in 2013 where Cambridge featured 60% as against WAEC's 21% application questions, generally there seems to be little or no difference in the proportion of higher cognitive questions fielded in Mathematics by UCLES and WAEC.

Data obtained from interviews and observations revealed virtually the same trend. Though few practical activities with concomitant products were observed in some of the schools visited [e.g. Prototype of Periscope, school magazine and story books written by Teacher and Students in the middle class school; books written by Teachers in the Public school; and liquid soap, disinfectant, and books written by a Teacher and a Student in the Mission Private School; while some of the schools did titration and few gas production], Teachers and Students predominantly have not been consistently engaging in real practical work over the years. Many of the Teachers and Students interviewed confirmed this assertion. For instance, in response to the question: '*How do you prepare for WAEC practical exams*? The students said: '*The past questions are used as guides and teachers provide specimens from the instruction sent by WAEC for the practical sessions*.' One of the Vice Principals, who was also a Chemistry teacher, informed the Researchers that the slot allotted in the scheme for practical work was few, barely twice in a term.

From the findings above, there are indications that real practical works that could birth indigenous productivity and development were lacking in many African training institutions. Learning Facilitators and Students interviewed adduced the following as some of the reasons for this trend: Lack of practical equipment and materials in some schools; low competence of Teachers in terms of skill for conducting real practical works; poor electricity and overloaded curriculum often leading to lack of time to do real practical work; over-population of students in public schools [e.g. a teacher currently teaches over 1000 students at the Final Year of the senior class in the public school visited]; and poor funding of public schools more because of the politicized 'Free' Universal Basic Education.

When pointedly asked, '*Do you agree with the notion that Teachers and Students focus more on topics and activities tested by WAEC?*' The response was a clarion 'YES' in all the schools visited. When further asked, '*Despite your current challenges, what will you do if WAEC begins to field more questions assessing application and practical oriented questions?*' Again the consistent response from everyone interviewed was, '*we shall be left with no choice than to study more around application questions and look for ways to do more practical work.*'

Stated below are samples of Development-oriented Achievement test questions proposed by the Author and extracted from Cambridge examination questions:

Physics

1. A micrometer is used to measure the diameter of a uniform wire [*Diagram of Micrometer gauge gripping a rod displayed*], *what is done to obtain an accurate answer?* [*Source*: Cambridge May 2013 Paper 1 Q 2];
2. Irregular power supply is a major problem in Nigeria today, from your knowledge of electricity generation, proffer a solution to this problem (Odukoya, 2014).

Chemistry

1. This term, you were taught the principle of *saponification*, explain in a step-wise fashion how you will produce soap for your household usage. State all challenges you will likely encounter and how you will overcome such (Odukoya, 2014).
2. Describe, with the aid of an equation, how ethanol is manufactured by fermentation (Cambridge May 2013 Paper 1 – Q B7e)

Biology

1. From your understanding of the factors responsible for growth in plants, explain how weed can be effectively controlled apart from using cutlass, uprooting or herbicide (Odukoya, 2014).
2. Crops can be grown under controlled conditions in large buildings. Describe and explain how such buildings can provide the conditions needed for maximum crop production (Cambridge May 2013 Paper 1 Q 6a).

Mathematics

1. The exchange rate is \$1 to €0.72. Eddie travels from the USA to Germany. He changes \$300 into euros (€). How many euros does he receive? (Cambridge May 2013 Paper 2 – Q 5a(i) UCLES (2013))
2. You are thinking of investing 1,000,000 naira that your uncle recently sent to you. If Treasury Bill offers 3% within a period of three months and your bank offers a fixed deposit interest of 11% per annum, decide on the best line of investment. Support your decision with clear mathematical calculations (Odukoya, 2014).

NEUROSURGEON LICENSING PROCESS

To become a Neurosurgeon in the United States, candidates are expected to take advanced courses in medical diagnostics and surgical practice. At the end of the training, candidates will also complete a residency program and get a medical license. All prospective medical doctors must pass the United States Medical Licensing Examination (USMLE) before practicing medicine.

The USMLE is a 3-step exam. **Step 1** is an 8-hour computerized exam that includes 322 questions, focusing on: Pharmacology; Microbiology; Anatomy; Medicine; Pediatrics; Obstetrics & Gynecology. **Step 2** is a 9-hour exam that features 8 sections of 44 multiple-choice questions that span: Medicine; Surgery; Pediatrics; Psychiatry; Obstetrics & Gynecology. **Step 3** is a 16-hour assessment that is administered over two days. Below are some of the sample medical questions:

1. A 32-year-old woman with type 1 diabetes mellitus has had progressive renal failure over the past 2 years. She has not yet started dialysis. Examination shows no abnormalities. Her hemoglobin concentration is 9 g/dL, hematocrit is 28%, and mean corpuscular volume is 94 μm. A blood smear shows normochromic, normocytic cells. Which of the following is the most likely cause?
    a.   Acute blood loss
    b.   Chronic lymphocytic leukemia
    c.   Erythrocyte enzyme deficiency
    d.   Erythropoietin deficiency
    e.   Immunohemolysis
    f.   Microangiopathic hemolysis
    g.   Polycythemia vera
    h.   Sickle cell disease
    i.   Sideroblastic anemia
    j.   β-Thalassemia trait

Ans: d

2. A 17-year-old boy was brought to the emergency department 30 minutes after being found with a "blank stare" and flat facial expression at a party. His pulse is 72/min, and blood pressure is 104/68mm Hg. He is sitting upright and appears catatonic. Physical examination shows rigidity. During the examination, he becomes hostile and attempts to assault the physician. This patient most likely ingested which of the following drugs?
    a.   Cocaine
    b.   Diazepam
    c.   Methamphetamine
    d.   Oxycodone
    e.   PCP (phencyclidine)

Ans: e

3.   A 14-year-old girl has had nausea, intermittent diarrhea, and a 2.2-kg (5-lb) weight loss over the past 4 weeks. Examination shows a migrating serpiginous pruritic perianal rash. Her leukocyte count is 8000/mm with 20% eosinophils. Which of the following tests is most likely to yield an accurate diagnosis?

a.   Blood smear
b.   Bone marrow biopsy
c.   KOH preparation
d.   Microscopic examination of the stool
e.   Skin snip

Ans: d

Source: USMLE (2019)

These sample questions shows that even multiple choice objective test formats can be used to assess higher levels of reasoning. These are hardly any recall or sole comprehension questions, though the higher cognitive questions naturally assess for the two lowest levels of cognitive abilities [i.e. recall and comprehension]. Further note that virtually all the questions assess real-life issues. For a life sensitive profession like Medicine, one should hardly expect anything less. The quality of examination questions is often directly related with the quality of learning and productivity. The singular act of publicly fielding development-oriented practice questions of this nature is apt to naturally incline students and learning facilitators to focus more on the same curriculum content and so provoke attendant productivity.

These are the kind of questions proposed for consistent usage in the DOPA model, especially in achievement, aptitude and performance tests. When these levels of questions are consistently presented in formative and summative examinations, students and teachers are apt to work along the same line at virtually any level of domain of education . In the long run, this is bound to promote national development.

These DOPA questions formats, when consistently applied in the training and certification process of IT project management students, are apt to produce more effective IT project managers that will provoke greater national development. This is the critical human factor that is expected to galvanize the development of IT project management and national development.

FINDINGS AND DISCUSSION

From the surmises so far, the following core findings are made:

1.   There is hardly any productivity and development drive, including IT project management, that is void of psychological assessment, and by extension human factor. The reason is apparent, as long as human beings are involved, psychological assessment is imperative.
2.   Almost in all cases, the assessment questions that provoke productivity and development tend to address real life issues and scenarios. This explains why virtually all the USMLE questions were real life patient scenarios. Teachings and assessments that adopt real life scenarios are apt to deliver more useful results in terms of productivity and development any day.
3.   Whenever real life scenarios are used in assessments, it is almost imperative that higher cognitive levels of reasoning – such as *application, analysis, synthesis, evaluation* and *creativity* – are tasked. These are the level of reasoning that naturally birth useful products and inventions.

4. The need for assessment and application of personality profiles in workplaces is also a recurrent issue. Virtually all jobs in workplaces have peculiar personality traits mix that make it to thrive. Correct early identification of such traits and allowing the information to guide the recruitment and retention process is crucial to business and project success.

As mentioned earlier, the core hypothesis that prompted this study is that *Learning Facilitators and Students tend to concentrate on topics that examining board repeatedly examine*. In other words, they dance to the rhythm of examinations. It was further noted that presently, Learning Facilitators and Students in many developing nations are not doing much of real practical work, when compared with their counterpart in developed countries, largely because their respective Examining Boards were not fielding enough true application/real practical questions that could provoke application, creativity, innovation and inventions. The hypothesis goes further to postulate that if the Examining Boards begin to consistently field more application questions, in a matter of years, the concerned developing nations will begin to evolve witty inventions that would translate to indigenous productivity and development.

The findings in this study tend to support the speculation that perhaps one of the secrets of development in developed countries like the United Kingdom could be the practice of Examining Boards like Cambridge in consistently fielding questions that assess higher domains of educational objectives as postulated by Bloom (1956). This inclination is apt to motivate Learning Facilitators and Students to tilt more towards higher level of reasoning while preparing for examinations. The short term and long term effect of such practice is increasingly better practical exercises leading to more productivity and development.

It is important to note that it is the *application* of the principles and laws in Physics, Chemistry, Biology and related science/technology subjects that birthed many of the goods and services that are enhancing standard of living around the world today. It is these inventions that make for human, capital and economic development worldwide (ILO, 2008). Of-course, application of social science principles also make for vital traits like peace and team cohesion, without which nothing works. These are the vital human factors necessary in effective IT program management.

From these findings in this study, it can be argued that one of the strong precursors of poor practical work in schools is not necessarily lack of materials or time but lack of *willpower*. It appears the 'willpower' can be ignited by examining boards via consistent fielding of more development-oriented questions that assesses higher levels of educational objectives, and especially application questions relating to real life issues. With such willpower in place, no 'mountain of challenge will be too high to surmount. Henry Ford, Thomas Edison, Wright Brothers, among other great inventors, are testimonies to this assertion.

It is imperative that examination bodies wake up to their responsibility. There are continuous dynamic changes in nature and nurture, from which literally all things are birthed, hence the need to constantly review and change the assessment systems. Any organization that refuses to move with the tide of time may be lost with time. With the advent of the ICT, there is clear information explosion all over the world. One cannot afford to be static, hence the urgent need to review current teaching and testing methods in developing countries like Nigeria as enunciated in the DOPA model.

CONCLUSION AND RECOMMENDATION

In this paper, an exploration of the potential of the DOPA model as it relates to personal, community and national development was made. The exercise suggests, among others, that sustainable development is hardly possible without concerted and consistent application of development-oriented psychological assessment. The application of psychological assessment within organizations and professions [such as IT Project Management] noted for productivities that make for national development is likely to achieve this feat. The DOPA model is apt to catalyze the development of the essential human factors required in IT project management, among others. It is therefore recommended that concerted effort should be made to consistently adopt the DOPA model in IT project management trainings because it addresses the essential human factors required for success in the field.

REFERENCES

APA. (2018). *Definition of Psychology*. Retrieved from http://www.apa.org/support/about-apa.aspx - 20/4/18

Baker, F. B. (1985). *The Basics of Item Response Theory*. Heinemann.

Bloom, B. (1956). *Taxonomy of Educational Objectives*. Handbook One.

UCLES, . (2013). *Cambridge International General Secondary Certificate Examination*. London: Cambridge Examination Board.

ILO. (2008). Skills for Improved Productivity, Employment Growth and Development. In *International Labour Conference Proceeding* (97th Session). Geneva: ILO.

McNurlin, B. (2009). *Information Systems Management in Practice* (8th ed.). Prentice Hall.

Odukoya, J. A. (2014). *Comparative Analysis of Cambridge O-Levels and WAEC O-Levels examination questions*. Unpublished Paper.

Odukoya, J. A. (2015). *Development Oriented Teaching Testing Model*. Unpublished Paper.

USMLE. (2019). *United States Medical Licensing Examination – Sample Questions*. Retrieved online: https://www.usmle.org/step-1/

Chapter 4
Skills and Competencies of Information Technology Professionals:
A Systematic Literature Review

Suchitra Ajgaonkar
Symbiosis International University, India

Netra Neelam
Symbiosis International University, India

ABSTRACT

Information technology (IT) is a vital source of economic growth across developed and developing countries. Skill gaps are significant barriers to technology adoption by many industries; therefore, this chapter reviews research studies sampling IT professionals to identify a whole gamut of IT professionals' skills and competencies. This systematic literature review comprises of exhaustive search for articles through Scopus database with empirical evidence or theoretical models meant for working IT professionals. Critical analysis of prominent papers is done to bring forth existing research categories (typology) and furnish generic as well as specific skills and competencies. This study attempts to become a resource for integration of IT professional capability research and a comprehensive report for researchers, practitioners, educators, and institutions. Tables containing list of publishing journals, country- and industry-wise article distribution, and prominent paper methodology are provided.

INTRODUCTION

Businesses are continually evolving in a fast paced environment resulting from advancements in technologies, newer business practices and ever changing social situations including geopolitics (Goles, Hawk, & Kaiser, 2008). It is now well-established through various sources that Information and Communication Technology (ICT) is immensely capable of transforming economies; therefore businesses need to invest

DOI: 10.4018/978-1-7998-1279-1.ch004

in IT infrastructure as it is a vital source of economic growth, both in developed and developing economies. ICTs drive social and economic development by generating employment at both global and local level (Global IT report, 2015; Jorgenson & Vu, 2005). In 2015, Economic and Social Affairs Department (United Nations) have claimed that within a decade, internet provision at households have increased twice as much, that gives 46% homes the ability to connect with the world using an online platform. This expansion affirms ICT as 'critical drivers' in the mission to accomplish sustainable development goals.

In 2018, Future of Jobs Report (World Economic Forum) have emphasized that significant skill gaps at local level have impacted negatively on adoption of technology in a range of industries. The report delineates ICT, aviation and financial services, a few among those facing the outcome of the skill gap menace. Consequently, IT professionals will have to upgrade their knowledge and skills to survive, adapt and thrive in the ever changing IT industry (Mahatanankoon, 2007).

In addition to the skill gap problem, the demographics of IT professionals are now seeing changes due to a mix of events such as: global outsourcing, retirements of earlier generations and decreased admissions to universities, this calls for changes in IT capabilities desired by IT function (Bullen, Abraham, Gallagher, Simon & Zwieg, 2009; Hawk et al., 2012). This is not limited to developed countries even developing countries need to address the skills gap, changes and upgradation at all levels. In-depth interviews conducted by Kong, Chadee and Raman (2013) revealed that in developing countries like India, students passing from universities are not industry ready and therefore organizations find it difficult to deploy them quickly on live projects, costing several months of training. Ironically, organizations loose these trained professionals in market competition. In light of this, universities and colleges need the right perspective from experienced IT professionals, especially skills and competencies required by organizations that could help students make the right career choices, and furthermore, individuals will continue upgrading to increase their marketability (Hawk et al., 2012).

Hawk et al. (2012) places an argument on the worldwide acceptance of the notion that IT professionals should be equipped with a 'combination of diverse skills' (p.3); however no research studies address the fundamental problem of identifying and grouping exact skills. This has resulted in the inability to consistently draw differences and similarities among skill categories across different periods of time, as a consequence IT skills research lacks integration and a summative theory construction.

This insight makes this systematic literature review an important step toward classifying IT skills and competency studies done on working IT professionals, and put forth a table of typologies of relevant research studies. The intention is to encourage future research to consider a unifying theory construction and testing.

ORGANIZATION OF PAPER

This literature review paper guides the reader with an understanding as to why this topic needs attention; as per author's knowledge, there is no such consolidated literature review till date. Further, the readers are informed about the steps involved in the review process along with full selection criteria of the relevant research papers. A list of typology of research papers along with its definitions gives a preview to subsequent analysis of the themes. Each theme describes findings relevant to the specific themes which benefits IT professional, as they develop an understanding of existing work on skills and competencies of IT professionals. Thereafter, limitations of this study is followed by a brief conclusion. Additionally, tables provide the list of Scopus indexed journals that have published these papers, an industry and country wise distribution of papers, and prominent paper methodology. This study attempts to become a resource for integration of IT professional capability research and a comprehensive report for researchers, practitioners, educators and institutions.

RESEARCH METHODOLOGY

Literature Search

Research papers that sample IT professionals and their skills and competencies were screened encompassing studies from all sectors. Only research articles and reviews from journals are selected, and the search is restricted to Scopus database. Therefore, all research papers included in this study are Scopus-indexed from peer-reviewed journals and not a part of grey literature.

Selection Process and Identification Criteria

The search is exhaustive using multiple keywords: 'Information technology professional', 'Career and information technology', 'Career and IT workforce', 'Career and IT personnel', 'IT personnel', 'IT workforce', 'Employability and information technology', 'IT Labor', 'Employability and IT Labor', 'Career and IT Industry', 'Employability and IT industry'. The keywords have matched title, abstract or keywords field in Scopus database hence obtained full reference. Furthermore, publication date is not restricted to avail a meaningful interpretation of important themes.

A total of 930 documents were retrieved from Scopus database by applying filters such as articles, reviews, journals and English language. EID numbers of documents were arranged in descending order in excel sheet and any duplicates and blank abstracts were removed, which retrieved 774 documents. Both the authors read the title and abstracts of each paper, further grouped them into relevant and non-relevant to our research study. Only those research papers were marked as relevant where samples included IT professionals. There are a huge number of papers that have sampled IT graduates and talk about industry demands, however this study aims to only include studies done specifically on working IT professionals. Working IT professionals share their work experience as well as IT and non-IT organizations share their perspective first hand, which is practical and of greater relevance. With this reason in mind, authors found 604 relevant research papers.

As a next step, authors read title and abstracts of research papers and grouped them on the basis of theme similarity. It included broader themes beyond just skills and competencies: skill development, gender, education, compensation, employability, organizational commitment etc. Further, themes were refined to narrow down the search criteria, so only research papers that included IT skills and competencies were picked. Research papers that focused on gender, compensation etc. did not fit the purpose of our study, therefore excluded.

Specific themes to classify research studies on skills and competencies of IT professionals were identified. The papers that studied any skills and competencies which enables better business outcome and /or describes skills and competencies that IT workforce should possess were found relevant. Thus 121 research papers were grouped together under relevant themes out of which 69 were found as important research papers to be included as part of our study; out of these 41 prominent papers with most citations or a necessary perspective have become part of the theme discussion and analysis.

Table 1. Typology (cluster of themes) and definitions

Typology	Definition
Variety of Skills	A list of skillset that vary with each other at construct level but are grouped as relevant to IT professional's repertoire
Competency model	A cluster of competencies expected from IT workforce to meet the business needs
Agility	Organization or individual's ability to cope with the ever changing external environment
Infrastructure capability/flexibility	Capability of IT professionals to build IT infrastructure flexible, so as to connect, adjust and modify software inside and outside of firms
Expertise	Learning to do better and gain mastery
Soft skills	A group of skills that enable effective work relationships other than technical skills and business related competencies
Social skills/capital	Informal mechanisms for interaction and collaboration for projects
Client / provider firm capability	Differing or converging IT professionals capability on account of their employment in client or IT provider firms
Interfirm capability	IT professionals build their careers as they move from one organization to another by gaining skills
Innovation	Ability to initiate new services and processes for maximizing firm's profitability and competitiveness
Knowledge sharing /transfer	Knowledge sharing, transfer or renewal capability of IT professionals
User / consumer understanding	Ability to understand user or customer needs and work with them to create useful infrastructure
Data oriented decision making	Ability to understand data oriented decision making for building analytics capability
Freelancer skills	Skills required to work on temporary projects or consultancy in a firm with contract relationship
Sustainability	IT professional's ability to reduce carbon footprint and energy wastage through integrated environment sustainability management practices
Technology / Tasks	A list of technologies that is the current and future trend on which individuals need to be skilled to remain employable

THEME DISCUSSION

Variety of Skills

A range of studies focus on the pressing importance of having a variety of skills by IT professionals to help them adapt to modern times. Gallagher et al. (2010) describes this as "law of requisite variety" (p.144) which is valued by today's employers because it serves many benefits; employees with variety of skills in their repertoire can work through complexity in problems, identifying significant opportunities and adapt quickly to perpetual changes.

More contribution to this variety of skills view comes from Kim et al. (2011), their study delineates the dimensions of IT expertise that includes technical skill, technology management, business, functional and interpersonal skills; IT expertise is required to facilitate evolution of infrastructure flexibility, however IT management capabilities mediate as they structure and control the IT experts for effective utilization.

To promote variety of skills view researchers sought to understand variety of technical skills and non-technical skills demonstrated by new entrants and mid-level employees, extending up to the level of CIO (Gallagher et al., 2010; Kappelman, 2016) Not restricting to core IT companies, researchers have investigated in manufacturing units; personal interviews of IT managers have revealed attributes and its significance in developing business knowledge and competence. The six attributes are: skills that support operational effectiveness; technology (tech savvy); proactive personality; responsiveness; ability to communicate; quality management; and being realistic (Jaska & Hogan, 2006);

At a national level, it is narrated that Japan's government have promulgated Information Technology Skill Standards (ITSS) that provides clearly organized list of abilities expected of IT professionals. An analysis of ITSS was performed through text mining technique that draws a skills update and reskill road map to enable diversion in career path or adapt to a job transition (El–Agamy & Tsuda, 2013).

Competency Model

Skill development requires an understanding of competencies expected from the workforce to meet the business needs; competency models can be developed not only for specific organizations but also for IT professionals across organizations. The workforce can benefit from knowing what competencies are required for IT professionals to be successful in the industry.

Ho and Frampton (2010) have developed a competency model by interviewing those who have important roles in IT architecture. The competency model consists of skills: analytical thinking and problem-solving, effectiveness of communication, conceptual and abstract thinking, managing situational politics; knowledge: technical know-how, knowledge update via experiential learning, comprehensive and contextual knowledge; self-concept, traits and motives. This research has introduced competency models for IT workforce in the literature; traditionally job analysis frameworks has been used which are task focused. IT professionals are often hired for projects in which teams are formed comprising different functional areas of the organization, therefore there is a need for broad professional competence framework, with behavioral expectancies clearly defined and not just aligning with specific set of tasks and responsibilities (Bassellier & Benbasat, 2004).

In this regard, Bassellier and Benbasat (2004) emphasized that IT professionals have a pressing need to work in collaboration with different functional areas; such an effort requires IT specialists to develop a common conceptual understanding and a language familiar to all functions, this unity should meet business requirements; profiling the broader expertise in IT professionals is instrumental for business partnerships, especially business competence. This justifies the need for a model of business competence for partnerships with clients.

Based on thorough literature review, Heidary et al. (2018) derived a competency model comprising of several competencies such as social, personal, subject, method and entrepreneurial competency, which were verified by experts.

Agility

By agility, we mean IT dependent organizational agility, which is defined by Neumann and Fink (2007) as the capability (organizational) to cope with the changes in its external environment; organizations need to respond by making changes in their strategy and leveraging operational efficiency in a quick and effective way.

Neuman and Fink (2007) being a prominent study highlights that capabilities of IT professionals is a vital source for building the organization wide IT infrastructure; it supports business processes to become dynamic in order to face uncertainties of the ever evolving external environment. Thus, this line of research confirms that technical and behavioral competencies of IT professionals have a positive outcome on the infrastructure capabilities, and that business knowledge may not be the crucial element. Behavioral competencies are important to develop relationships with business clients to plan, manage and execute via multidisciplinary approach.

Building on this research, Lowry and Wilson (2016) investigated IT agility as a positive service environment; their investigation reaffirms that the quality of services by IT professionals' leads to an agile environment; when employees perceive services provided by the IT of the organization as positive, it has an effect on organizational agility. Other relevant studies, have included variables such as human IT capability and knowledge management to relate to organizational agility (Panda & Rath, 2017; Panda & Rath, 2018)

Infrastructure Capability

To be agile it is imperative to be flexible, Chanopas et al. (2006) studied and defined IT infrastructure flexibility; the definition of IT infrastructure flexibility takes into account adaptation to external environment, but in order to do so, it involves more concepts such as information sharing, development of systems and perpetual operational efficiency.

For such flexibility, Byrd et al. (2004) confirms that IT professionals must demonstrate the capability of experimentation to build flexible information systems that brings competitive advantage. The three dimensions identified for infrastructure flexibility can be described as: connecting internal and external systems, sharing information types across varying technologies, and configuration and modifying of any software or hardware without difficulty, respectively (Byrd et al., 2004; Zhang & Ziegelmayer, 2009). It is noteworthy to say that, IT managers have an important role in developing organization's physical capabilities (services such as channeling client systems, IT security, data management, enabling applications, and offering infrastructure facility) to work on infrastructure projects, therefore managerial skills facilitate strategic and competitive gains (Fink & Neumann, 2009)

Zhang and Ziegelmayer (2009) have studied the impact of infrastructure flexibility and IT professional capability on IT responsiveness of Small and Medium Enterprises (SME); their literature review discussion summarizes SMEs struggle to sustain in ever changing and competitive business environment and build systems and processes to help adjust with market demands; authors confirm that SMEs use simple information systems to begin with. IT responsiveness is defined as IT capability to fulfill the demands by internal to fulfill the demands of internal as well as external environment. It encompasses several stakeholders: end-users support for work processes, managerial decision making, and working products for business process changes. The study corroborates that modularity dimension and IT professional's capability primarily showcasing relevant competencies drive IT responsiveness - it means that all stakeholders are satisfied with the outcome of the IT infrastructure; it further elaborates on the interdependency of each dimension of infrastructure flexibility.

Expertise

Professional expertise of IT professionals has been described by Morello (2005) whose conceptual framework is used in research in two developing nations, namely, Myanmar and Vietnam. Organizations across multiple sectors ranked each skill according to its current and future importance; IT professional's expertise include, IT infrastructure, managing information design, process and structure, client relationship and sourcing, and personal attributes. Authors further segregated roles into generalists, specialists and versatility (Lau et al., 2013; Lau et al., 2016). A lack of studies under this theme needs immediate attention; future research studies should focus on expertise development of IT professional's specific skills and competencies.

Soft Skills

Back in 2006, researchers note that companies have confirmed the essentiality of soft skills as an important characteristic sought in new entrants in the industry; especially important in placing low-skilled job seekers (Chapple, 2006).

Soft skills that have been traditionally valued at management levels specifically top levels, are now an essential skill at all levels of IT workforce including the service level. There is a growing concern among organizations for emotional intelligence and effective communication skills among IT professionals; researchers confirm that in the past, study of emotional intelligence and adaptation in terms of communication has been done only in relation with leadership studies, organizational or industrial psychology and generation studies. However, even service level employees require this at the optimal level to make their messages successfully accepted by the receiver (Hendon, Powell & Wimmer, 2017).

Dimensions of soft skills construct is extended further, a research based on Wagner and Sternberg taxonomy, studied IT practical intelligence with only four dimensions: managing tasks, career and self as well as others. This study compared expert and novice IT professionals; critical incidents were derived by interviewing 37 senior managers and further validated by 122 IT experts and novices. Researchers found that expert IT professionals scored better than novices by exceeding number of responses, utilizing lesser time to generate large repertoire of responses and that too of higher quality; thus showcasing differing levels of practical intelligence (Joseph et al., 2010)

In another important study, job advertisements were coded and nine skills were identified for job roles such as system analyst, and software designer, programmer and tester: raising communication standard, interpersonal understanding, analytical thinking, problem-solving ability, and demonstrating behaviors like being a team player, ability to organize data, quick learning, working independently; innovativeness, openness to new experiences and adaptability to situations (Ahmed et al., 2012)

Social Skills / Capital

Relationship between social and intellectual capital and organizational advantage – a theoretical model designed by Nahapiet and Goshal (1998) forms the basis of a case study by Reich and Kaarst-Brown (2003). The case study uses the theoretical model with some extensions to the model, namely the enablers and inhibitors.

King et al. (2005) researched upon socialization practices at corporates, they tried to examine its impact on IT professionals' adjustment in their organizational roles. Researchers stress that a variety of socialization tactics affect IT professionals differently, therefore one-size-fits all approaches may not be the best. IT professionals have already imbibed strong personal characteristics and practiced several skillset before they are employed by the organization; nevertheless, social capital helps an IT professional make the role adjustment. Specifically, socialization causes better role adjustment by reducing role conflict.

Social Networking Sites (SNS) are actively participating in organizational communication these days. Koch et al. (2012) investigated the implementation of an internal social networking site for a finance-based company to encourage engagement of newly joined IT professionals. The research used a case study approach utilizing the theory of positive emotions; it describes the impact of the newly implemented site on employees as well as the organization.

Study done by Schlosser et al. (2015) make us understand that social alignment between business and IT staff helps project based interaction as well as collaboration to run smoothly, which supports effective delivery of project work; not only this, the IT professionals also comprehend business practices. These informal mechanisms aligning social embeddedness through "joint documentation, joint meetings and joint trainings" (p.119-130) helps increase social alignment and facilitate knowledge transfer.

Further, there is empirical evidence to show that business senior management and IT staff must strengthen their relationships for business success and this facilitation should be treated as a business imperative. Manfreda and Indihar (2018) studied business and IT staff relationship using in-depth interviews followed by survey questionnaires to IT managers. Their interviews revealed that a gap prevails and this has implications for organizational performance in this digital era. Their survey results specify that trust and open communication with integrity and mutual cooperation has a positive impact on the knowledge base of managers; the more the IT managers become business oriented and more the top business executives value IT, the more effective is the relationship between the two. They then see each other as partners in business. The study applied social exchange theory to point out the need for social indicators for better business outcomes.

Client / Provider Firm Capability

IT organizations that provide IT services and products are called as providers and organizations who are the customers of these organizations, they are called clients; employees who work for both providers and clients need to satisfy demand for IT skills. This area of research have pointed out that both clients and provider firms draw from the same pool of talent; wherein some firms look for niche skills whereas others hire those with broader skill set and repertoire (Hawk et al., 2012).

A professional association called Society for Information Management (SIM) conducted a self-funded research project to comprehend IT skills desired by client and provider organizations globally. The two phases of research is detailed, in the first phase data were collected from client firms and in second phase from provider firms; the results of this project shows that a lot of skill demands from client firms converge with skill demands from provider firms. Client firms demand technical skill such as programming, system analysis and system design, from new hires at entry-level positions so that they can be absorbed in IT projects at an operational or infrastructure implementation level; soft skills also have become the foundation skills required for such roles. However, provider firms apart from technical and soft skills at entry-level desire project management skills; additionally, working with virtual teams and user relationship management are the most sought after skills. For mid-level employees, both provider as well as client firms, demand project management, business critical and client facing technical skills (Bullen et al., 2019). Provider firms demand greater project management skills whereas client firms demand finer business-oriented skills from employees; this difference can be owed to differing industry type or company objectives, therefore providers value customer relationships and clients do not place any such emphasis on managing relationships with providers (Hawk et al., 2012).

Interfirm Capability

Not only gaining skills in one single organization is the way to go forward, Bidwell and Briscoe (2010) have clarified that workers can now build their careers as they move from one organization to another gaining skills, building network and procuring positive image essential for jobs outside their immediate workplace. Authors further describe that IT professionals also show preference for working in certain companies in their early careers over others; this also depends on what career development opportunities each of the organizations have to offer them. In particular, individuals prefer to work in large organizations to develop skills base early on and later join "occupationally intensive industries" (p.1038) where they apply skills developed in large organizations. This interfirm mobility sets the trajectory for flow of knowledge and experience across organizations where some loose talent and some organizations gain talent. Interestingly, it is beneficial to IT professionals who take important decisions of transition for skill development appropriate to their career stage.

Not only interfirm mobility, but interfirm relationships are studied by researchers; interfirm relationships between two organizations conclude as strategic alliance and joint ventures. This collaboration between firms is highly complex and is affected by IT technical expertise as well as IT professional capabilities (Patrakosol & Lee, 2009).

Innovation

Kong (2013) defined innovation as a process where employees and departments initiate new services and redesign processes that gives the firm competitive advantage and in turn greater revenue. The author have emphasized that human resources are critical contributors to innovation especially in industries that are knowledge intensive and operate on employee contribution.

Fiet et al. (2017) states the value of systematic search and defines innovation as "the act of commercializing a promising idea" and can be extended as a planned action of search, discovery and development. To come up with a new venture proposal, entrepreneurs and technology managers, can find it useful to do systematic search to help them fulfill the criteria of a good fit, value and inimitability for a viable business project. This study used an experimental methodology, the results have practical importance to technology managers; managers can showcase effective entrepreneurial skills by following the stated theoretical model of discovery: look for information in domains in which they have prior experience or have a sound knowledge base, organize rich information into meaningful sets, formulate effective search strategies and create decision rules to venture.

In-depth interviews conducted by Kong (2013) uncovered many practice areas for innovation in IT: problems in IT organizations need creative resolution through improvement in business processes, value client-orientation and additional reengineering; employee's knowledge and capacity to quickly learn, in short agility, helps showcase 'domain expertise' (p.338) which is essential to achieve innovative practices and create sustainable business; it is expected to keep up high standards of quality services consistently; not limiting to paper work, any new knowledge or method that can be useful to existing clients should be proactively shared with clients.

Table 2. Sample of IT skills and competency related articles in this research paper

Journals	Articles = 69
ARPN Journal of Engineering and Applied Sciences	1
Behaviour and Information Technology	1
Career Development International	1
Communications of the ACM	3
Communications of the Association for Information Systems	3
Computers in Human Behavior	1
Data Base for Advances in Information Systems	1
Decision Support Systems	1
Electronic Journal of Information Systems in Developing Countries	1
European Journal of Information Systems	2
European Journal of Operational Research	1
Human Factors and Ergonomics In Manufacturing	2
Human Resource Management	1
Industrial Management & Data systems	1
Information and Management	3
Information Resources Management Journal (IRMJ)	1
Information Systems Management	2
Information Technology and People	1
Informing Science	1
International Journal of Bio-Medical Computing	1
International Journal of Business Information Systems	2
International Journal of Computer Applications in Technology	1
International Journal of Human Capital and Information Technology Professionals	2
International Journal of Information Management	1
International Journal of Information Quality	2
International Journal of Information Systems and Change Management	1
International Journal of Management Practice	1
International Journal of Pharmacy and Technology	1
International Journal of Urban and Regional Research	1
IT Professional	1
Journal of Cleaner Production	1
Journal of Computer Information Systems	1
Journal of Engineering and Technology Management - JET-M	1
Journal of Global Information Management	1
Journal of Global Information Technology Management	1
Journal of Industrial Engineering and Management	1
Journal of Information Technology	1
Journal of International Management	1

continued on the following page

Table 2. Continued

Journals	Articles = 69
Journal of Management and Organization	1
Journal of Management Information Systems	2
Journal of Organizational and End User Computing	1
Journal of Organizational Computing and Electronic Commerce	1
Journal of Research and Practice in Information Technology	1
Journal of the American Society for Information Science	1
Journal of the Association of Information Systems	3
Knowledge Management Research and Practice	1
Management Research News	2
Management Research Review	1
MIS Quarterly: Management Information Systems	1
Organization Science	1
Personnel Review	1
RAE Revista de Administracao de Empresas	1
Transportation Research Record	1

Knowledge Sharing / Transfer / Renewal

Knowledge sharing is looked upon as knowledge to be exchanged bi-directionally whereas knowledge transfer is disseminating pertinent knowledge in one direction. The study of knowledge sharing uses the theory of social interdependence wherein people interact with each other expecting goal, task and reward interdependencies; these interdependencies strongly impact knowledge sharing efforts during information systems development projects more than any other variable of relevance including project complexity, team size and contract type (Pee et al., 2010).

Knowledge transfer across clients and vendors were studied by Park et al. (2011), their study operationalized knowledge transfer as a process where clients gain, comprehend and use the knowledge residing with IT vendors to whom projects are being outsourced; factors affecting knowledge transfer comprised of behavioral indicators such as trust, integrity and benevolence.

The third subcategory identified under this theme is knowledge renewal, IT professionals will have to renew knowledge to meet consistently rising technological demands; researchers have found two typical career orientations – technical competence career orientation and the managerial competence career orientation, former strongly predicts renewal effectiveness. Specifically, professional activities have a larger impact whereas knowledge acquisition for structural organizational mechanisms have lesser impact on knowledge renewal of employees (Rong & Grover, 2009). Given this insight, it can be concluded that professional activities such as participation in professional conferences, building professional networks does enhance an IT professional's interest in knowledge renewal.

Table 3. Industry coverage of 41 articles analyzed

Industry type	Articles
Diverse (across various industries)	16
Banking & Finance	16
Manufacturing	12
IT services/ consulting/software development/	23
Telecommunication/media/advertising	8
Transportation/Tourism	9
Healthcare	7
Insurance	6
Real Estate	3
Government/municipalities	6

Table 4. Country wise distribution of 41 articles analyzed

Country	Articles
USA	21
Israel	2
Thailand	2
Australia, New Zealand	2
Myanmar, Vietnam	2
Canada	1
China	1
Germany	1
Japan	1
Korea	1
India	1
Iran	1
Malaysia	1
Singapore	1
Slovenia	1
Sweden	1
United Kingdom	1

User / Consumer Understanding

Employees who use the Information Systems are referred to as 'users' (Santhanam et al., 2007). Social identity theory is applicable here; IT professionals' should have the ability to understand user needs or consumer requirements for project development and implementation, for a cohesive work environment. Social identity is useful in explaining why responsiveness toward user needs can help achieve greater

Table 5. Typology and prominent paper details

Typology and no. of papers	Prominent papers	Citations in Scopus	Methodology
Variety of skills (9)	Kim et al., 2011	144	Field Survey, (N=243 directors and senior managers – IT and non-IT)
	Kappelman et al., 2016	9	Survey questionnaire (N=312) Society for Information Management (SIM) members
	Gallagher et al., 2010	39	Semi structured interview (N=104 academicians and senior IT managers)
Competency Model (4)	Bassellier & Benbasat, 2004	321	Questionnaire (N=109; IT professionals)
	Ho & Frampton, 2010	4	Semi structured interviews (N=14 IT architects)
	Heidary et al., 2018	5	N=3 Expert evaluation
Agility (4)	Neumann & Fink, 2007	131	Web-based survey (N=293 IT managers)
	Lowry & Wilson, 2016	17	Survey (N=400 IT managers and executives)
Infrastructure Capability (6)	Fink & Neumann, 2009	97	Survey (N=293; IT managers)
	Chanopas, 2006	44	Expert interviews (N=11) Field surveys (N=388)
	Byrd et al., 2004	40	Survey (N=207 executives)
	Zhang & Ziegelmayer, 2009	16	Survey (N=233 SME owners and managers)
Expertise (2)	Lau et al., 2013; Lau et al., 2016	4	Field Survey (N=29 organizations; CIO, IS manager, Project Manager)
Soft skills (4)	Joseph et al., 2010	51	Interviews (N=39) IT professionals (N=122)and IT students
	Ahmed et al., 2012	35	Surveys of job advertisements (N= Workopolis.ca; eurojobs.com; monsterindia.com; seek.com.au)
	Chapple, 2006	10	Surveys (N=298) jobseekers; in-depth interviews (N=93) training program graduates
	Hendon et al., 2017	4	Quantitative non-experimental correlational analysis (N=111)
Social Skill (12)	Koch et al., 2012	81	Case study with interviews (N=1 organization)
	King et al., 2005	28	Survey (N=93 firms, N=187 responses)
	Schlosser et al., 2015	20	Survey (N=132 US Bank managers)
	Reich & Kaarst-Brown, 2003	31	Case study (N=1)
	Manfreda & Indihar, 2018		Survey questionnaire (N=221 IT managers)
Client / provider firm capability (3)	Bullen et al., 2009	22	1st phase (N=104 senior executives – client companies); 2nd phase (N=126 providers)
	Hawk et al., 2012	11	Same as above
Interfirm Capability (2)	Bidwell & Briscoe, 2010	51	Telephonic Interview (N= 2369 IT professionals with IT major degree)
	Patrakosol & Lee, 2009	21	Survey (N=175 IT managers)
Innovation (3)	Kong et al., 2013	9	Semi-structured in-depth interviews (N=11 senior executives of ITSP)
	Fiet et al., 2007	25	Controlled Experiment (N=54 IT professionals)

continued on the following page

Table 5. Continued

Typology and no. of papers	Prominent papers	Citations in Scopus	Methodology
Knowledge Transfer (7)	Pee et al., 2010	77	Survey (N=105 Infrastructure System Development project teams)
	Park et al., 2011	43	Survey (N=87 projects; 338 responses -192 clients and 146 vendors)
	Rong & Grover, 2009	19	Survey (N=126 IT professionals)
Use / consumer understanding (9)	Santhanam et al., 2007	44	Participant Observation – qualitative coding and analysis (N=61 users, N=11 technical support staff)
	Gefen & Ridings, 2003	48	Survey (N=138; IT users)
	Lárusdóttir et al., 2014	14	Semi structured interviews (N=21; usability specialists, Scrum managers, team and business specialist)
Data oriented decision making (2)	Power, 2008	58	Literature review
	Vidgen et al., 2017	35	Delphi technique and semi-structured interviews (N=3 case organizations)
Freelancer skills (1)	Süß & Becker, 2013	3	Semi-structured interview (N=23)
Sustainability (3)	Wang et al., 2015	45	Survey (N=151 manufacturing firms; IT and business executives)
	Ojo et al., 2019	1	Survey (N=332, IT professionals in ISO14001 certified IT companies)
Technology/ Tasks (1)	Kim Lau et al., 1999		Survey (N=21; IT professionals)

support from new users who see IT projects as a genuine support for their day-to-day operations and processes. The study elaborates the inter-group dynamics between IT department and IT users, concluding that it increases acceptance of IT (Geffen & Ridings, 2003)

In a similar vein, researchers studied users and IT professional's interaction patterns but more specific to knowledge transfers between the two stakeholders and within them, namely intergroup communication between users and IT professionals, and intragroup communication within each of the two groups. The study examined workflow application in a bank that processed loan documents online and round the clock from any office. Training programs were conducted and a helpdesk support system established, the empirical evidence shows that users communicate both with IT professionals as well as other users, however what differs is the content of the knowledge shared; intergroup communication were of 'know-what and 'know-how' type whereas intra-users group communicated over 'know-why' (p.182) of the IT project. End user support remains an important tool that helps foster innovation, comprehend business processes and introduce newer business practices (Santhanam et al., 2007).

An extension of user centered approach is specified in the research on Scrum development process; IT professionals require the capability to do user-centric assessments over three dimensions of usability practices: effectiveness, efficiency and satisfaction along with subjective user experience. Semi-structured interview with Scrum teams have provided qualitative data, the interviews reveal that Scrum teams emphasize on collecting qualitative data from users, as it is difficult to collect and analyze quantitate data from users after each sprint because there are only minor changes between two sprints (Lárusdóttir et al., 2014).

Data Oriented Decision Making

There is theoretical literature available that details IT professional involvement and importance in business intelligence and developing data driven IT support systems to augment the power of taking decisions. Power et al. (2008) write in detail how IT professional's deployment on business intelligence projects support work processes such as 'operational performance' (p.153), these systems have special value to multinational organizations.

There is some empirical support for the claim that IT professionals are involved in projects for data –driven decision making. Vidgen et al. (2017) used Delphi technique to find that business analytic teams in organizations need IT professionals who are responsible for developing and configuring "data science solutions"; IT staff have to team up with data scientists and business analysts. Even though data scientists support data mining, data organization and build statistical models and business analysts utilize domain expertise, IT professionals are valuable in converting data into applications that can be used as products by decision makers. This meaningful conversion requires IT technical skills as well as data manipulation skills; therefore organizations need IT professionals with the ability to understand data-driven decision making for building their analytics capability.

Freelancer Skills

It should be noted that IT professionals also work as consultants, therefore work as freelancers; it is absolutely necessary for IT freelancers to gain competencies that are marketable. Süß and Becker (2013) confirm that there is dearth of literature on freelancer skills and competencies that make them employable; freelancers work on temporary projects and therefore require to exhibit agility to adapt to new situations about which they may not have any prior knowledge. What is seen as more important is understanding of organizational structure rather than only technical skills because freelancers have to deal with unfamiliar situations in variety of companies. The freelancer temporary employment is quite competitive as the study states that having expertise in niche area especially problem-solving skills enables an edge over other freelancers; those better at social competence helps network and collaborate with clients, also professional network is important for garnering more work and commission on projects. It is noteworthy to say that researchers found that training facility for freelancers is not provided by organizations.

Sustainability

Ensuring environmental sustenance is a major goal identified at the rise of millennium (United Nations Millenium Development Goals report, 2015); in this regard research on working IT professionals have taken a positive step.

Wang et al. (2015) have provided empirical evidence on how IT professional's competence impacts organization's environmental sustainability performance. The researchers have delineated the exact IT capabilities that will help integration of sustainability practices for environmental performance, these capabilities are grouped into technical infrastructure flexibility and integration with business. Most prominently, business related skills and IT technical skills are found to have major influence in meeting sustainability goals; ability to comprehend and identify business problems and working on it in an agile way is the key; when managers and executives strongly believe the critical nature of the sustainability problem it improves their usage of IT processes for the cause.

Similarly, Ojo et al. (2019) considers how cognitive evaluations about sustainable practices at workplaces influences environment management in firms; they confirm that IT professionals attitude toward sustainability is affected by knowledge and social influence; this tells us that sustainability beliefs and practices can be activated and sustained through bottom-up processes rather than just top-down influence. Green IT knowledge was measured by IT professional's knowledge about energy efficient devices, the belief that green energy can replace fossil fuels and nuclear energy, and can be relied upon as safe. Beliefs and knowledge about sustainability do emerge from social mechanisms in an organizations, when people engage in conversations about sustainability practices they are likely to be affected enough to act upon it.

Yadav and Bandopadhyay (2017) have contributed to sustainability research through a theoretical model on sustainability awareness throughout IT organizational hierarchies; they declare that efficient use of resources is a much desired management skill.

Technology / Tasks

Back in 1999, researchers have attempted to delineate technologies and tasks that were in trend at the time. This Singapore based study justified that businesses will benefit from the knowledge which kind of technologies are applicable now and will gain importance in future. They also analyzed different types of tasks: systems management, system development and support tasks; tasks and technologies are ranked according to their importance at the time and beyond 1999: LAN, WAN, UNIX among others are listed under categories such as system architecture, languages, databases telecommunications, networks among others (Lau, Ang & Winley, 1999) This study included this paper even though it is published in 1999 with nil citations, because it is important to do a contemporary research in this area. Authors share the perspective that even if this paper is old and may not find relevance in modern times, it could be debated and examined if technologies of importance can be listed by surveying organizations of today.

LIMITATIONS

Limited search to Scopus database only. Any articles appearing in conferences that emphasize on skills and competencies of IT professionals are unavailable. Also any articles that focus on other areas such as gender, organizational support, etc. do not meet the criteria for inclusion.

CONCLUSION

This systematic literature review delineates typology of research papers specifying skills and competencies expected from IT professionals. Many papers have focused on variety or diverse skills approach to skill development. Important papers have revolved around infrastructure capability and how KSAs help in building agile organizations. These organization centric studies enlist skill demands to meet business needs whereas themes like interfirm-capability and freelancer skills are specifically workforce centric studies. Soft skill as well as social skills are highlighted and focused on different dimensions of the construct, stating its significance for new entrants to the IT industry. Most of the papers are empirical in nature covering both qualitative and quantitative techniques from both developed and developing nations. IT professionals are employed in all kinds of industries as permanent and temporary employees within client and provider firms and therefore due coverage is given which reflects the comprehensiveness of our literature review. Majority of articles have collected data in United States of America, therefore more research is needed in this area in developing countries. However, significant research gaps appear and are mentioned within themes that are facing dearth of relevant studies.

REFERENCES

Achieving the Sustainable Development Goals through ICT. (2015, December). *United Nations Department of Economic and Social Affairs News.* Retrieved from https://www.un.org/development/desa/en/news/administration/achieving-sustdev-through-icts.html

Ahmed, F., Capretz, L. F., & Campbell, P. (2012). Evaluating the demand for soft skills in software development. *IT Professional, 14*(1), 44–49. doi:10.1109/MITP.2012.7 PMID:23397361

Bassellier, G., & Benbasat, I. (2004). Business competence of information technology professionals: Conceptual development and influence on IT-business partnerships. *Management Information Systems Quarterly, 28*(4), 673–694. doi:10.2307/25148659

Bennett, T. M. (2009). A study of the management leadership style preferred by it subordinates. *Journal of Organizational Culture, Communications & Conflict, 13*(2).

Bidwell, M., & Briscoe, F. (2010). The dynamics of interorganizational careers. *Organization Science, 21*(5), 1034–1053. doi:10.1287/orsc.1090.0492

Bullen, C. V., Abraham, T., Gallagher, K., Simon, J. C., & Zwieg, P. (2009). IT workforce trends: Implications for curriculum and hiring. *Communications of the Association for Information Systems, 24*(1), 9.

Byrd, T. A., Lewis, B. R., & Turner, D. E. (2004). The impact of IT personnel skills on IS infrastructure and competitive IS. *Information Resources Management Journal, 17*(2), 38–62. doi:10.4018/irmj.2004040103

Chanopas, A., Krairit, D., & Ba Khang, D. (2006). Managing information technology infrastructure: A new flexibility framework. *Management Research News, 29*(10), 632–651. doi:10.1108/01409170610712335

Chapple, K. (2006). Networks to Nerdistan: The Role of Labor Market Intermediaries in the Entry-level IT Labor Market. *International Journal of Urban and Regional Research, 30*(3), 548–563. doi:10.1111/j.1468-2427.2006.00674.x

El–Agamy, R., & Tsuda, K. (2013). Development of vision for IT engineers' required skills by analysis of ITSS applying text mining. *International Journal of Computer Applications in Technology, 48*(2), 162–172. doi:10.1504/IJCAT.2013.056021

Fiet, J. O., Norton, W. I. Jr, & Clouse, V. G. (2007). Systematic search as a source of technical innovation: An empirical test. *Journal of Engineering and Technology Management, 24*(4), 329–346. doi:10.1016/j.jengtecman.2007.09.001

Fink, L., & Neumann, S. (2009). Exploring the perceived business value of the flexibility enabled by information technology infrastructure. *Information & Management, 46*(2), 90–99. doi:10.1016/j.im.2008.11.007

Gallagher, K. P., Kaiser, K. M., Simon, J. C., Beath, C. M., & Goles, T. (2010). The requisite variety of skills for IT professionals. *Communications of the ACM*, *53*(6), 144–148. doi:10.1145/1743546.1743584

Gefen, D., & Ridings, C. M. (2003). IT acceptance: Managing user—IT group boundaries. *ACM SIGMIS Database: the DATABASE for Advances in Information Systems*, *34*(3), 25–40. doi:10.1145/937742.937746

Gonzalez, P. A., Ashworth, L., & McKeen, J. (2019). The CIO stereotype: Content, bias, and impact. *The Journal of Strategic Information Systems*, *28*(1), 83–99. doi:10.1016/j.jsis.2018.09.002

Hawk, S., Kaiser, K. M., Goles, T., Bullen, C. V., Simon, J. C., Beath, C. M., ... Frampton, K. (2012). The information technology workforce: A comparison of critical skills of clients and service providers. *Information Systems Management*, *29*(1), 2–12. doi:10.1080/10580530.2012.634292

Heidary Dahooie, J., Beheshti Jazan Abadi, E., Vanaki, A. S., & Firoozfar, H. R. (2018). Competency-based IT personnel selection using a hybrid SWARA and ARAS-G methodology. *Human Factors and Ergonomics in Manufacturing & Service Industries*, *28*(1), 5–16. doi:10.1002/hfm.20713

Hendon, M., Powell, L., & Wimmer, H. (2017). Emotional intelligence and communication levels in information technology professionals. *Computers in Human Behavior*, *71*, 165–171. doi:10.1016/j.chb.2017.01.048

Ho, S. Y., & Frampton, K. (2010). A competency model for the information technology workforce: Implications for training and selection. CAIS, 27, 5.

Ifinedo, P., & Olsen, D. H. (2015). An Empirical Research on the Impacts of organisational decisions' locus, tasks structure rules, knowledge, and IT function's value on ERP system success. *International Journal of Production Research*, *53*(8), 2554–2568. doi:10.1080/00207543.2014.991047

Jaska, P. V., & Hogan, P. T. (2006). Effective management of the information technology function. *Management Research News*, *29*(8), 464–470. doi:10.1108/01409170610692789

Jorgenson, D. W., & Vu, K. (2005). Information technology and the world economy. *The Scandinavian Journal of Economics*, *107*(4), 631–650. doi:10.1111/j.1467-9442.2005.00430.x

Joseph, D., Ang, S., Chang, R. H., & Slaughter, S. A. (2010). Practical intelligence in IT: Assessing soft skills of IT professionals. *Communications of the ACM*, *53*(2), 149–154. doi:10.1145/1646353.1646391

Kappelman, L. A., Jones, M. C., Johnson, V., McLean, E. R., & Boonme, K. (2016). Skills for success at different stages of an IT professional's career. *Communications of the ACM*, *59*(8), 64–70. doi:10.1145/2888391

Kim, G., Shin, B., Kim, K. K., & Lee, H. G. (2011). IT capabilities, process-oriented dynamic capabilities, and firm financial performance. *Journal of the Association for Information Systems*, *12*(7), 487–517. doi:10.17705/1jais.00270

Kim Lau, S., Yang Ang, A., & Winley, G. (1999). Alignment of technology and information systems tasks: A Singapore perspective. *Industrial Management & Data Systems*, *99*(6), 235–246. doi:10.1108/02635579910253788

King, R. C., Xia, W., Campbell Quick, J., & Sethi, V. (2005). Socialization and organizational outcomes of information technology professionals. *Career Development International*, *10*(1), 26–51. doi:10.1108/13620430510577619

Koch, H., Gonzalez, E., & Leidner, D. (2012). Bridging the work/social divide: The emotional response to organizational social networking sites. *European Journal of Information Systems*, *21*(6), 699–717. doi:10.1057/ejis.2012.18

Kong, E., Chadee, D., & Raman, R. (2013). Managing Indian IT professionals for global competitiveness: The role of human resource practices in developing knowledge and learning capabilities for innovation. *Knowledge Management Research and Practice*, *11*(4), 334–345. doi:10.1057/kmrp.2012.21

Lárusdóttir, M., Cajander, Å., & Gulliksen, J. (2014). Informal feedback rather than performance measurements–user-centred evaluation in Scrum projects. *Behaviour & Information Technology*, *33*(11), 1118–1135. doi:10.1080/0144929X.2013.857430

Lau, S. K., Winley, G. K., Lau, S. Y., & Tan, K. S. (2013). An exploratory study on the adoption and use of ICT in Myanmar. *The Electronic Journal on Information Systems in Developing Countries*, *59*(1), 1–31. doi:10.1002/j.1681-4835.2013.tb00417.x

Lau, S. K., Winley, G. K., Leung, N. K., Tsang, N., & Lau, S. Y. (2016). An exploratory study of expectation in IT skills in a developing nation: Vietnam. *Journal of Global Information Management*, *24*(1), 1–13. doi:10.4018/JGIM.2016010101

Lowry, P. B., & Wilson, D. (2016). Creating agile organizations through IT: The influence of internal IT service perceptions on IT service quality and IT agility. *The Journal of Strategic Information Systems*, *25*(3), 211–226. doi:10.1016/j.jsis.2016.05.002

Mahatanankoon, P. (2007). Exploring the impact of essential IT skills on career satisfaction and organisational commitment of information systems professionals. *International Journal of Information Systems and Change Management*, *2*(1), 50–68. doi:10.1504/IJISCM.2007.013881

Manfreda, A., & Indihar Štemberger, M. (2018). Establishing a partnership between top and IT managers: A necessity in an era of digital transformation. *Information Technology & People*, ITP-01-2017-0001. doi:10.1108/ITP-01-2017-0001

McLeod, J., Hare, C., & Johare, R. (2004). Education and training for records management in the electronic environment-the (re) search for an appropriate model. *Information Research*, *9*(3), 179.

Morello, D. (2005). *The IT Professional Outlook: Where Will We Go From Here?* Gartner, Inc. Retrieved from http://www.gartner.com/id=485489

Nahapiet, J., & Ghoshal, S. (1998). Social capital, intellectual capital, and the organizational advantage. *Academy of Management Review*, *23*(2), 242–266. doi:10.5465/amr.1998.533225

Neumann, S., & Fink, L. (2007). Gaining agility through IT personnel capabilities: The mediating role of IT infrastructure capabilities. *Journal of the Association for Information Systems*, *8*(8), 25.

Ojo, A. O., Raman, M., & Downe, A. (2019). Toward green computing practices: A Malaysian study of green belief and attitude among Information Technology professionals. *Journal of Cleaner Production*, *224*, 246–255. doi:10.1016/j.jclepro.2019.03.237

Panda, S., & Rath, S. K. (2017). The effect of human IT capability on organizational agility: An empirical analysis. *Management Research Review*, *40*(7), 800–820. doi:10.1108/MRR-07-2016-0172

Panda, S., & Rath, S. K. (2018). Information technology capability, knowledge management capability, and organizational agility: The role of environmental factors. *Journal of Management & Organization*, 1–27. doi:10.1017/jmo.2018.9

Park, J. Y., Im, K. S., & Kim, J. S. (2011). The role of IT human capability in the knowledge transfer process in IT outsourcing context. *Information & Management*, *48*(1), 53–61. doi:10.1016/j.im.2011.01.001

Patrakosol, B., & Lee, S. M. (2009). IT capabilities, interfirm performance, and the state of economic development. *Industrial Management & Data Systems*, *109*(9), 1231–1247. doi:10.1108/02635570911002298

Pee, L. G., Kankanhalli, A., & Kim, H. W. (2010). Knowledge sharing in information systems development: A social interdependence perspective. *Journal of the Association for Information Systems*, *11*(10), 1. doi:10.17705/1jais.00238

Power, D. J. (2008). Understanding data-driven decision support systems. *Information Systems Management*, *25*(2), 149–154. doi:10.1080/10580530801941124

Reich, B. H., & Kaarst-Brown, M. L. (2003). Creating social and intellectual capital through IT career transitions. *The Journal of Strategic Information Systems*, *12*(2), 91–109. doi:10.1016/S0963-8687(03)00017-9

Rong, G., & Grover, V. (2009). Keeping up-to-date with information technology: Testing a model of technological knowledge renewal effectiveness for IT professionals. *Information & Management*, *46*(7), 376–387. doi:10.1016/j.im.2009.07.002

Santhanam, R., Seligman, L., & Kang, D. (2007). Post implementation knowledge transfers to users and information technology professionals. *Journal of Management Information Systems*, *24*(1), 171–199. doi:10.2753/MIS0742-1222240105

Schlosser, F., Beimborn, D., Weitzel, T., & Wagner, H. T. (2015). Achieving social alignment between business and IT–an empirical evaluation of the efficacy of IT governance mechanisms. *Journal of Information Technology*, *30*(2), 119–135. doi:10.1057/jit.2015.2

Shin, B., & Kim, G. (2011). Investigating the reliability of second-order formative measurement in information systems research. *European Journal of Information Systems*, *20*(5), 608–623. doi:10.1057/ejis.2011.7

Süß, S., & Becker, J. (2013). Competences as the foundation of employability: A qualitative study of German freelancers. *Personnel Review*, *42*(2), 223–240. doi:10.1108/00483481311309393

The Future of Jobs Report. (2018). *The World Economic Forum*. Retrieved from http://www3.weforum.org/docs/WEF_Future_of_Jobs_2018.pdf

The Millennium Development Goals Report. (2015). *United Nations*. Retrieved from United Nations Millennium Development Goals website: https://www.un.org/millenniumgoals/2015_MDG_Report/pdf/MDG%202015%20rev%20(July%201).pdf

The World Economic Forum. (n.d.). *Global IT report 2015*. Retrieved from http://www3.weforum.org/docs/WEF_Global_IT_Report_2015.pdf

Vidgen, R., Shaw, S., & Grant, D. B. (2017). Management challenges in creating value from business analytics. *European Journal of Operational Research, 261*(2), 626–639. doi:10.1016/j.ejor.2017.02.023

Wagner, R. K., & Sternberg, R. J. (1985). Practical intelligence in real-world pursuits: The role of tacit knowledge. *Journal of Personality and Social Psychology, 49*(2), 436–458. doi:10.1037/0022-3514.49.2.436

Wang, Y., Chen, Y., & Benitez-Amado, J. (2015). How information technology influences environmental performance: Empirical evidence from China. *International Journal of Information Management, 35*(2), 160–170. doi:10.1016/j.ijinfomgt.2014.11.005

Yadav, S. S. K., & Bandyopadhayay, A. (2017). Communicating sustainability across the hierarchy of the organisation: A framework for the Indian ITeS sector. *International Journal of Management Practice, 10*(1), 17–29. doi:10.1504/IJMP.2017.080647

Zhang, J., Li, H., & Ziegelmayer, J. L. (2009). Resource or capability? A dissection of SMEs' IT infrastructure flexibility and its relationship with IT responsiveness. *Journal of Computer Information Systems, 50*(1), 46–53.

Chapter 5
Human Factors and Cultism Control in Social Media for Higher Education

Ambrose Agbon Azeta
Covenant University, Nigeria

Angela E. Azeta
FIIRO, Nigeria

Raymond Ativie
Covenant University, Nigeria

Felix Chidozie Chidozie
Covenant University, Nigeria

Sanjay Misra
https://orcid.org/0000-0002-3556-9331
Covenant University, Ota, Nigeria

Olufunmilola Amosu
FIIRO, Nigeria

ABSTRACT

The social media network is one of the trending platforms engaged for communication by students. Regrettably, this system has been used by persons to plan and commit cyber fraud and public vices. Some of the tertiary institutions including secondary and university in Nigeria have been turned to cultist environments resulting in killings and disorder amongst students in the school and environs. This is a situation that has continued to struggle with solutions in most higher institutions in the country, particularly in the government owned institutions. This obviously is a human factor issue that needs to be addressed. The objective of this study is to provide social media-based system that is integrated with anti-cultism component services towards combating cultism on campus. The platform will support interaction and learning on and off campus while at the same time helping to curtail cultism among students through filtering of keywords communicated on social media that are crime-based or cultism-related. In carrying out this study, appropriate research methods and implementation techniques such as modeling, design, server-side programming, database were deployed. The platform provides a dual platform that will enable active students to participate in learning, and also cultism control in the school system.

DOI: 10.4018/978-1-7998-1279-1.ch005

INTRODUCTION

The proliferation of secret cults in higher institutions in Nigeria and other parts of Africa can be traced back to the early 1950s (Chebli, Kallon, Harleston and Mansaray, 2007). The foundation of cultism was traced to confraternity, founded by a popular Nigerian and six others at the popular University of Ibadan in 1952. The confraternity was acclaimed to be peaceful, non-violent and protective as at them. However, in the 1980s, it grown into a secret cult whose activities has been described as violent behaviors. It is against this background that this paper enumerates the probable reasons and consequences of cultism in Nigerian institutions. The main causes of cultism in higher institutions were peer group influence; background of parents; societal vices; quality of educational standards; militarization of the Nigerian state; search for power and protection among others; lack of recreational amenities; (Ajayi, Ekundayo and Osalusi, 2010).

According to Oluwasanmi, Akande and Taiwo (2016), the major problems of cultism are the devastating environment created in our campus. Moreso, the activities of members of secret cult and their manner of operation is questionable going by the state of killings in our schools in modern times. Several lives have been truncated, or permanently maimed. Despite the approaches put up by the several institutions and arms of government for the purpose of minimizing the ugly menace of cultism, the menace on our schools campuses has refused to stop.

In the twenty-first century, the capability of students to take part in online learning is a key issue for stakeholders in the Nigerian educational system because of its attendant merits. As institutions continues to experience computer technology in service delivery, students have continued to engage in online network communication resources to commit crime and terrorism acts, particularly among innocent and easy going students' colleagues on campus. The act of terrorism is a term used to describe violence or other forms of harmful behaviour. Walter Laqueur in 1999 counted over hundred definitions of terrorism and concluded that the only distinctive attributes generally agreed upon is that terrorism has to do with aggression and the threat of hostility (Laqueur, 2003).

Cultism on campus involves students that have been convinced to believe that they could get respect and power by initiating themselves into precarious groups. Indeed, this has no benefits. Cultist groups include: Black Berret; The Black Nationalist of Ife; Black Axe Night; the Buccaneers, the Pirates Confraternity, the Eiye Confraternity, the Neo-Black Movement of Africa, the Vikings, the Mafia, the Black Cobra of Ife, Green Berret, and lately the Daughters of Jezebel. Cultism eradication in our institutions has been a major concern to many educational stakeholders and researchers since there are advancements in the number of students that enroll in cultism in tertiary institutions (Udoh and Ikezu, 2014). The advancement of social network websites in the last few decades has resulted in a new avenue for the security agencies to gain access to intelligence from criminals who utilize these websites. It is essentials for law enforcement agencies to identify the potentials and understand the various methods that cultism crime investigators cannot only access but also analysis this content towards enriching the cases (Jones, 2017).

In restraining cultism with the application reported in this paper, the users communicate with each other using the forum and voice interaction. Thereafter, their conversations are recorded and sent to a remote server where a detailed analysis of the threat keywords are stored and processed for further investigation. Short Message Service (SMS) is also sent to the system administrator when the system encounters a threat keyword. The anti-cultism system developed and discuss in this paper is a step towards providing succor to societal vices facing higher institutions in Nigeria. These vices are caused by human factors that need urgent attention. One of the limitations of the system is that the privacy of users is infringed upon and the fundamental human rights as specified in UN (2019) are violated. The monitoring of social media by any agencies would pose considerable risks to users' privacy and freedom of expression. Moreso, social media posts has the capability to reveal private details regarding an individual (Freedom of Expression, 2018).

The objective of this article is to report an anti-cultism social media educational system. The system will support interaction and learning on campus while at the same time helping to curb the menace of cultism on campus through filtering of communicated social media keywords that are cultism or crime-related, among the students. This study is an enhancement of a preliminary study on social media-based cultism control study reported in Azeta, Omoregbe., Ayo, Raymond, Oroge and Misra, (2014). This paper is organised as follows. The next section is a review of related literature highligting related works, previous efforts at curbing cultism and cultism control, human factors and national government. The proposed model and implementation is presented in section 3. The benefits of the system are contained in section 4, while section 5 concludes the article.

LITRATURE REVIEW

Related Works

Fayokun (2011) explored the origins and development of cults and explains the reasons why they continue to maintain their membership. The study concludes that campus cultism is due to economic, social, educational and political injustice, adding that cults catch the attention of students since the students have needs that influence them to associate with activist institution. The study ascertained that these influence must be addresses, arguing that, for any control to be effective, every step must address the needs that attract students to the cults.

The study by Ajayi, Ekundayo & Osalusi, (2010) examined the hazard of secret cults in the higher institutions in Nigeria. The origin of cultism was traced to the Seadog confraternity, founded by a popular Nigerian activist and six others at the foremost University of Ibadan in 1952. It was meant to be non-violent and peaceful. However, in the 1980s it graduated into a secret cult whose activities have been described by some bizarre and intense activities. To the best of the researcher's knowledge, the first cult-related violent attack leading to death happened in 1984 (Oguntuase, 1999). The challenges of the violence associated with cultism in higher institutions got to the hight with the ruthless massacre of five students of the Obafemi Awolowo University, Ile-Ife in the early hours of 10th July 1999.

The propagation of several secret societies has remained one of the most powerful instruments of attack on tertiary institutions in the country-Nigeria. The havoc being caused by these violent cultist menace in our institutions and other tertiary educational institutions has become a source of major concern to students, lecturers, parents, guardians, government and the society at large. There are incidents of cultist activities on our campuses with blood sucking and oath-taking ceremonies. Cases of house breaking, rapes and burglary involving sons and daughters of important personalities in the country are very common. It is believed that these despicable crimes are normally committed under the influence of hard drugs such as Indian hemp and cocaine. Dangerous weapons such as swords, axes, explosives, guns, spear, knives are reported to be freely engaged by the secret cult members. The university environment which should thrive through exchange of moral and intellectual ideas has suddenly been turn into a battle ground for violent crimes and activities.

The study by Chinwokwu (2013) examines the concept of terrorism and the predicament facing the Nigerian people in fighting domestic terrorism. The research also reports the efforts of government at keeping in check terrorism and the reasons those feedback are ineffective. Some suggestions were highlighted in the research as follows: policy reforms, harmonization of security operations, equipping and training of security personnel. Similarly, the case of cybergangs in social networks as violent platforms to impose and expose themselves was discussed in the study by Buoncompagni (2018). Newman (2009) explored a study on how the media including newspapers and broadcasters in the UK and US are responding to a wave of inclusive social media, and a historic shift in control towards achieving success stories. Okonkwo and Enem (2016) described the methods by which data mining techniques can be used law enforcement outfits in tracking the actions of cyber terrorists and their criminal behaviors. This study also examines the limitation of data mining in combating misdemeanor in Nigeria.

Previous Efforts at Curbing Cultism

Historical, several efforts have been put up at curbing cultism, including several reports, discussions and recommendations (Makanjuola,1999; ITePED 2011; Oguntuase, 1999; Oguntuase, 1999b; Ritchie, 1991; Robson, 1966; Olayiwola, 2013), on how best to curtain cultism in the tertiary institutions in the country, but very few studies have taken steps to provide a software solution to curb its menace in Nigerian institutions. The passion to provide a solution to radically reduce cultism problem in Nigerian schools is what motivated this novel platform. It is on this background that this article discusses the reasons and consequences of cultism in Nigeria.

The strategies towards building cultists free tertiary institutions in Nigeria are discussed in (Udoh and Ikezu, 2014) as follows: Students should be properly guided through guidance and counseling; Workshop should be organized during orientation of fresh students on the dangers of secret cult; Regular and routine check on possession of arms by the students should be carried out on campuses; High cost of education in Nigeria should be reduced; Establishment of tribunal to try cultists and if found guilty should be sentenced accordingly; and parents should monitor their children both in and outside the school and advice them regularly. Churches should have youth department with regular youth talks, that would give the youths the forum to vent their issues.

Smah (2001) examined the opinion and control of secret cult and the difficulties for quality living and learning in Nigerian institutions using the Universities in the Middle Belt Zone in the country as case study. The dilemma of secret cult invasion was observed to be disruptive and therefore requires a disruptive response in form of higher funding, decline in the brain drain experience and globalization of the academic background and principles. Cultism is not the only crime committed using Social Media as a platform of communication, other social media crimes platforms includes NW3C (2013): Burglary via Social Networking, Phishing & Social Engineering, Malware, Cybercasing the Joint, Identity Theft and Cyberstalking.

As a measure of tackling the menace of cultism, various institutions have mounted some form of publicity. But such publicity does not seem to yield positive results as it has been channeled to precise audience of only those who are august visitors to the institution (Ekeanyanwu and Igbinoba, 2007).

CULTISM CONTROL, HUMAN FACTORS, AND NATIONAL DEVELOPMENT

The article in Bouchard and Malm, (2016) discusses how the advancement of network analysis techniques has influenced research on crime and its control over the past two decades. The focus of human factors is on how people interact with tasks, with technologies, and with the environment, in order to better understand and evaluate these inter connections (Human factors, 2011). The study by Chinnah and Amabibi (2019) examined cultism and national development pointing its adverse effect to the development of the country. The paper made suggested on how cultism can be controlled in the society if sustainable development must be achieved; this includes the following: Parents should have full control of their children to teach them basic morality and societal values; There should be public sensitization, reorientation, and education of youths through useful program and workshop, seminar on the hazard of cultism; Provision of employment opportunities and empowerment program for the youth will help to deduce cultism since youths that are engaged will have little or no time to commit crimes; as they say idleness is the devil's workshop; and admittance into Nigeria universities should be based on merit. Some other measures of control includes among other things (Ezema, Ota and Abah, 2017) the following: provision of counseling, good education, importance on character building over educational achievements, effective organization of career talk at intervals, and mentoring of students.

According to Tayouri (2015), to be able to strengthen the human factor angle to social media menace, stakeholders should put in more efforts in education for students, starting as early as the first grade, at the time that the children are exposed to the world and internet. Remarkable approaches to cyber security training and mentorship should be taking into consideration, such as interactive video learning on games. But there should also be more efforts on scientific means of helping humans make smaller amount of errors and avoid being a cyber crime victim.

PROPOSED MODEL AND SYSTEM IMPLEMENTATION

Some of the functionalities in the application were modeled using the Unified Modelling Language (UML) to capture and provide a means to visualize, construct and document the artefacts of software systems (Bennett, Skelton, & Lunn (2005).

In this research, a social media e-learning system for use by students is described. It has forum, lecture uploads and downloads. As learners interact through the social media platform on the forum module, an agent is initiated to separate the sentences of conversation into tokens of words and each word is checked against a pool of threat keywords that relates to cultism. If the occurrence of keywords goes beyond a certain percentage threshold, a report pertaining to the IP address and location of the conversation is recorded and sent to the system administrator and authorities through SMS and voice message. Such information assist management to put certain areas under security surveillance. The voice part of the application records the interaction and conversation.

The activity diagram of Figure 1 shows the home page, login and registration page. Once a user successful log into the system, a menu containing the student, lecturer and administrator shows up. The users are able to access several modules of the system including forum, messages, upload/download, filter anti cultism keyword and validation. A logout process is initiated when a user is through with using the system.

Figure 1. A flowchart of ASEM system

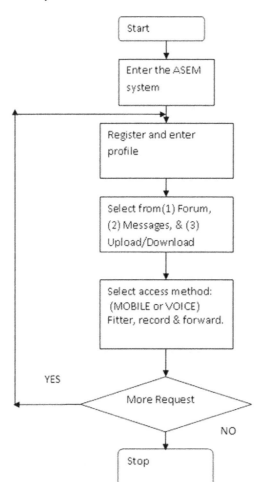

The system was developed using PHP scripting language for the web interface and SMS for the mobile interface. The database used as backend server was MySQL. Apache tomcat was used as a web server. Microsoft C# was used to develop the voice interface for the processing and transmission of voice messages.

The various modules of the system includes: login, students registration (Figure 1); lecture note uploads/downloads, forum, message, and update of status. To log into the system, a student, lecturer or administrator user has to first register if not a registered user. Thereafter, the different modules of the system including forum, messages, lecture upload/download, validation and flittering of cultism keywords would be available for selection. It is necessary for a user to logout after completing the usage of the system. The screen shots of the application are made up of the voice interface and web interface. The login page of Figure 2 is a web interface and is based on roles. The student, lecturer and administrator login provides access to different components of the system. Figure 3 and 4 are used by the lecturer to upload lecture and video notes respectively. The voice receiver in Figure 5 is a voice interface used to capture the conversation of would be cultism.

Figure 2. Collaboration diagram for the students

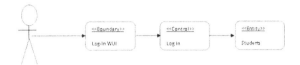

Figure 3. Activity diagram

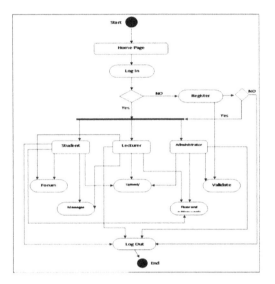

Figure 4. Login page

Figure 5. Student upload lecture note

The application provided through this paper will be particularly useful for educationist of primary and secondary schools, police in Nigeria, security operatives, territory institutions, military intelligence,, etc. The students make use of the web interface component of the application for forum, sending of messages, and download of lecture notes/video. Unknown to them, their conversations are recorded and forwarded to a remote server where some analysis of the threat keywords will be carried out for investigation. An SMS is also forwarded to the administrator when the system encounters a threat keyword. The system provides useful information that will assist school administrators to place surveillance on the locations where threat keywords are received.

PROJECT LOGIC PROCESS ANALYSIS

The flowchart in Figure 1 shows the Anti-cultism Social Educational Media (*ASEM*).

The user logs into the ASEM system and create a profile. He/she chooses from the menu options Forum, Messages and Upload/Download.

Collaboration Diagram displays an interaction organized around the objects and their links to one another. The collaboration diagram for student and lecturer case is shown in Figure 2. It shows the interaction for the student object which involves sending a forum message from the log-In WUI to the forum, where login users can access and send a reply to the message. The activity diagram describing student, lecturer and administrator processed is presented in Figure 3. Figures 4, 5, 6, 7 and 8 shown below explains the login processes, upload of lecture materials and Voice recorder.

Figure 6. Lecturer upload lecture note

Figure 7. Lecturer upload video

Figure 8. Voice receiver

The sequence of activities of the system shows login through the home page. Due registration is required before successful enterance into the system. There are three users of the system, the student, lecturer/instructor and administrator. Different roles are assigned to the users such as access to forum, messages, upload and download of resources, filtering of anti-culrism words, validation, and a lot more.

The login page of the school network home page is shown in Figure 4. A user pull down menu is required to be selected either as student, lecturer/instructor or administrator. Only registered users can access the system.

The student user can upload lecture notes as shown in Figure 5. A form is completed with all the required information before lecture upload can take place. Similarly, Figure 6 is used by the lecturers/ instructor to carry out lecture materials upload. Lecturers/instructors can also use Figure 7 to upload video materials unto the system.

The voice receiver is used to record online conversation of the users for security reasons.

The voice receiver is met to complement the online text conversation between two users.

Analytics is carried out on the text content of the conversation as well as the voice interaction that have been recorded during conversation.

BENEFITS OF THE SYSTEM

The proposed system will provide the following services:

- Interaction between student and lecturer.
- Reduction in the time taken to communicate.
- Provision of immediate updates for tracking friends and course mates.

Advantages of the proposed system to Staff / Faculty members:

- Online/real time communication with learners.
- Basic course management modules.
- Immediate entrance to information for counseling students.
- Simple accessible information for every facet of their carrier.

Advantages of the proposed system to Students:

- Web interface to courses, lecture notes and final year project
- Increased and flexible communication with lecturers access to alumni communities with
- current update of course mates data.
- Increased life-long learning opportunities.

CONCLUSION

In this research, an anti-cultism social media-based educational system using voice interface and web interface that will facilitate the control of cultism on campus through filtering of social media keywords that are cultism or crime related is provided. The platform will be useful for educational proprietors of mainly primary and secondary schools, Nigeria police, security operatives, tertiary institutions, military intelligence, etc.

The students make use of the web interface component of the application for forum, download of lecture notes/video, sending of messages. Unknown to the students, their discussions are recorded and sent to a remote server where a detailed analysis of the threat words are done and investigated. A short message service was be sent to the administrator when the system encounters a threat keyword. The system provides valuable information that will assist educationist and school administrators to keenly watch the locations where threat keywords are transmitted. In consideration for further studies, the following techniques will be fully engaged in the system design and implementation: Mobile-Azeta, Omoregbe, Misra, Adewumi, Olokunde, (2016), Voice- Azeta, Misra, Azeta, Osamor, (2019); DevOps- Azeta, Iboroma, Ige, Fawehinm,i, Ogunde (2018).

REFERENCES

Ajayi, I. A., Ekundayo, H. T., & Osalusi, F. M. (2010). Menace of cultism in Nigerian tertiary institutions: The way out. *Anthropologist, 12*(3), 155–160. doi:10.1080/09720073.2010.11891147

Azeta, A. A., Iboroma, D. A., Ige, O. O., Fawehinmi, O. A., & Ogunde, B. (2018). *A DevOps Software Architecture for Recommender Systems in Digital Library*. In 13th International Conference on eLearning (ICEL), Cape Town, South Africa.

Azeta, A. A., Misra, S., Azeta, V. I., & Osamor, V. C. (2019). Determining suitability of speech-enabled examination result management system. *Wireless Networks*, 1–8.

Azeta, A. A., Omoregbe, N. A., Ayo, C. K., Raymond, A., Oroge, A., & Misra, S. (2014). An Anti-Cultism Social Education Media System. Computer & Information Technology (GSCIT), 2014 IEEE Global Summit, 1-5. doi:10.1109/GSCIT.2014.6970097

Azeta, A. A., Omoregbe, N. A., Misra, S., Adewumi, A., & Olokunde, T. O. (2016). Adapted Cloudlet for Mobile Distance Learning: Design, prototype and evaluation. Frontiers in Artificial Intelligence and Applications, 282, 220-228.

Bennett, S., Skelton, J., & Lunn, K. (2005). *Schaum's Outlines UML* (2nd ed.). McGraw-Hill International.

Bouchard, M., & Malm, A. (2016). Social network analysis and its contribution to research on crime and criminal justice. *Oxford Handbooks Online.*

Chebli, C. M., Kallon, M. P., Harleston, K. K., & Mansaray, A. (2007). The Impact Of Cultism In Tertiary Education Institution Campuses: A Case Study Of Foural Bay College, Milton Margai College Of Education And Technology And Freetown Teachers College. Education Research Network for West and Central African (ERNWACA). Ernwaca Research Grants Programme 2007.

Chinnah, P. C., & Amabibi, F. (2019). Cultism And Sustainable National Development In Nigeria. *Economics And Social Sciences. Academic Journal*, *1*(2), 2019.

Chinwokwu E. C. (2013). Terrorism and the Dilemmas of Combating the Menace in Nigeria. *International Journal of Humanities and Social Science, 3*(4), 265-272.

Data Mining Techniques, Information Technology for People-Centered Development. (2011). Nigeria Computer Society (NCS).

Ekeanyanwu, N. T., & Igbinoba, A. (2007). The Media And Cultism In Nigerian Higher Institutions Of Learning: A Study Of Coverage, Treatment And Relevance. *International Journal of Communication*, (6).

Ezema, V. S., Ota, M. S., & Abah, G. O. (2017). Activities of Cultist and Measures for Eradicating Cultism among Secondary School Students in Nigeria: Implication for Child Development and Counselling. *European Journal of Social Sciences*, *55*(3), 254-261.

Fayoku, K. O. (2011). Campus Cultism in Nigeria's Higher Education Institutions: Origins, Development and Suggestions for Control. *Makerere Journal of Higher Education*, *3*(1).

Freedom Of Expression. (2018). The Human Rights Problem With Social Media Monitoring. *Accessnow*. Retrieved 11 August 2019 From Https://Www.Accessnow.Org/13503-2/

Human factors. (2011). Healthcare comes home: Chapter 3. In *What is human factors.* The National Academies Press.

Jones, K. R. (2017). *Law Enforcement Use of Social Media as a Crime Fighting Tool. Use Of Social Media As A Crime Fighting Tool* (Master's thesis). University of Oregon.

Laqueur, W. (2003). *No End to War: Terrorism in the Twenty-First Century.* New York: Continuum.

Makanjuola, O. A. (1999). *A Parent and A University Teacher Takes a Look at Cultism in Nigerian Tertiary Institutions.* NAS Annual Converge.

NW3C. (2013). *Criminal Use of Social Media.* National White Collar Crime Center.

Newman, N. (2009). *The rise of social media and its impact on mainstream journalism.* Working paper. Reuters Institute for the Study of Journalism.

Oguntuase, B. (1999c). Cultism and Violence in Higher Institutions of Learning in Nigeria. NAS Capone, University of Lagos.

Oguntuase, B. (1999a). *Open Letter to Nigerian Students on Campus Banditry.* Academic Press.

Oguntuase, B. (1999b). *Violence and Cultism in Tertiary Institutions: The Way Out.* NAS Annual Converge.

Okonkwo, R. O., & Enem, F. O. (2011). *Combating crime and terrorism using data mining techniques.* Nigeria Computer Society (NCS). Available online: http://www.ncs.org.ng/wp-content/uploads/2011/08/ITePED2011-Paper10.pdf

Olayiwola, O. O. (2013). Education Scenarios in Nigeria. *ABHINAV-International Monthly Journal of Research in Management and Technology, 2.*

Oluwasanmi, B. V., Akande, O. L., & Taiwo, O. E. (2016). Social Vices And The Effect Of Cultism Activities Among University Undergraduates Of Ekiti State University, Ado-Ekiti, Nigeria. *American Journal of Innovative Research and Applied Sciences.*

Ritchie, J. (1991). *The Secret World of Cults Angus & Robertson.* Academic Press.

Robson, J. (1966). *The College Fraternity and Its Modern Role. Menasha.* Banta.

Smah, S. O. (2001). *Perception and Control of Secret Cult and Gang-induced Difficulties for Quality Living and Learning in Nigerian Universities: The Case study of Universities in the Middle Belt Zone.* Centre for Development Studies University of Jos.

Tayouri, D. (2015). The human factor in the social media security –combining education and technology to reduce social engineering risks and damages. In *6th International Conference on Applied Human Factors and Ergonomics (AHFE 2015) and the Affiliated Conferences, AHFE 2015.* Elsevier. 10.1016/j.promfg.2015.07.181

Udoh, V. C., & Ikezu, U. J. M. (2014). Causes, Effects and Strategies for Eradicating Cultism among Students in Tertiary Institutions in Nigeria a Case Study of Nnamdi Azikiwe University Awka Anambra State, Nigeria. *Quest Journals Journal of Research in Humanities and Social Science, 2*(7), 12-20.

UN. (2019). United Nations Secretariat Guidelines For The Personal Use Of. *Social Medicine (Social Medicine Publication Group).*

Chapter 6
A Framework to Reduce the Human Factors for Analysis of Constraint Solvers in Project Management

Franklin Johnson
Universidad de Playa Ancha, Chile

Broderick Crawford
Pontificia Universidad Católica de Valparaíso, Chile

Ricardo Soto
Pontificia Universidad Católica de Valparaíso, Chile

Sanjay Misra
ⓘ https://orcid.org/0000-0002-3556-9331
Covenant University, Ota, Nigeria

ABSTRACT

Currently, there are multiple factors that affect the projects management. These factors may have different origins, but the human factor is still one of the main elements that affect decisions when managing a project. Another important factor is the use of software that supports these decisions and reduce the human factors. Given the complexity of current management problems, powerful software is needed to solve these problems. Constraint solvers are a kind of software that are based on a constraint approach. Currently there are different constraint solvers. Some are intricate software, and others are libraries for a programming language. This chapter presents a framework that allow to compare a constraint system based on the usability attributes of the solvers in order to reduce the human factors for the selection of the constraint solver. The authors show that it is possible to establish a comparison according to usability attributes, allowing to reduce the risks of decision making by the experts when working with a constrain solver in a project.

DOI: 10.4018/978-1-7998-1279-1.ch006

INTRODUCTION

The new applied problems, especially in the industrial area are increasingly difficult to solve. These problems use more data, and they are complexly related. This generates that complex mathematical models are needed for resolution. Given complexity of these models, these problems is not feasible to solve manually and it is necessary to use automatics systems to solve them (Ángel Vega-Velázquez, García-Nájera, & Cervantes, 2018). There is thus a strong need for use powerful software tools that using a simple user interface.

The project management is a kind of combinatorial problem and the human factors are a key element in managing a project. To reduce the costs associated with people in a project and their ability to perform assigned tasks, it can be controlled by systems that allow them to model their behavior and improve project management (Rahmanniyay & Junfang, 2018). In project management, the manager has to initiate, schedule, execute, control, and close the project; this involves a series of complex activities for the project manager (Radujković & Sjekavica, 2017). This is the reason why it is necessary to optimize these activities through a solver based on constraint programming.

Constraint Programming (CP) (Rossi, van Beek, & Walsh, 2006) is a powerful programming paradigm used for efficient problem solving, typically combinatorial problems. (Vianna, 2019; Kuchcinski, 2019). Under this paradigm, a problem is represented as a Constraint Satisfaction Problem (CSP), which corresponds to a mathematical model of the problem. The CSP mainly consist in a set of variables holding a domain and a set of constraints. CSPs are usually resolved by a constraint solver, which has a powerful search engine. The search engine finds a proper solution by building and exploring a search tree. The constraint solvers have different enumeration and propagation strategies, which are used in the resolution process of the problems (Soto et al., 2016).

Currently, there are different kinds of constraint solvers (Wallace, Schimpf, Shen, & Harvey, 2004), some of them are intricate software and others are libraries to extend the features of a programming language. In some cases, it is difficult to decide which constraint solver to use. A proper selection of a solver can be vital to a project. The project manager must have a constraint solver that suits your needs. In some cases, these can be simple, using a constraint solver as a black box, in which only it is sufficient to enter and tune different parameters. However, in other cases the developer will need a flexible system that allows him to develop more complex models, which is not available only by setting the solver.

Usability is a quality attribute to measure the ease with which a user interacts with the system. The system users generally have different levels of expertise and experience. In software engineering, usability is the degree to which a software can be used by specified consumers to achieve quantified objectives with effectiveness, efficiency, and satisfaction in a quantified context of use (ISO 9241-11 (1998) *Ergonomic requirements for office work with visual display terminals (VDTs) – Part 11: Guidance on usability. International).* The analyst may conduct a usability analysis. The usability includes methods of measuring usability, such as needs analysis and the study of the principles behind the perceived efficiency of an object. Usability differs from user satisfaction and user experience because usability does not directly consider usefulness or utility (Nielsen, 4 January 2012). Although this work is not a usability study, the authors use it as an important attribute to compare solvers, because a system with better usability attributes will reduce the risks associated with the end user. Even so, in the current literature contains few specialized papers on the usability of constraint programming systems. For the most part, studies are based on the performance, quantity and types of strategies implemented by the solvers (Soto et al., 2015) instead of the adaptability and ease of use of the constraint solvers

The main idea of this chapter is to present a way to reduce the human factors in project management when use a constraint system through a simple and objective framework to analysis of the usability of the constraint solver. The proposed framework is based on the usability attributes proposed by Nielsen (Nielsen, 4 January 2012). In this chapter, the authors try to measure attributes such as efficiency, ease-of-use, satisfaction, learnability, memorability. These attributes are essential for the usability analysis of a system. In order to test the usability of a specific constraint solver, the authors define the specific characteristics required and then a heuristic evaluation can be performed using the proposed framework.

This work shows that it is possible to establish comparison according to usability attributes, allowing to reduce the risks of decision making by the experts when working with a constrain solver in a project, allowing an analysis beyond the simple comparison of their internal attributes.

This chapter is organized as follows. Section 2 briefly presents the background of the project management and constraint solvers; section 3 presents the usability approach to reduce de human factors. Section 4 presents the usability framework to analysis of Constraint Solvers. The conclusions are presented in section 5.

BACKGROUND

The Project Management as a CSP

In project management, the manager has to initiate, schedule, execute, control, and close a project; this involves a series of complex activities for the project manager. These activities need to be optimized and they can be represented has a combinatorial problem, because for the same project may be a large number of possible and feasible plans, each with different cost and duration (Vukadinovic, Macuzic, & Djapan, 2018).

In literature, exist different adaptation of project management like a CSP. The Project Scheduling Problem (PSP) is a generic name for all kinds of problems in which it is necessary to program, optimally the time, cost and resources of the projects (Laalaoui & Bouguila, 2014). The Software Project Scheduling Problem (SPSP), which consists in making the adequate workers-tasks assignment that minimizes cost and duration for a software project (Reference Alba and Chicano 2007). The Resource-Constrained Project Scheduling (RCPSP) is a very popular problem in the literature (Brucker, Drexl, Mhring, Neumann, & Pesch, 1999) were a number of activities are to be scheduled. Each activity has a duration and cannot be interrupted. There are a set of precedence relations between pairs of activities, which state that the second activity must start after the first has finished.

Then a combinatorial problem can be modeled as a constraint satisfaction problem (CSP). A CSP is a mathematical problem determined by a set of variable, a set of domains for each variable, and a set of constraints, that determine the possible combinations of values of the variables. Formally, a CSP is defines by a triple $P = (X, D, C)$ where:

- X is a set of variables $X = (x_1, x_2, ..., x_n)$.
- D is a corresponding domains $D = (d_1, d_2, ..., d_n)$ such that $x_n \in d_i$, and d_i is a set of values for $i = 1, ..., n$.
- C is a set of constraints $C = (c_1, c_2, ..., c_3)$.

The classic CSP attempt to find the first solution that satisfies the whole set of constraints with the values assigned to the all variables, when the problem is an optimization problem an objective function is added which must be minimized or maximized. For example: a RCPSP can be defined as projects with limited resources in an environment which must process a set of activities subject to precedence constraints and resources, the latter being shared by several activities. The mathematical representation of a RCPSP is presented below.

- Set of activities $A = \{a_0, a_1, a_2, ..., a_n, a_{n+1}\}$
- Renewable resources limited set of $R = \{r_1, r_2, ..., r_m\}$
- Duration for each activity a_i con $i = (1, ..., n)$ represented by $d_i \geq 0$
- Amount of resources consumed $q_{ij} \geq 0$
- Maximum availability $Q_j \geq 0$ each resource $r_j \in R$ at each instant of time.
- Precedence Constraints $P_a \in A = \{a_1, ..., a_{n+1}\}$
- Each activity a_i cannot be initiated while predecessor activities P_i have not been finalized.
- Set of successor activities S_i for a_i activities being $i = \{1, ..., n+1\}$
- Set of start times for each activity $T = \{t_0, ..., t_{n+1}\}$
- Directed acyclic graph $G = \{A, E\}$ where $E = \{(a_i, a_j)/a_i \in P_a; a \in A\}$

The goal is to find a set of start times for each activity that meets the precedence constraints and availability of resources.

Additionally, an optimization criterion can be included such as duration of project and the problem can be converted into an optimization problem (Brucker, Drexl, Mhring, Neumann, & Pesch, 1999). Mathematically the RCPSP is represented by next model.

$$Min \ F_{n+1} \tag{1}$$

$$F_h \leq F_j - p_j \tag{2}$$

$$\sum_{j \in A(t)} r_{j,k} \tag{3}$$

$$k \in K; \ t \geq 0 \tag{4}$$

$$F_j \geq 0 \tag{5}$$

where $j = \{1, ..., n+1\}$

$h \in Pj$

Defined F_j as the completion of the activity j therefore in the mathematical formulation should be minimized F_{n+1} since $n+1$ It is the last activity. This is represented in the objective function presented in Equation. 1, used to define the quality of a solution (Fitness). The Equation 2 does satisfy the precedence constraint between activities since it shows that the completion of an activity h must be greater or equal to the completion of the activity j unless the predecessor activity. The Equation. 3 and Equation. 4 show the limits for each type of resource k and each time instant t, thus not allowing the demand for activities occurring at present does not exceed its capacity. Finally, the Equation. 5 defines the decision variables.

The general CSP can also be specialized in other categories e.g., depending on the values of the domains. As an example, a finite domain CSP stands for a CSP involving only integer values, a numerical CSP refers to CSP on reals.

Constraint Solvers

The constraint solvers (CP solvers) are a specialized Constraint Programming System that use a constraint programming approach to solve a Constraint Satisfaction Problem (Kim. Mariott, 1998; Gedik, Kalathia, Egilmez, & Kirac, 2018). For these a CP solver can use a constraint logic language, and constraint programming libraries. The CP solvers can use different kinds of strategies to solve a problem. To these end they implement sets of enumeration and propagation strategies.

A constraint solver uses an algorithm for solving constraints based on the constraint theory. The constraint solver stores the constraints that the problem has and puts them into the constraint store and then it tests their satisfiability, simplifies and if possible solves them.

When the constraint solver uses a constraint programming language, the solver should be able to perform: The Satisfiability test, where evaluates whether it is feasible to satisfy a constraint. The Simplification, where it transforms a constraint into a simpler constraint, but logically equivalent constraint. The Determination where evaluates that a variable in a constraint can only take a unique value, and the Variable projection elimination where eliminates a variable by projecting a constraint onto all other variables (Frühwirth & Abdennadher, 2005).

Commonly, to modelling and solving CSPs logical languages have been used. The logical languages are declarative and efficient. Nevertheless, there are various efforts to solve CSP using other kinds of languages, for this purpose several specialized library for the management of CP have been developed. These efforts to generate constraint-programming systems commonly referred as Constraint solvers have resulted in specialized compilers or libraries to implement Constraint Programming.

There are different constraint solvers, some of the most popular are: clp(FD) (Jaffar, Michaylov, Stuckey, & Yap, 1992), SICtus (Carlsson & Mildner, 2010), Eclipse (Niederlínski, 2014), Oz (Smolka, 2004), IMB Ilog CP solver (IBM company, 2006), B-prolog (Zhou, 2012), Choco (Choco Team, 2010), Comet (Hentenryck, 2005), Gecode (Gecode Team, 2006), JaCop (Kuchcinski & Szymanek, 2010), Minion (Gent, Jefferson, & Miguel, 2006), OscaR (OscaR Team, 2012), OptaPlanner (OptaPlanner Team (2014), Abscon (Lecoutre & Tabary, 2006), Mistral (Hebrard & Siala, 2007), CPHydra (O'mahony, Hebrard, Holland, & Nugent, 2008). The classification of Constraint solvers can be performed by different criteria. In this case, the authors classify according to: Constraint Logic programming languages, libraries to adapted to other programming languages, or constructed as specific solvers (Fernández & Hill, 2000).

Constraint Logic Programming Languages

The following describes some logical programming languages that use constrained programming. These systems are classified as Glass-Box and Black-Box. Since the distinction between the two is difficult to establish, the characteristics of each classification are presented first. The Glass-Box (Hentenryck, Saraswat, & Deville, 1998) languages provide very simple and primitive constraints, whose propagation scheme can be formally specified. The constraints are used to build high-level constraints, for each application. Moreover, the Black-Box languages provide a wide range of high-level constraints whose implementation is hidden from the user. These constraints perform specific tasks very efficiently. In these languages, it is difficult for a user to add new constraints, as these must be defined at a low level requiring a detailed knowledge of the implementation.

1. **Glass-Box Languages:** There are two types of glass-box languages. These differ in the way that constraint propagation may be defined: either using a single form of relational construct called an indexical or by means of special Constraint Handling Rules (CHR (Frühwirth, 1998).

An indexical is a reactive functional rule of the form X in R where X is a domain variable. R is a set-valued range expression of the form $t_1 \ldots t_2$ in which terms t_1 and t_2 denote singleton ranges, parameters, integers, combinations of terms using arithmetical operators or indexical ranges.

This constraint can be seen as an abstract machine for propagation-based constraint solving. It is possible to directly encode most of the higher-level Finite Domain constraints with this one basic constraint. Traditionally among these languages are clp(FD) (Jaffar, Michaylov, Stuckey, & Yap, 1992), and SICtus (Carlsson & Mildner, 2010).

On the other hand, the Constraint Handling Rules is a declarative programming language extension introduced in 1991 (Frühwirth & Raiser, 2011) by Thom Frühwirth. Originally designed for developing a prototype of constraint programming systems, CHR is increasingly used as a high-level general-purpose programming language. A CHR languages can define simplification and propagation over user defined constraints.

The application of consecutively CHRs allows solving the constraints defined by the user. Originally, CHRs were created to simplify the constraint languages, but it has spread to build CP solvers for particular applications and domains.

2. **Black-Box Languages:** A Black Box is a system such that the user sees only its input and output data: its internal structure or mechanism is invisible to him (Gent, Jefferson, & Miguel, 2006). This approach partially addresses the requirement for simplicity since the user does not have to be aware of (or modify or extend) embedded techniques and algorithms. However, a Black-Box constraint solver must have a default configuration that yields in most cases the best behaviour that could be obtained by fine-tuning of available options. This can be achieved by making the solver robust. One of the most popular black-box languages are Eclipse (Niederlínski, 2014.), Oz (Smolka, 2004), Ilog SOLVER (IBM company, 2006), B-prolog (Zhou, 2012).

Constraint Programming Libraries

The constraint programming libraries are a set of files and classes that make up a set of tools for developing constraint-based systems. These tools provide a constraint solver with all the features to solve a CSP problem through an imperative language (Kuchcinski, 2019).

The constraint programming library differs from constraint logic programming systems like CHIP (Dincbas, Van Hentenryck, Simonis, Aggoun, & Herold, 1988), Eclipse (Apt & Wallace, 2007) or SICStus Prolog (Carlsson & Mildner, 2010) in some topics such as imperative versus rule-based programming, stateful typed variables and objects versus logic variables and terms, no pre-defined search versus built-in depth-first search.

Constraint programming is often realized in imperative programming via a separate library. Some popular libraries for constraint programming are: Choco (Choco Team, 2010), Gecode (Gecode Team, 2006), IBM ILOG CP (IBM company, 2006), JaCop (Kuchcinski & Szymanek, 2010), OscaR (OscaR Team, 2012) among others.

Specialized Solver Systems

These systems correspond to a type of Black-Box system. They are developed using constraint-based logic programming languages or constraint programming libraries. These systems are specialized only in the resolution of CSP and they are closed systems. These systems try to free the end user from the complexity of solving the problem and only provide an interface to parameterize them. Some of these constraint solvers may be Abscon (Lecoutre & Tabary, 2006), Mistral (Hebrard & Siala, 2007), CPHydra (O'mahony, Hebrard, Holland, & Nugent, 2008).

A Usability Approach To Reduce De Human Factors

An innovative way of reducing human factors when deciding between different constraint systems, is introducing the concepts of usability to select the Solver that best suits the needs of the project. The usability refers to the user's experience when interacting with a system. A system with good usability is one that shows all the content in a clear and simple way to understand by the user, this is a fundamental aspect of the software. Jakob Nielsen (Nielsen, 4 January 2012), initially defined five basic attributes of usability: ease of learning, efficiency, retention in time, user error rates, and subjective satisfaction. Nielsen also defines ten principles of usability, which are useful and easy to verify.

USABILITY FRAMEWORK TO ANALYSIS OF CONSTRAINT SOLVERS

In the literature, there are not studies about usability in constraint solvers, just some works comparing constraint languages and constraint solvers (Fernández & Hill, 2000; Tulácek, 2009; Lazaar, Gotlieb, & Lebbah, 2012) have been presented. However, in all cases, there is an inherent difficulty in trying to compare different systems built it in different environments, languages, and paradigm. For this reason, authors propose a framework to simplify usability analysis of constraint solvers and make an objective evaluation based on the usability attributes proposed by Nielsen.

Table 1. List of usability principles by Nielsen

System visibility:	The system must keep users informed of what is happening, through reasonable periodic feedback.
Match between system and the real world	The systems must speak the language of the users, with words, phrases and familiar concepts for the user
User control and freedom	Users often choose options by mistake and clearly need to indicate an exit for those unwanted situations without having to go through extensive dialogues
Consistency and standards	Users do not have to guess that different words, situations or actions mean the same thing.
Error prevention	A careful design that prevents problems is better than good error messages
Recognition rather than recall	Make objects, actions and options visible. The user does not have to remember information from one party to another. The instructions for using the system must be visible or easily recoverable.
Flexibility and efficiency of use	Design a system that can be used by a wide range of users. Provides instructions when necessary for new users without hindering the path of advanced users
Aesthetic and minimalist design	Do not show information that is not relevant. Each piece of extra information competes with the important one and decreases its relative visibility
Help users recognize, diagnose, and recover from errors	To help users, error messages should be written in simple languages, indicate the problem accurately and show a solution
Help and documentation	The best system is the one that can be used without documentation, but always allows a help or documentation, this information should be easy to find, directed to the tasks of the users, list the concrete steps to do something and be brief.

The framework is based on the software technology evaluation methodology proposed by Brown and Wallnau (Brown & Wallnau), which seeks to identify the value added by technology through the establishment of a descriptive model in terms of its features of interest and their relationship and importance to its usage contexts. In our proposed only the first stage (descriptive design) of the Brown methodology is performed, providing a solid basis for the evaluation of solvers and a context for describing the features of interest. To develop a general framework for different constraint solvers, the author must establish some broad criteria, which are not subject to specific conditions. Furthermore, comparing different solvers is subjected to factors such as differences in modelling for each solver, different settings, among others (Wallace et al., 2004; Lecoutre, Roussel, & van Dongen, 2010). Thus do not consider runtimes, or number of backtracks. Authors will only establish a simple and clear mechanism to measure constraint solver according to the specific usability features that the evaluator needs.

The framework use the usability attribute proposed by Nielsen and the use of heuristic evaluation to test the usability using a standard test (Rauf, Troubitsyna, & Porres, 2019). This framework provides a methodology based on 2 stages; **Design stages,** at this stage the modelling of the test is carried out and the **Evaluation stage,** it is the application of heuristic evaluation. The framework is presented in Figure 1.

The Design stage suggests focusing on starting by modelling the usability of the constraint solver, using the usability measurement model based on a three-level hierarchy. This model defines the usability of constraint solver in terms of: Criteria, metrics and attributes. This can be seen in Figure 2.

First level: Definition of evaluation criteria. The criteria constitute the parameters for the evaluation of usability at the highest level (first level). The use of criteria refers to the use of a set of specific identifiers and primary characteristics, which allow a critical examination of a Constraint solver.

Second level: Definition of evaluation metrics. In this context, they are defined as two types of arguments; Attribute and measure of the attribute.

Figure 1. Stages of the framework

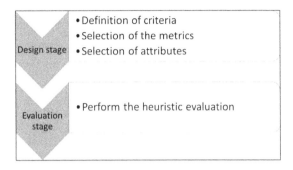

Figure 2. Model based on Criteria, Metrics, Attributes

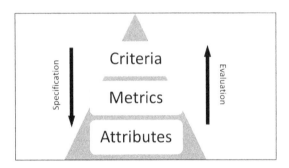

Third level: Definition of evaluation attributes. They are metrics that require the definition of attributes and must be declared qualitatively or quantitatively.

The Figure 2 allows us to visualize the relationship between the levels and processes of usability evaluation. If a solver has more heuristic evaluations made using the three-level hierarchy model, it will have greater usability. And from this new specification could be generated to modify the usability attributes of the solver. This last part is intended for future corrections and improvements that can be proposed to a solver.

Design Stage

In this stage, the authors determine the parameters for the measurement of usability. a set of criteria that allow us to evaluate the usability was defined. For each criterion a metric is applied and for each metric an attribute is measured. For the specific case of constraint solver, the authors have taken some criteria defined in the previous section and adapted to be measured according to the features of the solvers. The following criteria were defined; *Learning* (in Table 2), *Contents* (in Table 3), *Operability* (in Table 4), *Attractiveness* (in Table 5), and *Satisfaction* (in Table 6).

Table 2. List of metrics, and attributes associated to criteria learning

Criteria	Metrics	Attribute
Learning	Ease of learning	• Predictive
		• Familiarization
		• Synthetic.
	Help	• Consistency between the quality and quantity of help.
		• Context sensitive help
	Documentation	• Access to documentation / tutorials
		• Sufficiently explanatory and brief
	Effectiveness	• Create a CSP model without help / documentation
		• Solve a CSP without help / documentation
		• Minimization of execution errors

Table 3. List of metrics, and attributes associated to criteria contents

Criteria	Metrics	Attribute
Contents	Content to control the enumeration	• Data type and data structures
		• Variable selection heuristics
		• Value selection heuristics
	Content to control the propagation	• Definition of constraint
		• Create propagators
	Content for cooperation	• Integration and portability
		• input/output mechanisms

Evaluation Stage

At the end, of the design stage and once the evaluation guide has been defined, the heuristic evaluation can then be performed. In order to locate problems associated with usability, a heuristic evaluation can then be applied, which allows knowing in depth the constrain solver both functionally and its errors or possible improvements.

Heuristics Evaluation Tasks

Usability also used the heuristic evaluation (HE), HE is a usability engineering method "for finding usability problems in a user interface design by having a small set of evaluators examine the interface and judge its compliance with recognized usability principles (the "heuristics")". This method uses evaluators to find usability problems or violations that may have a deleterious effect on the ability of the user interact with the system. Typically, these evaluators are experts in usability principles, the domain of interest, or both. Nielsen and Molich (Nielsen & Molich, 1990) described the HE methodology as "cheap"', "intuitive"', "requires no advance planning"', and finally, "can be used early on in the development process"'. Often this methodology can be used in conjunction with other usability methodologies to evaluate user

Table 4. List of metrics, and attributes associated to criteria operability

Criteria	Metrics	Attribute
Operability	Modelling facility	• Definition of constraint
		• kind of constraint
		• Facility of reification.
		• Facility to define propagators
		• Facility to define value selection heuristics
		• Facility to define variable selection heuristics
	Ease of running a model	• By command line
		• By code embedding
		• By call of functions
	Easy to use	• Ease of installation
		• Simple and clear language
		• Allows selection for operating parameters
	Error tolerance	• Self-exploratory error messages
		• Minimize recovery time
		• Facilitates the correction to continue
		• Detection and warning of entry errors
	Understanding	• Interpretable interface functions
		• Clear explanation of input / output actions
		• Ease to understand the sequence of answers
		• Short messages and simple language
		• Clear functions that facilitate recall

Table 5. List of metrics, and attributes associated to criteria attractiveness

Criteria	Metrics	Attribute
Attractiveness	Attractiveness of the interface	• Aesthetically pleasing
		• Consistent presentation
		• Presentation of results in text and graphics
		• Combination of color / backgrounds
	Customize	• Customization of elements for modelling
		• Customizing elements to run CSP
		• Changeable elements in the interface

interfaces (Nielsen & Molich, 1989). To HE to be effective, that is, the greatest possible number of usability errors are found, it is recommended to perform a series of tasks, which are presented below:

1. Study previously the constraint solver to familiarize yourself with it
2. Determine the usability parameters established in the design phase.

Table 6. List of metrics, and attributes associated to criteria satisfaction

Criteria	Metrics	Attribute
Satisfaction	Reliability	• Texts and messages are easy to read
		• Simple and pleasant overall appearance
		• Allows access to help comfortably
		• The results are clearly presented
	Acceptability	• Update mechanisms
		• Multiple functionalities
		• On-line support

Table 7. Definition of Impact

Impact	Definition
Low (1)	Although it is recommended that the statement be fulfilled, its non-compliance does not imply confusion or error in the user. It would not give important usability problems.
Medium (2)	Failure to comply can cause not very serious problems of usability although it is convenient to solve them since it would facilitate the operation of the system.
High (3)	Produces significant problems of understanding and functionality in the system so it is essential that the problem is solved. It can cause serious usability problems.

3. Define, for each of the parameters, a series of questions to determine if they are met. Make an evaluation guide where each of the questions has the frequency with which the problem appears as well as its impact. The proposed criteria to estimate the impact of each of the questions is shown in the Table 6.
4. Perform the heuristic evaluation of the tool using the guide.

Then it is proposed to make a selection of users. The selection of users is a fundamental element in the evaluation process. In the selection can be considered users with knowledge of the constraint solver, given the specific use of this software.

Finally, in the framework a review and analysis of data is proposed. A systematic analysis of the data must be done in order to prepare a report detailing the problems and possible solutions applicable to solver.

As an example, the authors propose a simplified case of heuristic evaluation. For this, only the design of the learning criteria will be presented. The possible results for a testing CP solver are shown in Table 8.

Table 8 shows the result of an HE for Learning. The frequency corresponds to the number of observations (usability failures) made by the evaluator on that attribute. Then, the frequency is multiplied by the impact as a result the evaluation of that attribute is obtained. The sum of all the results is the evaluation of that criterion. A usability expert determines the impact value previously. In this case for Learning the HE value is 26, then a lower value of HE is better than a larger one.

Table 8. Example of HE on Criteria Learning

Criteria	Metrics	Attribute	Frequency	Impact	Result
Learning	Ease of learning	• Predictive	1	1	1
		• Familiarization	1	2	2
		• Synthetic.	1	1	1
	Help	• Consistency between the quality and quantity of help.	3	2	6
		• Context sensitive help	2	2	4
	Documentation	• Access to documentation / tutorials	1	3	3
		• Sufficiently explanatory and brief	2	2	4
	Effectiveness	• Create a CSP model without help / documentation	1	2	2
		• Solve a CSP without help / documentation	1	3	3
		• Minimization of execution errors	0	2	0
Result					26

CONCLUSION

The projects management is a highly complex activity, which must necessarily be supported by computer systems. Many management activities can be modeled as constraint satisfaction problems, and consequently solved by a constraint solver. To reduce the human factor when working with these solver, the authors propose a framework that allows selecting a solver according to its usability attributes.

Currently, there are varieties of constraint solvers. These can be of different types and cover different objectives. For this reason, it is difficult for a specialist to decide which solver to use in a particular project. On the other hand, there are no works that propose to evaluate any of these systems in terms of usability.

The main contributions of this work are a framework to evaluate different CP solver under a set of usability criteria. The framework is characterized by using two stages: a design stage, in which it is modelling the usability of the constraint solver, using the usability measurement model. This model defines the usability of constraint solver in terms of criteria, metrics and attributes. Later it is defined the evaluation stage which consists in conduct the experimental evaluation. In this phase a heuristic evaluation is performed. Evaluating a CP solver in terms of usability allows a better option to be taken by reducing the risks of use by a user. Consider usability in CP solvers is an unexplored area and much less associate it with project management.

ACKNOWLEDGMENT

Broderick Crawford is supported by Grant CONICYT/FONDECYT/REGULAR/1171243, Franklin Johnson is supported by Grant CONICYT/FONDECYT/INICIACION/11180524 and DGI/UPLA/ING 04-1819, Ricardo Soto is supported by Grant CONICYT/FONDECYT/REGULAR/1190129.

REFERENCES

Alba, E., & Chicano, F. (2007). Software project management with gas. *Information Sciences*, *177*(1), 2380–2401. doi:10.1016/j.ins.2006.12.020

Apt, K. R., & Wallace, M. (2007). *Constraint logic programming using eclipse*. New York, NY: Cambridge University Press.

Brown, A., & Wallnau, K. (1996). A framework for evaluating software technology. *Software, IEEE*, *13*(5), 39–49. doi:10.1109/52.536457

Brucker, P., Drexl, A., Mhring, R., Neumann, K., & Pesch, E. (1999). Resource constrained project scheduling: Notation, classification, models, and methods. *European Journal of Operational Research*, *112*(1), 3–41. doi:10.1016/S0377-2217(98)00204-5

Carlsson, M., & Mildner, P. (2010). *Sicstus Prolog - The First 25 years*. Academic Press.

Choco Team. (2010). *Choco: An open source java constraint programming library (Research report No. 10-02-INFO)*. École des Mines de Nantes.

IBM Company. (2006). *IBM ILOG CP*. Author.

Dincbas, M., Van Hentenryck, P., Simonis, H., Aggoun, A., & Herold, A. (1988). The Chip system: Constraint handling in Prolog. In E. Lusk & R. Overbeek (Eds.), *9th international conference on automated deduction* (Vol. 310, p. 774-775). Springer Berlin Heidelberg.

Fernández, A., & Hill, P. (2000). A comparative study of eight Constraint Programming Languages over the boolean and finite domains. *Constraints*, *5*(3), 275–301. doi:10.1023/A:1009816801567

Frühwirth, T. (1998). Theory and practice of constraint handling rules. *The Journal of Logic Programming*, *37*(1-3), 95–138. doi:10.1016/S0743-1066(98)10005-5

Frühwirth, T., & Abdennadher, S. (2005). *Principles of constraint systems and constraint solvers*. Academic Press.

Frühwirth, T., & Raiser, F. (Eds.). (2011). *Constraint handling rules: Compilation, execution, and analysis. Academic Press*.

Gecode Team. (2006). *Gecode: Generic constraint development environment*. Available from http://www.gecode.org

Gedik, R., Kalathia, D., Egilmez, G., & Kirac, E. (2018). A constraint programming approach for solving unrelated parallel machine scheduling problem. *Computers & Industrial Engineering, 121,* 139–149. doi:10.1016/j.cie.2018.05.014

Gent, I. P., Jefferson, C., & Miguel, I. (2006). Minion: A fast scalable constraint solver. In *Proceedings of ECAI 2006, riva del garda* (pp. 98 - 102). IOS Press.

Hebrard, E., & Siala, M. (2007). *Mistral 2.0. LAAS-CNRS.* Universite de Toulouse, CNRS.

Hentenryck, M. (2005). The comet programming language and system. *Principles and Practice of Constraint Programming - CP 2005, 11th International Conference,* 881-881.

Hentenryck, M., Saraswat, V., & Deville, Y. (1998). Design, implementation, and evaluation of the constraint language cc(FD). *The Journal of Logic Programming, 37*(1-3), 139–164. doi:10.1016/S0743-1066(98)10006-7

ISO 9241-11. (1998). *Ergonomic requirements for office work with visual display terminals (vdts) part 11: Guidance on usability. International.*

Jaffar, J., Michaylov, S., Stuckey, P. J., & Yap, R. H. C. (1992, May). The CLP(r) language and system. *ACM Transactions on Programming Languages and Systems, 14*(3), 339–395. doi:10.1145/129393.129398

Kim Mariott, P. S. (1998). *Programming with Constraints, An introduction.* MIT Press.

Kuchcinski, K. (2019). Constraint Programming in embedded systems design: Considered helpful. *Microprocessors and Microsystems, 69,* 24–34. doi:10.1016/j.micpro.2019.05.012

Kuchcinski, K., & Szymanek, R. (2010). *Jacop library user's guide.* Available from http://jacopguide. osolpro.com/guideJaCoP.html

Laalaoui, Y., & Bouguila, N. (2014). Pre-run-time scheduling in real-time systems: Current researches and artificial intelligence perspectives. *Expert Systems with Applications, 41*(5), 2196–2210. doi:10.1016/j. eswa.2013.09.018

Lazaar, N., Gotlieb, A., & Lebbah, Y. (2012). A CP framework for testing CP. *Constraints, 17*(2), 123–147. doi:10.100710601-012-9116-0

Lecoutre, C., Roussel, O., & van Dongen, M. (2010). Promoting robust black-box solvers through competitions. *Constraints, 15*(3), 317–326. doi:10.100710601-010-9092-1

Lecoutre, C., & Tabary, S. (2006). *Abscon 109 a generic CSP Solver.* Academic Press.

Niederlínski, A. (2014). *A gentle guide to Constraint Logic Programming via eclipse* [ksiazka]. Jacek Skalmierski Computer Studio.

Nielsen, J. (2012). *Usability 101: Introduction to usability.* Nielsen Norman Group.

Nielsen, J., & Molich, R. (1989, August). Teaching user interface design based on usability engineering. *SIGCHI Bull, 21*(1), 45–48. doi:10.1145/67880.67885

Nielsen, J., & Molich, R. (1990). Heuristic evaluation of user interfaces. In *Proceedings of the sigchi conference on human factors in computing systems* (pp. 249-256). New York, NY: ACM.

O'mahony, E., Hebrard, E., Holland, A., & Nugent, C. (2008). Using case-based reasoning in an algorithm portfolio for Constraint Solving. *Iris Conference on Artificial Intelligence and Cognitive Science.*

OptaPlanner Team. (2014). *OptaPlanner.* Available from http://www.optaplanner.org/

OscaR Team. (2012). *OscaR: Scala in OR.* Available from https://bitbucket.org/oscarlib/oscar

Radujković, M., & Sjekavica, M. (2017). Project Management Success Factors. *Procedia Engineering, 196*, 607–615. doi:10.1016/j.proeng.2017.08.048

Rahmanniyay, F., & Junfang Yu, A. (2018). A multi-objective stochastic programming model for project-oriented human-resource management optimization. *International Journal of Management Science and Engineering Management*, 1-9.

Rauf, I., Troubitsyna, E., & Porres, I. (2019). A systematic mapping study of API usability evaluation methods. *Computer Science Review, 33*, 49–68. doi:10.1016/j.cosrev.2019.05.001

Rossi, F., van Beek, P., & Walsh, T. (2006). *Handbook of Constraint Programming.* Elsevier.

Smolka, G. (2004). The development of Oz and mozart. In *Multiparadigm Programming in Mozart/Oz, second international conference, MOZ 2004, charleroi, Belgium, October 7-8, 2004, revised selected and invited papers* (p. 1). Academic Press.

Soto, R., Crawford, B., Olivares, R., Galleguillos, C., Castro, C., Johnson, F., ... Norero, E. (2016). Using Autonomous Search for Solving Constraint Satisfaction Problems via new modern approaches. *Swarm and Evolutionary Computation, 30*, 64–77. doi:10.1016/j.swevo.2016.04.003

Soto, R., Crawford, B., Palma, W., Galleguillos, K., Castro, C., Monfroy, E., ... Paredes, F. (2015). Boosting Autonomous Search for CSPs via Skylines. *Inf. Science, 308*, 38–48. doi:10.1016/j.ins.2015.01.035

Tulácek, M. (2009). *Constraint Solvers* (Bachelor thesis). Charles University in Prague.

Vega-Velázquez, M., García-Nájera, A., & Cervantes, H. (2018). A Survey on the Software Project Scheduling Problem. *International Journal of Production Economics, 202*, 145–161. doi:10.1016/j.ijpe.2018.04.020

Vianna, S. S. (2019). The Set Covering Problem applied to optimization of gas detectors in chemical process plants. *Computers & Chemical Engineering, 121*, 388–395. doi:10.1016/j.compchemeng.2018.11.008

Vukadinovic, S., Macuzic, I., Djapan, M., & Milosevic, M. (2018). Early management of human factors in lean industrial systems. *Safety Science.* doi:10.1016/j.ssci.2018.10.008

Wallace, M., Schimpf, J., Shen, K., & Harvey, W. (2004). On benchmarking Constraint Logic Programming platforms. Response to Fernandez and Hill's "A comparative study of eight constraint programming languages over the boolean and finite domains". *Constraints, 9*(1), 5–34. doi:10.1023/B:CONS.0000006181.40558.37

Zhou, N. (2012, January). The Language features and architecture of B-prolog. *Theory and Practice of Logic Programming, 12*(1-2), 189–218. doi:10.1017/S1471068411000445

Chapter 7
Skills for IT Project Management:
The View From EU Frameworks

Luis Fernández Sanz
https://orcid.org/0000-0003-0778-0073
University of Alcalá, Spain

María Teresa Villalba
https://orcid.org/0000-0003-0443-5979
Universidad Europea de Madrid, Spain

Vera Pospelova
Universidad de Alcalá, Spain

Manuel de Buenaga
Universidad de Alcalá, Spain

Ana Castillo
Universidad de Alcalá, Spain

Marián Fernández de Sevilla
Universidad de Alcalá, Spain

ABSTRACT

IT project management requires qualified staff capable of facing the rapidly changing conditions and even terminology of technology while managing large teams of people where main costs come from human work. A key factor for managing human side of IT is the understanding of the essential feature of people performance: skills. Capability to cope with this highly demanding field should firstly rely on clear and standardized frameworks for skills, not only the technical or hard ones but also the soft or behavioral ones, considered by employers as essential for employees' productivity. This chapter shows how the recent development of frameworks and standards in European Union (e.g. EN16234 or ESCO classification) is enabling the powerful exploitation of open big data from existing skills analysis systems for a more precise and solid determination of recommended skills for IT project management. The analysis will especially focus on the behavioral skills.

DOI: 10.4018/978-1-7998-1279-1.ch007

INTRODUCTION

Competences, skills, knowledge, job profiles, qualifications or occupations are some of the concepts most commonly used in the present within the IT profession. They can be easily found in all types of information written in e.g. job ads, training courses and CV of jobseekers. Ensuring that these terms are used consistently with a common language is essential for a correct match of needs between employers, job candidates and training providers. When the authors analyzed the case of European Union (EU), the main idea is that transnational coordination is a primary objective so this requires a common frame for all actors in ICT employment: that is a key, urgent and vital factor for the mobility of ICT people across borders. Consequently, EU has promoted different ICT competence frameworks to support a better coordination of the ICT job market where, as it happens in many other developed countries, companies are generally experiencing a shortage of qualified workers to cover their needs of digital transformation of businesses (Hüsing et al., 2015).

The efforts of EU in this area has led to a set of results in the shape of frameworks or competence models. The most relevant ones are the European e-Competence Framework (e-CF) (EN 16234-1, 2016), the European Competence, Skills, Qualification and Occupations (ESCO) classification (European Commission-1) and the European Foundational Body of Knowledge (BoK) (Oliver, 2012). These references try to capture the essence of the labor market and the opinion of stakeholders which can provide a standardized view of roles and occupations to all players in the talent field of ICT.

As a consequence, we can summarize that the aim of this chapter is to exploit these valuable assets of the above-mentioned skills frameworks to analyze which are the recommended skills profiles for those working in IT project management. This approach has the advantage of cumulating the work of hundreds of experts who worked on these models before. Moreover, as they establish a common language and model for working with the elusive field of skills categorization, these models enable the exploitation of sources of big open data to complement the profiles while capturing the reality of labor market. Our interest is not limited to the most technical skills required for effective IT project management. Employers have highlighted their interest in behavioral or non-cognitive skills as expressed in (Newton, Hurstfield, Miller, Page, & Akroyd, 2005): "employers are less demanding of technical skills, considering them trainable, if candidates exhibit employability and soft skills, and positive attributes" as stated citing the study by (Winterbotham, Adams, & Keuchel, 2002). As a consequence, we will analyze the so-called non-cognitive skills (NCS) by presenting the application of the exhaustive research done in the Skills Match project (www.skillsmatch.eu), customized to the area of IT project management. In the project, these skills are the cornerstone of a complete system for employability: the users can create their skills profiles, compared to the profile of target occupations and see which are the gaps where they can work with recommended online training resources to develop their weak points.

This chapter is organized as follows. The first section is devoted to the general underlying concepts and methodology of the work. The next three sections describe and analyze each of the mentioned frameworks (e-CF, ESCO and BoK) under the perspective of the IT project management occupations, profiles and skills. The next section illustrates how the impact and utility of these models within the IT project management area is. The authors will devote a full section to the NCS after that and the chapter will finish with a final section with conclusions and future works.

FOUNDATIONAL CONCEPTS AND METHODOLOGY

Our work with the skills and occupational side of IT project management is based on a simple set of steps as methodology to address the research questions. Our research questions can be expressed as follows:

- RQ1: can the EU skills frameworks be combined to generate a skills profiles of the IT project management area?
- RQ2: can the EU skills frameworks enable a NCS profile for the IT project management area?

The methodology for answering the questions can be described as follows:

- The first and preliminary step is the clarification of the underlying basic concepts which are essential in the area: occupation, skill, competences and knowledge. These are the basic bricks for a proper analysis of the existing frameworks.
- Once the comparison and analysis of the concepts is done, the foundations for comparing frameworks enable the analysis of each of them, firstly showing some of their strengths and weaknesses and then their application to the area of IT project management answering RQ1.
- Finally, we will segment the exploitation of skills profiles for IT project management to the NCS thus answering RQ2.

Following this idea of methodology, we firstly define the basic concepts required for the work. In reality, we can exploit the previous similar made by (Fernández Sanz, et. al., 2017) where the authors analyzed the definitions offered by the different frameworks and we are summarizing the findings in Table 1.

As it can be easily realised in the table, these concepts are compatible among the frameworks. From our point of view, the ESCO definitions are perfectly valid as reference for this chapter.

THE E-COMPETENCE FRAMEWORK (e-CF)

The European e-Competence Framework (e-CF) provides a common language to describe and support mutual understanding of the competences required and deployed by ICT professionals, including both practitioners and managers. In 2005, further to the recommendations of the European e-Skills Forum, the CEN ICT Skills Workshop members agreed that national ICT framework stakeholders as well as European ICT industry representatives should consider developing a European e-Competence Framework. ICT framework stakeholders met with representatives from European larger enterprises to carry out this initiative, encouraged and accompanied by the European Commission.

The e-CF version 1.0 was published in 2008 from the outcome of two years e-Skills multi-stakeholder, ICT and human resources experts' work from multiple organization levels. The e-CF version 2.0 was published 2 years later, with dimension 4 fully developed, and accompanied by an updated user guide and a newly developed methodology documentation. The e-CF framework became a standard for the ICT competences in Europe in 2016 (EN 16234-1, 2016) in what was informally considered its version 3.0. A new version of the standard, the so-called version 4.0, will be published in 2019 after a project for updating and refining it.

Table 1. Structure of the ESCO framework for ICT services

Concept	ESCO	e-CF	BOK	Comments
Occupation	Grouping of jobs involving similar tasks and which require a similar skill set.	A job profile provides a comprehensive description written and formal of a job	Same as e-CF	They refer to similar concepts
Competence	Proven ability to use knowledge, skills and personal, social and/or methodological abilities, in work or study situations and in professional and personal development.	Demonstrated ability to apply knowledge, skills and attitudes for achieving observable results.	Same as e-CF	They refer to similar concepts
Skill	Ability to apply knowledge and use know-how to complete tasks and solve problems	It is related to competences through some examples.		They refer to similar concepts. BOK does not consider this concept
Knowledge	Outcome of the assimilation of information through learning	It is related to competences through some examples.	High-level areas of knowledge that represent the base level starting ICT professionals should understand. Each knowledge area includes a list of items required as foundational knowledge necessary under that knowledge area.	They refer to similar concepts.

This framework is designed to fulfil the requirements of organizations and it is based on the following points:

- The e-CF expresses ICT competence.
- The e-CF is an enabler; it is designed to be a tool to empower users, not to restrict them, being them from private or public sector organization, ICT user or ICT supply companies, educational institutions, social partners or individuals.
- A competence can be a component of a job role, but it cannot be used as a substitute for similarly named job titles. Competences can be aggregated to represent the essential content of a job role or profile; moreover, one single competence may be assigned to a number of different job profiles.
- Competence is not to be confused with process or technology concepts. For example, Big Data or Cloud computing represent evolving technologies and they may be included in the e-CF dimension of knowledge and skills.

e-CF is structured through four dimensions that reflect different levels of business and human resource planning requirements in addition to job / work proficiency levels:

- **Dimension 1**: 5 e-Competence areas, derived from the ICT business processes: Plan, Build, Run, Enable and Manage. Plan, Build and Run are core areas whilst Enable and Manage are cross-cutting issues referred and related to the former. Each area includes a set of e-Competences.

- **Dimension 2**: A competence is a demonstrated ability to apply knowledge, skills and attitudes for achieving observable results. The e-Competences can then be adapted and customized into different business contexts such as e-commerce, e-health, e-banking, etc. According to dimension 2, 41 e-Competences have been identified and described in the e-CF 4.0:
  - PLAN
    - A.1. IS and Business Strategy Alignment
    - A.2. Service Level Management
    - A.3. Business Plan Development
    - A.4. Product/ Service Planning
    - A.5. Architecture Design
    - A.6. Application Design
    - A.7. Technology Trend Monitoring
    - A.8. Sustainable Development
    - A.9. Innovating
    - A.10 User Experience
  - B. BUILD
    - B.1. Application Development
    - B.2. Component Integration
    - B.3. Testing
    - B.4. Solution Deployment
    - B.5. Documentation Production
    - B.6. Systems Engineering
  - C. RUN
    - C.1. User Support
    - C.2. Change Support
    - C.3. Service Delivery
    - C.4. Problem Management
    - C.5. Systems Management
  - D. ENABLE
    - D.1.Information Security Strategy Development
    - D.2. ICT Quality Strategy Development
    - D.3. Education and Training Provision
    - D.4. Purchasing
    - D.5. Sales Development
    - D.6. Digital Marketing
    - D.7. Data Science and Analytics
    - D.8. Contract Management
    - D.9. Personnel Development
    - D.10. Information and Knowledge Management
    - D.11. Needs Identification
  - E. MANAGE
    - E.1. Forecast Development
    - E.2. Project and Portfolio Management
    - E.3. Risk Management

- E.4. Relationship Management
- E.5. Process Improvement
- E.6. ICT Quality Management
- E.7. Business Change Management
- E.8. Information Security Management
- E.9. IS Governance

Competences of version 4.0 are the results of a review of the 40 ones from version 3.0 completely updated in dimensions 2, 3 and 4, revising and/or enlarging content where it was meaningful after expert review and comments from a large set of stakeholders through direct meeting interaction, online surveys and workshops. The process resulted in three new competences (A.10. User Experience, C.5. Systems Management and D.7 Data Science and Analytics) while the competence D.5. Sales Development appear as a merge of three previous ones: Sales Proposal Development, Sales Management and Channel Management.

The dimension 3 with 5 proficiency levels (e-1 through to e-5) integrates four facets in version 4.0: influence, context complexity, autonomy and behavior. The dimension 4 is exemplificative and not pretend exhaustive samples of knowledge and skills related to each e-Competence. Knowledge and skills are related to competences through the most representative examples. They add value and context to the understanding and scope of each competence, but they are not a list or catalogue.

In summary, e-competences in dimension 1 and 2 are mainly presented from the organizational perspective. Dimension 3 offers a bridge between organizational and individual competences. Dimension 4, with its precise and specific skills and knowledges easily linkable to learning outcomes, can represent a bridge between organization competences and vocational training and qualifications. The 4-dimension structure of e-CF makes it particularly flexible and valuable for different uses. It provides a pragmatic competence overview of the European ICT labor market from the industry and public sector perspective. One additional feature provided by version 4.0 of e-CF is the addition of 7 transversals aspect for professional to be aware of and, if applicable, behaving proactively in: T1 Accessibility, T2 Ethics, T3 ICT legal issues, T4 Privacy, T5 Security, T6 Sustainability and T7 Usability. The standard will also present a set of annexes with links to other frameworks like ESCO (https://ec.europa.eu/esco/portal), DigComp (Carretero Gómez, et. al., 2017), SFIA (https://www.sfia-online.org/en/framework), etc.

The e-CF universe is complemented by additional technical documents. The most relevant one for our purpose of analyzing the recommended skills profile for IT project management is CWA 16458-1:2018, which describes 30 ICT Professional Role Profiles providing a generic set of typical roles performed by ICT Professionals in any organization, covering the full ICT business process. They represent roles, not occupations, so the descriptions are less detailed and less specific than job descriptions and offer a simple but flexible start point for applying e-CF to organizations and professionals.

Although the 30 profiles cover a wide range of professional activities, when analyzing them for the area of IT project management, the most evident related role is Project Manager, expressed as managing projects to achieve optimal performance and results. So, its mission is defining, implementing and managing projects from conception to final delivery, acting as responsible for achieving optimal results, conforming to standards for quality, safety and sustainability and complying with defined scope performance, costs, and schedule. Where applicable, the role involves deploying agile practices. The recommended profile of e-CF competences is the following one:

- A.4. Product/Service Planning Level 4: "Provides leadership and takes responsibility for, developing and maintaining overall plans".
- E.2. Project and Portfolio Management Level 4: "Manages complex projects or programmes, including interaction with others. Influences project strategy by proposing new or alternative solutions and balancing effectiveness and efficiency. Is empowered to revise rules and choose standards. Takes overall responsibility for project outcomes, including finance and resource management and works beyond project boundary".
- E.3. Risk Management Level 3: "Decides on appropriate actions required to adapt security and address risk exposure. Evaluates, manages and ensures validation of exceptions; audits ICT processes and environment."
- E.4. Relationship Management Level 3: "Manages simple multi-stakeholder, multi-disciplinary relationships."
- E.7. Business Change Management Level 3: "Evaluates change requirements and exploits specialist skills to identify possible methods and standards that can be deployed."

The other key item in EN16234 for IT project management is the competence E.2. Project and Portfolio Management Level 4 (mentioned in the role of Project Manager). It is described as set of activities including:

- Implements plans for a program of change.
- Plans, directs and manages a single or portfolio of ICT projects or services to ensure co-ordination and management of interdependencies.
- Orchestrates projects to develop or implement new, internal or externally defined processes to meet identified business needs.
- Defines activities, responsibilities, critical milestones, resources, skills needs, interfaces and budget, optimizes costs and time utilization, minimizes waste and strives for high quality.
- Develops contingency plans to address potential implementation issues.
- Delivers project on time, on budget and in accordance with original requirements taking into account changing circumstances.
- Creates and maintains documents to facilitate monitoring of project progress.

The examples of skills and knowledges shown for this competence are:

- Knowledge:
  - K1 a project methodology, including approaches to define project steps and tools to set up action plans
  - K2 technologies to be implemented within the project
  - K3 company business strategy and business processes
  - K4 development and compliance to financial plans and budgets
  - K5 IPR principles and regulation
  - K6 structured project management methodologies (e.g. agile techniques, DevOps)
  - K7 methods to plan and deliver benefits and business value (e.g. benefits mapping)

- Skills:
  - ○ S1 identify project risks and define action plans to mitigate
  - ○ S2 define a project plan by breaking it down into individual project tasks
  - ○ S3 communicate project progress to all relevant parties reporting on topics such as cost control, schedule achievements, quality control, risk avoidance and changes to project specifications
  - ○ S4 delegate tasks and manage team member contributions appropriately
  - ○ S5 manage external contracted resources to achieve project objectives
  - ○ S6 optimize project portfolio timelines and delivery objectives by achieving consensus on stakeholder priorities

The authors will later compare this information to the one coming from other European sources of information in Section "Common recommended skills for IT project management".

European Classification of Skills/Competences, Qualification and Occupation (ESCO)

ESCO is the multilingual classification of European Skills, Competences, Qualifications and Occupations. The European Commission services launched the project in 2010 with an open stakeholder consultation. ESCO is part of the Europe 2020 strategy.

The first version of ESCO was published on 23 October 2013, but it has been gradually developed focusing on sets of sectors to work in occupations, skills and knowledge. This continuous update is needed in order to reflect changes in the European labor market and in education and training. ESCO v1 was launched in 2017, after a complete revision carried out by the sectoral reference groups, groups of experts in each sector selected by the ESCO project secretariat after a public call for applications. The classification is now available free of charge to all stakeholders through the ESCO website[1].

The ESCO framework was mostly developed to link the gap between the labor market and the world of education and training. Thus, it is possible to minimize the detected mismatch between the skills of jobseekers and the needs of the companies.

The ESCO project is focused on the classification of European Skills, Competences, Qualifications and Occupations, which should be centered in occupational profiles showing the relationships between occupations, skills, competences and qualifications. These pillars are structured hierarchically and inter-related with each other.

ESCO is linked to relevant international classifications, standards and frameworks, such as The Statistical classification of economic activities in the European Community (NACE), the International Standard Classification of Occupations (ISCO) (International Labour Organization) and EQF (Council of the European Union, 2017) as some primary inspirational sources or references. However, specificity of some sectors like the one of ICT Services has leaded to decisions which have adjusted the initial common structure and procedures of creation. As an example, NACE classification of economic activity was suggested as guideline for the sectoral breakdown of occupations in all sectors. In the case of ICT Services was not considered as a good inspiration due to the fact that ICT occupations are transversal by nature and this classification would be not so meaningful.

The ESCO framework can be used to provide different services in several business cases:

- Bridging the communication gap between education and work. Effective communication and dialogue between the labor market and the education and training sector is vital, as the specific occupations, skills, competences and qualifications that people need change over time.
- Online matching of people to jobs. It helps employees to identify new career paths and show what transferable skills they have between occupations. ESCO can enhance recruitment by contributing to better competence-based job matching.
- Enabling mobility. Due to in almost all European countries, employment and career guidance services use different national classifications, mapping them to ESCO increases semantic interoperability. ESCO translates information between different classification systems, functioning as a hub.
- Supporting education and training in the shift to learning outcomes. The standardized terminology proposed by ESCO will facilitate the dialogue between labor market and education and training stakeholders within and across sectors and borders.
- Supporting skills intelligence and statistics. ESCO can serve as a basis for other types of research, such as benchmarking and cross-country comparison.

ESCO identifies and categorizes skills, competences, qualifications and occupations in a standard way, using standard terminology in all EU languages. The model is structured on the basis of three pillars representing a searchable database in 26 languages. These pillars are:

- **Occupations**: The ESCO occupations pillar contains occupation groups and occupations. An occupation is a grouping of jobs involving similar tasks and which require a similar skill set. An occupation group clusters occupations or occupation groups with common characteristics in a hierarchical way. The initial adopted scheme was the sectoral breakdown that is shown in Figure 1. The first level was structured into four categories: governance, management, development and operations. A second level was established under each category, except for ICT Governance because it involved a reduced number of occupations (Chief Information Officer, Chief Technology Officer, ICT Market Strategist, etc.). However, the final adopted structure is based on ISCO, the International Standard Classification of Occupations (International Labour Organization) which was implemented by many European countries in the past.
- **Skills/Competences:** The skills and competences pillar contain skills, competences, knowledge as well as skills and competence group concepts. It also includes other concepts that are frequently used to describe occupational profiles on the labor market, such as tools, materials, hardware, software and work contexts. Work context refers to concepts that can be used to describe the specific context of different jobs that belongs to the same occupation. Work context can, for example, describe a workplace, types of company, environmental conditions, products, technologies or business activities. Types of skills and competences:
  - Transversal skills and competences
  - Cross-sector skills and competences
    - Thinking
    - Language
    - Application of knowledge
    - Social interaction
    - Attitudes and values

- ○ Sector-specific skills and competences
  - ○ Occupation-specific skills and competences
  - ○ Job-specific skills and competences
- **Qualifications:** The qualifications pillar contains qualification groups and qualifications. A qualification is the formal outcome of an assessment and validation process which is obtained when a competent body determines that an individual has achieved learning outcomes to given standards. A qualification is defined by:
  - ○ Category:
    - ▪ National qualifications (indirectly via the EQF portal)
    - ▪ Qualifications awarded at national level but regulated at European level (directly in ESCO)
    - ▪ (International) qualifications, certificates and licenses linked to tasks, technologies (directly in ESCO)
    - ▪ (International) qualifications and certificates linked to occupations and sectors (directly in ESCO)
  - ○ Title.
  - ○ Awarding body
  - ○ Expiring date (optional)
  - ○ EQF level (optional)
  - ○ Definition (optional)
  - ○ Scope note (optional)

The pillars are interlinked to show the relationships between them. Occupational profiles show whether skills and competences are essential or optional and what qualifications are relevant for each ESCO Occupation. Alternatively, the user can identify a specific skill and see which occupation or qualification this skill is relevant to.

The structure of ESCO for ICT Services is summarized in Table 2. As commented, ESCO covers all sectors of economic activities so the global numbers for the whole ESCO structure are much higher: 2942 occupations and about 13485 skills and knowledge items. Everything adapted to 26 languages of the European Union.

When analyzing the information related to the area of IT project management, we can find the following items:

- Occupation: ICT project manager. It is described by mentioning its main tasks: "ICT project managers schedule, control and direct the resources, people, funding and facilities to achieve the objectives of ICT projects. They establish budgets and timelines, perform risk analysis and quality management, and complete project closure reports". Several alternative names have been

Table 2. Structure of the ESCO framework for ICT services

Profiles/occupations	111
Optional Skills/Knowledges	467
Essential Skills/Knowledges	631

identified for this occupation: IT projects manager, IT project manager, web projects manager, web project manager, ICT project managers. The recommended skill set for the occupation is the following one:

- ◦ Essential skills: apply conflict management, build business relationships, coach employees, create project specifications, estimate duration of work, identify legal requirements, manage ICT project, manage budgets, manage project information, manage staff, perform project management, perform resource planning, perform risk analysis, provide cost benefit analysis reports, recruit employees, train employees
- ◦ Essential knowledge: ICT project management, ICT project management methodologies, internal risk management policy, quality standards

THE EUROPEAN FOUNDATIONAL ICT BODY OF KNOWLEDGE (BoK)

The Body of Knowledge (known as BOK) is the complete set of concepts, terms and activities that compose a professional domain, known by the relevant learned society or professional association. The BoK often forms the basis for curricula for most professional programs, setting the essential competencies to get accredited before applying these principles in practice. There are a vast number of Bodies of Knowledge in each area of professional specialization and the ICT field is not an exception. However, despite its high acceptance, there is currently no global or European Body of Knowledge that is all encompassing, and which addresses all the ICT knowledge areas required by the industry. This situation is due to, in some cases, several countries have a national ICT BoK adapted to their national context. Besides it is possible to find different BOK on ICT field as outcome from different research projects, as happens with SWEBOK created by the IEEE Computer Society (IEEE Computer Society) and related to the software engineering discipline (Sicilia et al., 2005); with another shape, also the Computing Curricula, created by the ACM IEEE-CS joint committee is a well-known proposal of a set a curricular guideline on computer sciences (Draft, 2013).

These Bodies of Knowledge usually either structure the content adopting an industry point of view with the future employability of students in mind or take a purely educational point of view. The European Foundational ICT Body of Knowledge (IEEE Computer Society, 2014) claims to be the base level knowledge required to enter the ICT profession and acts as the first point of reference for anyone interested in working in ICT. BoK is linked to e-CF, since it was created after e-CF was well structured in version 3.0. A new project for updating it and linking to the new e_CF version 4.0 is planned for 2019.

The structure of the Foundational ICT Body of Knowledge could be described as an 'inverted T-model'. In this structure the horizontal axis shows the knowledge areas of the ICT domain, while the vertical axis corresponds to specific knowledge and skills to specialize in one domain. Its structure is summarized in Table 3.

The ICT BOK considers 12 areas and each area includes a:

1. List of items required as foundational knowledge necessary under this Knowledge Area.
2. List of references to the e-Competence Framework.
3. List of possible job profiles that require having an understanding of the Knowledge Area.
4. List of examples of specific Bodies of Knowledge, certification and training possibilities.

Table 3. Structure of the BoK framework

Job profiles	28
Knowledge	91
Areas	12
Competences	33

One of those areas is Project Management. The importance of this area is evidenced by the fact that "every IT project needs professional business managers capable of making effective and efficient project management decisions through the integration of specific knowledge, business understanding, and project management techniques supported by appropriate project management software" (European Commission, 2015). The area is linked to some role profiles from e-CF like Project manager, CIO or ICT Operations Manager as well as well-known knowledge, certification and training possibilities such as PRINCE2®, IPMA OR PMI certifications.

This approach should be supported by both quantitative and qualitative data relating to project planning, to evaluate alternative strategies for executing projects, to use a range of electronic and non-electronic tools to create a project plan, to understand the people, processes and procedures around organizing a project, including project contracts, risk management and people management. The area of Project Management also lists the following set of foundational knowledge items:

- Project management principles and concepts
- Project planning, monitoring and control
- Cost / financial management (including budget planning, etc)
- Fundamentals of econometrics
- Project management methodologies and tools
- Change management

COMMON RECOMMENDED SKILLS FOR IT PROJECT MANAGEMENT

As we can see, there are a wide set of skills and knowledge items recommended for the position of IT project manager and the competence of IT project management. The most evident link appears between BOK and e-CF as the first one directly connects the knowledge area of Project Management with three e-CF competences: E2 Project and Portfolio Management, A4 Product/Service Planning and C4 Problem Management. This information would be applicable to general IT project management activity, probably selecting the two competences E.2 and A.4 as the most directly linked to typical project management.

This can be contrasted to the expression of the role of IT project manager inserted in annexes of the new version 4.0 of the standard EN16234. The role profile previously published in CWA 16458:2018 (CEN, 16458-1) is confirmed with the next configuration of the standard so the recommended competences are:

- A.4. Product or Project Planning – Level 4
- E.2. Project and Portfolio Management – Level 4
- E.3. Risk Management – Level 3

- E.4. Relationship Management – Level 3
- E.7. Business Change Management – Level 3

When working with the relationship between ESCO and e-CF, we can compare the previous competences of e-CF with the set of skills and knowledge of ICT project manager occupation from ESCO. The following list shows the description of each of the five previous competences with the most similar items from the ESCO profile of ICT project manager:

- A.4. Product/Service Planning Level 4: "Provides leadership and takes responsibility for, developing and maintaining overall plans". ESCO: perform project management and perform resource planning
- E.2. Project and Portfolio Management Level 4: "Manages complex projects or programmes, including interaction with others. Influences project strategy by proposing new or alternative solutions and balancing effectiveness and efficiency. Is empowered to revise rules and choose standards. Takes overall responsibility for project outcomes, including finance and resource management and works beyond project boundary". ESCO: ICT project management, ICT project management methodologies and estimate duration of work, manage ICT project, manage budgets, manage project information
- E.3. Risk Management Level 3: "Decides on appropriate actions required to adapt security and address risk exposure. Evaluates, manages and ensures validation of exceptions; audits ICT processes and environment." ESCO: perform risk analysis, provide cost benefit analysis reports, internal risk management policy
- E.4. Relationship Management Level 3: "Manages simple multi-stakeholder, multi-disciplinary relationships." ESCO: build business relationships, apply conflict management, coach employees and manage staff.
- E.7. Business Change Management Level 3: "Evaluates change requirements and exploits specialist skills to identify possible methods and standards that can be deployed." ESCO: provide cost benefit analysis reports

There are still other skills from the ESCO profile which we cannot clearly be linked to the 5 e-CF competences: recruit employees, train employees, quality standards, create project specifications and identify legal requirements. These skills are more connected to other e-CF competences like D.3. Education and Training Provision, E.6. ICT Quality Management, etc.

This comparison can be easily appreciated in Table 4.

The similarities and some of the existing cross-references among the most relevant frameworks (E-CF, ESCO and BoK) are a good basis for their integration as it was already demonstrated in integrative framework described in (Fernández Sanz, et. al., 2017). However, we can see here that the match between EN16234 and ESCO is not perfect as there are some ESCO skills connected to other competences not explicitly mentioned in the core set of the IT project manager profile. This answers RQ1.

However, the degree of matching is high, and we can conclude that the set of the 5 e-CF competences and their associated ESCO skills represent the core set of skills recommended for the occupation of IT project manager. Obviously, it is always possible to add complementary skills or knowledge items as we have seen, even because ESCO considers not only the so-called essential skills but also possible

Table 4. Comparison of proposed skills for the IT project management area

EN16234 competences in profile	ESCO skills	Comment
A.4. Product or Project Planning – Level 4	perform project management perform resource planning	Good match between ESCO skills and e-CF competences
E.2. Project and Portfolio Management – Level 4	ICT project management ICT project management methodologies estimate duration of work manage ICT project manage budgets manage project information	Good match between ESCO skills and e-CF competences
E.3. Risk Management – Level 3	perform risk analysis provide cost benefit analysis reports internal risk management policy 1.	Good match between ESCO skills and e-CF competences
E.4. Relationship Management – Level 3	build business relationships apply conflict management coach employees and manage staff	Good match between ESCO skills and e-CF competences
E.7. Business Change Management – Level 3	provide cost benefit analysis reports	Good match between ESCO skills and e-CF competences
	recruit employees train employees quality standards create project specifications identify legal requirements	Connected to e-CF Competences not explicitly mentioned in the e-CF role profile: D.3. Education and Training Provision, E.6. ICT Quality Management,

optional ones which could be useful in particular situations or conditions for the occupation. The fact that the list of examples of skills and knowledge items listed for each competence of EN16234 is not aimed at being exhaustive also adds a possibility of finding additional recommendations. One relevant conclusion is that more work is required to achieve a better coordination of the two big EU references: ESCO and EN16234.

THE ADDITIONAL KEY ASPECT: NON-COGNITIVE SKILLS

The importance of non-cognitive skills comes from the high number of studies which correlate such skills with success in educational performance, employability, income and professional development or career e.g. (Brunello & Schlotter, 2011; Lippman, Ryberg, Carney, & Moore, 2015b; Lindqvist, Erik & Westman, Roine, 2009). But it also comes from the confirmation that "employers are less demanding of technical skills, considering them trainable, if candidates exhibit employability and soft skills, and positive attributes" as stated in (Newton, Hurstfield, Miller, Page, & Akroyd, 2005) citing the study by (Winterbotham, Adams, & Keuchel, 2002). Even more, the respondents interviewed for the study of (Newton et al., 2005) emphasized the need for well-developed soft skills in applicants to openings, and identified that soft skills were linked, in employers' minds, with positive characteristics and attributes. The reports also refer to (Costin, G.P., 2002) as he claimed that hard skill performance is often dependent upon soft skill capacity, primarily because learning itself is a soft skill.

One consequence of the increased focus on those skills, which are complementary to the specific technical skills for jobs, is reflected in the multitude of terms the experts and people use. The list includes names like 21st Century skills, life skills, essential skills, behavioral skills, non-cognitive skills, youth development assets, workplace or work readiness competencies, social emotional learning (SEL), transferable skills, employability skills, behavioral skills and character skills or strengths. The terms are not interchangeable; they point to different aspects of the world of these skills, and to different outcomes with which they are associated.

As explained in (Gutman & Schoon, 2016), the term "non-cognitive", however, creates a "false dichotomy" between cognitive abilities and what are often seen as psychosocial or soft skills". It is tempting to divide factors into two separated groups, but this division is not commonly agreed as a precise and practical categorization. Dichotomies such as technical/non-technical, hard/soft, cognitive/non-cognitive are more a simplified idea for informal work than a well-defined classification with formal definitions. The consequence is that there is little agreement even on whether 'non-cognitive skills' is the right way to describe the set of issues under discussion, and terms such as 'character skills', 'competencies', 'personality traits', 'soft skills', '21st Century skills' and 'life skills' are also widely used. Additional references are "socio-emotional skills," "transferable skills" or "21st-century skills" and one very well-accepted by experts: "behavioral skills". The name of NCS has been object of debate and analysis but, with all these considerations, the pragmatic definition of the NCS will refer to skills, behaviour, attitudes and personal qualities which enable a reflective ability of the individuals to effectively:

- react to and interact with their environment (social side)
- react to and interact with themselves (self-image, feelings and vision of the world)
- act and react to conditions and problems of their work when pursuing results (context and performance side), and
- effectively apply thinking methods and abilities to work (methodological side).

The authors have not distinguished between hard skills and NCS in the previous sections. However, as commented before, non-cognitive skills (NCS) are very relevant from the point of view of employers and deserve a specific analysis to clarify the complete skills set recommended for IT project management. One basic element to work with NCS is to have a common framework for managing the information. Unfortunately, after the extensive research carried out during the first phases of the project Skills Match[2], there is not standards or valid reference frameworks which enable a unified view of these skills, albeit the big number of contributions in literature and as reports from reputed organisms. So, the project Skills Match has created the NCSF, the Non-Cognitive Skills Framework, after an extensive work of research of hundreds of references and with the validation of experts in human resources management and recruitment.

Basically, the NCSF includes a set of 36 NCS which may be visualized in a structure of clusters as shown in Figure 1. It is supported by detailed descriptions of each skill, each one complemented by a non-exhaustive list of "buzzwords" which represent terms and expressions which are popular and common ways to contextualize each NCS in practical application. 774 words and expressions complement the descriptions of the NCS with an average of 21 per NCS. The 36 NCS of the framework have been mapped into the ESCO skills set by identifying their equivalent items, finally implemented in a set of 105 ESCO skills connected to the 36 NCS of the framework.

Figure 1. Optional structure of the NCSF represented as clusters in the shape of hive cells

Considering the NCSF as unified reference for NCS, the authors can now proceed to analyze the NCS recommended for IT project management. One of the advantages of our approach of using a model connected to ESCO is the possibility of exploiting the huge datasets provided by services and initiatives of the European Union as they use the references to ESCO, thus serving as universal link among the models. One of the best options is the Skills-OVATE (Skills Online Vacancy Analysis Tool for Europesystem) from CEDEFOP which offers detailed information on jobs and employer skill demands as requested in online job vacancies. The recently available version presents data from more than 32 million of vacancies collected between 1 July 2018 and 31 December 2018. Thousands of sources are covered including private job portals, public employment service portals, recruitment agencies, online newspapers and employer websites.

As Ovate portal stores big amount of data about ESCO skills and occupations, the authors will use the data from this portal in our study to find a relation between ESCO occupation skills and our NCS framework to see what employers require for IT project managers. It is important to mention that Ovate show data for group and not for specific position, this means that we could make a relation for the group and not for specific position. Using the existing relation between ESCO and the NCSF, the authors used

Ovate data to obtain groups of occupations for each ESCO skill connected to each NCS. With this link, we are capable of analyzing two different relevant options:

- Analysis of the relation between an occupation or group of occupations, in our case those connected to IT project management in general sense, and the demanded NCS for them
- Analysis of the occupations where the basic ESCO skills connected to project management such as "manage project information", "manage staff" and "manage project metrics". This analysis helps in realizing that project management skills are not restricted to occupations of project managers in the area of IT.

Referred to the first type of analysis, after extracting data from OVATE, we can realize, for example, that for the group of occupations 1330, "Information and communications technology service managers" (where traditional IT project managers and other project and service managers are classified) the NCS demanded by employers are the ones shown in Table 5. The table shows the NCS from the NCSF framework, its counterpart skill in ESCO and the percentage of job vacancies (for this group, the analyzed job vacancies are 163,530) which demand it.

In Table 5 we can appreciate that the three most demanded NCS skills for group 1330 are "adaptability", "organization" and "problem-solving".

The other analysis can show how some basic skills for project management can be present in different IT occupations.

Table 6 shows some of the project management skills that present in some of IT occupations. The highest result is obtained by the skill "manage staff", which is present in 14.4% of occupations in group "Information and communications technology service managers".

One final application of our NCSF framework is the use of buzzwords of the NCS (which complement their description) to make a deeper analysis of the occupation of "ICT project manager" by linking the skills suggested by ESCO portal for that specific occupation to NCS with the help of the buzzwords (see Table 7). This answers RQ2.

As we can see in Table 6, there is a massive presence of the NCS organization in the profile together with leadership, coaching conflict resolution or networking. This type of skills profile is clearly more focused on the organizational side of project managers than on the relational and people side although both are covered. This would reveal a certain bias to this part in the method of development of ESCO and the mindset of experts involved in it.

CONCLUSION AND FUTURE WORKS

In the past, the determination and management of the recommended skill sets for the professional activities in IT were more like an exercise of craftsmanship with spotted and very heterogeneous information which was not suitable for a systematic work. Now, the existence of consolidated skills frameworks and references, both general such ESCO or the NCSF or specialized in IT such as e-CF (EN 16234-1, 2016) or the BOK (European Commission, 2015) enable a more uniform and clearer playground where the existence of huge systems and database with extensive information from labor market and expert (such as OVATE or the own database of ESCO) can contribute with the power of open big data processing. This scenario leads to a new dimension in the management of IT professional talent with a bright future

Table 5. NCS relation for group 1330

NCS	ESCO	%
adaptability	adapt to change	82.10%
coaching	give advice to others	6.50%
communication	report facts	17.90%
customer focus	satisfy customers	1.60%
diligence	attention to detail	6.10%
diligence	make an effort	22.30%
diligence	work efficiently	2.60%
entrepreneurship	entrepreneurship	3.10%
leadership	lead others	13.10%
manage quality	manage quality	2.40%
motivate others	delegate activities	19.60%
motivate others	demonstrate enthusiasm	17.60%
motivate others	give advice to others	6.50%
motivate others	manage staff	14.40%
motivation	demonstrate enthusiasm	17.60%
motivation	work independently	18.30%
networking	persuade others	2.20%
organization	manage time	35.30%
positive attitude	demonstrate enthusiasm	17.60%
problem-solving	develop strategy to solve problems	34.60%
reliability	act reliably	2.70%
self-management	assertiveness	18.40%
teamwork	work in teams	15.30%

Table 6. Project management skills presence in IT occupations

Occupation group	Manage project information	Manage staff	Manage project metrics
Application programmers			4.4%
Database and network positions not elsewhere classified	5.5%		3.0%
Engineering professionals not elsewhere classified	5.5%	7.5%	1.9%
Information and communications technology service managers		14.4%	
Management and organization analysts	3.3%		
Software and application developers and analysts not elsewhere classified			9.4%
Software developers	2.1%		8.5%
Systems analysts	4.4%		
Web and multimedia developers	2.3%	5.6%	8.4%

Table 7. ICT project manager occupation related to NCS using Buzzwords

"ICT project manager" occupations in ESCO	Buzzword	NCS
apply conflict management	conflict management	conflict resolution
build business relationships	build relationships	networking
coach employees	coach	coaching
create project specifications	project management	organisation
estimate duration of work	time management	organisation
identify legal requirements	legal duty	respect privacy
manage ICT project	project management	organisation
manage budgets	project management	organisation
manage project information	project management	organisation
manage staff	people management	leadership
perform project management	project management	organisation
perform resource planning	project management	organisation
perform risk analysis	project management	organisation
provide cost benefit analysis reports	project management	organisation
recruit employees	project management	organisation
train employees	coach	coaching

of additional possible tools for an effective work. Obviously, there are limitations in this study as the sources of information are still evolving and some of the available datasets are still preliminary versions. Moreover, it is still required a deep analysis of existing big sets of information between ESCO and EN16234 using text mining techniques to improve the mapping between both of the, thus allowing a better combination of both for generating more precise occupation profiles. We are now working in this area once we have replicated the structure of both sources in a local integrated database which will serve as source for detailed text mining and matching.

As a simple example, this approach opens the possibility of also linking the available offer of training opportunities (e.g, MOOCs) to the required skills for specific occupations like IT project manager. This option has already been explored and successfully tested by the project Skills Match with automatic text mining procedures fed by data scraped from relevant MOOC repositories like MOOC-list[3]: it is possible to identify which courses are aimed at developing one or several NCS thus enabling existing or future IT professionals to develop such NCS for adjusting their skills profile to what is required by employers and labor market. We are already working in this line of activity having already analyzed thousands of online courses through semiautomated mechanism which combine automatics data collection from information repositories with text mining and semantic identification. Some preliminary results in the identification of courses for developing NCS have been already collected allowing us to develop a ranking of skills according to the availability of training opportunities to develop them.

ACKNOWLEDGMENT

This work has been partially funded by the project Skills Match, co-funded by European Commission Directorate General for Communications Networks, Content & Technology (DG CONNECT), Unit for Interactive Technologies, Digital for Culture and Education, under the grant agreement no. LC-00822001 (OKT2017).

REFERENCES

Carretero Gómez, S., Vuorikari, R., & Punie, Y. (2017). *DigComp 2.1: The Digital Competence Framework for Citizens with eight proficiency levels and examples of use*. Publications Office of the European Union.

CEN. (2018a). *CWA 16458-1:2018. European ICT professionals role profiles, Version 2 – Part 1: The 30 ICT profiles*. CEN.

CEN. (2018b). *EN 16234-1:2016. e-Competence Framework (e-CF) - A common European Framework for ICT Professionals in all industry sectors - Part 1: Framework*. CEN.

Council of the European Union. (2017). *Council Recommendation on the European Qualifications Framework for lifelong learning and repealing the Recommendation of the European Parliament and of the Council of 23 April 2008 on the establishment of the European Qualifications Framework for lifelong learning*. author.

Draft, S. (2013). *Computer Science Curricula 2013*. Academic Press.

European Commission. (2015). *e-Skills for ICT Professionalism. Creating a European Foundational ICT Body of Knowledge. European Commission*. ESCO: European Classification of Skills/Competences, Qualifications and Occupations. Retrieved July 2017, from https://www.ec.europa.eu/esco/portal/document/en/8e9cf30d-9799-4f95-ae29-e05c725b24c7

European e-Competence Framework. (n.d.). *e-CF 3.0 Profiling tool on-line*. Retrieved July 2017, from http://www.ecompetences.eu/e-cf-3-0-and-ict-profiles-on-line-tool

Fernández Sanz, L., Gómez Pérez, J., & Castillo Martínez, A. (2017). e-Skills Match: A framework for mapping and integrating the main skills, knowledge and competence standards and models for ICT occupations. *Computer Standards & Interfaces, 51*, 30–42. doi:10.1016/j.csi.2016.11.004

Hüsing, T., Korte, W. B., & Dashja, E. (2015). *e-Skills in Europe Trends and Forecasts for the European ICT Professional and Digital Leadership Labour Markets (2015-2020)*. Empirica Working Paper.

IEEE. Computer Society. (2014). Guide to the Software Engineering Body of Knowledge (SWEBOK(R)): Version 3.0. IEEE Computer Society Press.

International Labour Organization. (n.d.). *International Standard Classification of Occupations*. Retrieved July 2017, from http://www.ilo.org/public/english/bureau/stat/isco/

NACE. (n.d.). *Eurostat Statistics Explained*. Retrieved July 2017, from http://www.ec.europa.eu/eurostat/statistics-explained/index.php/Main_Page

Oliver, G. R. (2012). *Foundations of the Assumed Business Operations and Strategy Body of Knowledge (BOSBOK): an Outline of Shareable Knowledge*. Sydney: Darlington Press.

Sicilia, M. A., Cuadrado, J. J., García, E., Rodríguez, D., & Hilera, J. R. (2005). The evaluation of onto-logical representation of the SWEBOK as a revision tool. *Proceedings of the 9th Annual International Computer Software and Application Conference (COMPSAC)*, 26-28.

ENDNOTES

[1]   https://ec.europa.eu/esco/portal/home
[2]   http://skillsmatch.eu/
[3]   https://www.mooc-list.com/

Chapter 8
Human Factor in Designing an Elderly Care Ecosystem

Thais Andrea Baldissera
*FCT, NOVA University of Lisbon, Portugal
& Instituto Federal Farroupilha, Brazil*

Luis M. Camarinha-Matos
ⓘ https://orcid.org/0000-0003-0594-1961
FCT, NOVA University of Lisbon, Portugal

Cristiano De Faveri
FCT, NOVA University of Lisbon, Portugal

ABSTRACT

This chapter provides a brief overview of the demographic evolution and aging process, introducing a collaborative framework to assist senior citizens. The importance of supporting the age-related care needs, and the potential technologies for aging support are highlighted. A conceptual model for an elderly care ecosystem (ECE) and methods for care service personalization and evolution based on a collaborative environment are presented. To facilitate the consideration of human factors in the early design stage of ECE, a care need goals taxonomy and human-centered design principles are introduced. Customer, service, and service provider template profiles to design the elderly care ecosystem are proposed. Experimental results and feedback from lead users are presented and discussed. The goal of the ECE framework is to provide assistance in service recommendation (and adaptation) for the elderly care domain taking into account human factors.

DOI: 10.4018/978-1-7998-1279-1.ch008

INTRODUCTION

Current demographic trends show that the percentage of the elderly population is increasing significantly (Fengler, 2014; Gartner, 2018; Kearney, 2013). In continents, such as Europe, the current proportion of elderly is around 24% of the population, corresponding approximately to 175 million people, while young people are around 117 million (16%). In 2050, although Europe´s population tends to decrease, the number of seniors is expected to reach 27.2% of the population (Bureau, 2018). Such trends show that the population are living longer, staying healthy for more time, and consequently working for more years (Kearney (2013), (Bureau, 2018) and (WorldHealthOrganization, 2018). On the other hand, the number of births has declined worldwide in the past 20 years. The number of born alive babies reached 90 million in 1989. In 2010 only 73 million babies were born, and the trajectory has been moving steadily downward.

Age-related changes affecting perceptual capabilities (such as vision or hearing) and motor skills are especially problematic for older adults. Biological factors like physiological and cognitive declination are often strong causes for the loss of autonomy, and for physical limitations. In extreme cases, regular daily activities such as cooking, performing personal hygiene, housework's, etc., are often affected (Thakur et al., 2013).

The traditional way to deal with this problem requires intense care from family. Relatives need to actively participate in the aging process and support elderly. In this case, many people live with their family when they begin to lose capabilities. Those who remain living by themselves either care for themselves alone or require caregivers to assist them on daily activities. Alternatively, the elderly may stay in a nursing home, a solution that they typically hate. All these changes, can directly affect the senior´s life style (Thakur et al., 2013). The experience of aging can make people more demanding and grumpier, as they may not like this new lifestyle, or find that they are considered a burden to the family, suffering from depression and sadness moments. In this context, aging is a process that requires dedication of time (attentive care from family) and considerable financial resources.

When the objective is to keep seniors healthy and enjoying a high quality of life, specific care needs appear. Each individual elderly person may require focused services (e.g., care and assistance) according to his/her life context. In fact, characterizing a person as elderly involves more than age as a determinant factor. Singular elements of the aging process, such as life settings, individual capacities, and abilities, contribute to characterize an elderly person. As a result, a specific care service might be enough for an individual and very futile for another. This brings up the necessity of personalized and composite services in this sector.

The notion of personalized service typically involves a composition of various basic services, possibly offered by different providers, which together fit the needs of each individual (Baldissera et al., 2017b; Evenson & Dubberly, 2010; Hong et al., 2009; Lee, 2007). Therefore, customizing a (composite) service includes an understanding amongst customer and suppliers (and all other involved stakeholders) through which they share data to allow an adequate adaptation of the service offer (Baldissera et al., 2017a; Kwortnik Jr et al., 2009; Manoharan et al., 2015).

The idea of a collaborative business environment for elderly care can help in the integration of various services from different service providers (Afsarmanesh et al., 2012; Baldissera & Camarinha-Matos, 2016a; Camarinha-Matos et al., 2015). Likewise, finding the set of services and corresponding service providers that best cover the senior's lifestyle, needs, and desires is a challenge.

Although related approaches can be found in the literature, there is a lack of a comprehensive framework that manages the process of service composition and evolution for elderly care in a collaborative environment. Also, keeping the service always adapted to the continuous changes in lifestyle is a factor that adds more difficulty in overcoming this challenge (personalization and evolution of the service).

In this context, the main aim of this chapter is to devise an approach for assistance in service recommendation (and adaptation) for the elderly care domain considering the intervention of human factors.

Elderly Care Needs

The basic needs of people can be represented in a synthetic form in the well-known Maslow´s pyramid (Maslow, 1943) (Figure 1). The most fundamental level of needs is placed at the bottom of the pyramid, while the need of self-actualization is located on top. Maslow's model suggests that the most basic level of needs must be met before the individual desires (or focuses his/her motivation upon) the secondary or higher-level needs. On the other hand, the human behaviour is complex and involves parallel processes running at the same time. In the case of elderly, many different motivations from various levels of Maslow's hierarchy can occur at the same time and evolve with aging.

The aging process is responsible for changes at both biological and psychosocial levels. These age-related changes may impact several distinct aspects of older adults' lives and limit the extent to which they are able to perform certain activities (Kearney, 2013; Saarnio et al., 2017; Weicht, 2013). Physiological needs are the physical requirements for human survival. Age-related changes affecting perceptual capabilities (such as vision or hearing) and motor skills are especially problematic for older adults when trying to interact with actual technologies, like devices' screens and voice commands. Interacting with these technologies is almost mandatory for the daily activities, such as the use of ATMs or entering passwords for payments with credit cards.

Figure 1. Maslow´s adapted pyramid

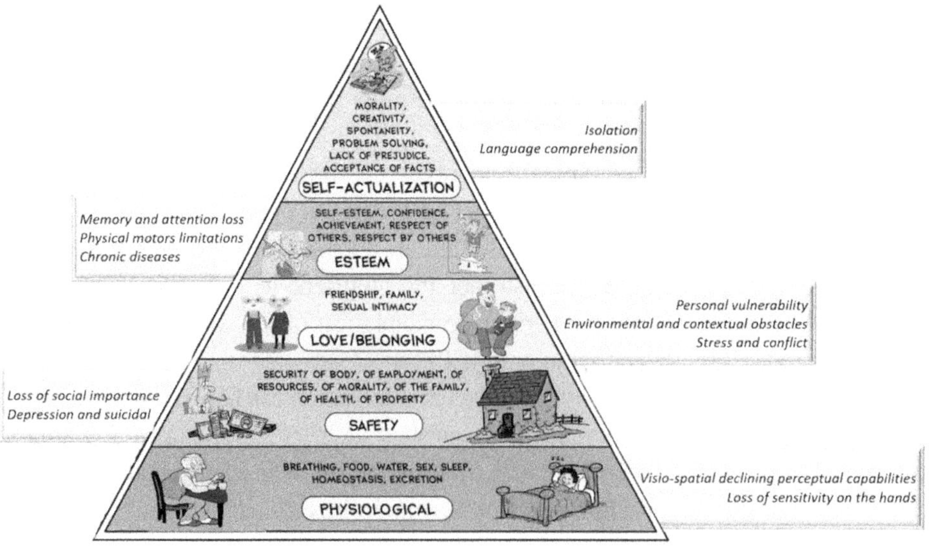

Biological factors such as physiological and cognitive decline are often strong factors for the loss of autonomy (Kearney, 2013; Thakur et al., 2013; Weicht, 2013). Also, physical motor limitations require support for mobility and transportation, and in extreme cases, chronic diseases may affect basic normal daily activities such as cooking, doing personal hygiene, house caring, etc.

Older adults can experience challenges while reading at close distances as a result of a condition known as presbyopia, the inability to focus effectively on near objects (Charness & Jastrzembki, 2009). Transitioning from light to dark environments or performing visual tasks under dim light can also be difficult (Park & Reuter-Lorenz, 2009). In general, seniors also experience a loss of static and dynamic visual acuity and yellowing of the lens, which decreases colour sensitiveness in the blue-to-green ranges (Charness & Jastrzembki, 2009).

Age-related changes in motor skills include slower response times, decrease in the ability to maintain continuous movements, disruptions at coordination, loss of flexibility and variability on movements (Czaja & Lee, 2009). The haptic processes can also suffer some changes, specifically the loss of sensitivity on the hands (Park & Reuter-Lorenz, 2009). These motor skills can greatly influence the perception that individuals get from interacting with technological systems.

Safety and security needs include personal security, financial security, health and well-being, a safety net against accidents/illness and their adverse impacts (Saarnio et al., 2017). Also, economic factors can influence directly on active aging, as one needs more money for health care, medicine, and prevention.

The level of human needs is interpersonal and involves feelings of belongingness. This need is especially strong in childhood and aging. The problems are further amplified by the reduction of the elder´s social network. For the older individual, the social component is one of the most important means towards well-being. However, in old ages, there are a number of factors that can inhibit the maintenance of relationships such as the death of friends and family, low interaction with professional colleagues, personal vulnerability, environmental and contextual obstacles, stress and conflicts (Crispim & de Sousa, 2010). The informal support of networks for the elderly as well as the involvement in social networks can be a good solution to minimize this situation (Camarinha-Matos et al., 2015; Gartner, 2018; HelpAgeInternational, 2018).

All humans need to feel that they are respected; this includes the need of having self-esteem and self-respect. Esteem represents the typical human desire of being accepted and valued by others. Being retired is often associated with a loss of social importance and power due to the disengagement of an active social role (Crispim & de Sousa, 2010; Munnell, 2011). This perceived lack of responsibilities and involvement in the society may induce an identity crisis and consequent loss of self-esteem and the feeling that she/he is a burden to her/his family (Maslow, 1943). Moreover, physical and cognitive changes that affect one's independence and autonomy can have psychologically distressing consequences. These changes can pose threats to one's ability to live safely and independently, leading to depression and the growing of suicidal rates (Kearney, 2013; Park & Reuter-Lorenz, 2009).

Memory and attention are some of the most important cognitive abilities that may suffer declination with aging. The capacity of short-term (or working) memory shows signs of declination with aging, and it is known that this affects many complex everyday tasks such as decision-making, problem-solving and planning of goal-directed behaviours (Park & Reuter-Lorenz, 2009). This situation is mainly due to the challenge older adults face when storing and managing large amounts of new information (Charness & Jastrzembki, 2009). However, unlike the working memory, the long-term memory (or semantic) is largely preserved in old age (Park & Reuter-Lorenz, 2009).

In general, attention is also affected by aging. Older adults have shown to face challenges in tasks that require divided attention across multiple input channels and are also more prone to being distracted by irrelevant information (Charness & Jastrzembki, 2009).

Two other relevant human skills are spatial cognition and language comprehension (Saarnio et al., 2017). The former is related to the ability of mentally manipulating images or patterns whereas the latter is the ability to interpret verbal information (Park & Reuter-Lorenz, 2009). Both these cognitive skills have shown to decline with age, and they can, along with memory and attention, affect the way elders perceive and interpret information.

Even though people tend to be aware of the physical age-related changes, social changes that occur in elder´s life are equally important (Misra et al.). These changes are presented in the next section.

In summary, the main changes in aging cover depression, memory loss, attention loss, autonomy loss, physical motors limitations, chronic diseases, visio-spatial declining perceptual capabilities, loss of sensitivity on the hands, decreased hearing, decreased vision, color sensitiveness, loss of flexibility and variability on movements, illness, feelings of belongingness and mental disorders (Saarnio et al., 2017; Weicht, 2013; Zinnikus et al., 2017).

Collaborative Networks Discipline

Historically, the use of technology has assisted organizations in many ways of doing business. The pervasive use of open distributed system, as observed with Internet-based solutions, enables efficient distributed businesses, rapid time to market, and cost-effective innovation in a globalized environment (Gartner, 2018). In highly dynamic domains, such as health and personal services, companies are challenged to be able to efficiently interplay with multiple organizations to compose personalized offers without losing competitiveness and quality in their services.

Typically, there are three networking levels involving multiple organizations, as shown in Figure 2 (Camarinha-Matos & Afsarmanesh, 2008b; Elliott, 2007). The first level represents networking and coordinated networking, which involves communication and information exchange for mutual benefit and the act of working together harmoniously. The next level explores cooperation, which involves information exchange and adjustments of activities, combined with sharing of resources for achieving compatible goals, and usually involves labour division among participants. The last level represents collaboration, which involves networking, coordination, cooperation, and mutual engagement of participants to solve a problem. This implies mutual trust, which takes time, effort, and dedication. The iteration and integration among participants grow as the degree of networking increases, and although the requirement is larger and also more difficult to reconcile, the best results generally happen as there is collaboration (Elliott, 2007).

The use of a collaborative environment offers a number of advantages to the engaged organizations including "survivability in a context of market turbulence, acquisition of a larger apparent dimension, access to new or wider markets and new knowledge, sharing risks and resources, joining of complementary skills, reaching high level of agility, and better achieving common goals" (Bititci et al., 2012; Camarinha-Matos et al., 2010a; Crispim & de Sousa, 2010).

In this context, a collaborative network (CN) is defined as *"an alliance constituted of a variety of entities (e.g. organizations and people) that are largely autonomous, geographically distributed, and heterogeneous in terms of their operating environment, culture, social capital and goals, but that col-*

Figure 2. Basic Networking Concepts – adapted from (Camarinha-Matos & Afsarmanesh, 2008b; El-liott, 2007)

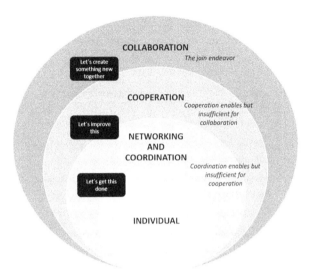

laborate to better achieve common or compatible goals, and whose interactions are supported by a computer network" (Camarinha-Matos & Afsarmanesh, 2008a).

Examples of business areas that have benefited from the adoption of the collaborative networks paradigm include the classical supply chain in automotive industry (Meyr, 2009; Sánchez & Pérez, 2005; Zhu et al., 2007), the agribusiness sector (FORAGRO, 2010; Ojijo et al., 2013; Volpentesta & Ammirato, 2013), the transport sector (Osório et al., 2010), smart grid sector (Camarinha-Matos, 2016; Cao & Zhang, 2011), water management (Hong et al., 2014; Romano & Kapelan, 2014), biodiversity data providers (Fuentes & Fiore, 2014), ICT and aging (Camarinha-Matos et al., 2010b; Plaza et al., 2011), etc. More specifically for the elderly care domain, examples can extend to home safety and care, localization and mobility assistance, health monitoring, rehabilitation and disabilities compensation, caring and intervention on medication or nutrition, learning support system, social and entertainment services, adjusted working spaces, intergenerational relations, assisted living facilities (e.g. with sensors, smart home appliances, and services robotics), senior intelligent villages, etc. (Camarinha-Matos et al., 2015).

Business Services And Business Ecosystem

The concept of "service" has been developed mainly in two areas: computer science and management. For the ICT community, a software or technical service represents a computational action executed in response to a trigger event. On the other hand, from the business perspective, business services add value to a customer (Baldissera & Camarinha-Matos, 2016b; Sanz et al., 2006; Xu & Wang, 2011). According to the same authors, it is logical to separate these two views, being worth noting that business service delivery is performed through business process execution. The activities of a business process can be done automatically (invocation of some software service) or manually (human-executed activities). Nevertheless, the concept of business service itself is not clearly defined, and different authors offer slightly different notions. Table 1 provides some definitions for business service.

Table 1. Business service descriptions

Business Services	Reference
"A change in the condition of a person, or a good belonging to some economic entity, brought about as the result of the activity of some other economic entity, with the approval of the first person or economic entity".	(Hill, 1977)
"Such a kind of specialized services and business operations mainly concerned with providing professional and specialized support for the business processes of other organizations, i.e., the clients".	(Bettencourt et al., 2005)
"A business activity, part of organization's business model, resulting in intangible outcomes or benefits".	(Baida et al., 2004)
"A specific set of actions that are performed by an organization".	(Sanz et al., 2006)
"Are present at a time T and location L if, at time T, the agent is explicitly committed to guaranteeing the execution of some type of action at location L, on the occurrence of a certain triggering event, in the interest of another agent and upon prior agreement, in a certain way".	(Ferrario & Guarino, 2009)
"Traditional services that feature higher inclusions of ICT and human capital adopt new techniques, new innovative business models, and new resource configurations patterns, thereby producing more added-value".	(Xu & Wang, 2011)
(In the elderly care domain) "Are equivalent to what is usually called care and assistance service: services provided to the end users which involve a number of software services and human intervention".	(Camarinha-Matos et al., 2013)

From the definitions presented in Table 1, it can be inferred that care and assistance services for elderly can be considered a kind of business service. The notion of business process corresponds to the management of services execution, involving both software services and manual services.

Figure 3 gives a structure to the notion of Care and Assistance Service in the Elderly Care Domain. Software services fundamentally represent software applications that define part of a system which can be "consumed" distinctly by numerous objects (Kohlborn et al., 2009). Thus, software services execute elements that perform business processes activities. Manual services correspond to services which involve some human interventions (Wang & An, 2010). Hence software services and manual services support the business process execution, materializing the notion of business service delivered to the customers (Kohlborn et al., 2009).

Currently, most initiatives on elderly care services have been focused on isolated and techno-centric services development, considering only a single service. However, in the elderly care domain, personalized services should cover the specific needs of each user, respecting the elderly individuality, and the evolution of limitations that come as the person and life environment change (Jula et al., 2014; O'Grady et al., 2010; Sanz et al., 2006). In this context, it is natural the need of combining multiple services and multiple providers to attend specific needs of an individual.

Figure 3. Care and assistance service in the elderly care domain

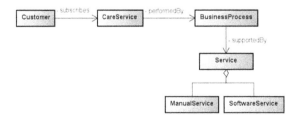

Complementary to the notion of a business service, a <u>business ecosystem</u> (and thus a care ecosystem as well) can be identified as a "*particular case of a virtual organizations breeding environment (VBE), which tries to preserve local specificities, tradition, culture, and frequently benefit from local government incentives, involving a complex interplay of collaboration and competition around producers, consumers, regulators, and support entities*" (Camarinha-Matos et al., 2010a; Camarinha-Matos et al., 2012).

An example of business ecosystem is given by the term Digital Business Ecosystem (Kearney, 2013), which is also inspired on biological ecosystem, but with a stronger emphasis on the technological support perspective. On the other hand, based on advances in the discipline of Collaborative Networks, and current demanding market challenges (better services and prices, market survival, increase of competitors, etc.), the term Collaborative Business Ecosystem (CBE) was introduced to emphasize the "collaborative environment" perspective (Baldissera & Camarinha-Matos, 2016b; Camarinha-Matos, 2013; Graça & Camarinha-Matos, 2015). A CBE supports organizations which must collaborate to overcome their weaknesses and strengthen their expertise and skills, to offer better integrated (composite) services and acquire competitive advantage with the focus on customer satisfaction.

A CBE is thus supposed to provide a variety of software services and manual services that can be combined to fulfill the needs of each customer. This requires proper management of business services composition and integration, as explained in the next Section. By adopting this approach, we can say that care and assistance services for elderly should (likely) result from the collaboration among various entities, possibly including governmental and non-governmental organizations, individual or cooperative professionals, family, friends, caregivers, etc., which in consequence calls for a supporting collaboration environment.

Care Services Composition, Personalization And Evolution

Building business solutions typically requires combining multiple available business services. A service composition is an aggregation of services (atomic or integrated) collectively composed to deliver a particular service pack (Kapitsaki et al., 2007). These composite (or integrated) services can be in turn recursively composed of other services into higher level solutions, (and so on), constituting an essential part of service provision. The novel (composite) service is adding value that was not existent in the atomic services.

In the CBE context, a single provider probably might not be able to cover all care needs of a customer, since a service provider typically has its area of service application and a customer typically may have needs (required services) of various areas. As such, service providers may get together in alliances aiming at the creation of composite services which can better meet the entire customer's care needs.

A <u>composite service</u> may thus involve several service providers, requiring various devices and a support infrastructure, depend on another service or resource, involve people and frequent information exchange, etc. (Baldissera et al., 2017a). Therefore, managing all these elements and relationships with efficiency is indeed a significant challenge.

The notion of <u>service personalization</u> means that a service is tailored to fit each individual (Evenson & Dubberly, 2010; Hong et al., 2009; Kwortnik Jr et al., 2009; LeadingAge, 2017; Lee, 2007). For several authors, e.g., (Kwortnik Jr et al., 2009; Lee, 2007; Manoharan et al., 2015), personalizing a service covers an agreement between customers and providers (and possibly other involved stakeholders) through which they share information to be organized intelligently and adaptively.

The effective establishment of a CBE requires, in fact, a proper understanding of the customers' profile in order to ensure that offered services are both competitive in market terms and relevant to the individuals. Some customers may require distinct types of care services to satisfy their particular needs, which lead to the notion of personalized services.

If the elderly and family are satisfied with the provided service, they feel like an exclusive customer and are inclined to keep loyalty towards the service provider (Lee, 2007). Collecting feedback information in this context can help service providers to deliver better-personalized services. Direct communication with customer representatives remains the most preferred channel for consumers and small companies with few customers. In this scenario, it is "easy" to personalize customers services (Manoharan et al., 2015). However, businesses (e.g., care service providers) with many customers need to seek multiple information sources to achieve personalization, using both human interventions and automatized mechanisms. These feedback acquisition transactions can be efficiently handled through ICT solutions like Internet of Things (IoT) devices and tele assistance (Alwan et al., 2007; Camarinha-Matos et al., 2015).

In the elderly care domain, it is primordial to understand the customer, her/his limitations, and longings, as well as the elderly living environment and associated stakeholders (Baldissera et al., 2017b). As a consequence, a personalized service package is likely to be provided by a number of providers working together, acting as a virtual organization.

Service evolution is the process of maintaining and evolving existing care services to cater for new requirements and technological changes (Wang et al., 2014). The CBE needs to constantly monitor the context and, for each new context change, to analyze the situation, plan the service evolution, and implement the evolution to fit that context.

An evolutionary ambient assisted living system is suggested by O'Grady et al. (2010) following this vision, but their focus is on a techno-centric evolution and adaptability of the system, and ignore the service providers and stakeholders. More recently, new developments appear to address user-stakeholders-centric services, combined with ICT, to offer services non-dependent of a place and time (Chiarini et al., 2013; Mukhopadhyay & Suryadevara, 2014; Xu & Wang, 2011).

Under this perspective, the notion of evolutionary service (Camarinha-Matos et al., 2015; Hong et al., 2009; LeadingAge, 2017; Millar et al., 2016; Xu & Wang, 2011) means that the provided service adapts to the customer's needs, environment and any changes that affect the customer's life context, as well as CBE demands, new regulations, and technological requirements.

In the literature, researchers present partial solutions for service composition (Afsarmanesh et al., 2012; Jula et al., 2014; Kapitsaki et al., 2007), service personalization (Baida et al., 2004; Baldissera et al., 2017b; Brown et al., 2002; Camarinha-Matos et al., 2015) and service evolution (Millar et al., 2016; O'Grady et al., 2010; Wang et al., 2014), mostly considering single service providers and comparison between isolated services (not combined with the service provider). In (Silva, 2018), service selection and ranking in cross-organizational business processes collaboration is considered. In this work, different parts of a business process are performed by different organizations (services providers in our approach). The focus of (Silva, 2018) is based on business strategies in the industrial sector. Our proposal is similar but emphasizes a user-centric view of elderly care (elderly profile and requirements) and integrates providers of different nature (regulators, support entities, and service providers) and categories (public, private, non-governmental, and mixed).

Elderly Care Ecosystem

An *Elderly Care Ecosystem (ECE)* is a particular case of a collaborative business ecosystem. It includes various elements of a collaborative environment (administration, broker, virtual organization, planner, and coordinator), and specific elements that characterize it as an "Elderly Care Collaborative Network", namely the seniors (customers), their requests and requirements, care needs, care services, and service provider entities, among others (Baldissera et al., 2017a; Baldissera & Camarinha-Matos, 2016a, 2016b). Figure 4 presents the partial (high-level) conceptual model of an ECE. The shaded part of the diagram represents common elements of a collaborative environment management system and the outside elements are those specific of the ECE.

- *ECEcosystem* represents the core entity in ECE. It is responsible for managing the entire ECE and guaranteeing that the execution policies established by the administrator (*ECEAdministration*) are enforced.
- *ECEAdministration* is the entity responsible for the ECE operation and evolution, which includes tasks such as registration of providers and customers, contract formalization, conflict resolution process, decision support management, etc.
- *ECEBroker* represents an ECE member that is responsible for identifying and acquiring collaboration opportunities.
- A *VirtualOrganization* (VO) represents a temporary alliance of organizations that share resources and skills and come together to deliver an integrated care service.
- *VOPlanner* represents a business integrator, who is responsible for planning, designing, and launching a new goal-oriented networks by creating new VOs. This role usually supports the response to an opportunity identified by an ECEBroker.
- A *VOCoordinator* is a person or an organization that manages a VO.
- Furthermore, the ECE environment domain diagram (see Figure 5) highlights four ECE subsystems: ECE Manager System, ECE Information System, ECE Personalization System, and ECE Evolution System, and the three phases involved in the operationalization of ECE: Preparation, Execution, and Monitoring.

Figure 4. ECE partial high-level conceptual model

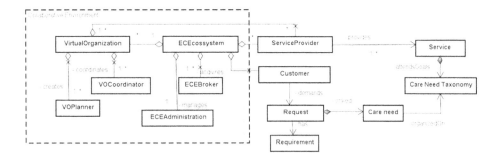

Figure 5. ECE Environment Domain Diagram

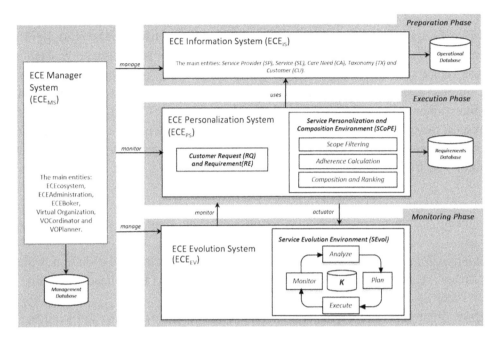

The *Preparation phase* corresponds to the creation of ECE and definition of its rules and functionalities within a collaborative environment. It involves representing the main body of information and knowledge, identifying the target audience, the involved stakeholders, namely partners in the various groups (support entities, regulation entities, private companies, governmental institutions, freelancing professionals, caregivers, etc.) which are members of ECE, ICT and human resources, business and management rules; and characterizing the available services. Based on a set of templates, this phase involves creating the taxonomy of care need goals, and identifying the service provider profile, service profile, and customer profile. The main subsystems responsible for the *Preparation phase* execution are *ECE Manager System* (ECE_{MS}) and *ECE Information System* (ECE_{IS}). ECE_{MS} is based on the pillar of collaborative networks. ECE_{IS} is more detailed in the next sections in the current chapter.

The *Execution phase* relates to the process of composition and personalization of services, including the ranking of the offered pairs (services and service providers). The main actuator subsystem at this stage is *ECE Personalization System* (ECE_{PS}) which involves the Service Composition and Personalization environment (SCoPE method). This method is based on three steps: scope filtering, service adherence calculation, and service composition and ranking, as detailed in next section.

The *Monitoring phase* resorts to the *ECE Evolution System* (ECE_{EV}) that supports the service evolution and monitoring. ECE_{EV} materializes the Service Evolution (SEvol) method. Considering the dynamic environment and stages of life, the *ECE broker* analyses the situation (in collaboration with the relevant stakeholders) and adapts the services to fit each new context. In this way, SEvol evolves an existing care solution to cope with the new phase of the customer's life (for instance, handling new or obsolete care needs, new customer inputs, technological changes, new strategies of service providers, etc.). The detailed process of the self-adaptive system approach for service evolution into ECE (ECE_{EV} and the SEvol method) is presented in next section.

Care Need Goals Taxonomy

A *Care Need* (CA) corresponds to current customer's wishes and care requirements. The proper identification of customer´s care needs as well as priorities is very important in order to find adequate care services. In general, a care need is expressed in natural language, which makes it notably difficult to automate the process of finding providers for a particular need (Chaudhari et al., 2016). Therefore, a care need requires a structured representation to support automation. We classify care needs in higher-level abstractions based on a taxonomy of care need goals (TX) (for which a partial example is shown in Figure 6).

Figure 6. Example of care need taxonomy (partial illustration)

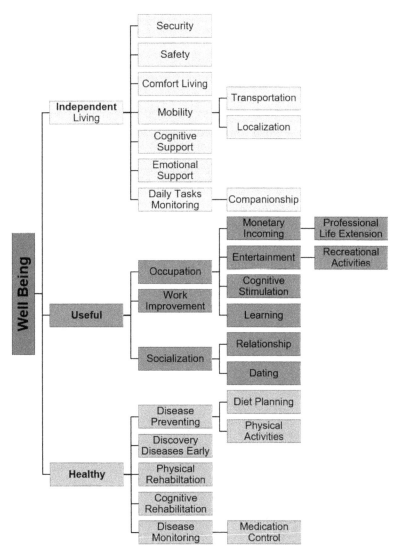

Each care need might be covered, to some extent (i.e. by some coverage level), by available care services in the ECE. Furthermore, each care need is associated with the impact it might have on another care need. An ECE has only one TX that is maintained by the *ECEAdministration*. It has the responsibility to remove, add, and update the TX for the proper execution of the ECE processes.

In the example shown in Figure 6, the main care needs goal for elderly is *Well Being* and its sub-needs are *Independent Living*, *Useful,* and *Healthy*. Considering the four life settings (proposed by the BRAID Project), we joined *Occupation in life* and *Recreation in life* into the single goal *Useful* (the same set of services), which for our purpose is enough.

Independent Living represents aspects of the elderly's life he/she would like to control during his/her aging. For example, controlling the walking capability by himself/herself or going shopping without depending on a family member. *Useful* represents the feeling of being connected and useful to the surrounding community by contributing to something larger than himself/herself. Finally, *Healthy* corresponds to health improvements and longevity, reducing the risks of disabilities.

These goals are essential to enable the elderly doing things he/she values most. These goals enable elderly people to age safely in a place that is adequate for them, continue their personal development and contribution to their communities, while retaining their autonomy and well-being during aging.

The main aspect related to the taxonomy is to be able to associate care needs and services at specific levels of the taxonomy tree in such way they can be processed by ECE. The upper the node is in the tree the more abstract the concept is. For example, if a care need is associated with the Mobility node, all services associated with this node are also supposed to attend its children Transportation and Localization nodes.

The concepts related to care needs and their detailed descriptions are shown in Figure 7 and Table 2 respectively.

Services are linked to nodes of the care needs taxonomy indicating the level of care needs they cover. It is however important to notice that the notion of "need's coverage" is not a binary concept; rather we can identify degrees of coverage. Therefore, ECE services have a coverage level regarding the care needs they are associated to. This level is expressed on a fuzzy scale (e.g. from *very low* to *very high*).

Figure 7. Care needs characterization diagram

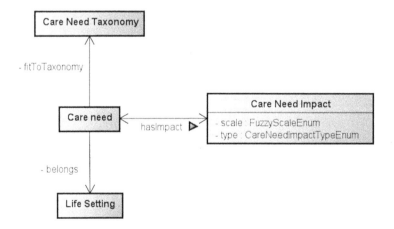

Table 2. Care need's elements

Class	Description
CareNeed	Representing current customer's care need. It is characterized by: name and description.
LifeSetting	Indicating which of the three areas to which care needs are associated: *Independent Living*, *Useful*, or *Healthy*.
CareNeedTaxonomy	The care needs taxonomy to which each care need is mapped to. It is composed of a hierarchy of nodes (care need goals).
CareNeedImpact	Indicating the impact that a care need might have on another care need. The impact can be a negative or positive influence (e.g. when a senior needs *Physical Support*, this situation influences negatively *Transportation*, and positively *Localization*). In addition, the impact level can be expressed on a fuzzy scale (e.g. from *very low impact* to *very high* impact).

This range is established based on a number of factors, including the field experts' experience, the customer's feedback, and indication of the service provider, or a combination of them (depending on the ECE management strategy).

ECE is assumed to provide an adequate taxonomy of services along with proper mechanisms to avoid unfair provider selection. For instance, discriminatory strategies can be induced when service providers only associate their services to high-level nodes to increase their chances of being selected during a bid process. To ensure fair play, ECE must consider multiple parameters for selection, such as reputation, the experience of the provider as a participant in the VO, its expertise, etc.

Personalization System

In the elderly care domain, personalization involves the analysis of the senior's life context. The organization responsible for delivering care and assistance services (in our case, the ECE) identifies specific requirements for the customer's context and builds (or composes) a service solution to fit the needs.

In this context, the SCoPE (Service Composition and Personalization Ecosystem) method is proposed to support the process of composing and personalizing services in a collaborative network environment for elderly care.

SCoPE (see Figure 8) is based on three main steps: *(i) scope filtering* - responsible for matching and excluding {service, provider} pairs based on the care need taxonomy, (ii) *adherence calculation* – resulting in the first rating of {service, provider} pairs based on adherence multidimensional matrix for a specific customer, and *(iii) service composition and ranking* - using strategies for service composition and offering a list of potential solutions.

In *Scope Filtering* (step 1), available services (and corresponding providers) that cover some of the customer's care needs are identified, excluding those that are unsuitable due to geographical restrictions, special conditions, unavailable resources, and other hard constraints. The {service, provider} pair must guarantee that the service attends some customer's care needs, ensuring a proper personalization and adapting to the feedback received from both the ECE, the VO partners, the customer and her/his relatives, certifying in this way a current service personalization.

The *Adherence Calculation* (step 2) identifies personal customer's requests and characteristics for service adherence evaluation taking into consideration cultural differences, religious constraints, social aspects, place of living, etc. *Adherence* represents a compatibility relation between the individual cus-

Figure 8. SCoPE method overview

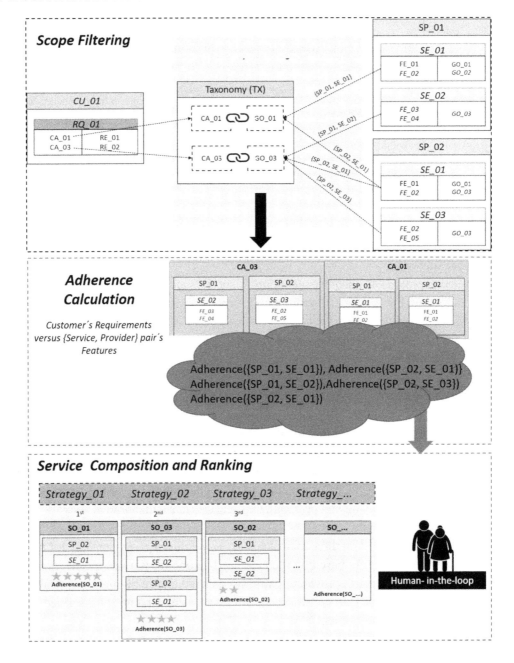

tomer and a solution fragment sp_{ij} (service s_i and respective provider p_j) and it is calculated by estimating four coefficients: *Closeness (CL)*, *Partial Adherence (PA)*, *Adherence (AD)*, and *Global Adherence (GA)*. *CL* is represented by a multidimensional matrix of the "proximity" between customer's requests and the features of the {service, provider} pair fragment. *PA* is an intermediate computation that refines the closeness based on criteria's weights ponderation. Finally, *AD* represents the resulting adherence according to the service's coverage level to each care need, and *GA* represents the adherence considering all care needs together.

Table *3* summarizes the *adherence calculation* process, including the goal, inputs, and outputs for each step.

Service Composition and Raking (step 3) uses strategies for achieving a personalized result. Traditional methods for service composition involve human judgments and frequent step-by-step interaction with the customer and service provider (a kind of service co-design). In our approach, we keep the human decision, but mainly for the final stage where the best solutions have already been found easing decision making. The service composition process can then proceed using the group of sp_{ij} fragments that have a reasonable *adherence* level. Various alternative composition methods can be considered, for instance with the purpose of adherence's maximization, number of services minimization or maximization, balanced number of providers, etc.

In the end, a customer's solution is presented through a vector representing the corresponding service and provider fragments (sp_{ij}) and their adherence (ad) to each care need k, the Global Adherence (GA) and cost of the solution, and the relation between adherence and cost.

Evolution System

In the elderly care ecosystem domain, and for each new context change, the proposed ECE Evolution System analyses the situation (in collaboration with the relevant stakeholders) and adapts the service to fit that new context. In other words, the developed Service Evolution (SEvol) method supports the solution evolution to cope with the new life stage. Under this perspective, the notion of evolutionary service (Baldissera & Camarinha-Matos, 2018; Brown et al., 2002; Hong et al., 2009; Marcos-Pablos & García-Peñalvo, 2019; O'Grady et al., 2010) means that the provided service is adapted to the senior's needs, and to any changes that affect the senior's life context.

Table 3. Steps of adherence calculation process

Adherence Calculation Process		Input	Output
Step 1. Criteria's weights definition Goal. Define criteria's weights		▪ Decision-making criteria ▪ selected by the customer.	▪ Vector of ▪ normalized weights: ▪ $W = \left\{ w_1, w_2, \ldots, w_{cri} \right\}$.
Repeated for each fragment sp_{ij}	**Step 2.** Closeness Calculation **Goal.** Calculate the closeness of each sp_{ij} fragment against the customer's requests	▪ sp_{ij} fragments features and customer's requests	
	Step 3. *PA calculation* **Goal.** Calculate the *Partial Adherence (PA)*, combining criteria's closeness and criteria's weights ponderation		▪ *PA* coefficient
	Step 4. *AD* vector calculation **Goal.** Calculate the *Adherence (AD)* combining the *PA* and the service coverage level about the customer's individual care needs.	▪ *PA* coefficient; ▪ Customer's care needs(CA); ▪ Service Coverage Level ▪ regarding the care need.	▪ *AD* vector ▪ $AD = \left\{ ad_1, ad_2, \ldots, ad_{ca} \right\}$
Step 5. GA matrix Calculation Goal. Calculate the *Global Adherence* (all care needs together) and build the solution fragments and care needs mapping		▪ *AD* vector	▪ *GA* multidimensional matrix

Following MAPE-K methodology, the SEvol method is based on a control loop composed of four main stages: (i) monitoring events that occur in the surrounding physical and social context (i.e., both context changes and messages exchanged between stakeholders); (ii) analyzing monitored data against solution requirements to identify need of adaptation; (iii) devising an evolution strategy that reconciles current solution with a new customer´s context; and (iv) enacting such strategy while minimizing disturbances caused by suggested solutions. These stages are identified in the i* rationale strategic model (see Figure 9) that provides an intentional description of processes in terms of process elements and the rationales behind them (Yu & Mylopoulos, 1995).

The main actor is *Evolution System* (A-04 in Figure 9) that is supported by additional elements of the model: *Context sensor* (A-01), *Agent* (A-02), and *Contextual actuator* (A-03). In more detail:

*Figure 9. Adapted i*rationale strategic model for the evolution system loop in ECE*

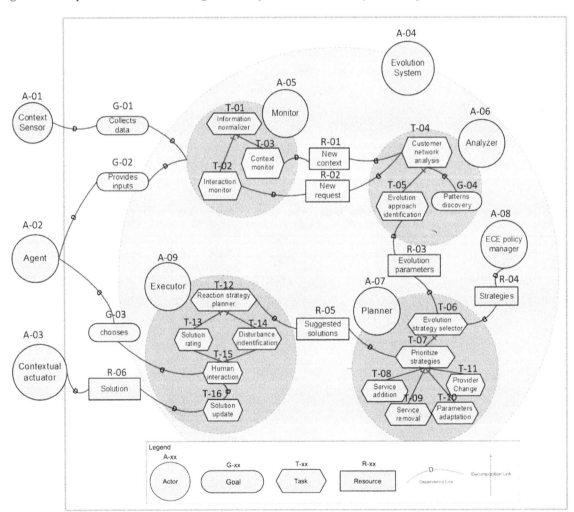

- *Context sensor* (A-01) is seen as a computational entity (hardware and software) providing raw data about the elderly environment. For instance, a bracelet that determines the current location of the customer or other stakeholders (e.g., who deliver/execute the care service), the sensor that determines the temperature and humidity levels in specific places, the smart communicator's automatic incoming/outgoing calls, etc.
- *Agent* (A-02) represents each of the actors who need to be monitored to ensure that they deliver according to their role in the ecosystem and send feedback about their acts. These agents may represent a senior, her/his guardian or caregiver, the coordinator of the virtual organization, VO (who manages the care service delivery for this senior), a service provider (which is part of a VO), etc. *Agents* are linked to the *Evolution System* (A-04) through inputs provision to identify a new request or through choices made in the human interaction. For instance, a substitution of a resource may be solicited by a service provider.

- *Evolution System* (A-04) provides the self-adaptation capabilities of our model. This actor is split into four sub-actors:
- Sub-actor *Monitor* (A-05) receives the information from agents (*Agent* (A-02)) and sensors (*Context Sensor* (A-01)). The inputs from the agents can be of several origins, for instance, from the customer and his/her family and guardian, or from the ECE, mainly originated in the Virtual Organization (VO) coordination, ECE management, or service provider. The inputs from sensors represent data about the elderly environment, for instance, information about senior's sleep analysis. Examples of outcomes are (i) the identified new care need, (ii) indication that a care need is no longer present, and (iii) indication that service changes the delivery parameters.
- Sub-actor *Analyzer* (A-06) receives, from *Monitor* (A-05), information about the current elderly context living (*New context* (R-01) or *New request* (R-02)) and observes the pattern identifying the solution parameters that need to evolve.
- Sub-actor *Planner* (A-07) selects evolution strategies to be adopted by the ECE policy manager (A-08), and ranks suggested solutions. The proposed solution evolution approach in ECE is based on (1) composition (or decomposition) of the current solution (*Service addition* (T-08) or *Service removal* (T-09)); (2) solution parameters change (*Parameters adaptation* (T-10)), for instance, delivery conditions; or (3) the change of the entity responsible for the care service delivery (*Provider change* (T-11)).
- Sub-actor *Executor* (A-09) changes the behavior of the managed resource using effectors based on the actions recommended by the *Planner* (A-07). Notice that evolution should not be considered a new personalization since it does not seek the better possible results from scratch, but instead seeks a satisfactory solution with the least possible disturbance to the customer (that is already used to the specific characteristics of current solution).

ECE Evaluation

To evaluate ECE a survey in terms of their applicability and utility considering an adaptation of the Technology Acceptance Model (TAM) methodology (Davis et al., 1989). TAM is focused on the intention to use a new technology or innovation. TAM was specifically developed to explain and predict the acceptance of information and communication technologies by potential users. The modified TAM is applied considering three contexts: *Technological, Organizational* and *Collaborative* environment.

An illustrate the use of the ECE by considering a scenario containing a hypothetical individual profile and her care needs, a set of providers available in the ECE as well as a set of services provided by these providers are used. During the application of the survey, we could have access to some questionnaires that companies apply to assess and build customers' profile. However, for a matter of confidentiality, we could not have access to real data. Thus, we built profiles based on public data available on companies' websites to reflect as close as possible real situations.

The questionnaire was tested with 95 elderly care professionals belonging to 17 distinct companies. The majority of the participants responded that they work exclusively with elderly for no more than three years, which shows that the profession of elderly caregivers has been fostered as the corresponding population grows. However, dedicated elderly care technologies for service personalization and evolution are still underutilized. All participants declared to not use any kind of software system to assist them on decisions of personalization and evolution of services. This is still a fundamentally manual process. Moreover, although the participants believe the ECE can contribute to improve their business and assist their customers better, they are still reluctant to fully adopt this kind of technology without a clear methodology for transition (manual to automated) and well-defined security and privacy policies. In particular, the latter is a strong concern declared by the participants.

Due to the high-competitive market, the organizations recognize they need to improve their processes and tools to provide services that can be personalized and evolve over time. One of the concerns these organizations have shown is regarding the multiple roles the organizations can assume in a collaborative network. Organizations that seem competitors today can become partners' tomorrow, form a virtual organization and expand their business. This demands well-established policies and maturity from the companies to play distinct roles in different business scenarios.

There is a perception that the concept of collaborative networks is known by the participants but using an earlier form - cooperative. Hence, the idea of collaborative network is not fully implemented. A quarter of the interviewed participants declared to know and use collaborative networks in their work. Nevertheless, it is natural to expect a certain level of skepticism when adopting new technologies like the ECE. However, the findings show the ECE had a strong acceptance in the researched community, having a positive impact in the nine dimensions considered in our survey.

CONCLUSION AND FUTURE DIRECTIONS

In this chapter, we analyzed several perspectives of human factors and highlighted their influence in designing core functionalities of an elderly care ecosystem under a collaborative environment perspective. The novel contributions of this work include a set of concepts, models, and methods to represent and provide personalized and evolutionary services for elderly care within the scope of a collaborative network environment. The original contributions appear at four different levels: concepts, models, and methods.

- **Concepts:** A set of concepts related to personalization and evolution of services for elderly care are discussed. By giving a formal description of the concepts, we provide base support for automated processes, including calculations such as *Closeness* and *Service Adherence*.

- **Models**: The concept of ECE is based on a computer-supported collaborative environment that allows the combination of services potentially involving multiple providers to seek better solutions for the senior's care needs.
- **Methods:** The SCoPE method is based on the match between the customer´s profile and the available {service, provider} pairs. The calculation of a service adherence index to a specific customer identifies suitable services and corresponding providers to attend him/her. SEvol is a method to build an adaptive and evolutionary system based on the MAPE-K methodology, supporting the solution evolution to cope with the new life stage in the elderly care domain. SCoPE and SEvol represent the two methods proposed in the ECE framework for service personalization and evolution respectively.

Concepts, methods, models and innovative concepts are all grounded into a set of existing studies on collaborative networks, aging process, technologies for aging support, adaptive systems, service evolution, care service composition and personalization, and collaborative business ecosystems. Various contributions to the background knowledge (collaborative networks, technologies and aging, collaborative business ecosystem, service composition and personalization, service evolution, and adaptive system area) occurred during the course of this work.

The outcomes of this chapter indicate that the proposed solutions are relevant in the target domain of human factors in the elderly care ecosystem. Nevertheless, this chapter also opens the opportunity for several new research directions, namely:

- **Taxonomy Improvements:** Improving the relationship between the care needs taxonomy and the services and customer request. Mapping customer's need and potential services is one of the greatest challenges when designing personalized services in the ECE. There is a multitude of parameters that may be considered to select a set of services in the ecosystem. Services should require distinct data to cover certain needs, thus, the matching process should be flexible enough to connect both sides (customer needs and offered services). In this sense, it is necessary to identify a richer common "language" that maps them to a taxonomy of services and care needs to get more accurate results.
- **Service Integration:** Service adaptation is challenging since many services can be dependent on each other, and there are various constraints that need to be observed before adaptating and enacting new services. There is a need to guarantee the adaptation does not interfere in other services currently under execution. Also, it is necessary to established methods to return the system to the previous state when the adaption does not achieve its goals.
- **Security, Privacy, and Other Non-Functional Requirements:** Security and privacy are one of the main concerns in modern systems. As observed by most of the participants of our survey, customers may hesitate in adopting solutions like the ECE due to security and privacy issues. In this sense, rigid security models need to be developed. We highlighted some open key aspects of service proposition requirements and challenges that should be overcome during the design and implementation of an ECE. It is not our intention to present a comprehensive list of concerns (e.g. cold start phenomenon, performance, fault tolerance, etc.).

ACKNOWLEDGMENT

The authors acknowledge the contributions of the Portuguese FCT-Strategic program UID/EEA/00066/2019 for providing partial financial support for this work.

REFERENCES

Afsarmanesh, H., Sargolzaei, M., & Shadi, M. (2012). A Framework for Automated Service Composition in Collaborative Networks. In L. Camarinha-Matos, L. Xu, & H. Afsarmanesh (Eds.), *Collaborative Networks in the Internet of Services* (Vol. 380, pp. 63–73). Springer Berlin Heidelberg. doi:10.1007/978-3-642-32775-9_7

Alwan, M., Wiley, D., & Nobel, J. (2007). *A program of the American Association of Homes and Services for the Aging (AAHSA)*. C. Foundation, Ed.

Baida, Z., Gordijn, J., & Omelayenko, B. (2004). *A shared service terminology for online service provisioning*. Paper presented at the 6th International Conference on Electronic Commerce, Delft, The Netherlands. 10.1145/1052220.1052222

Baldissera, T. A., & Camarinha-Matos, L. M. (2016a). Services Personalization Approach for a Collaborative Care Ecosystem. In H. Afsarmanesh, M. L. Camarinha-Matos, & A. Lucas Soares (Eds.), *Collaboration in a Hyperconnected World: 17th IFIP WG 5.5 Working Conference on Virtual Enterprises, PRO-VE 2016, Porto, Portugal, October 3-5, 2016, Proceedings* (pp. 443-456). Cham: Springer International Publishing. 10.1007/978-3-319-45390-3_38

Baldissera, T. A., & Camarinha-Matos, L. M. (2016b). Towards a Collaborative Business Ecosystem for Elderly Care. In M. L. Camarinha-Matos, A. J. Falcão, N. Vafaei, & S. Najdi (Eds.), *Technological Innovation for Cyber-Physical Systems: 7th IFIP WG 5.5/SOCOLNET Advanced Doctoral Conference on Computing, Electrical and Industrial Systems, DoCEIS 2016, Costa de Caparica, Portugal, April 11-13, 2016, Proceedings* (pp. 24-34). Cham: Springer International Publishing. 10.1007/978-3-319-31165-4_3

Baldissera, T. A., & Camarinha-Matos, L. M. (2018). *Services Evolution in Elderly Care Ecosystems*. Paper presented at the Working Conference on Virtual Enterprises.

Baldissera, T. A., Camarinha Matos, L. M., & DeFaveri, C. (2017a). Designing elderly care ecosystem in collaborative networks environment. *International Conference on Computing, Networking and Informatics*. 10.1109/ICCNI.2017.8123818

Baldissera, T. A., Camarinha-Matos, L. M., & DeFaveri, C. (2017b). Service Personalization Requirements for Elderly Care in a Collaborative Environment. In L. M. Camarinha-Matos, M. Parreira-Rocha, & J. Ramezani (Eds.), *Technological Innovation for Smart Systems, DoCEIS 2017* (pp. 20–28). Springer. doi:10.1007/978-3-319-56077-9_2

Bettencourt, L., Ostrom, A., Brown, S., & Roundtree, R. (2005). Client Co-production in Knowledge-intensive Business Services. In T. O. U.-S. Publications (Ed.), Operations management: a strategic approach (pp. 273–283). London, UK: Academic Press. doi:10.2307/41166145

Bititci, U., Garengo, P., Dörfler, V., & Nudurupati, S. (2012). Performance measurement: Challenges for tomorrow. *International Journal of Management Reviews*, *14*(3), 305–327. doi:10.1111/j.1468-2370.2011.00318.x

Brown, A., Johnston, S., & Kelly, K. (2002). *Using service-oriented architecture and component-based development to build web service applications*. Rational Software Corporation.

Camarinha-Matos, L. M. (2013). *Collaborative Business Ecosystems and Virtual Enterprises: IFIP TC5 / WG5.5 Third Working Conference on Infrastructures for Virtual Enterprises ... in Information and Communication Technology*. Springer Publishing Company, Incorporated.

Camarinha-Matos, L. M. (2016). Collaborative smart grids–A survey on trends. *Renewable & Sustainable Energy Reviews*, *65*, 283–294. doi:10.1016/j.rser.2016.06.093

Camarinha-Matos, L. M., & Afsarmanesh, H. (2008a). Classes of collaborative networks. In I. S. Reference (Ed.), *Encyclopedia of Networked and Virtual Organizations* (pp. 193–198). Academic Press. doi:10.4018/978-1-59904-885-7.ch026

Camarinha-Matos, L. M., & Afsarmanesh, H. (2008b). *Collaborative Networks: Reference Modeling*. Springer Science & Business Media.

Camarinha-Matos, L. M., Afsarmanesh, H., & Boucher, X. (2010a). The Role of Collaborative Networks in Sustainability. In L. Camarinha-Matos, X. Boucher, & H. Afsarmanesh (Eds.), *Collaborative Networks for a Sustainable World* (Vol. 336, pp. 1–16). Springer Berlin Heidelberg. doi:10.1007/978-3-642-15961-9_1

Camarinha-Matos, L. M., Afsarmanesh, H., & Ferrada, F. (2010b). *Collaborative networks approach to active ageing*. Paper presented at the 4th International Conference on Pervasive Computing Technologies for Healthcare (PervasiveHealth), Munich, Germany. 10.4108/ICST.PERVASIVEHEALTH2010.8866

Camarinha-Matos, L. M., Afsarmanesh, H., Ferrada, F., Oliveira, A. I., & Rosas, J. (2013). A comprehensive research roadmap for ICT and ageing. *Studies in Informatics and Control*, *22*(3), 233–254. doi:10.24846/v22i3y201301

Camarinha-Matos, L. M., Rosas, J., Oliveira, A. I., & Ferrada, F. (2012). A Collaborative Services Ecosystem for Ambient Assisted Living. In L. Camarinha-Matos, L. Xu, & H. Afsarmanesh (Eds.), *Collaborative Networks in the Internet of Services* (Vol. 380, pp. 117–127). Springer Berlin Heidelberg. doi:10.1007/978-3-642-32775-9_12

Camarinha-Matos, L. M., Rosas, J., Oliveira, A. I., & Ferrada, F. (2015). Care services ecosystem for ambient assisted living. *Enterprise Information Systems*, *9*(5-6), 607–633.

Cao, M., & Zhang, Q. (2011). Supply chain collaboration: Impact on collaborative advantage and firm performance. *Journal of Operations Management*, *29*(3), 163–180. doi:10.1016/j.jom.2010.12.008

Charness, N., & Jastrzembki, T. S. (2009). Geronthecnology. In P. Saariluoma & H. Isomaki (Eds.), *In Future Interaction II* (pp. 1–30). London: Springer.

Chaudhari, V. V., Dhawale, C., & Misra, S. (2016). *Sentiment analysis classification: A brief review*. Academic Press.

Chiarini, G., Ray, P., Akter, S., Masella, C., & Ganz, A. (2013). mHealth technologies for chronic diseases and elders: A systematic review. *Selected Areas in Communications. IEEE Journal on, 31*(9), 6–18.

Crispim, J. A., & de Sousa, J. P. (2010). Partner selection in virtual enterprises. *International Journal of Production Research, 48*(3), 683–707. doi:10.1080/00207540802425369

Czaja, S. J., & Lee, C. C. (2009). Information Technology and Older Adults. In A. Sears & J. A. Jacko (Eds.), *Human-Computer Interaction: Designing for Diverse Users and Domains* (pp. 18–30). CRC Press. doi:10.1201/9781420088885.ch2

Davis, F. D., Bagozzi, R. P., & Warshaw, P. R. J. M. s. (1989). *User acceptance of computer technology: a comparison of two theoretical models*. Academic Press.

Elliott, M. A. (2007). *Stigmergic collaboration: A theoretical framework for mass collaboration* (PhD). University of Melbourne. Retrieved from http://hdl.handle.net/11343/39359

Evenson, S., & Dubberly, H. (2010). Designing for service: Creating an experience advantage. In G. Salvendy & W. Karwowski (Eds.), *Introduction to Service Engineering* (pp. 403–413). John Wiley & Sons.

Fengler, W. (2014). *The End of the Population Pyramid*. Retrieved from http://www.economist.com/blogs/graphicdetail/2014/11/daily-chart-10

Ferrario, R., & Guarino, N. (2009). Towards an Ontological Foundation for Services Science. In D. John, F. Dieter, & T. Paolo (Eds.), *Future Internet --- FIS 2008* (pp. 152–169). Springer-Verlag. doi:10.1007/978-3-642-00985-3_13

FORAGRO. (2010). *Agriculture and rural prosperity from the perspective of technological research and innovation in LAC: FORAGRO Position 2010*. Retrieved from http://www.fao.org/docs/eims/upload/276851/foragro_presentation_english_f_1a.pdf

Fuentes, D., & Fiore, N. (2014). The LifeWatch approach to the exploration of distributed species information. *ZooKeys, 463*, 133–148. doi:10.3897/zookeys.463.8397 PMID:25589865

Gartner, I. (2018). *Gartner's 2018 Hype Cycle for Emerging Technologies Identifies Three Key Trends That Organizations Must Track to Gain Competitive Advantage*. Retrieved from http://www.gartner.com/doc/2847417?refval=&pcp=mpe#a-1321928256

Graça, P., & Camarinha-Matos, L. (2015). The Need of Performance Indicators for Collaborative Business Ecosystems. In L. M. Camarinha-Matos, T. A. Baldissera, G. Di Orio, & F. Marques (Eds.), *Technological Innovation for Cloud-Based Engineering Systems* (Vol. 450, pp. 22–30). Springer International Publishing. doi:10.1007/978-3-319-16766-4_3

Help Age International. (2018). *Global AgeWatch Index 2018*. Retrieved from http://www.helpage.org/global-agewatch/

Hill, T. P. (1977). On goods and services. *Review of Income and Wealth, 23*(4), 315–338. doi:10.1111/j.1475-4991.1977.tb00021.x

Hong, J., Lee, W., Ha Kim, J., Kim, J., Park, I., & Har, D. (2014). Smart water grid: desalination water management platform. In *Desalination and Water Treatment*. Taylor & Francis.

Hong, J., Suh, E.-H., Kim, J., & Kim, S. (2009). Context-aware system for proactive personalized service based on context history. *Expert Systems with Applications*, *36*(4), 7448–7457. doi:10.1016/j.eswa.2008.09.002

Jula, A., Sundararajan, E., & Othman, Z. (2014). Cloud computing service composition: A systematic literature review. *Expert Systems with Applications*, *41*(8), 3809–3824. doi:10.1016/j.eswa.2013.12.017

Kapitsaki, G., Kateros, D. A., Foukarakis, I. E., Prezerakos, G. N., Kaklamani, D. I., & Venieris, I. S. (2007). *Service Composition: State of the art and future challenges.* Paper presented at the 2007 16th IST Mobile and Wireless Communications Summit. doi:10.1109/ISTMWC.2007.4299297

Kearney, A. T. (2013). Understanding the Needs and Consequences of the Ageing Consumer. *The Consumer Goods Forum*. Retrieved from https://www.atkearney.com/documents/10192/682603/Understanding+the+Needs+and+Consequences+of+the+Aging+Consumer.pdf/6c25ffa3-0999-4b5c-8ff1-afdca0744fdc

Kohlborn, T., Korthaus, A., Taizan, C., & Rosemann, M. (2009). Identification and Analysis of Business and Software Services—A Consolidated Approach. *Services Computing. IEEE Transactions on*, *2*(1), 50–64. doi:10.1109/TSC.2009.6

Kwortnik, R. J. Jr, Lynn, W. M., & Ross, W. T. Jr. (2009). Buyer monitoring: A means to insure personalized service. *JMR, Journal of Marketing Research*, *46*(5), 573–583. doi:10.1509/jmkr.46.5.573

LeadingAge. (2017). *A Look into the Future: Evaluating Business Models for Technology-Enabled Long-Term Services and Supports.* Retrieved from http://www.leadingage.org/uploadedFiles/Content/About/CAST/CAST_Scenario_Planning.pdf

Lee, W.-P. (2007). Deploying personalized mobile services in an agent-based environment. *Expert Systems with Applications*, *32*(4), 1194–1207. doi:10.1016/j.eswa.2006.02.009

Manoharan, R., Ganesan, R., & Sabarinathan, K. (2015). Impac of Hosted Speech Technology for Health Care Service Providers through Call Centers. *Scholarly Research Journal for Interdisciplinary Studies*, *III*, 2712–2724.

Marcos-Pablos, S., & García-Peñalvo, F. J. J. S. (2019). *Technological Ecosystems in Care and Assistance: A Systematic Literature Review.* Academic Press.

Maslow, A. H. (1943). A theory of human motivation. *Psychological Review*, *50*(4), 370–396. doi:10.1037/h0054346

Meyr, H. (2009). Supply chain planning in the German automotive industry. In *Supply Chain Planning* (pp. 1–23). Springer Berlin Heidelberg. doi:10.1007/978-3-540-93775-3_13

Millar, S. L., Chambers, M., & Giles, M. J. H. E. (2016). *Service user involvement in mental health care: an evolutionary concept analysis.* Academic Press.

Misra, S., Banubakode, S. M., & Dhawale, C. A. (2014). *Novel user interface for text entry on touch screen mobile device for visually impaired users.* Academic Press. doi:10.1109/GSCIT.2014.6970122

Mukhopadhyay, S. C., & Suryadevara, N. K. (2014). Internet of Things: Challenges and Opportunities. In S. C. Mukhopadhyay (Ed.), *Internet of Things* (Vol. 9, pp. 1–17). Springer International Publishing. doi:10.1007/978-3-319-04223-7_1

Munnell, A. H. (2011). *What is the Average Retirement Age?* Retrieved from http://crr.bc.edu/wp-content/uploads/2011/08/IB_11-11-508.pdf

O'Grady, M. J., Muldoon, C., Dragone, M., Tynan, R., & O'Hare, G. M. (2010). Towards evolutionary ambient assisted living systems. *Journal of Ambient Intelligence and Humanized Computing, 1*(1), 15–29. doi:10.100712652-009-0003-5

Ojijo, N., Jakinda, D., & Annor-Frempong, I. (2013). *Tropical Agriculture Platform (TAP).* Retrieved from http://www.tropagplatform.org/

Osório, A. L., Afsarmanesh, H., & Camarinha-Matos, L. M. (2010). Towards a Reference Architecture for a Collaborative Intelligent Transport System Infrastructure. In L. Camarinha-Matos, X. Boucher, & H. Afsarmanesh (Eds.), *Collaborative Networks for a Sustainable World* (Vol. 336, pp. 469–477). Springer Berlin Heidelberg. doi:10.1007/978-3-642-15961-9_56

Park, D. C., & Reuter-Lorenz, P. (2009). The adaptive brain: Aging and neurocognitive scaffolding. *Annual Review of Psychology, 60*(1), 173–196. doi:10.1146/annurev.psych.59.103006.093656 PMID:19035823

Plaza, I., Martí, N. L., Martin, S., & Medrano, C. (2011). Mobile applications in an aging society: Status and trends. *Journal of Systems and Software, 84*(11), 1977–1988. doi:10.1016/j.jss.2011.05.035

Romano, M., & Kapelan, Z. (2014). Adaptive water demand forecasting for near real-time management of smart water distribution systems. *Environmental Modelling & Software, 60*, 265–276. doi:10.1016/j.envsoft.2014.06.016

Saarnio, L., Boström, A.-M., Hedman, R., Gustavsson, P., & Öhlén, J. (2017). Enabling at-homeness for residents living in a nursing home: Reflected experience of nursing home staff. *Journal of Aging Studies, 43*, 40–45. doi:10.1016/j.jaging.2017.10.001 PMID:29173513

Sánchez, A. M., & Pérez, M. P. (2005). Supply chain flexibility and firm performance. *International Journal of Operations & Production Management, 25*(7), 681–700. doi:10.1108/014435705 10605090

Sanz, J., Nayak, N., & Becker, V. (2006). Business services as a modeling approach for smart business networks. *IBM Research Devision Almaden Research Center RJ10381 (A0606-001)*, 1-16.

Silva, F. O. D. (2018). *Service selection and ranking in Cross-organizational Business Process collaboration (PhD).* Eindhoven: University of Technology of Eindhoven.

Thakur, M., Blazer, D., & Steffens, D. (2013). *Clinical Manual of Geriatric Psychiatry* (Vol. 1). USA: American Psychiatric Publishing.

Volpentesta, A. P., & Ammirato, S. (2013). Alternative agrifood networks in a regional area: A case study. *International Journal of Computer Integrated Manufacturing, 26*(1-2), 55–66. doi:10.1080/095 1192X.2012.681911

Wang, S., Higashino, W. A., Hayes, M., & Capretz, M. A. M. (2014). *Service Evolution Patterns.* Paper presented at the 2014 IEEE International Conference on Web Services. doi:10.1109/ICWS.2014.39

Wang, X. P., & An, Y. F. (2010). Building Flexible SOA-Based Enterprise Process Using Decision Services. Paper presented at the e-Business Engineering (ICEBE), 2010 IEEE 7th International Conference.

Weicht, B. (2013). The making of 'the elderly': Constructing the subject of care. *Journal of Aging Studies*, *27*(2), 188–197. doi:10.1016/j.jaging.2013.03.001

Xu, X., & Wang, Z. (2011). State of the art: Business service and its impacts on manufacturing. *Journal of Intelligent Manufacturing*, *22*(5), 653–662. doi:10.100710845-009-0325-3

Yu, E. S., & Mylopoulos, J. (1995). From ER To "aR"—Modelling Strategic Actor Relationships for Business Process Reengineering. University of Toronto.

Zhu, Q., Sarkis, J., & Lai, K. (2007). Green supply chain management: Pressures, practices and performance within the Chinese automobile industry. *Journal of Cleaner Production*, *15*(11–12), 1041–1052. doi:10.1016/j.jclepro.2006.05.021

Zinnikus, I., Bogdanovich, A., & Schäfer, R. (2017). *An Ontology Based Recommendation System for Elderly and Disabled Persons.* Academic Press.

Chapter 9
Human Knowledge and Expertise Platform for Managing Genomics Projects

Jitao Yang
Beijing Language and Culture University, China

ABSTRACT

Genomics has been used to more accurately support the realization of scientific research, personalized healthcare, and precision medicine. Professional knowledge and expertise are required to process the genomics project and laboratory workflows which include project enrollment, project and sample tracking, sample warehousing, nucleic acid extraction, library construction, concentration and peak map detection, pooling, sequencing, etc. Therefore, the digitizing management of projects and laboratory workflows is very important to support the handling of tens of thousands of samples in parallel. This chapter implements the human knowledge and expertise to a project and laboratory management platform, which can integrated manage the complex genomics projects, the laboratory workflows, the sequencing instruments, the analysis pipelines, and the genetic interpretation service. The platform can automate routine tasks, facilitate communication, optimize business procedures and workflows, process tens of thousands of samples parallelly, and increase the business efficiency.

DOI: 10.4018/978-1-7998-1279-1.ch009

INTRODUCTION

Advances in genomics have triggered a revolution in research and clinical therapeutics to facilitate understanding of the complex biological systems (e.g., single-nucleotide polymorphisms, copy-number variation) and diseases (e.g., Down syndrome, Edwards syndrome, Patau syndrome, breast cancer, lung cancer). The research and application of genomics require very complex business workflows, including project establishment, laboratory experiment, genome sequencing, bioinformatic analysis, genetic interpretation, report generation, and data release. Generally, the laboratory experiment costs the longest time in the genomics business workflow. The laboratory operations include sample warehousing, plasma separation (for blood samples), nucleic acid extraction, library construction, concentration and peak map detection, pooling, and etc. High throughput sequencing equipment, such as next generation sequencing (Metzker, 2010), third generation sequencing (TGS) (Rhoads, 2015), (McCarthy, 2010), or global screening array (GSA, 2019), are used to sequence the samples. The sequenced genomic data will be analyzed by bioinformatics pipelines, such as Genome Analysis Toolkit (GATK) (GATK, 2019). The analyzed genomic data will be interpreted by genetists using genetics databases, such as AutDB (AutDB, 2019), DisGeNET (Pinero, 2015), and OMIM (OMIM, 2019), (Amberger, 2017), to interpret the function, structure, and variation of genomic data.

The genomics business process is a complicated procedure that, human professional knowledge and expertise from project managers, laboratory staffs, bioinformatics engineers, genetists and IT engineers, are very important for providing successful genomics scientific research services.

A genomics sequencing center generally provides services for thousands of research, application and clinical customers (e.g., universities, institutions, small genomic data analysis companies, pharmaceuticals companies, and hospitals), handling hundreds of thousands of samples. This is a hard task for business management, not only for internal production, but also for customer services. Therefore, this chapter gives the design and implementation of a project and laboratory management platform.

The project management system has the modules of:

- contract management,
- invoice management,
- project management,
- sample management,
- sample verification, and
- data release.

The project management system will facilitate the communication with customers, automate the business process, and enhance the work efficiency, specifically, it has the functions of:

- enrolling project and sample information on-line or through mobile app (by sales or customers) before the post of samples to laboratory, so that the lab staffs can understand the project requirement, gather statistics of samples, and prepare the reagent and equipment for experiment;
- registering potential contracts and signing contracts;
- making out invoices based the requirement of customers;
- relieving the project management team from the burden of dealing with thousands of projects in parallel;

- helping project management team and customers to track sample information throughout the entire project life cycle;
- appointing experiment and sequencing tasks to laboratory staffs;
- assigning analysis tasks to bioinformatics engineers;
- distributing sequenced raw or fastq data and genetic reports to customers.

Additionally, a big genomics sequencing laboratory needs to accept and handle tens of thousands of sequencing samples in parallel, a laboratory information management system is necessary to be implemented to track the samples accurately, manage the molecular experimental procedures efficiently, and facilitate the collaboration of different departments in genomics business work-flows.

Therefore, this chapter also introduces a laboratory information management system, which is designed and developed specifically for genomics research laboratory that provides scientific research service including targeted DNA, transcriptome, targeted RNA, exome sequencing, and etc. The laboratory information management system can help laboratory to acquire samples from different sources (including hospitals, research institutes, agents and personal users), track samples throughout their whole business life cycles, implement Standard Operating Procedure (SOP), carry out complex routine operations step by step automatically following SOP, integrate with laboratory equipment, reduce errors, optimize procedures, process tens of thousands of samples in parallel, connect to storage system and high performance computing cluster, communicate with analysis engineers and analysis pipelines, automate genetic interpretation, and finally return sequencing data in raw or fastq (Cock, 2009) format and interpretation reports to customers through project management system.

The project management system and the laboratory information management system should be integrated and work together so that the project requirement and sample information could flow to the laboratory, and the sequencing data from the laboratory will be stored in storage system, analyzed by bioinformatics pipelines, interpreted by genetic interpretation system, and release genetic reports and sequence data to customers. This chapter introduces an integrated human knowledge and expertise platform that supports the full digitizing management of genomics service workflows.

BACKGROUND

Genomics scientific research business is a relatively new area, some of the top business management systems such as SAP Sales (SAP, 2019), Salesforce (Salesforce, 2019), Oracle Sales Cloud (Oracle, 2019) could only partially satisfy the business requirement of genomic data sequencing and analysis enterprises.

Laboratory information management system (LIMS) is a software-based solution supporting a modern laboratory's operations. A LIMS has been most adept at tracking experimental workflow, exchanging information with lab instruments, recording results, and providing search-able database. The application of a LIMS has evolved over the years from simple sample tracking to an enterprise core system that manages multiple aspects of a next generation sequencing (NGS) (Metzker, 2010) and third generation sequencing (TGS) (Rhoads, 2015), (McCarthy, 2010) genomics laboratory. Some of the laboratory information systems (Bath, 2011), (Grimes, 2014), (GeneSifter, 2019), (ProgenyLIMS, 2019), (IlluminaLIMS, 2019) are available but focus more on clinical genomics laboratory and require extensive modification to address the specific requirements of genomics laboratory which provides scientific research services. This

Figure 1. Project Work-flows of Genomics Scientific Research Service

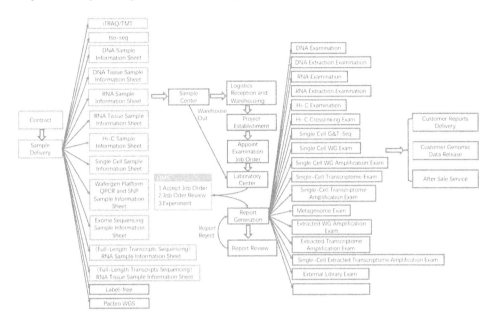

chapter therefore gives a web-based LIMS solution, which is robust for managing the large amounts of samples in parallel and flexible for the extension of new business line for new scientific research service.

The characteristics of modern genomics business, which requires the incorporating of professional knowledge and expertise from project managers, laboratory staffs, bioinformatics engineers, and genetists, are typically very different from those of traditional healthcare and clinical business. Extended from (Yang, 2018), this chapter gives the new integrated project and laboratory management solutions and platform.

PROJECT MANAGEMENT

Figure 1 describes the business process from potential contract enrollment to sample examination. The system is very complicated that, it supports multiple different business processes. When a potential contract was converted to contract, the customer can send his/her samples to the laboratory. The system can support multiple different types of samples such as DNA, DNA tissue, RNA, single cell, Hi-C (Berkum, 2010), and etc. Different samples will flow to different business processes. The sample center will notify the customers if the samples are received. The newly arrived samples will be stored in warehouse first, then the project management team will establish a project for the experiment and analysis of the samples following the agreement of the contract. The project management team will also appoint experimental job orders to the laboratory staffs. The lab staffs will accept and evaluate the job order and conduct the experiments. With the experiment results, the system will produce different reports for different samples. The reports will be delivered to customers for reviewing and deciding if the samples should continue to be arranged for the sequencing processes; if approved, the project management team will appoint library construction job orders to the laboratory staffs.

The function modules of the business management system are described below.

Contract Management

The contract management module has the following components.

- Potential contract enrollment, whose user is sales. For new customers, the sales could enroll customer information directly; for registered customers, the sales could enter sale's name, customer name, or customer organization to search the customer information. Wherever a new customer is enrolled, the customer information will be stored in the system for further reuse; the relation between sale and customer will be established. If experiment or sequencing solution is needed to provide for the customer, then the sale could submit the solution requirement to sale support department.
- Contract review. All the potential contracts submitted by sales will be reviewed by project management team in the company to evaluate and provide further support. The project management team can also add supplemental agreement.
- Customization evaluation. Some of the customers propose special experiment or analysis requirements which need to be evaluated by laboratory technical staffs or bioinformatics engineers. The evaluation team will proceed or reject the project and provide evaluation report. More customer and sample information will be enrolled with connection to the approved and signed contracts, and the system will open a cloud account automatically for customer to track the process of project, download sequence data, and access analysis report.
- Contract statistic, gathers statistics of contracts based on regions, samples, amount of money, and etc.
- Conversion rate, counts how many potential contracts have been finally signed, analyzes the reasons and designs marketing strategy for signing more customers.

Invoice Management

Invoice management includes the functions of invoice application, invoice records, accounts receivable confirmation, accounts receivable records, statistical report, invoicing approval process, and etc.

Project Establishment and Tracking

Based on the signed contract, a corresponding project will be established. Each project will describe clearly customer requirement, experiment requirement, analysis requirement, time table, data release methods (i.e., through portable hard drive, FTP, or cloud), etc.

In the project module, projects are listed with the properties of sale name, review date, submit date, contract name, customer name, customer organization, contract amount, invoice amount, received payments, etc. The user can search the project based on sale's name, contract ID, customer name, customer organization, and contract amount.

The user can also track the progress of the project by click the project status button, then a progress bar will demonstrate the status of each sample of the project, including logistics status, laboratory stages, sequencing time table, analysis pace and etc.

Sample Management

Sample management module allows customer and sales to enroll sample information respectively. In the project, the user should choose the type of sample first, then a corresponding sample information form will pop out with the existed contract information in the text-box, the user can further continue to choose analysis type, enter sample property, sample status, transportation requirement and so on, the user can also upload file for specific requirement. Generally, a project contains multiple samples, to ease the registration of samples by filling the sample form one by one on-line, the customer can organize sample data in excel following the template, and then upload the sample information excel to the system directly. The user can also modify or delete sample information on line in batch.

The customer should also describe sample transportation methods including: post by customer, deliver sample to laboratory, or collect from domicile.

The customer could communicate with project management team if further service is needed, and the project management team can also send information to customers if there are exception in samples.

If some of the samples are unconfirmed to the standards, then the project management team will send back the samples to customers.

Sample Verification

Each project has a list of samples, each sample has an ID. Select the samples for the same experiment and analysis aims, create a job order with parameters including experiment requirement and responsible lab staffs, then the job order will flow to the corresponding lab staffs. Generally, the job order will flow to a group, and the lab staffs could select to accept the job order and conduct the experiment. The job order could also be exported as excel file.

Through job orders, the workflow will flow from the project management team to laboratory team, and the sample experiment tasks will be transferred to and managed by laboratory information management system.

LABORATORY INFORMATION MANAGEMENT

The specific features of genomics scientific research service laboratory are the handling of multiple business lines as demonstrated in Figure 2 that the system could process in parallel more than eighteen different types of sample processing operations (such as DNA Detection, RNA Detection, Hi-C Detection, Single Cell Whole Genome Detection, Meta-Genome Detection, and etc.), separately. After the complex experimental steps, all the samples will be pooled and then sequenced together in the sequencing instrument; the sequence data will then be filtered and separated to different project directories waiting to be analyzed by different pipelines.

Before the samples' arrival at laboratory, the project and sample information will be enrolled into the project management system which could exchange data smoothly with LIMS. The sample information could be enrolled either by salesman who collaborates with hospitals and research institutions, or by

Figure 2. Laboratory Work-flows of Genomics Scientific Research Service

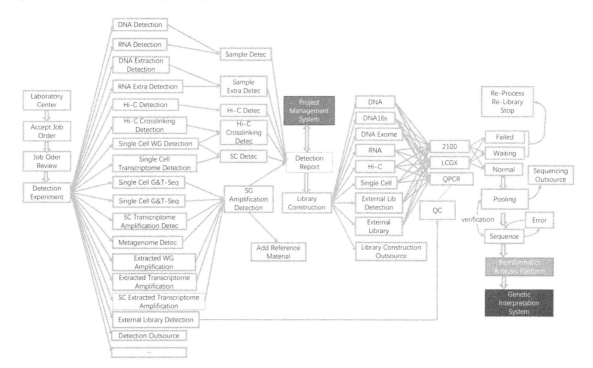

customers through web browser of personal computer or WeChat app. The project management team can arrange laboratory tasks ahead of the samples' arrival at laboratory, and the laboratory staffs will have adequate time to schedule the experimental tasks. All the enrollment modification operations are recorded by logs.

Samples are posted to the laboratory for sequencing from different areas distributed in the country and even in the world. Each sample's logistics information is tracked by project management system so that to avoid the loss of samples, the project management team will also have sufficient time to schedule the sequencing tasks in advance. When samples are arrived at laboratory, the two-dimensional bar-code will be scanned into system to markup that the samples are received. The system can help to check logistics status during the whole transportation process of a sample. If the sample was delayed or lost in logistics process, the corresponding person will be notified to deal with the event.

The business workflow of LIMS is demonstrated in Figure 2, some of the primary functions are described as follows.

Sample Detection

In genomics research lab, samples belong to different projects, when samples are arrived at laboratory, the bar-code of the sample will be scanned into system, then the sample will be connected to project information enrolled by the salesman or customers. According to project and sample information, the samples will be divided to different business processing lines including DNA Detection, RNA Detection,

DNA Extraction Detection, RNA Extraction Detection, Hi-C Detection, Hi-C Cross-linking Detection, Single Cell Whole Genome Detection, Single Cell Transcriptome Detection, Single Cell Transcriptome Amplification Detection, Meta-genome Detection, Extracted Whole Genome Amplification Detection, External Library Detection, and etc.

Detection Report Generation and Management

All the samples arrived at laboratory should be detected to verify if the samples meet the needs of sequencing. After the detection experiment, the lab staffs will use the system to produce detection reports that, different samples will receive different types of reports such as DNA report, DNA exome report, RNA report, Hi-C report, single cell report, and so on. The reports will be sent to project management team and further to customers to decide to continue the subsequent experiments or not.

Library Construction

The samples passed the detection will be further processed by the subsequent experiments, and then will be prepared for different types of library constructions including DNA, DNA 16s, DNA exome, RNA, Hi-C, single cell and etc. If the laboratory could not deal with some of the samples' library construction, the system also supports to transfer the sample to external laboratory for library construction.

Standard Operating Procedure

Standard Operating Procedure includes multiple important and complicated experimental steps, such as plasma isolation, nucleic acid extraction, 2100 detection, QPCR and etc. The system is also flexible to support to add new experimental operating procedure.

Pooling

Genomics pooling (Harakalova, 2011) is the efforts of preparing hundreds of sample individuals, so that the samples' genomic enrichment for regions of interest, are sufficient enough for deep sequencing. The system can efficient support this requirement and reduce a significant burden to experiment staffs.

Sequencing

After the pooling operations, the samples will be ready for sequencing by sequencing instruments (e.g., Illumina NovaSeq, HiSeq X Ten, PacBio). Generally, one sequencing instrument's running will be required to sequence as many samples as possible in parallel so that to minimize the cost of using sequencing reagents, therefore, the samples from different projects will be pooled together in the pooling process and sequenced in parallel. After sequencing, the sequenced data are stored in the storage system.

Quality Control and Reference Material Management

Quality is controlled in the whole genomics laboratory work flows, including experimental operation quality control, reagents quality control, sequencing data quality control, and etc. The system can also manage the reference material.

After sequencing, the filter and quality control pipelines will process the raw sequencing data and generate fastq data. The fastq data will be further separated into deferent project directories waiting to be analyzed by different genomics analysis pipelines which are implemented in the high-performance computing clusters.

To support the implementation of LIMS in enterprise, the system also has multiple administration, query and statistic modules.

For the proper functioning of LIMS, the fundamental data such as the detail data for experiment templates, barcode rules, agent information and pooling rules must be entered into the system through the master data management module.

Multiple instruments such as NovaSeq, MiSeq, HiSeq X Ten, HiSeq 4000, HiSeq2500 and NextSeq 500 are managed by the instrument management module, the instrument information such as location, valid time, detection time, maintenance time, running status, user manual and instructions are maintained in the system and could be queried from the system conveniently. The system will also notify the management staff when the instrument is near the maintenance or calibration time.

A user could have different roles and privileges in the system, the user's role, privilege, department, business, and data access and modification authority could all be configured flexibly.

Advanced data query and multidimensional data statistic and visualization functions have also been provided by the LIMS.

During the experiment, if some exceptions are found, then the lab staff could stop the sample experiment and return the exception information to project management team to decide if the experiment should continue or not, the project management team could also discuss with customers to give the decisions. The system supports to stop the sample experiment in batch and continue the sample experiment in batch.

If sample verification experiment has finished, then the lab staff will write sample verification report on-line, the report will be further reviewed by lab manager, and the system will generate final report in PDF or HTML 5 formats. The reports will also be accessible by project management team for review, and the approved reports will be distributed to customers to decide to continue the sequencing process or not.

GENETIC INTERPRETATION

After genomics analysis, the genomic data analysis result will be analyzed by the genetic interpretation system, which has a genetic interpretation knowledge database that established gene-disease associations based on the databases of AutDB (AutDB, 2019), DisGeNET (Pinero, 2015), OMIM (OMIM, 2019), (Amberger, 2017) and the other published scientific literatures. The genetic interpretation system can support the generation of dozens of different kinds of reports.

GENOMIC DATA RELEASE

Data release is an important function of the system, as mentioned above, a sequencing center can produce more than 20 Terabytes data every day, the sequenced data for personal customer can reach more than 100 Gigabytes for release, the sequenced data for enterprise or big laboratory customer are generally several Terabytes each day. Due to the limitation of Internet bandwidth, it is difficult to download big volume of data from the onsite data center of enterprise through Internet directly. Therefore, traditionally, the data are released to customer through hard disk, the bioinformatics engineers need to download the data from Network-Attached Storage (NAS) (Nagle, 1999) data storage system to hard disk and then post the hard disk to customers, the customers need to copy the data from hard disk to their own storage system and post the hard disk back to the sequencing center. This is complicated both for the sequencing center and the customers, also it's time consuming and uneconomical.

The project management system gives the big genomic data cloud (AliCloud, 2019), (OSS, 2019), (Docker, 2019), (ECS, 2019), (SLB, 2019), (RDS, 2019) release solution as described in Figure 3 that, when a project has been established, after the samples have been sequenced, the system will open a cloud account for customer and at the meantime creates a data storage directory for customer. After this, an email will be sent to bioinformatics engineers so that they will know where to upload the sequenced data, when the sequenced data have been uploaded and are ready to be downloaded, another email will be sent to customer including the cloud account information and cloud platform function descriptions to let the customers know how to download the sequenced and analyzed result data. Personal customer could download the small volume of data using FTP, enterprise customers could synchronize the large volume data to their regional cloud data centers, and connect their own data center to the cloud data centers with high speed fiber network.

SYSTEM DESIGN AND IMPLEMENTATION

The project management system and laboratory information management system were designed and developed separately in Java web technologies using the Spring (Spring, 2019) as domain layer, Spring MVC as application layer, Mybatis (MyBatis, 2019) as infrastructure layer, and the implementation is platform-independent. The platform framework provides the development APIs of authorization, access control, internationalization, database, log, UI (personal computer, WeChat and App), error process,

Figure 3. Genomic Big Data Release Work-flows

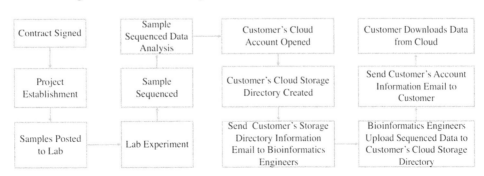

file storage, job scheduler, cache service, instant message work-flow, email notification, service load balance, and etc.

Tomcat is used as web servers; MySQL relational database management system, MongoDB (MongoDB, 2019), Network-Attached Storage (NAS), and Object Storage Service (OSS) (OSS, 2019) are used to store the structured data, semi-structured data, and files, respectively. The system architecture is described in Figure 4.

Since the system supports multiple different work-flows, therefore, a work-flow engine and a task schedule were developed.

Vue (Vue, 2019) is used as the frontend progressive framework, and the user interface was designed to adaptive to personal computer web browser and mobile phone automatically, with the support of HTML5, CSS, JQuery (JQuery, 2019), and bootstrap (Bootstrap, 2019). ECharts (ECharts, 2019) is used to show the dynamic complicated statistic charts.

The system was implemented in cloud environment and the system was developed to support computing and storage resources to scale elastically on demand. Web Application Firewall (WAF) was deployed to provide access and authority control. Hyper Text Transfer Protocol over Secure Socket Layer (HTTPS) was also implemented for the system to secure the data transfer.

SYSTEM INTEGRATION

It is important to connect the project management system with the laboratory information management system so that workflows from sales can flow to the laboratory smoothly. Figure 5 demonstrates the human knowledge and expertise platform that established to integrate the project management system and the laboratory information management system. Through job orders, the workflow will flow from the project management team to laboratory team, and the sample experiment tasks will be transferred from project management system to laboratory information management system. The data between the two systems are transferred through web service (Fielding, 2000) APIs and Json (Json, 2019). The laboratory

Figure 4. System architecture

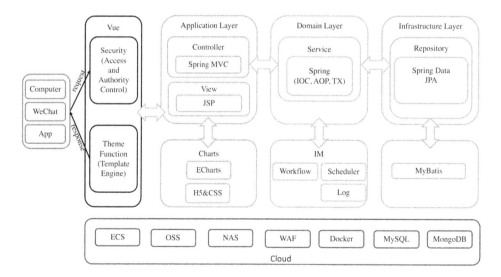

Figure 5. Human knowledge and expertise platform for genomics project and laboratory management

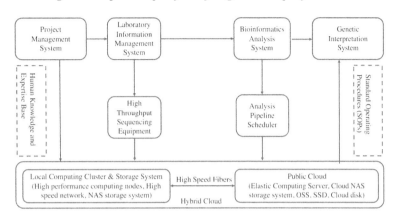

information management system was also connected to high throughput sequencing equipment so that to arrange the sequencing tasks. The LIMS can be configured to communicate with different sequencing platforms such as PacBio, Illumina NovaSeq, HiSeq X Ten, MiSeq, HiSeq, HiSeq 4000, HiSeq2500, NextSeq 500, Oxford Nanopore PromethION (PromethION, 2019) (Wouter, 2018) and could be configured to connect with other type of sequencing instruments.

After sequencing, the raw sequence data will be stored in local storage system, and the bioinformatics analysis pipelines will be notified to start to analyze the genomic data in parallel. The fastq data and analysis result data will be stored in storage system, and the analysis result data will be further processed by genetic interpretation system to generate genetic reports. Since the platform provides services for different organizations (such as universities, research institutions, companies, hospitals, and etc.), and different organizations require different report contents and formats, therefore, the genetic reports system can produce multiple different type of reports in PDF and HTML formats. The reports and the genomic data in fastq format will be sent to customers through the project management system. Because the platform integrates the systems together, therefore, the customers can track the full lifecycle status of each project and each sample through the project management system, such as if the sample has been received, the sample is processed in which step of the laboratory experiment, the sample genetic data is analyzed in which step of the pipeline, and etc.

All the systems and bioinformatics analysis pipelines have been implemented in the hybrid cloud environment. Due to there are large volume data to be uploaded to public cloud's storage system every day, the local computing data center is connected to public cloud's data center through high speed fiber. The public cloud can also provide computing nodes for the local computing cluster elastically.

The platform also supports the business management of multiple subcompanies.

HUMAN KNOWLEDGE AND EXPERTISE BASE

The success of the design and development of the platform for genomics project and laboratory information management, relies on the deep understanding of genomics business and genomics laboratory operation knowledge and expertise.

Different type of samples will have their independent business process, from the contract signing, laboratory operations, sequencing, data analysis, to genetic interpretation. The platform has stored multiple genomics business process knowledge base and experiment operation expertise base. As described in Figure 5, the platform has stored hundreds of business process procedures and laboratory experiment operation procedures, most of which have been formalized as standard operating procedures (SOPs). All the project management and service staffs, the laboratory experiment staffs and the bioinformatics engineers have to follow the SOPs to process the samples.

For instance, starting from the contract signing operation of the project management system, different samples to be sequenced will require different information sheets which include different parameters to describe the samples, the sequencing requirement, data analysis requirement, and etc. Therefore, the system has stored multiple knowledge sheets about different samples' parameters so that the sample and its description information can flow to the correct work flows to satisfy the standard operating procedure requirement, this will avoid the workflow error due to the information missing or un-qualified sample. Such as the Hi-C sample will be registered to the Hi-C Sample Information Sheet and will flow to the Hi-C Examination or Hi-C Crosslinking Examination; the Single Cell Sample Information Sheet will decide the single cell sample to flow to the Single Cell Whole Genome Examination, the Single Cell Whole Genome Amplification Examination, or the other operations.

In the laboratory experiment operation segment, because the genomics experiment is very complicated and easy to has errors, therefore, the platform has stored and can provide much more SOP guides for the laboratory staffs, so that the multiple experiment procedures could be executed correctly, quickly, and exactly. Such as the DNA sample will be processed following the DNA detection SOP, the RNA sample will be processed following the RNA detection SOP.

The platform is a big knowledge base of hundreds of genomics analysis pipelines that, based on the requirement, the sample's sequenced data will be analyzed by specific pipelines implemented in the platform.

As mentioned above, the platform also has a genetic interpretation knowledge base that established gene-disease associations so that to give genetic interpretations.

CONCLUSION

This chapter introduces a genomics project management platform which is composed by project management system and laboratory information management system. The platform has already been delivered on line and used by big genomics companies and laboratories. The project management system contains the human knowledge base of genomics project management and has the best practices from top genomics sequencing centers. This chapter describes clearly the workflows of genomics scientific research service business, from potential contract enrollment, signing new contract, project establishment and tracking, sample delivery, logistics monitoring, sample reception and warehousing, appointing experiment job order, report generation, report delivery to customer, to data release. This chapter describes these recent practical developments of genomics projects for scientific research service, identifies the important application scenarios, and a list of specific business scenarios are discussed and implemented into the project management system.

This chapter also introduces the solution of a web-based laboratory information system specifically for genomics scientific research service laboratory, which needs to accurately and efficiently handle tens of thousands of samples in parallel. The human knowledge base for laboratory management were implemented in the LIMS. In the LIMS, sample information is traceable from the enrollment, and the sample is tracked when it was posted to the laboratory. When the sample is arrived at laboratory, the arrival of the sample will be verified by scanning the barcode on the sample, and then the sample will be stored in refrigerator, and LIMS will record the sample's location in the refrigerator. The sample will be taken out for experiment by laboratory staff when she received detection order from project management team. Then, all the experimental operations will be recorded by the LIMS including DNA extraction, library construction, concentration and peak map detection, quality control, pooling, and sequencing. The sequenced data will be stored in NAS, and the LIMS will notify the bioinformatics engineers to filter, separate and analyze the sequenced data. The analyzed result will be transferred to genetic interpretation system to generate research or clinical reports.

The LIMS currently supports the sequencing platforms of PacBio, NovaSeq, HiSeq X Ten, MiSeq, HiSeq, HiSeq 4000, HiSeq2500, NextSeq 500, and could be configured for other type of sequencing instruments. The LIMS addresses most of the genomics research laboratory informationization needs that, the LIMS: brings accuracy tracking and accessibility to the samples in experimental steps, identifies sample quickly and reduces errors significantly in the whole experimental steps, accesses and queries data conveniently via the web rather than digging through files, integrates with laboratory instruments, provides advanced query and analysis capabilities, generates in-depth production statistic charts, shares experiment operating status and results with collaborators and clinicians, and controls experimental quality.

Further, the project management system and the laboratory information management system were integrated to work together to form a platform that provides the full management function for genomics service workflows. This chapter gives the leading project and laboratory management human knowledge and digitalizing solution for big genomic data sequencing and analysis centers.

ACKNOWLEDGMENT

This research was supported by the Science Foundation of Beijing Language and Culture University (supported by "the Fundamental Research Funds for the Central Universities") [grant numbers: 19YJ040010, 15YJ030001, 18YJ030006, 17YJ0302].

REFERENCES

AliCloud. (2019). *Alibaba Cloud (Aliyun)*. Retrieved from https://intl.aliyun.com

Amberger, J. S., & Hamosh, A. (2017). Searching Online Mendelian Inheritance in Man (OMIM): A Knowledgebase of Human Genes and Genetic Phenotypes. *Current Protocols in Bioinformatics*, *58*(1). PMID:28654725

Aut, D. B. (2019). *AutDB: a Genetic Database for Autism Spectrum Disorders*. Retrieved from http://www.mindspec.org/products/autdb/

Bath, T. G., Bozdag, S., Afzal, V., & Crowther, D. (2011). Lims Portal and BonsaiLIMS: Development of a lab information management system for translational medicine. *Source Code for Biology and Medicine*, *6*(1), 9. doi:10.1186/1751-0473-6-9 PMID:21569484

Berkum, N. L., Erez Lieberman-Aiden, E., Williams, L., Imakaev, M., Gnirke, A., Mirny, L. A., ... Lander, E. S. (2010). Hi-C: A Method to Study the Three-dimensional Architecture of Genomes. *Journal of Visualized Experiments*, (39): 1869. PMID:20461051

Bootstrap. (2019). *Bootstrap.* Retrieved from http://getbootstrap.com/

Cock, P. J. A., Fields, C. J., Goto, N., Heuer, M. L., & Rice, P. M. (2009). The Sanger FASTQ file format for sequences with quality scores, and the Solexa/Illumina FASTQ variants. *Nucleic Acids Research*, *38*(6), 1767–1771. doi:10.1093/nar/gkp1137 PMID:20015970

Docker. (2019). *Docker.* Retrieved from www.docker.com

ECharts. (2019). *ECharts.* Retrieved from https://ecomfe.github.io/echarts- doc/public/en/index.html

ECS. (2019). *Alibaba Cloud Elastic Compute Service (ECS).* Retrieved from https://intl.aliyun.com/product/ecs

Fielding, R. T. (2000). *Architectural Styles and the Design of Network-based Software Architectures.* PhD Dissertation.

GATK. (2019). *Genome Analysis Toolkit (GATK).* Retrieved from https://software.broadinstitute.org/gatk

GeneSifter. (2019). *GeneSifter Lab Edition.* Retrieved from http://www.cambridgesoft.com/services/SupportNews/details/?SupportNews=124

Grimes, S. M., & Ji, H. P. (2014). MendeLIMS: A web-based laboratory information management system for clinical genome sequencing. *BMC Bioinformatics*, *15*(1), 290. doi:10.1186/1471-2105-15-290 PMID:25159034

GSA. (2019). *Infinium Global Screening Array-24 Kit.* Retrieved from https://www.illumina.com/products/by-type/microarray-kits/infinium-global-screening.html

Harakalova, M., Nijman, I. J., Medic, J., Mokry, M., Renkens, I., Blankensteijn, J. D., ... Cuppen, E. (2011). Genomic DNA Pooling Strategy for Next-Generation Sequencing-Based Rare Variant Discovery in Abdominal Aortic Aneurysm Regions of Interest - Challenges and Limitations. *Journal of Cardiovascular Translational Research*, *4*(3), 271–280. doi:10.100712265-011-9263-5 PMID:21360310

Illumina, L. I. M. S. (2019). *Illumina LIMS.* Retrieved from https://support.illumina.com.cn/array/array_software/illumina_lims.html

JQuery. (2019). *JQuery.* Retrieved from http://jquery.com/

JSON. (2019). *Working with JSON.* Retrieved from https://developer.mozilla.org/en-US/docs/Learn/JavaScript/Objects/JSON

McCarthy, A. (2010). Third Generation DNA Sequencing: Pacific Biosciences' Single Molecule Real Time Technology. *Chemistry & Biology, 17*(7), 675–676. doi:10.1016/j.chembiol.2010.07.004 PMID:20659677

Metzker, M. L. (2010). Sequencing technologies - the next generation. *Nature Reviews. Genetics, 11*(1), 31–46. doi:10.1038/nrg2626 PMID:19997069

Mongo, D. B. (2019). *MongoDB*. Retrieved from https://www.mongodb.com/

MyBatis. (2019). *MyBatis*. Retrieved from http://blog.mybatis.org/

Nagle, D. F., Ganger, G. R., Butler, J., Goodson, G., & Sabol, C. (1999). Network Support for Network-Attached Storage. In *Proceedings of Hot Interconnects*. Stanford, CA: Stanford University.

OMIM. (2019). *OMIM: An Online Catalog of Human Genes and Genetic Disorders*. Retrieved from https: //omim.org/

Oracle. (2019). *Oracle Sales Cloud*. Retrieved from https://cloud.oracle.com/sales-cloud

OSS. (2019). *Alibaba Cloud Object Storage Service (OSS)*. Retrieved from https://intl.aliyun.com/product/oss

Pinero, J., Queralt-Rosinach, N., Bravo, A., Deu-Pons, J., Bauer-Mehren, A., Baron, M., ... Furlong, L. (2015). DisGeNET: A discovery platform for the dynamical exploration of human diseases and their genes. *Database (Oxford), 2015*(0), bav028. doi:10.1093/database/bav028 PMID:25877637

ProgenyL. I. M. S. (2019). *Progeny LIMS*. Retrieved from http://www.progenygenetics.com/lims/

PromethION. (2019). *Oxford Nanopore PromethION*. Retrieved from https://nanoporetech.com/products/promethion

RDS. (2019). Alibaba Cloud ApsaraDB for RDS (Relational Database System). Retrieved from https://intl.aliyun.com/product/apsaradb-for-rds

Rhoads, A., & Au, K. F. (2015). PacBio Sequencing and Its Applications. *Genomics, Proteomics & Bioinformatics, 13*(5), 278–289. doi:10.1016/j.gpb.2015.08.002 PMID:26542840

Salesforce. (2019). *Salesforce*. Retrieved from https://www.salesforce.com

SAP. (2019). *SAP Hybris Sales Cloud*. Retrieved from https://www.sap.com/products/crm-commerce/sales.html

SLB. (2019). *Alibaba Cloud Server Load Balancer (SLB)*. Retrieved from https://intl.aliyun.com/

Spring. (2019). *Spring Framework*. Retrieved from https://spring.io/

Vue. (2019). Retrieved from https://vuejs.org/

Wouter, D. C., Arne, D. R., Tim, D. P., Svenn, D., Peter, D. R., Mojca, S., ... Christine, V. B. (2018). Structural variants identified by Oxford Nanopore PromethION sequencing of the human genome. *bioRxiv, 434118*. doi:10.1101/434118

Yang, J. (2018). Business Management System for Genomics. In *Proceedings of the 9th IEEE International Conference on Information, Intelligence, Systems and Applications*. Zakynthos, Greece: IEEE.

Yang, J. (2018). Smart Laboratory Information System Accelerates Genomics Research. In *Proceedings of the 9th IEEE International Conference on Information, Intelligence, Systems and Applications*. Zakynthos, Greece: IEEE. 10.1109/IISA.2018.8633685

Chapter 10
Secure Human–Computer Interaction:
A Multi–Factor Authentication CAPTCHA Scheme

Emmanuel Oluwatobi Asani
https://orcid.org/0000-0002-6774-8529
Landmark University, Nigeria

Olumide Babatope Longe
American University of Nigeria, Nigeria

Anthony Jatau Balla
Landmark University, Nigeria

Roseline Oluwaseun Ogundokun
https://orcid.org/0000-0002-2592-2824
Landmark University, Nigeria

Emmanuel Abidemi Adeniyi
Landmark University, Nigeria

ABSTRACT

In this chapter, CAPTCHA was presented as a measure for secure human-computer interaction. A multi-factor CAPTCHA scheme that integrates facial recognition and real-time functionality as a secure verification mechanism to check the activities of bots that try to assume human status was designed, developed, and tested. The real-time functionality is premised on the human user's ability to complete trivial tasks which though simple for human is difficult to break by bots. This was motivated by the need to combat attackers' tendencies to beat existing CAPTCHA schemes through optical character recognition, image annotation, tag classifier, etc. Literature on a number of existing schemes was reviewed with a view to identifying gaps and establishing the research agenda. The system design and analysis were done using scalable design techniques. Implementation was done using Javascript and a set of APIs. The scheme was tested on an intel core i7 3GHz computer and further evaluated. Preliminary results and findings show a promising effectiveness and efficiency of the developed system.

DOI: 10.4018/978-1-7998-1279-1.ch010

INTRODUCTION

Human-Computer Interaction (HCI), also known as Human-Machine Interaction bothers on the study, design, development, and deployment of interactive systems and how humans relate with them, especially with a focus on functionality and usability (Jain and Sivaselvan, 2012). Thus, HCI considers activities and services offered by a system and how users can derive the maximum benefits accrued, to achieve specified goals in terms of ease of use and remembrance of how to use it, learnability, efficiency, error management and satisfiability (Brodić and Amelio, 2017).

Owing to its continued advances, ubiquity, and vast potentials, the internet has become a platform for the design, development, and deployment of Human-Computer Interactive (HCI) systems. Thus, there is an increasing need and demand for web-based HCI systems (Khalil, 2018). Consequently, HCI systems are susceptible to security issues plaguing internet technology and applications. This may explain the research interests in HCI security.

HCI security (HCI-Sec) studies the interaction between humans and machines as it relates to information security (Agathonos, 2016). Since, web-related resources are susceptible to security challenges such as Denial of Service, identity theft, phishing, XPath injection attacks and so on (Chaudhary *et al.,* 2015; Ajayi *et al.,* 2016; Jambhekar *et al.,* 2016; Omotosho *et al,* 2019), the aim of HCI-Sec, is to improve the security of information in HCI, while not compromising the usability of end-user applications (Garfinkel and Lipford, 2014; Asani *et al.,* 2018). HCI-Sec considers aspects of user authentication, e-mail security, device pairing, anti-phishing schemes, web privacy, mobile security among others (Lampson, 2009; Kainda et al., 2010; Weir et al., 2010; Larrocha *et al.,* 2011; Garfinkel and Lipford, 2014; Kanakaris *et al.,* 2019).

In this chapter, CAPTCHA is presented as an authentication scheme for secure Human-Machine Interaction. The study aims to present a multi-factor authentication captcha scheme based on facial authentication and human ability to complete trivial tasks. The objectives of the study are to develop a real-time CAPTCHA system, to embed a Facial authentication system for secondary authentication and finally to develop an integrated multi-factor authentication system.

BACKGROUND

HCI-Sec centers around the user's need for usable and secure computers (Satchell and Dourish, 2009; González-Pérez *et al.,* 2019). The objective is to prevent criminals or illegitimate users from gaining unauthorized access or compromising the system's security without compromising the system's usability. Thus, techniques for securing the systems must encompass elements of usability, because perceived difficulties often result in users resorting to practices that circumvent security or alternatively, users may seek easier to use, but insecure systems (Smith 2003; Kainda *et al.,* 2010). Faily and Fléchais, (2010) noted that users' biases and perception play a prominent role in the balancing of security and usability. Thus, they proposed the IRIS framework with an underlying model that integrates usability, requirements, and risk analysis. Osho *et al.,* (2019), highlighted the increasing demand for secure systems, without compromising effectiveness engendered by usability, convenience, and cost-effectiveness.

Kamoun and Halaweh (2012) conducted an empirical study on 247 subjects to investigate the relationship between interface design and how the system's security is perceived. Their work was based on the hypothesis that effective interface design would positively affect the perception of the security of the system. Their result confirmed their hypothesis of a positive correlation between interface design and security. Furthermore, they suggested that secure systems may not necessarily impede the systems' usability provided that important elements at the intersection of usability and security are considered. This work supports an earlier study on HCISec threat modeling.

While Sasse *et al.,* (2001) earlier posited that existing HCI design model sufficiently caters for potential security issues, Radke *et al.,* (2010) made a case for a robust model for HCI-Sec that integrate security requirements and all elements of usability. This is based on a study by Schechter et al (2007) that shows that HCI systems are susceptible to security issues due to users lapses. According to Kainda *et al.,* (2010), HCISec must differ from the generic security models and be adapted to suit the uniques demands of HCI by considering factors lying at the intersection of security and usability of systems. These include effectiveness, users' satisfaction, efficiency, social context, and security (see Figure 1).

Garfinkel and Lipford, (2014) identified CAPTCHA as a user-friendly authentication scheme for HCI-Sec; others include, text passwords, password managers, graphical authentication, biometrics, token-based authentication, mental computation, and one-time passwords and fallback and backup authentication. The usability goal of CAPTCHAs is to present a task that is difficult to perform by a computer, but easy enough to be completed by humans (Hidalgo and Alvarez, 2011). In a study to analyze the time taken for users to solve image based CAPTCHA as a case study for HCI, Brodić and Amelio, (2017), citing Baecher *et al.,* (2010) identified usability, security and practicality as the three key components of CAPTCHA. They were able to capture the psychology of users by drawing inference from their reaction (response time) to four different types of CAPTCHAs. They concluded that users finds CAPTCHAs that incorporate animated characters more usable.

CAPTCHA is a test that was created to tell humans apart from robots/computers. The test was created in a way to make most humans pass but not computers, these tests are often based on open artificial intelligence problems such as; the recognition of distorted text (Text-based CAPTCHA), identification of objects in images (Image-based CAPTCHA), recognition of content in an audio clip (Audio-based CAPTCHA) or simply by making common gestures to a camera (Motion-based CAPTCHA). CAPTCHA helps to combat identity theft.

Figure 1. Threat model for HCISec (Kainda et al., 2010)

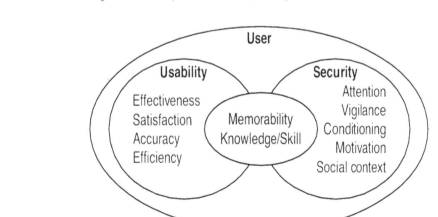

In spite of numerous research interventions, identity theft remains very rampant. Attackers continue to device innovative means of outsmarting authentication systems. Victims of identity theft have to cope with physical, social, emotional and financial consequences after the incidence. In 2017, over $16 billion was reportedly lost to identity theft (Javelin Strategy & Research, 2018). Existing authentication schemes such as facial authentication and CAPTCHA provide an extra layer of protection against identity theft but have both become liable to attackers due to recent advances in Artificial intelligence methods. According to Uzun et al. (2018), by presenting a randomly selected challenge embedded in a Captcha image, we can prevent the attacker from knowing what to expect in order to by-pass the system.

In this chapter, a multi-factor authentication scheme which depends on users' ability to complete trivial tasks and integrates Facial authentication is presented.

Classification of CAPTCHA

Hassan, W.K., (2016) classified CAPTCHA implementation for web services under two main approaches; the Optical Character Recognition (OCR) and the Non-Optical Recognition (Non-OCR). The OCR approach deals with text-based CAPTCHAs while the Non-OCR deals with audio and video-based CAPTCHAs.

Text-Based CAPTCHAs are the most commonly used, they are simple to develop. Text-based CAPTCHA deals with displaying groups of alphabetic, numeric or alpha-numeric characters to a user with slight modifications such as noise, scattering or rotation. These added modifications are to make it difficult for bots to read the characters. OCR Program is a common method used to break text-based CAPTCHA (Ying-Lien Lee and Chih-Hsiang Hsu, 2011). OCR programs achieve characters readability via three phases;

1. Pre-processing of the picture
2. Segmenting the picture, each segment should have only one character.
3. Identification of each character in each segment.

Some text-based CAPTCHA's in literature include Gimpy CAPTCHA (Greg Mori and Jitendra Malik, 2003), Ez-Gimpy CAPTCHA (Greg Mori and Jitendra Malik, 2003), Baffle Text CAPTCHA (Hassan, W.K., 2016), Pessimal Print CAPTCHA (Chen Li et al, 2010).

With text-based CAPTCHA, Users often face the problem of incorrect entry at first try. This may be due to the use of different lines, the use of multiple shapes, the use of multiple fonts, font size difference and the use of blurred characters. Additionally, text-based CAPTCHAs are attacked successfully using OCR techniques (Kaur and Behal,2014).

Image-Based CAPTCHA: In this type of CAPTCHA, users have to identify images by performing image recognition tasks. Users may have to interpret the given image(s), identify similarities or patterns and point certain objects. This is the most user-friendly CAPTCHA and it is fairly easier to pass, compared to text-based CAPTCHA (Bostik and Klecka, 2018). Image-based CAPTCHA was first proposed in Carnegie Mellon University and a prototype was developed called ESP Pix, other types of Image-Based CAPTCHA include Pix and Bongo CAPTCHA. Pix CAPTCHA uses an outsized database of photographic and animated pictures of daily objects. Users are to identify and match images relating to similar concepts from a set of images. Bongo contains two series of blocks namely; the left block series and the right block series. The blocks in the right series differ from those in the left, the test is for the user to identify each block's property that groups the two-block series apart (Kaur and Behal,2014). Image

CAPTCHA's are more secure compared with text-based CAPTCHA's, albeit, without considering users with visibility problems. It is also susceptible to Random guessing attack and Pictionary-based attack will break it easily (Raj et al, 2010). It also consumes space as image databases or servers are required to make the CAPTCHA. According to Lorenzi et al, (2012), image CAPTCHA such as SQ-PIX, ESP-PIX, and ASIRRA can all be broken by algorithms with an average of 70-75% accuracy, using classification and segmentation methods. Attackers use image recognition algorithms and heuristics to increase the probability of a successful solution. Also, image CAPTCHAs are quite vulnerable to Machine learning attacks (Jabed and Ranjan, 2013). Content-based picture retrieval and annotation techniques have been shown to be able to automatically find and name semantically similar images thereby making attacks more affordable. In conclusion, the image-based CAPTCHA is faced with usability challenges. Image CAPTCHA is impossible for humans with vision impairments, thus limiting the number of people able to pass it. This method is also very prone to attack by bots thereby rendering it not reliable.

Audio-Based CAPTCHA's: In this scheme, users are made to complete a test which involves recognizing and completing a task from an audio source. This is difficult because users have to a good grasp of the language and the accent of the audio source (Subramanyam and Priya, 2015). Unlike image-based CAPTCHA which relies solely on superior human perception, audio-based CAPTCHA relies on audio perception (Kulluru et al, 2016). Thus, this CAPTCHA is difficult, if not impossible to solve by humans with hearing impairments. In audio CAPTCHAs, a text is embedded and mixed in with surrounding noise, such as sound or unfamiliar chatter (Ahn et al, 2004). Although audio CAPTCHA is said to be analogous, the applications of this CAPTCHA is a bit different due to inherent changes in the interfaces used to remember and examine them. A major advantage of audio CAPTCHA is that it is a good solution for users with visual impairments. Tam et al, (2010) identified three techniques used to break audio CAPTCHA with up to 70% success rate; Mel-frequency cepstral coefficients (MFCC), perceptual linear prediction (PLP), and relative spectral transform-PLP (RASTA-PLP). MFCC is a very common speech representation scheme. MFCC utilizes Mel-frequency bands, which is more efficient in terms of estimating the frequencies humans can hear. Audio CAPTCHA's are not as user-friendly as text and image CAPTCHA. The availability of audio CAPTCHA is only in one language, the users are required to have an understanding of the language or else will have no chance of passing the test.

Video-Based CAPTCHA: This means of CAPTCHA prompts users to view a video; users will then have to correctly select a tag that best describes the video. The challenges are passed if the user selected tags are the same matches with the database of the ground truth tags of the video (Kluever and Zanibbi., 2009; Kwak et al, 2007). Video CAPTCHA cannot be broken using Optical Character Recognition program and provide greater security than Text-based CAPTCHA and Image CAPTCHA. Video CAPTCHA is also an easy solution for people with hearing impairments (Kaur and Behal, 2014). The major drawback of Video-based CAPTCHA's is that the files are often large, so downloading the media may be challenging.

DESCRIPTION OF DESIGN CONCEPT

Existing authentication schemes such as facial authentication and CAPTCHA provide an extra layer of protection against identity theft but have both become liable to attacks due to recent advances in artificial intelligence methods. In this chapter, a new authentication scheme is presented, which integrates facial recognition functionality and depends on users' ability to complete trivial tasks within a specified time.

The proposed system is a multi-factor authentication scheme that integrates Facial Authentication. The system will have a two-step authentication process, the primary step will be to solve an Image-based CAPTCHA in real-time while the secondary step will be Facial Recognition. The system is designed to validate human presence when signing up on an electronic mail platform.

After the user provides all the necessary information needed to sign up, they would be prompted to click the "I am not a robot" button on the requested webpage, and this will prompt an Image-based CAPTCHA that will have to be solved within 30 seconds or else the session will time out. Once the Image-based CAPTCHA has been solved, the browser will send a prompt to access the webcam of the computer. Once access is granted to the browser, a reCAPTCHA checker will pop up to detect the liveliness of the user that is being verified. Access is then granted to the human user once the Facial authentication algorithm has collected all relevant data and also upon passing the CAPTCHA test.

The system design process follows the linear-sequential life cycle waterfall engineering process model which spans from requirements modeling to acceptance testing.

Features of The System

The developed system will feature an Image-based CAPTCHA, a Webcam Input Feature and a Face detection Platform. The Image-based CAPTCHA feature is the first phase of the system. After the user is prompted to click the "I am not a robot" button, he/she will have to complete the shown Image CAPTCHA to verify that the user requesting the web service is a human. The system will then take input from the webcam which takes a live feed of the face of the user for Identification and Recognition. Tracking. js API was embedded to perform face detection. Tracking.js is a JavaScript library that brings a few machine vision algorithms, and a splash of related utilities, to the browser. The tracking library achieves feature extraction by Accelerated segment test, it finds corners on the parts of the image and saves it as distinct features. Face detection is primarily determined by the Viola-Jones Algorithm.

SYSTEM DESIGN

The Viola-Jones algorithm is one of the most widely used algorithms for face detection, because of its high training rate. It has a high true positive rate and it processes images quite fast. There are four main steps to achieve its goal of face detection; Haar feature extraction, Integral Image, AdaBoost Classifier learning, and Cascading Classifiers.

1. Haar features: This picture feature is used to discover human faces in images. Human faces consists of a pair of eyes, a mouth, and a single nose. These features can easily be compared using Haar features, principally used for face detection.
2. Integral Image: The idea of Integral image is made possible for quick feature extraction. Rectangle options are often computed in no time using an intermediate representation of the image that is named the integral image. The integral image computes a pixel value, in a very fast and effective method at every pixel.
3. AdaBoost Classifier learning: It is a machine learning algorithm that improves performance and feature selection.

4. Cascading Classifiers: This process combines the classifiers that promptly discard background openings so that more calculations can be performed on face-like regions.

The Viola jones algorithm for facial detection is presented below (Viola and Jones, 2001):

```
Input: original test image
Output: image with face indicators as rectangles
For i= 1 to num of scales in pyramid of images do
Downsample image to create image,
Compute integral image, image
For j= 1 to num of shift steps of sub-window do
For k= 1 to num of stages in cascade classifier do
For l= 1 to num of filters of stage k do
Filter detection sub-window
Accumulate filter outputs
End for
If accumulation fails per-stage threshold then
Reject sub-window as face
Break this k for loop
End if
End for
If sub-window passed all per-stage checks then
Accept this sub-window as a face
End if
End for
End for
The system design is implemented using; dataflow diagram, pseudo-codes and
flowcharts. The pseudocode of the image-based CAPTCHA is presented below:
User views captcha page:
User -> IP
Captcha-token = Scramble <- (Captcha-code + IP + Secret-code)
User <- Captcha-token
User solves the captcha, submits answer:
User -> IP, Captcha-code answer, Captcha-token
New token = Scramble <- (Captcha-code answer + IP + Secret-code)
IF Captcha-token = New token
User <- "Correct! You are a human."
ELSE
User <- "Incorrect, please try again."
```

Figure 2 describes the flow information in the system, while we present the flowchart of the system in Figure 3;

Figure 2. Data flow diagram of the CAPTCHA system

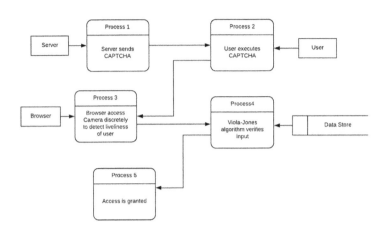

The system interface was developed using Hypertext Markup Language (HTML) and Cascading Style Sheets (CSS), while Javascript was used for the programming logic of the system. The Face Detection system was implemented using Tracking.js API.

Upon clicking the "I am not a Robot" checkbox, the system displays a reCAPTCHA to be solved by the user, this is shown in Figure 4. The reCAPTCHA must be solved within 30 seconds to continue with the registration of the new user, otherwise, it will time out.

Once the user has successfully solved the provided reCAPTCHA a reCAPTCHA checker will pop-up (see Figure 5). The reCAPTCHA checker is aimed at detecting the face of the acclaimed user, once a face is detected access is then granted.

SYSTEM EVALUATION

The Facial detection platform was subjected to photo attacks which are subject to two types of errors; the false rejection and false acceptance. The performance metric is measured by calculating the Half Total Error Rate $(HTER)$. It is calculated by the sum of the False Rejection Rate (FRR) and False Acceptance Rate (FAR) divided by 2, with the result in Percentage.

$$HTER(D) = \frac{FAR(D) + FRR(D)}{2}[\%]$$

In our evaluation, a dataset D of 80 photos were used. Handheld pictures were used for the presentation attack. Of the 80 handheld pictures, the system had a false acceptance of 5 images and a false rejection of 25 images while the rest were unidentified.

$False\ Acceptance = 5$

Figure 3. Flowchart of the proposed system

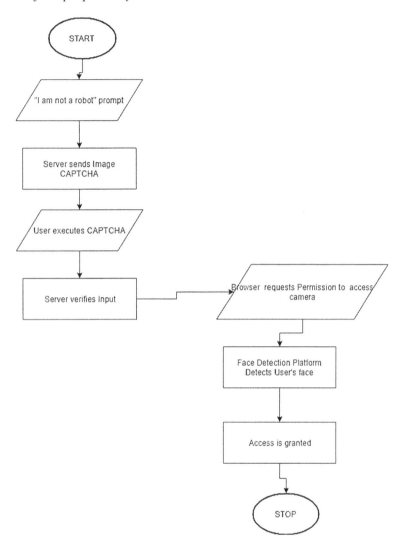

$$FAR = 5 / 80 = 0.0625$$

$$False\ Rejection = 25$$

$$FRR = 25 / 80 = 0.3125$$

$$HTER = \frac{0.0625 + 0.3125}{2}$$

$$HTER = 0.1875 = 18.75\%$$

Figure 4. reCAPTCHA

Figure 5. Face detection reCAPTCHA checker

$HTER$ results are sometimes presented using either Receiver Operating Characteristic (ROC) or Detection-Error Tradeoff (DET) graphs. $HTER$ is also presented in percentage. Primarily, FAR is plotted versus the FRR for different values of the threshold. Another widely used measure is to summarize the performance of the system by determining the Equal Error Rate (EER). This is defined as the point along the ROC or DET curve where the FAR equals the FRR.

For this evaluation the $HTER = 0.1875$, this means that photo attacks break the scheme at a rate of 18.75%. This mark is well below 50%, meaning that the system is efficient and effective.

Additionally, users' perception test was conducted on the CAPTCHA system using 100 respondents to validate the HCISec threat model discussed earlier (*Kainda et al., 2010*). Table 1 shows a summary of respondents' perception of the system. 85% of respondents attested to the system's ease of use.

Figure 6 shows that the reCAPTCHA has a 79% success rate within 10 seconds, 83% within 20 seconds and 93% before timeout. The average completion rate is 17.6 seconds.

The interface was evaluated for aesthetics. The result is shown in Fig 7.

Table 1. Users' perception of the CAPTCHA challenge

Survey Question	No. of Respondents that strongly agrees
The interface is easy to navigate	89
The CAPTCHA is easy to use	85
CAPTCHA task was completed before time-out	93
I prefer something more comfortable	17

Figure 6. Graphical representation of reCAPTCHA success rate

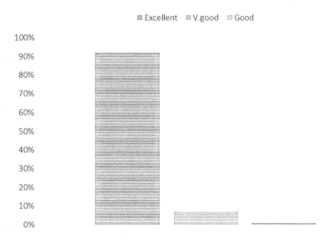

Figure 7. Graphical representation of users' perception of GUI

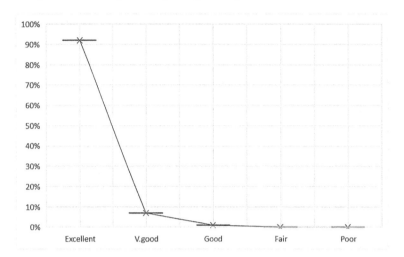

FINDINGS AND CONCLUDING REMARKS

This work outlined the use of a multi-factor CAPTCHA scheme for achieving secure Human-Computer Interaction. As highlighted earlier, the major challenge for CAPTCHA as it relates to HCI-Sec is to present a challenge that is easily solvable for humans but difficult for bots. By designing a scalable multi-factor scheme and adding time constraints for the reCAPTCHA challenge, the system can enhance the security of HCI with a score of 0.1875. Additionally, the challenge was completed within the first 10 seconds by the majority of respondents that tested the system. The average completion rate is 17.6 seconds with 8.93 seconds as the minimum solving rate. This performance is better than that of a similar system by Uzun *et al.,* (2018) which reported a minimum completion rate of 10.75seconds and 19.17 seconds average solving time. it is also better than the average solving time of image CAPTCHA's which is 9.8 seconds (Bursztei *et al.,* 2010). However, Uzun *et al.,* (2018) have a better overall solving rate of 96.2% compared to the system's 93% which is better than the average solving rate of image CAPTCHA's which is 71% (Bursztei *et al.,* 2010). The usability of the system is excellent based on users' perception.

In the future, additional research on breaking the facial authentication can be done to secure the system further. Also, researches should strengthen the current computer visual Library or seek to develop an even stronger one. In the future the multi-factor scheme created should be developed for a mobile app platform, this will help to provide discrete access to the webcam of the device.

REFERENCES

Agathonos, C. (2016). *Human-Computer Interaction And Security*. Academic Press.

Ajayi, P., Omoregbe, N., Adeloye, D., & Misra, S. (2016). Development of a Secured Cloud Based Health Information System for Antenatal and Postnatal Clinic in an African Country. Frontiers in Artificial Intelligence and Applications: Vol. 282. *Advances in Digital Technologies*. Doi:10.3233/978-1-61499-637-8-197

Asani, O., Omotosho, A., Omonigho, J., Longe, O. B., & Gbadamosi, B. (2018). A Real Time Gesture Engineered Captcha. *International Journal of Mechanical Engineering and Technology, 9*(12), 618–629.

Baecher, P., Fischlin, M., Gordon, L., Langenberg, R., Lutzow, M., & Schroder, D. (2010). CAPTCHAs: the good, the bad and the ugly. In F. C. Frieling (Ed.), *Sicherheit* (Vol. 170, pp. 353–365). LNI.

Bostik, O., & Klecka, J. (2018). Recognition of CAPTCHA Characters by Supervised Machine Learning Algorithms. *IFAC-PapersOnLine, 51*(6), 208–213. doi:10.1016/j.ifacol.2018.07.155

Brodić, D., & Amelio, A. (2017). Analysis of the Human-Computer Interaction on the Example of Image-Based CAPTCHA by Association Rule Mining. In L. Gamberini, A. Spagnolli, G. Jacucci, B. Blankertz, & J. Freeman (Eds.), Lecture Notes in Computer Science: Vol. 9961. *Symbiotic Interaction. Symbiotic 2016.* Cham: Springer. doi:10.1007/978-3-319-57753-1_4

Bursztein, E., Bethard, S., Fabry, C., Mitchell, J., & Jurafsky, D. (2010). How good are humans at solving CAPTCHA? *Proceedings of the 2010 IEEE Symposium on Security and Privacy*, 399-413. 10.1109/SP.2010.31

Chaudhary, S., Berki, E., Li, L., & Valtanen, J. (2015). Time Up for Phishing with Effective Anti-Phishing Research Strategies. *International Journal of Human Capital and Information Technology Professionals, 6*(2), 49–64. doi:10.4018/IJHCITP.2015040104

D'Souza, D., Polina, P., & Yampolskiy, R. (2012). Avatar CAPTCHA: Telling computers and humans apart via face classification. *Proceedings of Electro/Information Technology (EIT).* Doi:10.1109/EIT.2012.6220734

Faily, S., & Fléchais, I. (2010). Analysing and Visualising Security and Usability in IRIS. *2010 International Conference on Availability, Reliability and Security.* 10.1109/ARES.2010.28

Garfinkel, S. L., & Lipford, H. R. (2014). Usable Security: History, Themes, and Challenges. Usable Security: History. Themes, and Challenges. Academic Press.

González-Pérez, L. I., Ramírez-Montoya, M., & García-Peñalvo, F. J. (2018). User Experience in Institutional Repositories: A Systematic Literature Review. *International Journal of Human Capital and Information Technology Professionals, 9*(1), 70–86. doi:10.4018/IJHCITP.2018010105

Hassan, W. K. A. (2016). A Survey of Current Research on Captcha. *International Journal of Computer Science and Engineering Survey, 7*(3), 141–157.

Hidalgo, J. G., & Alvarez, G. (2011). CAPTCHAs: An Artificial Intelligence Application to Web Security. Advances in Computers, 83, 109–181.

Jain, S., & Sivaselvan, B. (2012). Usability Aspects of HCI in the Design of CAPTCHAs. *Proceedings of IEEE International Conference on Computational Intelligence and Computing Research 2012.* 10.1109/ICCIC.2012.6510223

Jambhekar, N. D., Misra, S., & Dhawale, C. A. (2016). Mobile computing security threats and solution. *International Journal of Pharmacy and Technology, 8*(4), 23075–23086.

Javelin Strategy & Research. (2018). *2018 Identity Fraud: Fraud Enters a New Era of Complexity*. Available online https://www.javelinstrategy.com/coverage-area/2018-identity-fraud-fraud-enters-new-era-complexity

Kainda, R., Flechais, I., & Roscoe, A. W. (2010). Security and Usability: Analysis and Evaluation. *2010 International Conference on Availability, Reliability and Security*, 275-282. 10.1109/ARES.2010.77

Kamoun, F., & Halaweh, M. (2012). User Interface Design and E-Commerce Security Perception: An Empirical Study. *International Journal of E-Business Research, 8*(2), 15–32. doi:10.4018/jebr.2012040102

Kanakaris, V., Lampropoulos, G., & Siakas, K. (2019). A Survey and a Case-Study Regarding Social Media Security and Privacy on Greek Future IT Professionals. *International Journal of Human Capital and Information Technology Professionals, 10*(1), 22–37. doi:10.4018/IJHCITP.2019010102

Kaur, K., & Behal, S. (2014). Captcha and Its Techniques: A Review. *International Journal of Computer Science and Information Technologies, 5*(5), 6341–6344.

Kaur, K., & Behal, S. (2014). CAPTCHA and its techniques: A review. *International Journal of Computer Science and Information Technologies, 5*(5), 6341–6344.

Khalil, I., Zahoor, K., & Amber, S. (2018). Human Computer Interaction and Security (HCI-Sec). *International Journal of Scientific & Engineering Research., 9*(4), 1549–1553. doi:10.14299/ijser.2018.04.04

Kluever, K. A., & Zanibbi, R. (2009). Balancing usability and security in a video CAPTCHA. *Proceedings of the 5th Symposium on Usable Privacy and Security 2009*. 10.1145/1572532.1572551

Kulluru, P. K., Shaikh, T., Bidwai, S., Mannarwar, A., & Shamlani, K. (2016). A Survey on Different Types of CAPTCHA. *IJCA Proceedings on National Conference on Advances in Computing, Communication and Networking ACCNET 2016*.

Kwak, H., Chew, M., Rodriguez, P., Moon, S., & Ahn, Y. Y. (2007). I Tube, You Tube, Everybody Tubes: Analyzing the World's Largest User Generated Content Video System. In *Proc. IMC 2007*. ACM Press.

Lampson, B. W. (2009). Privacy and security - Usable security: How to get it. *Communications of the ACM, 52*(11), 25–27. doi:10.1145/1592761.1592773

Larrocha, E. R., Minguet, J. M., Díaz, G., Castro, M., Vara, A., Martín, S., & Cristobal, E. S. (2011). Proposals for Postgraduate Students to Reinforce Information Security Management Inside ITIL®. *International Journal of Human Capital and Information Technology Professionals, 2*(2), 16–25. doi:10.4018/jhcitp.2011040102

Lee, Y. L., & Hsu, C. H. (2011). Usability study of text-based CAPTCHAs. *Displays, 32*(2), 81–86. doi:10.1016/j.displa.2010.12.004

Lorenzi, D., Vaidya, J., Uzun, E., Sural, S., & Atluri, V. (2012, December). Attacking image based captchas using image recognition techniques. In *International Conference on Information Systems Security* (pp. 327-342). Springer. 10.1007/978-3-642-35130-3_23

Mori, G., & Malik, J. (2003). Recognizing Objects in Adversarial Clutter: Breaking a Visual CAPT-CHA. *IEEE Computer Society Conference on Computer Vision and Pattern Recognition*. 10.1109/CVPR.2003.1211347

Omotosho, A., Asani, E. O., Fiddi, P., & Akande, N. (2019). Image and Password Multifactor Authentication Scheme for e-Voting. *Journal of Engineering and Applied Sciences (Asian Research Publishing Network)*, *14*(11), 3732–3740. doi:10.3923/jeasci.2019.3732.3740

Osho, O., Mohammed, U. L., Nimzing, N. N., Uduimoh, A. A., & Misra, S. (2019). Forensic Analysis of Mobile Banking Apps. In Lecture Notes in Computer Science: Vol. 11623. *Computational Science and Its Applications – ICCSA 2019. ICCSA 2019*. Cham: Springer. doi:10.1007/978-3-030-24308-1_49

Radke, K., Boyd, C., Brereton, M., & Nieto, J. G. (2010). How HCI design influences web security decisions. *Proceedings of the 22nd Conference of the Computer-Human Interaction Special Interest Group of Australia on Computer-Human Interaction - OZCHI '10*. 10.1145/1952222.1952276

Raj, A., Jain, A., Pahwa, T., & Jain, A. (2010). Picture captchas with sequencing: Their types and analysis. *International Journal of Digital Society*, *1*(3), 208–220. doi:10.20533/ijds.2040.2570.2010.0026

Satchell, C., & Dourish, P. (2009). Beyond the user: use and non-use in HCI. In *OZCHI 2009: Proceedings of the 21st Annual Conference of the Australian Computer-Human Interaction Special Interest Group (CHISIG) of the Human Factors and Ergonomics Society of Australia (HFESA)*. The University of Melbourne. 10.1145/1738826.1738829

Smith, S. W. (2003). Humans in the loop: Human-computer interaction and security. *IEEE Security & Privacy Magazine*, *1*(3), 75–79. doi:10.1109/MSECP.2003.1203228

Subramanyam, M., & Priya, V. (2015). A Study of Captcha Techniques and Development of SUPER Captcha for Secured Web Transactions. *International Journal of Applied Engineering Research*, *10*(21).

Tam, J., Simsa, J., Hyde, S., & Ahn, L. V. (2010). Breaking Audio CAPTCHAs. Advances in Neural Information Processing Systems, 1625-1632.

Uzun, E., Chung, S. P., Essa, I., & Lee, W. (2018). rtCaptcha: A Real-Time CAPTCHA Based Liveness Detection System. *Network and Distributed Systems Security (NDSS) Symposium 2018*. 10.14722/ndss.2018.23253

Viola, P., & Jones, M. (2001). *Rapid object detection was using a boosted cascade of simple features. Proc. of CVPR*.

Von Ahn, L., Blum, M., & Langford, J. (2004). Telling humans and computers apart automatically. *Communications of the ACM*, *47*(2), 56–60. doi:10.1145/966389.966390

Weir, C. S., Douglas, G., Richardson, T., & Jack, M. A. (2010). Usable security: User preferences for authentication methods in eBanking and the effects of experience. *Interacting with Computers*, *22*(3), 153–164. doi:10.1016/j.intcom.2009.10.001

Zeiler, M. D., Taylor, G. W., & Fergus, R. (2011). Adaptive deconvolutional networks for mid and high level feature learning. *2011 International Conference on Computer Vision, ICCV 2011*, 2018-2025. 10.1109/ICCV.2011.6126474

Chapter 11
CAD–Based Machine Learning Project for Reducing Human–Factor–Related Errors in Medical Image Analysis

Adekanmi Adeyinka Adegun
Landmark University, Nigeria

Roseline Oluwaseun Ogundokun
 https://orcid.org/0000-0002-2592-2824
Landmark University, Nigeria

Marion Olubunmi Adebiyi
 https://orcid.org/0000-0001-7713-956X
Landmark University, Nigeria & Covenant University, Nigeria

Emmanuel Oluwatobi Asani
 https://orcid.org/0000-0002-6774-8529
Landmark University, Nigeria

ABSTRACT

Machine learning techniques such as deep learning methods have produced promising results in medical images analysis. This work proposes a user-friendly system that utilizes deep learning techniques for detecting and diagnosing diseases using medical images. This includes the design of CAD-based project that can reduce human factor-related errors while performing manual screening of medical images. The system accepts medical images as input and performs segmentation of the images. Segmentation process analyzes and identifies the region of interest (ROI) of diseases from medical images. Analyzing and segmentation of medical images has assisted in the diagnosis and monitoring of some diseases. Diseases such as skin cancer, age-related fovea degeneration, diabetic retinopathy, glaucoma, hypertension, arteriosclerosis, and choroidal neovascularization can be effectively managed by the analysis of skin lesion and retinal vessels images. The proposed system was evaluated on diseases such as diabetic retinopathy from retina images and skin cancer from dermoscopic images.

DOI: 10.4018/978-1-7998-1279-1.ch011

INTRODUCTION

Automatic segmentation of the medical images is important in the detection of a number of diseases (Sharma, Anchal, & Shaveta Rani, 2016). Recently state-of-the-arts techniques such as deep learning have been applied in this segmentation processes. Computer-aided detection (CADe) and diagnosis (CAD) project for analysis medical images has evolved and is rapidly growing (Doi, K., & Huang, H. K., 2007). This includes the design of CAD techniques that ease the rigorous task of manual screening of medical images which is susceptible to human errors in disease diagnosis. Machine learning technique such as deep learning methods have produced promising results in medical images analysis. It has been shown that image analysis and segmentation carried out based on deep learning methods has produced improved results with a very high accuracy percentage as against the manual screening method that is characterized with human factor errors (Abràmoff, M. D., Garvin, M. K., & Sonka, M., 2010). This chapter proposes a human-friendly project that utilizes deep learning techniques for detecting and diagnosing diseases using medical images. The system accepts medical images as input and performs segmentation of the images. Segmentation process analyses and identifies the region of interest (ROI) of diseases from medical images. The proposed system was evaluated on diseases such as diabetic retinopathy from retina images and skin cancer from dermoscopic images. Retina vessels images and dermoscopic images datasets were used to test and evaluate the performance of the system. The output gave a promising result. This paper proposes better human interfacing tools for the proposed project in the future work.

RELATED WORKS

In the last decade, there have been a lot of research about the application of deep learning to medical image analysis. Some works have been particularly carried out in the segmentation process of medical image analysis state-of-the arts techniques. The performance of the deep learning projects has been compared with manual approach with so much human factors related errors. This section performs the review of related works in this aspect.

Deep learning method was utilized for detection and segmentation of colorectal liver metastases by (Vorontsov et al., 2019). They applied three-dimensional automated segmentations to resolve deficiencies of fully automated segmentation for small metastases and it was faster than manual three-dimensional segmentation. They compared the performance of fully automated and user-corrected segmentations with manual segmentations. Chen, L., Bentley, P., & Rueckert, D. (2017) proposed framework to automatically segment stroke lesions images. The framework was made up of two convolutional neural networks to evaluate the lesions detected in order to remove potential disease.

Vesal, S., Ravikumar, N., & Maier, A. (2018) proposed a convolutional neural network (CNN) project called SkinNet that employed dilated and densely block convolutions to incorporate multi-scale and global context information for skin lesion segmentation. Baur, C., Wiestler, B., Albarqouni, S., & Navab, N. (2019). combined the advantages of supervised and unsupervised methods into a novel framework for learning from both labeled & unlabeled data for the challenging task of White Matter lesion segmentation in brain MR images. They proposed a semi-supervised setting for tackling domain shift which is a known problem in MR image analysis. Chlebus et al., (2018) developed a fully automatic method for liver tumor segmentation in CT images based on a 2D fully convolutional neural network with an object-based post-processing step. The system was compared with human performance.

CNN architecture was used for blood vessel segmentation of fundus images (Xiancheng, et al.,2018) The architecture was derived from U-Net architecture that implemented an encoder-decoder architecture. A trainable Frangi-Net project was developed to perform segmentation of retinal images (Fu et al.,2017). A multi-scale convolutional neural network structure and label processing approach was applied for retinal vessel segmentation (Li et al., 2017). The method used two different scale image segments to generate input for two deep convolutional networks. Lastly, deep neural network (DNN) that uses max-pooling layers (MPCNNs) instead of subsampling or down sampling was also used for retina images segmentation (Melinščak, M., Prentašić, P., & Lončarić, S. 2015). The MPCNN mapped input samples into output class probabilities using hierarchical layers to extract features and fully connected layers to classify extracted features.

METHODOLOGY

Dataset

We evaluate our method on some publicly available databases namely:

1. Retinal image vessel segmentation dataset: DRIVE. The DRIVE (Digital Retinal Images for Vessel Extraction) (Staal et al.,2004) dataset consists of 400 color fundus photographs. The set of 400 images has been divided into a training set and a test set, both containing 200 images.
2. Skin lesion images ISIC dataset: The dataset used is repository in ISIC 2018 archive (Codella et al., 2017). The dataset contains 2600 samples in total. It consists of 2000 training samples in JPEG format and 600 testing samples. The original size of each sample was 700x900, which was rescaled to 256x256 for this implementation. The training samples include the original images and the corresponding ground truth label in PNG format.

Model Implementation

Software

The software used for the model implementation includes:

*   Python Version 3.5
*   Keras 2
*   Tensor flow backend
*   Scikit-image Version 0.14.1

Running Environment

The experimental platform is a PC equipped with an Intel Core i7 processor with ten (10) 3.4GHZ cores, 16GB memory and NVIDIA Tesla K40c GPU, and the operating system is Ubuntu 16.04.

General Architecture of the Proposed System

The proposed project utilizes Deep Convolutional Encoder-Decoder Model Architecture which adapts the popular U-Net model. The U-Net model implements a contemporary classification network into fully convolutional networks. It operates by learning from pixels to pixels in an end-to –end manner. Training image dataset and corresponding ground truth image dataset serves as the input into the system. These will be taken through the other sections of the system such as data preparation section and the learning and training section. Supervised form of training is employed here whereby the target goal in the form of the ground truth images is supplied together with the input images. After a period of training, the validation image data set will now be fed into the system for the expected predictions. The output data from the prediction will finally be compared with our target goals for accuracy and the performance metrics evaluated.

The architecture is composed of the following major sections:

Data Preparation

The training image data set and the corresponding ground truth image data set are used to train the model simultaneously. In this section, the images are first resized into the appropriate image size. The image sets are then resampled to remove every form of noise. The ground truth serves as the expected output and the training set serves as the input to train the system.

The sample training image data set and ground truth images for both the retina images and the skin lesion are illustrated in Figure 1, 2, 3 and 4 below.

Learning and Training

In this section, we have the encoder units and the decoder units.

Figure 1. A sample skin lesion training image data set

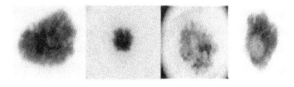

Figure 2. The corresponding skin lesion ground truth images

Figure 3. A Sample Retina Training Image Data Set

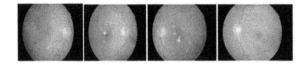

Figure 4. The corresponding retina ground truth images

Encoder

The encoder is made up of set of convolution layers and pooling layers. Features extraction from the input image takes place at the convolution layer and the pooling layers reduce the resolution of the image feature maps. In this model, the encoder applies rectified linear unit (RELU) activation function.

Each encoder uses the Max-pooling to translate invariance over small spatial shifts in the image and combine this with Subsampling to produce a large input image context in terms of spatial window. This method reduces the feature map size and this leads to image representation that is noisy with blurred boundaries. The restoration is done by decoder as the output image resolution must be the same as input image.

Decoder

The decoder ensures that the image resolution of image set from the encoder units is increased to the initial resolution status. It is also made up of set of convolution layers. Each of the layers in the decoder stage corresponds to the layer in the encoder i.e. for each of the encoders there is a corresponding decoder which up samples the feature map using the already stored max-pooling indices. Sparse feature maps of higher resolutions are then produced. These are fed through the training section to produce dense feature maps.

Prediction

The prediction section of this model is performed by predicting pixel-wise labels for an output which has the same resolution as the input image. The last part of the decoder is connected to a softmax classifier which classifies each pixel.

The sparse feature maps restored from the original resolution are then fed to the softmax classifier to produce the final segmentation.

Output

The final segmented images are generated at this section. These are stored with preds as the output name. The performance of the model is also evaluated at this section. The general layout of encoder-decoder architecture is illustrated with Figure 5.

Experimental Results and Analysis

The performance of the proposed model was evaluated and the results displayed below. The segmentation accuracy has been assessed by comparing the predicted results with the manual version. The final results of the validation image set used for testing segmentation are compared with the ground truth.

The metrics can be described as stated below:

- Intersection of Union: also known as Jaccard similarity coefficient, it can be described as similarity measure over two image sets.
- Sensitivity: also known as true positive rate (TPR) Sensitivity: This proportion of actual positives which are predicted positive. It can be defined as the proportion of examples which were predicted to belong to a class with respect to all of the examples that truly belong in the class.
- Dice Coefficient: also shows similarity measure and it is related to Jaccard index

Evaluation was done using Dice's coefficient and some other metrics, which are calculated as:

$$\text{Dice (A, B)} = \frac{|A \cap B|}{\left(|A| \cap |B|\right) \div 2} \tag{1}$$

Figure 5. General Layout Diagram of A proposed segmentation method for Medical Images analysis (Adeyinka et al. 2019)

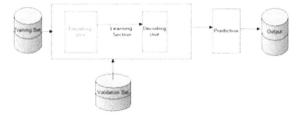

Table 1. Performance evaluation of the proposed model based on the specified metrics earlier discussed

Performance Metrics	Dice Coefficient (%)	Intersection of Union (%)	Positive Predictive Value (%)	Sensitivity (%)
Proposed model	82.23	72.23	96.5	96.5

$$PPV\ (A,\ B) = \frac{|A \cap B|}{|A|} \tag{2}$$

$$SENSITIVITY = \frac{|A \cap B|}{|B|} \tag{3}$$

$$IOU\ (A,\ B) = \frac{|A \cap B|}{|A| \cap |B|} \tag{4}$$

Where A denotes the segmented region and B denotes the manually labelled region, $|A \cap B|$ denotes the overlap area between A and B, AND $|A|$ and $|B|$ represent the areas of A and B respectively.

It can be shown that the results of the performance evaluation of the proposed model as stated above gave a reasonably high percentage of similarity and low level of diversity between the predicted results and ground truth results.

The final segmented output for the skin lesion images is presented in Figure 6 below.

The final segmented output for the retina images is presented in Figure 7 below.

Figure 6. The figure contains the project validation image set followed by the ground truth labels and the predicted skin lesion segmented images results from the proposed model

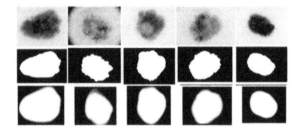

Figure 7. The figure contains the project validation image set and the predicted segmented retina images results from the proposed project model

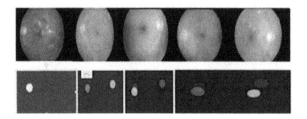

CONCLUSION

In this work, a CAD-Based Machine Learning Project for Reducing Human-factor Errors in Medical Image Analysis is proposed. A novel deep learning model for segmentation of medical images in order to detect diseases such as melanoma skin cancer, diabetic retinopathy, glaucoma, hypertension has thus been investigated. The review of the existing works was also carried out. The proposed model was evaluated and analyzed. This paper shows that the proposed project model gave a better performance over the manual approach of medical image analysis. This is as a result of errors due to human factors that has been eliminated in the automated approach. The encoder–decoder mechanism in this model can be improved on in the future works where ensemble methods with some other state-of-the arts techniques can also be explored. A more human friendly system can be developed in the future works.

REFERENCES

Abràmoff, M. D., Garvin, M. K., & Sonka, M. (2010). Retinal imaging and image analysis. *IEEE Reviews in Biomedical Engineering*, *3*, 169–208. doi:10.1109/RBME.2010.2084567 PMID:22275207

Adeyinka, A. A., Adebiyi, M. O., Akande, N. O., Ogundokun, R. O., Kayode, A. A., & Oladele, T. O. (2019, July). A Deep Convolutional Encoder-Decoder Architecture for Retinal Blood Vessels Segmentation. In *International Conference on Computational Science and Its Applications* (pp. 180-189). Springer. 10.1007/978-3-030-24308-1_15

Almotiri, J., Elleithy, K., & Elleithy, A. (2018). Retinal Vessels Segmentation Techniques and Algorithms: A Survey. *Applied Sciences*, *8*(2), 155. doi:10.3390/app8020155

Baur, C., Wiestler, B., Albarqouni, S., & Navab, N. (2019, May). Fusing Unsupervised and Supervised Deep Learning for White Matter Lesion Segmentation. In *International Conference on Medical Imaging with Deep Learning* (pp. 63-72). Academic Press.

Chen, L., Bentley, P., & Rueckert, D. (2017). Fully automatic acute ischemic lesion segmentation in DWI using convolutional neural networks. *NeuroImage. Clinical*, *15*, 633–643. doi:10.1016/j.nicl.2017.06.016 PMID:28664034

Chlebus, G., Schenk, A., Moltz, J. H., van Ginneken, B., Hahn, H. K., & Meine, H. (2018). Automatic liver tumor segmentation in CT with fully convolutional neural networks and object-based postprocessing. *Scientific Reports*, *8*(1), 15497. doi:10.103841598-018-33860-7 PMID:30341319

Codella, N. C., Gutman, D., Celebi, M. E., Helba, B., Marchetti, M. A., Dusza, S. W., ... Huang, H. K. (2007). Computer-aided diagnosis (CAD) and image-guided decision support. *Computerized Medical Imaging and Graphics*, *4*(31), 195–197.

Fu, W., Breininger, K., Würfl, T., Ravikumar, N., Schaffert, R., & Maier, A. (2017). *Frangi-Net: A Neural Network Approach to Vessel Segmentation*. arXiv preprint arXiv:1711.03345

Halpern, A. (2018, April). Skin lesion analysis toward melanoma detection: A challenge at the 2017 international symposium on biomedical imaging (isbi), hosted by the international skin imaging collaboration (isic). In *2018 IEEE 15th International Symposium on Biomedical Imaging (ISBI 2018)* (pp. 168-172). IEEE.

Li, M., Ma, Z., Liu, C., Zhang, G., & Han, Z. (2017). Robust retinal blood vessel segmentation based on reinforcement local descriptions. *BioMed Research International*. PMID:28194407

Melinščak, M., Prentašić, P., & Lončarić, S. (2015, January). Retinal vessel segmentation using deep neural networks. *10th International Conference on Computer Vision Theory and Applications (VISAPP 2015)*. 10.5220/0005313005770582

Sharma, A., & Rani, S. (2016, April). An automatic segmentation & detection of blood vessels and optic disc in retinal images. In *2016 International Conference on Communication and Signal Processing (ICCSP)* (pp. 1674-1678). IEEE. 10.1109/ICCSP.2016.7754449

Staal, J., Abràmoff, M. D., Niemeijer, M., Viergever, M. A., & Van Ginneken, B. (2004). Ridge-based vessel segmentation in color images of the retina. *IEEE Transactions on Medical Imaging*, *23*(4), 501–509. doi:10.1109/TMI.2004.825627 PMID:15084075

Vesal, S., Ravikumar, N., & Maier, A. (2018). *SkinNet: A Deep Learning Framework for Skin Lesion Segmentation*. arXiv preprint arXiv:1806.09522

Vorontsov, E., Cerny, M., Régnier, P., Di Jorio, L., Pal, C. J., Lapointe, R., ... Tang, A. (2019). Deep Learning for Automated Segmentation of Liver Lesions at CT in Patients with Colorectal Cancer Liver Metastases. Radiology. *Artificial Intelligence*, *1*(2), 180014.

Xiancheng, W., Wei, L., Bingyi, M., He, J., Jiang, Z., Xu, W., . . . Zhaomeng, S. (2018). Retina blood vessel segmentation using a U-net based Convolutional neural network. *Procedia Computer Science*.

Chapter 12
A Human–Centered Usability Evaluation of University Websites Using SNECAAS Model

Solomon Adelowo Adepoju
(iD) https://orcid.org/0000-0002-1128-4753
Department of Computer Science, Federal University of Technology Minna, Nigeria

Ishaq Oyebisi Oyefolahan
Department of Information and Media Technology, Federal University of Technology Minna, Nigeria

Muhammad Bashir Abdullahi
(iD) https://orcid.org/0000-0001-8200-2787
Department of Computer Science, Federal University of Technology Minna, Nigeria

Adamu Alhaji Mohammed
Department of Mathematics, Federal University of Technology Minna, Nigeria

Motunrayo O. Ibiyo
Department of Computer Science, Federal University of Technology Minna, Nigeria

ABSTRACT

One of the ways universities ensure constant touch with the human populace is through their websites. Therefore, websites must be engaging, interactive, easy-to-use, and provide users with the necessary information needed. Unfortunately, most universities have found this objective quite difficult to achieve. This chapter presents an evaluation the usability of six Nigerian university websites using a model which is based on seven usability criteria of speed, ease of use, navigation, content, aesthetic, accessibility, and security. The best six university websites based on webometric ranking were selected for the study with 233 participants via an online questionnaire using Google Docs. The overall results of the evaluation indicate that the usability of Nigerian university websites performed fairly well in ease of use, navigation, and aesthetic, averagely on speed and content, while the ratings based on accessibility and security are not very satisfactory.

DOI: 10.4018/978-1-7998-1279-1.ch012

INTRODUCTION

Many users today depend much on web application as a result of continuous growth in internet which has transformed the world into virtual market. Hence, the need arises for a highly dependable web applications even in the midst of growing competition among organisations (Esmeria & Seva, 2017). Website of an organisation serves as an access to its information, services and products (Daher & Elkabani, 2012). Through websites, the company's reach can be extended as it gives an overview of who, what and how the organisation carries out her activities. Therefore, website development process has to be done painstakingly and carefully in order to project the organisation properly.

One of the main aims of developing software application or website is to provide its users with a noble, satisfied and fulfilling services with good and exciting user experience (Boza, Schiaffino, Teyseyre, & Godoy, 2014). Among the myriads of organisation craving for good and usable websites usability is academic institutions in which universities belong. This class of websites is very important as it provides information for a wide category of audience like students, faculty, parents and many more (Adepoju & Shehu, 2014; Hasan, 2013; Nagpal, Mehrotra, Bhatia, & Sharma, 2015). The website of any academic institution plays a vital and prominent role in shaping its image. A university's website is expected to provide adequate, correct and timely information about the university and its activities to various stakeholders. Apart from this, it is to serve as a communication medium between the institution and students, staff, alumni, and guest (Jabar, Usman, & Awal, 2013). Furthermore, websites have been found to be one of the most utilized internet resources among the various ICT facilities used in universities. This is in addition to email services and web (Egoeze, Misra, Akman, & Colomo-palacios, 2014)

So, the usability of this type of website is very important. In order to achieve this good user experience, a software application or website should then be easy to use and learn. This attribute is commonly referred to as usability (González, Lorés, & Granollers, 2008). This implies that a very satisfying and pleasing user experience is highly needed from these websites that are been developed by different higher institutions.

According to International Organization for Standardization (ISO 9241-11), usability can be defined as "the extent to which a product, service or system can be used by specified users to achieve a specified goals with effectiveness, efficiency, and satisfaction in a specified context of use" (ISO, 2018). The user is the person who interact with the product (websites in this context), and the context of used refers to users, tasks, equipment (hardware, software and materials), and the physical and social environments in which a product. González et al.(2008) also indicated context of use to be "a picture of the actual state under which the interactive system or software application is being evaluated or is handled in normal functioning circumstances".

Generally, evaluation of websites can be done by considering it from credibility (Deedam, Thomas, & Taylor, 2018), quality (Anusha & Rama, 2016; Dominic, Jati, & Hanim, 2013), functionality (Calisir, Gumussoy, Bayraktaroglu, & Saygivar, 2011), accessibility (Al-faries, Al-khalifa, Al-razgan, & Al-duwais, 2013) and usability (Chamba-Eras, Jacome-Galarza, Guaman-Quinche, Coronel-Romero, & Jaramillo, 2017; Kaur, Kaur, & Parminder, 2016) point of view. The various evaluation aims at determining and evaluating the performance of the websites based on the metric defined in the evaluation. However, usability is seen as the most important evaluation that could be evaluated especially for academic websites.

This chapter therefore presents a comprehensive preliminary investigation into the usability of six Nigerian university websites which over the years have performed very well in webometric ranking. These are institutions with repeated good web presence over the years. This is aimed at knowing the performance of these university websites based on usability. The study also investigates if there is any similarity between webometric ranking obtained over the years and usability ranking results obtained in the study. The study also shows the usability ratings of all the websites used in the study.

LITERATURE REVIEW

In order to evaluate usability of websites, different approaches can be used which are user testing, tool-based testing, expert-based testing, analytical method, data mining techniques and multi criteria decision making approach testing among others (Adepoju & Shehu, 2014; Das & Patil, 2014; Nagpal et al., 2017).

User testing involves engaging users to evaluate the websites in order to discover the inherent problems in the websites. Expert based method which is also known as heuristic evaluation involves the use of expert to evaluate the websites based on a ser of predefined heuristics. Analytic methods entail the use of different models to predict usability, while data mining approach uses different classification algorithms to mine usability data. Multi criteria decision making approach entails the use of decision-making model to select, rank or prioritise some alternative websites based on some usability criteria.

To use any of these methods, different usability criteria or parameters have to be considered and measured. Due to the heterogenous view of usability, different criteria are being considered based on the view of the author and context of use. However, some of the common criteria are effectiveness, efficiency, ease of use, satisfaction, speed. learnability, credibility, navigation, content, operability, aesthetic, accessibility, stickiness and security (Cheng, 2015; Manian, Yurtchi, & Shadmehri, 2014).

Usability Evaluation of University Websites

Several authors from different countries in the past few decades have conducted research aimed at evaluating academic websites usability. While some focus on academic mobile digital and repositories library (Adewumi, Omoregbe, & Misra, 2016; Alasem, 2013; Jagero, Nhendo, Sithole, Takaingenhamo, & Guvava, 2014), others focus on mobile service (Al-khalifa, 2012). However, studies with specific focus on university websites include that of (Mustafa & Al-Zoua'bi, 2008) who evaluated nine Jordanian universities based on five usability criteria by using both questionnaire methods and automated toools. An acceptable level of usability was derived from the results. Hasan (2013) from the same country used heuristic evaluation to evaluate the usabilility of three Jordan universities.

Daher & Elkabani (2012) conducted usability evaluation study on the web portal of six Lebanese universities. Questionnaires were used to collect data based on Single Usability Metric (SUM) model which measures effectiveness, efficiency, satisfaction in relation to usability. The research was concluded by identifying the shortcomings of all the six-web portal and it was observed that content is the most important part of all web portals. Adepoju & Shehu (2014) study was conducted to determine the usability of Nigerian Federal universities by using three automated tools viz; Hera, A checker, and WAVE. The results of the evaluation showed that the none of the websites fully conform to the standards of accessibility as stipulated by Web Content Accessibility Guidelines (WCAG 2.0 and WCAG 1.0). Furthermore, Kiyea & Yusuf (2014) evaluated the usability of ten randomly selected Nigerian universities using

Webpage Analyser and HTML tool box. The result of the study also indicated that no website passed the evaluation from the two automated tools. A website evaluation model was developed to evaluate ten top ranking engineering universities in Asia with the results showing that the academic websites tested were partially usable (Manzoor & Hussain, 2012)

In another study, the usability of academic website of Uva Wellassa University, Sri Lanka was investigated by Jayathunga, Jayawardana, Wimaladharma, & Herath (2017). A Questionnaire which contains twenty usability criteria grouped under four categories was used. Descriptive statistical analysis and confirmatory statistical analysis were applied to analyse the data. The results showed that there exists a strong bond between usability and content and organization as well as web performance.

Boza et al. (2014) study focused on the use of a heuristic approach for usability evaluation using data mining techniques as a means to reduce cost and time consumed during usability assessment process. Apriori algorithm and J48 decision tree algorithm were used to analyse usability data obtained from thirty-five websites from diverse areas. The results indicated that the proposed method is able to mine out important patterns and show the relationship between the usability metrics under study.

Wardoyo & Wahyuningrum (2018) used the method of logarithmic fuzzy preference programming to evaluate the website quality of five university websites in Indonesia based on three usability and accessibility criteria of stickiness, backlink and web page loading time. The results obtained show that stickiness is most important factor that affect quality of the websites.

Websites Usability Models

Usability is one of the important quality factors in user interface design. This quality has attracted many researchers and hence different usability models have been proposed in literature for different products, services and systems. Some of the existing models found in literature are discussed as follows.

The ISO/IEC 9126 standard model which defined usability by five factors; understandability, learnability, operability, attractiveness and usability compliance (Botella et al., 2004). ISO 9241-11 standard model characterized usability based on efficiency, effectiveness and satisfaction of product, services and systems (Abran, Khelifi, & Suryn, 2003; Speicher, 2015). Nielsen in his model proposed that usability is to be measured based on effectiveness, efficiency, satisfaction, and learnability (Nielsen, 1994)

In the 2QCV3Q model, Mich, French, & Cilone,(2003) proposed a conceptual model that consists of seven dimensions to evaluate the quality of a website based on who-what-why-when-where- how and feasibility (with what means and devices). The model defines accessibility, navigability and understandability as usability factors.

McCall's model (also known as McCall's triangle of quality) is one of the software evaluation models which defines usability as product operation (basic functionalities), product revision (ability to change), product transition (ability to adopt new environment). Usability was defined under product operation and it comprises operability, training and communicativeness (McCall *et al.* (1977) cited in Shawgi & Noureldien, 2015)

Shawgi & Noureldien (2015) defines the high-level usability factors in the new usability measurement model (UMM) as accessibility, understandability, learnability, operability, attractiveness, and navigability, which are all defined in previous models, but not in one model.

Other usability models include Quality in use integrated (QUIM) model which defined usability in terms of efficiency, effectiveness, productivity, satisfaction, learnability, safety, trustfulness,, accessibility, universality and usefulness (Seffah, Donyaee, Kline, & Padda, 2006), Web Usability Evaluation Model

(WUEM) proposed by Manzoor & Hussain (2012) comprises web design, page design, accessibility and Navigation as its usability attributes. The enhanced usability model (EUM) comprises effectiveness, efficiency, satisfaction, learnability and security as criteria to measure usability (Abran et al., 2003). Table 1 shows the model in a tabular form for easy representation.

In addition to these, there are still some other factors on which usability depends as viewed by other authors. For example information content and navigation have been identified as the most important parameter in measuring usability according to the study conducted by Mehrotra, Pradesh, & Pradesh (2017). This is in addition to other factors, download speed, aesthetics, visual clarity, accessibility, ease of use, learnability and user interface design. These parameters when carefully examined fits into the major models discussed above.

In the light of this after extensive study, data gathering, analysis and interpretation, a new usability model which comprises speed, navigation, Ease of Use, Content, Accessibility, Aesthetic, and Security (SNECAAS) is proposed as shown in Fig 1. This is based on a framework earlier proposed by Adepoju, Oyefolahan, Abdullahi, & Mohammed (2018)

Speed is the amount of time it takes for the website to render or respond after a request has been made i.e. the load time. Navigation of a website measures the ability to detect and gain possession of appropriate information, menu, reports, options, and elements. Ease of Use refers to the ease at which the user uses and understands the structure, architecture and organization of the website. Content on the

Table 1. Usability evaluation models

Usability factor	McCall	ISO 9126-11	ISO 9241-11	Nielsen	2QCV3Q	UMM	WUEM	QUIM	EUM
Understandability		✓			✓	✓			
Learnability		✓		✓		✓		✓	✓
Operability/functionality	✓	✓				✓			
Attractiveness		✓				✓			
Usability compliance		✓							
Training	✓								
Communicativeness	✓								
Accessibility / readability					✓	✓	✓	✓	
Navigability				✓	✓	✓	✓		
consistency									
comment									
Web design							✓		
Page design							✓		
Security/privacy								✓	✓
organisation									
efficiency			✓	✓				✓	✓
effectiveness			✓	✓				✓	✓
productivity								✓	
satisfaction			✓	✓				✓	✓
universality								✓	

Figure 1. SNECAAS model structure

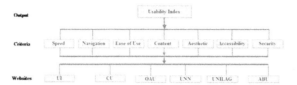

other hand refers to the textual, aural and visual information published on the website. Accessibility is the extent to which the website is compatible for use by people with disabilities. Simply put, it is availability of the websites to different categories of users without any form of discrimination. Aesthetic has to with attractiveness and look and feel of the website. This includes the design and color combination used in the website design. Lastly, based on ISO/IEC 9126 security, which is a sub-characteristic, is defined a set of software attributes which relates to its ability to prevent unauthorized access, whether accidental or deliberate to programs and data.

METHODOLOGY

The methodological steps used in carrying out the study is depicted in figure 2. The first step involved a comprehensive and detailed literature review in order to know the criteria to be used in the study. This also allow for the selection of the university websites to be used for the study. Thus it is ensured that quality and adequate data are gathered for use in the study. These steps are explained as follows.

Website Selection

The first step is the selection of the university websites to use for the study. At present Nigeria has close to 168 universities with all of them having functioning websites (NUC, 2019). More so, most of them have featured repeatedly on webometric ranking over the period of two years from 2016 to 2019 After a thorough analysis, six university websites which ranked very well over this period were selected for the study. Only six websites were selected in order to reduce the cognitive load of the human who are involved in the study (Cybermetrics, 2019) . Table 2 shows the selected websites and their URLs.

Figure 2. Methodological steps

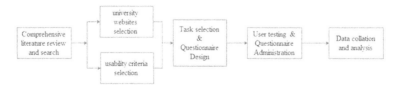

Table 2. University websites used for the study

	University name	URL	Acronym	2016 ranking	2017 ranking	2018 ranking	2019 ranking
1	University of Ibadan	www.ui.edu.ng	UI	1st	1st	1st	1st
2	Covenant university	www.covenant.edu.ng	CU	6th	2nd	2nd	4th
3	Obafemi Awolowo University	www.oauife.edu.ng	OAU	3rd	4th	3rd	3rd
4	University of Nsukka	www.unn.edu.ng	UNN	7th	3rd	4th	2nd
5	University of Lagos	www.unilag.edu.ng	UNILAG	2nd	6th	5th	6th
6	Ahmadu Bello University	www.abu.edu.ng	ABU	4th	7th	6th	5th

Usability Criteria Selection

The criteria used were selected based on comprehensive literature review of existing work in this area. This has been discussed in section 2. The author based the selection on criteria that have been covered in the same way as the existing model.

Task/User Testing and Questionnaire Design

To carry out the user testing, representative tasks to be performed on the websites must be selected. To do this, five representative tasks were identified for users to perform on each website. The identified tasks are:

1. View the mission and vision of the university
2. View a list of all the faculties in the school.
3. View a list of all the lecturers in the Electrical engineering department
4. Search for the university's academic calendar for the 2017/2018 session
5. Search for the latest news bulleting

To get users feedback from the test, an online questionnaire was designed using google docs. It comprises two sections. Section A is to collect data about the demography of the participants. Section B is grouped into seven items according to the numbers of criteria used. The total number of items in all is twenty-three. Users responses are rated from 1 to 5 based on five-point Likert scale of Strongly Disagree to Strongly Agree. The questionnaire was tested for both validity and reliability. Reliability with Cronbach's alpha value ($\alpha = 0.876$) was obtained. A total of 233 participants who are mostly students responded to the online questionnaire.

The proposed SNECAAS model structure used for the evaluation is depicted in figure 1 earlier and explained as follows.

The goal is to calculate and generate the usability index (UI) which ranges from 1 to 5. UI from 4-5 is rated as excellent, 3.5-3.99 as good, 3.0-3.49 as average, 2.5-2.99 as below average and 0-2.49 as poor.

Each website is evaluated based on each usability criteria and the result per criteria as well as on the overall results are then obtained.

The UI index is generated by obtaining the overall score per website based on all the criteria together.

RESULTS AND DISCUSSION

The demographic data of the participants in the study is shown in Table 3. It shows the sex, internet experience and age of participants used for the study. More male participants responded to the questionnaire than their female counterpart and most of the participants are within the age bracket of 21-25 years. This is because most of the participants are undergraduates.

Figure 3 shows the performance of each university across the seven criteria. All the universities performed very low on the security and accessibility criteria as half of the websites scored below the average score. This is due to the fact most users are not sure of the security features embedded in the websites as well as its accessibility options for the disabled.

On the other hand, Ease of Use criteria take the lead in the criteria rating with UNILAG websites coming first with a score that is far above the total average score. Likewise, CU, OAU and UI performed a bit above the average score for this criterion.

Navigation of the websites shows that ABU website performed below the average while others especially UNILAG performed very well among the users. CU and UNILAG websites speed are good compared to others that performed averagely. However, none scored excellent in this criterion. The trends obtained in this result is closely similar to that obtained in (Adepoju & Shehu, 2014) where UNILAG and OAU recorded less number or errors in their websites hence depicting better usability/

Figure 3. Performance of each university based on the criteria

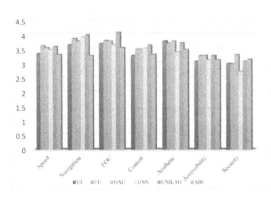

Table 3. Demographic data of the participants

Item	Option	Value
Sex	Male Female	148 85
Age	Below 16 16-20 20-25 26 and above	2 23 164 44
Internet experience	Expert Intermediate Novice	103 121 9

Further analysis of the result in Figure 4 shows that in the overall UNILAG obtained the highest usability score of 3.63, while OAU and CU followed with usability scores of 3.58 and 3.54 respectively. ABU obtained a score of 3.32 while UI and UNN are at par with scores of 3.41. However, on the average none of the websites performed excellent because none have a rating of 4.0 on all the criteria combined. This implies that only three of the six websites (UNILAG, OAU and CU) have scored good in overall usability.

Thus, the ranking obtained based on the overall usability score is in this order: UNILAG > OAU > CU > UNN >= UI > ABU. This ranking in comparison to the webometric ranking of Nigerian released from 2016 to 2018 (UI>CU>OAU>UNN>UNILAG>ABU) is a bit different. UNN and ABU retains their positions as 4th and 6th rank in both, while OAU and CU swap positions between 2nd and 3rd. UNILAG surprisingly take the lead in the overall usability rating with UI falling to 5th in the current usability rating. This implies that a good webometric ranking is not an indication of good usability in some cases.

Figure 5 shows the ranking of the criteria used in the study based on the performance by the websites. In overall, websites' Ease of Use, Navigation and Aesthetic were rated first, second and third respectively. This shows that the websites performed above average based on these criteria. However, speed and content are rated as average while accessibility and security were rated below average. This shows that while the EOU, navigation and aesthetic of the websites are to some extent designed fairly well. However, there is need for much improvement in both security and accessibility issues.

More worrisome is the fact that some websites do not have adequate and appropriate content to cater for the yawning of the users especially students. More so, the accessibility issue should be taking into

Figure 4. Overall Usability Score per university

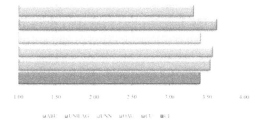

Figure 5. Criteria ranking across the websites

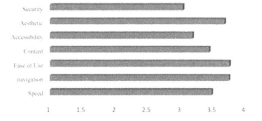

consideration as well. Many disable users cannot access these websites as expected because there is no provision for them. This has been the bane of many websites developed especially in developing countries in previous studies (Junaini, 2002; Al-faries et al., 2013; Deedam et al., 2018; Yerlikaya & Durdu, 2017)

The ranking order for the criteria is as follows: Ease-of-use, Navigation Aesthetic, Speed, Content, Accessibility, Security

CONCLUSION AND RECOMMENDATION

Academic websites and especially university websites usability evaluation have been of great interest to researchers till date. Though several models and methods with varied criteria have been proposed to be used by different authors, yet the peculiarity of this genre of websites still necessitate the need to come up with new ways of carrying out its evaluation especially from the usability point of view.

While great research efforts have been channeled into this in the developed countries to ensure the development of usable and accessible websites, most developing countries are lagging behind in this aspect. Hence, the need for this type of research to know the usability status of some high performing university websites in Nigeria. By using seven criteria of Speed, Navigation, Ease-of-use, Content, Aesthetic, Accessibility and Security, a SNECAAS model was proposed and validated.

Though the results show that the selected websites performed fairly well in the overall rating, it is of utmost concern that the issues of accessibility and security are still not well taken into consideration by the developers of these websites. This is despite the observation made by researches done previously in this regard (Adepoju & Shehu, 2014; Kiyea & Yusuf, 2014). The overall usability for the websites is still not good enough.

It therefore strongly recommended that adequate attention and measure should be taken by various stakeholders and universities managers to address the concern. Now that the world is a global village, many users have access to these websites at the tip of their fingers. Hence, great efforts should be channeled towards ensuring that they are up to the standard as expected. More so, enough and adequate resources should be channeled into acquiring state of the art hardware and software necessary for developing and hosting usable websites. Furthermore, the management of various universities should also ensure that adequate usability training is provided for the staff in charge of developing university websites. This will equip them with the necessary skills to develop a user centred websites which is a core area in Human Computer Interaction.

Future work will involve the use of integrated Multi Criteria Decision Making (MCDA) approach to rank the websites performance based on their usability as well as ranking the criteria to know their order of importance to the users as well as the experts. More so, the data obtained will be subjected to further mining and statistical analysis to reveal hidden patter, trends significance and correlations.

REFERENCES

Abran, A., Khelifi, A., Suryn, W., & Seffah, A. (2003). Usability Meanings and Interpretations in ISO Standards. *Software Quality Journal*, *11*(4), 325–338. doi:10.1023/A:1025869312943

Adepoju, S. A., Oyefolahan, I. O., Abdullahi, M. B., & Mohammed, A. A. (2018). Integrated Usability Evaluation Framework for University Websites. *I-Manager's Journal of Information Technology*, *8*(1), 19–27.

Adepoju, S. A., & Shehu, I. S. (2014). Usability Evaluation of Academic Websites Using Automated Tools. In *3rd International Conference on User Science and Engineering (i-USEr)* (pp. 186–191). Shah Alam, Malaysia: IEEE. 10.1109/IUSER.2014.7002700

Adewumi, A., Omoregbe, N., & Misra, S. (2016). Usability Evaluation of Mobile Access To Institutional Repository. *International Journal of Pharmacy & Technology*, *8*(4), 22892–22905.

Al-faries, A., Al-khalifa, H. S., Al-razgan, M. S., & Al-duwais, M. (2013). Evaluating the Accessibility and Usability of Top Saudi E- Government Services. In *7th International Conference on Theory and Practice of Electronic Governance* (pp. 60–63). Seoul: ACM.

Al-khalifa, H. S. (2012). A framework for evaluating university mobile websites. *Online Information Review, 2011*(2011). doi:10.1108/OIR-12-2012-0231

Alasem, A. N. (2013). Evaluating the Usability of Saudi Digital Library's Interface (SDL). In *World Congress on Engineering and Computer Science* (*Vol. I*, pp. 178–181). Academic Press.

Anusha, & Rama, N. (2016). A Novel Website Quality and Usability Evaluation Framework for Online Shopping Websites. *Indian Journal of Science and Technology, 9*(36). doi:10.17485/ijst/2016/v9i36/93821

Botella, P., Burgués, X., Carvallo, J. P., Franch, X., Grau, G., Marco, J., & Quer, C. (2004). ISO / IEC 9126 in practice: what do we need to know? *Software Measurement European Forum*.

Boza, B. C., Schiaffino, S., Teyseyre, A., & Godoy, D. (2014). An Approach for Knowledge Discovery in a Web Usability Context. In *Brazilian Symposium on Human Factors in Computing Systems* (*Vol. 13*, pp. 393–396). Foz do Iguaçu, Brazil: Academic Press.

Calisir, F., Gumussoy, C. A., Bayraktaroglu, A. E., & Saygivar, E. (2011). *Usability and Functionality : A Comparison of Key Project Personnel ' s and Potential users ' Evaluations*. World Academy of Science, Engineering and Technology.

Chamba-Eras, L., Jacome-Galarza, L., Guaman-Quinche, R., Coronel-Romero, E., & Jaramillo, M. L. -. (2017). Analysis of usability of universities Web portals using the Prometheus tool - SIRIUS. In *Fourth International Conference on eDemocracy & eGovernment (ICEDEG)* (pp. 195–199). IEEE. 10.1109/ICEDEG.2017.7962533

Cheng, I. (2015). *Factors Affecting the Usability of Educational Portals and their Influence on the Information Practices of Pre-Collegiate Educators*. Academic Press.

Cybermetrics. (2019). *Ranking of web of universities*. Retrieved from https://www.webometrics.info/en/africa/nigeria

Daher, L., & Elkabani, I. (2012). Usability Evaluation of Some Lebanese Universities Web Portals. In *International Arab Conference on Information Technology* (pp. 10–13). Academic Press.

Das, T., & Patil, S. R. (2014). A Review of Current Trends in Usability Evaluation Methods. *International Journal of Engineering Research & Technology*, *3*(9), 837–840.

Deedam, F. B., Thomas, E., & Taylor, O. E. (2018). *Accessibility and Usability Evaluation of State-Owned Universities Website in Nigeria*. Academic Press.

Dominic, P. D., Jati, H., & Hanim, S. (2013). University Website Quality Comparison by Using Non-parametric Statistical Test: A case study from Malaysia. *International Journal Operational Research*, *16*(3), 349–374.

Egoeze, F., Misra, S., Akman, I., & Colomo-palacios, R. (2014). An Evaluation of ICT Infrastructure and Application in Nigeria Universities. *Acta Polytechnica Hungarica*, *11*(9), 115–129. Retrieved from http://www.uni-obuda.hu/journal/Egoeze_Misra_Akman_Colomo-Palacios_55.pdf

Esmeria, G. J., & Seva, R. R. (2017). Web Usability : A Literature Review. In *De La Salle University Research Congress*. Retrieved from www.dlsu.edu.ph/conferences/dlsu-research-congress-proceedings/.../SEE-I-013.pdf

González, M. P., Lorés, J., & Granollers, A. (2008). Enhancing usability testing through datamining techniques: A novel approach to detecting usability problem patterns for a context of use. *Information and Software Technology*, *50*(6), 547–568. doi:10.1016/j.infsof.2007.06.001

Hasan, L. (2013). Heuristic Evaluation of Three Jordanian University Websites. *Informatics in Education*, *12*(2), 231–251.

ISO. (2018). *Ergonomics of human-system interaction -- Part 11: Usability: Definitions and concepts*. ISO. Retrieved from https://www.iso.org/standard/63500.html

Jabar, M. A., Usman, U. A., & Awal, A. (2013). Assessing The Usability Of University Websites From Users ' Perspective. *Australian Journal of Basic and Applied Sciences*, *7*(10), 98–111.

Jagero, P. N., Nhendo, C., Sithole, N., Takaingenhamo, C., & Guvava, N. (2014). An Assessment of the Usability of the Africa University Digital Library, Mutare, Zimbabwe. Academic Press.

Jayathunga, D. P., Jayawardana, J. M. D. R., Wimaladharma, S. T. C. I., & Herath, H. M. U. M. (2017). Usability Recommendations for an Academic Website : A Case Study. *International Journal of Scientific and Research Publications*, *7*(4), 145–152.

Junaini, S. N. (2002). Navigation Design and Usability Evaluation of the Malysian Public University Websites. In *Second National Conference on Cognitive Science* (pp. 181–189). Kuching.

Kaur, S., Kaur, K., & Parminder, K. (2016). Analysis of website usability evaluation methods. In *Computing for Sustainable Global Development (INDIACom), 2016 3rd International Conference on* (pp. 1043–1046). IEEE. Retrieved from http://ieeexplore.ieee.org/abstract/document/7724420/

Kiyea, C., & Yusuf, A. B. (2014). Usability Evaluation of Some Selected Nigerian Universities ' Websites. *International Journal of Computers and Applications*, *104*(3), 6–11. doi:10.5120/18180-9071

Manian, A., Yurtchi, B. S., & Shadmehri, N. (2014). Identifying & Prioritizing the Factors Influencing on Website Evaluation, A Content Analysis of Literature. *Management Researches in Iran, 18*(1).

Manzoor, M., & Hussain, W. (2012). A Web Usability Evaluation Model for Higher Education Providing Universities of Asia. *Science, Technology and Development, 31*(2), 183–192. Retrieved from https://opus.lib.uts.edu.au/bitstream/10453/118304/1/183-192.pdf

Mehrotra, D., Pradesh, U., & Pradesh, U. (2017). *Identification of Criteria Affecting the Usability of Academic Institutes Websites*. Academic Press. doi:10.4018/IJTD.2017070102

Mich, L., French, M., & Cilone, G. (2003). The 2QCV3Q Quality model for the analysis of web site requirements. *Journal of Web Engineering, 2*, 105–127.

Mustafa, S. H., & Al-Zoua'bi, L. F. (2008). Usability of the Academic Websites of Jordan's Universities An Evaluation Study. In *Proceedings of the 9th International Arab Conference for Information Technology* (pp. 31–40). Academic Press. Retrieved from https://faculty.psau.edu.sa/filedownload/doc-1-pdf-556f391937dfd4398cbac35e050a2177-original.pdf

Nagpal, R., Mehrotra, D., & Bhatia, P. (2017). The State of Art in Website Usability Evaluation Methods. In S. Saeed, Y. A. Bamarouf, T. Ramayah, & S. Z. Iqbal (Eds.), *Design Solutions for User-Centric Information Systems* (Vol. 1, pp. 275–296). IGI Global. doi:10.4018/978-1-5225-1944-7.ch015

Nagpal, R., Mehrotra, D., Bhatia, P., & Sharma, A. (2015). FAHP Approach to Rank Educational Websites on Usability. *International Journal of Computing and Digital Systems, 4*(4), 251–260. doi:10.12785/ijcds/040404

Nielsen, J. (1994). Usability inspection methods. *Conference Companion on Human Factors in Computing Systems - CHI '94*, 413–414. doi:10.1145/259963.260531

NUC. (2019, October). List of Approved Universities In Nigeria Federal. *National Universities Commission*. Retrieved from http://nuc.edu.ng/20th-october-2017-bulletin/

Seffah, A., Donyaee, M., Kline, R. B., & Padda, H. K. (2006). Usability measurement and metrics : A consolidated model. *Software Quality Journal, 14*(2), 159–178. doi:10.100711219-006-7600-8

Shawgi, E., & Noureldien, N. A. (2015). Usability Measurement Model (UMM): A New Model for Measuring Websites Usability. *International Journal of Information Science, 5*(1), 5–13. doi:10.5923/j.ijis.20150501.02

Speicher, M. (2015). *What is Usability? A Characterization based on ISO 9241-11 and ISO/IEC 25010*. Retrieved from http://arxiv.org/abs/1502.06792

Wardoyo, R., & Wahyuningrum, T. (2018). University Website Quality Ranking using Logarithmic Fuzzy Preference Programming. *Nternational Journal of Electrical and Computer Engineering, 8*(5), 3349–3358. doi:10.11591/ijece.v8i5.pp3349-3358

Yerlikaya, Z., & Durdu, O. (2017). Evaluation of Accessibility of University Websites : A Case from Turkey. In *International Conference on Human-Computer Interaction* (*Vol. 4*, pp. 663–668). Academic Press. 10.1007/978-3-319-58753-0_94

Chapter 13
Human Factors in Automated Analysis for Enterprise Models

Hector Florez

ⓘ https://orcid.org/0000-0002-5339-4459

Universidad Distrital Francisco Jose de Caldas, Colombia

ABSTRACT

Enterprise models are created for communicating and documenting the current state of the enterprise. However, these models can also be used for supporting analysis processes and are fundamental assets in project management. But, analysis is a process made by humans, and due to enterprise models that are complex and have a large amount of elements, analysis is usually a tough process. Then modeling tools might provide support for analysis. It is possible to offer this support through the use of automated analysis methods, which are algorithms for providing specific calculations based on the elements included in the model. The results of said automated analysis methods support decision-making processes. It is also possible to execute a sequence of analysis methods by the configuration of analysis chains. This chapter presents a proposal and strategy for analyzing enterprise models by the execution of automated analysis methods and automated analysis chains. This strategy is presented using enterprise models that conform to ArchiMate as modeling language.

INTRODUCTION

Information Technologies (IT) have become very important assets in enterprises for managing their business information, which is used by humans to achieve their business goals. IT components are modeled through enterprise models that might serve for different objectives such as analysis, communication, and documentation. When one enterprise model is used by humans to perform analysis processes in the organization, analysis results are the main input taken by humans to support decision making processes. Consequently, analysis processes have become a very important task and enterprise models must be able to include required information for performing desired analysis. Analysis is a complex human activity because it demands formulating hypotheses and finding solid insights to discover certain assessments of the enterprise (Florez, Sanchez, & Villalobos, 2016)þ. Typically, one human with the role of analyst

DOI: 10.4018/978-1-7998-1279-1.ch013

has the proper knowledge to manipulate these models in order to extract valuable information, which would be useful for evaluating the current state of the organization. Such information might be used in order to support decision making processes (Buckl, Matthes, & Schweda, 2009)þ. Normally, quality of analysis results depends on factors such as: 1) knowledge, skills, and experience of the analyst; 2) quality of models; and 3) granularity, completeness and level of detail of the information contained in models (Florez, Sanchez, & Villalobos, 2014a)þ. The implementation of automated analysis methods allows performing analyses by automating the operations for obtaining and calculating information. Based on these methods, it would be possible to use properly the model with all its elements and relations.

Moreover, some analyses can require different kinds of results that can be obtained by performing several different analysis methods. In this way, some analysis methods can have as inputs some information provided by other analysis methods. Then, analysts should be able to configure analysis chains composed by automated analysis methods in order to obtain a greater amount of results in the analysis process.

Nowadays, there are several tools that allow creating enterprise models. However, because of the size and complexity of the models, modeling tools do not present the complete model because it would not be properly visualized, but they present the model by partial views, which display the model with a reduced number of elements facilitating its manipulation by the analyst. Despite modeling using views is an excellent strategy for deploying enterprise models, this feature makes harder the analysis process for humans because required elements for one specific analysis can be scattered in more than one view. Therefore, it is useful for analysts performing automated business analysis methods that are algorithms, which based on the model, provide new business information that can be provided as facts or included in the model enriching it. Thus, business analysis methods support human analysis processes by providing knowledge regarding the enterprise. In addition, one model should be used for satisfying different analysis requirements by performing several analysis methods that can be executed individually or through the configuration of analysis chains.

However, not always the analyst can make business analyzes because of the lack of specific required information in models. Thus, automated business analysis methods require that the enterprise model to be analyzed have specific information in the elements or relations involved in the analysis method that is intended to be executed by the analyst. Then, it is desirable to extend the metamodel of the modeling language used for creating the enterprise models in order to ensure that the model includes proper and necessary information. This chapter presents a proposal for supporting automated analysis methods and analysis chains. This proposal has been created using ArchiMate as modeling language as well as includes a strategy for creating models based on supporting analysis requirements by extending the ArchiMate metamodel. Furthermore, the chapter presents a modeling tool, which is a model-based approach for creating, validating, and analyzing ArchiMate enterprise models.

This chapter has the following structure. The section *Background* describes concepts related to enterprise modeling and presents the related work. The section *Enterprise Analysis discuses* enterprise architecture analysis, which includes the description of analysis methods, strategy for creating and analyzing enterprise models, and analysis chains. Then, the section *Analysis Tool* presents a tool for the implementation of the strategy. Finally, the section *Conclusions* concludes the chapter.

BACKGROUND

Model Driven Engineering

Model Driven Engineering (MDE) offers standar concepts to understand the basic notions of metamodels and models. A model is a representation of a system, which is created for achieving a specific goal, while a metamodel is a specification model that abstracts a domain and provides statements in order to define rules that models in such domain must commit (Seidewitz, 2003). Thus, a metamodel is a formal description of a modeling language that allows in this context the construction of modeling and analysis artifacts (Florez & Leon, 2018; Sanchez & Florez, 2018)þ.

According to selic (Selic, 2003)þ, one model must offer the features: 1) abstraction by presenting a simplification of the system; 2) understandability, which implies that the model must be intuitive; 3) accuracy in order to provide a true representation of the system; 4) predictiveness, which means that the model must predict interesting properties of the system; and 5) inexpensiveness i.e., creating a model must be cheaper than the modeled system.

In addition, it is possible that one system is represented by different models. In this case, each model must represent specific aspects of the modeled system (Bézivin, 2005).

Enterprise Modeling

Enterprise modeling is the practice of using a modeling language to represent and describe elements and relations of an enterprise in a coherent way through an enterprise model (Jonkers et al., 2004)þ. The enterprise model must provide a holistic point of view of the organization in order to understand the organizational as well as the technological aspects of the enterprise. Normally, one enterprise model focuses on structural aspects, and serves for documentation, communication, analysis, discussion, and design purposes (Buckl, Buschle, Johnson, Matthes, & Schweda, 2011; Kurpjuweit & Winter, 2007)þ. Thus, an enterprise model is an abstract representation of the enterprise that includes enterprise concepts through typed elements, enterprise relations between elements and attributes that can be placed in elements or relations. In addition, enterprise models have a large number of elements and relations that represents the characteristics of the organization. Moreover, one enterprise model can be visualized through different points of view of the enterprise in order to present a fragment of the model, for a better understanding of the enterprise systems through proper abstractions. One enterprise model can vary depending on its purpose (e.g. documentation, communication, analysis); thus, it could be used not only for visualization and communication purposes, but for enabling analysis capabilities (Lankhorst, 2013)þ.

The modeling language structure is defined in one enterprise metamodel, which provides the abstract syntax of the Domain Specific Modeling Language (DSML) that includes the enterprise concepts and relations. The enterprise metamodel depends on the issues, requirements, and objectives of the enterprise. Nowadays, modeling languages allow modeling IT infrastructures and IT architectures (Frank, 2014a)þ through several domains (e.g., business process models, goal models, organizational models, architecture models). Thus, the enterprise model can have information from different domains, where each domain is represented by one specific metamodel.

Business Process Modeling Notation

Business Process Modeling Notation (BPMN) is a standard that allows modeling business process by providing a graphical notation for specifying business processes in a Business Process Diagram. BPMN was created by the Business Process Management Initiative (BPMI) (Owen & Raj, 2003; von Rosing, White, Cummins, & de Man, 2015)þ. The main goal of BPMN is to provide an understandable standard notation for all business users, while represent complex process semantics. Business users can be classified in three categories: a) business analysts, who model the business processes, b) technical developers, who implement the technology to run the modeled processes, and c) business people, who manage and monitor the implemented processes (White, 2004)þ. BPMN also provides execution semantics in order to be able to execute processes through the Business Process Execution Language (BPEL) and Business Process Execution Language for Web Services (BPEL4WS).

Enterprise Modeling Process

The enterprise modeling process is a complex task that involves several human actors such as domain experts and modelers. The result of the process is the enterprise model that abstracts the enterprise under study. Figure 1 presents the steps of the process.

In the first step, the domain experts produce some expectations about the enterprise. These expectations are determined based on enterprise requirements. These requirements might guide the expert, for identifying insights regarding the business issues and objectives. For the second step, the domain expert establishes one modeling language with the correspondent enterprise metamodel. The enterprise metamodel can be selected or created. Selecting the metamodel means that the domain expert has identified one standard modeling language that matches properly with the enterprise and purpose of modeling. Creating the metamodel means that the domain expert builds one metamodel specifically or the enterprise under study. However, building the metamodel can be supported by metamodels composition, where several desired concepts can be reused from existing modeling languages in order to facilitate the creation of the enterprise metamodel.

Figure 1. Modeling process

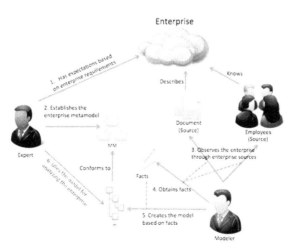

Once the metamodel is defined, the modeler is asked for creating the enterprise model. Thus, in the third step, the modeler observes and classifies the enterprises sources. Enterprise sources (e.g., employees, documents, meetings) are enterprise elements that can provide information regarding aspects of the enterprise. Based on the information provided by sources, in the fourth step, the modeler extracts, consolidates, and interprets facts. Based on these facts, the modeler identifies the enterprise structural elements and relations. In addition, the modeler classifies these elements and relations using the concepts and relations provided by the metamodel of the modeling language provided in the second step. The fifth step is the creation of the enterprise model. It implies a) creating the corresponding instances that represent the enterprise elements, b) creating relations between elements, and c) setting attributes in elements and relations (Florez, Sanchez, & Villalobos, 2014c)þ.

When the model is done, in the sixth step, the domain expert can use the model for making analysis. Usually, model analysis is performed by humans using minimal technological support because modeling tools are used just to access to the enterprise model information in an effective manner. Consequently, analysts have all the responsibility of finding new valuable information. Then, in large enterprise models, it is very likely to commit omissions and miscalculation (Florez et al., 2014a)þ. Nevertheless, in order to overcome said disadvantages, several works are focused on the creation of automated analysis methods, are implemented on top of some modeling tools for supporting the analysis processes.

Enterprise Models Characteristics

Usually, enterprise models have a large amount of elements and relations between elements that can be found in a typical organization. Moreover, creating a perfect enterprise model is not possible due to enterprise dynamics and sources limitations. Frequently, sources that provide enterprise information have divergent levels of reliability and accuracy. Thus, it is very likely to find various sources with conflict of interest, imprecise information, contradictory information, opposite points of view, lack of information, and even more situations that hinder the construction of the enterprise model (Florez, Sanchez, & Villalobos, 2014b)þ. Furthermore, it is very likely to find obsolete enterprise information, which is not possible to asses whether or not said information remains veracious. As a result, enterprise sources can be classified based on the characteristics of the information provided as follows (Florez, Sánchez, & Villalobos, 2013)þ:

1. Incorrect source that provide a value that is not true or is not usable
2. Imprecise source that provide a range of numeric values to one attribute that requires a specific numeric value.
3. Inconsistent source that provide several different values to one attribute or relation
4. Vague source that provide a linguistic value to one attribute that requires a specific numeric value
5. Uncertain source that provide a value with certainty degree.

Also, sometimes one source cannot provide information regarding one specific aspect of the enterprise, but such source should provide it. Then, the source observation can be considered as incomplete because it does not have any data to produce a useful fact.

As a result, when the enterprise model is used for analyzing the enterprise, human intervention is required. Although automated analysis methods provide additional information, an analyst must interpret the results provided by these automated analysis in order to decide its validity level. It is an additional important task for the analyst because the enterprise model can have wrong information in the elements that are involved in the automated analysis. In addition, automated analysis requires that the enterprise model satisfies some specific characteristics; then, it is necessary to use a proper modeling language that allows representing in the model, all desired elements of the enterprise.

Modeling Languages

Enterprise modeling languages can be classified as descriptive language, predictive language or a mixture of both (Johnson, Ullberg, Buschle, Franke, & Shahzad, 2013)þ. On the one hand, descriptive languages are used to obtain easy understanding of the enterprise. On the other hand, predictive languages are used to estimate future states of the enterprise. Commonly, one modeling language corresponds to a graphical language for facilitating communication and increasing understanding (Gómez, Sánchez, Florez, & Villalobos, 2014)þ.

There are several standardized modeling languages, which can model different enterprise domains. Some of the most used standardized modeling languages are: Business Motivation Model (BMM), which can express the intention of the enterprise; Business Process Model (BPM), which allows modeling of business processes; Business Process Execution Language (BPEL), which offers the required structure for the automated execution of business processes; ArchiMate, which allows representing all enterprise elements through different domains.

In particular, ArchiMate is a standard enterprise modeling language that allows creating enterprise models with different domains and points of view. In addition, it is extensible that allows including new typed elements, typed element's attributes, and typed relation's attributes, which is an important feature, when the model is intended to use for analyzing the enterprise. Also, ArchiMate is flexible, which allows including all kinds of information (e.g. imprecise, vague). As a result, ArchiMate can be considered as a good modeling language for analysis purposes.

Related Work

Several proposals are addressing on the analysis of enterprise models. Automated analysis methods can be classified in different categories (Buckl et al., 2009; Iacob & Jonkers, 2006)þ . The work presented in this chapter is comparable to quantitative and static analysis approaches.

Johnson et al. (Johnson, Lagerström, Närman, & Simonsson, 2007)þ present an approach to perform enterprise architecture analyses based on influence diagrams. In this context, an influence diagram is an extension of Bayesian networks that graphically represents causal relations between nodes, where each node represents a variable with a number of states. The extended influence diagram is combined with enterprise architecture scenario models for the purposes of enterprise architecture analysis. Similar to this proposal, the work presented in this chapter is based on the extension of the enterprise model.

Razavi et al. (Razavi, Shams Aliee, & Badie, 2010)þ propose including additional information of quality attributes. This feature is also posible in the proposal presented in this chapter. This approach is based on Analytical Hierarchy Process (AHP) to help decision makers of an enterprise to decide about different scenarios according to their level of quality attribute achievement. Each quality attribute is composed of several criteria and sub-criteria which are specified in the quality attribute general scenario.

Närman et al. (Närman, Johnson, & Nordstrom, 2007)þ propose a metamodel that supports the creation of enterprise architecture models amenable to a range of the following quality attribute analyzes: Maintainability, Security, Reliability, Usability, Efficiency, Interoperability, Suitability, and Accuracy. This work shows that, in order to perform certain kinds of analysis, metamodels have to be adapted.

The work of Johnson et al. (Johnson, Johansson, Sommestad, & Ullberg, 2007)þ propose a tool for analyzing enterprise architecture models. This tool allows the creation of enterprise information system scenarios through enterprise architecture models. In addition, it generates quantitative assessments of the scenarios. Such assessments can be of various quality attributes, such as interoperability, performance, information security, availability, maintainability, usability, accuracy, and functional suitability. This proposal has interesting similarities with the approach presented in this chapter because it allows including additional information in the model by quality attributes and based on this information it is possible to produce assessments.

Buckl et al, (Buckl et al., 2011)þ propose a meta-language built on the Meta Object Facility (MOF) for satisfying requirements of enterprise architecture analysis. The meta-language addresses enterprise architecture requirements by providing means of the values of certain attributes that are dependent on other attributes' values, without creating the need to provide dependency rules.

Frank (Frank, 2014b)þ proposes Multi-perspective Enterprise Modeling (MEMO), which is an approach to represent different perspectives of the enterprise. MEMO offers a framework that includes common abstraction of enterprises. The enterprise perspectives are represented by the languages: 1) Strategy Modeling Language (MEMO-SML) for including concepts from strategic planning; 2) Organization Modeling Language (MEMO-OrgML) that serves to model organizational concepts; and 3) Object-Oriented Modeling Language (MEMO-OML), which allows the specification of information. MEMO architecture contains the specification and integration of modeling languages. The architecture is extensible by updating the metamodels or the meta-metamodels for specific purpose modeling. It allows the specification of additional languages and the creation of enterprise analysis methods.

Buckl et al. (Buckl et al., 2009)þ present an analysis classification inspired in different contexts and developed based on the literature. This classification presents five dimensions: 1) Body of Analysis, which refers to the nature of the information to be analyzed; 2) Time Reference, which makes EA analysis based on an existing architecture or a planned architecture; 3) Analysis Technique, which can be expert-base, rule-based, or indicator-based; 4) Analysis Concern, which corresponds to the needs to fulfill functional requirements of the organization; and 5) Self Referentiality, which analyses the complexity of the model.

ENTERPRISE ANALYSIS

Based on Byrne (Byrne, 1997)þ, analysis is the process of transforming mere facts into reasoned facts in order to provide the information needed to solve a problem using solid arguments. In the enterprise modeling context, some enterprise elements such as models, catalogs, matrices and diagrams are used for representing these facts (Speckert, Rychkova, Zdravkovic, & Nurcan, 2013)þ . Based on Johnson (Johnson, Johansson, et al., 2007)þ, enterprise analysis is the application of property assessment criteria on enterprise models. This means that, given a property and a criterion for assessing that property, doing model analysis requires evaluating said criteria using the information available in the model.

However, most of the modeling tools for enterprise modeling (e.g., tools based on ArchiMate) are mainly focused on the visualization and modeling aspects than in the analysis of the resulting models. As a result, analysts have to perform their analysis task in a mostly manual fashion. In addition, enterprise models have become very big and complex because they are intended to include more details and to incorporate other domains. The use of views and viewpoints has allowed to decrease the complexity of models; however, it presents a disadvantage regarding to the risk of losing the holistic view of the enterprise which is very important in the enterprise architecture practice (Rozanski & Woods, 2011)þ.

Automated Business Analysis Methods

Automated analysis is defined as the process of extracting and manipulating data contained in the enterprise model using automated mechanisms (Benavides, Segura, & Ruiz-Cortés, 2010)þ in order to support optimization, diagnosis, finding out caused problems, and decision making processes across different areas of one organization (Kohlhammer, May, & Hoffmann, 2009; Lankhorst, 2013)þ. Nowadays, the analysis problem resides in identifying methods and models that can transform data into reliable and comprehensible knowledge.

Automated business analysis methods are algorithms that allow obtaining information from the enterprise model for obtaining desirable knowledge about the organization (Florez, Sánchez, & Villalobos, 2016) þ. Moreover, they might be used to include certain data in the enterprise model through the execution of instructions stated in the analysis method. This analysis methods might be used to 1) obtain results based on the information placed in the model or 2) enrich the model augmenting it with elements, relations, elements' attributes, or relations' attributes in order to provide new useful information.

Automated business analysis methods demand that the enterprise model offers enough and proper information about a system under study. These methods imply that the enterprise model needs to include specific required information in the elements or relations that are used by the analysis. Then, the metamodel of the modeling language must be extended (e.g. including new attributes in one or several elements or in one or several relations) according to the set of analysis methods that the analyst might select.

For example, consider that an organization has an enterprise model that conforms to ArchiMate as modeling language. In addition, consider that the analyst requires to know the number of business processes associated to business roles. In this case, one automated analysis method can provide this information, where output correspond to facts with details regarding the amount of business processes associated, and the percentage of business process associated regarding the total amount of business processes. In a second example, the analyst requires to determine which devices are impacted or affected by one requirement based on the devices' availability. The requirement establishes the minimum value of availability that the devices must accomplish. In this case, the ArchiMate metamodel must be extended including the following attributes: 1) *conditionAttribute* with the type *String* in the concept *Requirement*; 2) *conditionOperation* with the type *String* in the concept *Requirement*; 3) *conditionValue* with the *Double* in the concept *Requirement*, where the value must be between 0 and 1 and 4) *availability* with the type *Double* in the concept *Device*, where the value must be between 0 and 1. This analysis method requires that the modeler sets the value of the attribute *availability* in the concept *Device*. The analysis method draws new relations named from the requirement to the devices that satisfies the condition provided by the correspondent attributes. This analysis method enriches the model because new relations are automatically added in the elements that conforms to the concept *Requirement*. For a third example, one analysis method intends to calculate the availability of all application components based on the availability of the devices that support it. The ArchiMate metamodel must be extended including the following attributes: 1) *availability* with the type *Double* in the concept *ApplicationComponent* and 2) *availability* with the type *Double* in the concept *Device*, where the value must be between 0 and 1. This analysis method requires that the modeler sets the value of the attribute *availability* in the concept *Device*. As a result, once the analysis method is executed, it enriches the model because new information is automatically added in the elements that conforms to the concept *ApplicationComponent*.

Enterprise Analysis Process

Automated analysis methods can augment the model with new concepts, relations, and attributes, which are not define in the metamodel of the modeling language (e.g., ArchiMate). Then, the metamodel of the modeling language must be extended (Florez, Sanchez, Villalobos, & Vega, 2012)þ. Therefore, there is the need to have several different extended metamodels in order to create the model with the proper information for performing the desired analysis method.

After the modeling process is completed, the business analysis process can be performed through the steps specified in Figure 2. In the first step, the analyst selects the analysis method that is intended to be performed. The extended metamodel of the Domain Specific Modeling Language (DSML) is generated as second step. In the third step, the analyst validates that the model has the required information for performing the desired analysis method. As fourth step, the analyst executes the selected analysis method using an *Analysis Engine*, which uses the model and input parameters provided by the analyst for generating the needed results. For the fifth step, according to the analysis method executed, the *Analysis Engine* might produce two results. On the one hand, it might produce facts, which are information calculated with all elements under study included in the model. On the other hand, it might enrich the model, which implies including new elements, relations, elements' attributes, or relations' attributes; In the sixth step, based on the results produced by the *Analysis Engine*, the analyst interprets the facts and the enriched model. Finally, once the analyst has interpreted the results produced by the *Analysis Engine*, he can communicate those results interpretation through *Assessments* that are used for decisions making in the enterprise (Florez et al., 2014a)þ.

Figure 2. Analysis process

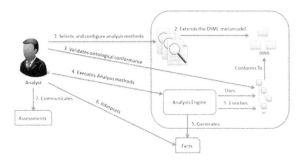

Analysis Chains

Analysis over large organizations is very complex because it requires to take into account a large number of elements. In addition, it is possible that the analyst desires to perform one analysis that requires the execution of more than one analysis method. In this case, one analysis method may require results (i.e., outputs) provided by the previous analysis method. As a result, one analysis can be performed by one analysis chain, which is the composition of various automated analysis methods, where each analysis method provides outputs that can be used as input for the following analysis method in the analysis chain. Outputs of analysis methods are very important because in terms of the analysis processes, each output generates cumulative value. Thus, analysis chains presents a sequential value creation process composed by different interdependent value activities (Porter, 2008)þ. Each value activity requires some inputs and resources (e.g., human resources and technological resources) in order to create information or specific assets that contribute to the achievement of one common goal. In addition, Porter also defines value activities like *building blocks* (Porter, 2008)þ, which is a term introduced in *Service Oriented Architecture* in order to denote the service as its fundamental element. Then, one analysis method can be expressed as a service and the analysis chain as a service orchestration, which coordinate the execution of several independent analysis methods. As a result, the analysis chain can be represented by a flow that integrates and synchronizes multiple analysis methods.

The analysis chains process, which is presented in Figure 3 has some different steps than the analysis process described above. In this case, in the first step the analyst selects one analysis method; later, he selects another analysis method that depends on the results provided by the first analysis method selected. In addition, in the fourth step, when the analyst executes the analysis chain, the analysis engine executes the first analysis method generating the corresponding facts and enriching the model; however, in this case, the analysis engine executes sequentially all analysis methods that belong to the analysis chain configured by the analyst.

For instance, based on ArchMate as DSML, business processes are supported by one or several application components that are hosted in one or several devices. Then one business process can be fail if one of the application components that support it is not available. Also, one application component can be affected if one or several devices that support it are offline. As a result, analysts can establish the availability of all application components in the model, based on the availability of the devices that support them. Moreover, analysts can establish one index of fault susceptibility of all business processes,

Figure 3. Analysis process

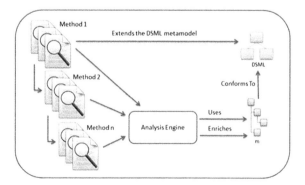

based on the availability of the application components that support them. In this case, the correspondent ArchiMate metamodel must be extended including the attributes: 1) *faultSusceptibility* with the type *Double* in the concept *BusinessProcess*, 2) *availability* with the type *Double* in the concept *Application-Component*, and 3) *availability* with the type *Double* in the concept *Device*. The modeler must include the real availability value for all devices in the model. Thus, it is possible to execute one analysis chain that includes on analysis method for calculating the availability for all application components in the model, and based on the results of the previous analysis method, the analysis chain includes another analysis method for calculating the fault susceptibility for all business processes in the model. After executing the analysis method, each element in the model that conforms to *ApplicationComponent* and *BusinessProcess* will include the correspondent calculated values in the correspondent attributes.

A TOOL FOR SUPPORTING AUTOMATED ANALYSIS

As part of this research work, a modeling and analyzing tool based on ArchiMate as modeling language has been created. This tool is a graphical modeling editor based on Eclipse Modeling Framework (EMF)[1] and Graphical Modeling Framework (GMF)[2]. Furthermore, the project EuGENia[3] was used to facilitate the creation of the required GMF components. In the editor, all elements are drawn with rounded squares that include the correspondent icon and color established in the ArchiMate specification; all relations have the graphical representation established in the specification as well; and all attributes, which can belong to elements or relations, are displayed through an additional tab in the properties view. The tool is also capable of validating the model providing assistance to the user, in order to determine if the model fulfils the required information for running the desired automated analysis method. This validation is supported by Epsilon Validation Language (EVL)[4]; thus, when the desired analysis method is selected, the tool generates an EVL script that is used for validating the model. Figure 4 presents a screenshot of the modeling tool and shows the Business Cooperation View of the ArchiSurance Case Study (Jonkers, Band, & Quartel, 2012)þ.

Automated Analysis Methods

After the modeling phase is finished, the analyst can execute any available analysis method. The modeling tool allows selecting the analysis method through a wizard as shown in Figure 5, which is used to make two basic questions: the main concept involved in the desired analysis and the specific analysis method to be invoked. In addition, the wizard presents information regarding the attributes or relations for each related ArchiMate element that the analysis method require or will create. After selecting the analysis method, the tool updates the ArchiMate metamodel in order to generate the correspondent extension and the validation scripts in order to verify that the model accomplishes the requirements for the selected analysis method. In addition, after performing the analysis method, the modeling tool presents the results of the process in one tab called Analysis Result and enriches the enterprise model when the analysis method is intended to do it.

Examples described in the subsection *Automated Business Analysis Methods* have been created in order to illustrate the way in which the modeling tool manages the automated analysis methods. Figure 6 presents a model for the first example, which is intended to determine the level of participation of all business roles in business processes. This method calculates the number of business processes that are

Figure 4. Screenshot of the tool

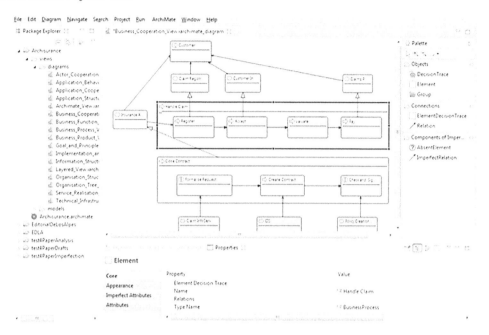

Figure 5. Wizard for selecting analysis methods

Figure 6. Model for analysis method: participation of business role

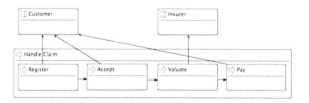

used by each business role regarding the total amount of business process in the model. After performing the analysis method, the results are presented as shown in the Figure 7. The results present in one table each business role with the percentage of participation and the related business processes. This analysis method only provide facts that contains information regarding the involved elements.

In the second example, one requirement establishes the minimal value of availability for devices. In this case, the modeling tool extends the ArchiMate metamodel and updates the validation scripts in order to include a) the attribute *availability* in all devices of the model and b) the required attributes in the requirement for establishing the condition that is intended to be evaluated in all devices. After performing the analysis method, one association relation is created for each device that fits with the requirement. Figure 8 presents the model after performing the analysis method, which has been enriched with new relations. Figure 9 presents the attributes of the requirements through one tab in the properties view, which has been created to visualize properly elements' and relations' attributes of the model. Figure 10 presents the results of the analysis method including necessary details. In this example, the attributes *conditionAttribute*, *conditionOperation*, and *conditionValue* determines that this requirement points out all devices that have an availability lower than *0,95%*. The results of the analysis show that the devices *DataBase Server* and *Windows Server* satisfies the availability condition of the requirement, and the device *NAS File Server* does not have assigned availability. Then, the analysis method creates three associations from the requirement *Min Availability* to each mentioned devices.

Figure 7. Analysis method results: participation of business role

Figure 8. Model for analysis method: requirement over devices

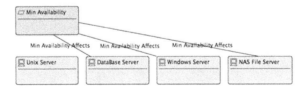

Figure 9. Model Attributes for Analysis Method: Requirement over Devices

Figure 10. Analysis Method Results: Requirement over Devices

Analysis Chains

The modeling tool allows configuring analysis chains based on enabled analysis methods. After the model is created, the analyst can configure one analysis chain selecting the desired analysis methods through one wizard presented in Figure 11. Initially, the wizard presents all enabled analysis methods. Once the first analysis method is selected, the wizard provides the list of viable analysis methods. If there is just one analysis method selected, viable analysis methods are those that need as input any output provided by the selected method. For instance, if an analysis method calculates one attribute (e.g., availability) in one specific element type (e.g., application component), one viable analysis method should require requires this attribute to calculate further information. However, if there are selected more than one analysis method, viable analysis methods are those that need as input any output provided by any selected method. The wizard also presents information regarding the attributes or relations for each related ArchiMate element that each selected analysis method require or will create.

The example presented in the subsection *Analysis Chains* is used here. In this example, the analyst desires to determine the fault susceptibility of all business processes based on the availability of application components that support them. However, availability information is included only in devices, which are used by application components. Then, the analysis chain is composed by two automated analysis methods already created. The first analysis method calculates the availability of each application component based on the availability of all devices that support them. The example has four devices,

Figure 11. Wizard for selecting analysis chains

which must have the attribute *availability*. Then, this analysis method calculates the availability for the application components *CRM, Policy Data Management*, and *Financial Application*. The second analysis method calculates the fault susceptibility for the business processes *Register, Accept, Valuate*, and *Pay* based on the availability of all application components (already calculated) that support them. Figure 12 presents one example of model that can be used for applying this analysis chain while Figure 13 presents the results after performing the analysis chain. The results show each calculation made in the model with details about the associated elements.

Analysis Conformance Validation

When the analysis method or analysis chain is selected, the ArchiMate metamodel is extended; as a result, the tool must validate that the model conforms to the extended metamodel. Figure 14 shows the result of the validation process. In this example, the application component *Policy Data Management* does not have the attribute *availability* required to perform the analysis method *Fault Susceptibility* for business processes. Then, the validation engine places a warning informing the problem.

Figure 12. Model for Analysis Chain

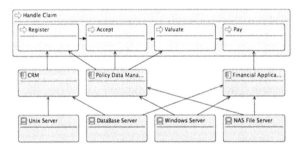

Figure 13. Analysis Chain Results

Figure 14. Analysis method validation

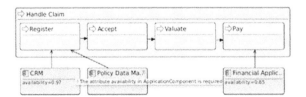

CONCLUSION

Enterprise modeling analysis is a very important task in organizations because it provides knowledge that can be use for improving several aspects of the business. However, enterprise modeling tools usually are not suited for supporting analysis. In this paper, we have presented a strategy to support automated analysis methods. This strategy is based on the possibility for extending the metamodel of the DSML by including elements that specific analysis methods require. Based on the extended metamodel, it is possible to execute automatic analysis methods, which provide results that can be included in the model.

The paper also discuses analysis chains, which are the composition of several automated analysis methods. Analysis chains are used for helping architects to deal with the complexity of performing strategic analysis over large enterprise models. In addition, the proposal enables the reuse of automated analysis methods in order to extend the capabilities for facing new desired analyses.

The strategy was instantiated in a modeling tool, which provides automated analysis methods for ArchiMate models, and offers a framework for the development of additional methods. The tool also offers a framework for creating an executing analysis chains based on the existing automated analysis methods. This tool has the capability of handling models that only partially conform to the metamodel, and the capabilities to handle the results of the analyses, which may be used to enrich the models.

REFERENCES

Benavides, D., Segura, S., & Ruiz-Cortés, A. (2010). Automated analysis of feature models 20 years later: A literature review. *Information Systems*, *35*(6), 615–636. doi:10.1016/j.is.2010.01.001

Bézivin, J. (2005). On the unification power of models. *Software & Systems Modeling*, *4*(2), 171–188. doi:10.100710270-005-0079-0

Buckl, S., Buschle, M., Johnson, P., Matthes, F., & Schweda, C. M. (2011). A meta-language for Enterprise Architecture analysis. *Enterprise, Business-Process and Information Systems Modeling*, 511–525.

Buckl, S., Matthes, F., & Schweda, C. M. (2009). Classifying enterprise architecture analysis approaches. *Enterprise Interoperability*, 66–79.

Byrne, P. H. (1997). *Analysis and science in Aristotle*. SUNY Press.

Florez, H., & Leon, M. (2018). Model Driven Engineering Approach to Configure Software Reusable Components. *International Conference on Applied Informatics*, 352–363. 10.1007/978-3-030-01535-0_26

Florez, H., Sánchez, M., & Villalobos, J. (2013). Embracing Imperfection in Enterprise Architecture Models. *CEUR Workshop Proceedings*, *1023*, 8–17.

Florez, H., Sanchez, M., & Villalobos, J. (2014a). Extensible Model-based Approach for Supporting Automatic Enterprise Analysis. *18th IEEE International Enterprise Distributed Object Computing Conference (EDOC)*, 32–41. 10.1109/EDOC.2014.15

Florez, H., Sanchez, M., & Villalobos, J. (2014b). iArchiMate: A Tool for Managing Imperfection in Enterprise Models. *18th IEEE International Enterprise Distributed Object Computing Conference Workshops and Demonstrations (EDOCW)*, 201–210. 10.1109/EDOCW.2014.38

Florez, H., Sanchez, M., & Villalobos, J. (2014c). Supporting drafts for enterprise modeling. *2014 IEEE 9th Computing Colombian Conference (9CCC)*, 200–206.

Florez, H., Sanchez, M., & Villalobos, J. (2016). A catalog of automated analysis methods for enterprise models. *SpringerPlus*, *5*(406), 1–24. PMID:27047732

Florez, H., Sánchez, M., & Villalobos, J. (2016). Analysis of Imprecise Enterprise Models. *International Workshop on Business Process Modeling, Development and Support*, 349–364.

Florez, H., Sanchez, M., Villalobos, J., & Vega, G. (2012). Coevolution Assistance for Enterprise Architecture Models. *Models And Evolution (ME 2012) Workshop at The ACM/IEEE 15th International Conference on Model Driven Engineering Languages And Systems (MoDELS 2012)*.

Frank, U. (2014a). Enterprise modelling: The next steps. *Enterprise Modelling and Information Systems Architectures*, *9*(1), 22–37. doi:10.100740786-014-0003-6

Frank, U. (2014b). Multi-perspective enterprise modeling: Foundational concepts, prospects and future research challenges. *Software & Systems Modeling*, *13*(3), 941–962. doi:10.100710270-012-0273-9

Gómez, P., Sánchez, M., Florez, H., & Villalobos, J. (2014). An approach to the co-creation of models and metamodels in Enterprise Architecture Projects. *Journal of Object Technology*, *13*(3), 2:1. doi:10.5381/jot.2014.13.3.a2

Iacob, M.-E., & Jonkers, H. (2006). Quantitative analysis of enterprise architectures. *Interoperability of Enterprise Software and Applications*.

Johnson, P., Johansson, E., Sommestad, T., & Ullberg, J. (2007). A Tool for Enterprise Architecture Analysis. *11th IEEE International Enterprise Distributed Object Computing Conference*, 142–142.

Johnson, P., Lagerström, R., Närman, P., & Simonsson, M. (2007). Enterprise architecture analysis with extended influence diagrams. *Information Systems Frontiers*, *9*(2–3), 163–180. doi:10.100710796-007-9030-y

Johnson, P., Ullberg, J., Buschle, M., Franke, U., & Shahzad, K. (2013). P 2 AMF: predictive, probabilistic architecture modeling framework. *International IFIP Working Conference on Enterprise Interoperability*, 104–117.

Jonkers, H., Band, I., & Quartel, D. (2012). *The ArchiSurance Case Study*. The Open Group Case Study (Document Number Y121).

Jonkers, H., Lankhorst, M., Van Buuren, R., Hoppenbrouwers, S., Bonsangue, M., & Van Der Torre, L. (2004). Concepts for modeling enterprise architectures. *International Journal of Cooperative Information Systems*, *13*(03), 257–287. doi:10.1142/S0218843004000985

Kohlhammer, J., May, T., & Hoffmann, M. (2009). Visual analytics for the strategic decision making process. In *GeoSpatial Visual Analytics* (pp. 299–310). Springer. doi:10.1007/978-90-481-2899-0_23

Kurpjuweit, S., & Winter, R. (2007). Viewpoint-based Meta Model Engineering. *Proceedings of the 2nd International Workshop on Enterprise Modelling and Information Systems Architectures*, 143–161.

Lankhorst, M. (2013). *Enterprise architecture at work: Modelling, communication and analysis.* Springer. doi:10.1007/978-3-642-29651-2

Närman, P., Johnson, P., & Nordstrom, L. (2007). Enterprise Architecture: A Framework Supporting System Quality Analysis. *11th IEEE International Enterprise Distributed Object Computing Conference (EDOC 2007)*, 130–130. 10.1109/EDOC.2007.39

Owen, M., & Raj, J. (2003). *BPMN and business process management.* Introduction to the New Business Process Modeling Standard.

Porter, M. E. (2008). *Competitive advantage: Creating and sustaining superior performance.* Simon and Schuster.

Razavi, M., Shams Aliee, F., & Badie, K. (2010). An AHP-based approach toward enterprise architecture analysis based on enterprise architecture quality attributes. *Knowledge and Information Systems*, *28*(2), 449–472. doi:10.100710115-010-0312-1

Rozanski, N., & Woods, E. (2011). *Software systems architecture: working with stakeholders using viewpoints and perspectives.* Addison-Wesley.

Sanchez, D., & Florez, H. (2018). Model driven engineering approach to manage peripherals in mobile devices. *International Conference on Computational Science and Its Applications*, 353–364. 10.1007/978-3-319-95171-3_28

Seidewitz, E. (2003). What models mean. *Software, IEEE*, *20*(5), 26–32. doi:10.1109/MS.2003.1231147

Selic, B. (2003). The pragmatics of model-driven development. *IEEE Software*, *20*(5), 19–25. doi:10.1109/MS.2003.1231146

Speckert, T., Rychkova, I., Zdravkovic, J., & Nurcan, S. (2013). On the Changing Role of Enterprise Architecture in Decentralized Environments: State of the Art. *Enterprise Distributed Object Computing Conference Workshops (EDOCW), 2013 17th IEEE International*, 310–318.

von Rosing, M., White, S., Cummins, F., & de Man, H. (2015). *Business Process Model and Notation-BPMN.* Academic Press.

White, S. A. (2004). Introduction to BPMN. *IBM Cooperation, 2*(0), 0.

KEY TERMS AND DEFINITIONS

Analysis Chains: Composition of various automated analysis methods, where each analysis method provides outputs that can be used as input for the following analysis method.

ArchiMate: Domain Specific Modeling Language to describe and visualize enterprise model with a holistic point of view.

Automated Analysis: Process of extracting and manipulating data contained in the enterprise model, using automated mechanisms, in order to support diagnosis, finding out caused problems, optimization, and decision-making processes across different areas of one organization.

Automated Business Analysis Methods: Algorithms that allow extracting information from the model in order to obtain knowledge about the enterprise.

Enterprise Analysis: Process of transforming mere facts into reasoned facts in order to provide the information needed to solve a problem using solid arguments.

Enterprise Modeling: Practice to create, maintain, and use models in order to represent certain aspects of the enterprise.

Modeling Language: Structure that includes the enterprise concepts and the enterprise relations.

ENDNOTES

1   http://www.eclipse.org/modeling/emf/
2   http://www.eclipse.org/modeling/gmp/
3   http://www.eclipse.org/epsilon/doc/eugenia/
4   http://www.eclipse.org/epsilon/doc/evl/

Chapter 14
Artificial Intelligence, Other Minds, and Human Factor Development:
The Fate of Man in the World of Machines

Ikedinachi Ayodele Power Wogu
Rhema University, Nigeria

Comfort Olushola Roland-Otaru
Independent Researcher, Nigeria

Jesse Oluwafemi Katende
Covenant University, Ota, Nigeria

Hosea Abalaka Apeh
University of Abuja, Nigeria

Ayotunde Elegbeleye
Covenant University, Ota, Nigeria

Nkechi J. Ifeanyi-Reuben
Rhema University, Nigeria

Sanjay Misra
https://orcid.org/0000-0002-3556-9331
Covenant University, Ota, Nigeria

ABSTRACT

While the majority of scientists agree that artificial intelligence (AI) technology have provided excellent platforms for inventing tools beneficial for enhancing man's quality of life on earth, there are a host of others who have identified existential and ontological hazards associated with the proliferation of super-intelligent machines (SIM), now utilized for virtually every human endeavor. The Marxian alienation theory was adopted for the study while Creswell's qualitative and Marilyn's ex-post facto research design approaches were adopted as viable methodologies for the study. Justifiable grounds by which existentialist scholars continue to promote the 'extinction risk threat' and the impending job annihilation theory were identified. Scientists and existentialist scholars are therefore enjoined to urgently identify pathways for aligning the goals of SIM with those of mankind.

DOI: 10.4018/978-1-7998-1279-1.ch014

INTRODUCTION

Background to the Study

Artificial Intelligence (AI) as a field of study among contemporary scientists, is founded on the supposition that the feature of 'Intelligence'- a feature initially believed to be typical and solely associated with beings known as *Homo sapiens* alone - is today, also possible to simulate and duplicate in non-living things such as artifacts and machines. The acceptance of this notion among scientists and scholars of AI research from the beginning of this dispensation, has raised philosophical, ontological and existential questions about the nature of the mind in individuals who are perceived as the only class of beings capable of partaking in the feature of 'intelligence'. This reality for scholars like McCorduck, raises vital questions about the bounds of scientific proclamations and endeavours, which have been exemplified, discussed and presented in scientific fictions, mythologies, and in philosophical debates for decades now (McCorduck, 2004; Wogu, Olu-Owolabi, Assibong, Apeh, Agoha, Sholarin, Elegbeleye... & Igbokwe, 2017).

Today, however, the argument has gone beyond whether machines possess a mind of their own or whether they can indeed think for themselves. The real challenge for scholars seems to be that these machines are developing to the point of acquiring super-intelligent capabilities in the nearest future, to the disadvantage of man. Scholars like Fallenstein, Benya in his work (Marquart, 2017), corroborate this when he noted that:

...intelligent machines have transformed and are presently at the verge of acquiring super-intelligent capabilities, a scenario feared would grant machines the domineering advantage with which to relegate its human counterpart to unimaginable conditions and situations, a scenario feared would take place earlier than was initially expected (Marquart, 2017).

This fear calls on contemporary researchers and scholars of AI to seek out ways of preventing machines from possessing 'super human intelligence' in the future, which is feared would lead to the eventual and total annihilation of the job of mankind. A resultant consequence of this situation would lead to the eventual taking e over of the place of man's jobs in virtually all life's endeavours. This fear is further personified in the words of Moshe Vardi's when he exclaimed that:

Machines have already automated millions of routine working-class jobs in manufacturing industries. And now, AI is learning to automate non-routine jobs in transportation and logistics, legal writing, financial services, administrative support, and healthcare...humans have never competed with machines that can outperform them in almost anything. AI threatens to do this, and many economists worry that society won't be able to adapt from its consequence... (Davey, 2017).

The above situation notwithstanding, it is important to note that the 21st century has witnessed a host of technological advances and innovations especially in the information and Communications Technology (ICT) sector with regards to education, (Ghafourifar, 2017 and Wogu, 2019). Machines for instance, are now able to analyze and calculate complex figures and issues as can be witnessed in the Google search algorithms (Hawking, Tegmark, Russell, & Wilczek, 2014). These same innovations have now given machines the capacity to play and defeat humans in games of chees and in the very complex game of poker (Wogu, 2011; Kasparove, 1996 and RileyMar, 2017). There is also the innovations that have given machines the ability to possess and display the human like feature of facial recognitions, which is now available in virtually every modern devise. The same intelligent systems and technology is what is used today to power self-driving cars and other powerful and complex systems capable communicating with each other (Wogu, 2019). These were features that were generally believed would not be possible to accomplish in machines in a very long time. From the above examples, however it is clear that innovations in technology in the 21ˢᵗ century has gone beyond man's expectations. This scenario is believed to have inlfeunce the opinion of Max Tegmark when he opined that:

Everything we love about civilization is a product of intelligence, so amplifying our human intelligence with artificial intelligence has the potential of helping civilization flourish like never before – as long as we manage to keep the technology beneficial… Technology is thus giving life the potential to flourish like never before… or to self-destruct. Let's make a difference (Tegmark, 2016, p. 1).

The Problematique of the Research

The main problem which initiated the writing of this chapter emerged from various advanced studies (Marquart, 2017; Davey, 2017) conducted by AI researchers on the fate of man in view of rising innovations and inventions now prevalent and made possible via AI technology, a scenario which many believe would herald the a situation described as *the extinction risks theory (it is a theory that foresees a time when human and their place in the labour industries would become extinct as a result of machines' ability to simulate virtually all the jobs and the role of mankind in the order of things via the platform of super-intelligence systems which they are beginning to acquire)*, a scenario which most social science and medical scientist infer, could have psychical and ontological consequences on the mental state of persons, especially those who fall in the category of those who must exchange their labour for a means of sustenance and livelihood, to the owners of the means of production. The problems raised here, studies reveal (Davey, 2017; Tegmark, 2016), cut across various endeavours and sectors of life like in: economics, job polarization, contingent labour and education. However, the under listed issues constitute some of the specific problems that motivated the study conducted in this chapter:

1. The rise in the number of literature which presents proofs of an impending AI threat to the *beingness* of mankind in the nearest future, amides the various advantages of innovations in AI.
2. The prevalence of the feelings of ontological lacks propelled by the drastic suffering and feeling of alienations which mankind experience as a result of the rising ability of intelligent machines to simulate various verity of man's jobs in the industry, a scenario observed to exert existential consequence on man's place as the being that must works to live and sustain its self here on earth.
3. Advances in innovations of IA technology has initiated an inimical rise in the number of jobs that have suffered from the impact of the 'massive job annihilation' taking place in industries of industrialized nations of the world..

Research Objectives for the Chapter

In view of the issues identified in the above context as the problems initiating the conduct of this research, the authors of this chapter are poised to evaluate critically, most of the contending arguments raised for and against the extinction risk theory which mankind fears, is beginning to have drastic effect on most automated jobs in the manufacturing industry. However, in more specific terms, the authors of this chapter are guided by the following objectives:

1. To identify, interrogate and evaluate the various arguments presented so far - for and against - the *scary extinction risk theory* with the view to ascertaining the validity of the claims on either side.
2. The chapter analyzes and seeks to identify in specific terms, the degree and classes of Marxian Alienations which man is perceived to experience as a result of the adoption of innovations in AI technology for daily life's endeavours in the industries and so on.
3. The authors would evaluate the claims of job annihilation presumed to be taking place in most of the industrialized nations of the world and evaluate the consequences of this supposed job annihilation, which is occasioned as a result of the adoption of innovations in AI technology for manufacturing industries.

Method Adopted for the Chapter

The chapter adopts the Marxian Alienation's Theory (Cox, 1998) as the theoretical platform for the chapter because the theory provides viable platforms for appropriately evaluating the degree and classes of estrangement people experience as a result of dwelling and working in a stratified society of social classes. An estrangement perceived to be initiated by the adoption of AI innovations for manufacturing industries by their capitalist owners. Creswell's mix-method research approach (Creswell, 2003) which favors the combined or separate use of both qualitative and quantitative research designs for analyzing contending arguments and data existing in the subject areas of this study, was adopted. Marilyn's *ex-post facto* research design (Marilyn, 2013) was utilized since the chapter largely relied and utilized data and analysis of findings obtained from previously conducted studies on the subject matter of the chapter. Deriders' deconstructive method (Balkin, 1987) for critically analyzing the meaning of terms issues in the social science and in philosophy, was also adopted for the research since the approach aids researchers to interrogate the meanings and rational provided for the various arguments, concepts and issues proposed and discussed so far about the existential and ontological risks which AI technology is believed to exerts on mankind.

Relevance and Justifications for the Chapter

Accepted that the issues identified above are the problems which initiated the study in this chapter, and considering the fact that these issues are considered fundamental and germane to contemporary scholars, there is thus an urgent need for existentialist scholars to attempt finding viable answers to some of the fundamental questions that have been raised over the years about the role of AI technology in the life of man, even in these contemporary times. Some of the questions in this category include:

1. Will AI technology provide new jobs commensurate with the ones it had destroyed thus far?
2. Would this same technology be able to provide jobs soon enough so as to hasten the transition from job 'A' to job 'B' effectively?
3. What will become the fate of workers who lose their place of work to the skills and ingenuity displayed by super-intelligent machines in the manufacturing industries?

The relevance of these questions and the need to find solution to them, affirms and justifies the timeliness and essence for attempting to address this questions and other issues raised in the chapter.

REVIEW OF RELATED LITERATURE AND THEORETICAL ANALYSIS

Artificial Intelligence (AI) and Other Minds

The term AI has often been used or referred to the general abilities machines and artifacts have for analyzing and processing data intelligently in ways that makes it possible for them (machines) to be able to learn and understand new materials and knowledge, often utilized for solving problems beneficial to man (Wogu, 2011; Wogu, Misra, Assibong, Olu-Owolabi, Maskeliunas & Damasevicius, 2019; Uhuegbu, Ukpokolo & Wogu, 2011). The advent of AI machines in the 21st Century have shaken the very foundations of what scholars are prepared to believe is meant by 'intelligence'. As such, scientist like B.F. Skinner observed that the issues at stake have gone beyond that of whether machines have mind or not. The real issue, he opines, is the question of whether humans really utilize the minds they believe to possess efficiently…"? (Lawhead, 2003).

Artificial Intelligence as a field of study emerged in response to the awareness and consciousness which machines have acquired over the years. On the other hand, Computer science is the branch of study which preoccupies itself with AI related studies. It also preoccupies itself with the designing of intelligent agents (Poole, Mackworth, & Goebel, 1998; Wogu, *et al*, 2017; Wogu, Misra, Assibong, Ogiri, Maskeliunas, & Damasevicius, 2018; Wogu, Misra, Olu-Owolabi, Assibong, Udoh; Ogiri; Maskeliunas…. & Damasevicius, 2018; and Wogu, 2010). Intelligent agents on the other hand are perceived as systems that are conscious of their environment, hence, thy take actions on their own to maximize its success rate (Russell & Norvig, 2003). Defining Artificial Intelligence - the man who coined the term 'AI' in 1956 - 'John McCarthy', opined that the discipline is all about the engineering and science of designing and using intelligent machines' (Crevier, 1993). The point emphasized here is that AI can be suitably perceived as that branch of science and engineering which focuses on aiding machines and artifacts to address complex issues via the simulations of humanlike intelligence through written algorithms in ways that computers can process. The study of AI has among other things, become a breath taking subject that is full of optimism. Irrespective of the hitches the discipline has suffered over the years, AI has emerged as a field of technology that seeks to provide solutions to the multifaceted issues inherent in the field of science, engineering and technology for the benefit of man.

Accepted that the mind is the seat of intelligence which human beings use to process information and solve problems, machines, in the same vein, are observed to behave in a manner typical to those of human intelligence, because they are presumed to possess the feature referred to as mind. Artifacts and machines which belong to this group (metaphysics and ontology), are stratified under the category of artifacts and machines which possess what scientists chose to refer to as 'Other Minds' (McCorduck,

2004). Some of the fundamental questions raised in this field of study include: How are artifacts able to acquire mental states, from where they are perceived to attain the abilities to behave in the same way individuals behave (intelligently)? Pertinent questions of this nature are the kind of questions (issues and problems) described as the problems of 'other minds', (Wogu, 2011) which is a sub set of the field of Ontology and Artificial Intelligence. Of the several questions that have been raised in these fields of study, the emphasis for this study focused on analyzing the questions that border on the kind of relationships that exists between innovations in AI technology and the harmful consequences it exerts on mankind.

Pros and Cons of Innovations in AI Technology

Studies (Bryant, 2014; Hawking, Tegmark, Russell & Wilczek, 2014) reveal that today's computers have gone beyond possessing intelligent capabilities to becoming conscious (intentionality) and super-intelligent machines with the ability to cultivate and maintain a mind of their own to the disadvantage of man (Marquart, 2017; Bryant, 2014; Griffin, 2015; Russell, 2015; Tegmark, 2016; Hawking, Tegmark, Russell & Wilczek, 2016). The abilities discovered in AI technologies have long gone beyond the realm of fiction and mythology. Studies indicate that via AI platforms, programs have successfully been written for automated trading systems in the finance industry, self-driving cars in the manufacturing industry, pace-making machines in the health industry, facial recognition devices in the information technology sector, the list goes on and on. However, irrespective of the clear advancements and advantages which AI technologies have brought the way of humans, scholars like Steven Hawking (Hawking, Tegmark, Russell & Wilczek, 2016), refused to be clouded by the seeming merits inherent in intelligent machines and devises powered by AI technology. Consequently, he, on a note of caution, asserted that:

'The successful creation of innovations powered by Artificial Intelligence, is indeed, the biggest event in the history of mankind. Sadly, this same feat might turn out to be the last major event before man goes into extinction by virtue of the hazards associated with these AI innovations. Man must therefore figure out ways of avoiding these hazards' (Hawking, Tegmark, Russell & Wilczek, 2016).

Apart from the opinion of Hawking from the Future of Life Institute (FLI). Other researchers like (Marquart, 2017; Azuela, Gerhard, Jean, & Cortés, 2005; Tegmark, 2016; Andrews, 2017 and Davey, 2017) were of the opinion that 'innovations in AI are fundamental to advancing the condition and quality of man's life on earth. For Tegmark, (Tegmark, 2016), he remarked that: 'While scholars at FLI, are disposed to recognizing the beneficial potentials inherent in AI technology, they are also quick to identify the fact that these AI systems have the potential to unintentionally or intentionally become hazardous to man in its line of duty'. He thus, reiterated the need for contemporary researchers in this area of study to extended and advance their research in the area of creating necessary awareness about the pros and cons of AI so that all concerned would be equipped with the knowledge they need both for policy formulations and for researchers and users of AI technology. This move he believes would better prepare all concerned with the likely hazards known to be associated with some of the products and devices emanating from AI technology in the future (Tegmark, 2016).

One of the areas where AI technology is perceived to be dangerous is in areas where it's been designed to be autonomous in its operation. Thus, where the need arises to perhaps, alter or change their operations, it (the machines) has been known to see such external attempts to alter its mode of operation, as a threat to its normal way of operation. Any such interference with its modus of operation would be perceived as an attempt to prevent it from attaining its initial goal and objectives. In situations like this, AI machines could unintentionally bring harm to mankind and its creator while attempting to prevent any external body from altering its mode of operation. Hence Prof. Hawking laments: "Artificial intelligence machines could kill us because they are too clever... Such computers could become so competent that they kill us by accident" (Griffin, 2015). Hawking perceives that the real risk with AI technologies is the fact that they will become extremely good at accomplishing their assigned tasks. However, where these tasks are not aligned with those of their human counterparts, most scholars believes that such situations will spell trouble or doom for mankind (Griffin, 2015).

Artificial Intelligence and the Alienation of the Human Psyche

Alienation is perceived as the kind of mental separation which individuals are forced to suffer from when they are denied an aspect of their essence as beings in the world. This scenario is often occasioned by man's position and place in a highly classified social class system (Cox, 1998). The theory, among other things, offers humanist researchers, the theoretical platforms for examining and evaluating the kind of relationships that transpires between persons as a consequence of their business interactions with other beings in nature. The interaction in questions is believed to be one of the main factors responsible for his predicament, one in which he seems totally subsumed by the forces of nature he had – through various labour processes - put in place to serve his purpose (Cox, 1998).

Alienations of the human psyche could be perceived as one of the scenarios or predicaments that emanate from occasions where, the reckless deployment of innovations in AI technology - in certain areas of human endeavour – have dehumanizes man such that he is displaced from his *beingness* (the knowledge of self-fulfillment which man gets from actualizing his existence when he succeeds in doing what make him happy, satisfied and fulfilled, for instance) to the point where it causes him/her onto-logical and or existential harm (Russell, 2015; Hawking, Tegmark, Russell & Wilczek, 2014; Marcus, 2013; Hendry, 2014; Armstrong, 2014). The most profound of one of the consequences arising from such reckless adoption of AI technology, is perhaps, the fear that super-intelligent machines present to the mind of the individuals (human psyche). This kind of fear - to existentialist scholars - is known as 'the extinction risk threat' (the fear that the presence of intelligent machines in the industries translates to the extinction of human jobs and soon, 'human beings' from the labour market) (Armstrong, 2014). In the light of this, Stuart Armstrong opined that 'what humanity must fear is the ability for super-intelligent machines to desire to replace man on account of their (man's) inefficiency and lack of precision when it comes to meeting targets and goals. The way AI machines see it, 'man has failed to live up with the required intelligence essential for daily functioning and productivity' (Armstrong, 2014). Armstrong thus suggests that contemporary thinkers ought to occupy themselves with the thought of how to retain their existential relevance before machines decide to remove them from the scene and fully take over their responsibilities.

Scholars from the social sciences tend to associate ontological and existential problems emanating from threats orchestrated by the arising adoption of AI technology with the Marxist Alienation theory (Cox, 1998). This is because the labour force behooves on the human nature as the only viable avenue through which its daily needs can be met. Marx further argues that without the labour of the individual, human nature would not function smoothly the way it is expected to function. The labour process for

Marx is thus the process through which the worker changes the worlds he lives in. Inversely, the changes he put in place, unwillingly sets into motion the need for introducing innovations into the processes of production for the purpose of enhancing the products from his labour and his way of life. By so doing, the labour of the individual initiates a sets of changes, developments and transformations in his society (Cox, 1998).

The advent of innovations in AI, adopted and utilized in manufacturing industries have unfortunately, changed the statuesque man was used to. Consequently, it now appears that the labour of man is no longer a prerequisite for changing the world for the betterment of man. This is so because capitalist's economies have - in the bid to cut down cost and maximize profit - changed the processes in the production line with the innovations and tools formulated from AI technology, which were created by man himself. Tools that produce more at little or no cost to the owners of the means of production. Tools that, from all indication, have put man in a not too comfortable spot. Scholars believe that 'mankind have never before, been put on such a spot, as a result of the creation of his own labour. Never before has the creation of his hand so threatened the ontological and existential essence of his being. Commenting on the above issue, Judy Cox laments: 'Never before have we felt so helpless in the face of the forces we ourselves created' (Cox, 1998).

Responding to Karl Marx's question on the essence of human labour, the chapter argues that when man finds himself in a situation where he begins to compete with the very works of his hand (AI technology), a technology that have been proven to produce more, faster and at lesser cost than the original creator could possibly muster, he is left with no choice than to become alienated from the works of his hand and his nature. This scenario exposes him to various other types/classes of alienation which were clearly defined in Karl Marx theory of Alienation: (i) **Alienation of the worker from his work and his product.** This class of Alienation portrays a scenario where the worker is estranged from the works of his hands to the extent that he is not able to enjoy the satisfaction or benefits that comes from the product and labour of his own hands, as a result of the condition of labor put in place by the capitalist himself. (ii) **Alienation of the worker from the act of production**. This type of alienation makes reference to the kind of estrangement that emerges as a result of the helpless situation which the worker is exposed to since the product of his hands are reduced to the value of insufficient wages which the capitalist pays for the product produced by the worker. Such wages have been known to be insufficient for the worker to buy the goods for himself. (iii) **Alienation of the worker from what Karl Marx called "their Gattungswesen (species-essence).** This scenario describes the kind of estrangement that distorts the psychology/mind of the worker. The worker in this case suffers from a kind of dehumanization from the conditions which the capitalist expose the worker to, during the cause of production. (iv) **Alienation from human nature**. This kind of estrangement takes place when the capitalist succeed in pitching the worker against his fellow worker when he the capitalist introduces and uneven wage stratification among workers that tends to cause them to rise and compete for even smaller wages as a result of a scarcity of jobs in the labour market (Gouldner, 1984; Dictionary of Philosophy, 1984).

AI AND EXISTENTIAL RISK THREATS IN AMERICA'S LABOUR FORCE

Studies among scholars likes (Andrews, 2017; Davey, 2017; and Tegmark, 2016) revealed that one of the topmost issues discussed amongst existentialists and ontological scholars in America is the threat AI technology poses on the labour force around the globe, especially in industrialized societies of the world.

Figure 1. Work distribution in the US
Source: IPUMS-CPS/University of Minnesota. Credit: Quoctrung Bui/NPR

Figure 2. US productivity, GDP, employment & income: 1953-2011
Source: (Centus Beauro, Bureau of labour Statistics, 2012).

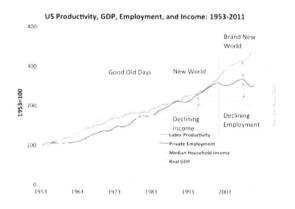

This reality is re-enforced by the fact that an unprecedented number of workers lose what philosophers refer to as, 'their *beingness*' (the essence for which they [humans] exist as human beings on earth) as a result of the various classes of alienation orchestrated by the widespread use of AI innovations which have in-turn, boosted ongoing industrial revolution amongst capitalist all over the world (Davey, 2017; Tegmark, 2016). The rise in the use of AI technology in manufacturing industries have increased the number of factory workers who lose their roles and relevance on the production line, hence they lose their jobs to technology and machines. The situation expressed in the above context and as further ex-emplified in (Figure 3.) adds credence to Moshe Vardi's fears when he noted that:

The future of work is now...! The impact of technology on the labor force have become clearer as the days go by. Machines have already automated millions of routine working-class jobs in manufacturing. And now, AI technological devices are learning to automate non-routine jobs in transportation and logistics, legal writing, financial services, administrative support and healthcare (Davey, 2017).

Figure 3. US manufacturing is the largest sector; 2014 gross output in trillion dollars
Source: BEA

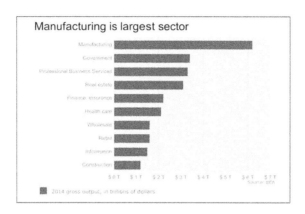

The existentialist's are troubled by the fact that a continuous rise in the adoption of AI innovations for manufacturing industries would destroy more jobs in this century, as indicated in the data presented in (Figure 2.) & (Figure 4.). Both diagrams vividly illustrates that, despite the fact that the rise in GDP is sustained for jobs with little or no automation, individuals in manufacturing industries who get their jobs automated every now and then, tend to lose their jobs while productivity in GDP continues to rise in these sectors. While few displaced skilled individuals get new jobs after a while, thereby remaining employed, majority of the unskilled are thrown into the streets and out of job. It is the view of most economists that all those displaced and thrown out from their jobs won't be able to comprehend the degrading existential and ontological reality they will be faced with, when the times comes (Davey, 2017).

Figure 4. US real manufacturing output vs. employment 1974-2014
Source: Daniel Miessler. (2014). US manufacturing is as strong as ever https://danielmiessler.com/blog/u-s-manufacturing-is-as-strong-as-ever-we-justneed-way-fewer-people-to-do-it/

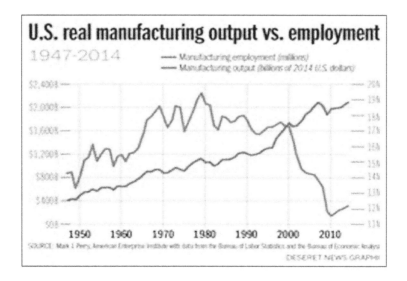

The information in (Figure 1.) illustrations the scenario that is found in the US labour force. It identifies the various classes of job distribution and those states with high automation density. The diagram in (Figure 3.) signifies the various classes of job specification in the US and how the manufacturing industry is the largest sector with the greatest number of labour force employed per time. However, it is the sector experiencing the greatest degree of job annihilation threat, as a result of the massive automation of most of its jobs.

SUMMARY OF FINDINGS

For the purpose of exhausting the discussions on the influence and effect which ongoing simulations and automation of human jobs in the manufacturing industries is having on workers in America's labour force, and for the purpose of identifying the classes of alienation at play in different scenarios, the authors at this point, present a summary of findings and results obtained from the various studies and analysis considered for the objectives of this study:

1. A survey conducted in 2013 about the nature of jobs in the US, indicated that 47% of America's labour force were engaged in jobs with high risk of being automated in a decade or two from now as indicated in (Figure 1).[Class I, II and III of Marxian Alienation is evident in this case].
2. The past 30 years in the Rust Belt regions of America, had witnessed a loss of over 8 million jobs with the rising adoption of AI technology in the manufacturing industry alone. This loss of jobs was identified as one of the factors that crippled the US economy, thus leaving a class of workers within the age ranges of 25 - 54 with no college education, out on the streets with no jobs. This is exemplified in (Figure 2. & Figure 4.)[class I, II, III & IV of Marxian Alienation is evident in this case]
3. The most common and lucrative job in the US is the Truck driving job. This also stands to be lost soon with the rising automation of the role of drivers in industries and outside the industries with the invention of the intelligence that power self-driving cars and automobiles. See (Figure 1.), (Figure 2.), (Figure 3.), & (Figure 4.) for details. The class of Alienation experienced by those affect by this AI innovations is the (Class III & IV Alienation).
4. In Detroit, three of the largest companies in 1990 with an estimated worth of $65 Billion, had 1.2 Million persons as her labour force. However, in 2016, three Silicon Valley largest companies, with the estimated worth of $1.5 Trillion, only had 190,000 people in her work force (Davey, 2017). From this results, it appears that as companies become larger and make more money, fewer human labour is required, a situation made possible by the massive automations and adoption of AI technology. The data in (Figure 2.) & (Figure 4.) adds credence to this argument. The classes of Alienation at play here are those of (Class II & IV Alienation).

From the findings made in the above context, scholars like (Davey, 2017; Armstrong, 2014; Price & Tallinn, 2012; Muehlhauser and Koch & Russell, 2014) are convinced that the massive adoption of innovations in AI technology is poised to eventually annihilate most human jobs sooner than it's been predicted to take place. This invariably will increase the number of the unemployed in the society as exemplifies clearly in (Figure 4). Other scholars like (Davey, 2017; Tegmark, 2016) believe this scenario might eventually lead to the situation where people will rise up in a great revolution. The remarks by Andrew McAfee, in a closing statement presented at the end of the 2017 Asilomar AI Conference (Wogu, Olu-Owolabi, Assibong, Apeh, Agoha, Sholarin, Elegbeleye… & Igbokwe, 2017), corroborates the idea that man would soon reach the point where they would rise up in revolution against the eventual birthing of the era where the role and duties of man is taken over by super-intelligent machines.

RECOMMENDATIONS

In view of the findings made so far from the analyses of the various studies considered for the objectives highlighted for this chapter, the authors of this chapter deem the following recommendations germane to addressing the challenges associated with the rising innovations emanating from AI and super-intelligent technologies:

1. The authors of this chapter join their voices with those of other scholars like: Steve Wozniak, Stephen Hawking and Bill Gates, who have expressed troubling concerns in international conferences, high impact journals, workshops, books and other kinds of media platforms, with a view to raising adequate awareness about the extinction risks theory looming over mankind. AI researchers would thus, be fostering a healthy future if the start now to work together to find answers to the complex questions of how they (AI technologies) and mankind can co-exist (Marquart, 2017).
2. 21st Century scholars and scientists of AI research are enjoined to strive together in ensuring that future inventions and research in AI technology would be such that the goals of AI technology and super-intelligent machines would align with those of mankind. Programs that drive these super-intelligent machines should be designed in such a manner that they will be amenable to control, irrespective of the degree independence they may have as machines.
3. The need to control human scientific and technological research endeavours at all levels, especially in AI research and in AI technology labs, accentuates the relevance of adopting the 23 AI Ashimolar Principles. It's soon implementation would help reduce the chances of producing scientist who will birth machines capable of acquiring the autonomy that will allow them run amok and eventually take over man's job totally.
4. Schools and universities must begin to prepare their students and graduates to remain relevant even in an era of ever increasing innovations in the world of AI technology. Those already in the work force must, as a matter of necessity, upgrade their skills with essential training in advanced skills and certifications that would increase their relevance and job opportunities alongside rising AI innovation .

CONTRIBUTION TO KNOWLEDGE

Findings and observations made so far in this research, gave the authors reasons to believe that the thesis presented in this chapter - when published and its content assimilated and implemented by all concerned - would make the following pertinent contributions to the world of knowledge:

1. The findings made from this study goes a long away to further affirm and justify the 'extinction risks threat'. The study affirms that these claims indeed, are more real than an over exclamation, as most scholars have presumed it to be. Thus, all concered must necessarily begin to take steps towards addressing the matters arising from this study, since it is no longer a myth.

2. The study at present, is the most recent account on the nature and degree of alienations which mankind and indeed, the labour force in America is currently experiencing. As such, the study provides up-to date data and information on matters arising from the rising adoption of innovations in AI technology, as adopted and implemented by owners of US based manufacturing industries.

3. Data gathered from the studies and analysis conducted in this research, further highlight and presents and up to date information on the degree of job annihilations taking place in US manufacturing industries, to the detriment of mankind. These current data would come in handy for policy evaluations and for future research in related areas.

4. The study for the first time in Nigeria and indeed Africa, brings to the fore, the 'job annihilations' and 'extinction risk threat' theory which has so far humbled existentialist researchers in America. There is therefore the need for African scholars and existentialists researchers in the field of AI and related fields, to join forces with their counterparts in advanced countries in research labs all over the world, to find ways of aligning the goals of machines with those of mankind.

CONCLUSION

Despite the identifiable achievements of AI innovations in the 21st century, the future of mankind without prejudice to current realities, could be described as one which will eventually become miserable to him, especially considering the rate at which advances in AI technology are massively automating human jobs in American industries.

Studies conducted in this chapter affirmed that, since intelligence is a quality that grows over a period of time, and since it was established that today's machines have acquired a mind of their own, then the ability for these machines to attain an increasing capacity for acquiring super-intelligent capabilities would in fact take place no sooner than anticipated. Thus, studies in this area of research needs to be taken seriously since data gathered in this study so far, revealed that the process of job annihilation has already began and its gaining an alarming speed worthy of note.

The present state of affairs of workers in America's labour force, (the high rate at which the majority of the work force in American industries have lost their jobs to IA machines simulations/automation) indicates that there is a rising proportion of persons in the labour force who are daily experiencing various classes of the Marxian alienation as a result of rising adoption of AI innovations for her manufacturing industries. Thus, more time and research needs to be devoted to finding ways of aligning the goals of AI with those of mankind.

REFERENCES

Andrews, A. (2017). Alexander Peysakhovich's theory on artificial intelligence. *Pacific Standard Magazine*. Retrieved from https://psmag.com/magazine/alexander-peysakhovich-30-under-30

Armstrong, S. (2014). Artificial intelligence poses 'extinction risk' to humanity says Oxford University's Stuart Armstrong. *Huffington Post UK*. Retrieved from http://www.huffingtonpost.co.uk/2014/03/12/extinction-artificial-intelligence-oxford-stuart-armstrong_n_4947082.html

Azuela, J., H., S., Gerhard, R., Jean, S., & Cortés, U. (2005). *Advances in artificial intelligence theory*. Center for Computing Research of IPN.

Balkin, J., M. (1987). Deconstructive practice and legal theory. *Yale L.J., 96*(15).

Bryant, M. (2014). 'Artificial intelligence could kill us all'. Meet the man who takes that risk seriously. *The Next Web (TNW) Online publication*. Retrieved from https://thenextweb.com/insider/2014/03/08/ai-could-kill-all-meet-mantakes-risk- seriously/#.tnw_hVchaHqU

Cox. J. (1998). An introduction to Marx's theory of alienation. *International Socialism: Quarterly Journal of the Socialist Workers Party, 5*(79).

Creswell, J. W. (2003). *Research design: Qualitative and quantitative approaches*. Thousand Oaks, CA: SAGE.

Crevier, D. (1993). *A.I, The tumultuous search for artificial intelligence*. New York, NY: Basic Books.

Davey, T. (2017). Artificial Intelligence and the Future of Work: An Interview With Moshe Vardi. *Future of Life*. Retrieved from https://futureoflife.org/2017/06/14/artificial-

Dictionary of Philosophy. (1984). Alienation. In The Dictionary of Philosophy (2nd ed.). Academic Press.

Ghafourifar, A. (2017). 14 ways AI will impact the education sector. *Entefy*. Retrieved from https://venturebeat.com/2017/07/23/14-ways-ai-will-impact-the-education-sector/

Gouldner, A. W. (1984). *The two Marxisms*. New York: Oxford University Press.

Hawking, S., Tegmark, M., Russell, S., & Wilczek, F. (2014). Transcending complacency on Super-intelligent machines. *Hoffpost*. Online publication. http://www.huffingtonpost.com/stephen-hawking/artificial-intelligenceb5174265.html

Hendry, E. R. (2014). What happens when artificial intelligence turns on us? *Smithsonian.com*. Retrieved from http://www.smithsonianmag.com/innovation/what-happens-when- artificial-intelligence-turns-us-180949415/

Independent News. (2015). Retrieved from http://www.independent.co.uk/life-style/gadgets-and-tech/news/stephen- hawking-artificial-intelligence-could-wipe-out-humanity-when-it-gets-too-clever-as-humans-a6686496.html

Kasparove, G. (1996). The day I sensed a new kind of intelligence. *Time Magazine*. Retrieved from http://content.time.com/time/subscriber/article/0,33009,984305-1,00.html

Lawhead, F. W. (2003). A case for artificial intelligence. In Philosophical Journey: An interactive approach (2nd ed.). McGraw Hill.

Marcus, G. (2013). Why we should think about the threat of Artificial Intelligence. *The New Yorker*. Retrieved from http://www.newyorker.com/tech/elements/why-we-should-think-about-the-threat-of-artificial-intelligence

Marilyn, K. (2013). *Ex-post facto research: Dissertation and scholarly research, Recipes for success*. Seattle, WA: Dissertation Success LLC. Retrieved from http://www.dissertationrecipes.com/wp-content/uploads/2011/04/Ex-Post-Facto-research.pdf

Marquart, S. (2017). Aligning super intelligence with human interests. *Future of Life*. Retrieved from https://futureoflife.org/2017/07/18/aligning-superintelligence-with- human-interests/

McCorduck, P. (2004). 'Machines who think': 25th Anniversary Edition. *RAQ Online*. Retrieved from http://www.pamelamc.com/html/machines_who_think.html

Muehlhauser, L., Koch, C., & Russell. (2014). *On machine super- intelligence. Machine Intelligence Research Institute (MIRI)*. Online publication of MIRI: https://intelligence.org/2014/05/13/christof-koch-stuart-russell- machine- superintelligence/

Poole, D., Mackworth, A., & Goebel, R. (1998). *Computational intelligence: A logical approach*. Oxford University Press.

Price, H., & Tallinn, J. (2012). Artificial intelligence- Can we keep it in the Box? *The Conversation: Academic rigour, journalistic flair*. Retrieved from http://theconversation.com/artificial-intelligence-can-we-keep-it-in-the-box-8541

RileyMar, T. (2017). *Artificial intelligence goes deep to beat humans at poker*. Retrieved from http://www.sciencemag.org/news/2017/03/artificial-intelligence-goes-deep-beat-humans-poker

Russell, S. (2015). This artificial intelligence pioneer has a few concerns. *Quanta Magazine*. Retrieved from https://www.wired.com/2015/05/artificial-intelligence-pioneer-concerns/

Russell, S., & Norvig, P. (2003). Artificial Intelligence: A modern approach (3rd ed.). Prentice Hall.

Tegmark, M. (2016). Benefits and risks of artificial intelligence. *Future of Life*. Retrieved from https://futureoflife.org/background/benefits- risks-of-artificial- intelligence/

Uhuegbu, C., Ukpokolo, I., & Wogu, I. A. (2011). Advances in the History and Philosophy of Science. Lulu Enterprise, Inc.

Wogu, I. A. (2010). Ancient Greek Philosophers and their Philosophy. In I. A. Wogu (Ed.), *A Preface to Logic, Philosophy and Human Existence* (pp. 14–62). Lagos, Nigeria: *Pumack Educational Publishers*.

Wogu, I. A. P. (2011). *Problems in Mind: A new approach to age long problems and questions in philosophy and the cognitive science of human development*. Pumack Nigeria Limited Education Publishers.

Wogu, I. A. P., Misra, S., Assibong, P. A., Ogiri, S. O., Maskeliunas, R., & Damasevicius, R. (2018). Super-Intelligent machine operations in 21st century manufacturing industries: A boost or doom to political and human development? In *Towards Extensible and Adaptable Methods in Computing*. Springer Nature Singapore Plc. Ltd. Retrieved from https://link.springer.com/chapter/10.1007/978-981-13-2348-5_16

Wogu, I. A. P., Misra, S., Assibong, P. A., Olu-Owolabi, E. F., Maskeliunas, R., & Damasevicius, R. (2019). Artificial Intelligence, Smart Classrooms and Online Education in the 21st Century: Implications for Human Development. *Journal of Case on Information Technology, 21*(3). Retrieved from https://www.igi-global.com/article/artificial-intelligence-smart-classrooms-and-online-education-in-21st-century/227679?camid=4v1

Wogu, I. A. P., Misra, S., Olu-Owolabi, F. E., Assibong, P. A., & Oluwakemi, D. (2018). Artificial intelligence, artificial teachers and the fate of learners in the 21st century education sector: Implications for theory and practice. *International Journal of Pure and Applied Mathematics, 119*(16), 2245-2259. Retrieved from https://acadpubl.eu/hub/2018-119-16/issue16b.html https://acadpubl.eu/hub/2018-119-16/2/232.pdf

Wogu, I. A. P., Olu-Owolabi, F. E., Assibong, P. A., Apeh, H. A., Agoha, B. C., Sholarin, M. A., . . . Igbokwe, D. (2017). *Artificial intelligence, alienation and ontological problems of other minds: A critical investigation into the future of man and machines.* Retrieved from https://www.scopus.com/record/display.uri?eid=2-s2.0-85047079881&origin=resultslist&sort=plf-f&src=s&st1=ICCNI+&nlo=&nlr=&nls=&sid=02fcb90c5e2fe9f02e52574629f67b0d&sot=b&sdt=b&sl=12&s=CONF%28ICCNI+%29&relpos=51&citeCnt=0&searchTerm=

Wogu, I. A. P., Sanjay Misra, J., Assibong, P. A., Adewumi, A., Maskeliunas, R., & Damasevicius, R. (2018). A critical review of the politics of artificial intelligent machines, alienation and the existential risk threat to America's labour force. *Lecture Notes in Computer Science, 10963*, 217-232. Retrieved from https://link.springer.com/chapter/10.1007/978-3-319-95171-3_18

Chapter 15
The Politics of Domestic Violence Laws Against Women and the Dignity of Womanhood:
An Appraisal of Human Factor Issues in Emerging Polities

Ikedinachi Ayodele Power Wogu
Rhema University, Nigeria

Ayotunde Elegbeleye
Covenant University, Ota, Nigeria

Kalu Uche Uwaoma
Rhema University, Nigeria

Charles Nathaniel Chukwuedo
Federal College of Education Technology, Asaba, Nigeria

Morris Edogiawere
Igbenigiong University, Okada, Nigeria

Chidiebere Aguziendu
Covenant University, Ota, Nigeria

Sanjay Misra
https://orcid.org/0000-0002-3556-9331
Covenant University, Ota, Nigeria

ABSTRACT

Studies on domestic violence against women (DVAW) reveals that the patriarchal and socio-cultural mindset of Nigerians, which tend to dignify the roles of men over women, thus encumbering the full implementation of the laws designed to protect the dignity of womanhood, is at the crux of factors militating against women. With the culture violence theory as theoretical framework for the study, Marilyn's ex-post-facto research method was adopted since the chapter utilized data gathered from previously analyzed studies on the subject of DVAW. Socio-cultural and the lackadaisical behavior of politicians were identified as pertinent factors influencing the rising cases of DVAW recorded, despite the presence of the Violence Against Persons Prohibition Act (VAPPA) laws that prohibit violence against persons in states, a factor impeding most women from attaining their full potential and dignity in African societies. The need to strengthen and increase sensitization about the essence of VAPPA laws and what women and girls stand to achieve by its enforcement were emphasized.

DOI: 10.4018/978-1-7998-1279-1.ch015

INTRODUCTION

Background to the Study

Domestic Violence Against Women' (DVAW) has since become an age long phenomenon (Kaur & Garg, 2008) discussed more frequently among human right's scholars, lawyers and activists for over a century now. Hence, issues concerning DVAW are known to cuts across race, religions, culture, and international boundaries with rising cases in the number of women and children who are placed in harm's way every day (Oyediran & Abanihe-Isiugo, 2005; Abayomi, Kolawole & Olabode, 2013). Most scholars argue that reports about cases of DVAW and several other kinds of abuse have become a menace which has eaten deep into the fabric of nations where these cases are rampant. It is reported that this kind of violence is responsible for more of the sudden death cases recorded among women in contemporary societies around the globe (Abayomi, Kolawole & Olabode, 2013). The scenario is worse off for women and young girls living in war torn and crisis infested areas. Such women are more prone to losing their dignity and womanhood to all kinds of violence. Some of the types of violence women are confronted with in include: gang rap, intimidation, all kind of sexual harassments, often leading to the use of women and young girl as instruments of war by rebel's forces that are opposed to the government (Oyediran & Abanihe-Isiugo, 2005). Other kinds of domestic violence meted on women include: female genital mutilation, various forms of physical abuses, forced marriage, sexual assault, and so on (Oyediran & Abanihe-Isiugo, 2005).

The menace of DVAW seems to persist because it has become more like a norm or an acceptable way of life by many African cultures that are largely founded on patriarchal lines. Hence, these cultures accept some forms of violence as measures and avenues for discharging some form of disciple to erring wives and women under their care (Aihie, 2009). Viewed from this perspective, DVAW becomes a function of the very low perception and position which the women folks fall into, considering the hierarchy or status which women in African societies are accorded in their cultures and communities. It has thus been argued that in societies where there are clear cut roles assigned to each gender in a male dominated society, the women folks are often not equipped to protect themselves from the kind of abuse that are often directed at them by their male counterparts. Hence, the World Health Organization (WHO, 2002) observed that husbands who commit battery on their wives do so under the guise of exercising their cultural giving rights by law, to subjugate and conquer their wives any time they fall out of line and go beyond their boundaries in the family or in the society (Kaur & Garg, 2008; Hart, 2015). This kind of violence against the womenfolk is often perceived as the prerogative of the husband to discipline his wife who by nature, is prone to behaving in ways regarded as inimical and a threat to the position of the man who by nature and traditions, is heads of the family in virtually every society. Consequently, such gross acts of indiscipline must be curbed by the husband with appropriate sanctions (Oyediran & Abanihe-Isiugo, 2005; Aihie, 2009).

Would this factor explain why the rate of DVAW in African and in Nigeria in particular, continues to increase? Going by the recent report by CLEEN Foundation who conducted a survey in 2013 on the frequency of the cases of reports on DVAW, the summary of their survey results indicates that the past three years had witnessed an increase (21% in 2011 to 30% in 2013) in the number of cases of DVAW recorded in the country alone (CLEEN, 2013). This implies that Nigeria have one of the highest rates of cases of DVAW in the African continent. Could the lackadaisical behaviour of politicians in the African continent be one of the causes for the rising cases of DVAW reported so far? Could this explain why the 2015 Violence Against Persons Prohibition Act (VAPPA) laws of Lagos State, have not really taken any strong footing towards addressing the issues of DVAW? Do cultural factors largely explain why most women, rather endure the situation they find themselves in, instead of fight to preserve their dignity in a male dominated world? Are religious and cultural factors responsible for why most African women are contented with the cruelty they are exposed to from the hands of their male counterparts? These critical questions regarding the issues of DVAW in Nigeria, its causes and effects on the dignity of womanhood, constitutes the central issues which this chapter seeks to find answers to. The urgent need to address the rising inimical trend in Nigeria and beyond, justifies the timeliness of the study conducted in this chapter.

The *Problematique* of the Paper

The central issue before the chapter is the problems of understanding and addressing the factors that continues to render of no effect, all the efforts made towards abating the rising trends of DVAW, even in presence of the recently promulgated VAPPA laws in Lagos state. However, in more specific terms, the problems that promoted the writing of this chapter include:

1. The fact that recent studies revealed that the patriarchal and cultural nature of the African polity largely encourages the high level politicking militating against the full enforcement of the recently enacted VAPPA laws in Nigeria.
2. The trend of events with regards to the rising cases of DVAW, if not checked, would soon totally annihilate whatever is left of the dignity of womanhood and the rights of the girl child in Africa and in Nigeria in particular.
3. Results of recent studies (Oyediran & Abanihe-Isiugo, 2005; Hart, 2015; Ogunjuyigbe, Akinlo and Ebigbola, 2005) revealed that a majority of women in African and in Nigeria (Eti-Osa LGA) are more inclined to believing that DVAW has become an African cultural phenomenon that have come to stay, hence they tend to endure their plight rather than to crying out, with a view to seeking out viable ways of preventing the continued sacrilege meted on the dignity of womanhood in the 21st century.

Aims and Objectives of the Study

In the light of the above issues identified as factors which necessitated the writing of this chapter, the authors are poised to, among other things, interrogate the factors militating against the full implementation and enforcement of the 2015 VAPPA laws in Nigeria. However, in more specific terms, the under listed points consist of some of the main objectives which the authors of this chapter are poised to achieve:

1. To identify and interrogate the most prevailing factors militating against governments' inability to enforce the 2015 VAPPA laws in a patrimonial culture such as Nigeria's and in Eti-Osa LGA in particular.
2. The authors seek to identify and propose more viable ways of curbing the rising menace of the cases of DVAW in Nigeria and in Eti-Osa LGA in particular.

3. The chapter seeks to construct and promote effective and efficient path ways of sensitizing women and the girl child about the existence of this laws and how and why they must continue to seek out ways of sustaining and upholding the dignity of womanhood by all means, irrespective of cultural settings and laws which they may find themselves.

Theory and Methodology for the Study

With the 'culture violence theory' (Wolfgang, & Ferracuti, 1976) adopted as the theoretical framework to guide the analysis intended to be carried out later in the for the chapter, the authors largely relied on Marilyn's ex-*post facto* research design and method (Marilyn, 2013) since the chapter largely relied and utilized data and analysis of findings obtained from previously analised studies on the subject matter of domestic violence against women. Creswell's mix-method approach (Creswell, 2003) which allows for a combination or the separate use of qualitative and quantitative research designs for gathering and analyzing data obtained from focused group discussion (FGD) and private interview sessions, was utilized to obtain most of the data adopted in this chapter, since the methods favour the attainment of the objectives earmarked for this chapter. In all, these methods were instrumental for interrogating and attaining the factors that continues to impede the enforcements of the 2015 VAPPA laws and policies in Nigeria. Derrida's deconstructive and reconstructive method (Balkin, 1987) of analyzing deeper meanings of concepts and arguments was also utilized for the various studies conducted in the chapter.

Relevance and Justification for the Study

The need to identify and addresses the factors responsible for the poor nature of results obtained from recent studies and surveys which depicts a sharp rise in the number of cases of DVAW in the country, even in the presence of the newly promulgated VAPPA laws of Lagos state, justifies the urgent need for conducting this present study. The need to de-lopotomise the minds of women and the girl child who from studies conducted by (Oyediran, & Abanihe-Isiugo, 2005; CLEEN, 2013; Arisi, 2011), are observed as beginning to get accustomed to the fact that, men from the African cultural setting have every religious and cultural rights to subjugate the female folk as they please, especially when it is clear that a bride prize had already been paid over the head of the women concerned, as captured in studies by (Oyediran, & Abanihe-Isiugo, 2005; CLEEN, 2013; Arisi, 2011). This fact, these studies reveal, are some of the reasons why most women have freely given up on the efforts directed at gaining back any iota of the sense of dignity amongst most women of the 21st century.

LITERATURE ON DOMESTIC VIOLENCE AGAINST WOMEN

Conceptual Clarifications

Violence is largely perceived as a universal scourge that eats deep into the heart of every known community, hence, its presence threatens the health, the state of mind and the lives of everyone in the community were such violence exists. It has been projected that over 1.6 million lives are lost annually as a result of violent *activities* (Chamberlain, 2018). Violence has also been projected to be one of the main causes of death among people within the ages of 15-44 year old. Due to its frequency, most scholars (Chamberlain, 2018; Washburn, 2018) now consider the phenomenon of DVAW as a common feature which human nature cannot do without, hence it has been perceived as a common feature of human existence that would always need to be responded to but not necessarily to prevent (WHO, 2002). This perhaps explains why most scholars find the concept of violence notoriously difficult to conceptualize since as a phenomenon, "it is multi-faceted, socially constructed and highly ambivalent" (Haan, 2008). Scholars like David Richie defined violence as "an act of physical hurt often deemed legitimate by the performer and illegitimate by (some) witness" (Haan, 2008). It has also been perceived as the exertion of force or power over other persons by certain other person, an agency, or a social process which tends to deny some individuals their humanity or by limiting them from actualizing their full potentials (Haan, 2008).

Domestic Violence Against Women

Domestic violence is perceived as a kind of conflict or clash that could ensure between house hold members or extended family members, a scenario that could manifest either through inflicting physical harm, sexual assault, or the fear of being inflicted with physical harm. The class of persons that could be involved with this kind of violence include: Parent-children relations, adult people related by blood and those not related by blood, those dating or in a relationships leading to marriage, former spouses, household members and other category of members in the family. The kind of abuse that constitutes domestic violence include: Blame, Jealousy, Isolation, Intimidation, Threats and Coercion, Economic abuse, Emotional abuse, Sexual abuse and Physical abuse.

Violence against women on the other hand is often perceived as a form of violation and discrimination of the rights of women to act and exercise freely, their fundamental human rights' in the society. Consequently, the lives of those affected are plunged into deep misery with their lives cut short. Numerous number of women today live in fear and pain arising from scares created by several forms of violence in the world today. Examples of violent actions that could cause pain or harm to the women folk include: suffering, coercion, mental, physical or sexual harm, threat to life and a denial of liberty (Foster, & Dyer, 2010). Put mildly, the notion of domestic violence has an array of meanings without no specific authoritative meaning ascribed to it. Put more mildly, violence against women in developed nations of the world is recognized as a public health problem because its effect on women has more far reaching consequences on the mental and physical state of the woman and the girl child. (Krantz, & Garcia-Moreno, 2005).

Forms of Domestic Violence Against Women

The following examples are some of the forms of violence which scholars have done extensive studies on: 'Human Trafficking' which manifest in two different ways: Labour trafficking and Sex trafficking (Foster & Dyer, 2010) and 'Sexual violence' which often comes in the form of sexual assault or rap (Reitan, 2001). Another form of violations against women include: Female genital mutilation (Mandara, 2004). This could occur in either four different ways: (1) The partial or total removal of the clitoris, (2) There is the excision of the clitoris and the labia minora. In most cases, labia majora have been removed in the process. (3) This involves the narrowing of the Vagina opening through the creation of a covering seal. The process in known as 'Infibulation'. (4) The fourth type is associated with any kind of excruciating exercise (poking, piercing and cutting of the labia or the clitoris or any exercise that could bring harm to the delicate contents/tissues in the vagina which will ultimately bring harm upon it. The most common form of female genital mutilation is the process where the labia minora and the clitoris is removed. Studies (Mandara, 2004) reveal that this process accounts for over 80% of all known cases recorded in places like Nigeria, Mali, Northern Kenya, Ethiopia and Southern Egypt (Kaur & Garg, 2008). Of the listed countries above, Nigeria is known to have the highest number of cases of female genital mutilation, largely because of her teaming population (Okeke, Anyaehie, & Ezenyeaku, 2012). Sexual violence and abuse however, seems to constitute a large portion of some of the recorded cases of spousal violence (Kaur & Garg, 2008).

Another form of DVAW include: Honor killing, a scenario where the lives of women are forcefully taken from them on account of protecting one family, ethnic, religious or societal honor or the other (Mayell, 2002; Sharma, 2016). It is important to note that this practice cut across virtually all communities and most predominant religions. For instance, women have been killed for getting pregnant outside marriage. Such acts, for certain customs and religion, is a violation of their codes of conduct. To these cultures and religions, the death sentence is usually the penalty for this kid of act. Most times, while the victims (the women) are punished for bringing dishonor to the family, society, and so on, those men responsible for perpetrating such acts with these women, go unpunished (Kulwicki, 2002). Other forms of DVAW worthy of note in this chapter include: Sexual Harassment, often directed against the women folk. It is globally perceived to be an offensive act that violates the fundamental human rights' of women. It also violates their dignity in so many ways (Abe, 2012). Where this form of harassment takes place in the work place, it's been known to exert certain emotional and psychological pressure on the women folk, thus hampering their productivity and performance (Idris, Adaja, Audu, & Aye, 2016).

Theoretical Framework for the Study

Series of theories have been propounded by scholars researching on the subject of DVAW, with a view to understanding and explaining the nature and behaviours of men who wilfully commit the crime of violence against women. Some of the most prominent theories in this field of study include: Feminist theory, Culture of violence theory and the Social learning theory. For want of space, only a few of these theories shall be discussed in this chapter.

Of the three theories reviewed for this paper, the Culture violence theory was considered most appropriate and suitable a theory for the projections, analysis and evaluations intended in this study. While the 'Feminist Theorists' focus on the structure of violence which is influenced by a male dominated society, which largely wilds its power on gender (Jasinski, 2001), the 'Social Learning Theory' on the other hand, which was proposed by Albert Banura in the early 70's, suggests that violence is learned from various contexts of socialization in and outside the family. Thus, persons who have witnessed several scenarios of violence and the purpose and effect it has on its victims, are inclined to presume that violence is a tool for getting anticipated results and goals in and around the family setting (Jasinski, 2001).

Of the theories reviewed for this paper, the culture violence theory which largely posits that violence is a learned behaviour (Glick, 2005), was adopted for this chapter. In other words, there are certain accepted values norms and certain accepted attitudes which exist and are accepted by certain groups of people which tends to embrace violence as part of the life style of the group in questions. Put differently, the idea of violence to such subcultures are regarded as a way of life. This very theory tends to justify why violent behaviours are condoned and acceptable among a sect or class of people (Glick, 2005). This chapter thus adopts this theory seeing that it largely accounts for the nature and types of violence experienced in African and Nigeria in particular. The theory in this chapter is thus adopted for inter-rogating the nature of violence witnessed in the Nigerian context.

AN OVERVIEW OF THE DOMESTIC VIOLENCE LAWS AGAINST WOMEN IN LAGOS STATE

Background to Eti-Osa Local Government Area (LGA) of Lagos State

The area designated as Eti-Osa (LGA) of Lagos state, is a division of Lagos State Nigeria. The entire division comprise four Local Government Development Areas (LGDA): Iru Victoria Island LGDA, Eti-Osa West LGDA, Eti-Osa East LGDA, Ikoyi-Obalande LGDA, in no particular order. It is important to note that within the area designated as Eti-Osa LGA, lies several thriving areas of Lagos such as Lekki Port and Victoria Island. It is on record that before the capital city of Lagos was moved to Abuja, Eti-Osa LGA served alongside Lagos Island as the capital city of Nigeria. The city's last estimated population was placed at: 283,791, with a distribution of 124,933 for males and 158,858 for the females (Tukool, 2018; Naijasky 2014).

An Analysis of the Domestic Violent Laws of Lagos State

While it is clear that every community or state has standard rules, codes and regulations designed to guide her conducts, with a view to ensuring the peaceful co-existence of all the members of the society - irrespective of the social status, sex, religious affiliation or economic status in the society - Domestic violence laws of Lagos state are laws and regulations designed to prescribes and regulates the behaviour of every citizen of Lagos state in their domestic environment (Falana, 2013). By this laws and codes, the interest and concerns of the less privileged and those vulnerable to domestic violence arising from psychological, socio-economical, or physical weakness, are protected. The prohibition against domestic violence for Lagos state was made by the Lagos State Government and it came into force on 18th May, 2007. This law was the first of its kind to be made in the whole 36 states (Chijoke, & Abifarin, 2013). These laws were largely designed to protect people against any or all forms of violence in homes or outside the home environment. More importantly, the law seeks to remove perpetrators from the environment so they would no longer be able to cause more harm. The law provides financial support to victims of domestic violence who may not be able to afford the cost for seeking redress in courts (Falana, 2013).

Violence Against Person's Prohibition Act (VAPPA), 2015 of Lagos State

The need to strengthen the laws on domestic violence lead to the enactment of the act: the 'Violence against Person's Prohibition Act (VAPPA) of Lagos state'. The bill bearing this law was passed into law by the House of Representatives and the Senate in 2013 and 2015 respectively. The bill was later signed into law by the President on the 28th of May, 2015, hence, it is now regarded as the VAPPA laws of 2015 (LawPavalion, 2014). The VAPPA laws was designed to eliminate all forms of violence in the private and public sector, it prohibits all forms of violence against persons, hence, it provides maximum protection to all those vulnerable to any form of domestic violence. It also provide effective remedies for victims and appropriate punishments for perpetrators (Onyemelukwe, 2015). Writers like (Onyemelukwe & Okekeogbu, 2017) observed that one of the advantages of this law is that it broadened the whole idea and definition of what violence used to be perceived as initially. The 'Act' presently defined acts of violence as: *...violence means any act or attempted act, which causes or may cause any person physical, sexual, psychological, verbal, emotional or economic harm, whether this occurs in private or public life, in peace time or in conflict situations.* So far, only states like Jigawa State, Ekiti State, Ebonyi State and Lagos State have taken steps to adopt similar laws on domestic violence against women. After a review of all the various attempts some states have made in the past to enact laws against domestic violence such as: female genital mutilation, harmful widowhood practice, the 2015 VAPPA laws of Lagos state, (Onyemelukwe & Okekeogbu, 2017) believes, it is a more comprehensive law with a wider coverage of legislation against domestic violence.

Some Known Causes of Domestic Violence

Several known causes of domestic violence were identified during the cause of this study. For lack of space, the authors of this chapter have chosen to discuss the following: (1) Weak legal framework and government policies on domestic violence, (2) Low level education on the part of victims involved, (3) the problem of poverty, cultural and social norms issues in the society.

Weak legal framework and government policies on domestic violence: The violence against persons' prohibition act (VAPPA) was passed into law on May, 2015. However, before this time, the law first spent 11 years at the National Assembly from 2002 to 2013 when it finally got to the House of Representatives where it was finally passed by the House on 14th day of March, 2013 (Eze, 2017). The senate later passed it into law in 2015. In all, the bill had taken 13 long years to go from one legislative arm of government to the other before it eventually got signed into law by the President on the 28th day of May, 2015. However, several studies (Onyemelukwe & Okekeogbu, 2017; Eze, 2017) conducted on the provisions of the law, seem to reveal that, as long as 13 long years was spent processing this laws, a law which the authors of this chapter would later argue, was found to be traversed by lots of loop holes which in many ways, has influenced the rise in the cases of DVAW in Nigeria.

Some of the provisions of this laws, for instance, give accused persons the leverage from where they can easily escape punishments. Thus, instead of really protecting women from domestic violence, the laws tends to encourage incidents of domestic violence against women. A good instance of this scenario can be found in section [55 (1) d] of the penal code of Nigeria. There the laws tends to empower men to correct their wives, earing children, servants, pupils in schools (Aguziendu, 2017). Hence, victims of cases of violence who make efforts to report cases of violence to appropriate agencies for the purpose of redress, are often blamed for the incident leading to the said violent acts. As such, the reports of such cases of violence have often been trivialized and the victims blamed and sent home to go and sort things out with their family. Since matters of this nature were regarded as private matters by the agencies where the cases are reported to, they strive to treat the matters from these perspectives (Eze-Anaba, 2010). Arising from this, there is no gain saying the fact that the patriarchal predispositions of the Nigerian culture and society have continued to have strong influence on the processes of formulating, interpreting and implementing the laws and policies associated with domestic violence against women.

Low level education on the part of victims involved: The poor orientation of according less education to the girl child and more to the males, due largely to cultural and religious reasons (Bakare, 2013), to some extent, accounts for the poor education of the girl child and by implication, the feminine gender. The fact that very few are aware of the value of education in the development of its citizens, and by implication, the nation, is a major factor impeding the training of the girl child. The question arising from deep cultural and traditional African belief systems, which has enhanced this scenario include: why spend much on a child that would be married off to another family? Why spend more on persons whose role are largely that of rearing and raising children? (Makama, 2013). It is from this perspective that the authors of this chapter are inclined to infer that the lacking of appropriate education for the girl child, is one of the factors associated with the rising rate of domestic violence cases among women in Nigeria (Abayomi, Kolawole & Olabode, 2013).

The problem of poverty: While accepting that the definition of poverty is relative, it is a factor that is influenced by the income of the individual or group of individuals in question (Kanayo, 2014). Viewed from a materialistic point of view, people are termed poor when they do not have what it takes (mental, physical or material resources) to meet their daily needs (Spicker, 1999). Persons who fall into this category tend to lack the ability to work with dignity in the society (Kanayo, 2014). Studies (Ucha, 2010 & Agbugah, 2015) conducted for the subject of this chapter, tends to show that "about 71% (percent) of Nigerians live on less than $1 per day and about 92% live on less than $2 per day". With a statistics of this nature on poverty in Nigeria, many scholars are inclined to argue that the anger and frustrations emerging from the harsh conditions associated with poverty, is largely responsible for the rising rate of spousal domestic violence cases in Nigeria and another parts of the world (Eze-Anaba, 2010; Agbugah, 2015).

PRESENTATION AND ANALYSIS OF DATA

Methodological and Ethical Considerations for the Study

The authors largely relied on Marilyn's ex-*post facto* research design (Marilyn, 2013) since the chapter basically relied and utilized data and analysis of findings obtained from previously analised studies on the subject matter of domestic violence against women. It is important to also highlight the fact that Creswell's mix-research method which allows researchers to either combine or separately use quantitative or qualitative methods of gathering and analyzing data obtained from interviews and focused group discussion (FGD) sessions, (Creswell, 2003) was also used for gathering the analysis obtained from the data and studies adopted for this study, directed largely at interrogating the prominent factors impeding the full implementation of the 2015 VAPPA laws in all the 36 states of Nigeria and in Eti-Osa LGA of Lagos state in particular.

It is important to note at this juncture that the rights and privacy of women and all others who participated in the studies from where valuable data and analysis were adopted for this research (NDHS, 2013; NPC, 2014), was taken into consideration. This is because the authors understand that the collection of such reliable and valid data void of ethical bias, usually poses particular challenges. Especially were the study in question involved collecting very sensitive data/information about intimate violent disposition from spouse and close family relatives. Consequent on this situation, three ethical considerations were called into play in designing the questionnaire used for the various studies. (1) The 'Kish Grid' was built into the question structure for the research, (Kish, 1965), (2) Informed consent was obtained from all the participants via the feeling of forms, while they were assured of the privacy of their contribution to the study. (3) The domestic violence module was only administered where the privacy and safety of the participants were assured. Where there were uncertainties about such security and privacy, the interview was cancelled. In all, data form 27,634 women were gathered from the studies (NDHS, 2013; NPC, 2014) considered for this research. Efforts were made to ensure that there was an adequate sub-sample representation of all the representative that participated in the study, nationally.

The studies considered for this study largely evaluated cases of domestic violence committed by spouse and by close family relatives. To this effect, data was gathered from married and unmarried women via questionnaires and interviews (Evaluation Briefs, 2008). The pilot studies conducted for this research reveals that intimate spousal violence is one of the most common type of violence against women, hence the spouse/partner violence was given more attention than any other kind of violence through the shortened version of the 'Conflict Tactics Scale' (CTS) (Straus, 1990). The USAID assisted research outlines the various kinds of questions that were used during the study conducted by (NDHS, 2013; NPC, 2014):

Does (did) your (last) husband/partner ever:

1. Say or do something to humiliate you in front of others?
2. Threaten to hurt or harm you or someone else close to you?
3. Insult you or make you feel bad about yourself?

Does (did) your (last) husband/partner ever do any of the following things to you?

1. Push you, shake you, or throw something at you?
2. Slap you?
3. Twist your arm or pull your hair?
4. Punch you with his fist or with something that could hurt you?
5. Kick you, drag you, or beat you up?
6. Try to choke you or burn you on purpose?
7. Threaten or attack you with a knife, gun, or any other weapon?
8. Physically force you to have sex with him even when you did not want to?
9. Physically force you to perform any other sexual acts you did not want to?
10. Force you with threats or in any other way to perform sexual acts you did not want to? (NDHS, 2013; NPC, 2014).

Where the participants response was a 'yes' a follow up question of the frequency of the event occurring in the past 12 months preceding the time of interview was required from the respondents. Where the response to questions i-iii is a 'yes' response, then the researchers inferred a heavy presence of emotional violence at play in the lives of the respondents. In the same vein, where the response to question iv-x got 'yes' responses, then the researchers where more inclined to affirm the case of physical violence on the part of the respondents. However, where a 'yes' response was recorded for question xi-xiii, the case of sexual violence is naturally established (NDHS, 2013; NPC, 2014).

Analysis of Data Generated from Qualitative and Qualitative Field Study

The data in (Table 1) indicates that domestic violence cuts across all cultural and socio-economic backgrounds. It also reveals that 28% of women between the ages of 15-49 have experience one form of violence or the other from the time they clocked 15 years old. The data in the table also reveals the percentage of women who in the past 12 months preceding the time the study was conducted, had experienced one form of domestic violence or the other. The study revealed that the experience of violence also varies from one religious group to the other. For instance, 44% of women who fall into the category of Catholics and Protestant women, have a higher probability of reporting cases of domestic violence than from women who fall into the category of other religious groups. Muslim women however, were discovered to only have 13% of domestic violence cases reported during the period in question.

Those in the rural areas are likely to report lesser cases of domestic violence compared to their counterparts in the urban areas (24% vs 33%). Worthy of note also is the fact that the study observed that there were notable variations in the degree of violence recorded in different zones of the country. For instance, data in (Table 1) indicates that the proportion of women who experienced violence from age 15 in the South Southern parts of Nigeria (Lagos and the environs), was far higher (52%) than the proportion of women from the ages of 15 in the North Western parts of the country, who experienced as low as (7%) physical violence. The same pattern was observed when close attention was drawn to the degree of violence believed to have taken place within the 12 months preceding the study by (NDHS, 2013; NPC, 2014) (19% vs 3%) respectively.

Another factor observed to have had great influence on the proportion of physical violence experienced by women is their educational background. The study revealed that women who did not attend school were less likely to experience physical violence compared to those with more educational qualifications. The same study observed a similar pattern that women with higher financial status tend to be more prone to experiencing physical violence than those who had less access to wealth. The data in (Table 1) revealed that Lagos state, from the other states listed amongst the South Western States of the country, had the highest percentage of women who experience physical violence alongside women from Oyo State. The study revealed that, of the array of perpetrators listed during the study, 36% - 52% of women were willing to affirm that the most violence actions they experienced came from their husbands/former husband or partner.

Data and results of the study presented in (Table 2) revealed that physical violence alone constitute one of the highest forms of violence that women experience yearly. A combination of physical and sexual violence however, indicated higher results among other forms of violence experienced by women from the ages of 15-49 years. Hence over 30% of women reported that they had experienced either sexual or physical violence during the 12 months preceding the period of conducting the research. There is however no substantial variation in the forms of violence experienced in this category by age. Data in (Figure 1) however, captures the specific forms of violence which most scholars allude, have tampered with their dignity as human beings of the opposite sex.

Data in (Figure 1) also revealed that the most common spousal physical violence /abuse that women have suffered in the hands of their husbands /spouse is the 'hand slaps'. 13% of women in the category under investigation, affirmed that this is the most common form of abuse, followed by pushing and violent shaking of the woman's body (7%). The most common emotional spousal violence takes place when husbands or partners insult and verbally abuse their women in public or make them feel very bad about her body or herself esteem.

Table 1. Percentage of women who experience physical violence

Percentage of women age 15-49 who have experienced physical violence since age 15 and percentage who experienced violence during the 12 months preceding the survey, by background characteristics, Nigeria 2013

Background characteristic	Percentage who have experienced physical violence since age 15[1]	Percentage who experienced physical violence in the past 12 months			Number of women
		Often	Sometimes	Often or sometimes[2]	
Age					
15-19	26.5	1.6	13.2	14.9	5,417
20-24	29.1	1.7	9.2	10.8	4,813
25-29	27.6	1.8	8.5	10.3	5,034
30-39	30.0	1.8	9.6	11.4	7,233
40-49	25.1	1.3	6.8	8.1	5,137
Religion					
Catholic	44.0	1.8	16.0	17.9	3,007
Other Christian	43.6	2.6	14.5	17.1	9,885
Islam	13.3	0.8	4.6	5.5	14,340
Traditionalist	36.3	8.4	14.7	23.0	258
Missing	36.2	1.0	11.3	12.4	140
Marital status					
Never married	34.9	1.4	12.6	14.0	6,438
Married or living together	24.6	1.5	8.4	10.0	19,925
Divorced/separated/ widowed	42.3	4.5	11.7	16.3	1,272
South West					
Ekiti	25.8	2.9	9.7	12.6	236
Lagos	43.9	2.9	12.1	15.0	1,365
Ogun	22.8	0.6	10.2	10.8	629
Ondo	43.7	4.8	15.8	20.6	575
Osun	12.8	0.4	3.6	4.1	556
Oyo	48.0	4.0	12.1	16.1	1,121
Education					
No education	11.8	1.0	4.6	5.6	10,479
Primary	36.5	2.6	13.3	15.9	4,809
Secondary	38.6	2.1	14.0	16.1	9,841
More than secondary	35.6	0.7	5.2	6.0	2,505
Wealth quintile					
Lowest	12.8	1.0	5.4	6.4	5,069
Second	23.3	1.7	9.7	11.4	5,275
Middle	30.0	2.2	11.3	13.5	5,301
Fourth	33.1	1.9	10.8	12.7	5,683
Highest	37.0	1.4	10.1	11.5	6,307
Total	27.8	1.6	9.5	11.2	27,634

Note: Total includes 63 cases with missing information on employment
[1] Includes violence in the past 12 months. For women who were married before age 15 and who reported physical violence by a spouse, the violence could have occurred before age 15
[2] Includes women for whom frequency in the past 12 months is not known

Source: Adopted with permission from (NDHS, 2013) USAID funded Survey

Table 2. Percentage of forms of violence among women

Age	Physical violence only	Sexual violence only	Physical and sexual violence	Physical or sexual violence	Number of women
15-19	22.7	1.8	3.8	28.3	5,417
15-17	22.4	1.7	3.3	27.3	3,370
18-19	23.3	2.1	4.5	29.9	2,047
20-24	22.6	2.1	6.4	31.2	4,813
25-29	21.1	1.9	6.6	29.5	5,034
30-39	23.8	1.5	6.2	31.5	7,233
40-49	19.9	1.5	5.2	26.6	5,137
Total	22.2	1.8	5.6	29.6	27,634

Percentage of women age 15-49 who have ever experienced different forms of violence by current age. Nigeria 2013

Source: Adopted with permission from (2013 NDHS), A USAID funded Survey

Figure 1. Specific forms of physical & sexual violence committed by spouse
Source: Adopted with permission from (2013 NDHS) USAID funded Survey

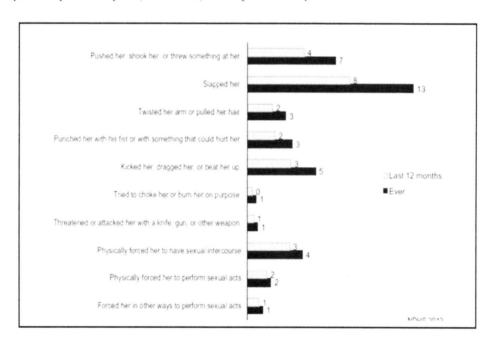

Before closing discussion in this section, it important to also note that most cases of violence recorded are not synonymous with the level of education women in this area may have. For instance, the study discovered that the education of women and their experience of violence is not consistent. In the case of the specific forms of violence analised in (Figure 1), most cases of violence where recorded amongst women with primary and secondary education, against those who did not have such educational background. As discussed in the previous section, women who were disposed to having more wealth were found to be prone to experiencing more of the spousal orchestrated forms of violence as discussed in (Table 1).

The Effect of Domestic Violence Perpetrated on Women

While physical and emotional effects are some of the most prevailing consequences and outcomes of domestic violence perpetrated - mostly by spouse/husbands and closest family relations (NDHS, 2013; NPC, 2014) - the data in (Table 3) reveals most of the prominent causes and consequences of harm that could arise from the survey conducted on domestic violence.

Physical kinds of abuses were identified to have taken place and more prominently, amongst the South Western women and among most Protestants and Catholic women with little or no educational background and with a high percentile of income (NDHS, 2013; NPC, 2014). As such - in no particular order - deep wounds; broken head, bones, teeth or nose, arising from a physical beating of the spouse, are some of the examples of the kinds of violence women in the study had encountered. Other kinds of physical harm often inflicted on women via domestic violence include: bruises, cuts, harm or aches. In all, the data in (Table 3) indicates that 30% of women sustain any of the injuries listed, while 27% of the participants allude to have suffered from bruises, cuts or aches, arising from spousal violence. 12%

Table 3. Types of injuries caused by domestic violence

Percentage of ever-married women age 15-49 who have experienced specific types of spousal violence by types of injuries resulting from the violence, according to the type of violence and whether they experienced the violence ever and in the 12 months preceding the survey, Nigeria 2013

Type of violence	Cuts, bruises, or aches	Eye injuries, sprains, dislocations, or burns	Deep wounds, broken bones, broken teeth, or any other serious injury	Any of these injuries	Number of ever-married women who have ever experienced any physical or sexual violence
Experienced physical violence[1]					
Ever[2]	26.5	11.8	6.0	30.2	3,062
In the past 12 months	28.8	13.3	6.6	33.0	1,969
Experienced sexual violence					
Ever[2]	23.4	13.0	7.2	28.6	1,008
In the past 12 months	21.8	12.9	7.1	27.3	782
Experienced physical or sexual violence[1]					
Ever[2]	24.1	10.7	5.4	27.4	3,425
In the past 12 months	25.2	11.6	5.7	29.0	2,314

Note: Husband/partner refers to the current husband/partner for currently married women and the most recent husband/partner for divorced, separated, or widowed women.
[1] Excludes women who reported violence only in response to a direct question on violence during pregnancy
[2] Includes violence in the past 12 months

Source: Adopted with permission from USAID funded Survey

of the participants on the other hand, alluded to have gotten eye injuries, burns, dislocations or sprains during such violent encounters. Those who acquired either of these bruises from sexually related violence were 29%. In all, the study recorded that 27% of women who had even experienced domestic violence, got either of the listed injuries in the process of various violent encounters with their spouse.

On the other hand, emotional injuries abound which the study observed, constitutes a major part of the consequences and effect arising from domestic violence. Examples of the recorded instances noted in the study include: when several women/spouse comment on the degree of humiliation they are often subjected to by their spouse in front of others, a case where the spouse threatens to hurt a partner or a close relative of the partner or other scenarios where the spouse insults the other and make them feel pretty bad about themselves. Recent studies by (Krug, Dahlberg, Mercy, Zwi & Lozano, 2002) suggests that 'physical violence in relationships are often accompanied by various kinds of psychological abuse, most of which comes via sexual abuse by the spouse'.

FURTHER DISCUSSION OF FINDINGS AND CONCLUSION

Matters Arising from Data Analysis

While a majority of the data discussed in the (NDHS, 2013; NPC, 2014) study focused on domestic violence issues in the whole of Nigeria, sections of the study clearly captured the statistics and data on the degree of domestic violence inherent among the South Western women of Nigeria, the women of Lagos state, and by implication, women from Eti-Osa LGA of Lagos State. The data in (Table 1) for instance, clearly analyses the various cases and forms domestic violence data captured from each of the 6 states in the South Western region of Nigeria. The findings from the analysis of data indicates that Lagos state is second to Ekti State, which recorded the second largest percentages of various forms of domestic violence perpetrated among women by their spouse.

The sample size utilized for further analysis on the participants domiciled in Eti-Osa LGA was determined using Taro Yamane's formula:

$$n = \frac{N}{1 + N\left(e\right)^2}$$

where n is the required sample size of the population under study, N is the entire populations while E stands for sample error assumed to be 5% $= 0.05$. The populations of Eti-Osa LGA is placed at:

$$n = \frac{283791}{1 + 283791\left(0.05\right)^2} = n = \frac{283791}{1 + 283791\left(0.0025\right)} = n = \frac{283791}{710.4775}$$

A study conducted by (Aguziendu, 2017) argued that some of the reasons identified for the high rate of the various forms of domestic violence noted to be inherent amongst participants in Eti-Osa LGA of Lagos state and in the Lagos environs, were largely a function of the poor knowledge women have about their right's to dignity as free beings in every community. The lack of education and sensitizations on the rights of women and the laws that have been enacted to protect them from further harm and abuse by their spouses etc., is identified as one of the factors behind the continuous increase in the number of domestic violence cases recorded in states.

This authors of this chapter wish to note at this point that the 2015 VAPPA laws in its present form, have not adequately deterred acts of violations in recent times, going by the rising number of the various forms of domestic violence offences perpetrated against women in Eti-Osa LGA, in recent times, (12 months interval preceding the time data was collected for the study). The study by (Aguziendu, 2017) is corroborated by (Goodmark, 2018; and Chamberlain, 2018), who - while hosting an interview about his book - opinioned that similar laws on domestic violence against women's act (VAWA) enacted in the US, are unlikely to deter domestic violence from taking place. In the same vein, there are scholars who argue that criminalizing domestic violence, as the present 2015 VAPPA laws is observed to do, tends to aggravate some of the factors that initiates scenarios of violence in the first instance (Goodmark, 2018). Below are a few of the instances and arguments that sustains this point:

1. The VAPPA law for instance, suggests prison terms of up to 4 years to those convicted of domestic violence. Consequently, men who are incarcerated often go through traumatic moments in prison. Upon their release, they are not able to re-integrate back into society. Persons with such traumatic experience are often more liable to committing more acts of domestic violence.
2. Where domestic violence is totally accepted as a criminal offence, the frequency of domestic violence would no sooner than later, turn criminal of everybody in the society. A society of individuals with such high criminal records would not find jobs easily. Jobless people in turn, become more prone to committing more acts of domestic violence.

Summary of Findings

The following comprise of some of the key findings which were made from this study:

1. The patriarchal and cultural inclinations of Africans and indeed, the religious and ethnic affiliations of Nigerian people's, continues to be one of the most prevailing factors militating against government's inability to fully implement, legislate and enforce the 2015 VAPPA laws in all the various sectors and states in Nigeria.
2. Criminalizing the acts of domestic violence against women – as is the case in the present 2015 VAPPA laws - studies indicates, does not really deter perpetrators of the acts of domestic violence from committing more acts of domestic violence, it rather has a way of increasing the number of cases recorded each year.
3. The educational status and level of awareness among the women in Eti-Osa LGA has not really deterred the number of cases of domestic violence among women and girls within the ages of 15 - 49 years age bracket, as considered for this study.
4. As much as 28% of women between the ages of 15 – 49 years old affirmed to have experienced some form of physical violence since they clocked 15 years old. 11% of this number indicated to have experienced physical violence within the last 12 months preceding the time of the adopted (NDHS, 2013; NPC, 2014; NPC & ICF, 2014) surveys.
5. The study revealed that as high as 45% of women who reside within the Eti-Osa LGA of Lagos state, and who experience either of the forms of domestic violence, never really disclosed their

plight and experiences to third parties nor did they seek any kind of help necessary for victims of domestic violence. This decision, studies revealed, were highly influenced by cultural and religious factors.

6. Data analised and adopted from the (NDHS, 2013; NPC, 2014) study, revealed that over 7% of females (between the ages of 15 – 49) residing in the Eti-Osa LGA, who also participated in the study, were reported to have had, at least one experience of sexual violence during their life time.

RECOMMENDATIONS

In the light of the above findings, the authors of this chapter deem it necessary to suggest the following recommendations as germane for addressing the challenges associated with DVAW in Eto-Osa LGA and by implication, Nigeria:

1. Preventing violence should go beyond being partisan. Hence, government should provide legislations and enforce laws that would rather target, recruit and rehabilitating offenders through designing groundbreaking programs that would aid in changing abusive behaviours among individuals than criminalize such perpetrators as is the case with the present state of the VAPPA laws.

2. While the 2015 VAPPA laws are generally considered a step in the right direction, the laws in its present form is far from developing a balanced policy for addressing intimate partner violence in Nigeria. Efforts should therefore be made to ensure that the laws are modified to be able to accommodate and address contemporary realities.

3. Most states in Nigeria are yet to adopt and begin implementation of the 2015 VAPPA laws. Thus, government should ensure that every other state in the federation adopts and begin rapid implementation of the 2015 VAPPA laws in its current form.

4. An analysis of the 2015 VAPPA laws indicates that the laws in its present form, relies heavily on the criminal systems, hence, it does not do much about addressing the main causes of intimate violence amongst partners, which include: Unstable communities, adverse trauma arising from various childhood experiences and economic distress to mention but a few. Funds that go into empowering the criminal systems to fight offenders, could rather go into designing training programs that would economically empower the class of persons disposed to this kind of violence. Such funds could also provide anti-violence education for the most vulnerable class of persons (young women and girls) who are most affected by domestic violence.

Contribution to Knowledge

The authors of this chapter are convinced that the study conducted here would make immense contributions in the following ways:

1. This chapter for the first time interrogated and analysis the main causes of domestic violence against women in Nigeria and more closely, amongst the women of Eti-Osa LGA, with the view to understanding why the cases of DVAW continues to rise, despite the adoption of the 2015 VAPPA laws in Lagos State.

2. The study provided vivid and current data on DVAW that would be relevant for policy formulation which will in turn, improve the state of women (the dignity of womanhood) experiencing all the various forms of violence discussed in the chapter.
3. The chapter identified the weaknesses in the present 2015 VAPPA laws and suggested ways of making the laws more effective at addressing contemporary issues surrounding DVAW in Eti-Osa LGA, Lagos State and Nigeria as a whole.
4. The study identified pertinent steps that would aid curbing the menace of DVAW in Eti-Osa LGA, Lagos State and Nigeria as a whole, that is, where such steps are urgently adopted and implemented by the federal government.

CONCLUSION

Against the initial trend of politicizing the issues of DVAW laws, government needs to set up structures and laws into motion that would facilitate addressing current issues surrounding the rising trend of domestic violence cases against women in Nigeria. This has become an issues that cannot be over emphasized in the 21st century. While legislations directed at protecting the dignity of womanhood and educating women and young girls have been passed into law and adopted by a few state in Nigeria, there are still a lot other states that are yet to adopt or implement the necessary laws designed to protect vulnerable women from all forms of violence discussed in this chapter. Government should, as a matter of urgency and necessity, enforce the implementation of these domestic violence laws in all the 36 state in Nigeria, as this would enhance and increase the efforts made towards improving the already down trodden dignity of womanhood in Eti-Osa LGA and in Nigeria as a whole.

The lapses observed to be inherent in the present 2015 VAPPA laws are identified as part of the factors that continues to influence the rise in the cases of domestic violence perpetrated against women in Eti-Osa LGA of Lagos State and in Nigeria as a whole. Thus, there is a strong agitation for government and policy makers to upgrade the present laws to meet with present realities.

ACKNOWLEDGMENT

This research received no specific grant from any funding agency in the public, commercial, or not-for-profit sectors. However, it received the support and permission of the following organizations for the use of the data, tables, figures and charts that were used to prepare the arguments made for the objectives of this chapter.

1. Nigeria Demographic and Health Survey (**NDHS**). Their report summarized the findings of the **2013** Nigeria Demographic and Health Survey

2. National Population Commission (**NPC**) [Nigeria] and ICF International. (2014).

REFERENCES

Abayomi, A. A., Kolawole, C., & Olabode, T. (2013). Domestic Violence and Death: Women as an Endangered Gender in Nigeria. *American Journal of Sociological Research*, *3*(3), 53–60.

Abe, I. (2012). Defining and awareness of sexual harassment among selected University students in Lagos metropolis, Nigeria. *Journal of Emerging Trends in Educational Research and Policy Studies*, *3*(3), 1–3.

Agbugah, F. (2015). *Poverty is the main cause of violence against women in Nigeria: Noi Polls*. Retrieved 2nd March, 2017 from http://venturesafrica.com/poverty-is-the-main-cause-of-domestic-violence-in-nigeria-noi-polls/

Aguziendu, C. (2017). *Domestic violence law against women in Eti-Osa LGA* (Unpublished thesis). Department of Political Science & International Relations, Covenant University, Ota, Ogun State, Nigeria.

Aihie, O. N. (2009). Prevalence of domestic violence in Nigeria: Implications for counselling. *Edo Journal of Counselling, 2*(1). Retrieved 17th March, 2017 from the website https://www.ajol.info/index.php/afrrev/article/viewFile/69290/57319

Arisi, R. O. (2011). Cultural violence and the Nigerian woman. *An International Multidisciplinary Journal, Ethiopia*, *5*(4), 369–381.

Bakare, K. A. (2013). Low level of education in Nigeria: Causes and solution. *Information Nigeria*. Retrieved 1st March, 2017 from http://www.informationng.com/2013/02/low-level-of-education-in-nigeria-causes-and-solution.html

Balkin, J. M. (1987). Deconstructive practice and legal theory. *Yale L.J., 96*(15).

Chamberlain, S. (2018). *Preventing violence isn't partisan: Time to reauthorize violence against women act. The Hill*. Retrieved on the 25th of October, 2018 from https://thehill.com/blogs/congress-blog/civil-rights/406597-preventing-violence-isnt-partisan-time-to-reauthorize

Chijoke, O. J., & Abifarin, O. (2013). *An appraisal of protection against domestic violence law of Lagos state, 2007*. Retrieved 3rd November, from http://abuad.edu.ng/an-appraisal-of-protection-against-domestic-violence-law-of-lagos-state-2007/

CLEEN Foundation. (2013). National Crime Victimization Surveys. *National Crime Victimization and Safety Survey*. Retrieved from cleenfoundation.blogspot.com/2013/10/public-presentation-of-findings-of.html

Creswell, J. W. (2003). *Research design: Qualitative and quantitative approaches*. Thousand Oaks, CA: SAGE.

Evaluation Briefs. (2008). *Data collection method for program evaluation questions*. Retrieved 7th February, 2017 from https://www.cdc.gov/healthyyouth/evaluation/pdf/briefly.pdf

Eze, U. L. (2017). *The violence against person's prohibition act, 2015*. Retrieved 8th March, 2017 from https://donlaz.wordpress.com/20

Eze-Anaba, I. (2010). Domestic violence and legal reforms in Nigeria: Prospects and challenges. *Cardozo Journal of Law and Gender*, *14*(21), 15–18.

Falana, F. (2013). A law to provide protection against domestic violence and for connected purposes. Lagos: Women Empowerment and Legal Aid (WELA).

Foster, S., & Dyer, C. (2010). *Ending violence against women and human trafficking: A Guide to new strategies.* Retrieved from http://www.ncdsv.org/images/GlobePartnerendVAW_EndVAWTrafficking-Toolikit_3-2010.pdf

Glick, L. (2005). *Criminology.* Retrieved 19th February, 2017 from http://catalogue.pearsoned.co.uk/samplechapter/020540278X.pdf

Goodmark, L. (2018). *The violence against women act is unlikely to deter domestic violence — here's why.* The conversation .com Flipboarad.

Haan, D. W. (2008). *Violence as an essential contested concept: Violence in Europe.* New York: Springer New York.

Hart, B. (2015). *A shame of Nigeria: Statistics of violence against women.* Retrieved 3rd November, 2016 from www.naija.com/430683-every-fourth-nigerian-woman-suufers-domestic-violence https://www.unicef.org/nigeria/.../Nigeria-demographic-and-health-survey- 2013.pdf

Idris, H., Adaja, J., Audu, S., & Aye, G. A. (2016). Analysis of the causes and the effects of sexual harassment on the performance of female employees in some selected organizations in Kogi state, Nigeria. *International Journal of Democratic and Development Studies, 2*(2), 31–34.

Jasinski, J. L. (2001). Theoretical explanations for violence against women. In *Sourcebook on violence against women.* New Delhi: SAGE Publications. Retrieved 3rd March, 2017 from https://books.google.com.ng/books?hl=en&lr=&id=v7n5zP3uKn8C&oi=fnd&pg=PA5&dq=how+subculture+of+violence+theory+explain+domestic+violence+against+women&ots=DHMEdnggP3&sig=9Ngztb0RSYS-rjH0diXZBo1-Pzi8&redir_esc=y#v=onepage&q&f=false

Kanayo, O. (2014). Poverty incidence and reduction strategies in Nigeria: Challenges of meeting 2015 MDG targets. *Journal of Economics, 5*(2), 201–217. doi:10.1080/09765239.2014.11884997

Kaur, R., & Garg, S. (2008). Addressing domestic violence against women: An unfinished agenda. *Indian Journal of Community Medicine, 33*(2), 73–76. doi:10.4103/0970-0218.40871 PMID:19967027

Kish, L. (1965). *Survey sampling.* New York: John Wiley and Sons Inc.

Krantz, G., & Garcia-Moreno, C. (2005). Violence against women. *Journal of Epidemiology and Community Health, 59*(10), 818–821. doi:10.1136/jech.2004.022756 PMID:16166351

Krug, E. G., Dahlberg, L. L., Mercy, J. A., Zwi, A. B., & Lozano, R. (Eds.). (2002). World report on violence and health. Geneva, Switzerland: World Health Organization.

Kulwicki, A. D. (2002). The practice of honor crimes: A glimpse of domestic violence in the Arab world. *Issues in Mental Health Nursing, 23*(1), 136–138. doi:10.1080/01612840252825491 PMID:11887612

LawPavalion. (2014). *The violence against persons' prohibition act, of 2015.* Retrieved from Lawpavilion.com on the 11th December, 2018. https://lawpavilion.com/blog/the-violence-against-persons-prohibition-act-2015/

Makama, G. A. (2013). Patriarchy and gender inequality in Nigeria: The way forward. *European Scientific Journal, 9*(17), 140-145.

Mandara, M. U. (2004). Female genital mutilation in Nigeria. *International Journal of Gynaecology and Obstetrics: the Official Organ of the International Federation of Gynaecology and Obstetrics, 84*(3), 291–298. doi:10.1016/j.ijgo.2003.06.001 PMID:15001386

Marilyn, K. (2013). *Ex-post facto research: Dissertation and scholarly research, Recipes for success.* Seattle, WA: Dissertation Success LLC. Retrieved from http://www.dissertationrecipes.com/wp-content/uploads/2011/04/Ex-Post-Facto-research.pdf

Marilyn, K. (2013). *Ex-post facto research: Dissertation and scholarly research, Recipes for success.* Seattle, WA: Dissertation Success LLC; Retrieved from http://www.dissertationrecipes.com/wp-content/uploads/2011/04/Ex-Post-Factoresearch.pdf

Mayell, H. (2002). Thousands of women killed for family "honor". *National Geographic News.* Retrieved January 25, 2015 from http://news.nationalgeographic.com/news/2002/02/

Naijasky. (2014). *History of Eti-Osa Local Government Area.* Retrieved 1st March, 2017 from http://naijasky.com/eti-osa/137/history-of-eti-osa-local-government-area/3273/

National Population Commission (NPC) [Nigeria] and ICF International. (2014). *Nigeria Demographic and Health Survey 2013.* Abuja, Nigeria: NPC and ICF International.

NDHS. (2013). *This report summarizes the findings of the 2013 Nigeria Demographic and Health Survey (NDHS), implemented by the National Population Commission.* NPC.

Ogunjuyigbe, O. P., Akinlo, A., & Ebigbola, A. J. (2005). Violence against Women: An examination of men's attitudes and perceptions about wife beating and contraceptive use. *Journal of African and Asian Studies, 40*(3), 219–229. doi:10.1177/0021909605055070

Okeke, T. C., Anyaehie, U. S. B., & Ezenyeaku, C. C. K. (2012). An overview of female genital mutilation in Nigeria. *Annals of Medical and Health Sciences Research, 2*(1), 70–73. doi:10.4103/2141-9248.96942 PMID:23209995

Onyemelukwe, C. (2015). *Overview of the violence against persons (prohibition) act, 2015.* Centre for Health, Ethics, Law and Development. Retrieved 9th March, 2017 from http://domesticviolence.com.ng/wp-content/uploads/2015/12/OVERVIEW-OF-THE-Violence-Against-Persons-Prohibition-ACT-2015.pdf

Onyemelukwe, C., & Okekeogbu, I. (2017). *The violence against persons (prohibition) act: A CHELD Brief.* CHELD. Retrieved on the 9th March, 2017 from http://cheld.org/wp-content/uploads/2012/04/Violence-Against-Persons-Prohibition-Act-2015-A-CHELD-Brief.pdf

Oyediran, A. K., & Abanihe-Isiugo, C. U. (2005). Perceptions of Nigerian women on domestic violence: Evidence from 2003 Nigeria Demographic and Health Survey. *African Journal of Reproductive Health, 9*(3), 39–41. PMID:16485585

Reitan, E. (2001). Rape as an essentially contested concept. *Hypatia, 6*(2), 43–66. doi:10.1111/j.1527-2001.2001.tb01058.x

Sharma, K. (2016). Understanding the concept of honor killing within the social paradigm: A theoretical perspective. *ISOR Journal of Humanities and Social Science, 21*(9), 125–127.

Spicker, P. (1999). *Definitions of poverty: Twelve clusters of meaning*. Retrieved 23rd February, 2017, from http://dds.cepal.org/infancia/guide-to-estimating-child-poverty/bibliografia/capitulo-I/Spicker%20 Paul%20(1999)%20Definitions%20of%20poverty%20eleven%20clusters%20of%20meaning.pdf

Straus, M. A. (1990). Measuring intra-family conflict and violence: The conflict tactics (CT) scales. Academic Press.

Tukool. (2018). *All you need to know about Eti-Osa LGA, Lagos State*. Retrieved from: https://tukool. com/know-nigeria/know-about-lagos/know-about-eti-osa/#The_Government_Of_Eti-Osa

Ucha, C. (2010). Poverty in Nigeria: Some dimensions and contributing factors. *Global Majority E-Journal*, *1*(1), 46–48.

Washburn, K. (2018). *Violence against women act at risk of lapsing*. Open secret.org. Center for responsive policies. Retrieved from on October, 25th https://www.opensecrets.org/news/2018/10/vawa-at-risk-of-lapsing/

Wolfgang, M. E., & Ferracuti, F. (1976). *The subculture of violence: towards an integrated theory in criminology*. London: Tavistock. Retrieved from https://lib.ugent.be/en/catalog/rug01:000505954

World Health Organization. (2002). *World report on violence and health: Summary*. Geneva: World Health Organization. Retrieved 15th February, 2017 from, http://www.who.int/violence_injury_prevention/violence/world_report/en/summary_en.pdf?ua=1

Chapter 16
Impact of Human Interaction in Agile–Oriented Content Delivery in Learning Environments

Salman Abdul Moiz

https://orcid.org/0000-0001-9294-0275

University of Hyderabad, India

ABSTRACT

In this chapter, a linear process model is proposed for outcome-based education. Then an agile-based approach is presented that aims to integrate the Instruction design and student assessment to improve the quality of design and delivery. An agile process model suitable for virtual learning environments is proposed. The agile project management artifacts that include a content story, test plan, etc. are being used in the education domain. There is a need for human interaction in the teaching and learning process to improve the outcomes. The feedback generated after the student assessment process will help in improving the process of content designing and delivery in subsequent increments. The proposed agile model for the virtual learning environment is adapted for a graduate course offering. Based on the continuous assessments and feedbacks, various instructional methods are used for the delivery of the course. The results show that there is an improvement in student's grades, learning outcomes, and there is a considerable reduction in failures and dropout rates.

DOI: 10.4018/978-1-7998-1279-1.ch016

INTRODUCTION

Learning is a means of acquiring knowledge and ethical values. The major actors of the education system are the learner and the Instructor. Taxonomy of the delivery mechanisms depends on the geographical location of the teacher and the learner. The teaching method adopted in a classroom is known as face-face teaching. The primary goal of the education system is to ensure that learners gain the required outcomes. Virtual learning has become a vital element of the digital world because of its ubiquitous nature. Content can be accessed anywhere, anytime, anyplace, and from any device. The primary preamble for e-learning today is whatever is the technology used; learning is a vital element. E-Learning generally takes place in a real-time environment. It can be synchronous, asynchronous, or blended. Blended learning is supposed to be effective in the majority of courses.

Irrespective of the learning adopted, the content design and delivery have to follow a well-defined process. Several e-learning processes are available in the literature. Most of the e-learning processes are plan driven in nature where each phase is defined and frozen. The changes to the content design and delivery are not possible during development, or it requires a majority of rework. There are some agile approaches proposed, but it doesn't give the incremental feedback for the design and delivery of e-content.

According to Sharp & Lang (2018), there is a potential of agile methods to improve the teaching and learning process. Further, there is a need for systematic research on the use of agile methods for course development. Chun's(2004), ATLM uses agile methods for the successful delivery of technical courses. There is a need for a generic agile framework for the content delivery mechanism. D'Souza & Rodrigues (2015) presents extreme pedagogy approach to improve student learning continuously. However, there is a need to define a process satisfying these principles in learning environments.

In this chapter, the authors propose linear and agile based approaches for outcome-based education. Motivated by Agile based software development (Schawber-2001), this chapter presents templates for stories and test planning. This chapter also introduces the Agile-based process model relevant to the virtual learning environment as the traditional agile method can't be directly applicable to the e-learning environments.

This chapter also presents a simulation of an agile model for virtual learning by changing the delivery methods based on the continuous feedback from the learners. It is to note that student performance improved from one increment to another. The analysis of learners feedback states that it increased their confidence as the course progressed. Incorporating this model may drastically reduce the dropout rate if it is used in the asynchronous mode of learning and helps to transform a passive learner to an independent learner.

The remaining part of this chapter contains the following sections. The second section specifies various approaches used in eLearning for managing quality. The third section introduces to instructional methods and assessment mechanisms. The fourth section describes the linear and agile based process models for outcome-based education. This section also presents an agile model for the virtual learning environment. This section introduces, content story template and the testing templates relevant to content delivery methods for outcome-based education. The authors also address Content and change management processes. The fifth section specifies the results achieved by realizing the agile model for the virtual learning environment, and the final section presents the conclusion and future directions.

RELATED WORK

Traditional education process models are plan-driven, and the assessments are in the form of formative and summative assessments. Learners give feedback at the end of the course, which may be used to improve the content design and delivery for subsequent course offerings. According to Uppal et al. (2018), a satisfactory e-learning experience is possible only when more services are offered apart from the learning material. An extended SEQ VQUAL model compares customer expectation and customer experience, which helps at a later stage after content design and delivery. Chatterjee (2016) proposed a quality assurance method for e-learning quality, which uses the Kirkpatrick model. They introduced several parameters to design and assess various building blocks of the e-learning system. However, it still follows a linear approach, and such measures don't help the learner of that course.

Rahman et al. (2017) propose that the user satisfaction system and information quality influences the e-learning system quality. The results of short and long distance learning students are compared to see the outcome of service and quality of the portal. However, this work lacks a realistic scenario of outcome-based education, and the quality assessment is carried out in the last phase. Esfijani (2018) proposes a review of measures of quality of online education by considering 112 publications between 2000 and 2017. It reports that there is a lack of evidence for outcome-based approaches for measurement of quality indicators. Pipan et al. (2014) proposed the extended method of group assessment of Learning Management Systems. They used the services of three experts in the technology domain to evaluate the same LMSs against five criteria, and individual decisions are taken to record the group decision finally. However, the emphasis is to measure the quality of the Learning Management system. Bari et al. (2014) present the existing quality standards and frameworks for e-learning systems. It also states that though ISO/IEC 19796-1 is a quality standard which applies to specific stakeholders needs. According to Rossi et al. (2014), process management in the area of education is as important as process management in other domains. The process of education domain has to incorporate a feedback mechanism for continuous improvement. Khan et al. (2006) proposed a holistic approach for creating, deploying, and maintaining the P3 model (People-Process-Product), which uses a modular approach.

As per the extreme programming practices, one of the principles states that "people not process" i.e people are more important than the process (Corriea et al 2019). The feedback of the people results in better realization and adoption of the process being followed.

Zamudio et al (2017), states that traditional requirements engineering issues can be solved using Agile methods. The same can be adopted in learning envriomnets by mapping the educational domain requirements to an agile method.

The existing process and quality models proposed in the domain of education are linear. In the proposed linear models, the learners give feedback at the end of the course. This approach doesn't help the learner in achieving the course objectives. In this chapter, an agile based approach for outcome-based education is proposed, which adopts the iterative and incremental way of content design and instructional delivery. The proposed method helps in continuous feedback which is adaptable to the changing needs of the learners concerning content design and delivery.

INSTRUCTIONAL METHODS AND ASSESSMENT

In the last few decades, teaching and learning processes have become prominent in the educational domain. Though the higher educational institutes have adopted the best practices, a very less percentage of graduates are employable. Further, in the virtual learning environment, the dropout rates are high. The basic building blocks of the education system are teaching, learning, assessment, and pedagogy. The terms instructional methods and content delivery is used interchangeably in this chapter. According to Dash(2013) study on students, about 56% of learners agreed that practical session is more interesting than the theory sessions and about 45% of learners feels that the teaching method lacks interest. According to Ganyaupfu(2013), student-centric learning environment produces better outcomes than that of teacher-centric learning paradigms. It reports that the dropout rates considerably may decrease due to this transition. Learning through inquiry, design, creativity, problem-solving, and action-based learning is the need of the present times.

The instructional method that engages learners in the teaching-learning process is known as active learning. Active learning helps the learner to involve in learning by doing. Further collaborative and cooperative learning are primary factors for a transition from passive to an active learner. In a collaborative learning group of learners work together for a common goal, whereas cooperative learning is a structured learners group working together, yet they are assessed individually (David et al. 2013). Problem-based learning is an Instructional method in which problems given to learners are discussed throughout the course delivery to gain a skill of problem-solving (Prince 2004).

According to William (2013), "Assessment is the central part of effective instruction." It bridges the teaching and learning process. It is used to assess whether learners were engaged in intended learning. Learners are assessed at various levels using blooms taxonomy so that they gain the desired skills. According to Dixson (2016), there exist several classroom assessments which include a formative, summative, quiz, etc. Formative and summative assessments are being used to asses the learners in virtual learning or e-learning environments. Formative assessment is applicable for continuous improvement and the summative assessments for measuring learning outcomes. If the performance of the learner is below certain specified threshold limits, the learner retakes the test. The learner is made aware of the areas of improvement. Summative assessment is used to evaluate the learning outcomes of a course. The final grade of the learner includes both formative and summative measures.

AGILE BASED CONTENT DELIVERY

The process models supported in education domain and the process management frameworks follow a linear approach. The generic phases of the content design and delivery are Planning, Designing, Development, and Evaluation. In most of these approaches, the feedback is the final artifact. In ADDIE [Branch et al. 2009], SCORM and other models, the linear method is used to realize the basic building blocks of the education domain. The phases in a direct approach include content planning, content design, content delivery, evaluation, and feedback. The student or learner is the primary stakeholder in the education system. Continuous feedback from the learners will help the improvement of the process. However, learners are not involved in regular input in the traditional education system, and it becomes more difficult in virtual learning environments. In a virtual learning environment, since a learner is a virtual learner, it becomes more difficult to involve them in providing a learner-centric approach. Traditionally in the linear models, feedback, and the performance of the students is used to improve the content, design, and delivery for the subsequent batches of students of same course offerings. The basic building blocks of the education system viz., teaching and learning, evaluation, and feedback can be realized in an iterative and incremental approach. The content design phase can be implemented in short increments and can be tested and verified to improve the same content, and the feedback can be fruitful in developing the content of the next iteration.

Similarly, there are several content delivery methods. In the higher education system, a single delivery method may not be appropriate to realize all the objectives of the course. Hence it is proposed to achieve the content delivery by following an iterative and incremental approach. In the proposed method, feedback of stakeholders is used at regular intervals for the continuous improvement of content delivery based on several factors.

The scope of this section is to first introduce to the agile framework of the outcome-based education system, then specifying an agile approach for the content delivery for proper nurturing and evaluation

Linear Process Model for Outcome-based Education

Effective teaching and learning process is often possible by following the practices of outcome-based education. Each program is expected to have Program-Educational Objectives (PEOs) and Program Specific Outcomes (PSOs). PEOs specifies the objectives that the program is preparing learners to achieve. PSOs defines the indicators that describe what the learner should be able to meet at the end of the course. The performance of a learner is measured and graded based on the degree of satisfying the particular outcomes. Each course consists of objectives *CObi* and Course outcomes *COi*. For each course objective, there may be several measurable outcomes. The degree of conformance of learning outcomes for each learner is measured.

Program, $P = <PEOs, PSOs>$

Course, $C = \{C_1, C_2, C_3, \ldots C_n\}$

Course Objectives, $COb_i = \{COb_{i1}, COb_{i2}, \ldots Cob_{in}\}$

Course Outcomes, $CO_i = \{CO_{i1}, CO_{i2}, \ldots Co_{in}\}$

Each course contains several modules, and each module consists of objectives and outcomes. The module objectives and module outcomes are subsets to course objectives and course outcomes for that course. Formative assessment is done to assess the learners to see the degree of conformance to the module outcomes. Summative assessment is carried out to measure the degree of compliance of course outcomes by the learner. The intermediate artifacts in outcome-based education involve content development and delivery. A linear approach is generally adopted to realize the goals of outcome-based education.

In the linear approach of outcome-based education (Figure 1), for a given course, its objectives and outcomes are defined. Subsequently, the goals and targets of the individual modules are listed. The content for each module is developed to meet the module objectives, and the degree of conformance of module outcomes by learners is measured. At the end of each module, formative assessments are conducted to know the degree of compliance of a learner to the specified results. The actual time taken to complete a

Figure 1. Linear model for outcome-based education

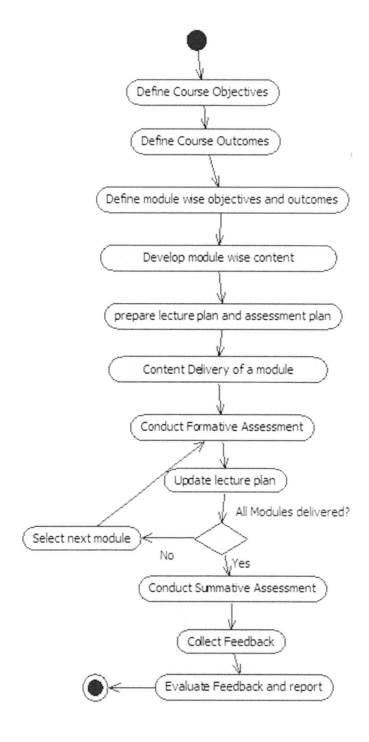

particular module or lesson is recorded in the lecture plan.. Once all modules are delivered and assessed a formative assessment is made to know the degree of conformance of the course outcomes. Feedback is collected and reported to help in improving the given course offering in the future.

Analysis of Linear Model for Outcome-Based Education

The linear model of outcome-based education is applied to classroom learning, virtual learning, or even to a blended learning environment. This model is suitable as long as both stake holder's, i.e., the instructor and the learner are clear about the objectives, outcomes, delivery mechanisms adopted, and assessment strategies. However since this model is linear, any changes required in design and development of course content, course delivery or assessment strategy will be known only at the end of the course through feedback given by the learners.

The instructor uses a single and common Instructional delivery mechanism for all modules of a given course. However, based on the content, various delivery methods may be adopted. To adequately realize the learning outcomes, the decision about the delivery method chosen should be taken by both teachers and learners to satisfy the learning outcomes.

In a virtual learning environment, the dropout rate is high as the learner is not capable of adapting to the same delivery method for all modules of a course. This problem may not be severe in the classroom or blended learning as the instructor may sense the feeling of learners and may adopt different learning methods. However, even in such cases, the required delivery mechanism is not planned. Hence there is a need for an approach to realize the outcomes of a particular course such that the learners can satisfy the course outcomes effectively.

Agile Process for Outcome-Based Education

In the linear model of outcome-based education, the feedback is either taken at the end of the course or is collected twice during the course offering. However, the learner has no role in requesting for changes in course design and delivery until the end of the course. An agile based approach for outcome-based education is proposed to address this issue. The transition in learner's roles from passive to the active learner, reproducer of knowledge to the producer and dependent to autonomous learner requires a transformation in teaching, learning, and evaluation processes. This transition is expected to operate in a changing the environment as the learners may not be satisfied with the same design and delivery method for the entire content.

In higher education, there may be scenarios where particular course objectives require changes due to the current demands of the industry. For example, the learner may request to introduce a specific topic in the course which needs modifications to the objectives of the course. In such cases, the linear approach will not be feasible. The changes to the few goals are possible in autonomous institutions. Even in cases where a specified course curriculum is adopted, an instructor can add the new goals as this may contribute to "beyond curriculum" delivery, which is a part of outcome-based education. Hence there is a need for a process model for an education system that helps in making changes based on learner's feedback. These changes are possible if the content designing and delivery spans in small steps called increments.

Motivated by the Scrum Agile method (Schwaber and Beedle, 2001), this section presents an agile approach for outcome-based education. It is an incremental mechanism wherein each objective is realized

Figure 2. An incremental approach to outcome-based Education

Content Planning	Content Deigning	Content Delivery	Evaluation	Feedback
Obj$_1$				
Obj$_2$	Obj$_1$			
Obj$_3$	Obj$_2$	Obj$_1$		
Obj$_4$	Obj$_3$	Obj$_2$	Obj$_1$	
Obj$_5$	Obj$_4$	Obj$_3$	Obj$_2$	Obj$_1$

across content planning, design, delivery, evaluation, and feedback in a series of iterations called increments. The following figure (Fig. 2) represents the incremental approach to outcome-based education.

In the Content planning phase, the course objectives and outcomes are formulated. The course objectives and outcomes may be further grouped into module objectives and outcomes. Each of the goal or objective corresponds to an increment. In the next phase, the content designing activity begins for the selected course objective(s). Parallelly content planning for the next goal begins. There is a need to prioritize the course objectives based on the learner's capability. In the current changing environment, it may not be adequate to follow a strict chronological order of course curriculum unless it is also arranged based on the logical order of course objectives.

The process of content planning, designing, delivery, evaluation, and feedback can be interleaved to realize each of the objectives. The next step after content planning is content design and delivery. For a given purpose, the instructor develops the content, and a suitable method is used to deliver the content to the learner.

In the evaluation phase, each learner is assessed against the degree of conformance of each of the outcomes, and learner gives the feedback for that phase. The feedback will help the content manager to plan the following objectives, which are either in content planning or designing. This feedback will also help in planning and outlining the other goals of the course. It is to be noted that the evaluation of each outcome is to be realized by developing assessment plans at various levels of blooms taxonomy (Anderson et al. 2013). The learner has to be assessed by framing questions at different levels for each of the specified outcomes.

The proposed model uses an incremental and iterative approach. The significant advantage of the progressive model is to manage the changes in course planning, design, and delivery. Learners feedback can be used to plan subsequent modifications. The modification to delivered content can be taken up in the next cycle.

Outcome-Based education systems can use the following basic principles of agile methods (Sommerville, 2011):

- Customer Involvement: Leaner is the primary customer of an education system. Learners are expected to be intimately involved in choosing the design and delivery methods for a given content. Their role is to provide and prioritize the new objectives and evaluate the current goals for the continuous feedback

- People do not Process: In spite of the learner's involvement, the content developers are independent to develop the content in their proven ways without being pressurized by the customary processes.

- Embrace Change: The changes in the design and delivery of the current module or other modules is possible. Continuous changes in the design and delivery of the course are possible.

- Maintain Simplicity: Attempt is made to simplify the complex task and adopt a lean approach my removing unwanted activities.

The incremental approach to outcome-based education and the underlying agile principles can be applied to face to face teaching or blended mode of instruction. However, it may not be possible for learner's involvement in all the phases in virtual learning environments. Traditionally in virtual learning environments, the content planning and content development phase are completed well before the commencement of a course. However, in the agile approach, content design and development is in small iterations called increments. This approach helps in making learning exciting and thereby reducing the dropout rates.

The following figure (Fig. 3) describes the agile process for the outcome-based education system.

Figure 3. Agile oriented process for outcome-based education

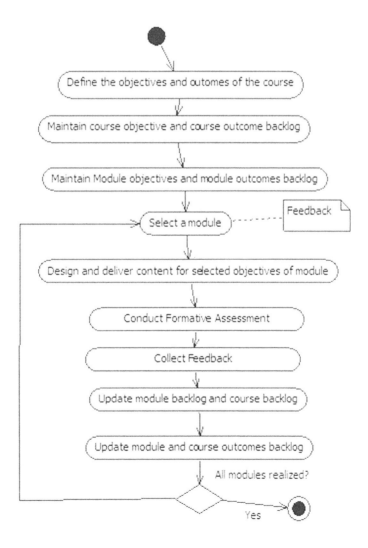

In the agile oriented process for outcome-based education, once the course objectives and outcomes and decided in the content planning phase, they are stored in course objective backlog and course outcome backlog databases. The backlog database indicates the goals and outcomes of the given course. A course generally consists of several modules, and each module is associated with module objective backlog and module outcomes backlog, respectively.

The module wise objectives stored in the module backlog database has to be realized. The content for the said module objectives has to be designed and delivered. Once the module delivery is completed, an assessment is conducted to evaluate learners on the outcomes stated in the module outcome database. Feedback is collected from the students, which can be used to improve the design and delivery of subsequent increments. The backlog databases are updated. The updated databases specify the pending modules and curriculum. It also updates the priorities of the objectives to be realized based on the feedback received from the learners.

The backlog databases will help the content managers to monitor the progress of the curriculum development and delivery. Each increment feedbacks can help to modify the subsequent increments that help in enhancing the quality of the learners.

Agile Project Management

To reduce the time for content planning, development, and delivery, cross-functional teams may be used. As specified in Figure 2, content planning, development, delivery, and assessment activities are carried out in a pipeline by forming separate teams. When one of the objectives is in the delivery phase, the second would be under development, and the third objective will be in the planning phase, each is taken up by separate teams in a pipeline. (Mundra et al 2013)

A story in agile oriented development represents a subset of features of the system. In the education domain, each objective or content story consists of several tasks. Table 1 specifies the content story template.

According to Burra et al (2013), for each crative process there shoud be corresponding creative roles. In the context of educational domain certain creative roles are assigned namely Content manager, Content Planner, Content Developer and a Content Tester.

A course comprises of several objectives and each of which is associated with a story id. The course content development and the delivery follows an incremental approach in a pipeline, i.e., when the content developer is developing the course content, the content planner may plan for the subsequent content increment at the same time. It may be noted that content developer may also use a learning management

Table 1. Content story template

Story id	As a \<type of user\>	I want to \<perform some task\>	So that I can \<achieve some goals\>
1.	Content manager	Define course objectives Prioritizes objectives	Course outcomes are met
2.	Content Planner	Plan each task and manage	Course content delivery is as per schedule
3.	Content developer	Develop each task	Each task is successfully realized
4.	Content tester	Verify each of the outcomes	The course outcomes are met

system to create the content and configure the same according to the needs. The team for the realization of objectives as content stories consists of 4-5 members known as content Sprint team. The entire team is involved in the design and development of each content story. The content planner schedules and manages each task, content developer develops those small tasks, and the content tester ensures that the learner satisfies the course outcomes.

One of the principles of agile systems is "test first development." The test cases of each task are planned well before proceeding for the development of the content for that objective. There are two advantages to this principle. Firstly the developed material can be tested for required quality before content delivery. Secondly, the degree of conformance to the course outcomes can be assessed. Table 2 presents the test plan template.

Test case id is assigned to test a given objective for a particular course identified by course name. A short description of the goals to be tested is specified. Each outcome may have to be tested with several test cases identified by Test#, T_Date specifies the date on which the test is scheduled. The action to be tested and its actual and expected outcome are recorded. In general, if the expected and actual outcomes matches, the test case passes; otherwise, it Fails. However, in the educational domain, the result cannot be a Boolean value. Instead, we need the degree to which the expected outcomes confirm. A threshold can be set to decide on the acceptability of the degree of the actual result. If the degree of actual result is less than the threshold for several learners, then there is a need to modify the design, delivery, and assessment activities for that objective. Also, the feedback from the student concerning the expected outcomes will help in resolving the issues with content design and delivery.

Analysis of Agile Process for Outcome-Based Education

The agile based model for outcome-based education will succeed if there is an involvement of learners. If the learners are biased or are not interested in giving the feedbacks, this model may fail. However, adoption of the agile process for outcome-based education increases the productivity of the learners.

The main advantage of the agile-based model is that the priority of the course objectives can be modified or new course objectives can also be included during the design and delivery of the course.

Though this model is suitable for classroom or blended mode, it may not be directly applied to the virtual learning environment as the learner can't be involved in all the phases of the incremental model because of its virtual presence. In virtual learning environments, it is assumed that the course planning and content development is completed before commencing the course. The agile process can be applied to realize content delivery with regular feedback from the learners. This feedback will help the instructor to adopt an appropriate content delivery mechanism.

Table 2. Content test plan template

Course name:			Test case id:		Version:	
Description:			Written by/date:		Tested by/date:	
Test #	T_Date	Action/Task	Expected outcome	Actual outcome	Pass?	Degree

Figure 4. Agile oriented process for content delivery

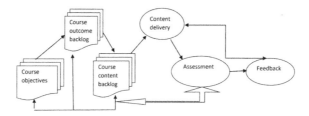

Agile Content Delivery Process in Virtual Learning Environment

The agile model presented in the previous section involves interleaving of several activities like content planning, design, and development, delivery, evaluation, and feedback. Based on the feedback from learners, subsequent iterations, or increments may be modified. However, in a virtual learning environment, all these activities can't be interleaved.

In an agile based content delivery process, the content planning and content designing phases are completed first. The artifacts from these phases are course objectives, course outcomes, and course content databases. The content delivery process is divided into various increments specifying the mechanisms of content delivery of the respective course objective.

In a virtual or e-learning environment, content planning and design are completed before the course delivery begins. Three artifacts namely course objectives, outcomes, and contents backlog are created before launching the course. On the one hand, virtual learning delivery can help learners to take courses from across the globe, which is developed and delivered by experts in their respective field. On the other hand, it lacks student interest, and it is often seen that the dropout rate is high in a virtual learning environment. One of the reasons for the increase in dropout rate is due to the same delivery method adopted for the entire course, and the feedback is usually collected at the end of the course.

In the agile oriented process for content delivery in a virtual learning environment, the instructors begin the first module by introducing its objectives, outcomes, and delivery mode used. The content is then delivered, and at the end of the module or submodule, a formative assessment is conducted. Before collecting the feedback, the instructor introduces the following modules objectives and delivery mechanism planned with justification. The feedback is then received. The feedback form involves questions specific to the completed module and the delivery mechanism proposed for the upcoming module. The feedbacks are thoroughly analyzed, and accordingly, the content delivery technique is selected for the next module.

This approach uses a hybridization of the linear and agile approach. Content planning and content designing are realized linearly. The increments are planned for content delivery, evaluation, and feedback. Figure 5 specifies a partial feedback form which deals with the content delivery queries.

It is evident from the feedback form that learners response to the current delivery mechanism is assessed first. This will help the content manager to make changes to the delivery mechanism used to realize the initial modules. Before collecting the feedback, the objectives, outcomes, and delivery mechanism to be adopted in the next module is presented to the learners. The learners can suggest changes in the delivery mechanism. This approach helps the instructor to select the appropriate delivery mechanism. It is observed that this process makes learning more interesting, and the number of students completing the course with a better degree of knowledge may increase.

Figure 5. Feedback form template

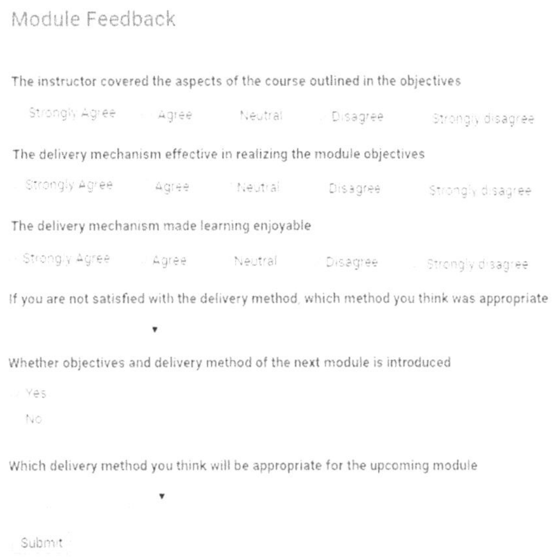

Module Feedback

The instructor covered the aspects of the course outlined in the objectives

  Strongly Agree   Agree   Neutral   Disagree   Strongly disagree

The delivery mechanism effective in realizing the module objectives

  Strongly Agree   Agree   Neutral   Disagree   Strongly disagree

The delivery mechanism made learning enjoyable

  Strongly Agree   Agree   Neutral   Disagree   Strongly disagree

If you are not satisfied with the delivery method, which method you think was appropriate

            ▼

Whether objectives and delivery method of the next module is introduced

  Yes

  No

Which delivery method you think will be appropriate for the upcoming module

            ▼

Submit

EXPERIMENTATION AND RESULTS

The agile based process model for dynamic selection of instructional methods based on learners feedback is applied to a course offered to graduates and undergraduates. The applicability of the proposed agile model is tested on three modules of the course. About 45 students have enrolled for this course. To incorporate all scenarios of learning environment, the blended mode of learning was adopted in the said course.

In the first phase, the objectives of the first module, its expected outcomes, and the planned instructional method are briefed to the learners. The instructional method selected during the delivery of the first module was learning by example. In this approach, mostly the learner is passive but was introduced with the concepts with the help of real-time examples. After completion of the module, the learners were assessed on each of the outcomes. The formative assessment contained questions at three levels viz., remembering, understanding, and analyzing.

After completion of the first module's assessment, the student is introduced to second module goals, its outcomes, and the planned instructional method. In the second module, the delivery method chosen was a case study method. Then the feedback is collected from the learners. It is observed that almost all the learners were happy with the selected content delivery mechanism for the second module.

In the second phase, after completion of the second module, learners were assessed for each of the outcomes. The formative assessment contained questions at three levels viz. applying, analyzing, and evaluating. The performance of the candidates from the first assessment to that of the second is analyzed. The following state transition matrix specifies, the grade transitions of learners from the initial evaluation to the second. Rows in the figure define the grades earned in the initial assessment, and the columns of the matrix represent grades of other evaluation. Each cell value specifies the number of students whose grades changed from the initial assessment to the second. For example, cell (D, C) value is 9, which indicates that nine students whose grade was D in the first assessment got grade C in the second assessment.

The matrix specified in Figure 6 is an upper triangular matrix. It is to observe that there is no degradation in the grades of the learners. It is to note that in a few scenarios, there is no improvement in grades of learners from the first to the second assessment.

It is observed in Figure 6, that most of the students have improved their grades. After completion of the formative assessment of the second module, the objectives, outcomes, and the proposed instructional method was again briefed to learners. The feedback from learners is collected after completion of the module. The instructional process planned for the third module was problem-based learning. However, most of the learners were interested in learning by doing as they would like to realize the objectives of the third module practically. Based on the feedback of learners, the instructional method was changed.

After completion of the third module, learners were being evaluated for each of the outcomes of the unit. The formative assessment contained questions at three levels viz., analyzing, evaluating, and creating. The performance of learners from the second assessment to that of the third module is analysed.

The characteristic of the above transition matrix is that it is also an upper triangular matrix. It is evident from Figure 7 that most of the learners have improved their grades from the second assessment to the third assessment. With the comparison of the two transition matrices, it is to note that learners in lower grades have reduced. For example, (F, F) and (F, D) transitions in Figure 6 are eight and eight, respectively. The same change in Figure 7 is eight and seven, respectively.

Further, it is to note that the learners felt that learning is enjoyable. At the end of the first module, 60% of learners felt that learning is enjoyable. This percentage was raised to 80% after completion of the second module and further to 95.5% by the end of the third module.

The results show that the performance of the leaners was average at the end of the first module, and further, only 60% of the leaners indicated that learning is enjoyable. Learners do not much appreciate passive learning. Alternatively, the learners enjoyed the case study and problem-based learning.

Figure 6. State transition matrix representing the transition of grades from first to the second assessment

	F	D	C	B	B+	A	A+
F	8	8	1	0	0	0	0
D	0	3	9	1	2	0	0
C	0	0	2	2	3	0	0
B	0	0	0	0	2	1	1
B+	0	0	0	0	0	1	0
A	0	0	0	0	0	1	0
A+	0	0	0	0	0	0	0

Figure 7. State transition matrix representing the transition of grades from second to the third assessment

	F	D	C	B	B+	A	A+
F	0	7	0	1	0	0	0
D	0	2	3	3	4	0	0
C	0	0	3	1	3	3	1
B	0	0	0	0	2	1	0
B+	0	0	0	0	3	4	0
A	0	0	0	0	0	1	2
A+	0	0	0	0	0	0	1

Finally, a summative assessment was conducted to check the degree of conformance to learning outcomes. The results indicate that the degree of compliance of learning outcomes is higher as compared to the linear approach. Through analysis on learners who couldn't improve their grades to better levels is carried out. It is to note that such learners have issues in the understanding of some part of content and questions in assessment due to the knowledge of language and grammar.

The traditional outcome-based education system doesn't possess continuous feedback. For the same set of students, the linear model of design and delivery is used to compare their performance with that of an agile approach. It is observed that in most of the case student performance didn't improve in a linear model. Further, as students involvement is minimal, the feedback was not taken from learners regularly. Learners in the final feedback requested for a modified delivery mechanism which couldn't be incorporated in the current course.

CONCLUSION AND FUTURE DIRECTIONS

Washington Accord and its affiliate organizations introduce best practices to improve the quality of education. The National Board of Accreditation in India has introduced outcome-based educational pedagogy in higher educational institutes. However, because of the several limitations like tight course schedule, it is challenging to take feedbacks regularly for the continuous improvements of the teaching-learning process. In this chapter, the authors propose a linear and agile based process model for outcome-based education. The Agile Project management framework is also recommended to manage the artifacts of iterative and incremental development.

The use of Learning Management Systems and ICT tools have increased exponentially in the last decade. However, at the same time, the dropout rate has also increased considerably. The most important aspect is the acceptability of the content and the time schedules of a particular course. Agile-based content development for virtual learning is proposed to address these issues. The proposed approach gives continuous feedback, and accordingly, next set objectives are planned to dynamically select an instructional method which is acceptable by the learners. The proposed model is applicable for a course spread across a semester, and the results show that the student's performance has mostly improved from one increment to the other. Further, the feedback also shows the high motivational levels of the learners.

The agile based method can also be applied explicitly for content development to enhance the quality of the course material. In the same way, student feedback can incorporate changes dynamically. In the future, the agile process may include the input of learners and the self-appraisal of the instructors to gain the confidence of both instructor and learner. In general, it may result in a win-win model for all stakeholders of the education system. The proposed model can be better realized by continuous interaction between instrutors and learners which are instances of a human. The continuous feedback of learners helps in improving the content delivery mechanisms.

The proposed model is implemented effectively, and it helps learners in realizing course outcomes and also enjoy the learning methods adopted. This method may fail if it lacks proper planning. An adequate work break down structure is needed to realize the agile model within the given time frame. Further, the proposed agile model may fail if the learner is not interested in being involved during the content design and delivery process.

REFERENCES

Anderson, L. W., David, R. K., Peter, W. A., Kathleen, A. C., Meyer, R. E., Pentrich, P. R., . . . Wittrock, M. C. (2013). A Taxonomy for Learning, Teaching & Assessing. Pearson New International Edition.

Bari. (2014). Quality Frameworks and Standards in E-Learning Systems. *International Journal of the Computer, the Internet and Management, 22*(3), 1-7.

Branch, M. R. (n.d.). *Instructional Design: The ADDIE approach.* Springer Verlag.

Chatterjee, C. (2016). Measurement of E-Learning Quality. *3rd International Conference on Advanced Computing and Communication Systems*, 38-42.

Chun, A.H.W. (2004). The Agile Teaching/Learning Methodology and Its e-Learning Platform. *Lecture Notes in Computer Science, 3143.*

Correia, A., Gonçalves, A., & Misra, S. (2019). Integrating the Scrum Framework and Lean Six Sigma. *Lecture Notes in Computer Science, 11623.*

D'Souza, M. J., & Rodrigues, P. (2015). Extreme Pedagogy: An Agile Teaching-Learning Methodology for Engineering Education. *Indian Journal of Science and Technology, 8*(9), 828–833. doi:10.17485/ijst/2015/v8i9/53274

Dash, S. K., Patro, S., & Behera, B. K. (2013). Teaching Methods and its Efficacy: An Evaluation by Students. *Journal of Indian Acad Forensic Med, 35*(4), 321–324.

David, M., & Colleen, A. (2013). *Effectiveness of active learning in the arts and science.* Humanities Department Faculty Publications & Research paper 45.

De la Barra, C.L., Crawford, B., Soto, R., Misra, S., & Monfroy, E. (2013). Agile Software Development: It Is about Knowledge Management and Creativity. *Lecture Notes in Computer Science, 7973.*

Dixson, D. D., & Worrell, F. C. (2016). Formative and Summative Assessment in the Classroom. *Journal of Theory into Practice, 55*(2), 153–159. doi:10.1080/00405841.2016.1148989

Dylan, W. (2013). Assessment: The Bridge between Teaching and Learning. *Voices from the Middle, 21*(2), 15–22.

Esfijani, A. (2018). Measuring Quality in Online Education: A Meta-synthesis. *American Journal of Distance Education, 32*(1), 57–73. doi:10.1080/08923647.2018.1417658

Ganayaupfu, E. M. (2013). Teaching Methods and Students Academic Performances. *International Journal of Humanities & Social Sciences Inversion, 12*(9), 29–35.

Khan, B. H., & Joshi, V. (2006). E-Learning Who, What & How? *Journal of Creative Communications, 1*(1), 61–75. doi:10.1177/097325860500100104

Mudra, A., & Misra, S. (2013) Practical Scrum-Scrum Team: Way to Produce Successful and Quality Software. *IEEE Proceedings on 2013 13th International Conference on Computational Science and its Applications*, 119-123.

Peters & Pedrycz. (2012). *Software Engineering: An Engineering Approach*. Wiley India.

Pipan, M., Arch, T., Srdjevic, Z., Srdjevic, B., & Balaban, I. (2014). Group Assessment of Learning Management Systems. *33rd International Conference on Organizational Science Development*, 564-570.

Prince, M. (2004). Does Active Learning Works? A Review of the Research. *Journal of Engineering Education*, *93*(3), 223–231. doi:10.1002/j.2168-9830.2004.tb00809.x

Rahman & Hamed. (2017). E-Learning Service Quality. *International Conference on Research and Innovation in Information Systems*, 1-6.

Rossi, R., & Mustaro, P. N. (2014). Process Management for e-learning Quality. *International Journal of Information and Education Technology (IJIET)*, *4*(4), 302–307. doi:10.7763/IJIET.2014.V4.418

Schawber, K., & Beedle, M. (2001). *Agile Software Development with Scrum*. Englewood Cliffs, NJ: Prentice Hall.

Sharp, J. H., & Lang, G. (2018). Agile in Teaching and Learning: Conceptual Framework and Research Agenda. *Journal of Information Systems Education*, *29*(2), 45–52.

Sommerville. (2011). *Software Engineering* (9th ed.). Addison-Wesley.

Uppal, M. A., Ali, S., & Gulliver, S. R. (2018). Factors determining e-learning service quality. *British Journal of Educational Technology*, *49*(3), 412–426. doi:10.1111/bjet.12552

Zamudio, L., Aguilar, J. A., Tripp, C., & Misra, S. (2017, July). A Requirements Engineering Techniques Review in Agile Software Development Methods. *Lecture Notes in Computer Science, 1408*, 683-698.

Chapter 17
Impact of Social Media on Consumer Purchase Intention:
A Developing Country Perspective

Anil Kumar

https://orcid.org/0000-0001-9057-6043

VNS Group of Institutions, Bhopal, India

Nagendra Kumar Sharma

https://orcid.org/0000-0002-6698-8926

Graphic Era University, Dehradun, India

ABSTRACT

In the current scenario, social media play a key role for the customers because the content generated by users through social media has a great influence on their purchase intention. The objective of this study is to examine the impact of social media factors that influence the student's purchase intention through social media. Three factors, namely trust, perceived usefulness, and social commerce construct, were tested and examined the impact on purchase intention of the students. Data were gathered from 240 undergraduate and postgraduate students. Structural equation modelling was used to get the results from the data. The outcomes of the data analysis show that majorly prevailing factor that influences the purchase intention of young consumers was consumer trust via social media interface. Further, that is followed by social commerce construct and perceived usefulness. Furthermore, it has also been found that all the constructs are positively associated with purchase intention. In the end, practical implications, limitations, and future research scope of this study were discussed.

DOI: 10.4018/978-1-7998-1279-1.ch017

INTRODUCTION

"Social media refer to the online platforms and tools that people use to share opinions and experiences including photos, videos, music, insights and perceptions with each other" (Turban et al.2009). The Social Media plays an important role in current digital era because of the technology. Many users are able to share their content online and exchange different information with the general public and their close one. The current period is the internet intensive era that gives a wonderful opportunity to interact with many people on a single platform and that too without meeting them physically (Gruzd et al. 2011). In the present era, the social media environment is viewed by customers in a new way, especially in a commercial way. Its development and the emergence of online purchasing facility have turned customers into consumers. Customers consider social media websites as a service medium, where they can engage on real-time bases (Leggat, 2010) to remain updated all time with the content on social media. Due to this reason and its importance, Google has changed the algorithm of their search system to facilitate customers to see the updated content first (Freidman, 2011). A study conducted by Info-graphics, found that almost fifty percent of the users using Twitter and Facebook are engaged in discussing about the products and suggesting other users about their experiences. They usually do all these commercial activities once they associated with the brand on their social media pages (Jackson, 2011).

On the basis of the previous studies in the field of social media, there is no doubts that social media makes a better path for consumers to intend towards a successful purchase. Social media platforms or other internet based communities are one of its kind of web based technologies that enable users to interact and spread valuable information among desired groups (Lu & Hsiao 2010). In this way, social media is used as a tool for the marketer. Marketers take this advantage and design marketing strategy to turn them into potential customers. From the consumer's point of view, the social media environment is very easy and convenient for people looking for a product or service. Thus the role of social media has changed the system of communication among customers and marketers (Hennig-Thurau et al., 2004) and the social media play the most important role as a medium of communication(Dahnil et al., 2014). SNSs become the centre point for electronic commerce activities where consumers make social connections and participate virtually in real time (Mueller et al. 2011).

The context of the research is chosen as India because, India's internet user base, India is second largest after China. The internet user growth in India is expected to be three times the world average, growing at a CAGR of ~20%. India and will add ~400 million users in the next five years. India is also home to the world's second-largest user base for social media giants like Facebook and LinkedIn (NASSCOM report 2016). A report made by Ernst and Young LLP (Jan'2016) *on "Future of Digital Content Consumption in India (FDCCI)"*states that, Smartphone penetration in India is expected to grow to 520 million by 2020, making India one of the largest smartphone economies in the world. Broadband penetration will increase from 14% today to 40% by 2020.

Thus, these figures are good reasons to carries out this study on social media. We have taken three important constructs as social commerce construct, trust and perceived usefulness and examine the impact on purchase intention of an individual. The objectives of the study were to examine the relationship among social commerce constructs, perceived usefulness, and trust and purchase intention while another one is to examine, how social commerce construct gives impact on consumer trust in m-commerce and e-commerce. The study made its best effort to establish the relationship between consumer trust and perception lead usefulness.

The paper contains literature review section, where the hypotheses are also proposed based on the literature evidences in the area of social media. A theoretical framework was also added to understand the associations among the variables. Further, the study is followed by research methodology section, data analysis and results. In the end, discussion, conclusion, limitations of the study were presented. Future research and scope were also discussed in the end of the paper.

LITERATURE REVIEW

The theoretical analysis with the help of previous studies serves as the platform to develop, describe and elaborate the relationship among the variables seems relevant and identified through observation, interviews and the review of the literature (Sekaran & Bougie, 2009). Kaplan and Haenlein (2010) defines social media as "*a group of Internet-based applications that build on the ideological and technological foundations of web 2.0, and allow the creation and exchange of user-generated content*". In its phase of inception due to expansion of network infrastructure, social media platform was used by mostly youngster to play several web based games and entertainment (Laudon & Traver, 2016). Social media platform contains many network based tools like, Facebook, Twitter, YouTube and Bloggers etc. that are available for an individual to use as a medium for them to participate. Each tool has its own user base and helps them to develop purchase intention. In the present study, the research model is influenced by Technology Acceptance Model (TAM) that was proposed by Davis (1986). The imperative assumptions behind TAM, was the purchase intention of the consumers mediated by consumer trust, perceived usefulness and social commerce factors. Therefore, in the study TAM was adopted as it is a suitable model to explain the relationships such as purchase intention lead by social media factors in the study (Gillenson & Sherrell, 2002; Moon & Kim, 2001).

Consumer Trust

Consumer trust is awfully vibrant in nature and played an imperative position among all web based transactions. In this way, it is significant to reveal the background of a consumer's trust associated to its perceived usefulness and purchase intention of an individual. In the online environment, people have complete freedom to publish and express their feelings towards certain products or services without disclosing the real identity (Ng, 2013). Eagly & Chaiken (1993) found that the impact of a message depends on the number of positive attributes the communicators possess and therefore depend on the users to determine the trustworthiness of the contributors in order to either adopt or reject the information presented. Information received from highly trusted sources is perceived to be useful and reliable, and thereby facilitates knowledge transfer (Ko et al., 2005). In the present scenario, customers exchange the shopping experiences on social media with the people and enforce web vendors to add functions for customers to review and rate the products. The online web vendor continuously improves the quality of their websites and the available services to enhance buyers' trust. Social media provides a platform where people can discuss online, get advice from trusted individuals and then plan to purchase them (Rubel, 2005). Trust is an important element of social capital and necessary to maintain relations (Mayer et al., 1995). The customer intention to purchase products online influenced by the trust in the website of the products (Kim et al., 2008) because trust brings satisfaction to the consumers and help in reducing the searching cost (Gulati, 1995). The trust on product recommendation through social media stimulus the purchase intention and the user may purchase such products (Gordon, 2007). Since trust in social media influences the intensity of networking (Ulusu et al., 2011).This will bring trusted relationship. Previous studies in E-commerce strongly related the trust with the disclosure of information about shoppers (Metzger, 2004) and intention to purchase (Lumsden & MacKay, 2006). From the past study, it was confirmed that consumers' product recommendations had an impact on consumer purchasing behaviour (Chevalier and Mayzlin, 2006). Several researchers have shown the direct positive relationship between trust and purchase intention (Bhattacherjee, 2002; McKnight et al. 1998).

Perceived Usefulness

A perceived usefulness can be understood as the level where, an individual makes its belief that after using a specific system he or she can achieve a better growth and work performance in his/her personal life (Davis, 1989; Gefen & Straub, 2000). In the past several empirical studies provide the evidence that perceived usefulness positively affected the attitude towards using information enabled systems (Venkatesh and Bala, 2008; Venkatesh and Davis, 2000). In the virtual environment, new ideas and opinions are shared by the users about the products and services. The perceived usefulness is predicted on the basis of its relevance, timeliness and accuracy. It is thus necessary to have only the relevant, timely, up-to-date and accurate information in the online community to take better decisions (Dunk, 2004, Wixom and Todd, 2005). People would judge individual perception of these opinions about the usefulness to help them to make a better purchase decision. Thus if members of social networking sites think that a comment or like is useful, they will have greater chances to accept the comment and take suitable purchase decision. Previous studies indicated that perceived usefulness positively affects the purchase intention (Sin et al., 2012; Lee et al., 2011; Cho & Fiorito, 2009; Ahn et al., 2007).

Social Commerce Constructs

Social commerce involves multiple disciplines, including marketing, computer science, sociology and psychology etc. Social interactions of consumers create social word of mouth which ultimately brings trust among the people. In the present scenario, it was claimed by the researchers that through social media platforms such as forums and communities, ratings and reviews, and referrals and recommendations consumer become sociable. These social platforms are social commerce constructs. The consumers and e-vendor develop the personal relationships during the process. From the past study about the social commerce construct, it was found that that customer feedbacks and ratings promote a higher level of trust (Ba & Pavlou, 2002). Social commerce facilitates the consumers' ratings and reviews, and recommendations and referrals through social media. Ratings and reviews help customers to see the friends' reviews and make a suitable decision of purchase. The people join virtual communities for information exchange, and it has a direct influence on customer behaviour (Ridings & Gefen, 2004). Previous research shows that reviews by a third party significantly influenced the purchase intention of consumers (Chen & Xie, 2005). Social commerce constructs also have an influence on trust. Previous studies show that customer ratings influenced the level of trust, which resulted in the form of increase in sales (Swamynathan et al., 2008). In fact, positive ratings have a strong influence on trust formation (Ba & Pavlou, 2002). This study also found that social context is the other factor that influences trust (Weisberg et al., 2011). Previous research shows that social presence increases the level of trust (Gefen & Straub, 2004) and that social presence can be achieved by social commerce constructs.

In order to understand these constructs more closely a table (Table-1) of theoretical review was prepared that shows the significant outcomes of the previous studies.

Thus, it can be concluded that prospective consumers show purchase intention that is influenced by the recommendations of the connected users such as friends, peers and family on web based community called social network. It develops trust because they understand and know each other. Following hypotheses were formulated in the study that is based on the previous significant research papers. A theoretical model was also proposed in the study as shown in the fig.1. The model is empirically tested in the study and validated by the significant research findings.

H1: Trust has a positive impact on the perceived usefulness of an individual.
H2: perceived usefulness has a positive impact on purchase intention of an individual.
H3: Trust has a positive impact on purchase intention of an individual.
H4: Social commerce constructs have a positive impact on an individual trust.
H5: Social commerce constructs have a positive impact on purchase intention of an individual.

RESEARCH METHODOLOGY

The research design is descriptive in nature because there is clear tested hypotheses that enable a researcher to get statistical findings and concludes the results (Malhotra, 2004). The study conducted a survey on Pharmacy, Management and Engineering students in Bhopal MP India in order to validate the proposed model. University students were selected because the current generation of young adults are

Table 1. Significant findings of previous studies

Author(s)	Parameters	Significant Findings
Eagly & Chaiken (1993); Ko et al. (2005); Rubel (2005); Kim et al., (2008); Ulusu et al., (2011); Ng, (2013); Lin et al., (2018).	Consumer Trust	Social media platform develops consumer trust based on the experimental purchase via shared experiences. The increasing developing trust towards use of social media among consumers is fruitful for developing consumer trust towards brands and perceived usefulness.
Venkatesh and Davis (2000); Ahn et al. (2007); Venkatesh and Bala (2008); Cho & Fiorito (2009) Sin et al. (2012); Alalwan (2018).	Perceived Usefulness	According to several studies it is found that perceived usefulness is one of the imperative factor which leads to purchase intention. It is also found in a study that the positive customer attitude is based on perceived usefulness lead by online advertising
Gefen & Straub (2004); Ridings & Gefen (2004); Chen & Xie (2005); Swamynathan et al. (2008); Weisberg et al. (2011); Bai et al. (2015); Chen et al (2017).	Social Commerce Constructs	Social commerce contains several key benefits such as social support, behavioural change based on positive influences and other social factors. The overall findings indicate that social commerce leads to better trust and consumer purchase intention.
Ng (2013); Balakrishnan et al. (2014); See-To & Ho (2014); Bai et al. (2015); Gunawan & Huarng, (2015); Zhu et al. (2016); Alalwan, (2018); Chen & Chang (2018); Kim et al. (2018); Sokolova, K. & Kefi, H. (2019).	Purchase Intention	Source credibility, perceived usefulness and social influence leads to purchase intention. On the other hand it is found in the studies that social capital is a strong factor leading to purchase intention. However, perceived value, satisfaction, rating results, reviews and quality of information are significant factors for explaining purchase intention.

Figure 1. Proposed research model

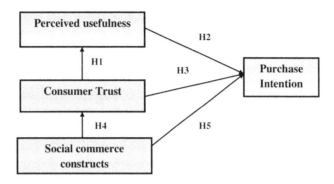

frequent users of online social networks (Wilcox and Stephen, 2013) and also are much more likely to use these sites than adults of thirty or older (Lenhart et al., 2010). The study is conducted with the help of well designed structured questionnaires administered to students. These participants are from different states of India residing in Bhopal, Madhya Pradesh for pursuing their studies. A stipulated measurement instrument i.e. a questionnaire was developed considering five point Likert type scale where, 1 stands for Strongly disagree and 5 stands for strongly agree. The items in the measurement scale were adopted from the previous studies. (Gefen & Straub, 2004; Lin & Lu, 2011; Hajli, 2015; McKnight, et al., 2002). Regular users of facebook, Twitter, Linkedin and Whatsapp etc. were the target respondents of the study. A total of 400 paper questionnaires were distributed and received only 240 usable questionnaires for analysis. Participants ranged from 16 to 30 years old. The youth were selected as targeted respondents because India has the relative advantage at present over other countries in terms of distribution of youth population. As per India's Census 2011, the total youth population is 422 million. India is expected to have 34.33% share of youth in total population by 2020. The demographic profile of the respondents is shown in Table 2.

Before running Partial Least Square- Structured Equation Modeling (PLS-SEM) to test the model and hypotheses, for purifying and validating the measures, we first conducted an exploratory factor analysis (EFA). All the items loaded properly on their intended scale except two items of social media that were deleted because they loaded very low on the intended construct. The factor analysis was carried out to identify the factors determining purchase intention of the respondent. Data were analyzed using SPSS 20 software. The students were asked to rate the items on a five-point scale according to their experience. The test of the validity of data was examined with the help of a Kaiser- Meyer-Ohlin (KMO) measure of sample adequacy and Barlett's test of sphericity. The value of KMO more than 0.7, is the acceptable threshold value for data reduction i.e. factor reduction (Cerny & Kaiser, 1977; Hair et al., 2010). These two tests satisfied the validity of data for factor analysis (Table 3). To determine the number of variables, only the Eigenvalues greater than or equal to 1 were considered (Guttman 1954; Kaiser 1960).

Table 2. Demographic profile of respondents

	Age Group			Education background of the students			Gender	
	16-20	21-25	Above 25	BE	Pharmacy	Management	Male	Female
No of respondents	62	151	27	62	47	131	189	51

Table 3.

KMO and Bartlett's Test		
Kaiser-Meyer-Olkin Measure of Sampling Adequacy.		.802
Bartlett's Test of Sphericity	Approx. Chi-Square	1831.959
	Df	136
	Sig.	.000

RESULT ANALYSIS

PLS-SEM was applied for analysis in the study. PLS-SEM has become an effective tool for survey-based research because It is also useful for the low sample size and it does not require normality treatment. It provides conformist estimates of every path coefficients (Henseler et al., 2009; Hair et al., 2011).

PLS path models give two types of results in the form of measurement model and structural model. One is showing the relationship between latent variables whereas other one Shows the association between a latent variable and its literature based concepts (Ringle et al., 2010).

The Measurement Model Estimates

The reliability and validity of the constructs in the study were analyzed to verify the model of the study (Hulland, 1999). While considering reliability and validity of the measurement model, CR (composite reliability) was found more than 0.70 i.e. threshold value (Wasko & Faraj 2005).

After getting the output of the data analysis it was found that the internal consistencies are more than 0.70 in both the measurement i.e. CR and Cronbach's alpha value. In this way the results indicates that the data is reliable (Naylor et al. 2012). The results of reliability meaausres shown in Table-3. The convergent validity has been also checked to verify the validity of the measurement scale which was done with the help of average variance extracted (AVE) where, the value of AVE must be above 0.50 (Wixom & Watson 2001; Wasko & Faraj 2005). The table-3 shows, that the composite reliability of various dimensions is higher than 0.7; Average Variance Extracted (AVE) is higher than 0.5. Thus the convergent validity of the construct is considered adequate.

As per the criteria of Fornell and Larcker (1981), discriminant validity was also tested. Here, in the study it was found that the value of AVE is greater than its shared variance in comparison to another construct and hence it also confirms dicriminant validity established and shown in Table 5.

The Structural Model

The association between exogenous and endogenous that are latent variables shown with the help of structural model (Hulland, 1999). The explanatory power of the structural model based on squared multiple correlations (R^2) and path coefficient (β) values. Where R^2 shows the percentage of variance, an endogenous depicts in the model, whilst the path coefficients show the strengths of relationships between constructs (Chin, 1998). $R^2$of endogenous is considered as substantial = 0.26, moderate =0.13 and weak=0.02 (Cohen et al., 2003). In this study, the proposed research model explained 41.7% of the variance in the purchase intention due to trust, which is considered to be the good in terms of explanatory

Table 4. The convergent validity

Items	Factor Loadings	Composite Reliability	Average Variance extracted	Cronbach Alpha
T2	0.647	0.869	0.625	0.80
T3	0.827			
T4	0.824			
T5	0.848			
PU1	0.923	0.926	0.807	0.88
PU2	0.913			
PU3	0.858			
SCC1	0.529	0.806	0.515	0.67
SCC2	0.793			
SCC3	0.727			
SCC4	0.789			
PI1	0.812	0.88	0.602	0.83
PI2	0.633			
PI3	0.871			
PI4	0.591			
PI5	0.917			

Table 5. Discriminant validity

Constructs	Perceived Usefulness	Purchase Intention	Social commerce constructs	Trust
Perceived Usefulness	**0.898**			
Purchase Intention	0.264	**0.776**		
Social commerce constructs	0.193	0.493	**0.718**	
Trust	0.191	0.561	0.395	**0.791**

power. The social commerce construct having 30.4% variance in the purchase intention and Perceived usefulness has the least variance in purchase intention. Those constructs having highest β value indicates significant construct and vice-versa that can be seen in table-6, the direct effect of trust on purchase intention (0.417) is higher than the social commerce constructs on purchase intention (.304). This shows that trust is more important than social commerce construct in intention to purchase the products. It is also clear that effect of social commerce constructs on trust (.395) is stronger than the purchase intention (.304). Thus trust is the most significant construct while social commerce constructs is the second most influential construct. The perceived usefulness is though useful in making the purchase decisions but its influence is least.

Table 6. Path coefficient

Constructs	Perceived Usefulness	Trust	Purchase Intention
Perceived Usefulness			0.126
Social commerce constructs		0.395	0.304
Trust	0.191		0.417

Table 7. Significance levels 0.05 (2-tailed test)

Hypothesis	t-value	p value
H1: Trust has a positive impact on the perceived usefulness of an individual.	2.813	0.005
H2: Perceived usefulness has a positive impact on purchase intention of an individual.	2.39	0.017
H3: Trust has a positive impact on purchase intention of an individual.	9.503	0.000
H4: Social commerce constructs have a positive impact on an individual trust.	10.477	0.000
H5: Social commerce constructs have a positive impact on purchase intention of an individual.	4.644	0.000

Figure 2. Bootstrapping results significance levels 0.05 (2-tailed test)

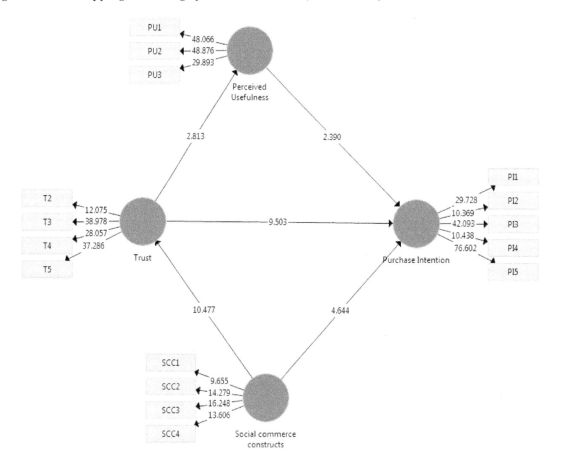

Goodness of Fit (GoF) of the Model

In order to check the Goodness of Fit (GoF) of the model a method adopted by Tenenhaus et al. (2005) was considered. In this method the AVE and value of R^2 were considered. The value was found 0.52 which indicates a good model fit as per the standards suggested by Wetzels et al. (2009).

Hypotheses Testing

To test the hypotheses, the significance level of the the various associations were checked which was based on the t-statics found with the help of PLS bootstrapping. Table-7 shows the results of the hypotheses and observed values of the t. Table-6 shows that every hypothesis used in the study are accepted. The final version of the model after bootstrapping shown in figure-2.

The Mediation Effect

The mediation effect of perceived usefulness and trust on purchase intention was tested in this section. The method employed by Baron and Kenny (1986) is applied for testing the mediating effect. Baron and Kenny (1986) suggested the following steps. We first test the mediating effect of perceived usefulness.

Step1. This step shows that the Trust (T) as an independent variable is correlated with the dependent variable purchase intention (PI).

$$PI = a + b \, (T) \hspace{6cm} \text{(Model1)}$$

Step2. This step shows that the Trust (T) as an independent variable is correlated with the mediating variable perceived usefulness (PU).

$$PU = a + b \, (T) \hspace{6cm} \text{(Model2)}$$

Step3. This step shows that the mediating variable perceived usefulness(PU) affects the dependent variable purchase intention(PI) and controlling the independent variable Trust(T).

$$PI = a + b \, (PU) + c(T) \hspace{5cm} \text{(Model3)}$$

Now we test the mediating effect of Trust

Step1. This step shows that the social commerce construct (SCC) as an independent variable is correlated with the dependent variable purchase intention (PI)

$$PI = a + b \, (SCC) \hspace{6cm} \text{(Model 4)}$$

Step2. This step shows that the social commerce construct (SCC) as an independent variable is correlated with the mediating variable trust.

$$T = a + b \ (SCC) \hspace{4cm} (Model5)$$

Step3. This step shows that the mediating variable trust (T) affects the dependent variable purchase intention (PI) and controlling the independent variable social commerce construct.

$$PI = a + b \ (T) + c \ (SCC) \hspace{3cm} (Model\ 6)$$

Table 8 Presents the results of the regression analysis of the all six models as shown above. Models 1 and Model 2 show that independent variable trust (T) affects both the dependent variable PI and mediating variable PU. Similarly, model 4 and Model 5 show that independent variable SCC significantly affects both the dependent variable PI and the mediating variables T. Model 3 shows that both T and PU significantly affect PI. It implied that the PU partially mediates the relationship between trust (T) and purchase intention (PI). Similarly, Model 6 shows that both SCC and T significantly affect PI implying that the trust (T) partially mediates the relationship between SCC and PI. This is well supported by previous studies (Ganguly et al.,2010; Hong & Cha,2013).

DISCUSSION

In this paragraph, the findings are discussed as follow.

We have hypothesized that "Trust has a positive impact on the perceived usefulness of an individual". From the analysis the hypothesis is satisfied (t =2.813 p =.005). This is well supported by the previous studies (Kim et al., 2008; Gulati, 1995). Trust brings satisfaction to the consumers and helps in reducing the searching cost (Gulati, 1995). Thus it can be concluded that Trust has a positive impact on the perceived usefulness of an individual.

We have hypothesized that "perceived usefulness has a positive impact on purchase intention of an individual". From the analysis the hypothesis is satisfied (t = 2.39 p =.017). This is well supported by the previous studies (Sin et al., 2012; Cho & Fiorito, 2009; Ahn et al., 2007, Lee et al., 2011). (Dunk, 2004, Wixom and Todd, 2005) concluded that relevant, timely & up-to-date information in the online community help in better decision making. In this way, it is concluded that there is a positive impact of perceived usefulness on consumer purchase intention.

Table 8. Mediation effect of perceived usefulness and trust results

Model	Dependent Variable	Independent Variable	B	SE	T	P-value	Adj R²	F
1	PI	T	0.543	0.077	9.969	0.00	.292	99.378
2	PU	T	0.169	0.156	2.644	0.009	0.024	6.989
3	PI	T	0.512	0.077	9.468	0.00	0.321	57.576
		PU	0.183	0.032	3.380	0.001		
4	PI	SCC	0.469	0.062	8.191	0.000	0.217	67.087
5	T	SCC	0.400	0.045	6.725	0.000	0.156	45.227
6	PI	T	0.423	0.080	7.520	0.000	.365	69.643
		SCC	0.300	0.061	5.334	0.000		

We have hypothesized that "Trust has a positive impact on purchase intention of an individual". From the analysis the hypothesis is satisfied (t =9.503 p =0.00). The findings are well supported by the previous studies (Pavlou, 2003; Gefen and Straub, 2004). Chen and Barnes (2007) found that trust is an important factor in influencing purchase intention. When a consumer has a higher degree of trust, the consumer will elicit a higher degree of purchase intentions (Gefen and Straub, 2004). Thus it can be concluded that there is a positive & significant relationship between trust and purchase intention.

We have hypothesized that " The Social commerce constructs have a significant positive impact on an individual trust". From the analysis the hypothesis is satisfied (t =10.48 p =0.00). This is well supported by the previous studies (Swamynathan et al., 2008; Weisberg et al.2011). Social context & social presence are the factors that increase the level of trust in social media platforms (Weisberg et al., 2011; Gefen & Straub, 2004). Thus it can be concluded that there is a positive & significant relationship between Social commerce constructs and trust.

We have hypothesized that "The Social commerce constructs have a strong significant positive impact on purchase intention of an individual". From the analysis the hypothesis is satisfied (t = 4.64, p =0.00). This is well supported by the previous study (Chen & Xie, 2005). Kim and Srivastava (2007), examined the social impact on online customers and their purchasing decisions. They found that social factors significantly impact customers' purchase intention. Thus it can be concluded that there is a positive & significant relationship between Social commerce constructs and purchase intention.

In the study we have also examine the mediating role of trust in purchase intention as well as mediating role of perceived usefulness. The findings suggest that trust and perceived usefulness partially mediates the purchase intention.

CONCLUSION

This study examined the impact of trust, social commerce construct and perceived usefulness on purchase intention among Indian students. The outcomes showed that three imperative factors, i.e. trust, social commerce construct and perceived usefulness significantly & positively affect the purchase intention. Furthermore, It has also been examined the impact of social commerce construct on trust and the impact of trust on perceived usefulness. The results supported all the five hypotheses formulated in the study.

The empirical findings suggested that respondents' trust and their purchase intentions were two important factors enhancing the willingness to purchase the socially-recommended products from the website. It is also supported by past study (Kim et al., 2008; McKnight et al., 2002). Consumers' trust in product recommendations had a direct and significant positive effect on purchase intentions (Hsiao et al., 2010) and it has been also proved in the study.

The findings of the study strongly advocates that the respondents of the study have a strong faith towards social media that helps them in taking buying decision via suggestions and recommendations of their social media friends. This concept is proved in the study i.e. positive relationship between social commerce and purchase intention.

The results give some practical implication to the social sites owners as to how social commerce constructs can help in developing the trust and gives a strong impact on consumer purchase intention. The implications of the present study are that in this work we propose a new model given the new concepts in social media. This research develops the literature of social media by introducing trust, perceived usefulness and social commerce construct through an empirical study. This research also discusses how these constructs can influence purchase intention in this era of globalisation.

No work is said to be perfect so as this research is not without limitations. One of the research limitations is that the study used a five-point Likert-scale. The future research should test the scales using a seven-point Likert-scale to get better results. Another limitation of this study is regarding the respondents. Only students of professional courses were selected as respondents thus the results cannot be generalised. The future study can be expanded to all kind of people as responded with a bigger sample size and more cities should be included.

REFERENCES

Ahn, T., Ryu, S., & Han, I. (2007). The impact of Web quality and playfulness on user acceptance of online retailing. *Information & Management, 44*(3), 263–275. doi:10.1016/j.im.2006.12.008

Alalwan, A. A. (2018). Investigating the impact of social media advertising features on customer purchase intention. *International Journal of Information Management, 42*, 65–77. doi:10.1016/j.ijinfomgt.2018.06.001

Ba, S., & Pavlou, P. A. (2002). Evidence of the effect of trust building technology in electronic markets: Price premiums and buyer behavior. *Management Information Systems Quarterly, 26*(3), 243–268. doi:10.2307/4132332

Bai, Y., Yao, Z., & Dou, Y. F. (2015). Effect of social commerce factors on user purchase behavior: An empirical investigation from renren. com. *International Journal of Information Management, 35*(5), 538–550. doi:10.1016/j.ijinfomgt.2015.04.011

Balakrishnan, B. K., Dahnil, M. I., & Yi, W. J. (2014). The impact of social media marketing medium toward purchase intention and brand loyalty among generation Y. *Procedia: Social and Behavioral Sciences, 148*, 177–185. doi:10.1016/j.sbspro.2014.07.032

Bhattacherjee, A. (2002). Individual trust in online firms: Scale development and initial test. *Journal of Management Information Systems, 19*(1), 211–241. doi:10.1080/07421222.2002.11045715

Cerny, C. A., & Kaiser, H. F. (1977). A study of a measure of sampling adequacy for factor-analytic correlation matrices. *Multivariate Behavioral Research, 12*(1), 43–47. doi:10.120715327906mbr1201_3 PMID:26804143

Chen, A., Lu, Y., & Wang, B. (2017). Customers' purchase decision-making process in social commerce: A social learning perspective. *International Journal of Information Management, 37*(6), 627–638. doi:10.1016/j.ijinfomgt.2017.05.001

Chen, C. C., & Chang, Y. C. (2018). What drives purchase intention on Airbnb? Perspectives of consumer reviews, information quality, and media richness. *Telematics and Informatics, 35*(5), 1512–1523. doi:10.1016/j.tele.2018.03.019

Chen, Y., & Xie, J. (2005). Third-party product review and firm marketing strategy. *Marketing Science, 24*(2), 218–240. doi:10.1287/mksc.1040.0089

Chen, Y. H., & Barnes, S. (2007). Initial trust and online buyer behaviour. *Industrial Management & Data Systems, 107*(1), 21–36. doi:10.1108/02635570710719034

Chevalier, J. A., & Mayzlin, D. (2006). The effect of word of mouth on sales: Online book reviews. *JMR, Journal of Marketing Research, 43*(3), 345–354. doi:10.1509/jmkr.43.3.345

Chin, W. W. (1998). The partial least squares approach to structural equation modeling. *Modern Methods for Business Research, 295*(2), 295-336.

Cho, H., & Fiorito, S. S. (2009). Acceptance of online customization for apparel shopping. *International Journal of Retail & Distribution Management, 37*(5), 389–407. doi:10.1108/09590550910954892

Cohen, J., Cohen, P., West, S. G., & Aiken, L. S. (2003). *Applied Multiple Regression/Correlation Analysis for the Behavioral Sciences* (3rd ed.). Mahwah, NJ: Lawrence Erlbaum Associates, Publishers.

Dahnil, M. I., Marzuki, K. M., Langgat, J., & Fabeil, N. F. (2014). Factors influencing SMEs adoption of social media marketing. *Procedia: Social and Behavioral Sciences, 148*, 119–126. doi:10.1016/j.sbspro.2014.07.025

Davis, F. D., Jr. (1986). *A technology acceptance model for empirically testing new end-user information systems: Theory and results* (Doctoral dissertation). Massachusetts Institute of Technology.

Davis, F. D. (1989). Perceived usefulness, perceived ease of use, and user acceptance of information technology. *Management Information Systems Quarterly, 13*(3), 319–340. doi:10.2307/249008

Dunk, A. S. (2004). Product life cycle cost analysis: The impact of customer profiling, competitive advantage, and quality of IS information. *Management Accounting Research, 15*(4), 401–414. doi:10.1016/j.mar.2004.04.001

Eagly, A. H., & Chaiken, S. (1993). *The psychology of attitudes.* Harcourt Brace Jovanovich College Publishers.

Ernst & Young LLP. (2016). *On Future of Digital Content Consumption in India.* Author.

Fornell, C., & Larcker, D.F. (1981). Evaluating structural equation models with unobservable variables and measurement error. *Journal of Marketing Research, 18*(1), 39-50.

Freidman, A. (2011). *Freshness Update + Social Media = Happy Users.* Retrieved from http://searchengineland.com/freshnessupdate-social-media-happy-users-102880

Ganguly, B., Dash, S. B., Cyr, D., & Head, M. (2010). The effects of website design on purchase intention in online shopping: The mediating role of trust and the moderating role of culture. *International Journal of Electronic Business, 8*(4-5), 302–330. doi:10.1504/IJEB.2010.035289

Gefen, D., & Straub, D. W. (2004). Consumer trust in B2C e-Commerce and the importance of social presence: Experiments in e-Products and e-Services. *Omega, 32*(6), 407–424. doi:10.1016/j.omega.2004.01.006

Gillenson, M. L., & Sherrell, D. L. (2002). Enticing online consumers: An extended technology acceptance perspective. *Information & Management, 39*(8), 705–719. doi:10.1016/S0378-7206(01)00127-6

Gordon, K. T. (2007). *Looking for ways to get people talking about your products? The new social shopping trend can help you build buzz.* Academic Press.

Gruzd, A., Wellman, B., & Takhteyev, Y. (2011). Imagining Twitter as an Imagined Community. *The American Behavioral Scientist, 55*(10), 1294–1318. doi:10.1177/0002764211409378

Gulati, R. (1995). Does familiarity breed trust? The implications of repeated ties for contractual choice in alliances. *Academy of Management Journal, 38*(1), 85–112.

Gunawan, D. D., & Huarng, K. H. (2015). Viral effects of social network and media on consumers' purchase intention. *Journal of Business Research, 68*(11), 2237–2241. doi:10.1016/j.jbusres.2015.06.004

Guttman, L. (1954). Some necessary conditions for common-factor analysis. *Psychometrika, 19*(2), 149–161. doi:10.1007/BF02289162

Hair, J. F., Ringle, C. M., & Sarstedt, M. (2011). PLS-SEM: Indeed a silver bullet. *Journal of Marketing Theory and Practice, 19*(2), 139–151. doi:10.2753/MTP1069-6679190202

Hajli, N. (2015). Social commerce constructs and consumer's intention to buy. *International Journal of Information Management, 35*(2), 183–191. doi:10.1016/j.ijinfomgt.2014.12.005

Hennig-Thurau, T., Gwinner, K., Walsh, G., & Gremler, D. (2004). Electronic Word-of-Mouth Via Consumer Opinion Platforms: What Motivates Consumers to Articulate Themselves on the Internet? *Journal of Interactive Marketing, 18*(1), 38–52. doi:10.1002/dir.10073

Henseler, J., Ringle, C. M., & Sinkovics, R. R. (2009). The use of partial least squares path modeling in international marketing. *Advances in International Marketing, 20*, 277-319.

Hong, I. B., & Cha, H. S. (2013). The mediating role of consumer trust in an online merchant in predicting purchase intention. *International Journal of Information Management, 33*(6), 927–939. doi:10.1016/j.ijinfomgt.2013.08.007

Hsiao, K. L., Chuan-Chuan Lin, J., Wang, X. Y., Lu, H. P., & Yu, H. (2010). Antecedents and consequences of trust in online product recommendations: An empirical study in social shopping. *Online Information Review, 34*(6), 935–953. doi:10.1108/14684521011099414

Hulland, J. (1999). Use of partial least squares (PLS) in strategic management research: A review of four recent studies. *Strategic Management Journal, 20*(2), 195–204. doi:10.1002/(SICI)1097-0266(199902)20:2<195::AID-SMJ13>3.0.CO;2-7

Jackson, N. (2011). *Infographic: Using Social Media to Build Brand Loyalty.* Retrieved from: http://www.theatlantic.com/technology/archive/2011/07/infographic-using-social-media-to- uild-brand-loyalty/241701/

Kaiser, H. F. (1960). The application of electronic computers to factor analysis. *Educational and Psychological Measurement, 20*(1), 141–151. doi:10.1177/001316446002000116

Kaplan, A. M., & Haenlein, M. (2010). Users of the world, unite! The challenges and opportunities of Social Media. *Business Horizons, 53*(1), 59–68. doi:10.1016/j.bushor.2009.09.003

Kim, D. J., Ferrin, D. L., & Rao, H. R. (2008). A trust-based consumer decision-making model in electronic commerce: The role of trust, perceived risk, and their antecedents. *Decision Support Systems*, *44*(2), 544–564. doi:10.1016/j.dss.2007.07.001

Kim, J., Kang, S., & Lee, K. H. (2018). How social capital impacts the purchase intention of sustainable fashion products. *Journal of Business Research*. doi:10.1016/j.jbusres.2018.10.010

Kim, Y., & Srivastava, J. (2007, August). Impact of social influence in e-commerce decision making. In *Proceedings of the ninth international conference on Electronic commerce* (pp. 293-302). ACM. 10.1145/1282100.1282157

Ko, D. G., Kirsch, L. J., & King, W. R. (2005). Antecedents of knowledge transfer from consultants to clients in enterprise system implementations. *Management Information Systems Quarterly*, *29*(1), 59–85. doi:10.2307/25148668

Laudon, K. C., & Traver, C. (2016). E-Commerce 2016: Business, Technology, Society. Pearson Higher Ed.

Lee, H. H., Fiore, A. M., & Kim, J. (2006). The role of the technology acceptance model in explaining effects of image interactivity technology on consumer responses. *International Journal of Retail & Distribution Management*, *34*(8), 621–644. doi:10.1108/09590550610675949

Leggatt, H. (2010). *Rebuild Brand Loyalty with Social Media*. Retrieved from: http://www.bizreport.com/2010/08/price-sensitiveshoppers-still-seeking-out-deals.html

Lenhart, A., Purcell, K., Smith, A., & Zickuhr, K. (2010). *Social Media & Mobile Internet Use among Teens and Young Adults. Millennials*. Pew Internet & American Life Project.

Li, C. Y. (2017). How social commerce constructs influence customers' social shopping intention? An empirical study of a social commerce website. *Technological Forecasting and Social Change*.

Lin, K. Y., & Lu, H. P. (2011). Why people use social networking sites: An empirical study integrating network externalities and motivation theory. *Computers in Human Behavior*, *27*(3), 1152–1161. doi:10.1016/j.chb.2010.12.009

Lin, R., van de Ven, N., & Utz, S. (2018). What triggers envy on Social Network Sites? A comparison between shared experiential and material purchases. *Computers in Human Behavior*, *85*, 271–281. doi:10.1016/j.chb.2018.03.049 PMID:30078937

Lu, H. P., & Hsiao, K. L. (2010). The influence of extro/introversion on the intention to pay for social networking sites. *Information & Management*, *47*(3), 150–157. doi:10.1016/j.im.2010.01.003

Lumsden, J., & MacKay, L. (2006, August). How does personality affect trust in B2C e-commerce? In *Proceedings of the 8th international conference on Electronic commerce: The new e-commerce: innovations for conquering current barriers, obstacles and limitations to conducting successful business on the internet* (pp. 471-481). ACM. 10.1145/1151454.1151526

Malhotra, N. K. (2004). *Marketing research: An applied orientation*. Prentice-Hill.

Mayer, R. C., Davis, J. H., & Schoorman, F. D. (1995). An integrative model of organizational trust. *Academy of Management Review*, *20*(3), 709–734. doi:10.5465/amr.1995.9508080335

McKnight, D. H., Choudhury, V., & Kacmar, C. (2002). The impact of initial consumer trust on intentions to transact with a web site: A trust building model. *The Journal of Strategic Information Systems*, *11*(3-4), 297–323. doi:10.1016/S0963-8687(02)00020-3

Metzger, M. J. (2004). Privacy, trust, and disclosure: Exploring barriers to electronic commerce. *Journal of Computer-Mediated Communication, 9*(4).

Moon, J. W., & Kim, Y. G. (2001). Extending the TAM for a World-Wide-Web context. *Information & Management*, *38*(4), 217–230. doi:10.1016/S0378-7206(00)00061-6

Mueller, J., Hutter, K., Fueller, J., & Matzler, K. (2011). Virtual worlds as knowledge management platform–a practice-perspective. *Information Systems Journal*, *21*(6), 479–501. doi:10.1111/j.1365-2575.2010.00366.x

Naylor, R. W., Lamberton, C. P., & West, P. M. (2012). Beyond the "like" button: The impact of mere virtual presence on brand evaluations and purchase intentions in social media settings. *Journal of Marketing*, *76*(6), 105–120. doi:10.1509/jm.11.0105

Ng, C. S. P. (2013). Intention to purchase on social commerce websites across cultures: A cross-regional study. *Information & Management*, *50*(8), 609–620. doi:10.1016/j.im.2013.08.002

Pavlou, P. A. (2003). Consumer acceptance of electronic commerce: Integrating trust and risk with the technology acceptance model. *International Journal of Electronic Commerce*, *7*(3), 101–134. doi:10.1080/10864415.2003.11044275

Ridings, C. M., & Gefen, D. (2004). Virtual community attraction: Why people hang out online. *Journal of Computer-Mediated Communication*, *10*(1), 00. doi:10.1111/j.1083-6101.2004.tb00229.x

Ringle, C. M., Sarstedt, M., & Mooi, E. A. (2010). Response-based segmentation using finite mixture partial least squares. In Data Mining (pp. 19-49). Springer. doi:10.1007/978-1-4419-1280-0_2

Rubel, S. (2005). *Trends to watch. Part II: social commerce–micro persuasion*. Academic Press.

See-To, E. W., & Ho, K. K. (2014). Value co-creation and purchase intention in social network sites: The role of electronic Word-of-Mouth and trust–A theoretical analysis. *Computers in Human Behavior*, *31*, 182–189. doi:10.1016/j.chb.2013.10.013

Sekaran, U., & Bougie, R. J. (2016). *Research methods for business: A skill building approach*. John Wiley & Sons.

Sin, S. S., Nor, K. M., & Al-Agaga, A. M. (2012). Factors Affecting Malaysian young consumers' online purchase intention in social media websites. *Procedia: Social and Behavioral Sciences*, *40*, 326–333. doi:10.1016/j.sbspro.2012.03.195

Sokolova, K., & Kefi, H. (2019). Instagram and YouTube bloggers promote it, why should I buy? How credibility and parasocial interaction influence purchase intentions. *Journal of Retailing and Consumer Services*. doi:10.1016/j.jretconser.2019.01.011

Swamynathan, G., Wilson, C., Boe, B., Almeroth, K., & Zhao, B. Y. (2008, August). Do social networks improve e-commerce?: a study on social marketplaces. In *Proceedings of the first workshop on Online social networks* (pp. 1-6). ACM. 10.1145/1397735.1397737

Tenenhaus, M., Vinzi, V. E., Chatelin, Y. M., & Lauro, C. (2005). PLS path modeling. *Computational Statistics & Data Analysis, 48*(1), 159–205. doi:10.1016/j.csda.2004.03.005

Turban, E., King, D., & Lang, J. (2009). *Introduction to electronic commerce.* Upper Saddle River, NJ: Pearson Education, Inc.

Ulusu, Y., Durmus, E. S., & Yurtkoru, D. (2011). Personality, privacy and trust issues in virtual society. New perspective of contemporary marketing, Athens.

Venkatesh, V., & Bala, H. (2008). Technology acceptance model 3 and a research agenda on interventions. *Decision Sciences, 39*(2), 273–315. doi:10.1111/j.1540-5915.2008.00192.x

Venkatesh, V., & Davis, F. D. (2000). A theoretical extension of the technology acceptance model: Four longitudinal field studies. *Management Science, 46*(2), 186–204. doi:10.1287/mnsc.46.2.186.11926

Warner, C. (2018). *10 Social Media Usage Statistics You Should Know (and What They Mean for Your Marketing Strategy).* Retrieved from https://www.skyword.com/contentstandard/marketing/10-social-media-usage-statistics-you-should-know-and-what-they-mean-for-your-marketing-strategy/

Wasko, M. M., & Faraj, S. (2005). Why should I share? Examining social capital and knowledge contribution in electronic networks of practice. *Management Information Systems Quarterly, 29*(1), 35–57. doi:10.2307/25148667

Weisberg, J., Te'eni, D., & Arman, L. (2011). Past purchase and intention to purchase in e-commerce: The mediation of social presence and trust. *Internet Research, 21*(1), 82–96. doi:10.1108/10662241111104893

Wetzels, M., Odekerken-Schröder, G., & Van Oppen, C. (2009). Using PLS path modeling for assessing hicrarchical construct models: Guidelines and empirical illustration. *Management Information Systems Quarterly, 33*(1), 177–195. doi:10.2307/20650284

Wilcox, K., & Stephen, A. T. (2013). Are close friends the enemy? Online social networks, self-esteem, and self-control. *The Journal of Consumer Research, 40*(1), 90–103. doi:10.1086/668794

Wixom, B. H., & Todd, P. A. (2005). A theoretical integration of user satisfaction and technology acceptance. *Information Systems Research, 16*(1), 85–102. doi:10.1287/isre.1050.0042

Wixom, B. H., & Watson, H. J. (2001). An empirical investigation of the factors affecting data warehousing success. *Management Information Systems Quarterly, 25*(1), 17–41. doi:10.2307/3250957

Zhu, Z., Wang, J., Wang, X., & Wan, X. (2016). Exploring factors of user's peer-influence behavior in social media on purchase intention: Evidence from QQ. *Computers in Human Behavior, 63,* 980–987. doi:10.1016/j.chb.2016.05.037

Chapter 18
The Role of Human Resource Management in Enhancing Organizational Information Systems Security

Peace Kumah
Ghana Education Service, Ghana

ABSTRACT

Emerging human resource management (HRM) practices are focusing on background checks, training and development, employer-employee relations, responsibility and accountability, and monitoring of information systems security resources. Information systems security ensures that appropriate resources and adequate skills exist in the organization to effectively manage information security projects. This chapter examined the role of HRM in enhancing organizational information systems security. Using importance-performance map analysis, the study found training, background checks, and monitoring as crucial HRM practices that could enhance organizational information systems security. Moreover, four indicators, consisting of training on mobile devices security; malware management; background checks; and monitoring of potential, current, and former employees recorded high importance but with rather low performance. Consequently, these indicators should be improved. On the contrary, the organizations placed excessive focus on responsibility, accountability, and employee relations.

INTRODUCTION

Human resource management (HRM) practices are day-to-day activities including recruitment and selection, performance appraisal (Khan, 2010), training and development (Katuo & Budhwar, 2006), career planning management, compensation (Ahmad & Schroeder, 2003), and internal communication (Oladipo & Adbulkadir, 2011). Human resource management plays a vital role in organizations through performance of administrative HR functions such as recruitment, training, promotion, welfare services, performance appraisal, salary administration, and collective bargaining, and retention of employees

DOI: 10.4018/978-1-7998-1279-1.ch018

(Asare-Bediako, 2011). HRM practices are strategic tools for gaining higher employee performance (Khan, 2010). For organizations to achieve their set goals, strategic plans to invest in employee knowledge, skills and abilities are crucial (Battaglio et al., 2017). Human resource management practices must be strategic in measuring current workforce capacities (Goodman et al., 2015) and in assessing the prudent use of human resources (Selden, 2009). Therefore, it is important for organizations to incorporate human capital into the organization's strategic planning by investing in the workforce (Selden, 2009).

Without strong security controls, businesses risk the possibility of financial loss, legal liability, reputation harm (Amarachi, Okolie & Ajaegbu, 2013), and the effect on national security (Okewu et al., 2018). Therefore, emerging information systems security research is discovering ways to improve organizational security by motivating employees to engage in more secure security behaviors using HRM practices (Boss et al., 2015). Information security management system is a collection of policies concerned with information technology related risks (Amarachi, Okolie & Ajaegbu, 2013). Information security management system aims at implementing the appropriate measures in order to eliminate or minimize the impact that various security related threats and vulnerabilities might have on an organization (Amarachi, Okolie, & Ajaegbu, 2013).

Human resource management practices can address the problem of the human-oriented factors. Human resource management practices of employee recruitment and selection, training and development, performance monitoring and appraisals are very important to improve organisational performance (Naz, Aftab, & Awais, 2016). Investing in training and development can motivate staff and support the growth of the organisation (Leidner & Smith, 2013). Information systems security and data privacy training can serve as critical controls for safeguarding organisation's information resources (Baxter, Holderness, & Wood, 2016). Safa et al. (2018) identify lack of employees' awareness, negligence, resistance, disobedience, apathy and mischievousness as the root causes of information security incidents in organisations. As a result, Odun-Ayo et al. (2017) propose a framework for enhancing human resources in addressing information security. Thus, to achieve the best results, security training and awareness programs should be regularly evaluated so that corrective actions can be taken (Rantos, Fysarakis & Manifavas, 2012).

In addition, employee relations are seen by employers as critical in achieving job performance through employee involvement, commitment and engagement (Radhakrishna & Raju, 2015). Moreover, employee monitoring is a significant component of employers' efforts to maintain employee productivity (Ford et al., 2015). Employee background checks are important to ascertain criminal records, character, and fitness of the employee (Sarode & Deore, 2017). Furthermore, employee's accountability can improve information security (Vance, Lowry, & Eggett, 2013). However, accountability can have both positive and negative effect on work behavior (Ossege, 2012). Enhancing information systems security by focusing on human resource management practices has not received much attention by researchers. Using Importance-Performance Map Analysis (IPMA) (Ringle & Sarstedt, 2016), this chapter aims at exploring the role of HRM practices in improving organizational information systems security. In particular, the chapter (a) discusses the use of IPMA, (b) identifies the HRM practices that can improve the performance of organisational information systems security and (c) the specific HRM indicators that can enhance organisational information systems security

BACKGROUND

Information Systems Security

Information systems security is a global concern (Ikenwe, Igbinovia, & Elogie, 2016; White, Hewitt, & Kruck, 2013). It involves protection of information assets from unauthorized access, accidental loss, destruction, disclosure, modification, or misuse (Tassabehji, 2005). Information security involves managing risks related to the use, processing, storage, transmission of information or data and the systems and processes used for those purposes (Yalman & Yesilyurt, 2013). Information security is a multi-disciplinary area involving professional activity of developing and implementing technical, organisational, human-oriented security mechanisms in order to keep information systems free from threats (Cherdantseva & Hilton, 2013). As a result of increasing dependency on information technology (IT) systems and emerging security threats and vulnerabilities relating to privacy, identity theft, and cybercrime, the role of IT professionals become crucial for maintaining security of information resources (Khao, Harris, & Hartman, 2010).

Information systems security breaches may result in loss of sensitive information and productivity which may lead to huge financial liabilities, adversely affecting the reputation of the organisation (Abawajy, 2014). Information security needs to become an organisation-wide and strategic issue, taking it out of the IT domain and aligning it with the corporate governance approach (Amarachi, Okolie, & Ajaegbu, 2013). Au and Fung (2019) suggested that IT Governance practices can improve knowledge dissemination of information security within organizations. Balozian, Leidner and Warkentin (2019) suggested that managers' participation in the information systems policy decision-making process could motivate lower-level employees toward policy compliance.

Information technology professionals are facing challenging tasks analysing, designing, and deploying solutions to protect information resources. Notwithstanding, previous studies acknowledge that human factors are the major sources of many security failures (Abawajy, 2014; Driscoll & McKee, 2007; Furnell & Thomson, 2009; Komatsu, Takagi, & Takemura, 2013). Human beings are vulnerable to a wide range of security attacks, which range from deliberate violation of security policy to circumvention of physical and technical security controls (Stewart, Tittel, & Chapple, 2005). Moreover, people underestimate the likelihood of the occurrence of security breaches (Herath & Rao, 2009). It is important to understand the employees' personal attitudes, norms and beliefs and the link between compliance and rewards/punishment (Cram, D'Arcy & Proudfoot, 2019).

One of the key challenges in information security management is to understand how human factors affect the outcomes of information security in an organisation (Hu et al., 2012). Organisations are taking measures to ensure the security of information (Yalman & Yesilyurt, 2013). However, organisations invest inefficiently in information technology security measures (Zhao, Xue, & Whinston, 2013), while human attitude was identified as having significant impact on compliance with security policy (Zhang, Reithel, & Li, 2009). Thus, technological security solutions alone are ineffective at reducing security breaches. According to Angst, Block, D'Arcy and Kelley (2017), information technology (IT) security investments are effective at reducing the incidence of data security breaches when they are balanced with institutional factors. According to Herath and Rao (2009), organisational commitment, social influence, and threat perceptions about the severity of breaches effect employees' attitudes toward policy compliance.

Burns et al. (2017) established the relationship between organisational insiders' psychological capital with information security threat and coping appraisals. Self-control is a major factor influencing individual behaviour towards information security (Hu, West, & Smarandescu, 2015). Moreover, suspicion plays a role between users' normal working behaviors and their ability to change that behavior to detect and react to cyber attacks (Hirshfield et al., 2019). Khan and AlShare (2019) found significant difference in employees' information security policy violation with respect to perceived privacy, subjective norms, perceived severity of penalty, and organizational security culture.

Organisations should measure their information security performance in order to make the right decisions (Bernik & Prislan, 2016) and channel resources to areas of high importance that will lead to high security performance. A recent study showed that a high level of information security performance is mostly dependent on measures aimed at managing employees (Bernik & Prislan, 2016). Managing employees' security behaviors for better information security performance will require security training and development programs, creating employee relations, background checks and monitoring, and accountability.

Security Training and Development

Training and development is a planned process and the most important tool that exposes employees to new knowledge, higher level of skills and technologies for higher performance (Subramaniam, Shamsudin, & Ibrahim, 2011). Blair (2007) emphasized the importance of investment into training and development as it can give competitive advantage to organizations. According to (AL-Qudah, Osman, Ab Halim, and Al-Shatanawi (2014), training and development can be used to improve the capabilities of employees and to promote organizational commitment towards the attainment of organizational goals. Furthermore, Hassan (2016) concluded that training and development plays significant role in organizational performance. Also, Saifalislam, Osman and AlQudah (2014) and Sattar, Ahmad and Hassan (2015) proposed positive and significant relation between training and development and employee performance. Koh (2018) examined the Influence of Human Resource Management Practices on Employee Performance in the Manufacturing Sector in Malaysia. Data was collected through survey from 161 manufacturing sector in Malaysia. The regression analysis indicated significant positive relationship between training and development and employee performance. The study, therefore, suggested that training and development is the most critical factor that influences employee performance.

Misra and Khurana (2018) stressed the need for enhancing the employability skills of information technology professionals. Investing in training and development can motivate staff and support the growth of the organisations (Leidner & Smith, 2013). While lack of security training often lie behind many contemporary breaches (Lacey, 2010), security education enables skilled professionals and ensures adequate security awareness among end users (Kaspersky & Furnell, 2014). Abawajy (2014) evaluated the effects of various information security awareness delivery methods that could improve end-users' information security awareness and behavior. By conducting experiments on information security awareness using three different methods: text-based, game-based and video-based, the study suggested that a combined delivery methods of improving end-users' information security awareness and behaviour are better than individual security awareness delivery method (Abawajy, 2014). A related study determined the impact of cyber threat education and awareness intervention on changes in user security behaviour (McCrohan, Engel, & Harvey, 2010). The study was based on protection motivation theory and an experimental was performed by using undergraduate business school students. McCrohan, Engel and Harvey (2010) found that when users are educated of the threats to e-commerce and trained about proper security practices, their behavior could be changed to enhance information security. Hence, security and assurance should be a core component of the curriculum for all information security and business students (White, Hewitt, & Kruck, 2013).

Moreover, a survey conducted on 196 undergraduate students in a business college to investigate students' understanding and attitudes toward information security suggested that when universities provide easily accessible security training programs to students, information security improves (Kim, 2014). In a related study, Da Veiga (2016) determined the influence information security policy had on the information security culture by comparing the security behavior of employees who read the policy to those who did not. An empirical study was conducted at four intervals over eight years across 12 countries using a validated information security culture assessment (ISCA) questionnaire. The overall information security culture was significantly more positive for employees who had read the information security policy compared with employees who had not. Employees' information security training can improve adherence to security policies when employees are shown the reasons behind the written policies (Ramakrishna & Figueroa, 2017). Accordingly, organisational security education, training and awareness efforts influence employees' threat and coping appraisals (Posey, Roberts & Lowry, 2015).

Employer-Employee Relationship

The most critical asset in organizations is the people. It is therefore important for organizations to have keen interest in managing employer-employee relationships. Employer- employee relationship enhances commitment, job satisfaction and engagement that eventually improve organizational outcome employer-employee relationships employer-employee relationships (Klaas, Olson-Buchanan & Ward, 2012; Bashshur & Oc, 2015). For example, Bhattacharya, Trehan and Kaur (2018) established the importance of psychological contract amongst the employer and employees. Bhattacharya et al. (2012) stated the need to pay attention to employer-employee relationship to enable their businesses to grow. Empirical studies on the impact of employer-employee relationships on business growth revealed positive relationship between employer-employee relationships and business growth (Dumisani, Chux, Andre & Joyc, 2014).

Employee relations are seen by employers as critical in achieving job performance through a focus on employee involvement, commitment and engagement. The emphasis of employee relations is now focussed on relationship with individual employees (Radhakrishna & Raju, 2015). Organisational commitment is a means by which information security threats become personally relevant to employees (Posey, Roberts, & Lowry, 2015). A previous study revealed that IT employees were treated with only moderate fairness/justice by the organisations, however, their commitment to their organisation was fairly high (Patrick, 2012). It was found that organisational justice significantly influenced organisational commitment of IT employees. The results of this study provided considerable insight into the IT employees' perceptions of fairness could promote commitment (Patrick, 2012). Also, D'Arcy and Greene (2014) examined the influence of security-related and employment relationship factors on employees' security compliance decisions. Data were collected using two online surveys that were administered at separate points in time. The study found that security culture is a driver for employees' security compliance in the workplace and that employee's feeling of job satisfaction influences security compliance intention (D'Arcy & Greene, 2014).

Background Checks and Monitoring

According to Stringer (2009), recruitment remains a critical element for effective implementation of HRM practices. The role of HRM in every organization is to identify, select and recruit suitable employees. The Society for Human Resource Management (SHRM) indicated that background checks are important tool that employers must use to reduce the risk of a negligent hiring (SHRM, 2012). Sarode and Deore (2017) emphasized that it is critical for HR mangers to conduct background checks on potential employees to avoid recruiting wrong people. Background checks for the IT professionals and every individual in other sectors is crucial for all organizations (Valentine, 2014). Freeman (2013) concluded that background check gives great advantage to employers as people who may engage in workplace violence, defraud, steal or unreliable and untrustworthy are eliminated. Furthermore, a meta-analysis of some studies revealed significant correlation between background check and employee behavior (Aamodt, 2015).

Background checks of potential employee have become essential task for HR personnel so that the organisation could avoid recruiting the wrong persons (Sarode & Deore, 2017). Hughes, Keller, & Hertz (2010) discussed issues of higher education institutions' policies and procedures with regard to background checks for students, staff, and faculty in light of homeland security concerns. Brody and Cox (2015) emphasized the need for thoroughness and accuracy of background checks and security clearance investigations. Brody (2010) explored the various methods available when conducting a pre-employment screening investigation in attempt to hire honest employees, those less likely to commit fraud against their organisation. Using interviews with experts in the area of background investigation services, the study recommended that organisations should consider performing other screening techniques before hiring an employee. Brody (2010) cautioned that merely relying on the most basic background check may lead to the hiring of the wrong employee, one likely to commit fraud. Besides, employees are increasingly monitored concerning their behaviors and actions. The use of monitoring systems has been advocated for improved performance, increased productivity, and reduced costs (Holt, Lang, & Sutton, 2017). Without effective monitoring disgruntled employees can expose valuable business trade secrets or engage in corporate espionage or sabotage (Ford et al., 2015). They may render the organisation to several risky situations (Rigon et al., 2014). Therefore, it is importance to analyse the strength, weakness, opportunity and threat in service delived by employees (Misra & Adewumi, 2015).

Sreejith and Mathirajan (2016) developed criteria for continuous employee performance evaluation of Information Technology organizations. Monitoring an employee's behaviors and actions is an essential HR practice. Monitoring improves employee-employer relationships, enhances employee competence, ensures that employees comply with safety regulations, improves performance and increases production rates (Durden, 2019). Monitory system ensures accountability, enhances planning and organizational performance. Without effective monitoring employees will lose focus by engaging in illegal activities (Alampay & Hechaniya, 2010) and discontented employees can reveal trade secrets or sabotage projects (Ford et al., 2015).

Responsibility and Accountability

Employees should be accountable to and be responsibility for preventing security breaches. According to Styles and Tryfonas (2009), employees are duty-bound to consider the security of the computing and information resources they interact with. Accountability makes employees answerable for accomplishing a goal or assignment (U.S. Office of Personnel Management, n.d). It often connotes punishment or negative consequences of punishing employees, creating fear and anxiety in the work environment. But accountability can produce positive and valuable results. When used constructively, it can improve employee performance, enhance participation and involvement, increase feelings of competency, enhance commitment to the work, improve creativity and innovation, and produce higher employee morale and satisfaction with the work (U.S. Office of Personnel Management, n.d). Accountability should focus not only on punishment but also reward. Parker (2008) remarked that without security rewards and sanctions in all employee job performance appraisals, any attempt to secure information assets in an organisation is purely cosmetics. Thus, those who control security, those who are constrained by it, and those who use and possess the assets must be sufficiently motivated to make it work (Parker, 2008).

In a recent study, Zaman and Saif (2016) found that perceived accountability has a significant positive relationship with job performance. Thomson and van Niekerk (2012) showed how employee apathy towards information security can be addressed through the use of existing theory in social sciences. Based on goal-setting theory, the study suggested that employees' performance of their roles and responsibilities can contribute towards organisational culture of information security (Thomson & van Niekerk, 2012). To understand security behaviour by developing a security behaviour typology based on the concepts of discipline and agility, Harnesk and Lindström (2011) undertook a case study to analyze security behaviors. The study found that security behaviour can be shaped by discipline and agility and that both can exist collectively if organisations consider the constitutional and existential aspects of information security (IS) management. Vance, Lowry, and Eggett (2013) presented a new approach for reducing access policy violations. Drawing from the theory of accountability, the study identified four system mechanisms that heighten an individual's perception of accountability: identifiability, awareness of logging, awareness of audit, and electronic presence (Vance, Lowry, & Eggett, 2013). Safa et al. (2019) proposed deterrence as the mitigating factor for reducing insider threat to information systems resources. Deterrence discourages employees from engaging in information security misbehaviour and the severity of sanctions significantly influence individuals' attitudes from information security misconduct (Safa et al., 2019).

MAIN FOCUS OF THE CHAPTER

Explaining Importance-Performance Map Analysis

The chapter explains the principles underlying and procedures involved in using IPMA. The first step in creating an importance-performance map (IPM) requires selecting the target construct of interest in the PLS path model (Ringle & Sarstedt, 2016). Reviewing studies on the use of partial least squares structured equation modelling (PLS-SEM) (Hair et al., 2012; Ringle et al., 2012; Sarstedt et al., 2014) reveals that information security researchers basically rely on the standard PLS path model analysis, ignoring the Importance-Performance Map Analysis (IPMA). IPMA provides guidance for the prioritization of managerial activities of high importance but require performance improvements (Ringle & Sarstedt, 2016). It is particularly useful for generating additional findings and conclusions from the standard PLS-SEM. Thus, in this study IPMA is used to evaluate the level of importance organisations attach to each of the HRM factors and indicators, which can improve information security performance.

Consider the PLS path model in Figure 1 with five constructs (C_1 to C_5). In PLS path model in Figure 1, C_5 represents the key target construct. C_5 is directly predicted by C_1 to C_4. Also, C_1 has indirect effect on C_5 via C_2, C_3, and C_4. To perform Importance-Performance Map Analysis, the PLS path model in

Figure 1. Concept of path model of IPMA

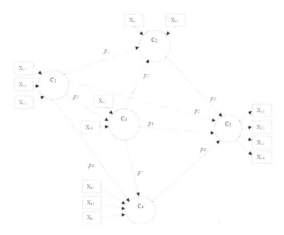

Figure 1. Concept of Path Model of IPMA

Figure 1 will be transformed into IPMA grid as shown in Figure 2 with two dimensions – importance and performance dimensions. The addition of the predecessor constructs' (C_1 to C_4) direct and indirect effects yields their total effects on C_5. This represents the importance dimension in the IPMA (Ringle & Sarstedt, 2016). On the other hand, the constructs' average latent variable scores represent the performance dimension in IPMA. The higher values indicate a greater performance and vice versa (Ringle & Sarstedt, 2016). Also in Figure 1, x_{ij} (for example x_{11}, $x_{22,}$ x_{42}) represents the indicators of the constructs C_i and p_i (p_1 to p_9) represents the path coefficients.

Now, the two dimensions can be plotted graphically by placing the total effects (Importance dimension) on the x-axis and the rescaled latent variable scores (re-scaled on a range from 0 to 100), representing the Performance dimension on the y-axis. This results in an Important-Performance Map in Figure 2. Moreover, the two dimensional IPMA model is further divided into four quadrants. To achieve this, two lines are drawn on the Importance-Performance Map. The vertical line is the mean importance value and the horizontal line is the mean performance value of the constructs. Thus, these two lines divide the Importance-Performance Map into four areas with importance and performance values below and above the average (Figure 2). Generally, when analyzing the Importance-Performance Map, constructs appearing in the lower right area (i.e. Quadrant I) are of the highest interest to achieving improvement in the target construct (C_5), followed by the higher right (i.e. Quadrant II), lower left (i.e. Quadrant III) and, finally, the higher left areas (i.e. Quadrant IV) (Ringle & Sarstedt, 2016).

The four quadrants (Figure 2) are generally referred to as *concentrate here (Quadrant I)*, *keep up the good work (Quadrant II)*, *low priority (Quadrant III)*, and *possible overkill (Quadrant IV)*. The constructs and indicators that fall within the quadrants can be interpreted as below (Ringle & Sarstedt, 2016).

Quadrant I (High Importance/Low Performance). The constructs or indicators that fall within this quadrant represent key areas that need to be improved with top priority.

Quadrant II (High Importance/High Performance). All constructs or indicators that fall within this quadrant are the strength of the organisations.

Quadrant III (Low Importance/Low Performance). Any of the constructs or indicators that falls within this quadrant is not important to the organisations.

Figure 2. Relative importance-performance regions

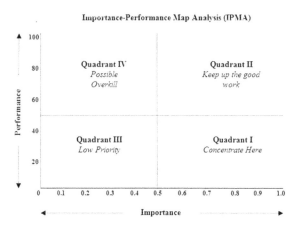

Figure 2: Relative Importance-Performance Regions

Quadrant IV (Low Importance/High Performance). This denotes constructs or indicators that are overly emphasized by the organisations. Organisations, instead of continuing to focus in this quadrant, should allocate more resources to deal with constructs or indicators that fall within *Quadrant I*.

Importance-Performance Map Analysis (IPMA)

Specifically, to further explain the concept, Figure 3 and Figure 4 demonstrate IPM for both constructs and indicators respectively. In Figure 3, C_1 is particularly important to improve the performance of the target construct C_5, as it falls within the *Quadrant I* (High Importance/Low Performance). More precisely, a one-unit point increase in C_1's performance increases the performance of C_5 by the value of C_1's total effect on C_5. Thus, in Figure 3, the performance of C_1 is relatively low; there is therefore substantial room for improvement, making this construct particularly relevant for managerial actions. Moreover, to generate IPM for indicators, individual data points in the Importance-Performance Map are derived from indicator mean values and their total effect on a particular target construct, C_5. As can be observed

Figure 3. Constructs - IPMA on the target construct, C5

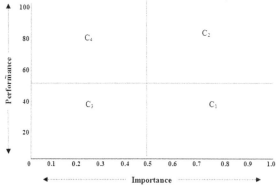

Figure 3: Constructs - IPMA on the Target Construct, C5

Figure 4. Indicators - IPMA on the target construct, C_5

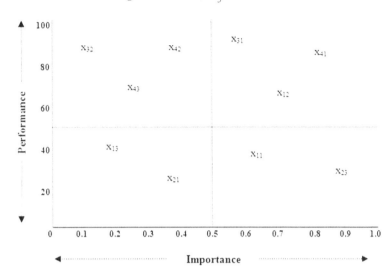

Figure 4: Indicators - IPMA on the Target Construct, C_5

in Figure 4, x_{11}, x_{23} have the highest importance but low performance values (Quadrant I). Thus, these indicators will require management attention to improve their performance in order to enhance the performance of the target construct, C_5.

Assessing HRM and Information Systems Security Model

A structured survey questionnaire was used to collect data from Information Security Officers, Chief Information Officers, IT Managers, IT Specialists, and other IT staff in organizations in assessing the model. When using IPMA, three requirements must be met (Ringle & Sarstedt, 2016). Firstly, the latent variable scores should be re-scaled on a range of 0 and 100, thus requiring that all indicators in the PLS path model should use a metric or quasi-metric scale (Sarstedt & Mooi, 2014). Secondly, all the indicator coding must have the same scale direction. The minimum value of an indicator must represent the worst outcome and the maximum value must represent the best outcome of the indicator (for instance 1 represents *strongly disagree* and 5 *strongly agree*). Otherwise, conclusion cannot be drawn that the higher latent variable scores represent better performance. Accordingly, the current study used a metric with 5 likert scale which can be scaled between 0 and 100. Thirdly, regardless of the measurement model being formatively or reflectively, the outer weights estimates must be positive. Negative outer weights might be a result of high indicator collinearity and these indicators should be removed from the analysis (Hair et al., 2017). To meet this requirement, all the items whose outer weights were negative have been removed (see Table 1).

Moreover, the blindfolding and bootstrapping techniques were used. The blindfolding procedure was used in assessing the predictive relevance (Stone-Geisser's Q^2 value) of the structural model (Geisser, 1974; Stone, 1974). According to Hair et al. (2014), a Q^2 value larger than zero for the reflective endogenous latent variable indicates the path model's predictive relevance. Table 2 showed the structural model's predictive relevance. Also, bootstrapping was performed. It is a nonparametric procedure that allows

Table 1. Validity, reliability and descriptive statistics

Constructs	Indicators	Outer Weight > 0	Mean	SD	Cronbach Alpha
SECURITY TRAINING AND AWARENESS					
ST01	Employees are given periodic training on security policies.	0.272	3.95	.997	
ST02	Employees are trained to keep mobile devices secured.	0.362	3.53	.925	
ST06	Employees are trained to be suspicious of any software that arrives in the mail, even though it may appear to be packaged and sent by trusted persons or vendors.	0.290	3.25	.984	.778
ST10	Employees have been made aware of the fact that mass produced and mass distributed software could still contain targeted malware.	0.361	3.40	.954	
EMPLOYER-EMPLOYEE RELATIONSHIP					
ER01	The organisation makes fairness and good faith in the treatment of employees a priority.	0.732	3.87	.803	
ER02	The organisation provides adequate mechanisms for employees to express their grievances without penalty and for them to see those grievances being conscientiously addressed.	0.017	3.60	.755	
ER03	The organisation handles re-deployment/down-sizing in a manner that minimizes hostile feelings on the part of former employees.	0.117	3.64	.774	.849
ER04	The organisation offers a procedure which allows employees to report attempts by outsiders to extort their organisation in circumventing security.	0.251	3.72	.718	
ER05	If an employee is going through a period of great difficulties in his or her personal life, there is a policy for temporarily reducing that employee's responsibilities for critical systems and access to critical systems.	0.053	3.73	.815	
BACKGROUND CHECKS AND MONITORING					
BC02	If an employee is promoted to a considerably higher level of responsibility and access, a new background check is carried out.	0.477	3..35	.973	
BC03	Background screening is carried out for of potential and third parties.	0.359	3.18	.845	.811
BC04	An effort is made to track the current whereabouts of former employees who were deeply acquainted with critical systems and procedures.	0.333	3.25	1.045	
RESPONSIBILITY AND ACCOUNTABILITY					
SA02	All employees are required to sign confidentiality and intellectual property agreements.	0.291	3.34	.862	
SA06	Information security policies defined the proper use of e-mail, internet access, and instant messaging by employees.	0.689	3.53	1.058	.696
SA11	Employees are given adequate incentives to report security breaches and bad security practices.	0.237	3.51	.817	
INFORMATION SECURITY					
BEC06	Information is generally disseminated throughout the organisation on a need-to-know basis.	0.298	3.75	.692	
BEC07	Areas of responsibility are distributed among employees in such a way that a single employee cannot carry out a critical operation without the knowledge of other employees.	0.329	3.47	.768	
BEC08	The employee's physical and electronic access logs are periodically reviewed to identify access patterns that are not motivated by normal work responsibilities.	0.301	3.73	.725	.790
BEC09	Employees are required to take periodic vacations, so that ongoing activities they might otherwise be able to conceal would be noticed by their temporary replacements.	0.346	3.70	.808	

testing the statistical significance of various PLS-SEM results, such as path coefficients, Cronbach's alpha, and R^2 values (Hair et al., 2017). The results from bootstrapping with 5,000 samples using the no sign change option and the 95 percent confidence intervals showed that all the path coefficients were statistically significant (Table 3). More specifically, TRAINING, MONITORING, ACCOUNTABILITY, and RELATIONSHIP each has significant and positive effects on INFORMATION SECURITY. Thus, the bootstrapping results demonstrated that all total effects on the target construct, INFORMATION SECURITY, were significant.

Table 2. Stone-Geisser's Q² value

Constructs	SSO	SSE	Q² (=1-SSE/SSO)
ACCOUNTABILITY	954	672.471	0.295
INFORMATION SECURITY	1,272	920.981	0.276
MONITORING	954	742.136	0.222
RELATIONSHIP	1,590	1,352.801	0.149
TRAINING	1,272	1,272.000	-

Table 3. Path coefficients and statistical significance

Constructs	Sample Mean	Standard Deviation	Path Coefficients	T Statistics	*p*-values
ACCOUNTABILITY -> INFORMATION SECURITY	0.180	0.077	2.333	2.333	0.020
MONITORING -> ACCOUNTABILITY	0.334	0.059	5.713	5.713	0.000
MONITORING -> INFORMATION SECURITY	0.242	0.064	3.804	3.804	0.000
MONITORING -> RELATIONSHIP	0.383	0.067	5.691	5.691	0.000
RELATIONSHIP -> INFORMATION SECURITY	0.290	0.054	5.280	5.280	0.000
TRAINING -> ACCOUNTABILITY	0.485	0.056	8.718	8.718	0.000
TRAINING -> INFORMATION SECURITY	0.135	0.054	2.501	2.501	0.012
TRAINING -> MONITORING	0.576	0.035	16.461	16.461	0.000
TRAINING -> RELATIONSHIP	0.247	0.062	3.856	3.856	0.000

Observably, in Table 1, Table 2, and Table 3, the requirements of the measurement model assessment have been met. The outer weights were above zero. Those items below zero were removed from further analysis. The instrument validity and reliability requirements were fulfilled. The predictive relevance via blindfolding technique was also fulfilled. Through the bootstrapping results, the structural model also showed that all the constructs had significant effect on the target construct. Instrument reliability and validity were also tested via Cronbach's alpha and outer loadings. According to Hair et al. (2017), items with outer loading less than zero should be removed from further analysis. Consequently, items whose outer loadings were less than zero were removed from the study (see Table 1). Moreover, the Cronbach's alpha shows the reliability coefficients of the measures: Security Training and Awareness (.778), Employer-Employee Relationship (.849), Background Checks and Monitoring (.811), Responsibility and Accountability (.696), and Information Security (.790) (see Table 1). Apart from Responsibility and Accountability, all the measures were all found to be far above the threshold of 0.7 (or higher) and were considered acceptable according to Nunally's (1978) guidelines. Based on these, the study proceeded to create Importance-Performance Map.

Determining HRM Practices for Enhancing Information Systems Security

The IPMA technique produced the structural model and Important-Performance Map (Figure 5) to identify the important HRM practices that can improve the performance of organisational information security. Table 4 and Figure 5 show the path coefficients and the performance values of the constructs. Table 5 shows the direct, indirect, and the total effects (the Importance dimension) together with the Performance values (re-scaled between 0 and 100). These values were used to create the graphical representation of the Importance-Performance Map (Figure 6). The Important-Performance Map utilises unstandardized total effects for the importance-dimension (x-axis) and the re-scaled performance values of the latent and manifest variables on the performance dimension (y-axis).

Figure 6 reveals that two direct predecessors of INFORMATION SECURITY, MONITORING and TRAINING, have a particularly high importance but relatively low performance (Quadrant I). Observably, TRAINING construct has considerably higher importance than the MONITORING construct. Managerial actions should therefore prioritize improving the performance of security TRAINING. Moreover, the importance of MONITORING was relatively high but its performance was relatively low. Attention also needs to be paid on improving the performance of MONITORING, which can be achieved by focusing on the predecessor construct of MONITORING, which is TRAINING. On the other side, the result showed that too much attention has been paid to RELATIONSHIP (Quadrant IV). This denoted that RELATIONSHIP constructs was overly emphasized by the organisations. Instead of continuing to focus on RELATIONSHIP, organisations should allocate more resources to increase the performance of TRAINING and MONITORING. Surprisingly, ACCOUNTABILITY fell within Quadrant III, indicating low importance and performance.

Table 4. Performance / index values and path coefficients

Constructs	LV Index Values	Performances	ACCOUNTABILITY	INFORMATION SECURITY	MONITORING	RELATIONSHIP
ACCOUNTABILITY	3.477	61.933		0.134		
INFORMATION SECURITY	3.660	66.499				
MONITORING	3.261	56.537	0.323	0.178		0.313
RELATIONSHIP	3.801	70.015		0.252		
TRAINING	3.516	62.904	0.507	0.106	0.616	0.214

LV – Latent Variable

Figure 5. Structural model of importance-performance analysis

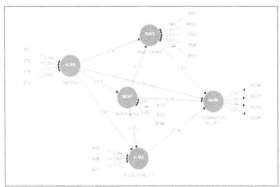

Figure 5: Structural Model of Importance-Performance Analysis

Table 5. Direct, indirect, and total effects of importance-performance construct values

Predecessor Construct	Direct Effect on Security	Indirect Effect on Security	Total effect on Security/ Importance	Performance
ACCOUNTABILITY	0.134	-	0.134	61.933
MONITORING	0.131	0.169	0.300	56.537
RELATIONSHIP	0.252	-	0.252	70.015
TRAINING	0.023	0.390	0.413	62.904
Average			0.275	62.847

Notes: All effects denote unstandardized effects.

Figure 6. IPM constructs on information security

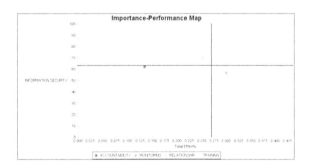

Determining HRM indicators for Enhancing Information Systems Security

In the previous section, TRAINING and MONITORING were identified as very important for improving information security performance. However, to gain more specific information as to which key training and monitoring indicators will increase the performance of organisational information security, the indicator level Importance-Performance Map Analysis was performed. Table 6 shows the total effects

(Importance dimension) and the information security (performance dimension) values at the indicator level. These values were used to create the indicator level Importance-Performance Map, as shown in Figure 7. The four quadrants on the IPM is made possible using the mean level of importance of 0.073 and the mean level of performance of 63.051, indicated by the vertical and the horizontal lines on the map.

In Quadrant I, *Concentrate Here*, the respondents perceived the attributes within this region as highly important, but their performance was very low. From the map (Figure 7), six key indicators/attributes were found that could improve information security performance. These are classified under the two constructs:

Table 6. Importance-performance indicator values

Indicators	Total Effect (Importance)	Information Security (Performance)
BC02	0.119	58.648
BC03	0.103	54.403
BC04	0.077	56.132
ER01	0.153	71.698
ER02	0.004	64.937
ER03	0.025	65.881
ER04	0.059	68.082
ER05	0.011	68.239
SA02	0.035	58.491
SA06	0.068	63.365
SA11	0.030	62.736
ST01	0.084	73.742
ST02	0.121	63.208
ST06	0.091	56.132
ST10	0.117	60.063
Average	0.073	63.051

Figure 7. IPM indicators on information security

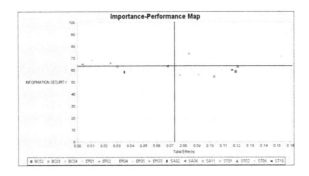

Security Training

- ST02 Employees are trained to keep mobile devices secured.
- ST06 Employees are trained to be suspicious of any software that arrives in the mail, even though it may appear to be packaged and sent by trusted persons or vendors.
- ST10 Employees have been made aware that mass distributed software could contain targeted malware.

Monitoring

- BC02 If an employee is promoted to a considerably higher level of responsibility and access, a new background check is carried out.
- BC03 Background screening is carried out for potential and third parties (suppliers, contractors, building maintenance personnel).
- BC04 An effort is made to track the current whereabouts of former employees who were deeply acquainted with critical systems and procedures.

Moreover, the following two indicators fell within Quadrant II (High Importance/High Performance). These indicators are the strength of the organisations. The indicated that the organisation must "keep up good works" in these areas to maintain security performance.

- ST01 Employees are given periodic training on security policies.
- ER01 The organisation makes fairness and good faith in the treatment of employees a priority.

On the contrary, seven indicators of EMPLOYEE RELATIONS and EMPLOYEE ACCOUNTABIL-ITY constructs were categorised as low importance but high performance, as they fell within Quadrant III and Quadrant IV respectively. The indicators are listed below.

Employee Relations

- ER02 The organisation provides adequate mechanisms for employees to express their grievances without penalty and for them to see those grievances being conscientiously addressed.
- ER05 If an employee is going through a period of great difficulties in his or her personal life, there is a policy for temporarily reducing that employee's responsibilities for critical systems and access to critical systems.
- ER03 The organisation handles re-deployment and down-sizing in a manner that minimizes hostile feelings on the part of former employees.
- ER04 The organisation offers a procedure which would allow employees to report attempts by outsiders to extort their organisation in circumventing security.

Accountability

- SA02 All employees are required to sign confidentiality and intellectual property agreements.
- SA06 Information security policies defined the proper use of e-mail, internet access, and instant messaging by employees.
- SA11 Employees are given adequate incentives to report security breaches and bad security practices.

SOLUTIONS AND RECOMMENDATIONS

The study identified security training, background checks and monitoring as the major HRM practices that can improve the performance of information security in organisations. Managerial actions should therefore prioritize improving training, background checks and monitoring. While lack of security training often lie behind many contemporary breaches (Lacey, 2010), investing in training and development can motivate staff and support the growth of the organisation (Leidner & Smith, 2013). HRM practices on security policy compliance found training for career development as positively associated with employees' behavioral intent to comply with security policy (Youngkeun Choi, 2017). Hence, information security training effectively reduces employees' non-compliance (Hwang et al., 2017). Security training, at the indicator level, ST02 ("Employees are trained to keep mobile devices secured") has a relatively high importance when focusing on information security, but required some room for performance improvement. Hence, performance improvements can focus on offering high-quality security trainings to provide users with the skills and knowledge they need to protect the mobile devices (Yaokumah, 2016). Similarly, other indicators, ST06 and ST10, focussed on employee training on malware. This should be given particular attention regarding improving the information security performance.

Moreover, the background checks and monitoring of the current employees, third parties, and former employees were found as important HRM practices that can improve the performance of organisational information security. A thorough and accurate background checks and security clearance investigations (Brody & Cox, 2015) can help an organisation to hire honest employees, those less likely to commit fraud against the organisation (Brody, 2010). Likewise, employee monitoring systems can improve performance, increase productivity, and reduce costs (Holt, Lang, & Sutton, 2017). In particular, at the indicator level, BC02 ("If an employee is promoted to a considerably higher level of responsibility and access, a new background check is carried out") has a relatively high importance but required performance improvement. Similarly, the BC03 ("Background screening is carried out for potential employees and third parties - suppliers, contractors, building maintenance personnel") and BC04 ("An effort is made to track the current whereabouts of former employees who were deeply acquainted with critical systems and procedures") required performance improvement. Thus, further improvement efforts should be concentrated on mobile devices security, malware, monitoring and background screening of current and former employees, including third party contractors.

Two indicators were found to be the strength of the organisations as they have attained the highest importance and performance levels in the organisations. These are ST01 ("Employees are given periodic training on security policies") and ER01 ("The organisation makes fairness and good faith in the treatment of employees a priority"). Accordingly, the organisations should continue to provide regular security training on security policies to the employees. Employees' information security training enhances adherence to security policies (Ramakrishna & Figueroa, 2017) and influences employees' threat and coping appraisals (Posey, Roberts, & Lowry, 2015). Besides, fairness in treating employees positively influences information security behaviour. Employees' perceptions of fairness promote commitment (Patrick, 2012).

On the contrary, two HRM practices, Employee Relations and Accountability were found to be of low importance but with high performance. This signified that these two constructs were overly emphasized by the organisations. Thus, accountability might not have remarkable impact on employees' security compliance behavior (Abed & Roland, 2016). Rather, instead of continuing to focus in employee relations and accountability, organisations should allocate more resources for security training programs, background checks and employee monitoring.

FUTURE RESEARCH DIRECTIONS

The significance importance of security training, background checks and monitoring on improving information security offer an important opportunity for information security management practices. Organisations can improve information security by channelling resources from less important activities and invest them in security training, background checks and monitoring. Besides, before applying IPMA, this study demonstrated the concept and the use of importance-performance map analysis. By combining the analysis of the importance and performance dimensions of the IPMA, the study allowed the IT and HR leaders to identify and prioritize HRM practices and indicators that were most important for improving the performance of the organisations' information security. The study also provided guidance for the formulation of information security strategy that could accurately allocate resources to maximise a high return on security investment.

The findings extended information security research literature by showing how HRM practices (training, background checks and monitoring) can play a major role in improving information security. Our results provided one of the few empirical validations of information security to be recognized as a multi-disciplinary issue as conceptualized through HRM practices. In addition, the study extended information security research by considering the role of employee relations and accountability from the HRM literature. However, some HRM practices were not included in the current study. For example, including remuneration and rewards might further enhance information security literature. Moreover, because HRM practices may differ among the organisations, future research using a multi-group analysis that allows for contrasting group results might produce an insightful finding.

CONCLUSION

In this chapter, the IPMA technique was discussed and applied to measure HRM practices from the perspective of IT professionals to identify priority areas for the allocation of resources to improve the performance of organisational information security. A survey was conducted on the IT professionals' perceptions to identify areas of importance and performance of HRM practices. Using IPMA technique, the study identified security training, background checks and monitoring as highly important that needed to be improved in order to enhance organisational information security performance. Two indicators (periodic training in adherence to security policy and fairness in treating employees) were found to have attained the highest importance and performance levels in the organisations. In terms of key indicators for specific management actions, attention needed to be paid to: (a) training to keep mobile devices secured, b) training on malware, (c) tracking of the whereabouts of former employees who were deeply acquainted with critical systems and procedures, and d) background checks on employee promoted to a considerably higher level of responsibility and system access. Organisations need to consider allocating resources to training, background check and monitoring.

REFERENCES

Aamodt, M. G. (2015). Using background checks in the employee selection process. In C. Hanvey & K. Sady (Eds.), *Practitioner's Guide to Legal Issues in Organizations*. New York: Springer. doi:10.1007/978-3-319-11143-8_4

Abawajy, J. (2014). User preference of cyber security awareness delivery methods. *Behaviour & Information Technology*, *33*(3), 237–248. doi:10.1080/0144929X.2012.708787

Abed, J., & Roland, W. H. (2016). Understanding deterrence theory in security compliance behavior: A quantitative meta-analysis approach. *SAIS 2016 Proceedings*. Retrieved from http://aisel.aisnet.org/sais2016/28

Ahmad, S., & Schroeder, R. G. (2003). The impact of human resource management practices on operational performance: Recognising country and industry differences. *Journal of Operations Management*, *21*(1), 19–25. doi:10.1016/S0272-6963(02)00056-6

AL-Qudah, M. K. M., Osman, A., Ab Halim, M. S., & Al-Shatanawi, H. A. (2014). The effect of human resources planning and training and development on organizational performance in the government sector in Jordan. *International Journal of Academic Research in Business and Social Sciences*, *4*(4).

Alampay, E. A., & Hechanova, R. M. (2010). Monitoring employee use of the internet in Philippine organizations. *The Electronic Journal on Information Systems in Developing Countries*, *40*(5), 1–20. doi:10.1002/j.1681-4835.2010.tb00287.x

Amarachi, A. A., Okolie, S. O., & Ajaegbu, C. (2013). Information security management system: Emerging issues and prospect. *IOSR Journal of Computer Engineering.*, *12*(3), 96–102. doi:10.9790/0661-12396102

Angst, C. M., Block, E. S., D'Arcy, J., & Kelley, K. (2017). When do IT security investments matter? Accounting for the influence of institutional factors in the context of healthcare data breaches. *Management Information Systems Quarterly*, *41*(3), 893–916. doi:10.25300/MISQ/2017/41.3.10

Asare-Bediako, K. (2011). *Human resource management in Ghana lacks strategic focus*. Ghana News Agency. Retrieved from http://www.ghananewsagency.org/social/human-resource-management-in-ghana-lacks-strategic-focus—27174

Au, C. H., & Fung, W. S. (2019). Integrating knowledge management into information security: From audit to practice. *International Journal of Knowledge Management*, *15*(1), 37–52. doi:10.4018/IJKM.2019010103

Balozian, P., Leidner, D., & Warkentin, M. (2019). Managers' and employees' differing responses to security approaches. *Journal of Computer Information Systems*, *59*(3), 197–210. doi:10.1080/088744 17.2017.1318687

Bashshur, M. R., & Burak, O. C. (2015). When voice matters: A multilevel review of the impact of voice in organizations. *Journal of Management*, *41*(5), 1530–1554. doi:10.1177/0149206314558302

Battaglio, P., Goodman, D., & French, P. E. (2017). Contracting out for municipal human resources: Analyzing the role of human capital in the make or buy decision. *Public Administration Quarterly*, *41*(2), 297–333.

Baxter, R. J., Holderness, D. K. Jr, & Wood, D. A. (2016). Applying basic gamification techniques to it compliance training: Evidence from the lab and field. *Journal of Information Systems*, *30*(3), 119–133. doi:10.2308/isys-51341

Bernik, I., & Prislan, K. (2016). Measuring Information Security Performance with 10 by 10 model for holistic state evaluation. *PLoS One*, *11*(9), 1–33. doi:10.1371/journal.pone.0163050 PMID:27655001

Bhattacharya, C. B., Sen, S., & Korschun, D. (2012). Using corporate social responsibility to win the war for talent. *MIT Sloan Management Review*, *49*, 37–44.

Bhattacharya, S., Trehan, G., & Kaur, K. (2018). Factors Determining Psychological Contract of IT Employees in India. *International Journal of Human Capital and Information Technology Professionals*, *9*(1), 37–52. doi:10.4018/IJHCITP.2018010103

Blair, D., & Sisakhti, R. (2007). Sales training: what makes it work? *T & D Magazine*. Retrieved from www.astd.org/astd/Publications/TD_Magazine/2007_pdf/August/0708ExecSum.htm

Boss, S. R., Galletta, D. F., Lowry, P. B., Moody, G. D., & Polak, P. (2015). What do systems users have to fear? Using fear appeals to engender threats and fear that motivate protective security behaviors. *Management Information Systems Quarterly*, *39*(4), 837–864. doi:10.25300/MISQ/2015/39.4.5

Brody, R. G. (2010). Beyond the basic background check: Hiring the "right" employees. *Management Research Review*, *33*(3), 210–223. doi:10.1108/01409171011030372

Brody, R. G., & Cox, V. L. (2015). Background investigations a comparative analysis of background checks and federal security clearance investigations. *Business Studies Journal*, *7*(1), 84–94.

Bumgarner, J., & Borg, S. (2007). *US-CCU Cyber-Security Questionnaire*. US-CCU (Cyber Consequences Unit) Cyber-Security Check. Retrieved from www.usccu.us

Burns, A. J., Posey, C., Roberts, T. L., & Lowry, P. B. (2017). Examining the relationship of organisational insiders' psychological capital with information security threat and coping appraisals. *Computers in Human Behavior*, *68*, 190–209. doi:10.1016/j.chb.2016.11.018

Cherdantseva, Y., & Hilton, J. (2013). Information security and information assurance. The discussion about the meaning, scope and goals. In F. Almeida & I. Portela (Eds.), *Organisational, Legal, and Technological Dimensions of Information System Administrator*. IGI Global Publishing.

Choi, Y. (2017). Human resource management and security policy compliance. *International Journal of Human Capital and Information Technology Professionals*, 8(3), 14. doi:10.4018/IJHCITP.2017070105

Cram, W. A., D'Arcy, J., & Proudfoot, J. G. (2019). Seeing the Forest and the Trees: A Meta-Analysis of the Antecedents to Information Security Policy Compliance. *Management Information Systems Quarterly*, 43(2), 1–24. doi:10.25300/MISQ/2019/15117

Cybercrime Unit. (2016). *Government will fight Cyber Crime*. Retrieved from http://cybercrime.gov.gh/?p=313

D'Arcy, J., & Greene, G. (2014). Security culture and the employment relationship as drivers of employees' security compliance. *Information Management & Computer Security*, 22(5), 474–489. doi:10.1108/IMCS-08-2013-0057

Da Veiga, A. (2016). Comparing the information security culture of employees who had read the information security policy and those who had not: Illustrated through an empirical study. *Information & Computer Security*, 24(2), 139–151. doi:10.1108/ICS-12-2015-0048

Driscoll, C., & McKee, M. (2007). Restorying a culture of ethical and spiritual values: A role for leader storytelling. *Journal of Business Ethics*, 73(2), 205–217. doi:10.100710551-006-9191-5

Dumisani, X., Chux, G. I., Andre, S., & Joyce, N. (2014). The Impact of Employer-Employee Relationships on Business Growth. *Journal of Economics*, 5(3), 313–324. doi:10.1080/09765239.2014.11885007

Durden, O. (2019). *The advantages of monitoring employees*. Retrieved from https://smallbusiness.chron.com/advantages-monitoring-employees-18428.html

EEOC vrs Freeman (2013). *Court Slams EEOC on Background Check Lawsuit No. 09-CV-2573*. Retrieved from https://www.employmentlawspotlight.com/2013/08/court-slams-eeoc-on-background-check-lawsuit/

Ford, J., Willey, L., White, B. J., & Domagalski, T. (2015). New concerns in electronic employee monitoring: Have you checked your policies lately? *Journal of Legal, Ethical & Regulatory Issues*, 18(1), 51–70.

Furnell, S., & Thomson, K. L. (2009). From culture to disobedience: Recognizing the varying user acceptance of IT security. *Computer Fraud & Security*, 2(2), 5–10. doi:10.1016/S1361-3723(09)70019-3

Geisser, S. (1974). A Predictive Approach to the Random Effects Model. *Biometrika*, 61(1), 101–107. doi:10.1093/biomet/61.1.101

Goodman, D., French, P. E., & Battaglio, R. P. Jr. (2015). Determinants of local government workforce planning. *American Review of Public Administration*, 45(2), 135–152. doi:10.1177/0275074013486179

Hair, J. F., Hult, G. T. M., Ringle, C. M., & Sarstedt, M. (2014). *A primer on partial least squares structural equation modeling (PLS-SEM)*. Thousand Oaks, CA: Sage.

Hair, J. F., Hult, G. T. M., Ringle, C. M., & Sarstedt, M. (2017). *A primer on partial least squares structural equation modeling (PLS-SEM)*. Thousand Oaks, CA: Sage.

Hair, J. F., Sarstedt, M., Ringle, C., & Mena, J. A. (2012). An assessment of the use of partial least squares structural equation modeling in marketing research. *Journal of the Academy of Marketing Science*, 40(3), 414–433. doi:10.100711747-011-0261-6

Herath, T., & Rao, H. R. (2009). Protection motivation and deterrence: A framework for security policy compliance in organisations. *European Journal of Information Systems*, *18*(2), 106–125. doi:10.1057/ejis.2009.6

Hirshfield, L., Bobko, P., Barelka, A. J., Costa, M. R., Funke, G. J., Mancuso, V. F., & Knott, B. A. (2019). The role of human operators' suspicion in the detection of cyber attacks. Cyber Law, Privacy, and Security: Concepts, Methodologies, Tools, and Applications, 1482-1499.

Holt, M., Lang, B., & Sutton, S. G. (2017). Potential employees' ethical perceptions of active monitoring: The dark side of data analytics. *Journal of Information Systems*, *31*(2), 107–124. doi:10.2308/isys-51580

Hu, Q., Dinev, T., Hart, P., & Cooke, D. (2012). Managing employee compliance with information security policies: The critical role of top management and organisational culture. *Decision Sciences Journal*, *43*(4), 615–659. doi:10.1111/j.1540-5915.2012.00361.x

Hu, Q., West, R., & Smarandescu, L. (2015). The Role of Self-Control in Information Security Violations: Insights from a Cognitive Neuroscience Perspective. *Journal of Management Information Systems*, *31*(4), 6–48. doi:10.1080/07421222.2014.1001255

Hughes, S., Keller, E. W., & Hertz, G. T. (2010). Homeland security initiatives and background checks in higher education. *New Directions for Institutional Research*, *2010*(146), 51–62. doi:10.1002/ir.342

Hwang, I., Kim, D., Kim, T., & Kim, S. (2017). Why not comply with information security? An empirical approach for the causes of non-compliance. *Online Information Review*, *41*(1), 2–18. doi:10.1108/OIR-11-2015-0358

Ikenwe, I. J., Igbinovia, O. M., & Elogie, A. A. (2016). Information Security in the Digital Age: The Case of Developing Countries. *Chinese Librarianship*, *42*, 16–24.

Javad, A., & Weistroffer, H. R. (2016). Understanding Deterrence Theory in Security Compliance Behavior: A Quantitative Meta-Analysis Approach. *SAIS 2016 Proceedings*. Retrieved from http://aisel.aisnet.org/sais2016/28

Karlsson, F., Åström, J., & Karlsson, M. (2015). Information security culture – state-of-the-art review between 2000 and 2013. *Information & Computer Security*, *23*(3), 246–285. doi:10.1108/ICS-05-2014-0033

Kaspersky, E., & Furnell, S. (2014). A security education Q&A. *Information Management & Computer Security*, *22*(2), 130–133. doi:10.1108/IMCS-01-2014-0006

Katuo, A., & Budhwar, P. (2006). Human resource management systems and organizational performance: A test of a mediating model in the Greek manufacturing context. *International Journal of Human Resource Management*, *17*(7), 1223–1253. doi:10.1080/09585190600756525

Khan, H. U., & AlShare, K. A. (2019). Violators versus non-violators of information security measures in organizations - A study of distinguishing factors. *Journal of Organizational Computing and Electronic Commerce*, *29*(1), 4–23. doi:10.1080/10919392.2019.1552743

Khan, M. A. (2010). Effects of human resource management practices on organizational performance - An empirical study of oil and gas industry in Pakistan. European Journal of Economics. *Finance and Administrative Sciences*, *24*, 157–175.

Khao, B., Harris, P., & Hartman, S. (2010). Information security governance of enterprise information systems: An approach to legislative compliant. *International Journal of Management and Information Systems*, *14*(3), 49–55.

Kim, E. B. (2014). Recommendations for information security awareness training for college students. *Information Management & Computer Security*, *22*(1), 115–126. doi:10.1108/IMCS-01-2013-0005

Klaas, B. S., Olson-Buchanan, J. B., & Anna-Katherine, W. (2012). The determinants of alternative forms of workplace voice: An integrative perspective. *Journal of Management*, *38*(1), 314–345. doi:10.1177/0149206311423823

Koh, R. J. (2018). The Influence of human resource management practices on employee performance in the manufacturing sector in Malaysia. *International Journal of Human Resource Studies, 8*(2).

Komatsu, A., Takagi, D., & Takemura, T. (2013). Human aspects of information security: An empirical study of intentional versus actual behavior. *Information Management & Computer Security*, *21*(1), 5–15. doi:10.1108/09685221311314383

Lacey, D. (2010). Understanding and transforming organisational security culture. *Information Management & Computer Security*, *18*(1), 4–13. doi:10.1108/09685221011035223

Leidner, S., & Smith, S. M. (2013). Keeping potential job-hoppers' feet on the ground. *Human Resource Management International Digest*, *21*(1), 31–33. doi:10.1108/09670731311296492

McCrohan, K. F., Engel, K., & Harvey, J. W. (2010). Influence of awareness and training on cyber security. *Journal of Internet Commerce*, *9*(1), 23–41. doi:10.1080/15332861.2010.487415

Miller, D. (2017). *Importance of School Monitoring And Evaluation Systems*. Retrieved from http://leansystemssociety.org/importance-of-school-monitoring-and-evaluation-systems/

Misra, R. K., & Khurana, K. (2018). Analysis of Employability Skill Gap in Information Technology Professionals. *International Journal of Human Capital and Information Technology Professionals*, *9*(3), 53–69. doi:10.4018/IJHCITP.2018070104

Misra, S., & Adewumi, A. (2015). An Analysis of the Suitability of Cloud Computing Services in the Nigerian Education Landscape. *Proceeding of IEEE International Conference on Computing, Communication and Security*, 1-4. 10.1109/CCCS.2015.7374203

Naz, F., Aftab, J., & Awais, M. (2016). Impact of Human Resource Management Practices (HRM) on Performance of SMEs in Multan, Pakistan. *International Journal of Management. Accounting & Economics*, *3*(11), 699–708.

Nunnally, J. C. (1978). *Psychometric theory* (2nd ed.). New York, NY: McGraw-Hill.

Odun-Ayo, I., Misra, S., Omoregbe, N., Onibere, E., Bulama, Y., & Damasevičius, R. (2017). *Cloud-Based Security Driven Human Resource Management System. In Frontiers in Artificial Intelligence and Applications* (Vol. 295, pp. 96–106). Advances in Digital Technologies.

Okewu, E., Misra, S., Sanz, L. F., Maskeliūnas, R., & Damaševičius, R. (2018). An e-Environment System for Socio-economic Sustainability and National Security. *Problemy Ekorozwoju*, *13*(1), 121–132.

Oladipo, J. A., & Abdulkadir, D. S. (2011). Strategic human resource management and organizational performance in the Nigerian manufacturing sector: An empirical investigation. *International Journal of Business and Management, 6*(9), 46–56.

Ossege, C. (2012). Accountability – are we better off without it? *Public Management Review, 14*(5), 585–607. doi:10.1080/14719037.2011.642567

Overseas Security Advisory Council (OSAC). (2012). *Ghana 2012 OSAC crime and safety report.* Retrieved from https://www.osac.gov

Parker, D. B. (2008). Security accountability in job performance. *Information Systems Security, 3*(4), 16–20. doi:10.1080/10658989509342474

Patrick, H. A. (2012). Commitment of information technology employees in relation to perceived organisational justice. *IUP Journal of Organisational Behavior, 11*(3), 23–40.

Posey, C., Roberts, T. L., & Lowry, P. B. (2015). The impact of organisational commitment on insiders' motivation to protect organisational information assets. *Journal of Management Information Systems, 32*(4), 179–214. doi:10.1080/07421222.2015.1138374

Radhakrishna, A., & Raju, S. R. (2015). A study on the effect of human resource development on employment relations. *IUP Journal of Management Research, 14*(3), 28–42.

Ramakrishna, A., & Figueroa, N. (2017). Is seeing believing? Training users on information security: Evidence from Java Applets. *Journal of Information Systems Education, 28*(2), 115–122.

Rantos, K., Fysarakis, K., & Manifavas, C. (2012). How effective is your security awareness program? An evaluation methodology. *Information Security Journal: A Global Perspective, 21*(6), 328-345.

Rigon, E. A., Westphall, C. M., dos Santos, D. R., & Westphall, C. B. (2014). A cyclical evaluation model of information security maturity. *Information Management & Computer Security, 22*(3), 265–278. doi:10.1108/IMCS-04-2013-0025

Ringle, C. M., & Sarstedt, M. (2016). Gain more insight from your PLS-SEM results: The importance-performance map analysis. *Industrial Management & Data Systems, 116*(9), 1865–1886. doi:10.1108/IMDS-10-2015-0449

Safa, N. S., Maple, C., Furnell, S., Azad, M. A., Perera, C., Dabbagh, M., & Sookhak, M. (2019). Deterrence and prevention-based model to mitigate information security insider threats in organisations. *Future Generation Computer Systems, 97*, 587–597. doi:10.1016/j.future.2019.03.024

Safa, N. S., Maple, C., Watson, T., & Von Solms, R. (2018). Motivation and opportunity based model to reduce information security insider threats in organisations. *Journal of Information Security and Applications, 40*, 247-257.

Saifalislam, K. M., Osman, A., & AlQudah, M. K. (2014). Human resource management practices: Influence of recruitment and selection, and training and development on the organizational performance of the Jordanian Public University. *Journal of Business and Management, 16*(5), 43-46.

Sarode, A. P., & Deore, S. S. (2017). Role of third party employee verification and background checks in HR management: An overview. *Journal of Commerce & Management Thought, 8*(1), 86–96. doi:10.5958/0976-478X.2017.00005.2

Sattar, T., Ahmad, K., & Hassan, S. M. (2015). The role of human resource practices in employee performance and job satisfaction with mediating effect of employee engagement. *Pakistan Economic and Social Review, 53*(1), 81–96.

Selden, S. C. (2009). *Human capital: Tools and strategies for the public sector.* Washington, DC: CQ Press. doi:10.4135/9781483330754

Sreejith, S. S., & Mathirajan, M. (2016). Identifying Criteria for Continuous Evaluation of Software Engineers for Reward and Recognition: An Exploratory Research. *International Journal of Human Capital and Information Technology Professionals, 7*(4), 61–78. doi:10.4018/IJHCITP.2016100105

Stewart, J. M., Tittel, E., & Chapple, M. (2005). *Certified Information Systems Security Professional (Study Guide)* (3rd ed.). San Francisco: Sybex.

Stone, M. (1974). Cross-Validatory Choice and Assessment of Statistical Predictions. *Journal of the Royal Statistical Society. Series A (General), 36*(2), 111–147.

Styles, M., & Tryfonas, T. (2009). Using penetration testing feedback to cultivate proactive security amongst end-users. *Information Management & Computer Security, 17*(1), 44–52. doi:10.1108/09685220910944759

Subramaniam, C., Shamsudin, F. M., & Ibrahim, H. (2011). Linking human resource practices and organisational performance: Evidence from small and medium organizations in Malaysia. *Journal Pengurusan, 32*, 27–37. doi:10.17576/pengurusan-2011-32-04

Syamala, D. B., & Dasaraju, S. R. (2014). *A suggested conceptual framework for employee background Check.* ICBPEM, Knowledge Partner.

Tassabehji, R. (2005). Information security threats: From evolution to prominence. In *Evcyclopedia of Multimedia Technology and Networking (Margherita Pagani).* Idea Group Inc. doi:10.4018/978-1-59140-561-0.ch058

Thomson, K., & van Niekerk, J. (2012). Combating information security apathy by encouraging prosocial organisational behaviour. *Information Management & Computer Security, 20*(1), 39–46. doi:10.1108/09685221211219191

U.S. Office of Personnel Management. (n.d.). Retrieved from https://www.opm.gov

Valentine, R. L. (2014). *Human Resource Management. Stanford, CA: Cengage Learning. SHRM.*

Vance, A., Lowry, P. B., & Eggett, D. (2013). Using accountability to reduce access policy violations in information systems. *Journal of Management Information Systems, 29*(4), 263–290. doi:10.2753/MIS0742-1222290410

White, G. L., Hewitt, B., & Kruck, S. E. (2013). Incorporating global information security and assurance in I.S. education. *Journal of Information Systems Education, 24*(1), 11–16.

Yalman, Y., & Yesilyurt, M. (2013). Information Security Threats and Information Assurance. *TEM Journal*, *2*(3), 247–252.

Yaokumah, W. (2016). The influence of students' characteristics on mobile device security measures. *International Journal of Information Systems and Social Change*, *7*(3), 44–66. doi:10.4018/IJISSC.2016070104

Zaman, U., & Saif, M. I. (2016). Perceived accountability and conflict management styles as predictors of job performance of public officials in Pakistan. *Gomal University Journal of Research*, *32*(2), 24–35.

Zhang, L., & McDowell, W. C. (2009). Am I really at risk? Determinants of online users' intentions to use strong passwords. *Journal of Internet Commerce*, *8*(3–4), 180–197. doi:10.1080/15332860903467508

Zhao, X., Xue, L., & Whinston, A. B. (2013). Managing interdependent information security risks: Cyberinsurance, managed security services, and risk pooling arrangements. *Journal of Management Information Systems*, *30*(1), 123–152. doi:10.2753/MIS0742-1222300104

Chapter 19
The Business Transformation and Enterprise Architecture Framework:
Holistic Skills Design and Evolution (HSD&E)

Antoine Trad

IBISTM, Croatia

ABSTRACT

The HSD&E activities are supported by a central decision-making system (DMS) (in which a HR subsystem is included), knowledge management system (KMS), and an enterprise architecture project (EAP). The chapter's proof of concept (PoC) is based on a business case from the insurance domain where the central point is the capacity of the selected manager skillset to successfully start and finalize a BTP or an EAP (or simply a project). The PoC shows the selection process of a manager's skillset to transform the traditional insurance enterprise into an agile and automated enterprise. Projects are managed by managers, who are (or should be) supported by a methodology and a framework that can estimate the risks of failure of a project; at the same time, they should be capable of managing the implementation project processes.

BACKGROUND

The riskiest CSF in a *Project* transforming a traditional business environment (BE) into a lean and automated BE, is the role and skills/human factors of the *Manager* and his capabilities in managing the implementation phase of the *Project*. The basic skills set and education background of a *Manager* has not been sufficiently investigated in a holistic manner in order to design and define the right skills set; and that is the main chapter's goal (Trad & Kalpić, 2013a); by holistic the authors refer to a generic or cross-functional approach. *Manager* skills/human factors set that has to manage the complex imple-

DOI: 10.4018/978-1-7998-1279-1.ch019

mentation phase of a *Project* that requires a specific set of DMS, KMS, EA, design and implementation skills. The *Project*'s Implementation Phase (PIP) is the major cause of high failure rates (CapGemini, 2009). Analysing the failure rates, the authors have found that only around 12% of BEs successfully finish *Projects* (Tidd & Bessant, 2009). Therefore, there is a tremendous need for more research on the *Manager* skills set that needs holistic EA and implementation skills for the PIP. The knowledge gap was acknowledged and confirmed, due to the fact that the existing literature and various methodologies treating *Projects* offer practically no insight into the skills set/human factors of the *Manager* as an Architect of Holistic Business System (AofHBS or simply a *Manager*) (SAP, 2013a); Actual *Projects* are reliant on business schools accountants skills sets... Holistic approach and managing PIP complexity requires a mixed method that is mainly based on a hyper-heuristics model. The AofHBS must be capable of transforming the BE's Information and Communication Systems (ICS) and to exploit the technologies in order to successfully conduct the *Project*. Such *Manager*s and organizations need holistic methodologies, like SAP's BTP2 or even better, the one proposed by the authors, that encompasses Enterprise Architecture (EA), HR activities, and the management of *Projects* (Uhl & Gollenia, 2012). Using Google Scholar to match the combinations of the keywords: 1) *Manager* and DMS; 2) *Manager* and EA; 3) EA and DMS… shows that the authors and their unique framework have a total lead (Trad & Kalpić, 2019a). This chapter shows that the *Manager* is an AofHBS with holistic or cross-functional skills, is mainly a holistic technocrat, which opposes business schools' approach, to use cheap interface and brutal accountants, who are schooled to deliver tuned balance sheets, with no understanding of complex environments (The Economist, 2000).

The AofHBS manages *Projects* that involve complete digitization of value chains and business processes automation, and enables a traditional BE to create new business models and hence business excellence. A capable *Manager* can make transformed BEs like Cisco Systems, Dell Computer and many others report important financial gains due to *Projects* (Barua, Konana, Whinston, & Yin, 2001). This research phase uses the Trad Kalpić Methodology and Framework (*TKM&F*), as shown in Figure 1 (Trad & Kalpić, 2018f), which is based on CSFs from various areas like EA, DMA, business processes, accountancy, enterprise skills….

This chapter presents a set of HHFD&EP managerial recommendations and combines needed fields, like Knowledge Management (KM), applied mathematical models, EA, information technology management, HR management and business transformation. Integrating a HHFD&EP should be a fundamental strategic *Project*'s goal (Trad & Kalpić, 2018a, 2018b; Cearley, Walker & Burke, 2016), where Figure 2 is fundamental to understand the whole research project and it is used in the whole book.

The proposed HHFD&EP uses the *TKM&F* that is based on the Research and Development Project (RDP) of intelligent neural networks (Trad & Kalpić, 2018a). The HHFD&EP is agnostic to any specific application field, as shown in Figure 3, and is based on the Architecture Development Method (ADM) (The Open Group, 2011a).

The used EA method and its ADM are central to implement *Projects,* where the HHFD&EP is used for the *Manager*'s selection, evolution and training (Trad & Kalpić, 2017b; Trad & Kalpić, 2017c; Thomas, 2015; Tidd, 2006). In *Projects*, the *Manager*'s role is important and his or her (in further text – his) actions are supported by a a DMS as shown in Figure 4.

The HHFD&EP uses a holistic approach, as shown in Figure 5, where it uses skills set CSFs (Daellenbach & McNickle, 2005; Trad & Kalpić, 2016a).

The authors will try to prove that a qualified technocrat's skills set would be a base for the AofHBS (Farhoomand, 2004); who needs to be assisted with by a DMS (Trad & Kalpić, 2013c; Oduh, Misra,

Figure 1. The research framework's concept (Trad & Kalpić, 2016a)

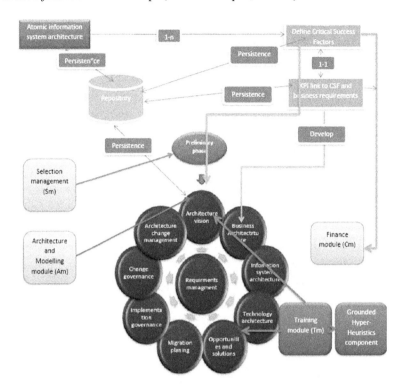

Figure 2. The research framework's interaction flow (Trad, 2018a)

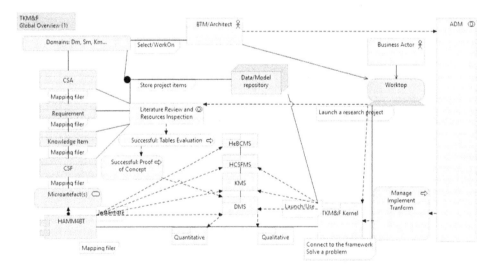

Figure 3. The research framework's architecture method's interface (The Open Group, 2011a)

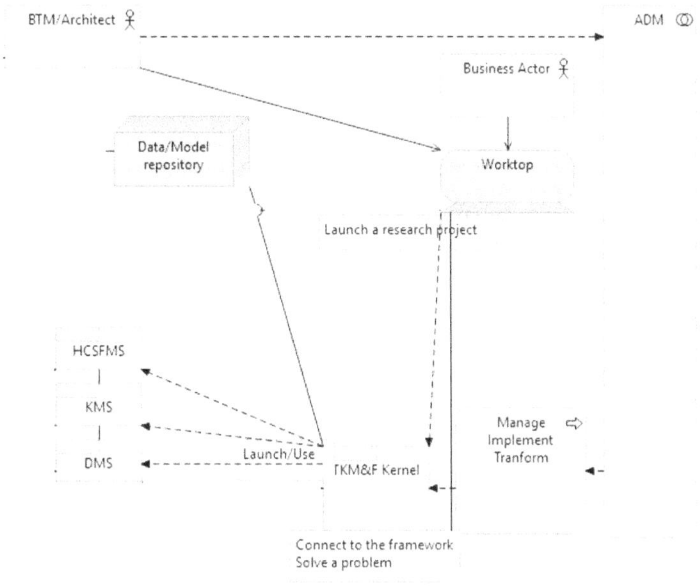

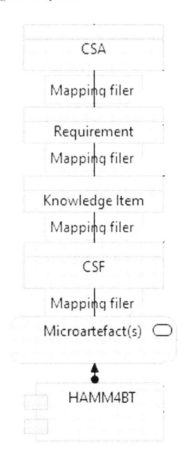

Figure 4. Business decision management system

Figure 5. Interaction with factors

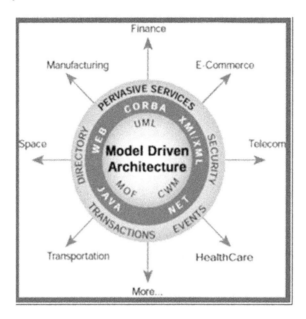

Damaševičius, Maskeliūnas, 2018) Cloud Based Simple Employee Management Information System: A Model for African Small and Medium Enterprises. In: Rocha Á., Guarda T. (eds) Proceedings of the International Conference on Information Technology & Systems (ICITS 2018). ICITS 2018. Advances in Intelligent Systems and Computing, vol 721. Springer, Cham). *Projects* lack a holistic approach to support the HHFD&EP and that is this work's focus (Thomas, 2015; Cearley, Walker & Burke, 2016; Trad & Kalpić, 2016b). HHFD&EP recommendations can be applied by *Project's* stakeholders (Desmond, 2013) that uses *TKM&F* microartefacts (Johnson & Onwuegbuzie, 2004; Trad & Kalpić, 2017b; Trad & Kalpić, 2017c; Trad & Kalpić, 2018a). The RDP is based on a mixed methodology and is unique (Easterbrook, Singer, Storey & Damian, 2008); where this chapters tries to prove the HHFD&EP' feasibility through a Research Question (RQ).

THE RESEARCH PROCESS

Projects failure rates are high and are constantly increasing (Bruce, 1994) that is due to the complexity encountered in the PIP (CapGemini, 2009); to enhance the success rate, the authors propose the *TKM&F* that is unique and can be considered as a pioneering approach. *TKM&F* recommends linking a Mathematical Model (MM) to all levels of the *Project*, as shown in Figure 6 (Trad & Kalpić, 2018b; Agievich, 2014), including the CSF based HHFD&EP (Tidd & Bessant, 2018).

The Applied Research Framework

The HHFD&EP can be applied to various types of *Projects* (Trad 2018c, 2018d) and is a part of the Selection management, Architecture-modelling, Control-monitoring, Decision-making, Training management, *Projects* management, Finance management, Geopolitical management, Knowledge management, Imple-

Figure 6. Presents levels of project's interaction (Trad & Kalpić, 2017b; Trad, & Kalpić, 2017c)

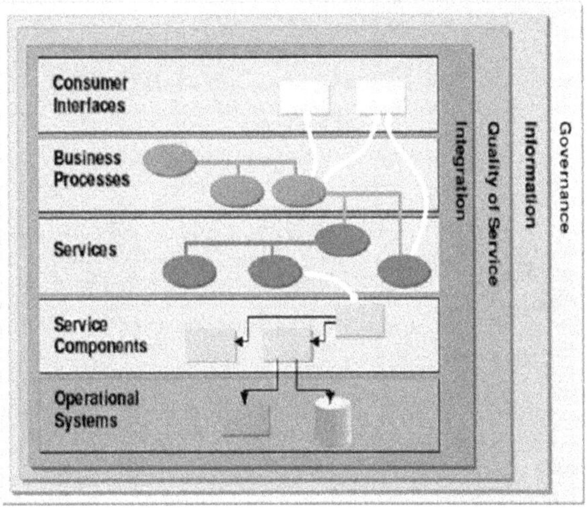

mentation management and Research management Framework (SmAmCmDmTmPmFmGmKmImRmF, for simplification reasons, in further text the term *TKM&F* will be used). This chapter's RQ is: "Which business transformation managers' skills and evolution schemes are optimal for the implementation phase of business transformation and enterprise architecture projects?" (Trad, 2011a; Trad & Kalpić, 2011a). This chapter's RQ was formulated after a literature review process.

The Research's Literature Review and Gap

The knowledge gap was acknowledged, mainly because the existing literature, on failure rates and on various methodologies treating *Projects*, offer practically no insight into the skills set of the *Manager* as an AofHBS; which can setup *Project*s and can manage their PIP (SAP, 2013a; Trad & Kalpić, 2013b; Trad & Kalpić, 2013c). This RDP inspects the *Manager*'s skills set, which is mainly based on the Aof-HBS model that makes it unique.

The Research's Uniqueness

The uniqueness of this research promotes a holistic unbundling process, the alignment of standards and strategies to support *Projects* (Farhoomand, 2004). The uniqueness of this research project is based on its holistic approach that combines: 1) *Project*; 2) HMM; 3) software modelling and architecture; 4) business engineering; 5) financial analysis; 6) *Manager* skills set and evolution schemes; 6) EA; and 7) it offers a methodology and Framework.

Review's and Check of the Critical Success Factors/Critical Success Areas

The HHFD&EP promotes the transformation through the use of Critical Success Area (CSA) that contains a set of CSFs, where a CSF is a set of Key Performance Indicators (KPI), where each KPI corresponds to a single *Projects* requirement and/or an item that can be a skills set requirement or skill that has a column in each evaluation table (Putri & Yusof, 2009; Peterson, 2011;Trad & Kalpić, 2018f). As shown

Figure 7. The factors interaction in the TKM&F

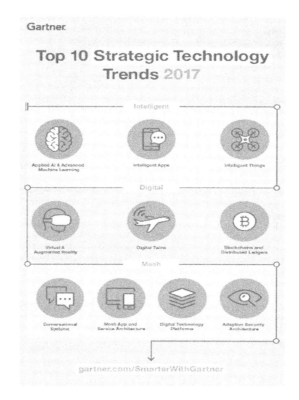

in Figure 7, a *Project* starts with the first phase called the feasibility phase to check the basic CSFs, to check if the *Project* makes sense; it ends with success or failure. Based on the HHFD&EP literature review and related evaluation processes, the most important extracted CSFs that are used and evaluated using defined rules (Trad & Kalpić, 2018f).

THE BUSINESS CASE

Managing the Business Case

HHFD&EP uses an Applied Case Study (ACS), developed by the Open Group as a reference study, it presents the possibilities to implement *Projects*' components and is related to an insurance company named ArchiSurance (Trad & Kalpić, 2018f); in this chapter it is used to check the HHFD&EP.

Integrating Critical Success Factors

A CSF is measurable and mapped to a weighting that is roughly estimated in the first iteration and then tuned through ADM iterations, to verify the AofHBS skills set and evolution schemes, using the DMS; where a holistic business and enterprise architecture CSFs are essential (Felfel, Ayadi & Masmoudi, 2017). The main issue here is how to define the background and selection aspects for such a skills set; and how to interrelate the different business/EA skills (KPMG, 2014).

The Architecture Development Method and Projects

This RDP focuses on the design of *Projects'* integration and presents the influence of HHFD&EP to select the *Manager*. In the actual age of distributed intelligence, complexity, knowledge, economy and technology (Gardner, 1999). HHFD&EP offers a pattern that includes a hyper-heuristics tree that supports a wide class of problem types, and it is a major benefit (Markides, 201), where the DMS offers a set of AofHBS skills sets (Trad, Kalpić & Fertalj, 2002; Trad & Kalpić, 2014d; Oduh, Misra, Damaševičius, Maskeliūnas, 2018). The *TKM&F's* parts, must synchronize with the ADM that are shown in Figure 8.

The Business Case Study's Critical Success Factors

Based on the CSF review process, the important business case's CSFs that are used and evaluated

As shown in Table 1, the result's aim is to prove or justify that the HHFD&EP' business case and how it can be used with the PoC. The next CSA to be analysed is the holistic MM's integration.

The Research Section's Link to the Applied Mathematical Model

This section's deduction is that HMM is crucial for the RDP's credibility. Where it is the basis for its mathematical model and structure.

THE APPLIED MATHEMATICAL MODEL

The Mathematical Model's Basics

The HHFD&EP uses a CSF based HMM that is an abstract model containing a proprietary Mathematical Language (ML) that can be used to automate, transform and implement the behaviour of the HHFD&EP. The HMM nomenclature that is presented to the reader in Figure 9, in a simplified form, to be easily understood, on the cost of a holistic formulation of the model.

Figure 8. Business architecture phases (The Open Group, 2014b)

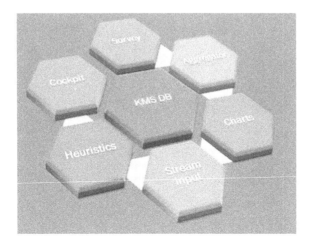

Table 1. The applied case study's critical success factors that have an average of 8.63.

AMM4BT

rncRequirement	$= KP I$	(1)
CSF	$= \Sigma\ KPI$	(2)
CSA	$= \Sigma\ CSF$	(3)
Requirement	$= \bigcup$ rncRequirement	(4)
(e)neuron	$=$ action+ rncInteligenceArtefact	(5)
mcArtefact	$= \bigcup$ (e)neurons	(6)
rncEnterprise	$= \bigcup$ mcArtefact	(7)
(e)Ellterprise	$= \bigcup$ rncEnterprise	(8)
mcArtefactScenario	$= \bigcup$ mcArtefactDecisionMaking	(9)
IntelligenceComponent	$= \bigcup$ mcArtefactScenario	(10)
OrganisationalIntelligence	$= \bigcup$ InteligenceComponent	(11)
AMM4BT	$=$ ADM+ OrganisationalIntelligence	(12)

Figure 9. The applied mathematical model's nomenclature (Trad, & Kalpić, 2017a)

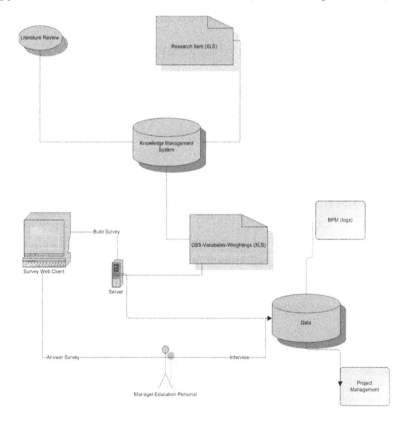

As shown in Figure 9:

- The symbol $\sum$ indicates summation of weightings/ratings, denoting the relative importance of the set members selected as relevant. Weightings as integers range in ascending importance from 1 to 10.
- The symbol U̲ indicates sets union.
- The proposed HMM enables the possibility to define *Project* as a model; using CSFs weightings and ratings.
- The selected corresponding weightings to: CSF ϵ { 1 … 10 }; are integer values.
- The selected corresponding ratings to: CSF ϵ { 0.00% … 100.00% } are floating point percentage values.

A weighting is defined for a HHFD&EP CSF and a rating for a KPI.

The Applied Business Transformation Mathematical Model

The HMM can be modelled after the following formula for Business Transformation Mathematical Model (*BTMM*) that abstracts the *Projects*:

HMM = Weigthing$_1$ * HMM_Qualitative + Weigthing$_2$ * HMM_Quantitative (1).

HMM = $\sum$ HMM for an enterprise architecture's instance (2).

(*BTMM*):

BTMM = $\sum$ HMM instances (3).

The objective function of the *BTMM*'s formula can be optimized by using constraints and with extra variables that need to be tuned using the HMM. The variable for maximization or minimization can be, for example, the *Project's* success, costs or another CSF. For the HHFD&EP PoC the success will be the main and only constraint and success is quantified as a binary 0 or 1. where the objective function definition will be:

Minimize risk *BTMM* (4).

The *BTMM* is the combination of a *Project* methodologies and a holistic mathematical model that integrates the enterprise organisational concept, information and communication technologies (Lazar, Motogna & Parv, 2010).

As shown in Figure 10, the HMM is a part and is the skeleton of the *TKM&F* that uses microartefacts' scenarios to support HHFD&EP requests (Kim & Lennon, 2017).

The HHFD&EP components interface the DMS and KMS, as shown in Figure 11, to evaluate, manage and map CSFs for selection activities; if the aggregations of all the *Project's* CSA/CSF tables is exceeds the defined minimum the *Projects* continues to its second part, the HHFD&EP PoC.

Figure 10. The framework's components and its mathematical model

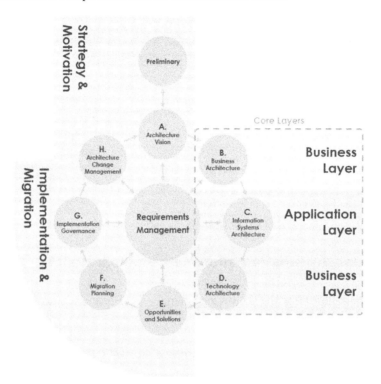

Framework's Applied Mathematical Model Integration

The *Project's* initialization phase generates the needed CSFs and hence creates the types skills set issues to analyzed.

The HMM is a part and is the skeleton of the *TKM&F* that uses microartefacts' scenarios to support HHFD&EP requests (Agievich, 2014).

The Mathematical Model's Integration Critical Success Factors

Based on the HHFD&EP review process and the most important CSFs that are evaluated as follows:

As shown in Table 2, the result's aim is to prove or justify that HMM is mature and possible to be used for the HHFD&EP and can be used for the PoC. The next CSA to be analysed is the holistic management of the ICS.

The Research Section's Link to the Information and Communication System

This section's deduction is that the ICS' unbundling is a crucial process for the BE.

Figure 11. The decision making interface

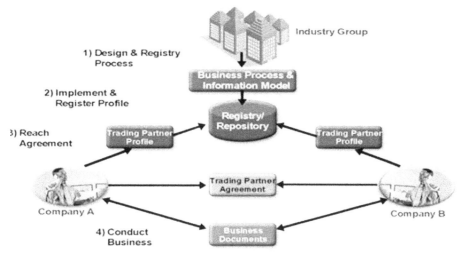

Table 2. The critical success factors that have an average of 9.15

Critical Success Factors	HMM - KPIs	Weightings
CSF_BusinessCase_Modelling	ComplexNeedsUnbundling ▾	From 1 to 10 08 Selected
CSF_BusinessCase_FactorsIntegration	ComplexClassification ▾	From 1 to 10 08 Selected
CSF_BusinessCase_References	LimitedSilos ▾	From 1 to 10 08 Selected
CSF_BusinessCase_ArchitectureDevMethod	Integrated ▾	From 1 to 10 10 Selected
CSF_BusinessCase_Technologies	UniquePlatform ▾	From 1 to 10 09 Selected
CSF_BusinessCase_Governance	Advanced ▾	From 1 to 10 09 Selected
CSF_BusinessCase_Transformation_TKM&F	NoDifference ▾	From 1 to 10 10 Selected
CSF_BusinessCase_AofHBS_Extension4HR	ComplexProfile ▾	From 1 to 10 08 Selected

valuation

THE KMS' INTEGRATION IN THE INFORMATION AND COMMUNICATION TECHNOLOGY SYSTEM

Distributed Unit of Work

Microartefact granularity and responsibility for a given MM scenario is a complex undertaking (Kim & Lennon, 2017); added to that there is the implementation of the "1:1" mapping and classification of the transformed microartefacts, as shown in Figure 12; where each resource passes from one component to the other with a mapping concept. The EA concept uses methodologies like The Open Group's Architecture Framework's (TOGAF) ADM that supports a set of the *TKM&F's* and HHFD&EP (Neumann, 2002).

Figure 12. The framework's microartefact interactions

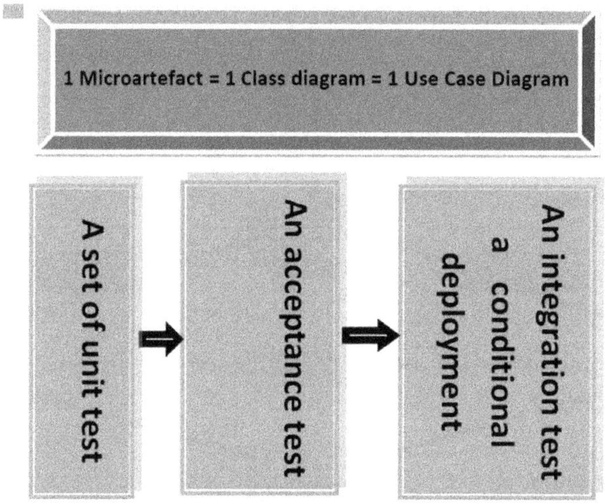

1 Microartefact = 1 Class diagram = 1 Use Case Diagram

A set of unit test → An acceptance test → An integration test a conditional deployment

Architecture and Technology Standards

A *Manager* must have the skills to manage agile *Project* and especially its PIP; where an adequate mapping concept is used to integrate standards (OASIS, 2014); that is a recommendation. The strategy is enabled by the establishment of an ADM based iterative model that can map *Project's* microartefacts in a linear "1:1" manner (The Open Group, 2011b), as shown in Figure 13.

The scope's difficulty and complexity lie in capability of a BE to synchronize the *Project's* vision with its capabilities (Trad & Kalpić, 2015b).

Figure 13. The iterative architecture development process (The Open Group, 2011a)

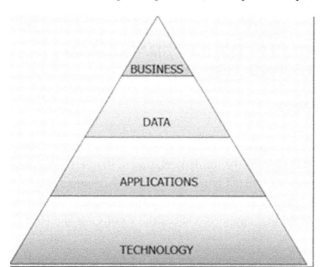

Project Strategy

The *Manager* must be capable of integrating the *TKM&F's* using a pseudo bottom-up approach that is based on Service Oriented Architecture (SOA) concept that is described in Capgemini's SOA framework, as shown in Figure 14 (Gartner, 2005).

Holistic Qualification Procedures

Figure 15 shows actual immaturity of design, development, qualification and operations for *Projects* that still are in an infancy age, or simply chaotic. Tools for implementation environments are still confronted with serious project issues. These problems show that tools are still inappropriate for large enterprise intelligent systems and the authors recommend the use HHFD&EP CSF based patterns (Gartner, 2013).

Figure 14. Services integration (The Open Group, 2011c)

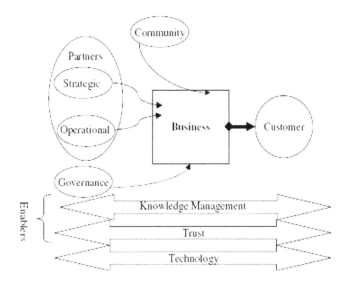

Figure 15. The decision making based systems' evolution (Gartner, 2013)

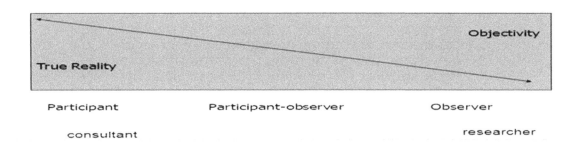

Resources, Artefacts and Factors Management

The *Manager* must have the capacity to manage the *TKM&F's* repository that maps HHFD&EP CSFs to types of *Project's* resources, as shown in Figure 20. This mapping concept associates CSFs, resources and microartefact scenario instances to HHFD&EP requests (The Open Group, 2011a).

The Information and Communication System's Critical Success Factors

Based on the review process and factors' evaluation, the most important HHFD&EP ICS CSFs are evaluated as follows:

As shown in Table 3, the result's aim is to prove or justify that it is possible to implement a HHFD&EP which interacts with the ICS that enables the next CSA to be analysed, which is the integration of the ADM in the environment.

The Research Section's Link to the Architecture Development Method

This section's deduction is that the ICT and other fields are dependent on an EA paradigm and therefore the ADM is crucial for the integration of the HHFD&EP.

Figure 16. The knowledge management subsystem

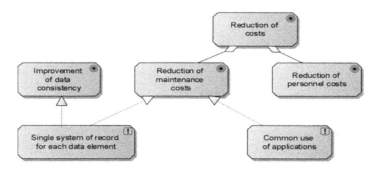

Table 3. The critical success factors that have an average of 9.10

Critical Success Factors	HMM - KPIs	Weightings
CSF_HMM_TKM&F_Integration	StableTested	From 1 to 10. 09 Selected
CSF_HMM_InitialPhase	RobustTested	From 1 to 10. 10 Selected
CSF_HMM_PoCPhase	StableTested	From 1 to 10. 10 Selected
CSF_HMM_Qualitative&Quantitative	Complex	From 1 to 10. 07 Selected
CSF_HMM_Final_BusinessSystem	VerifiedModel	From 1 to 10. 09 Selected
CSF_HMM_ADM_Integration	Synchronized	From 1 to 10. 09 Selected
CSF_HMM_SkillsEvolutionConcept_Interfacing	StableTested	From 1 to 10. 10 Selected

valuation

THE INTEGRATION WITH THE ARCHITECTURE DEVELOPMENT METHOD

The ADM is a method that recommends a set of phases and iterations to develop the *Project's* architecture; it designs parts of the transformed system interfaces and other deliverables also with other internal (like the HHFD&EP) and market frameworks. The HHFD&EP defines a set of basic EA requirements for skills set's selection, training and evaluation; that are stored in the *TKM&F* KMS database, as shown in Figure 17 (Trad & Kalpić, 2014e).

Architecture Phases

As shown in Figure 18, the ADM manages the *Project's* development iterations; in this section the authors present ADM's phases and the HHFD&EP' interactions:

- The preliminary phase selects the relevant CSFs and interactions.
- The architecture vision and business architecture phases interactions.
- The information system architecture phase's interactions.
- The technologies architecture phase's interactions.
- The requirements management and tests phase's interactions.

Business Architecture

The *Manager* must use the *TKM&F* ao apply standards that deliver added value and robustness to *Projects*. In order to move towards a just-enough business architecture that is known as the target or final interaction architecture as shown in Figure 19, where the important adjacent domains are clearly shown and the others are blurred because of their low level of importance (OASIS 2006).

The traditional business architecture layers that are shown in Figure 20, represent a silo model of the fundamental components. These four components are very hard to melt down into an agile BE and holistic EA (Trad & Kalpić, 2015a).

Figure 17. The knowledge management system item

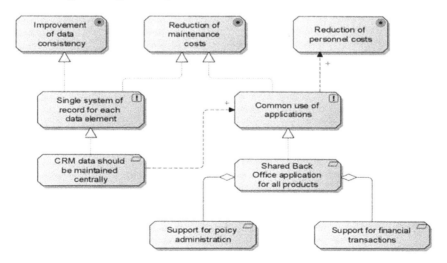

Figure 18. The architecture method's interaction

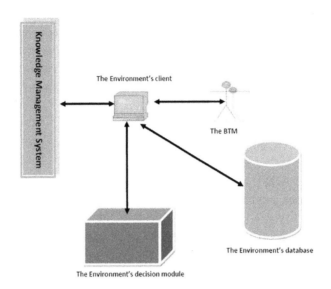

Figure 19. The business interaction architecture (OASIS, 2006)

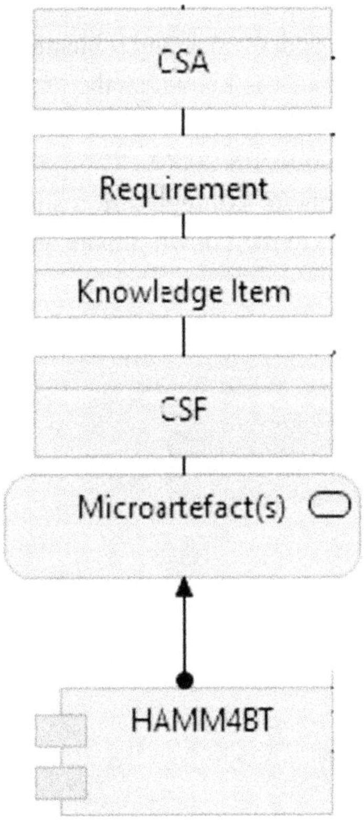

Figure 20. Traditional architecture levels (The Open Group, 2011a)

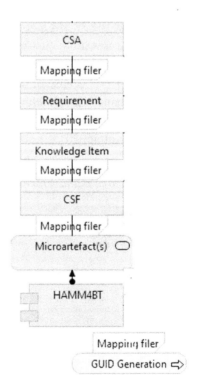

The Architecture Development Method Critical Success Factors

Based on the literature review and CSF evaluation process, the most important ADM's CSFs are evaluated to the following:

As shown in Table 4, the result tries to prove or justify that it is possible to integrate and automate the ADM's interaction with the HHFD&EP; and the next CSA to be analysed is the holistic management of the KMS.

The Research Section's Link to the Electronic Knowledge Management System

This section's deduction is that the HHFD&EP can be integrated in the *Projects* and a holistic ADM. Now follows the HHFD&EP interfacing the KMS.

THE HOLISTIC ELECTRONIC KNOWLEDGE MANAGEMENT SYSTEM

The Holistic Electronic Knowledge Management

The *Manager* must be capable of managing project Knowledge Items (pKI); where pKIs and microartefact scripts are responsible of the manipulation of intelligence and they control various knowledge processes. The KMS supports the HHFD&EP underlying mechanics to manage pKI microartefacts. The *Manager* is responsible for designing pKI's extraction using holistic systemic approach (Daellenbach & McNickle, 2005; Trad & Kalpić, 2016a). A HHFD&EP interfaces the KMS to enable an efficient search process (Trad, 2018c).

Table 4. The critical success factors that have an average of 9.60

Critical Success Factors	HMM - KPIs	Weightings
CSF_ICS_IntegrationProcesses	MatureSupported	From 1 to 10. 09 Selected
CSF_ICS_Operations&Choreography	SimpleAutomated	From 1 to 10. 09 Selected
CSF_ICS_DesignProcess	SimpleSupported	From 1 to 10. 09 Selected
CSF_ICS_McLifecycle	ExistingProcedures	From 1 to 10. 10 Selected
CSF_ICS_RAD_BusinessProcess	ComplexEnvironments	From 1 to 10. 08 Selected
CSF_ICS_Tests	ExistingTests	From 1 to 10. 10 Selected
CSF_ICS_StorageRepository	Supported	From 1 to 10. 08 Selected
CSF_ICS_Mapping	Supported	From 1 to 10. 09 Selected
CSF_ICS_HSD&E_StandardsIntegration	Supported	From 1 to 10. 09 Selected
CSF_ICS_HSD&E_Strategy	Supported	From 1 to 10. 10 Selected
CSF_ICS_HSD&E_Security	Integrated	From 1 to 10. 10 Selected

valuation

The Holistic Knowledge Strategy

An HHFD&EP interfaces the KMS/pKI, where sets of AofHBS skills set are stored (Trad & Kalpić, 2017a; Trad & Kalpić, 2017b; Trad & Kalpić, 2017c). The interface strategy is included in the architecture roadmap and the *Manager* must select tools for the KMS management (Alhawamdeh, 2007), as shown in Figure 21.

The Knowledge Management Success Factors

Based on the literature review, the most important knowledge CSFs that are used are:

The Modules Chained Link to the Intelligence Support or Decision System

The KMS' integration result prove that it is possible to implement an HHFD&EP to interface the DMS.

THE INTEGRATION WITH THE DECISION MAKING SYSTEM

A Complex Process

AofHBS skills design is supported by the HHFD&EP' selection, training and evaluation using the DMS (Şeref, Ahuja, & Winston, 2007; Oduh, Misra, Damaševičius, & Maskeliūnas, 2018). The DMS' results are presented as a set of possible solutions or possible AofHBS skills sets (SAP, 2013a). The best solution proposes the right skills set in relation to the selection, evaluation and training activities.

Figure 21. Knowledge management and the business environment

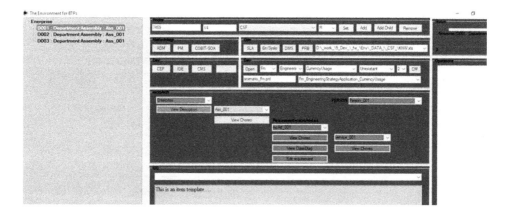

Table 5. The critical success factors that have an average of 9.00

Critical Success Factors	HMM - KPIs	Weightings
CSF_ADM_CSF_Initialization&Setup	MatureStatus	From 1 to 10 10 Selected
CSF_ADM_IntegrationProcesses	StandardSupported	From 1 to 10 09 Selected
CSF_ADM_Phases	Supported	From 1 to 10 10 Selected
CSF_ADM_Requirements	MappingAutomated	From 1 to 10 09 Selected
CSF_ADM_HSD&E_Architecture	FullySupported	From 1 to 10 10 Selected

valuation

A Risky Process

HHFD&EP, KMS and DMS integration may face problems due to complex CSF evaluation process that implies that the analysis and management of risk is one of the important pre-requisites to ensure the success of HHFD&EP activities. The HHFD&EP uses the DMS risk management capabilities (Hussain, Dillon, Chang & Hussain, 2010).

The Decision Making Process

The decision making process is supported by the HMM formalism that uses a holistic approach for delivering a set of AofHBS possible skills set in form of solutions (Daellenbach & McNickle, 2005). The HHFD&EP interfaces the DMS, in which various skills sets are selected and tuned, using selected CSF sets for skills sets that are orchestrated by the HMM's choreography engine.

The Decision Making System's Critical Success Factors

Based on the literature review and evaluation processes, the most important DMS's CSFs that are used are evaluated to the following:

As shown in Table 6, the result tries to prove or justify that it is possible and even mature to implement a holistic and distributed DMS using the HMM formalism and that will be presented in the HHFD&EP section.

Table 6. The critical success factors that have an average of 9.00

Critical Success Factors	HMM - KPIs	Weightings
CSF_KMS_ICS_Integration	FullySupported	From 1 to 10 10 Selected
CSF_KMS_pKI_Mapping	ComplexToImplement	From 1 to 10 08 Selected
CSF_KMS_Patterns	Implementable	From 1 to 10 10 Selected
CSF_KMS_HSD&E_Integration	Implementable	From 1 to 10 09 Selected
CSF_KMS_HSD&E_AccessManagement	StandardIntgeration	From 1 to 10 09 Selected
CSF_KMS_HSD&E_ProfileMatching	ComplexToImplement	From 1 to 10 08 Selected

valuation

The Research Section's Link to the Holistic Skills set

This chapter's conclusion based on CSFs, is that the analysis of the HHFD&EP will be executed.

THE HOLISTIC PROFILE

Basics

The *Manager* should have a deep understanding of *Projects* and their integrated DMS that is the first step towards the application of a transformation process. He needs also in-depth knowledge of: 1) electronic lean business environment architectures; 2) integrated development environments; 3) business people integration, 4) agile project management; and 5) coordination of computer engineers. The AofHBS acts as business and information systems solution designer and implementation architect (SAP, 2013a, 2012a).

The Skills Set's Role

Manager skills set and profile have an enormous impact on the concrete PIP of *Projects*, where the managerial aspects of such *Projects* are not well defined. Currently there is no business or enterprise architecture set of recommendations and educational curriculum for such skills sets (Trad, 2011a; Laudon, K., & Laudon, 2011). There is an essential need for more research on the AofHBS' skills sets and role for increasingly competitive BEs.

Architecture Skills

The HHFD&EP can help executive management select a *Manager* for the *Project's* PIP, in any of its stage of development; that helps also in the maintenance of the resulting BE. The *Manager* manages mechanistic BEs that will be challenged to use their *Project* results in order to change their business operations, re-engineer their ICS, or to re-schedule various tasks of project management plans (Pham, Misra, Huynh, & Ahuja, 2019); which could result in automating tasks that might have been performed manually in the past (Trad, & Kalpić, 2001).

Architecture Framework Usage and the Role of an Enterprise Architect

Meta-management and business integration require a *Manager* skills set who must be an avant-garde innovation project manager. The *Manager* must be an excellent agile project manager, who is capable of implementing a very light version of the disciplines TOGAF, service and processes. The use of processes will enhance the management of knowledge and help in the selection of an *Manager*. Such need for a specific skills set requires a special educational curriculum. Future *Manager's* need to have the ability to deeply understand each company's unique enterprise architecture, and to swiftly identify *Project* steps and to effectively implement them into their business processes as the basis for a future sustainable profitable enterprise. According to the latest Gartner Study, "the ability to apply versatile and extensive methodological skills in managing business processes is the number one business priority for successful entrepreneurial activities" (Trad, & Kalpić, 2014e, 2014g). The implementation of this managerial recommendations in the real world is done by the training of the selected AofHBS who should have had at least, the minimal needed experiences before.

Needed Experience

This RDP is also based on the authors' experiences in various domains of business engineering and respective EA/ICS consultancy. In their carriers, the authors have often encountered *Projects* with serious problems having high rates of failure. This fact motivated them to pursue this RDP and contribute to this endemic problem related to complex *Projects* in mechanistic BEs; and to promote the optimal *Manager* skills set. The difficulty lies in the duration of *Projects* that take many years to be finalized.

The complex activity of interconnecting the company's business processing nodes that is known as unbundling, is extremely complex and in general it causes major resistance; consequently it may cause *Projects* to fail (Farhoomand, Lynne, Markus, Gable, & Khan, 2004). The HHFD&EP offers a selection and training framework, where the training part is supposed to enhance the *Manager*'s knowledge by adopting holistic skills set.

Holistic Characteristics

The *Manager* must have a holistic skills set and the most important recommendation is that he has cross-functional skills (CapGemini, 2007). The preferred basic skills set is a flexible and intelligence-based person, who is able to transform the BE and is also capable of exploiting the inter-related avant-garde technologies in order to successfully conduct *Projects*. Managing of complex skills and educational concepts, requires a mixed method that is mainly based on action research; a hyper-heuristics model (Trad, & Kalpić, 2014e, 2014g). The implementation in the real world is done by the HHFD&EP selection of the right *Manager* that has this main quality and has been proven in industry.

Needed Hands-on Skills

The *Manager* must have extensive skills in *Project*'s and especially PIPs, his empirical hands-on skills must encompass: 1) knowledge of business architectures and business process management; 2) automated business environments; like mechanistic BEs (Krigsman, 2008); 3) agile project management; 4) knowledge management integration; 5) organizational concepts; 6) management sciences methodologies; 7) enterprise architecture; and 8) other concrete *Project* implementation artefacts (Trad, & Kalpić, 2014e, 2014g).

Figure 22. The synergy between real world experience and research outcomes (Trad, & Kalpić, 2011)

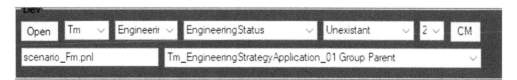

Business Modelling and Integration

The *Manager* must have extensive knowledge of business process modelling in *Project*s to manage the implementation of the existing business scenarios, into an automatized set of business processes. These process setups insure that the *Manager* rationalizes the enterprise's business scenarios and enable inter-enterprises eco-systems development through the business enterprise architecture framework.

Business Infrastructure Integration

The *Manager* must have extensive knowledge of business infrastructure integration in *Project*s to manage the implementation of the existing platform nodes, into an automatized and highly available BE infrastructure. This process is set up, to insure that the *Manager* can rationalize the BE's platform nodes and to enable intranet and extranet business communication through the EA framework's control. For various BEs that are transformed into mechanistic entities; with a generic business driven approach, where the business infrastructure implementation is a very important factor to glue its ICS to the external world, and to give it the needed leanness (Trad, & Kalpić, 2014e, 2014g).

The Role of Soft Skills

The subject of soft skills management is a subject to many writings and research projects, that is why in this paper the authors do not treat how does the *Manager* manage the human factor, and the staff's para-psychological, behavioural and cultural aspects. The implementation of this managerial recommendation in the real world is done by the selection of a right *Manager* who has this very important soft qualities.

The Holistic Skills set's Critical Success Factors

Based on the literature review and evaluation processes, the most important HHFD&EP's CSFs that are used are evaluated to the following:

As shown in Table 7, the result tries to prove or justify that it is possible and even mature to implement a HHFD&EP.

Table 7. The critical success factors that have an average of 9.00

Critical Success Factors	AHMM4T enhances: KPIs	Weightings
CSF_DMS_ComplexSystemsIntegration	Supported	From 1 to 10. 09 Selected
CSF_DMS_HSD&E_Interfacing	Supported	From 1 to 10. 09 Selected
CSF_DMS_KMS_Interfacing	IntegrationEnabled	From 1 to 10. 10 Selected
CSF_DMS_DMP	IntgeratesAsKernel	From 1 to 10. 10 Selected
CSF_DMS_HolisticApproach	Supported	From 1 to 10. 08 Selected
CSF_DMS_Manager_ProfileOptimization	Supported	From 1 to 10. 08 Selected

valuation

The Research Section's Link to the Proof of Concept

This chapter's deduction is that, the selected and evaluated CSFs, based on the presented of seven tables that this RDP justifies the following phase, which is the PoC's implementation.

THE PROTYPE INTEGRATION

The ACS is an insurance management system that has an archaic ICS, a mainframe, claim files service, customer file service.

Application Portfolio Rationalization Scenario, Data Unification

This HHFD&EP PoC, uses the ArchiSurance ACS; to select the AofHBS and uses a structured pool of CSFs to satisfy the HHFD&EP requirements, as shown in Figure 23 that can be considered as the base sets of CSAs.

Setup and Critical Success Factors of the Architecture Method's Phases

The HHFD&EP's needed skills for:

- phase A or the Architecture Vision phase, needs architecture roadmap; as shown in Figure 24.
- Phase B or the Business Architecture phase, needs *Project's* target architecture and requirements definition.
- Phase C or the Gap Analysis phase, needs for modelling a target application landscape.

Figure 23. Transformation goals (Jonkers, Band & Quartel, 2012)

Figure 24. Goals and principles (Jonkers, Band & Quartel, 2012)

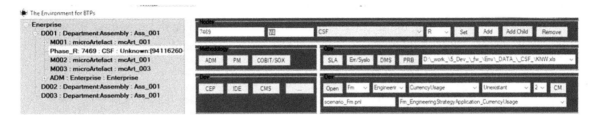

- Phase D or the Target Technology Architecture and Gap Analysis phase needs the final *Project's* infrastructure design.
- Phases E and F, Implementation and Migration Planning, needs the transition architecture, proposing possible intermediate situation and evaluates the *Project's* status (Pham, Misra, Huynh, & Ahuja, 2019).

This PoC focuses on the *Manager*'s capability to make a common application architecture, a goal that can be seen in Figure 24.

The Proof of Concept

The chapters' PoC is implemented using the authors' *TKM&F*. The PoC is based on the HMM's instance and the HHFD&EP interfaces the DMS that uses the skills set CSFs, That is an example for this chapter, it is presented and evaluated in Tables 1 to 8 as shown in Figure 25.

The required skills have mappings to specific *Projects* resources like CSFs, as shown in Figure 26.

The used microartefacts are designed using EA methodologies and the HHFD&EP concept defines relationships between the HHFD&EP requirements and microartefacts, using global unique identifiers, as shown in Figure 27.

The PoC is achieved by using the *TKM&F* client's interface that is shown in Figure 28; where the starting activity is to structure the organizational part.

Once the development setup interface is activated, the NLP interface can be launched to implement the needed microartefact scripts to process the defined six CSAs. After starting the *TKM&F's* graphical interface, the sets of CSFs are selected, in this case for training *Manager*s, as shown in Figure 29.

Then follows the CSF attachment, for training *Manager*s, to a specific node of the *TKM&F's* graphical tree, as shown in Figure 30; to link later the microartefacts.

From the *TKM&F* client's interface the ML development setup and editing interface can be launched to develop the microartefacts that are related to the CSF, responsible for training *Manager*s, as shown in Figure 31.

These scripts make up the intelligence basis and the HMM's instance set of actions that are processed in the background to support services to be used in microartefacts. The HMM uses services that are called by the DMS actions, that manage the edited mathematical language script and flow, for training *Manager*s, as shown in Figure 32.

This research's HHFD&EP instance, the HMM and its related CSFs, for training *Manager*s, were selected as demonstrated previously, as shown in Figure 33.

Figure 25. The TKM&F sequence of phases

```
// Microartefct: Tm Operations
//

debug = on

[mcArt_Def] TmOperations

// Variable declaration
//
var v1 = 11; // CSF for Training Minimization
var v2 = 12; // CSF for Fast Problem Solving
var v3 = 0;  // Problem Solving Value


// EXEC_NNSCENARIO scenario
// QUANTIFY    quantifyFn 70 quantify CSV

MessageBox START


LABL0:

// Microartefct
//
MessageBox LABL0
[mcArt_aservice] TmCalculate Activity.poolOfActivitiesDefs.calcAssets 120 30
MAPPING SLA=T REQ=T AUD=T LOG=F CSF=T:0,1 CPU=1 WTU=0,8 WTL=0,8
QUALIFY qualifyFn 60 Heuristics Exec
QUANTIFY quantifyFn 70 Factorial Exec
var1 = retval
MessageBox retval
TESTS UNIT
if retval > 0 then goto LABL1 else LABL5
```

Figure 26. The TKM&F microartefacts concept

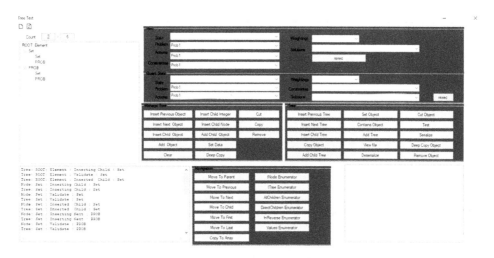

Once the microartefact is ready, the CSF and NLP files are configured as shown in Figure 33. In this chapter's seven tables and the result of the processing of the first initial phase, as illustrated in Table 8, shows clearly that the HHFD&EP can be used in *Projects*. HHFD&EP is not an independent component and is bonded to all the *Project's* overall architecture, hence there is a need for a holistic approach.

Figure 27. The TKM&F's global unique identifiers interaction

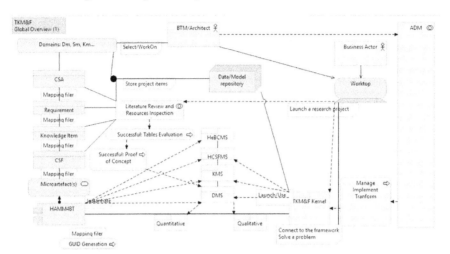

Figure 28. The TKM&F's client interaction

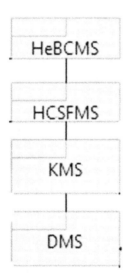

Figure 29. The TKM&F's factor setup interface

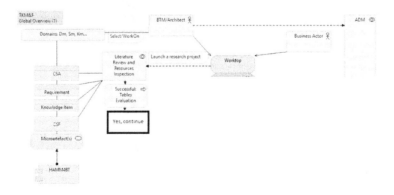

Figure 30. The TKM&F's factor setup interface

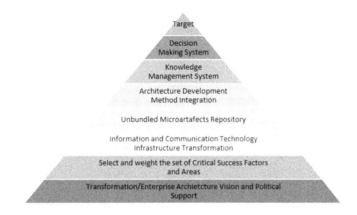

Figure 31. The edited mathematical language script and flow

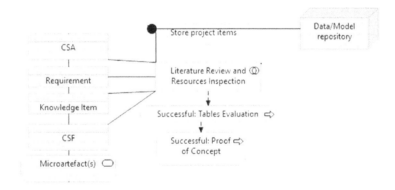

The *TKM&F* and hence the HMM's main constraint to implement the HHFD&EP is that CSAs for simple *Projects* components, having an average result below 8.5 will be ignored. In the case of the current CSF evaluation an average result below 7.5 will be ignored. As shown in Table 8, this fact keeps the CSAs (marked in green) that helps to make this work's conclusion; and drops the ones in red. The result 6.06 means that the HHFD&EP integration is mature and can be used in all types of *Projects, where* the complexity is integrating the HHFD&EP in *Projects* that must be done in multiple transformation sub-projects (small iterations), where the first one should try to define the basic AofHBS and iterate the reach the right skills set.

SOLUTION AND RECOMMENDATIONS

The managerial recommendations are needed for finding the solutions to enable HHFD&EP. The HHFD&EP CSFs are the result of the literature review and the surveys outputs and are used in the hyper-heuristics research model. In this article, the focus is on the *Manager* skills set, capabilities and

Figure 32. The heuristics tree configuration

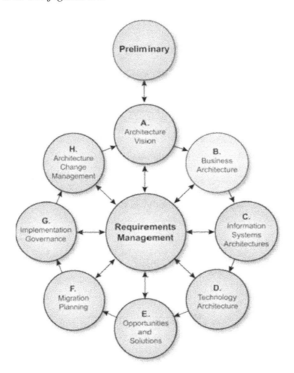

Figure 33. The TKM&F's components' interaction

CSA Category of CSFs/KPIs	Influences *Projects*	Average Result
The Applied Case Study Integration	CredibleButComplex ▾	From 1 to 10. **8.63**
The Usage of the Architecture Development Method	FullyIntegrated ▾	From 1 to 10. **9.60**
The Information and Communication Technology System	Transformable ▾	From 1 to 10. **9.10**
The Mathematical Model's Integration	IsApplicable ▾	From 1 to 10. **9.15**
The Decision Making System	Implementable ▾	From 1 to 10. **9.00**
The Holistic Knowledge Making System	Implementable ▾	From 1 to 10. **9.00**
The HSD&E Concept	Implementable ▾	From 1 to 10. **9.00**

Evaluate First Phase

educational prerequisites. These characteristics and prerequisites are needed to holistically manage the design PIPs. The research tris to define the optimal skills set and his educational curriculum, which should be adequate for the finalization of *Projects*. There has been a lot developed and written on enabling success in *Projects*, but the authors propose to inspect why they fail in the PIP. That is mainly due to the *Manager* lack of knowledge in managing business integration and implementation and the non-existence of an adequate training and educational curriculum. Because of very high score, above 9,

Table 8. The holistic factor management system research's outcome, is 9.06

Critical Success Factors	HMM - KPIs	Weightings
CSF_HSD&E_BasicSystemsIntegration	Supported	From 1 to 10. 09 Selected
CSF_HSD&E_Architecture_Skills	Supported	From 1 to 10. 09 Selected
CSF_HSD&E_ProfileRoles	ManagementEnabled	From 1 to 10. 09 Selected
CSF_HSD&E_DMP_ForProfileSearching	Intgerated	From 1 to 10. 10 Selected
CSF_HSD&E_HolisticApproach	Supported	From 1 to 10. 09 Selected
CSF_HSD&E_TKM&F_Support	Intgerated	From 1 to 10. 10 Selected
CSF_HSD&E_RoleOfExperience	Analyzable	From 1 to 10. 09 Selected
CSF_HSD&E_HandsOn_Skills	Auditable	From 1 to 10. 08 Selected
CSF_HSD&E_Soft_Skills	Auditable	From 1 to 10. 08 Selected
CSF_HSD&E_BusinessModellingIntegration_Skills	Supported	From 1 to 10. 09 Selected
CSF_HSD&E_BusinessInfrastructureIntegration_Skills	Supported	From 1 to 10. 09 Selected

Valuation

Table 8 shows that the HHFD&EP implementation is not a risky transformation process and that today the *TKM&F* is ready and the only methodology and framework that can in parallel construct *Projects*, EAPs, MMs, KMS, DMS' and *Projects*. The resultant technical and managerial recommendations are:

- A HHFD&EP concept must be established and tried to check its feasibility and it should replace traditional obsolete factors evaluation mechanisms.
- The *Project*'s technical PIP, is the major cause of high failure rates in (e)transformations, therefore there is a need for an optimal architecture pattern and a qualified *Manager*.
- The *Manager* must be an architect and a technocrat, who is capable of supporting and designing the transformation process of the enterprise (Trad & Kalpić, 2013b; Trad & Kalpić, 2014d; Farhoomand, Lynne, Markus, Gable & Khan, 2004).
- The *Manager* must have extensive experience in (e)Business transformation projects: the *Project*'s PIP is the main cause of high failure rates (Neumeier, 2009; Capgemini, 2007; Capgemini, 2009).
- The *Manager* must be an agile project manager, who is capable of implementing a light version of an EA framework and of management of process models (Uhl & Gollenia, 2012).
- The *Manager* must have cross-functional skills (The Economist, 2000); such a person can be described as flexible and adaptable, capable of managing complexity. (Uhl & Gollenia, 2012; The Open Group, 2011b; The Open Group, 2011c).
- Knowledge gap; the literature review proved the existence of a knowledge gap between the traditional management skills and educational prerequisites for *Projects* (Trad, Kalpić, 2013).
- Evolutionary Mixed Method; this research uses an evolutionary research model in order to create the initial *Manager* skills set and educational prerequisites (Trad, A., Kalpić, 2013).
- The *Project* PoC and interviews delivered the research's recommendations on how to select and educate *Manager's* (Trad & Kalpić, 2014).
- Managerial recommendations, benefits and framework uses a qualitative hyper-heuristics model, which confirmed the survey outcomes; and delivered the managerial recommendations and benefits. The *Project* research project proposes a concrete framework on how to select, train and evaluate a *Manager*.

HHFD&EP managerial recommendations, and the *TKM&F*, round up the approach needed for the complex PIP. The *Manager's* skills set selection pattern, defines the *Manager's* skills set and educational prerequisites that round up a selection and educational capacities, on how to select and train a *Manager*.

FUTURE WORK

The future work and its related research and development processes, will continue to tune the *TKM&F* and will work more specifically on the decision module's evolution; mainly focusing on neural networks algorithms.

CONCLUSION

The most important managerial recommendation that was generated by the previous research phases was that the *Manager* must be an architect of adaptive business systems. The PoC was based on the CSAs/CSFs links to a specific *Projects* resources and the reasoning model evaluated the selected CSFs. The deduced result implies that an attempt of HHFD&EP based transformation can be successful. In this chapter, the focus is on the optimal *Manager's* skills set to holistically manage the design and PIP of a *Project*. There has been a lot developed and written on enabling success in transformation projects, but the authors propose to inspect why *Manager*s fail in the PIP of a *Project*. That is mainly due to the *Manager's* lack of knowledge in managing business integration and implementation and the non-existence of adequate business enterprise architecture integration for such research question. The most important findings in this phase are: 1) The *TKM&F* PoC and interviews proved the approach and delivered the recommendations on how to select and educate *Manager*s (Farhoomand, Lynne, Markus, Gable, & Khan, 2004) and EA integration, benefits and framework. In a meta-managerial business driven coordination, the information technology is a commodity used to glue the various business components (Uppal & Rahman, 2013). There has been a lot of development and research work on the reasons for success or failure in *Projects*, but the authors propose to inspect the holistic aspects *Projects*. The managerial recommendations are offered to help *Manager*s to decrease the high failure rates and are a result of the resources review, surveys outputs, interviews, simulation and prototyping. The *TKM&F* supports the *Manager* by using the HHFD&EP pattern and delivers a set of managerial recommendations for *Projects*.

ACKNOWLEDGMENT

It was our great pleasure to prepare this chapter and its experiment. Now our greater hopes are for readers to receive some small measure of that pleasure and support for his project.

REFERENCES

Agievich, V. (2014). *Mathematical model and multi-criteria analysis of designing large-scale enterprise roadmap*. PhD thesis.

Alhawamdeh, M. (2007). The Role of Knowledge Management in Building E-Business Strategy. *Proceedings of the World Congress on Engineering and Computer Science 2007.*

Barua, A., Konana, P., Whinston, A., & Yin, F. (2001). *Managing E-Business Transformation: Opportunities and Value Assessment. Center for Research in Electronic Commerce.* The University of Texas at Austin.

Blackburn, R., & Rosen, B. (1993). Total quality and human resources management: lessons learned from Baldrige Award-winning companies. *Academy of Management Perspectives, 7*(3).

Bruce, C. (1994). *Supervising literature reviews.* UK. In O. Zuber-Skerritt & Y. Ryan (Eds.), *Quality in postgraduate education.* Kogan Page.

CapGemini. (2007). *Trends in Business transformation - Survey of European Executives.* CapGemini Consulting and The Economist Intelligence Unit.

CapGemini. (2009). Business transformation: From crisis response to radical changes that will create tomorrow's business. A Capgemini Consulting survey.

Cearley, D., Walker, M., & Burke, B. (2016). *Top 10 Strategic Technology Trends for 2017.* Academic Press.

Daellenbach, H., McNickle, D., & Dye, S. (2012). *Management Science - Decision-making through systems thinking* (2nd ed.). Palgrave Macmillan.

Desmond, C. (2013). Management of change. *IEEE Engineering Management Review 41*(3).

Felfel, H., Ayadi, O., & Masmoudi, F. (2017). Pareto Optimal Solution Selection for a Multi-Site Supply Chain Planning Problem Using the VIKOR and TOPSIS Methods. *International Journal of Service Science, Management, Engineering, and Technology.* Doi:10.4018/IJSSMET.2017070102

Gardner, H. (1999). *Intelligence Reframed: Multiple Intelligences for the 21st Century.* New York: Basic Books.

Gartner. (2005). *External Service Providers' SOA Frameworks and Offerings: Capgemini.* Gartner.

Gartner. (2013). *Scenario Toolkit: Using EA to Support Business Transformation.* Gartner Inc.

Gunasekare, U. (2015). *Mixed Research Method as the Third Research Paradigm: A Literature Review.* University of Kelaniya.

Hussain, O., Dillon, Th., Chang, E., & Hussain, F. (2010). Transactional risk-based decision making system in e-business interactions. *International Journal of ComputSystSci & Eng, 1,* 15–28.

Johnson, R., & Onwuegbuzie, A. (2004). *Mixed Methods Research: A Research Paradigm Whose Time Has Come.* Sage Journals.

Jonkers, H., Band, I., & Quartel, D. (2012a). *ArchiSurance Case Study.* The Open Group.

Kim, J., & Lennon, Sh. (2017). *Descriptive Content Analysis on E-Service Research. International Journal of Service Science, Management, Engineering, and Technology.* doi:10.4018/IJSSMET.2017010102

KPMG. (2014). *Over 90 Percent Of U.S. Companies Are Changing Existing Business Models: KPMG Survey.* Retrieved from http://www.kpmg.com/us/en/issuesandinsights/articlespublications/press-releases/pages/over-90-percent-of-us-companies-are-changing-existing-business-models-kpmg-survey.aspx

Krigsman, M. (2008). *Business change failures: 9 success tips.* Retrieved from http://www.zdnet.com/blog/transformationfailures/business-change-failures-9-success-tips/1080

Lanubile, F., Ebert, C., Prikladnicki, R., & Vizcaíno, A. (2010). Collaboration Tools for Global Software Engineering. *IEEE Journals & Magazines, 27*(2).

Laudon, K., & Laudon, J. (2011). *Management Information Systems* (11th ed.). Prentice Hall.

Markides, C. (2011, March). Crossing the Chasm: How to Convert Relevant Research Into Managerially Useful Research. *The Journal of Applied Behavioral Science, 47*(1), 121–134. doi:10.1177/0021886310388162

Neumann, G. (2002). Programming Languages in Artificial Intelligence. In Encyclopaedia of Information Systems. Academic Press.

Neumeier, M. (2009). *Innovation Workshop: Brand Strategy + Design Thinking = Transformation.* Pearson.

OASIS. (2006). The Framework for eBusiness. An OASIS White Paper. *The OASIS ebXML Joint Committee For OASIS.* Retrieved from www.oasis-open.org

OASIS. (2014). *ISO/IEC and OASIS Collaborate on E-Business Standards-Standards Groups Increase Cross-Participation to Enhance Interoperability.* Retrieved from https://www.oasis-open.org/news/pr/isoiec-and-oasis-collaborate-on-e-business-standards

Oduh, I. U., Misra, S., Damaševičius, R., & Maskeliūnas, R. (2018). Cloud Based Simple Employee Management Information System: A Model for African Small and Medium Enterprises. *Advances in Intelligent Systems and Computing, 721.* 10.1007/978-3-319-73450-7_12

Peterson, S. (2011). *Why it Worked: Critical Success Factors of a Financial Reform eProjects in Africa. Faculty Research Working Paper Series.* Harvard Kennedy School.

Pham, Q. T., Misra, S., Huynh, L. N. H., & Ahuja, R. (2019). Investigating Enterprise Resource Planning (ERP) Effect on Work Environment. In Lecture Notes in Computer Science: Vol. 11623. *Computational Science and Its Applications – ICCSA 2019. ICCSA 2019.* Cham: Springer. doi:10.1007/978-3-030-24308-1_50

Putri, N., & Yusof, S. M. (2009). Critical success factors for implementing quality engineering tools and techniques in malaysian's and indonesian's automotive industries: An Exploratory Study. *Journal Proceedings of the International MultiConference of Engineers and Computer Scientists., 2,* 18–20.

SAP. (2012a). *Business Process Management Business Transformation Academy.* SAP.

SAP. (2013a). GBTP: Global Business Transformation Manager Master Certification (SAP Internal). Business Transformation Academy.

Taleb, M., & Cherkaoui, O. (2012, January). Pattern-Oriented Approach for Enterprise Architecture: TOGAF Framework. *Journal of Software Engineering & Applications, 5*(1), 45–50. doi:10.4236/jsea.2012.51008

The Economist. (2000). A survey of E-management-How to be an e-manager. *The Economist.*

The Economist. (2000). Inside the machine. A survey of E-management. *The Economist.*

The Open Group. (2011a). *Architecture Development Method.* The Open Group. Retrieved from http:// pubs.opengroup.org/architecture/togaf9-doc/arch/chap05.html

The Open Group. (2011b). *TOGAF 9.1.* The Open Group. Retrieved from http://www.opengroup.org/ subjectareas/enterprise/togaf

The Open Group. (2011c). *Enterprise Architecture Standards.* Retrieved from http://www.opengroup. org/standards/ea

Thomas, A. (2015). *Innovation Insight for Microservices.* Retrieved from https://www.gartner.com/ doc/3157319/innovation-insight-microservices

Tidd, J. (2006). *From Knowledge Management to Strategic Competence* (2nd ed.). London, UK: Imperial College. doi:10.1142/p439

Tidd, J., & Bessant, J. (2009). *Managing Innovation, Integrating Technological, Market and Organizational Change* (4th ed.). Wiley.

Tidd, J., & Bessant, J. (2018). *Managing Innovation: Integrating Technological, Market and Organizational Change* (6th ed.). New York: Wiley.

Trad, A. (2011a). *The Selection and Training Framework* (Thesis). GEM, Grenoble, France.

Trad, A. (2013). *COSC 3750 - DSS, Decision Support Systems – Labs results.* Geneva, Switzerland: Webster University.

Trad, A. (2018a). *The Business Transformation Framework's Resources Library. Internal project.* IBISTM.

Trad, A. (2018b). *The Transformation Framework Proof of Concept. Internal project and paper.* IBISTM.

Trad, A. (2018c). The Transformation Framework's Resources Library. IBISTM.

Trad, A. (2018d). *The Transformation Framework Proof of Concept.* IBISTM.

Trad, A., & Kalpic, D. (2001). *Building an extensible markup language (XML) based Object Mapping System (OMS).* IEEE.

Trad, A., & Kalpić, D. (2011a). The "Selection, Training, Follow and Evaluation (STF), for Manager's in Business Innovation Transformation Projects - The Human Factor". *Conference on Information Technology Interfaces.*

Trad, A., & Kalpić, D. (2013a). *The Selection and Training Framework (STF) for Managers in Business Innovation and Transformation eProjects - The Design and Implementation of the Research Model. 3rd position Award.* IMRA.

Trad, A., & Kalpić, D. (2013b). *The Selection, and Training framework (STF) for Managers in Business Innovation Transformation eProjects - The Literature Review. IEEE 2013.* Centeris.

Trad, A., & Kalpić, D. (2013c). The Selection, and Training Framework (STF) for Managers in Business Innovation Transformation eProjects -The Skills set. *Conference on Information Technology Interfaces.*

Trad, A., & Kalpić, D. (2014a). *The "Selection and Training Framework" (STF) for Manager's in Business Innovation Transformation eProjects" / The mathematical model.* EUROPMENT, Conference.

Trad, A., & Kalpić, D. (2014b). *The Selection and Training Framework (STF) for Managers in (e)Business Innovation Transformation eProjects - Managerial Recommendations.* Centeris, Portugal: IEEE.

Trad, A., & Kalpić, D. (2014c). The Selection, and Training Framework (STF) for Manager's in Business Innovation Transformation eProjects. *Mathematical Modelling.*

Trad, A., & Kalpić, D. (2014d). *The Selection and Training Framework (STF) for Managers in Business Innovation and Transformation eProjects - The Skills set of a Business Transformation Manager.* IMRA.

Trad, A., & Kalpić, D. (2014e). *The Selection and Training Framework (STF) for Managers in Business Innovation and Transformation Projects – The TOGAF recommendations.* Venice, Italy: EUROPMENT.

Trad, A., & Kalpić, D. (2014g). *The Selection and Training Framework (STF) for Managers in Business Innovation and Transformation Projects – The educational recommendations.* Zagreb, Croatia: EDEN.

Trad, A., & Kalpić, D. (2015a). *The Selection, Control, Decision making and Training Framework for Managers in Business Innovation and Transformation eProjects-Decision making model.* EUROPMENT Conference.

Trad, A., & Kalpić, D. (2015b). *The Selection, Control, Decision making and Training Framework for Managers in Business Innovation and Transformation eProjects- Managerial Recommendations for enterprise architecture.* EUROPMENT Conference.

Trad, A., & Kalpić, D. (2015c). Transformation Framework Proposal for Managers in Business Innovation and Business Transformation eProjects-Intelligent atomic building block architecture. Centeris-Elsevier.

Trad, A., & Kalpić, D. (2016a). *The (e)Business Transformation Framework for (e)Commerce Architecture-Modelling Projects. In Encyclopaedia of E-Commerce Development, Implementation, and Management.* IGI-Global.

Trad, A., & Kalpić, D. (2016b). *A Transformation Framework Proposal for Managers in Business Innovation and Business Transformation Projects-A heuristics decision module's background.* Oxford, UK: ABMR.

Trad, A., & Kalpić, D. (2017a). *An Intelligent Neural Networks Micro Artefact Patterns' Based Enterprise Architecture Model.* IGI-Global.

Trad, A., & Kalpić, D. (2017b). *A Neural Networks Portable and Agnostic Implementation TKM&F for Business Transformation eProjects. The Basic Structure.* Annecy, France: IEEE.

Trad, A., & Kalpić, D. (2017c). *A Neural Networks Portable and Agnostic Implementation TKM&F for Business Transformation eProjects. The Framework.* Annecy, France: IEEE.

Trad, A., & Kalpić, D. (2017d). A Neural Networks Portable and Agnostic Implementation *TKM&F* for Business Transformation eProjects- The Basic Structure. *IEEE Conference on Computational Intelligence.*

Trad, A., & Kalpić, D. (2017e). *The Business Transformation and Enterprise Architecture Framework / The London Inter Bank Offered Rate Crisis - The Model.* Cambridge, UK: ABMR.

Trad, A., & Kalpić, D. (2018a). *The Business Transformation Framework and Enterprise Architecture Framework for Managers in Business Innovation-Knowledge and Intelligence Driven Development (KIDD). Encyclopaedia.* IGI-Global.

Trad, A., & Kalpić, D. (2018b). *The Business Transformation Framework and Enterprise Architecture Framework for Managers in Business Innovation- Knowledge Management in Global Software Engineering (HKMS). In Encyclopaedia of E-Commerce Development, Implementation, and Management.* IGI-Global.

Trad, A., & Kalpić, D. (2018c). *The Business Transformation An applied mathematical model for business transformation-The applied case study. Encyclopaedia.* IGI-Global.

Trad, A., & Kalpić, D. (2018d). *The Business Transformation An applied mathematical model for business transformation- The Research Development eProjects Concept (RDPC). Encyclopaedia.* IGI-Global.

Trad, A., & Kalpić, D. (2018e). *The Business Transformation An applied mathematical model for business transformation-Introduction and basics. Encyclopaedia.* IGI-Global.

Trad, A., & Kalpić, D. (2018f). *An applied mathematical model for business transformation-The Holistic Critical Success Factors Management System (HCSFMS). In Encyclopaedia of E-Commerce Development, Implementation, and Management.* IGI-Global.

Trad, A., & Kalpić, D. (2019a). *The Trad-Kalpić Methodology and Framework. Total lead in business transformation and enterprise architecture projects-A google scholar analysis.* IBISTM.

Trad, A., Kalpić, D., & Fertalj, K. (2002). Proactive monitoring of the information system risk and quality. *Information Technology Interfaces, 2002. ITI 2002. Proceedings of the 24th International Conference.*

Uhl, L., & Gollenia. (2012). *A Handbook of Business Transformation Management Methodology.* Gower.

Uppal, M., & Rahman, T. (2013). *Business Transformation Made Straight-Forward.* QR Systems Inc.

ADDITIONAL READING

Farhoomand, A. (2004). *Managing (e)Business transformation.* Palgrave Macmillan. doi:10.1007/978-1-137-08380-7

Farhoomand, A., Lynne, M., Markus, M., Gable, G., & Khan, H. (2004). *Managing (e)Business Transformation: A global Perspective.* Palgrave Macmillan. doi:10.1007/978-1-137-08380-7

Chapter 20

Human Factors That Lead Successful Implementations of ERP Systems:
Guidelines for IT Project Managers of Higher Education Institutions

Gabriela Gerón-Piñón
https://orcid.org/0000-0003-0259-6963
University of Monterrey, Mexico

Pedro Solana-González
https://orcid.org/0000-0001-5606-1476
University of Cantabria, Spain

Sara Trigueros-Preciado
University of Cantabria, Spain

Daniel Pérez-González
https://orcid.org/0000-0002-1469-220X
University of Cantabria, Spain

ABSTRACT

Although Latin America has exhibited lately the largest growth in terms of ERP adoption rate worldwide, there is a gap in the literature focused in examining the success and underlying causes of such adoptions. After an extensive literature review, the authors found little evidence of studies oriented to the study of human factors in ERP projects in higher education institutions (HEIs) in the region, which is the aim of this study. It is known that the success of these projects is limited, and that the failure rate is high (between 60% and 90%). Therefore, it is worth identifying the human factors that may serve as reference for the HEIs that are planning to implement these systems. This work compiles the experiences of experts who have participated in projects at universities in Latin American countries, establishing a set of unique features and the specific factors to lead successful ERP projects.

DOI: 10.4018/978-1-7998-1279-1.ch020

INTRODUCTION

Higher Education Institutions (HEIs) in Latin America are facing the global trends that are affecting education: revenue pressure; austerity; accountability and outcomes; operation efficiency; education access and readiness; global learning; digital transformation; students' higher expectations; and maintaining a relationship with the community among others. Latin America is an emerging, young and changing region. A recent report on higher education (Brunner & Miranda, 2016) shows the changing landscape and the speed with which this sector is changing in most of these countries where the number of students is over 24 million, that represents 11.5% of the student population worldwide.

In the region, there are currently about 11,000 institutions; 4,220 universities and 6,648 non-university higher education institutions (Brunner & Pedraja, 2017). In Latin America, expenditure for student (US$ 2,380) is lower than in developed countries. Private expenditure finances 50% of the total enrollment. Several countries have also relied extensively on private providers to meet the growing demand for higher education, resulting in massive expansion of the number of private HEIs (Segrera, 2010).

Because of the above conditions, Higher Education in Latin America has specific challenges, mainly as a result of the social and economic differences: institutions that previously had only one campus have expanded their operations in several countries; private education is predominant because public education does not meet the massive social demand; a severe reduction in government funding; limited scientific research; emergence of new interdisciplinary areas of knowledge that are replacing traditional curricula; and the rise of evaluation and accreditation mechanisms (Guajardo et al, 2018).

Following the example of large corporations, HEIs are continuously reviewing and improving their management and administration systems. The concerns HEIs face are similar to those of a wide range of organizations (Rabaa'i, 2009). Without any doubt HEIs are involved in the current technology trends. Topics such as cloud computing, Software as a Service (SaaS), mobile technologies, analytics, among others, are on the daily agenda of Information Technologies (IT) areas. Although Latin America has exhibited lately the largest growth in terms of ERP adoption rate worldwide, there is a gap in the literature focused in examining the success and underlying causes of such adoptions there (Maldonado & Sierra, 2013).

The ERP systems are often the largest software application adopted by universities with significant amounts allocated to their implementation. The main aim of ERP implementation in universities is to provide schools and colleges with an increased ability for research and teaching at the reasonable and low cost. These multi-functional systems are designed to streamline almost every aspect of how institutions operate. Simply put, an ERP integrates institutional data and processes through one system. The benefits of an education ERP systems are: cost effective; better organization of data; data is secured; more automated administration; a quicker management process; and more focus on education (Rani, 2016).

Little research has been conducted about ERPs in a university environment, compared with other enterprise environments (ALdayel et al., 2011). The research on ERP system in HEIs is still limited and in the immature stage, hence little is known about the success factors for the adoption stage of ERP systems (Soliman & Karia, 2017). There is little evidence of studies focused in Latin America HEIs.

Jacobson et al. (2007) sustain that Latin America holds the largest compound annual growth rate in ERP spending (21%) at least until 2011. The lack of a more fully developed IT culture might explain the region's lagging international competitiveness. Although ERP-based solutions also appear to be gaining acceptance among Latin America companies, in many cases such solutions are inadequate, because of the many obstacles preventing ERP from being implemented according to the needs of individual companies. Most of the firms in Latin America lack a formal organizational structure or even personnel qualified in specialized tasks required for IT (Maldonado & Sierra, 2013).

A considerable investment is required, for both the initial acquisition and the ongoing support, while the return on investment (ROI) is obtained in the medium or long term. In the United States, according to Swartz & Orgill (2001), some HEIs spend over $20 million USD to implement these complex software products. Projects that can take two, three, or more years to be implemented.

Therefore, is highly relevant for HEIs that are considering decisions or are about to start an ERP implementation project, to understand the conditions required for this type of project. Since there is evidence that many ERP implementation projects achieve limited success and the failure rate is high, between 60% and 90% as research has showed (Xu et al., 2010). For that reason, is imperative to identify the ERP implementation's best practices in the region that help managers to lead successful projects.

Kvavik et al. (2002) conducted studies to evaluate the ERP's benefits in higher education; these studies concluded that ERP systems were implemented to improve services for students, faculty and staff. However, 50% of these implementations went over both budget and timeline schedules. Research in Australian higher education has reported a series of problems with ERP implementations that appear unique to universities (von Hellens, Nielsen & Beekhuyzen, 2005). This makes it more important to minimize the ERP failure in the Higher Education and focus the research specific in Latin America. Maldonado & Sierra (2013) sustain that few existing research pieces addressing the ERP topic in developing regions and affirm that there exist differences in critical success factors not only among regions, but also among established and recognized factors.

This work aims to identify the Human Factors of ERP implementations in HEIs in Latin America, through a compilation of the experience of experts who have participated in projects in countries in the region. It is intended that this research will serve as a reference for institutions that are seeking the implementation of these systems, and that it will also serve as guide for IT Project Managers to start such projects and ensure the understanding of the conditions required that will help them to have a successful project.

Human Factor is a body of knowledge about human abilities, human limitations, and other human characteristics that are relevant to the IT project management domain. It can be divided into three areas: physical ergonomics, cognitive ergonomics and organizational ergonomics. This research is based fundamentally on the levels of cognitive ergonomics (top management engagement and support, communication and change management, project manager experience and specialized consultants) and organizational ergonomics (team commitment, efficient decision making, project governance and people who will operate the system).

The outline of this study is as follows: in the first section an introduction is presented. In the second section a literature review of ERP systems in HEIs and Human Factors of ERP implementations are included. Third section explains in detail the research methodology used for this investigation. The fourth section presents results and discussions of interviews with experts about the key human factors main barriers that these projects face. The chapter ends with conclusions of this study, its limitations and future lines of research.

LITERATURE REVIEW

ERP Systems and HEIs

Higher education is undergoing fundamental changes more than ever. Universities are forced to look for new sources of funding and enter into partnerships with private companies, competition is increasingly assuming the characteristics of an open market. All these changes indicate that higher education is being gradually transformed into a specific type of industry. Higher education institutions that want to succeed in these changed circumstances must begin to behave more like profit-oriented organizations. They have to understand their business processes and, more importantly, know how to enhance and manage their business performance (Serdar, 2010).

Enterprise Systems are large-scale, real-time, integrated application-software packages that use the computational, data storage, and data transmission power of modern information technology to support processes, information flows, reporting, and business analytics within and among complex organizations (Seddon, Calvert & Yang, 2010). Core modules in ERPs for higher education are considered financial management, human resource management and student module (Chaushi, Chaushi & Ismaili (2018).

Pollock & Cornford (2004) suggest that universities share similarities with manufacturing organizations but recognize that universities have specific and unique administrative needs. Traditional ERP systems address basic business administrative functions such as HR (Human Resource), Finance, Operations & Logistics and Sales and Marketing applications. Yet, the higher education sector requires unique systems for: student administration, course/unit administration, facilities (timetabling) requirements, and other applications, which are not part of traditional ERP. There is an explicit recognition that universities are different: they have components not found in other organizations (students).

Universities are complex organizations, with specific characteristics and clearly differentiated from any other type of organization that conditions their organizational culture: objectives that are confusing and difficult to measure; marked disciplinary and cultural diversity, both internal and external; differences among the faculty staff, administrative and service staff that make it difficult to solve problems. In sum, the environment in which universities develop is highly complex, changing and demanding (Bartell, 2003). Many of the difficulties for incorporating technologies are related to the current HEIs' organizational models (Durall Gazulla et al., 2012). However, the differences between universities and organizations are apparent; universities use ERP systems for academic purposes, but organizations use ERP systems for business purposes. Furthermore, ERP is more critical in the higher education sector because faculty, staff and students interact with major educational and administrative activities through ERP (Abugabah & Sanzogni, 2010).

According to Lang & Pirani (2014), more than 95% of the U.S. institutions have a Student Information System. These systems rank among the oldest and most customized of institutional ERP systems. LISTedTECH (2017) reported that around 4,000 universities in U.S. and Canada have implemented the following Student Information Systems: 1,080 Banner from Ellucian; 565 College from Ellucian; 575 Peoplesoft from Oracle; 554 Campus Nexus from Campus Management; 480 Jenzabar; 147 CAMS; 109 Populi; 144 PowerCampus from Ellucian; 87 Vision and 78 SONIS. Unfortunately, this data is not available for Latin American HEIs.

At HEIs, the circumstances that called for moving to an ERP included: a redundant, disorganized database structure; inaccurate data; difficulty in reporting and sharing information; dependence on manual processes and human interventions; problems in providing seamless customer service among offices;

difficulty complying with reporting requirements; heavy reliance on the computing center staff; and lack of capacity for process improvements. ERP systems promise to increase operational efficiency, improve customer service, and help enforce an institution's business rules (Powel & Barry, 2005).

There are many reasons that attract universities to implement ERP systems including: global trends, growth in student numbers, a competitive education environment, quality and performance requirements. These require the Higher Education sector to evolve and replace the existing management and administration systems with ERP systems which provide many management tools and facilities that guarantee the efficiency and accessibility for all users.

In recently years, large companies have invested and developed ERP systems to meet the specific functionalities required for academic administrations that contain their main processes: recruitment, admissions, academic records, courses, registration, class schedules, location management, faculty, accounts receivable and graduation among others. According to Schindel (2018), some of the largest sellers of EPR systems in higher education are: Oracle, Peoplesoft, SAP, Workday as well as others have cloud-based ERP system offerings. G2 (2019) published a quadrant with the best Student Information Systems: Oracle (PeopleSoft system), Ellucian (Banner, PowerCampus and Colleague systems), SAP (SAP for Higher Education and Research), Salesforce (Salesforce for Higher Ed), Workday (Workday Student), Jenzabar (SONIS and ONE), and Campus Management (Campus Nexus). In Latin America the most important ERP vendors are: Oracle (PeopleSoft), Ellucian (Banner and PowerCampus) and SAP (Campus Solutions). Besides, there are other local vendors such as OCU and ERP University.

The integration of cloud computing to ERP applications have created several challenges including difficulty in planning an ERP systems project, matching new with old ERP applications, building new IT infrastructure without budget approval as well as issues related to cloud computing such as privacy, security, reliability, access, and regulation (Suo, 2013).

Human Factors of ERP Implementations in HEIs

Critical Success Factors of ERP in different industries have been thoroughly studied. Ram & Corkindale (2014) examined the literature of 627 referred papers published between 1998 and 2010 on ERP, from which 236 papers were related to Critical Success Factors on ERP. An in-depth research of ERP implementation processes carried out by Zarei & Naeli (2013) found out that five critical success factors: project management, top management supports, business process reengineering, and change management and training were highly interdependent. Ali & Miller (2017) presented a comprehensive structured literature review of implementation in large enterprises between the period 1989 and 2014. There is relatively little attention and studies that measure ERP success or failure in Higher Education (Rabaa'i, Bandara & Gable, 2009; Nizamani et al., 2017; Soliman & Karia, 2017).

Appendix shows the studies found in Higher Education worldwide. ERP implementation practice has proven that making this review provides a good understanding of the elements that contribute to the success (or failure) and also provide a solid base for planning these projects giving a guide to identify the key success factors that need more focus. Implementing an ERP system often uses a waterfall development process approach. There are major stages that occur during each implementation. Ehie & Madsen (2005) developed a 5-stage model to represent a standard ERP implementation. This model follows these major stages: 1) Project Preparation, 2) Business Blueprint, 3) Realization, 4) Final Preparation, and 5) Go Live and Support.

Okland (1990) defined Critical Success Factors as: "What the organization must accomplish to achieve the mission by examination and categorization of the impacts". Verville, Bernardas & Halingten (2005) claimed that one single critical factor by itself will not ensure the success of an Enterprise System acquisition process, but rather it is a mixture of critical factors that will result in the desired outcomes.

Implementing an ERP system is not an inexpensive or risk-free venture. In fact, 65% of executives believe that ERP systems have at least a moderate chance of hurting their businesses because of the potential for implementation problems (Cliffe, 1999). To provide valuable insights into ERP, identifying the critical factors are the most important issue in achieving quality and success (Saygili, Ozturkoglu, & Kocakulah, 2017).

In terms of Human Factors for successful ERP implementations, much research recognizes that human resources play a critical role in the success or failure of an IT project (André et al., 2011). There are also theories taking into consideration the Human Factor such as: need of the owners, users and stakeholders, the project team; team building; communication; motivation; ambition; and leadership (Lent & Pinkowska, 2007).

El-Sabaa (2001) analyzed 126 projects and identified project manager essential skills. Results of his research show that human (soft) skills (according to the research recognized among others as communication, coping with situation, delegating, mobilizing mental and emotional energy) are the most important and the most essential project manager skills.

Furthermore, ERP projects' implementations are complex and risky; the risks in such projects can be mitigated through many ways such as communicating with and involving stakeholders, as well as good project management; the most important point to be considered includes the barriers in communication channels through implementing projects, as it can limit the development of knowledge and make it difficult to develop ERP projects, because of the gap between the needs of the stakeholders and what is available in the organizations (Andersson, 2016).

Effective communication is way to create a healthy relationship between external ERP systems experts and organizational members. The more efficient communication during, before, and after the ERP project, the more the project manager understands the outcome that the organization leader wants to achieve (Hasibuan & Dantes, 2012). Communication is one the most critical success factors in ERP implementation projects.

On the other hand, human resource management, as defined by William & Taylor (2010), includes all aspects of managing the project teams that are working together on a project. It was found that there is a strong relationship between the team members' qualifications and how the team is composed and the success of implementing ERP, so hiring qualified employees is very important to provide the project with the required individuals who are suitable for the project (Dezdar & Ainin, 2011).

Amid et al. (2012) clarify the importance of the project team competence and dedicated resources. The time management also has a large share of the literature related to ERP projects. The average time for ERP system implementation is between six months and two years (Aloini et al., 2007).

What makes the projects that implements ERP different from others is the method of implementing the project processes in many areas including the scale, complexity, users' participation and cost (Ziemba & Oblak, 2013). Information systems initiatives are change projects because they come with a lot of changes, some of which makes employees resist them (Cameron & Green, 2015). Assimilation of a standard ERP system to an organization is difficult. User involvement seems to be the crux of the matter (Pries-Heje, 2008).

IT projects are still facing a high rate of failure because the importance of change management is not yet fully incorporated in information systems projects. Most information systems projects have technical successes but still face organizational failures due to the behavioral challenges and organizational cultures towards the introduction of new information systems. There is lack of change management methods and skills amongst IT professionals on how to deal with various organizational challenges that negatively impact on the success of information systems-initiated change. Wognum et al. (2004) attributed 90% of information systems failures to behavioral challenges and organizational cultures towards information systems.

As ERP systems have evolved, they have become increasingly important as a way of leveraging transaction data for building decision support and analytics applications (Holsapple, Sena & Wagner (2019). Mathrani & Mathrani (2013) found that ERP data transformation is a holistic process that not only includes the essential data and technology factors, but also includes organizational strategy deployment, business process management, and development of skills and proficiency levels of IT professionals.

Finally, consultants in ERP system implementation play that high role. They could provide support to help plan a successful ERP project. Experts are well trained in ERP implementation methods and usually, have real system implementation experience. These consultants could increase better communication and the better understanding of the use of the ERP systems (Lapiedra et al., 2011).

As part of this research an extensive literature review was conducted of papers related to this topic, looking at those specific articles that analyzed this problem in depth and provided best practices in ERP implementations, but also looking at those that referred to implementations in higher education. As a result, the articles selected are presented in Appendix I. All these researches served as a base for the designing of the experts' interview giving a deep reference regarding the Human Factors that is the aim of this study. Table 1 summarizes the most critical success factors found in the literature review.

METHOLODOGY

In this work, a qualitative research was carried out based on interviews with experts. The requisite for selecting these experts was that they had participated in at least one successful implementation of an ERP at a HEI. It was decided to engage with experts who have performed at different levels and roles within an organization (manager, project managers, implementation team members, technical users, consultants and final users) following the suggestion of Boynton & Zmud (1984), considering that success factors are different for each group.

The interviews with experts were conducted by telephone and Skype. Twenty-three experts were interviewed, and they reported that participated in academic, financial, human resources and alumni systems implementations in Latin American countries: Argentina, Brazil, Chile, Colombia, Costa Rica, Dominican Republic, Ecuador, Honduras, Mexico, Panama, Peru, Puerto Rico, Uruguay and Venezuela.

Given that the researchers have in average over 20 years of experience in higher education, it was decided to engage with experts that worked in the most representative software providers companies in Latin America, such as Ellucian, SAP, OCU and Oracle. Besides, international companies with operations in the region like Neoris, Riemann Venture, Grupo TI and others participated in the study.

The interview consisted in questions related to the topic of inquiry, identifying the HEI-specific Human Factors and barriers. The questions were validated previously with some experts to secure accuracy and understanding of the purpose of the research.

Table 1. Critical success factors found in the literature review

1. Top management support. 2. Project team competence. 3. Inter-departmental cooperation. 4. Clear goals and objectives. 5. Project management. 6. Inter-departmental communication. 7. Management of expectation. 8. Project champion. 9. Vendors' support. 10. Careful package selection. 11. Data analysis and conversion. 12. Dedicated resources. 13. Use of steering committee. 14. User training on software. 15. Education on new business processes. 16. Business Process Analysis. 17. Minimal customization. 18. Architecture choices. 19. Change management. 20. Partnership with vendors. 21. Use of vendors' tool. 22. Use of consultant.

Source: Own elaboration

The following questions served as guidelines for the interviews:

1. Which are the factors that you consider critical for an ERP system implementation at a HEI to be successful?
2. Give me any examples in connection with the critical success factors?
3. Can you sort the previously mentioned critical success factors by relevance?
4. Which are in your opinion the main barriers for successfully ERP system implementation projects at HEIs?

An exhaustive classification and analysis process of the information collected was performed. The data resulting from the interviews were detailed classified and analyzed seeking to keep the content, language and experience of the interviewees. The information was also validated with the experts to avoid miss-understandings.

RESULTS AND DISCUSSION

Twenty-one critical success factors were identified by the experts. Table 2 presents the list of factors with the number of experts that mentioned each one.

Eight Human Factors out of the twenty-one were identified as result of this research. Table 3 enlists the most important Human Factors for an ERP implementation.

These Human Factors are described below to provide details that may serve as guidelines for IT Project Managers at HEIs that are interested in these projects. Besides, specific examples from the experts are included as reference in real life implementations.

Table 2. Critical Success Factors identified by the experts

Critical Success Factor	Number of experts
Top management engagement and support (executive sponsor with decision making power).	20
A committed multidisciplinary team, with experience in the institution and its processes.	17
Project communication and change management.	16
Clear project expectations (deliverables).	14
Project is aligned to the institution's strategy.	13
ERP fulfils the institution's requirements.	9
Standardized critical processes (that can be modelled within the ERP).	9
Project planning (scope and timeline).	7
Financial planning (budget during the project, and once it is completed).	6
Capacity to innovate and improve the processes.	6
Project Manager with experience and provided with decision-making capabilities.	5
Give weekly follow-up to the project advances (progress feedback).	5
Identify who will operate the new system.	4
Project governance.	4
Communicate that the ERP project is not just an IT initiative, it's an institutional project.	4
External specialized consultants support.	4
System modifications because of external requirements.	3
Efficient decision making.	2
Adopt the ERP system standard processes without any modifications.	2
Integration with the current ecosystem.	2
IT support.	1

Source: Own elaboration

Top Management Engagement and Support

Top management needs to exhibit specific leadership behavior to motivate and inspire other managers and employees, resolve conflicts and rebalance powers, and reward desirable conducts at different phases of the project. This is one of the most important Human Factors for an ERP implementation. It is very important that, from the system selection stages, the top management has a clear understanding on the ERP implementation repercussions at the institutional level. There must be a fully engaged executive committee, and such engagement must come right from the institution's president.

Is critical for management to take the first step to implementation the ERP systems in the organization since they need to understand the management equipment for implementing ERP system and the organization that will support the organizations leaders to determine the project budget and timeline.

Top management must articulate the goals for the benefits that the institution gains by implementing ERPs and must play a role in organization functionality, business processes, and organization

Table 3. Human factors identified by the experts

1. Top management engagement and support.
2. A committed multidisciplinary team.
3. Project communication and change management.
4. Efficient decision making.
5. Project Manager with experience and decision-making capabilities.
6. Identify who will operate the new system.
7. Project governance.
8. External specialized consultants support.

Source: Own elaboration

boundaries that should be implemented. The top manager must support and motivate the stakeholders to communicate and be involved in the implementation. Top management needs to understand how the new IT technologies can be used in the institution, proving a tactical and strategic plan to the senior management, and understanding the strength and the weakness of the technologies that are available to be used in the institution.

Also, top management has to provide the necessary resource requirement for the implementation and act as a leader to help in the success of the ERP system and ensure the implementation of the ERP system is meeting the institution's requirements. Top management require strong leadership skills that will provide the necessary authorization to achieve success implementation of ERP systems.

Top management leaders have to change the entire organization's business process, with a holistic view, accurate estimation, and management of the entire implementation process, in order to support the ERP system project to be successful.

To illustrate top management engagement and support, here are some real cases shared by the experts:

The president continually followed on the project progress. During the server's installation stage, there was a problem in a server that would cost $20,000 dollars and the IT area had no budget that year to buy it and it was going to postpone the project for next year. The president found out and authorized to buy the server since they would not expose a strategic project for this. The decision was made in a timely manner and the project went ahead

The project was led by the president under the policy of using the processes that the system included as best practices, always emphasizing that if thousands of universities do things in a way why they have to be different. With this guideline, the IT Director took ownership of the project and presented the project to the Board of Directors and involved the Human Resources Director and Provost to be the project leaders

The implementation team did not want to change the processes, so the president became involved in the decision-making process when the prerequisites of the academic courses had to be defined, taking the decision to do it as the system proposed it, giving his approval to the Provost. He was very clear with the implementation team that there were no additional resources to make changes, so the guideline was to implement the system as it was given, that is why they had acquired it because it contained the best practices in the industry

During the implementation the owner of the university met every Wednesday with the Project Manager to track the project progress and know if something was necessary. The university knew that he was involved in the project, so the estimated times for the project were achieved

The president appointed the Vice-president of Finance, someone who was not in IT, to be the leader of the project. Every Saturday the president went to see the advances and on Monday he solved any situation that required it. He gave full support to the Vice-president to make the decisions that were necessary during the project

The rector of the university had a technological background, so he was very involved in the project, he not only knew the university, but also the technology. He was at the kickoff event of the project and met weekly with the team. The phrase he had was blunt "the one who does not agree with system to step aside," which caused many people to move from area. Also, his signal was "what is not in the system, does not exist", he was an example of the commitment that existed in the project

The project had the executive sponsorship of the president and his first level of management. It is a small university, but the president made sure that his team had the details of the decisions that were made and that they knew the reasons for the changes

A Committed Multidisciplinary Team

Appointing a proper implementation team is substantial for correctly implementing and configuring the processes to operate within the ERP. The team assigned to the implementation needs to be deeply acquainted with the institution and its processes, to be experienced in the institution-specific practices, and to show an open attitude to innovations and change. All successful implementation projects have in common that their respective implementation teams were 100%, full time engaged in the project. During the implementation they were supported for their daily activities by other staff members.

The quality of personnel involved in the project is very critical for project success and is dependent upon the skills and experience of the project team. The team members should be selected with a balance between members with business experience within the organization and external experts with specialties in ERP in order to be able to measure the operational level according to the following: is the project will deliver on time, on budget, and with user's satisfaction.

Here are some examples of how institutions selected their implementation teams:

A strong implementation team was selected so that the consensus and implementation could be achieved. The Directors of Information Technology, Finance, Auditing and Deans were involved. The implementation team must be committed full-time

Key users were identified to participate in the project. Some Academic Directors and those responsible for the registration and school processes participated during the implementation. A Committee was established so that changes in the system could be approved after the go live

It was important to identify from the beginning the people who would be willing to standardize processes and optimize them, as well as those who would be in conflict or with a strong resistance to change. When the project was started during the BPA (Business Process Analysis), the reaction of the people was studied in such a way that allies of the project and key people who had to participate were identified

Some Deans were selected to participate in the project, but when they attended the operational meetings, they showed little interest. The Project Manager spoke with the president to tell him that it was important to change the team and bring people who knew the processes and were involved in the operation. It is important to have full commitment of the people who will implement the system the time to participate in the project

It was decided that the Director of Registration to be dedicated exclusively to the project for one year. An interim was hired during the implementation. The implementation team was 100% focused on this project

The implementation team was made up of 48 people. Among them were the Deans, Academic Secretaries of the different Departments, Technical Staff and the Registration area. All of them actively participated in the definition of the new processes and the rules of the study plans that would operate in the system. The implementation team was 100% focused on the project for one year

In the implementations there is a lot of rotation of the implementation teams so many projects have not been successful. Process engineers who do not belong to the university have also been hired for the project, but since they lack knowledge of business processes and rules, the projects have also failed. It is important that the implementation team know the current processes, the objectives of the project and have their own decision-making capacity

Project Communication and Change Management

Change management includes stakeholder management, communication, end-user education and training and after go-live operation support. The project strategic goals must be promoted and communicated from the institution's top management down. A responsible area should be appointed for managing change within the institution, and for informing, training, and sharing the ERP implementation results, as the system is deployed.

Change management is always a constant factor when a new information system is implemented since it will always bring changes to the already existing business processes. However, it is critical for the end users to clearly understand the benefits of the new system as this will reduce the amount of resistance.

Effective communication is a challenging and important task in ERP implementation project, and it has to be started in the early stage on ERP implementation projects. Effective communication creates an understanding and agreement on how ERP functions would be used in the institution and the outcomes across the organization with each different stage of the implementation. Communication between stakeholders must start in the early stages of the system implementation to understand the purpose and the goals for implementation.

Communication is way to create a healthy relationship between external ERP systems experts and organizational members. The more efficient communication during, before, and after the ERP project, the more the project manager understands the outcome that the organization leader wants to achieve.

Below are some strategies that universities implemented in this regard:

The functional team promoted the creation of a Web page of the project where the new services that would be provided to the students and to the administrative part of the Web were shared within the university. The students and employees were continually informed of the progress of the project and it was a leverage tool for the live performance because an expectation had already been generated

An external company was hired to implement a methodology to manage change. They mapped the processes in their initial state and defined where they wanted to go. In the initial state, the expectations, dates of the interviews and gaps were recorded. Critical users who were not willing to change were identified and a clear map of the staff was established defining focused actions and training for them

In the university the main opposition of the project were the teachers, so they selected a teacher who did not know how to use the computer for the tests. They taught him from using the computer and then using the system, so they showed that if the teacher could, then the others could not say no. The idea was to involve teachers so that they could give their opinions and thus feel they were participants in the project

During the implementation an expectation management campaign was carried out because the staff that was going to operate the system had a lot of time in the institution. A weekly circular was implemented to promote the system, the benefits it would bring. Once implemented, they also continued sharing the achievements that were obtained

"It is important to be tactful, not to confront people, to be patient and to position the people who participate in the project in their new situation. We must remind them how things were done differently, that the documentation of the new process is done by the same team, as well as the manuals and the new documentation that is generated. Change management is psychological rather than technical. It is important to tell them that the team is becoming an important nucleus of the university, what has been seen is that the people who participate in these types of projects become key persons of the university, which is a natural step. It is important that people understand their own development in this type of projects. The team that implements the ERP becomes a critical point of the university".

It is important that the project has a name, logo, that the marketing office disseminates internally in a staggered manner

The basis of change management was to develop a plan that included the internal sale of the project from an initial phase of implementation and then an external sale. This plan was developed between the project leader and the Human Resources area, with the aim that the whole institution felt part of the project, for that they put a name that represented what was going to be done in order to create identity, this name was "Classroom". A plan was developed where different activities were activated at certain times. Part of the change management process was to involve many people (functional users) in a system simulation with real cases previously created by the functional team of the project. Another important point was the creation of a Web site, an email, a chat and a telephone line were assigned where the users could at any time consult questions about the project, operational doubts or download information about the processes of the institution. At the same time, it was the source of information for project news, new features that were incorporated, the website remained for a long time

Efficient Decision Making

The implementation team will need a process in place to easily make decisions with autonomy, depending of their authority, as needed or reach out to top management in the most efficient way. The required internal structures must be created so decisions needed are swiftly taken during the project execution.

The lack of this process is reflected in these two real stories:

The implementation project lasted 6 years precisely because from the beginning it was defined that the decisions had to be made in a consensual manner, so it was slow, it was not clear who was the project leader, many changes were requested in order to attend to the requests of the participants, all this for 4 and a half years. When a new president arrived, he became aware of this situation, changed the imple-

mentation team and established the policy that the system would remain as it was. He was directly involved so that the decisions were taken immediately so that the project would go on being a success story

It is important that the decisions during the project are taken within 72 hours after they are identified, or the implementation is considerably delayed. In one university, all the cases that require decision are analyzed at departmental level, so the project instead of taking 1 year as planned, have decided that it will take 4 years

Now, let's review other cases:

The leader of the project held weekly meetings with the Steering Committee to report progress and pending points where decisions had to be made. It also established a direct line with the software provider where they had preferential response times. If anything was required, he would attend the provider's offices in Miami to request support, for example, when the consultants found gaps in the system, they would send him to a more specialized consultant to help them. The people knew about the commitment of the organization and that commitment permeated throughout the institution

The president had a close involvement with the implementation team. They could go to his office so that the necessary decisions could be made in a timely manner. The president is one of the owners of the university, so the necessary disciplinary decisions were made to reach the necessary agreements

During the implementation, a decision had to be made regarding the schedules, since the schedules were defined according to the availability of part-time professors to teach classes, so there were very crazy schedules. The decision was to continue doing it in the system as they had been doing or adopting the best system practice of 1-hour on Monday, Wednesday and Friday and 1 hour and a half on Tuesday and Thursday. The fear they had was that the teachers were going to leave, but the rector made the decision and they changed to modules. Nothing happened, the teachers lined up at the new schedules and did not leave. It was a case of success because when optimizing its academic offer, it was no longer necessary to build a new building, there was plenty of room in the building, so they built offices in the available rooms. Another decision they made was the review of why they charged before and analyzing the process they realized that it had once been defined as a strategy to pay bonuses, so they needed the money in December. They decided to change the system and charge only a minimum entry fee to all students and then the courses were selected. That decision was taken by the Provost and it was also very successful and well received by the students

Project Manager with Experience and Decision-Making Capabilities

A critical factor for the assigned Project Manager is to be experienced in higher education so he/she is capable of preserving the project's leadership and coordination, and for helping both the ERP provider's team and the institution implementation team –coaching-. It is essential that the Project Manager is recognized by the institution, and that he/she is provided with decision making capabilities and the required confidence, so he/she can take action. Also, the Project Manager must have direct communication with the institution's top management, so he/she is able to inform of any situation requiring its attention.

The most important individual who has the power for making projects successful is the Project Manager since he/she has the responsibility of putting the project team in their undersigned tasks and must make sure that those people have knowledge about their tasks. The project manager should make sure that all the resources needed for the project to be completed are in place.

A major part of human resource management is monitoring and tracking of allocating resources and the ongoing task during a project, especially if any overloaded team member may be less motivated to give the best performance in the work.

Some recommendations and experiences from the experts are:

From the beginning of the project, the president appointed the IT Director as the Project Manager, removed him from his role as Director and gave him the power to lead the implementation team. During the implementation, the decisions were taken by the implementation team and the IT Director informed the president on a weekly basis of what the new processes would be like. The president published the policy of the new process and in this way was institutionalized and formalized in the university

Main functions of a good Project Manager are: 1) Administrative activities of the project (plan, agendas, deviations from the project, etc.); 2) Control of project risks (scale the problems and decisions that should be taken to the established channels); 3) Coaching of the team (system provider and the implementation team); 4) Direction and coordination of the project to achieve the objectives. It is essential that all these functions are carried out in a timely manner in each project

Top management should give an open letter to the Project Manager to talk about the project, it is important to establish this open channel

Every week the Project Manager met with the CIO and the president to follow up on the project and support the necessary decisions to achieve the objectives

Identify Who Will Operate the New System

Prior to the implementation kickoff, all roles and individuals who will operate the new system are identified. Those who will operate the new system are properly identified and engaged in the system configuration, during the implementation.

The commitment from the final user is an important factor in information systems projects. The organization must be committed and be in a position to adopt the new system after deployment, for instance, the users must clearly define the expectations and be committed to them. It is essential that the implementation team understands the expectations of business divisions for the successful implementation of projects.

Training with a focus on the new business processes, technical aspects of the system and end user needs is a key part of successful ERP system implementation. Some examples explain this Human Factor for successful projects:

When the go live was going to be done, the Department leaders were told that now they were going to operate the system instead of Registration to manage the groups, they wanted to do it since they could now operate the system directly and not depend on other areas to give attention to their students

Massive meetings were held at the venues when the modules were being launched. They gathered the academic and administrative staff in the main hall to share the progress and inform them of the changes that were taking place, indicating that the changes would no longer be reversed and the benefit it would have for the university

The planning of the project was made aligned with the strategy of the university and it was communicated within the institution, since everyone's participation was required, and everyone would be affected

Once the objectives were clear, it was explained to the final users how the project would be carried out and provided support, training and project leadership. A global deployment was made with a common implementation team that contributed its experience

Managing expectations is also a factor to consider, users think that many of their current problems will disappear that will be all automatic, almost magical and in reality, that rarely happens

It is important to manage people expectations. The stakeholders must understand what the tools or systems can do to make it clear what they can achieve. At the beginning of the project, the practice is to show the team responsible for the university what the system can do, decide what can be useful, in order to identify what can be done and what cannot be done

Each school and department were visited by someone from the functional team to align expectations and clarify doubts. Subsequently, a project launch was made in each of the venues, with the presence of the rector and the deans supporting the project and showing their commitment for this to work properly. Subsequently, the technological support area that the institution had in the previous system was trained to support the operation

Project Governance

It is important to establish an Executive Committee in charge of providing communication, coordination and guidance, and making the required decisions during the ERP implementation. According to the experts, it is advisable to have a Project Manager with the ERP provider, and a Project Manager from the institution. Both of them must work together in a coordinated way, supervising the completion of the defined activities towards the achievement of the provided goals. Such structuring enables governance-specific organization, which enables communication lines to be clearly defined.

The importance given to both top management support and Project Manager is a clear indication that implementation of enterprise wide systems are very different from normal software development projects. ERP projects are actually business transformation projects, rather than straightforward large software development projects and their implementation will significantly change work processes and organisational structures, together with the daily activities of the majority of staff. Because the business transformational nature of ERP systems, their failure is more likely to be due organisational, social or even political reasons that than to technical or software-based causes. Governance is about providing strategic direction, planning and controlling projects and people, and is delegated to project leaders (project governance), those responsible for IT (IT governance) and senior executives (organisational governance) by the Board of Directors.

IT governance is an integral part of organisational governance because it provides direction, through the implementation of an IT strategy. Individuals and committees who take responsibility for IT governance will also have an important role in any ERP system implementation through the following activities: assessing IS infrastructure risk; ensuring adequate infrastructure; providing the project with adequate visibility; building in transparency; overseeing IT infrastructure partner relationship management; providing a forum to which to escalate changes to project costs, timelines, etc,; establishing a clear process for exception handling; providing or ensuring the existence of a project champion to share a global view of the project with the project team and project benefits with the business stakeholders.

This is a recommendation from one of the experts:

In the teams there must be transparency in the communication and a power to empower the project. Rules of coexistence should be established, such as dancing if you are late for a meeting or making a piggy bank for not having complied with something. Communication must be constant and not wait until the scheduled meeting if what has happened is transcendental. The indicator that the team is engaged is when someone finishes their job and offers to help another team member.

External Specialized Consultants Support

Successful implementations engaged with external consultants specialized in higher education-specific processes, who can generate trust among the implementation team. This trust creates an environment of certainty that makes it easier to guide the team towards making the changes in the processes and in the institution's way of operating, in cases where these are necessary, based on best practices.

The success of ERP implementation by using excellent consultant knowledge could change the outcome. A knowledgeable and experienced consultant can help the company implement an ERP system that is aligned with the institution's process needs. External consultants play a crucial role in the success of ERP system implementation. Consultants provide extensive support and work during the implementation process that allows institutions to reach the project goals. ERP systems consultants, however, must have a good understanding of uniqueness of their current clients. Moreover, consultants have to be team players, knowledgeable in the field, and hold excellent communication and interpersonal skills. The presence of well-qualified consultants is essential to perform a complete and successful ERP implementation.

Some examples highlighting the importance of engaging with specialized consultants:

Before starting any project in which, he participated as a Consultant, he carried out a Business Process Analysis even though the university had not hired these services. With this process analysis, he tried to involve the president and the important members of the university to see how they were doing their processes and to identify if they were doing it well and efficiently. The important thing was to position each of the participants in their processes and have the same knowledge as a starting point for the implementation

It is essential to have specialized consultants that generate trust, it is easier to create those changes if you win the confidence of the implementation team. It is important that you are a senior consultant with experience in higher education processes

Table 4. Barriers for ERP successful implementation projects at HEIs

Barrier	Human factor that acts as moderator
Resistance to change.	Project communication and change management.
Lack of a single team properly acquainted with the processes.	A committed multidisciplinary team, with experience in the institution and its processes.
Lack of Top Management and institutional commitment.	Top Management engagement and support (executive sponsor with decision making power).
The ERP implementation is not positioned as an institutional project led by the President.	Project communication and change management.
Lack of a well-positioned project leader.	Project Manager with experience and provided with decision-making capabilities

Source: Own elaboration

The consultant was a person with proven experience in the implementation of similar systems in other universities. This allowed him to gain the credibility of the team and also to guide them even though they claimed to be a different university. The consultant acted many times as a mediator between the Project Manager of the university and the Project Manager of the supplier company

Before starting the ERP project, the institution decided that it is important to define the strategy, because even though they had it written, nobody was following it, so a consultancy was carried out to define the plan, objectives, government, resources, communication and establishment of a change management strategy for an adequate transition. The medium and long-term institutional strategy was established and then the IT strategy that supported it. With this clarity the Council committed and supported the project. The planning of the project was made aligned with the strategy of the university and it was communicated within the institution, since everyone's participation was required and everyone would be affected

Barriers for ERP projects successful

In the last phase of the research, it was deeper in knowing the most important barriers that hinder the process of implementing an ERP. Table 4 shows the results from the expert opinion collected data, sorted by relevance. Additionally, Human Factors that act as moderators of each barrier are included.

The first barrier that ERP implementation projects face is resistance to change. The experts commented that the fear and misunderstanding within the institution when an ERP implementation is underway leads the institution's staff to object to the project and block its activities. On this concern, the human factor is essential for pulling a project through at a HEI, since these projects require the engagement of all levels within the organization as previously commented, for everyone will be impacted by the new processes. Honest and effective communication during ERP implementations may reduce user resistance.

It is essential to recognize these barriers in order to focus efforts on surmounting them. Resistance to change, for instance, is mitigated by *"project communication and change management"* which must be carried out in parallel to the ERP implementation throughout the institution. The obstacle about the lack of a single team properly acquainted on the processes is surmounted by creating *"a committed multidisciplinary team, with experience on the institution and its processes"*.

FUTURE RESEARCH DIRECTIONS

For future research it is recommended to make this study by university type, because as was noted previously, in Latin America the percentage of private HEIs is large and are different in their operation, financial capacity and management compared to public HEIs. Besides, it is recommended to apply the study considering a sample of experts and universities in different geographic areas or focusing on a country, to be able to generalize the results in the higher education sector or perform in-depth analysis in a given country.

CONCLUSION

This study was conducted focusing on a subject where there is such little evidence in the existing literature on what the Human Factors of ERP implementations in HEIs. The relevance of this research is that for the first time an article is focused in Latin America, a young region in which just a few HEIs have implemented ERPs. Therefore, it was very attractive and enriching to produce this paper that may serve as reference for IT Project Managers that are planning to implement these projects and help to make them successful.

Research recognizes that human factors play a critical role in the success or failure of an IT project. This study identifies 8 human factors that need to be considered for successful ERP implementation projects: 1) top management engagement and support; 2) a committed multidisciplinary team; 3) project communication and change management; 4) efficient decision making; 5) Project Manager with experience and decision-making capabilities; 6) identify who will operate the new system; 7) project governance; and 8) external specialized consultants support. Each human factor was described with detail providing real examples by the experts to provide insights to IT Project Managers of the initiatives that can be implemented in their institution.

It is very important for any professionals that have not previously worked amid the higher education environment to recognize these features making HEIs unique, in such a way that understanding these characteristics and bearing them in mind enable the IT Project Managers to take the right steps for addressing them. The discovery about decision making by consensus, which was mentioned by 13 experts, highlights the importance of establishing an infrastructure and mechanisms enabling *"efficient decision making"* which is essential for a successful ERP implementation, as it is known that several projects stagnated after a pending decision was left to the next scheduled academic committee meeting.

The experts emphasized the importance of cultural aspects, essentially highlighting the importance of relationships between people. Since universities' life develops among a political environment, it is important to get closer to all the people that would be somehow affected by an ERP project and convince them; you must win them over; both the project and its results must be explained to them, for the opposition of those even at lower hierarchical levels can seriously affect the project. The experts' recommendation is to identify those against the project right at its first stages, when the processes are being reviewed and designed. Once the individuals against the project are identified, special activities must be carried out with them as part of the project's risks identification, so actions can be made on the issue.

One important finding that was recognized by the experts is that the implementation team must be 100% focused on the project. Projects that have been successful are those where the implementation team was focused and dedicated to the project, and during this time the top management supported them with additional personnel responsible for assisting them in their daily activities, also giving them the confidence that their job was safe, and in many cases people involved in the implementation became key persons at the institution, so in addition to recognition by the project, they had growth and promotion opportunities inside the institution. It is not enough to involve key people; it is essential to allocate them full time.

As was demonstrated in the analysis, the identified barriers can be mitigated if the HEIs commit with the Human Factor identified in this research since 4 of the 8 most important Human Factors act as moderators.

REFERENCES

Abdellatif, H. J. (2014, September). ERP in higher education: a deeper look on developing countries. In *2014 International Conference on Education Technologies and Computers (ICETC)* (pp. 73-78). IEEE. 10.1109/ICETC.2014.6998905

Abugabah, A., & Sanzogni, L. (2010). Enterprise Resource Planning (ERP) System in Higher Education: A literature Review and Implications. *International Journal of Humanities and Social Science*, *5*(6), 395–399.

Al-Hadi, M. A., & Al-Shaibany, N. A. (2017). Critical success factors (CSFs) of ERP in higher education institutions. *International Journal (Toronto, Ont.)*, *7*(4), 92–95.

ALdayel, A. I., Aldayel, M. S., & Al-Mudimigh, A. S. (2011). The Critical Success Factors of ERP implementation in Higher Education in Saudi Arabia: A Case Study. *Journal of Information Technology & Economic Development*, *2*(2), 1–16.

Ali, M., & Miller, L. (2017). ERP system implementation in large enterprises–a systematic literature review. *Journal of Enterprise Information Management*, *30*(4), 666–692. doi:10.1108/JEIM-07-2014-0071

Aloini, D., Dulmin, R., & Mininno, V. (2007). Risk management in ERP project introduction: Review of the literature. *Information & Management*, *44*(6), 547–567. doi:10.1016/j.im.2007.05.004

Althonayan, M., & Althonayan, A. (2017). E-government system evaluation: The case of users' performance using ERP systems in higher education. *Transforming Government: People. Process and Policy*, *11*(3), 306–342.

Althunibat, A., Al-mahadeen, B. M., Altarawneh, F., & Al–Qarem, F. A. (2019, April). The Acceptance of using Enterprise Resource Planning (ERP) System in Higher Education: A Case Study of Jordanian Universities. In *2019 IEEE Jordan International Joint Conference on Electrical Engineering and Information Technology (JEEIT)* (pp. 315-318). IEEE. 10.1109/JEEIT.2019.8717451

Amid, A., Moalagh, M., & Ravasan, A. Z. (2012). Identification and classification of ERP critical failure factors in Iranian industries. *Information Systems*, *37*(3), 227–237. doi:10.1016/j.is.2011.10.010

Andersson, A. (2016). Communication barriers in an interorganizational ERP-project. *International Journal of Managing Projects in Business*, *9*(1), 214–233. doi:10.1108/IJMPB-06-2015-0047

André, M., Baldoquín, M. G., & Acuña, S. T. (2011). Formal model for assigning human resources to teams in software projects. *Information and Software Technology*, *53*(3), 259–275. doi:10.1016/j. infsof.2010.11.011

Andrianto, A. (2019, April). Impact of Enterprise Resource Planning (ERP) implementation on user performance: Studies at University of Jember. *Journal of Physics: Conference Series*, *1211*(1), 012040. doi:10.1088/1742-6596/1211/1/012040

Bartell, M. (2003). Internationalization of universities: A university culture-based framework. *Higher Education*, *45*(1), 43–70. doi:10.1023/A:1021225514599

Bhamangol, B., Nandavadekar, V., & Khilari, S. (2011). Enterprise resource planning (erp) system in higher education, a literature review. *International Journal of Management Research and Development*, *1*(1), 1–7.

Bhattacharya, P. (2016). Strategizing and innovating with enterprise systems: The case of a Public University. *Journal of Cases on Information Technology*, *18*(2), 1–15. doi:10.4018/JCIT.2016040101

Boynton, A. C., & Zmud, R. W. (1984). An assessment of critical success factors. *Sloan Management Review*, *25*(4), 17–27.

Brunner, J. J., & Miranda, D. (2016). *Educación Superior en Iberoamérica. Report 2016.* Santiago, Chile: CINDA.

Brunner, J. J., & Pedraja Rejas, L. (2017). Challenges to higher education governance in Ibero-America. *Ingeniare. Revista Chilena de Ingeniería*, *25*(1), 2–4. doi:10.4067/S0718-33052017000100002

Cameron, E., & Green, M. (2015). *Making sense of change management: A complete guide to the models, tools and techniques of organizational change.* Kogan Page Publishers.

Chaushi, B. A., Chaushi, A., & Ismaili, F. (2018, May). ERP systems in higher education institutions: Review of the information systems and ERP modules. In *2018 41st International Convention on Information and Communication Technology, Electronics and Microelectronics (MIPRO)* (pp. 1487-1494). IEEE.

Chondamrongkul, N. (2018). ERP implementation in university: A case study in Thailand. *International Journal of Business Information Systems*, *27*(2), 177–192. doi:10.1504/IJBIS.2018.089109

Chuang, C. (2016, March). The Critical Success Factors for ERP Implementation in Higher Education. In *Proceedings of International Academic Conferences* (No. 3305901). International Institute of Social and Economic Sciences. 10.20472/IAC.2016.021.008

Cliffe, S. (1999). ERP implementation. *Harvard Business Review*, *77*(1), 16–17. PMID:10345391

Cua, F., & Reames, S. (2013). Theory versus application: A study to determine the right choice in deploying an enterprise resource planning (ERP) system. *International Journal of Information Systems in the Service Sector*, *5*(4), 47–62. doi:10.4018/ijisss.2013100104

Dezdar, S., & Ainin, S. (2011). Examining ERP implementation success from a project environment perspective. *Business Process Management Journal*, *17*(6), 919–939. doi:10.1108/14637151111182693

Durall Gazulla, E., Gros Salvat, B., Maina, M. F., Johnson, L., & Adams, S. (2012). *Perspectivas tecnológicas: educación superior en Iberoamérica 2012-2017.* Academic Press.

Ehie, I. C., & Madsen, M. (2005). Identifying critical issues in enterprise resource planning (ERP) implementation. *Computers in Industry, 56*(6), 545–557. doi:10.1016/j.compind.2005.02.006

El-Sabaa, S. (2001). The skills and career path of an effective project manager. *International Journal of Project Management, 19*(1), 1–7. doi:10.1016/S0263-7863(99)00034-4

Fadelelmoula, A. A. (2018). The effects of the critical success factors for ERP implementation on the comprehensive achievement of the crucial roles of information systems in the higher education sector. *Interdisciplinary Journal of Information, Knowledge, and Management, 13*, 21–44. doi:10.28945/3942

Gallagher, K. P., Worrell, J. L. J., & Mason, R. M. (2012). The negotiation and selection of horizontal mechanisms to support post-implementation ERP organizations. *Information Technology & People, 25*(1), 4–30. doi:10.1108/09593841211204326

Guajardo, P. H., Mato, D., Grimaldo, H., Gacel-Ávila, J., Lemaitre, M. J., Guarga, R., & Ramírez, R. (2018). *Tendencias de la educación superior en América Latina y el Caribe 2018.* Academic Press.

Hasibuan, Z. A., & Dantes, G. R. (2012). Priority of key success factors (KSFS) on enterprise resource planning (ERP) system implementation life cycle. *Journal of Enterprise Resource Planning Studies, 2*, 1–15. doi:10.5171/2011.122627

Holsapple, C., Sena, M., & Wagner, W. (2019). The perceived success of ERP systems for decision support. *Information Technology Management, 20*(1), 1–7. doi:10.100710799-017-0285-9

<eref>G2. (2019). Best Higher Education Student Information Systems. Retrieved from https://www.g2.com/categories/higher-education-student-information-systems</eref>

Jacobson, S., Shepherd, J., D'Aquila, M., & Carter, K. (2007). The ERP market sizing report, 2006–2011. *AMR Research, 29.*

Karande, S. H., Jain, V. K., & Ghatule, A. P. (2012). ERP implementation: Critical success factors for Indian Universities and higher educational institutions. *Pragyaan Journal of Information Technology, 10*(2), 24–29.

Kitto, S., & Higgins, V. (2010). Working around ERPs in technological universities. *Science, Technology & Human Values, 35*(1), 29–54. doi:10.1177/0162243908329535

Kvavik, R. B. R., Katz, R. N., Beecher, K., Caruso, J., & King, P. (2002). The Promise and Performance of Enterprise Systems for Higher Education. *EDUCAUSE Center for Applied Research, 4*, 1–7.

Lang, L., & Pirani, J. A. (2014). *Adapting the Established SIS to Meet Higher Education's Increasingly Dynamic Needs. CDS Spotlight Report. ECAR Research Bulletin.* EDUCAUSE.

Lapiedra, R., Alegre, J., & Chiva, R. (2011). The importance of management innovation and consultant services on ERP implementation success. *Service Industries Journal, 31*(12), 1907–1919. doi:10.1080/02642069.2011.556189

Lent, B., & Pinkowska, M. (2007). *Human Factor–The key success factor of ICT project management.* Information Systems Architecture and Technology.

Leyh, C., Gebhardt, A., & Berton, P. (2017, September). Implementing ERP systems in higher education institutes critical success factors revisited. In *2017 Federated Conference on Computer Science and Information Systems (FedCSIS)* (pp. 913-917). IEEE. 10.15439/2017F364

LISTedTECH. (2017). *Student Information System Software By Total Enrollment.* Retrieved from https://www.listedtech.com/blog/student-information-system-software-total-enrollement

Maldonado, M., & Sierra, V. (2013). User satisfaction as the foundation of the success following an ERP adoption: An empirical study from Latin America. *International Journal of Enterprise Information Systems*, *9*(3), 77–99. doi:10.4018/jeis.2013070104

Mathias, B., Oludayo, O., & Ray, M. (2014). Identifying Critical Success Factors: The case of ERP Systems in Higher Education. *The African Journal of Information Systems*, *6*(3), 1.

Mathrani, S., & Mathrani, A. (2013). Understanding the Transformation Process Success Factors in Enterprise System Implementations: An IT Professional's Perspective. *International Journal of Human Capital and Information Technology Professionals*, *4*(1), 9–21. doi:10.4018/jhcitp.2013010102

Nizamani, S., Khoumbati, K., Ismaili, I. A., Nizamani, S., Nizamani, S., & Basir, N. (2017). Testing and validating the ERP success evaluation model for higher education institutes of Pakistan. *International Journal of Business Information Systems*, *25*(2), 165–191. doi:10.1504/IJBIS.2017.083682

Okland, J. S. (1990). *Total Quality Management- Text with Cases.* Oxford, UK: Butterworth-Heinemann.

Pollock, N., & Cornford, J. (2004). ERP Systems and the university as a "unique" organization. *Information Technology & People*, *17*(1), 31–52. doi:10.1108/09593840410522161

Powel, W. A., & Barry, J. (2005). An ERP Post-Implementation Review: Planning for the Future by Looking Back. *EDUCAUSE Quarterly*, *28*(3), 40–46.

Pries-Heje, L. (2008). Time, attitude, and user participation: How prior events determine user attitudes in ERP implementation. *International Journal of Enterprise Information Systems*, *4*(3), 48–65. doi:10.4018/jeis.2008070104

Qian, L., Schmidt, E. K., & Scott, R. L. (2015, December). ERP pre-implementation framework for Higher Education Institution: A case study in Purdue University. In *2015 IEEE International Conference on Industrial Engineering and Engineering Management (IEEM)* (pp. 1546-1550). IEEE. 10.1109/IEEM.2015.7385906

Rabaa'i, A. A. (2009). Identifying critical success factors of ERP Systems at the higher education sector. *Third International Symposium on Innovation in Information & Communication Technology.*

Rabaa'i, A. A., Bandara, W., & Gable, G. G. (2009). ERP Systems in the Higher Education Sector: A Descriptive Case Study. *Proceedings of the 20th Australasian Conference on Information Systems.*

Ram, J., & Corkindale, D. (2014). How "critical" are the critical success factors (CSFs)?: Examining the role of CSFs for ERP. *Business Process Management Journal, 20*(1), 151–174. doi:10.1108/BPMJ-11-2012-0127

Rani, S. (2016). A Review of ERP Implementation in Higher Education Institutions. *International Journal of Advanced Research in Computer Science and Software Engineering, 6*(6), 542–545.

Sabau, G., Munten, M., Bologa, A.-R., Bologa, R., & Surcel, T. (2009). An evaluation framework for higher education ERP systems. *WSEAS Transactions on Computers, 8*(11), 1790–1799.

Saygili, E. E., Ozturkoglu, Y., & Kocakulah, M. C. (2017). End Users' Perceptions of Critical Success Factors in ERP Applications. *International Journal of Enterprise Information Systems, 13*(4), 58–75. doi:10.4018/IJEIS.2017100104

Schindel, K. (2018). *An analysis of implementing an ERP system in a higher education institution.* Academic Press.

Seddon, P. B., Calvert, C., & Yang, S. (2010). A multi-project model of key factors affecting organizational benefits from enterprise systems. *Management Information Systems Quarterly, 34*(2), 305–328. doi:10.2307/20721429

Segrera, F. L. (2010). *Trends and Innovations in Higher Education Reform: Worldwide, Latin America and the Caribbean.* Berkeley, CA: Center for Studies in Higher Education.

Serdar, A. M. (2010). Performance management and key performance indicators for higher education institutions in Serbia. *Perspectives of Innovations, Economics and Business, 6*(3), 120–124.

Shakkah, M. S., Alaqeel, K., Alfageeh, A., & Budiarto, R. (2016). An investigation study on optimizing enterprise resource planning (ERP) implementation in emerging public university: Al Baha university case study. *Iranian Journal of Electrical and Computer Engineering, 6*(4), 1920–1928.

Shatat, A. S. (2019). The Impact of ERP System on Academic Performance: A Case Study Approach. *Journal of Information & Knowledge Management*, 1950018.

Shoham, S., & Perry, M. (2009). Knowledge management as a mechanism for technological and organizational change management in Israeli universities. *Higher Education, 57*(2), 227–246. doi:10.100710734-008-9148-y

Soliman, M., & Karia, N. (2017). Antecedents for the Success of the Adoption of Organizational ERP Among Higher Education Institutions and Competitive Advantage in Egypt. *Technology & Applied Science Research, 7*(3), 1719–1724.

Suo, S. (2013). *Cloud implementation in organizations: Critical success factors, challenges, and impacts on the IT function* (Doctoral dissertation).

Swartz, D., & Orgill, K. (2001). Higher Education ERP: Lessons Learned. *EDUCAUSE Quarterly, 24*(2), 20–27.

Ullah, Z., Al-Mudimigh, A. S., Al-Ghamdi, A. A. L.-M., & Saleem, F. (2013). Critical success factors of ERP implementation at higher education institutes: A brief case study. *Information (Japan)*, *16*(10), 7369–7378.

Vathanophas, V., & Stuart, L. (2009). Enterprise resource planning: Technology acceptance in Thai universities. *Enterprise Information Systems*, *3*(2), 133–158. doi:10.1080/17517570802653800

Verville, J., Bernadas, C., & Halingten, A. (2005). So you're thinking of buying an ERP? Ten critical factors for successful acquisitions. *Journal of Enterprise Information Management*, *18*(6), 665–677. doi:10.1108/17410390510628373

von Hellens, L., Nielsen, S., & Beekhuyzen, J. (Eds.). (2005). *Qualitative case studies on implementation of enterprise wide systems*. IGI Global. doi:10.4018/978-1-59140-447-7

Wanko, C. E. T., Kamdjoug, J. R. K., & Wamba, S. F. (2019, April). Study of a Successful ERP Implementation Using an Extended Information Systems Success Model in Cameroon Universities: Case of CUCA. In *World Conference on Information Systems and Technologies* (pp. 727-737). Springer. 10.1007/978-3-030-16181-1_68

Waring, T., & Skoumpopoulou, D. (2012). An enterprise resource planning system innovation and its influence on organisational culture: A case study in higher education. *Prometheus (United Kingdom)*, *30*(4), 427–447.

William Dow, P. M. P., & Taylor, B. (2010). *Project management communications bible* (Vol. 574). John Wiley & Sons.

Wognum, P. M., Krabbendam, J. J., Buhl, H., Ma, X., & Kenett, R. (2004). Improving enterprise system support—A case-based approach. *Advanced Engineering Informatics*, *18*(4), 241–253. doi:10.1016/j.aei.2005.01.007

Xu, L. X. X., Yu, W. F., Lim, R., & Hock, L. E. (2010, July). A methodology for successful implementation of ERP in smaller companies. In *Service Operations and Logistics and Informatics (SOLI), 2010 IEEE International Conference on* (pp. 380-385). IEEE.

Zarei, B., & Naeli, M. (2013). Critical Success Factors in Enterprise Resource Planning Implementation: A Case-Study Approach. In M. Haab & S. Cramer (Eds.), *Enterprise Resource Planning Systems in Higher Education* (pp. 10–21). IGI Global. doi:10.4018/978-1-4666-4153-2.ch002

Ziemba, E., & Oblak, I. (2013). Critical success factors for ERP systems implementation in public administration. In *Proceedings of the Informing Science and Information Technology Education Conference* (pp. 1-19). Informing Science Institute. 10.28945/1785

KEY TERMS AND DEFINITIONS

Cloud Computing: Paradigm that allows computer services to be offered over a network, allowing users and organizations to remotely use and access hardware and software across the Internet. From the user's point of view, a browser is used to connect to an application that the cloud service provider owns and maintains, and the user must pay for the use of certain services or functionalities.

ERP Implementation: Normally is viewed as stages of life-cycles with five phases: problem identification and motivation (define the specific problem and its value), definition objectives for an ERP solution (what is possible and feasible), design and development (new constructs and models), demonstration (how to support the use activity), and evaluation (how the system responds to the problem).

Higher Education Institutions (HEIs): Universities, colleges, and further education institutions offering and delivering higher education. Include traditional universities and professional-oriented institutions, which are called universities of applied sciences or polytechnics. An educational institution in any State that admits as regular students only persons having a certificate of graduation from a school providing secondary education and is legally authorized within such State to provide a program of education beyond secondary education; provides an educational program for which the institution awards a bachelor's degree, or awards a degree that is acceptable for admission to a graduate or professional degree program, subject to review and approval by the Secretary; and is a public or other non-profit accredited institution.

Software as a Service (SaaS): Software distribution model in which all underlying infrastructure, middleware, software, and application data are located in the IT provider's data center, accessed via Internet from a client. SaaS allows users to connect and use cloud-based applications over the Internet, offering a software solution that is leased to a cloud service provider using a pay-for-use model.

APPENDIX

Table 5. Literature review on Success Factors of ERP implementations in HEIs

Author(s)	Country	Objective of the study
Rabaa'i (2009)	Australia	Through an extensive literature review, the researcher found a large number of articles that provide answers to the question: "What are the key critical factors for ERP implementation success".
Rabaa'i, Bandara & Gable (2009)	Australia	This teaching case illustrates how the contextual factors contribute to the success or failure Enterprise systems at Queensland University of Technology.
Sabau et al. (2009)	Romania	This paper examines the application of ERP software in Romanian Universities and made a SWOT analysis for implementing an ERP system. Also, the authors proposed a comparison framework of ERP solutions for higher education management using as starting point the requirements of a Romanian University.
Shoham & Perry (2009)	Israel	This study examines the organization-wide technological changes that have infiltrated every aspects of life at all universities that are part of the higher education system in Israel during the last 7 years. Also, proposes a model for managing organization-wide technological changes in universities on the basis of the existing mechanism, using knowledge management strategies for the purpose of change management.
Vathanophas & Stuart (2009)	Thailand	Identify the factors associated with computing satisfaction for existing legacy systems and the perceptions of usefulness and ease of use of an ERP system for Thai university staff.
Abugabah & Sanzogni (2010)	Australia	The paper is divided into two parts, the first part focuses on ERP literature in higher education at large, while the second focuses on ERP literature in higher education in Australia.
Kitto & Higgins (2010)	Australia	This article explores the work-arounds through which an ERP software system is implemented within an Australian University. While resistance is significant, the process of working around a technology can have ambiguous effects in terms of how users-in this case academics-are governed and govern themselves.
ALdayel et al. (2011)	Saudi Arabia	This paper explores and analyses the existing literature on ERP implementation and attempts to identify the critical success factors for a successful implementation of an ERP in HEIs in Saudi Arabia.
Bhamangol, Nandavadekar & Khilari (2011)	India	This paper aims at the impact of in- house and vendor or consultant's specific groups and different skill sets for implementing ERP Systems in Higher Education. The researcher also focuses on benefits, security check lists and percentage of customization of Educational ERP system, based on ERP system literature review in Higher Education.
Gallagher, Worrell & Mason (2012)	United States of America	The study is a replicated case study based on interviews with project leaders in nine universities judged to have successful PeopleSoft ERP implementations.
Karande, Jain & Ghatule (2012)	India	Identify the critical success factors for a successful implementation of an ERP in HEIs in India. This article has contributed to academic research by producing the observed evidence to support the theories of critical success factors and ERP implementation success.
Waring & Skoumpopoulou (2012)	United Kingdom	This paper adds to the debate through a longitudinal case study of an integrated information system implementation undertaken within a large UK university. The system was introduced into a university in 2006 and the focus of the research has been on culture change within the SITS environment.
Cua & Reames (2013)	Australia	This paper discusses the critical use and lessons learned from the single case model while implementing an ERP system at a leading university and discusses the case system inclusive of the grounded case theory, diffusion of innovation theory, innovation-process theory and their application during the ERP system implementation.
Ullah et al. (2013)	Saudi Arabia	Analyze the ERP system implementation in HEIs and find out the critical success factors of ERP system implementation in the literature. Also, the paper discusses a brief case study of King Saud University is been presented.
Abdellatif (2014)	Egypt and Bahrain	This research highlights the potential for implementing Enterprise Resource Planning (ERP) system in higher education institutions, recommends some best practices from Oracle solutions for universities, and discusses the situation of ERP in developing countries accompanied with a case study from a university in a developing country.
Mathias, Oludayo & Ray (2014)	Africa	The researchers identify ten critical success factors influencing the effective implementation of ERP systems in HEIs in Africa.
Qian, Schmidt & Scott (2015)	United States	This study focuses on the OnePurdue – SAP software pre-implementation phase. The study provides a framework for ERP system pre-implementation in a higher education institution.
Bhattacharya (2016)	Australia	This case discusses a globally renowned and highly ranked public University based in Australia and its journey of adopting an Enterprise System. The case further illustrates how the organization, enabled by its Enterprise Systems, achieved both operational efficiency as well as managed to retain its position at the top end of the academic market through innovation and better strategic decisions.
Chuang (2016)	United States	The objective of this study is to identify the critical success factors for ERP implementation in higher education. The study outcome contributes practical advice to both academics and practitioners. The information gathered in this study identifies the critical success factors that can serve as foundation to engage ERP implementation in higher education.
Shakkah et al. (2016)	Saudi Arabia	The study focused on the level of Campus ERP implementation and the level of awareness against the ERP implementation in education industries, identify perceptions of implementing Campus ERP and identify the barriers of implementing Campus ERP. The respondents are at the private institution of higher learning with University and College University status.

continued on the following page

Table 2. Continued

Author(s)	Country	Objective of the study
Althonayan & Althonayan (2017)	Saudi Arabia	This research aims to evaluate the impact of ERP systems on higher education (HE) from the perspective of stakeholders' performance.
Al-Hadi & Al-Shaibany (2017)	Yemen	This study confirms that ERP is suitable for any group of organizations that have same organizational structure, data flow, business process structure, and industry. The authors recommend Yemeni government should start thinking to provide the HEIs system of their public universities through the integrated ERP to reduce the cost, increase control on university's operations, and effective process management.
Nizamani et al. (2017)	Pakistan	A questionnaire based online survey approach is used to collect data from 323 respondents. Findings of the paper result in a refined model for analyzing success of ERP implementation. By employing this model, the paper also reports on the success and failure of ERP implementation.
Soliman & Karia (2017)	Egypt	This article contributes to the development of the theoretical framework of the successful implementation of the ERP system to explain the competitive advantage of HEI by merging information system (IS) success and diffusion of innovation (DOI) theories with the success factors for the adoption stage of ERP systems.
Chondamrongkul (2018)	Thailand	A case study in a Thai university that implements ERP system, which shows how selected critical success factors are taken into practice throughout implementation process. The study shows software learnability as a significant challenge that causes problems in the post-implementation phase.
Fadelelmoula (2018)	Saudi Arabia	The aim of this study is to examine the effects of certain critical success factors for the implementation of ERP Systems on the comprehensive achievement of the crucial roles of Computer-Based Information Systems.
Schindel (2018)	United States	The goal of this paper is to identify the unique challenges of rolling out such a system in a Higher Education environment at a large U.S. University. The research studies implementations in Texas A&M, Washington, Louisiana State and Iowa State universities.
Althunibat et al. (2019)	Jordan	The main purpose of this study is to determine the factors that affect the acceptance of using ERP by Jordanian universities, by evaluating through the questionnaire survey, in order find the most appropriate and prepared universities that willing to adopt ERP system in Jordan.
Andrianto (2019)	Indonesia	This study aims to determine whether the implementation of ERP in University of Jember has an impact on the performance of employees (lecturers) and in order to generate conclusions in the form of evaluation of the application of ERP in the University of Jember better.
Shatat (2019)	Oman	This research paper investigates the impact of ERP system on academic performance at Sohar University. A survey questionnaire is distributed to several academic stakeholders to investigate the impact of ERP system on academic performance within the University context.
Wanko, Kamdjoug & Wamba (2019)	Cameroon	This paper studies case of successful implementation of ERP system in the higher education sector in Cameroon. A model was based on the information system success model (ISSM) by Delone and Mclean. Results of the study showed that ISSM is well suited for studying a successful ERP implementation for universities, particularly in the Cameroonian environment. They also indicated that the feeling of belonging to an organization, work satisfaction and the perception of technological innovation are strongly influenced by the use of a university ERP system and the satisfaction that a user can draw from this use.

Source: Own elaboration

Chapter 21
Virtual Collaboration Tools for Project Managers:
A Study of Human and Technological Factors

Tomislav Rozman

https://orcid.org/0000-0001-9738-7253

BICERO Ltd., Slovenia

ABSTRACT

This chapter examines virtual collaboration tools from the perspective of project managers of EU-funded projects. The chapter overviews virtual collaboration tool types, users types, and their motivation to use the chosen tool alongside the human factors. The authors have observed 40 EU project managers, who have managed 244 EU projects. Despite of the abundance of modern, web-based, and mobile tools, project managers are still not familiar with the advantages of cloud-based document systems and communication tools. Factors such as un-friendliness, security concerns, and lack of IT skills prevent more wide usage of virtual collaboration tools. Live meetings are still perceived as the most efficient channel for distributing and receiving project tasks, but they are closely followed by virtual meetings using the communication software. The authors propose a standardized process of including virtual collaboration tools to distributed project teams. Their experiences show that strong leadership and defined process increase the usage of IT tools and consequently the success of EU-funded projects.

DOI: 10.4018/978-1-7998-1279-1.ch021

INTRODUCTION

Imagine you are a project manager of an EU project, coordinating an international team. You are aware of the fact, that the single most significant factor affecting the success of a project is the communication ability of the project manager (Zulch, 2014).

How can you live up to such expectations when project participants come from various cultures (Dafoulas & Macaulay, 2002; Gibbs, Sivunen, & Boyraz, 2017) and organizations, they speak different languages (Lockwood, 2015) and they are used to different ways of knowledge sharing (Almeida & Soares, 2014)? They have various beliefs and statuses within their organizations. Project partners use their own documentation and communication information systems and processes used within their organizations. For shared project purposes, yet another documentation and communication system is usually selected. Project partners' knowledge and motivation to use such systems may vary significantly.

The question is: Is it possible to achieve smooth and effective collaboration of a virtual team and timely finalization of tasks, and eventually reach project objectives in such a complex environment?

The authors of this paper are involved in the management of virtual project teams on a daily basis and struggle with similar issues as described in the literature. They are especially interested in the IT aspect of virtual teams' management: shared documentation and IT-supported communication. Cloud-based document management tools (such as Google Drive, Dropbox, SharePoint, Office 365 and similar) have been used for a decade and are quite mature in technological and usability terms. Nevertheless, their adoption and usage are still limited, which is surprising, because improving document management increases the project management efficiency (Eloranta, Hameri, & Lahti, 2001). Similarly, in the age of modern communication tools (email, sound & video conferences, chats, social media platforms), the selection of appropriate communication channels for different project management tasks is still an issue.

Firstly, we will present existing literature on the following topics: virtual teams, distributed teams, document management and similar. Then, we will present a typical EU project environment. Next, we will present the problem which is in the focus of our research: collaboration between project team members using online tools. We will summarize the types of project document management in 9 patterns. Next, we will present the results of the research (survey). These results include answers from various project participants and their attitude towards various communication tools and techniques. The results (descriptive statistics) were analyzed using pivot tables.

In the end, the results are discussed and guidelines for project managers are presented.

The results were used to create guidelines for project managers and reference processes for document and communication management, which are presented in the last chapter.

RELATED WORK

Virtual, Distributed Teams and Project Networks

Managing virtual teams is tightly integrated with the effective usage of information technology (Olariu & Aldea, 2014). Electronic communication is ranked the highest among effective communication methods in some researches (Zulch, 2014) that were done among construction, occupational health, environment, safety, finance and claims managers in non-virtual teams. Managing distributed teams requires a different set of competencies than a collocated team (Seshadri & Elangovan, 2019b). Effective leadership is a must for distributed teams, where role clarity, communication satisfaction and effectiveness are even more important as in collocated teams.

Based on the vast research within the project management area, the large share of knowledge-intensive projects performed by virtual teams struggles with serious issues (Ayoko, Konrad, & Boyle, 2012). Those issues can negatively influence achieving project objectives, communication and relations between team members.

(Harej & Horvat, 2007) state that a virtual team is defined by the degree of online communication, not the geographical dispersion. A temporary team is established for a specific time-limited project, whereas a permanent team is established for long-term tasks (such as open-source development community).

In contrast, other authors (Guzmán, Ramos, Seco, & Esteban, 2010) state the difference between virtual and traditional teams: members work at different geographical locations, they come from different cultures, have different teamwork practices, speak different languages, knowledge management and distribution is different and time difference makes agenda management difficult. Same authors also emphasize (among others) problems related to virtual teams: ineffective management of shared knowledge among different team members causes duplication and inconsistency.

Moreover, (Ale Ebrahim, Ahmed, & Taha, 2009) identified 12 factors which influence the virtual teams. The same authors compiled a comprehensive literature review on this topic and defined a virtual team as geographically dispersed, driven by a common purpose, enabled by communication technologies and involved in the cross-boundary collaboration. Other characteristics of virtual teams are: they are not permanent teams, the team size is small, the members are knowledge workers and may belong to different companies. Other authors offer similar definitions (Hertel, Geister, & Konradt, 2005; Joinson, 2002; Shea, Sherer, Quilling, & Blewett, 2011), (Watkins, 2013).

The main advantage of a virtual team is its agility. At the same time, those teams are especially vulnerable to mistrust, communication issues, conflicts and power struggles. (Ale Ebrahim et al., 2009) also compiled a list of advantages and disadvantages of virtual teams. Some of a virtual team's disabling factors are addressed in this research, such as requirements for complex technological applications, task-technology fitness, technophobia, training.

Project networks thus maintain a stable core of project team members while at the same time dynamically tapping into the expertise within the personal networks of members as necessary (Cummings & Pletcher, 2011). When the task is non-routine, this set-up often increases the chance of success of a project. A project network combines the advantages of the project team with those of the personal network. EU projects can be viewed as a special type of project networks. Core members of an EU project represent the core of the project team, while their associates/assistants and sub-contractors represent non-core contributors of the project network.

We are aware of the fact that trust is very difficult to develop and maintain in a virtual team (Huls, Piggott, & Zwiers, 2014), because of different barriers (Kimble, 2011) in culture, time and geography. These barriers are sometimes called *distance* (Seshadri & Elangovan, 2019a). It is therefore even more important to select the adequate technological solution to support and not to diminish trust in project teams. Thorough research of VT development in the last ten years (Gilson, Maynard, Young, Vartiainen, & Hakonen, 2015) found different results for the impact of technology use in virtual teams: from no effect to better overcoming of teamwork challenges. It recommends more investigation and attention to newer technological solutions, which is what we are doing specifically for EU funded projects.

Software development projects in virtual teams are especially common. For example, most of the open-source software is being developed in virtual teams. Several authors have researched the performance of the virtual software development team. (Colomo-Palacios, Casado-Lumbreras, Soto-Acosta, García-Peñalvo, & Tovar, 2014) found out that the performance of such projects is lower than in-house projects. One of the main reasons for the lower performance of a team is a lack of attention of virtual project manager to development tasks.

(Colomo-Palacios, Casado-Lumbreras, Soto-Acosta, Misra, & García-Peñalvo, 2012; Misra, Colomo-Palacios, Pusatli, & Soto-Acosta, 2013) discusses the role of people in GSD (global software development). Challenges in GSD virtual teams can be summarized as communication, knowledge management, coordination, collaboration, socio-cultural distance and lack of trust challenges. Authors propose several ideas to overcome these challenges such: investment in people, promotion of mobility and improvement of the software development process.

(Colomo-Palacios, Soto-Acosta, García-Peñalvo, & García-Crespo, 2012) performed a research (focus group and Delphi study) with special attention on packaged software development. Their main conclusion is that people are still the most important resource in SW development, regardless of the type of software. Therefore, the transparency of competences, reporting and quality process are the areas which need to be well managed in distributed software development teams.

Virtual project teams are here to stay and growing (Shea et al., 2011). For example, 145,463.81 M € are spent on EU projects in a single year (EU_comission, 2014). A big part of this funds (e.g. 17,551.69 M € for Competitiveness and for growth and jobs) are managed in virtual teams. To ensure more optimal expenditure of EU project funds, the management of project teams should be improved.

The existing literature mainly explores key success factors for managing project teams but skips the technological dimension and its relations to the project team members' motivation.

Factors Affecting the Performance of a Project and Virtual Teams

(Ebrahim, 2015) identified the main groups of factors, which influence the effectiveness of virtual teams. He found out that the 'knowledge worker' and 'process' group of factors positively relates to the effectiveness of the virtual team while the 'technology construct' group of factors relates to it in a negative way. (Salaheldin, Sharif, & Al Alami, 2010) describe the driving and resisting forces within project management software implementation. Their research on the effect of various factors on the success of project implementation (understanding of the business case, objectives, management support, defined plan etc.). The effect of the usage of PM tools is only partially addressed in this research.

Acceptance of Cloud-Based Document Management Tools

Online collaboration platforms have existed since the very beginnings of the internet, for example, PLATO in 1973 (Woolley, 1994), which was the predecessor of the wide-spread system Lotus Notes. With the advancement of Web 2.0 in 2004 (O'Reilly, 2005), real-time sharing and syncing platforms emerged, such as Google Docs.

The academic research in the field of contemporary, especially cloud-based document management systems (Gilson, 2015) and its usage for collaborative project work is slowly growing. For example, a search using keywords 'google docs' in Mendeley returns around 400 results and Emerald Insight returns 190 results. A partial research on the usage of Google Docs within a specific domain has been done by: (Mansor, 2012) – collaboration between academics, and (Blau & Caspi, 2009; Suwantarathip & Wichadee, 2014; Watson, 2006; Zhou, Simpson, & Domizi, 2012) – collaboration between students for the writing tasks. User acceptance of Google Docs within the organizational setting has been investigated by (Tan & Kim, 2015). They found out that the perceived usefulness and satisfaction positively affect the intention to continue using such tools.

The majority of the researchers agree that even in 2019 the digital collaboration is diverse, relevant and challenging, which is also the main topic of the book edited by (Riemer & Schellhammer, 2019).

The goal of this research is to explore the behaviour of project managers of virtual teams in relation to supporting IT tools. From the literature review, we can conclude that a lot of research has already been done, but it mainly focuses on different aspects of project management, IT tools and factors influencing the effectiveness of the communication. Our focus is on the usage of IT tools for managing EU funded projects, which are usually performed by virtual teams.

EU Projects

EU projects are usually long-term relationships between organizations. For example, the three-year project actually means that the organization is joining in project-related relationships for a much longer period (up to nine years) from proposal preparation to the end of the possible evaluation period (Horvat, Harej, & Rozman, 2006). Web-based collaboration tools are considered as enablers for successful cooperation, which is of the utmost importance in such long periods (Schwarz, 2005).

Numerous programs and funding opportunities (EU_Commision, 2014) exist for different types of activities. Different types of organizations can apply for funding. The main characteristics of EU co-financed projects (like Lifelong Learning – Leonardo da Vinci, FP7 or the latest Erasmus+ and Horizon 2020), which are considered in this article, are:

- duration: 1-3 years
- types of projects: research, development of innovation, transfer of innovation, partnerships, knowledge alliances and similar
- a number of partners (organizations): min. 3, average 8, max. 12 with 1-5 people/ partners
- location of partners: minimum 3 different EU countries (core partners) and other countries (associated partners), but generally more than that (typically 4-5)
- partners' organization type: private companies, public organizations, NGOs, academic institutions, associations etc.
- partners' organization size: micro to medium companies
- expected project results: mostly intellectual outputs like research reports, events, training materials, courses, e-content, software, new processes and services
- project organization: network/virtual team
- project scope: multidisciplinary

The skills and characteristics of a successful project manager, associated with EU projects like Lifelong learning – Leonardo Da Vinci have been already characterized to some extent by (Draghici & Draghici, 2013). The authors have analyzed project managers, who are directly or indirectly associated with projects that contribute to the development of training courses under ECQA (European Certification and Qualification Organization). Within this survey, they have found out that the most common managerial style is based on the Germanic culture encouraging rational plan development and control of changes; it focuses on the processes and the background of the project manager is mainly in IT sector. This research does not include operational or IT details of project management, which is described in our research.

EU funded projects and specifically diverse research networks positively impact on the commercial impact of their innovation, which was described in a study of 603 collaborative projects by (Nepelski, Van Roy, & Pesole, 2019).

Patterns of Collaboration in a Project Using Document and Communication Tools

The possibility to access distributed and distinct computing resources can bring substantial advantages to project management. Cloud computing is particularly useful to support a lean and digitalized approach to project management (Nicoletti, 2012).

Cloud-based document management systems are used for intellectual outputs (documents, spreadsheets, presentations, schemes …) exchange within knowledge-intensive projects. For several years our project partners report the usage of Google Drive, Dropbox or proprietary document management systems with mixed success. According to our experience, document management within a project team can be summarized in at least 9 patterns [Figure 1].

The first and simplest pattern is represented by local editing of files and their exchange by the email system. The second pattern is represented by a traditional file server, which enables central storage of files, with no locking mechanism. The third pattern of document management is represented by CVS,

Figure 1. Different models of cloud /other document management systems usage patterns [1]

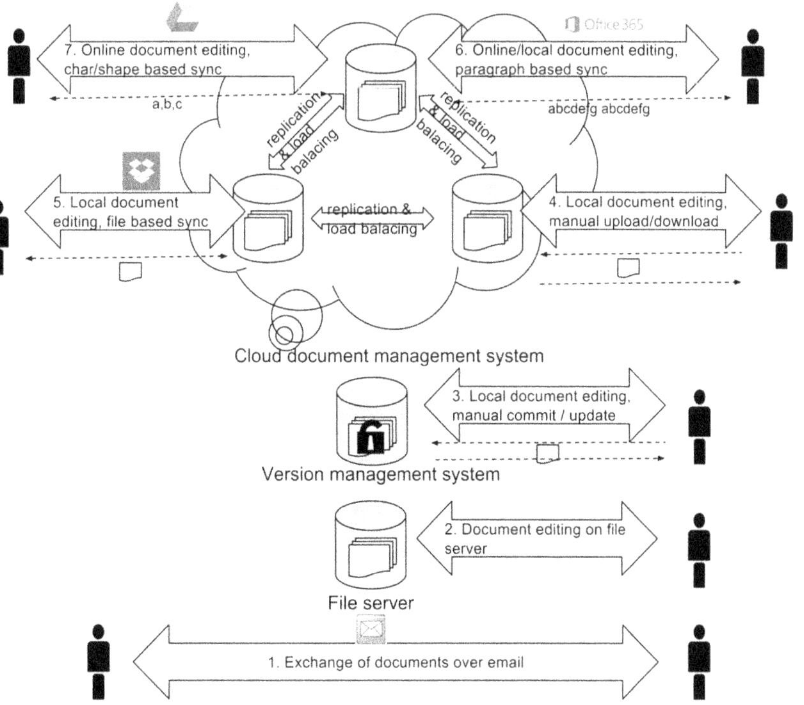

Subversion or similar system, which allow versioning, committing, updating and branching of files. Some examples of the fourth pattern are SharePoint, Blackboard, Moodle, or any other web-based system which allows manual document uploading and downloading. Examples of the fifth pattern are Office365 and Microsoft SharePoint, which allow paragraph-based online editing. Examples of the sixth pattern include Google Drive (local sync client), Dropbox and OneDrive, which allow automatic synchronization of the files. Examples of the seventh pattern are Google Drive/Docs system, Draw.io or similar, which allow simultaneous real-time editing of the documents. The eighth pattern could be represented by cloud project management tools, which also include event, task and project portfolio management. The ninth pattern includes social messaging.

Other tools for online project management, which include event/task management and social messaging (e.g. Wiggio, Teambox, Manymoon, BaseCamp etc.[2]), were omitted from the research. Nevertheless, these tools could be interesting candidates for future research, because within this research we have found out their efficiency for task distribution is on-pair with e-mail communication [Figure 10].

Document management does not eliminate the need for proper communication between project partners. Communication patterns and channels have been well known for quite some time (Katz & Tushman, 1979), but what we wanted to find out is which channel is the most efficient for assigning and accepting project tasks.

Communication within an EU project virtual project team is usually performed using different channels. There is less face-to-face communication (except on yearly meetings) and more e-communication. The communication can be asynchronous (e-mail, chat) or synchronous (chat, voice (e.g. skype), phone, video conference (many-to-many), webinar (one-to-many). Those communication channels are the only way of the project manager to reach project members, therefore it is useful to know which one is the most appropriate for which situation. The effectiveness of different communication channels was addressed in our research.

Research Questions And Hypotheses

The main research question is: Which factors influence the usage of modern document management and communication (D&CM) tools for managing virtual teams in EU projects?

Specific research questions are:

- **RQ1:** Is the usage of D&CM tools influenced by demographics (age, location, education …)?

Based on these research questions, hypotheses were formulated:

- H1. The majority (>½) of projects performed by virtual teams uses some kind of IT-supported documentation management system
- H2. Younger project managers from private companies prefer using cloud-based document management tools
- H3. The most effective communication channels for assigning and accepting project tasks are those with IT support

Within this article, we will mostly tackle the collaboration and communication aspects of project management. We will look at the factors that are related to collaboration and communication tools, such as messaging systems (e-mail, skype) and document management systems (Google Drive, SharePoint, Dropbox, proprietary systems).

Our research focuses on collaboration using online tools within virtual project teams. We are especially interested in temporary virtual project teams, which are common in EU co-financed projects.

RESEARCH DESIGN

The Context

A typical project, as observed here, is usually led by the main partner (contractor) and coordinator, who are not necessarily the same person. Project team members usually meet face-to-face twice per year. Therefore, most of the communication and collaboration is performed on-line.

The team usually consist of the following roles: project manager, quality manager, developers, teachers, administrative staff and technical staff, all from different organizations. Therefore, the term 'project network' could be used instead of 'project team'.

For the best collaboration, the team should use central storage for documents and results, which are produced within the project. But as we will see from the results, the majority of projects still exchanged documents exclusively via e-mail.

The online cloud-based document management systems have a lot of advantages over exchanging files using e-mail. Those advantages are a single point of document storage, less document duplication, the proper (automatic) version management, better document visibility, less time wasted for local classification and storage, better information circulation, better collaborative work etc.

We wanted to find out, what are the reasons behind the low acceptance rate of online document management systems.

In addition to document management tools, we were interested in online communication platforms. Since teams are geographically dispersed, we wanted to find out, which communication medium is suitable for task assigning and accepting.

We were interested in the influence of personal characteristics (self-starter, leader, being part of the hierarchy, motivation for participation in the project) to the usage of online collaboration platforms. We also wanted to know if the usage of online collaboration platforms is influenced by age or the type of organization that project members come from.

Our research was motivated by our own work: we (authors) are project managers and are dealing with these issues daily.

At the beginning of our research, we suspected that acceptance of cloud-based IT tools for project management and communication depends on the age of the project team members. The younger generation (up to the age of 40) should be more inclined to use the tools mentioned above. But this theory was rejected by the fact that some of the older project team members have no problems using IT tools for project management. The next thought was: does it depend on the type of the organization? Each project manager who was interviewed had their own personal limiting factor of the usage of IT tools for collaboration.

Therefore, we started our research in 2014 by preparing a short article, which was posted on the LinkedIn platform. We asked project managers: "Why do people resist using shared, cloud-based document management systems (such as Google Drive/Dropbox/Office365)?[3]" The received free-text answers were grouped in the following groups:

- I don't understand cloud-based DMs
- I'm afraid of losing the files
- I'm concerned about my privacy
- Lack of knowledge (caused by generation gap)
- I don't know how to use it
- The DM system is not safe

The participants' answers became the starting point for broader research, where we conducted a survey and asked project managers about their motivation to use modern cloud-based IT tools for collaboration. We wanted to find out which are the factors influencing acceptance, therefore we asked the research participants about their demographics, experiences, motivation, self-drive and similar.

RESEARCH DESIGN

Our research includes qualitative (observation and interviewing EU project managers) and quantitative techniques (web survey). This kind of methodological triangulation gives a more balanced picture of the situation. To establish a preliminary set of factors that influence the effectiveness of virtual teams in project management, the authors have conducted preliminary research. Firstly, the authors have been collaborating in EU projects for more than a decade and have been observing collaboration processes from within. Next, the authors have queried social networks (LinkedIn) and gathered responses from fellow project managers regarding the usage of cloud-based document management systems for project management tasks.

Design overview is shown in [Figure 2].

Preliminary Research

Within the preliminary qualitative research, the authors observed a small set of EU project managers for several years (field research - direct observation). The result of those observations and interviews is a set of factors which influences the effectiveness of project management in a virtual team. The main research question was: *What is the main reason for the poor performance of a virtual project team?* Each project manager had their own view of the reasons for poor performance and cooperation. For example, some older project managers thought that age is a limiting factor for effective use of online document management tools, while others thought that the difficulty of using the tools hinders their usage the most. The initial set of factors is shown in [Figure 3].

As we can see from [Figure 3], there is no clear consensus among project managers on which factors influence the effectiveness of collaboration in virtual teams. As it seems, the effectiveness itself is a term whose meaning depends on the observer.

Figure 2. Research design

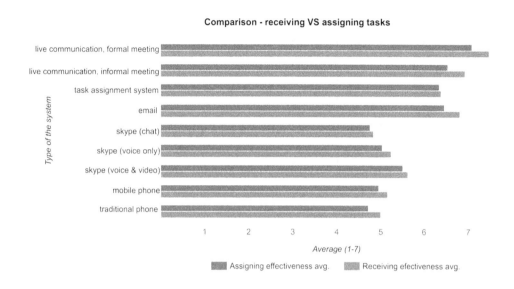

Figure 3. Initial set of factors

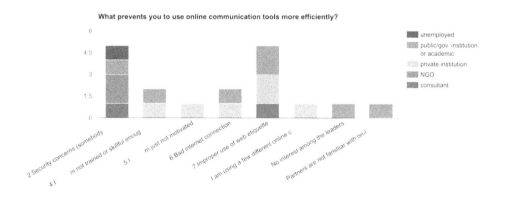

A Survey

Using a web survey, we gathered data about project participant demographics (country, age, type of organization, educational background), experiences with project management (proposal preparation and coordination, the number of coordinated/collaborated/ administered projects), types of projects (source of financing, hierarchical structure), motivation (self-starter, being part of an organizational structure, leadership, motivation for participation). The most important questions included technology-related issues of collaboration and communication platform usage (main collaboration/communication platform, its effectiveness, user-friendliness, obstacles for usage). In addition, we asked the participants, which factor is the most influential when assigning or receiving tasks. We also asked the participants about their self-drive, their motivation to participate in the most recent project and their leadership abilities.

Sampling and Validity of the Research

We used non-probability accidental sampling. We selected the participants for the survey from the authors' personal networks of current or past project partners. This type of sampling was used because we were mostly interested in collaboration improvement within our own project partners networks. We extended the target group by posting a request to participate in the survey within a LinkedIn group, which is dedicated to EU project management. We are aware that the conclusions of this research are difficult to generalize to all project managers in the EU but that was not our primary intention.

The survey was constructed using Google Forms and invitations were sent by e-mail and posted to LinkedIn groups. 44 persons who managed 244, partnered in 544 and administered 484 EU projects participated in this research. The full population of EU project managers is difficult to determine; there are currently more than 55 EU programmes (EU_Commision, 2014) which comprise a large number of projects. Those calls/projects have various duration and funding. There is no summary information about the total number of EU projects granted per year for all calls. For example, only Horizon 2020 published 173 calls in the year 2014/2015 (EU_commision, 2015).

Analysis

The data gathered was analyzed using Google sheets and IBM SPSS Software. First, we conducted a univariate analysis and then we used bivariate analysis to investigate the correlation between the variables. Descriptive statistics were prepared using simple statistics (averages etc.). For the data summarization, pivot tables were used. Correlations were discovered using Pearson's' correlation coefficient.

There were no missing data to handle, because all questions, which used the 7-level Likert scale, were mandatory to answer. The answers to open questions were classified in groups (coded).

Demographics

Demographic data: age group (40% were born 1971-1980, 20%: 1961-1970, 22%: 1981-1990, 14%: 1944-1960) [Figure 4]; country of the respondents: France, Netherlands, Italy, Slovenia, UK, Romania, Iceland, Bulgaria, Spain, Belgium); organization type: 36% private institution, 28% public institution,

Figure 4. Who manages EU projects by age groups

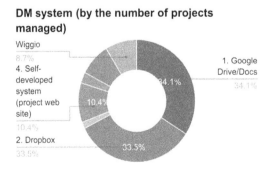

14% independent consultants, 11% NGOs, 11% others; educational background: 36% economics, 14% social sciences, 6% education, 22% technical sciences, 8% informatics.

Most projects overall are managed by the generation 1961-1970 (generation X).

If we take a closer look, we notice, that most project managers in private organizations belong to the generation 1944-1960 (generation 'baby boomers') [Figure 5]. If we focus only on consultants, most of them are from generation X. Public/academic organizations show an interesting distribution: approximately one-third of the sample is from 1944-1960, another third from 1961-1970 and the last third from the 1971-1980 generation.

Millennials (1980-2000) are underrepresented in all types of organizations except in private institutions.

Education background of the survey participants [Figure 6]: 32% technical sciences, 43% economics, 7,7% law, 7,7% social sciences and other. We have separated informatics and technical sciences catego-

Figure 5. Who manages EU projects by types of organizations

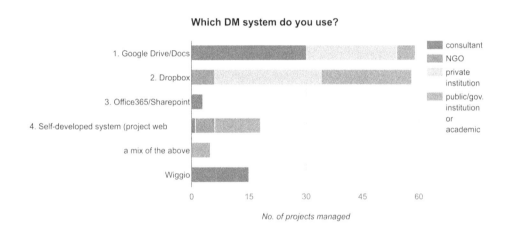

Figure 6. Education background of EU project managers

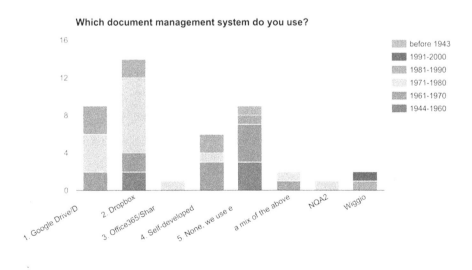

ries to determine if there is any correlation with educational background and IT systems usage. Most projects are managed by persons with an economics background, out of which most are from generation 1944-1960 [Figure 7].

Experiences: 66% of participants have already prepared a full proposal, 30% have collaborated in one and 5% have not been involved in proposal preparation yet. 72% have coordinated preparation of a project proposal and 28% have not.

Project organization [Figure 8]: A majority of projects followed a network type of project organization (60%), followed by a hierarchical organization (39%) and a mix of those (the remaining).

A network type of organization (as expressed by lead partners) is more common in Bulgaria, Italy and Slovenia whereas strict hierarchical organization is more common in Belgium [Figure 9]. Overall, most teams are organized as networks.

Figure 7. Education background and age groups of EU project managers

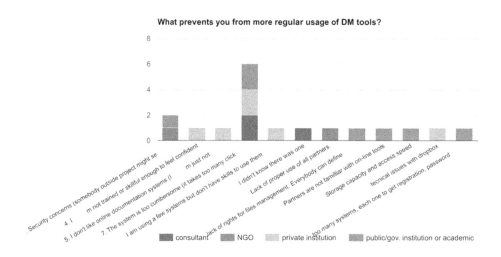

Figure 8. Project organization

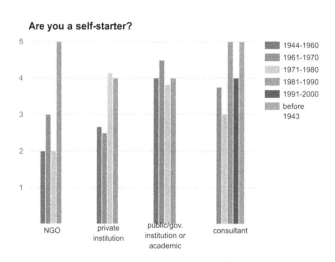

Figure 9. Demographics structure of survey participants by countries

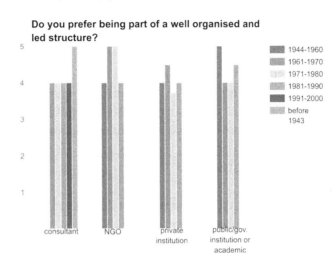

This complies with the findings of (Hoch & Kozlowski, 2014), who have found out that shared leadership (including a non-hierarchical organization) is significantly related to virtual team performance.

Receiving and Assigning Tasks Efficiency

As we see from [Figure 10], live communication and formal meeting still present the most efficient communication channels, closely followed by a live informal meeting. Surprisingly, e-mail is the third most efficient system for task assigning/receiving, closely followed by dedicated task assignment system.

It is not surprising that synchronous communication channels are perceived as most effective. **More interesting is the observation that asynchronous electronic communication channels (like e-mail**

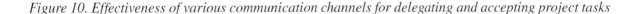

Figure 10. Effectiveness of various communication channels for delegating and accepting project tasks

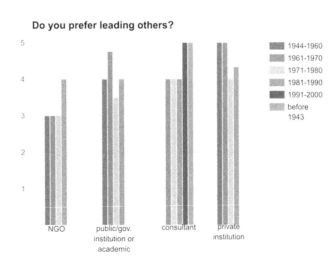

& task assignment system) are more effective as synchronous (skype, mobile, traditional phone). With focus only on asynchronous electronic communication channels, **skype with voice and video is considered as the most effective.**

There are subtle differences between different communication channels and assigning/receiving tasks, which are considered not significant (comparison of red/blue bars).

If we focus only on the use of communication tools, results [Figure 11] show that most users are concerned with security and improper use of web etiquette. Nevertheless, meetings (live or virtual) are still one of the most effective communication means, which was also researched by (Misra & Akman, 2014).

Document Management System

Many projects are still being managed without a shared documentation system (32%). Among others [Figure 12], Google Drive and Dropbox are the most used systems with an approximately equal share (GDrive-34.1% and Dropbox 33.5%).

If we observe only those answers, which use some kind of document management (DM) and group them by user types [Figure 13], we find out that **Google Drive is mainly used by project managers, which work as consultants or come from private organizations**. The reason could be in this product's attractive pricing, quick learning curve and broad product coverage. Public, governmental and academic institutions mainly use Dropbox or a self-developed system.

An analysis of DM systems usage by age groups shows that generations 1961-1970 and 1944-1960 are less keen to use the cloud-based DM system [Figure 14].

The two main obstacles for using cloud-based DM systems are: 1. the system is too cumbersome (it takes too many clicks to perform a task) and 2. security concerns. Other responses are presented in [Figure 15].

Figure 11. What prevents effective usage of online communication tools

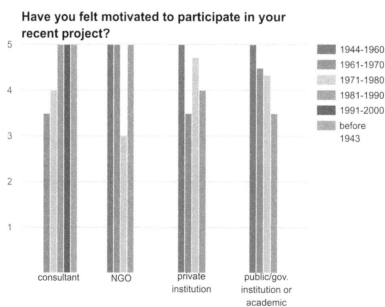

Figure 12. Which DM systems EU project managers use

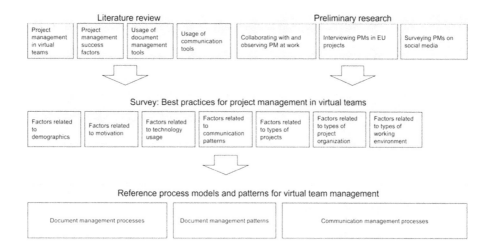

Figure 13. Which DM systems EU project managers use (by types of organizations)

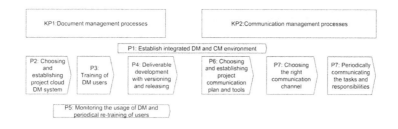

Figure 14. Which DM systems EU project managers use (by age groups)

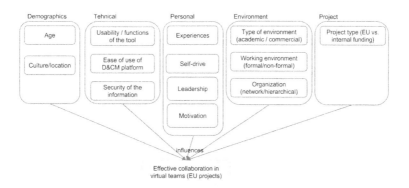

Figure 15. What prevents effective usage of document management tools

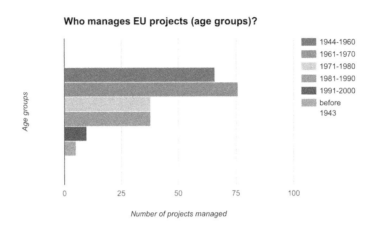

Motivation and Leadership of EU Project Managers

We asked our participants questions about motivation and leadership: 1. Do you consider yourself as a self-starter? 2. Do you prefer being part of a well-organized and led structure? 3. Do you prefer leading others? and 4. Have you felt motivated to participate in your recent project?

The results [Figure 16] show that most persons from the group of consultants consider themselves as self-starters, persons from the age groups 1981-1990 and before 1943 alike.

Most people from NGOs prefer to be part of a well-organized and led structure [Figure 17].

Persons who prefer leading others are mostly from private institutions and consultants [Figure 18]. An analysis by the age group shows the persons born before 1943 and between 1991 and 2000 prefer leading others. Persons born on 1971-1980 least prefer leading others, which is a very interesting result.

Figure 16. Leadership attitude: self-starter

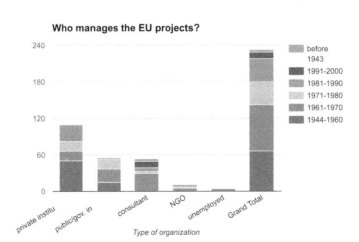

Figure 17. Leadership attitude: organization structure

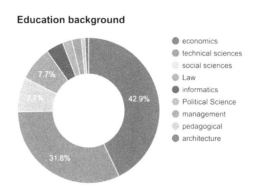

Figure 18. Leadership attitude: leading others

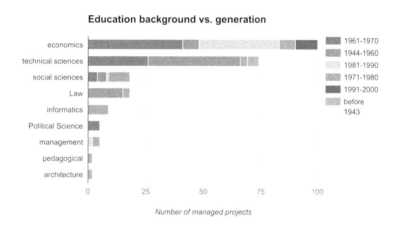

Most motivated to participate in a recent project were persons from NGOs and private institutions [Figure 19].

An analysis of correlations between variables showed that project managers who consider themselves as self-starters were also motivated to participate in their most recent project (Pearson's coefficient 0,327* at 0.05 level, 2-tailed).

Open Comments from Participants

From the free-text answers we could extract and summarize the following useful information: 1. complex systems can cause problems in temporary project settings (e.g. people were unhappy with the enforcement of Wigglio tool), 2. exchanging documents (only) via e-mail is not recommended because of poor

Figure 19. Leadership attitude: motivation to participate in a project

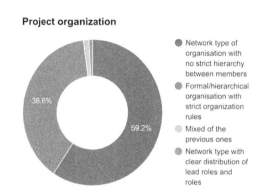

Project organization

● Network type of organisation with no strict hierarchy between members
● Formal/hierarchical organisation with strict organization rules
● Mixed of the previous ones
● Network type with clear distribution of lead roles and roles

38.6%

59.2%

version history tracking capabilities, and 3. training of project partners for efficient usage of DM tool is strongly advised.

RESULTS

Hypotheses

H1. The majority (>½) of projects performed by virtual teams uses some kind of IT-supported documentation management system

The hypothesis is confirmed. We have found out that 64% of survey participants use some kind of cloud-based documentation system for project management.

H2. Younger project managers from private companies prefer *using cloud-based document management tools*

The hypothesis is partially confirmed. We have found out that in generations 1971 and younger, the share of participants who do not use any of the cloud DM systems is almost zero. In generation 1944-1961-, almost half of the participants do not use any DM system, and in generation 1961-1970 approximately a quarter of the participants do not use any of DM systems.

H3. The most effective communication channels for assigning and accepting project tasks are those with IT support

The hypothesis is not confirmed. We have found out that live communication (formal and informal) is still most effective for assigning and receiving project tasks.

Suggestions for Better Document and Communication Management

The results derived from our research are a set of reference processes, DM patterns and recommendations, which need to be in place to ensure effective project management of virtual teams. [Figure 20] shows a high level of key process areas and processes which need to be established for effective document and communication management.

[Table 1] shows suggestions for project managers which can be used for deployment of D&CM processes. These processes were tested in case studies, which are presented in the next chapter.

POST-RESEACH CASE STUDIES

Since our first research of factors that influence the usage of collaborative tools in 2016, the findings have been used in some new international projects. These case studies are presented from the perspective of one of the participating project partners (BICERO Ltd.). Most of the projects were co-funded by the EU Commission, programme Erasmus+ KA2 Strategic partnerships. All projects included the following activities: market analysis, curriculum development, learning materials development, e-learning platform development, performing the online courses and preparing manuals for the trainers (Rozman, Maio, & Alexeeva, 2019). Project partners were diverse: companies, NGOs, associations, training centres, faculties, consultancies. Partners were also diverse regarding collaboration tools usage experiences. Some authors (Seshadri & Elangovan, 2019a) use the term *distance* (spatial, temporal, configurational, cultural, subjective, social, psychological, psychic) instead of *diversity*.

In our case, a 'project partner' means an organization with 2-5 directly involved project participants, which makes approx. 12-30 directly involved people, from project assistants to developers and university professors. DM and CM tools were used in addition to in-person project meetings every 6 months.

Figure 20. Reference process models for document and communication management within virtual project teams

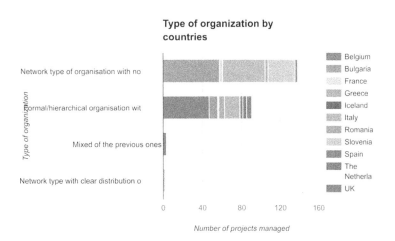

Table 1. Suggestions for process deployment

Process	Suggestions for process deployment
P1: Establish integrated DM and CM environment	If the team is well trained, has cooperated and used integrated D&CM system before, the introduction of an integrated system could be a good solution. If not, the introduction of a new integrated system can be a burden (e.g. see results from our research chapter *Open comments from participants*). Sometimes less is more (e.g. combining simple DM with e-mail task delegation).
P2: Choosing and establishing project cloud DM system	Choose the DM system for a project team considering patterns presented in [Figure 1]. For example, if the majority of project deliverables are in the form of files, a cloud-based repository with local file synchronization is a good solution (e.g. Dropbox). If you expect that collaborative work on the same deliverables (e.g. documents, spreadsheets, presentations) will be performed, choose Google Drive or Office 365. Establish a repository, grant access rights. Consider edit/read-only access for different members. Establish an initial folder structure. Dedicate one person as a document manager.
P3: Training of DM users	Allocate some time at the project kick-off meeting to perform initial training of project team members. Then, train core team members using videoconference and screen sharing. Perform individual training (one-on-one) if necessary. Employ social learning (e.g. learning from most IT literate in the partner groups)
P4: Versioning and releasing	Develop deliverables using versioning and releasing rules. Team members who have no background in software development, usually have difficulties managing versions. Standardize and set up rules (within configuration management plan) for file naming, classifying, versioning and releasing. Train users explain how automatic history preservation of files works (if used). Avoid branching of deliverables development, because it takes a lot of effort to merge them. Instead, introduce shared files to develop (e.g. shared training content presentation or shared spreadsheet for status tracking).
P5: Monitoring the usage of DM and periodical re-training of users	A dedicated person must periodically track what is happening in the documentation system. This includes monitoring of activity (e.g. Google Drive Activity stream), monitoring of file naming, classification, content, duplicates. Without regular monitoring, your DM repository will quickly become a mess. Use the insights of DM monitoring for re-training of users.
P6: Choosing and establishing a project communication plan and tools	Establish a communication plan which includes events, source, destination, frequency of communication and communication channels. Consider the findings from our research (see chapter Receiving and assigning tasks efficiency). Choose appropriate tools, e.g. Skype for virtual meetings, Doodle for planning communication events, GoToMeeting for webinars, e-mail or task assignment system for task distribution etc.
P7: Choosing the right communication channel	For each communication event, choose the appropriate communication channel. Consider the findings from our research (see chapter Receiving and assigning tasks efficiency). For the most important events (e.g. kick-off meeting), use live communication. Combine formal and informal communication. Example: Perform a formal project kick-off meeting in the morning and plan socializing activities for the afternoon and evening. For regular task distribution, use e-mail or task assignment system. Avoid using phone and chat tools for distributing tasks. People do not consider them effective; the message can get lost easier than in an e-mail. Synchronous channels (e.g. phones) are effective for resolving issues and getting quick feedback and less for distributing tasks.
P7: Periodically communicating the tasks and responsibilities	If no task management system is used, the project manager should periodically communicate the status of the tasks (open, closed, cancelled ...). Also, a simple shared spreadsheet – a list of tasks with statuses will work if updated regularly. Keep it simple, but don't oversimplify.

Case 1: 2-Year Project enGaging[4] (2015-2017), 6 Partners from 6 Countries (SLO, ITA, CRO, UK, PT, BG)

A document management tool used: Google Drive, Dropbox
Communication tool used: Skype, email
Degree of shared document system usage: poor
Main issues: document circulation outside of DM, version issues
Possible reason: No clear leadership, duplicate DM tool usage

Within this project, 2 document management systems were used: Google Drive and sometimes Dropbox. The main reason for such a situation was frequent changes in the project management team and unfamiliarity with DM tools capabilities. Dropbox system didn't prove itself effective, because some project partners had full account quotas and couldn't sync the shared documents.

Some partners refused to use collaborative editing in Google Docs documents. Frequent conversions between MS Office and Google Docs format caused some document design issues. Frequent project team's members caused some issues related to the transfer of the ownership of the Google Drive documents.

At least one team members had strong experiences and skills to manage DM issues, which softened the project manager's lack of experience to manage DM and communication issues. The processes from [Figure 20: Reference process models for document and communication management within virtual project teams] were not followed, especially steps 1-6, which caused mentioned issues.

Case 2: 3-Year Project SUCCEED[5] (2016-2019), 6 Partners from 6 Countries (LUX, BE, ITA, ES, SLO, RO)

A document management tool used: OnlyOffice
Communication tool used: OnlyOffice, Skype, GoToMeeting, WhatsApp, email
Degree of shared document system usage: good
Main issues: vague folder structure, minor version issues, minor document conversion issues, lost changes
     when editing simultaneously
A possible reason for good project collaboration: Strong leadership, clear communication and leading
     by example

Within this project, the OnlyOffice cloud-based DM and CM system was enforced from the beginning of the project. Project manager clearly stated that the only acceptable document flows are within the OnlyOffice system and allowed no exchange of documents via email. She also led by example – all deliverables related to the project were circulated via OnlyOffice. Moreover, all communications related to the project were done in OnlyOffice Discussion threads and Chat. Task status is being communicated by email and OnlyOffice built-in Tasks functionality.

Overall, the usage and communication using OnlyOffice were good and contributes to the successful project execution.

The processes from [Figure 20: Reference process models for document and communication management within virtual project teams] were followed closely, except the 4th step.

Case 3: 2-year Project TeachSUS[6] (2018-2020), 6 Partners from 3 Countries (RO, SLO, HU)

A document management tool used: Google Drive

Communication tool used: Skype, email

Degree of shared document system usage: good

Main issues: none so far, minor issues related to the ownership and access to the Google Drive

A possible reason for effective collaboration: Strong leadership and leading by example

Within this project, Google Drive is being used for document storage and collaborative editing. The project's folder structure was initially set and closely follows the project proposal structure (Work packages, Intellectual Outputs, Events, Meetings and Dissemination became the main document folders). The project manager proactively stores all project-related documents within the system and no documents are sent by email. Other project partners follow this behaviour which ensures the effective use of shared document storage. Task status and progress is being communicated by email, which causes some minor difficulties about an overall overview of the task statuses.

The processes from [Figure 20: Reference process models for document and communication management within virtual project teams] are followed closely, except the steps 3, 4 and 6.

Case 4: Ongoing Project of the International Association Management[7], 30+ Partners from Almost all EU Countries

A document management tool used: SharePoint

Communication tool used: Skype, GoToMeeting, Email

Degree of shared document system usage: low

Main issues: the SharePoint system is being used only for document storage, rarely for the exchange.
    Difficulties at collaborative work.

Possible reasons: Technical limitations of the system, low motivation for the usage

Within this project, SharePoint is being used for document storage and collaborative editing. The project's folder structure was initially set by the association president. The usage of the system is encouraged by the manager, but it is used mainly by the manager to distribute documents. Collaborative editing was tested, but due to the synchronization issues was abandoned. Other functionalities of the system (messaging) are not being used.

Case 5: 1-Year Editorial Project of the Online Magazine, 20+ Writers, 5 Editors, 2 Proofreaders (SLO)

A document management tool used: Google Drive / Docs

Communication tool used: Skype, email

Degree of shared document system usage: high

Main issues: people's attitude towards collaborative editing

Possible reasons: Non-IT educated collaborators

Within this project, Google Docs is being used for a writer's article storage and collaborative editing and review process. The project's folder structure was initially set by the main editor. The usage of the system is encouraged and enforced by the main editor. After initial friction, all writers of the articles accepted the collaborative editing process (the communication between authors, editors and proofreaders through Google Docs changes and comments). Collaborative real-time editing is heavily used without any issues. The editor-in-chief performed one-on-one training with each of the collaborators. This is one of the rare cases where all factors for successful virtual collaboration were aligned.

It is evident from mentioned case studies that successful collaboration within the distributed project team is closely related to the DM and CM tool usage. Leadership and leading by example are the main factors which ensure all team uses the selected tools. Following the steps from the suggested process model also prevents issues in relation to DM and CM in international projects. We can summarize our observation of the factors to three most evident (a combination of technological, organizational and human-related): ***right IT tools**, **leadership** and *defined process*.

DISCUSSION AND FURTHER WORK

The results of our research are interesting: the biggest obstacles for more efficient usage of online communication tools are bad online collaboration etiquette, security concerns and lack of skills. Results also show that live communication is still the most efficient method to delegate tasks, closely followed by e-mail or dedicated task assignment systems. Therefore, we suggest project managers use multiple channels for communication. Live meetings should be held at the major milestones (e.g. at project kick-off or intermediate reporting). E-mail (or other types of asynchronous) communication should be used for delegating packages of tasks to team members if no other tool is available. Synchronous communication should be used for daily operation, micromanagement and quick resolving of issues, which need immediate feedback. The communication system should be used simultaneously with the online documentation system.

The biggest obstacle for more efficient usage of online document management systems is user (un-) friendliness (the system is too cumbersome/it takes too many clicks). Before conducting the research, we speculated that security concerns will be the major obstacle for online document management systems. Interestingly, respondents evaluated security concerns with a relatively low score of importance.

We have also found out that there is no consensus about which obstacle prevents more efficient usage of DM and communication tools the most. But we gathered a set of possible obstacles, which can be studied by the project manager or configuration/documentation manager when choosing the DM system for a virtual project team.

After the initial research, have studied some cases of virtual collaboration using and observing different DM and CM tools and leadership styles. We have found out that three main factors are associated with efficient virtual collaboration: 1. Mature and well tested IT tool 2. Good leadership to common goal and 3. Defined process of collaboration tool usage.

Despite the drawbacks detected in DM tools usage, we believe that cloud-based DM systems for project management provide many advantages: transparency of work, easy insight into the history of changes, easier version management and, most importantly, simpler collaboration. These advantages are drawbacks by some: insight in document changes can be understood as a breach into a person's privacy and a threat to intellectual property. Moreover, when collaborating in real-time, a person's incompetence can be spotted more easily. Is this the issue most of us are afraid of?

REFERENCES

Ale Ebrahim, N., Ahmed, S., & Taha, Z. (2009). Virtual Teams: A Literature Review. *Australian Journal of Basic and Applied Sciences, 3*(3), 2653–2669. doi:10.2139srn.1501443

Almeida, M. V., & Soares, A. L. (2014). Knowledge sharing in project-based organizations: Overcoming the informational limbo. *International Journal of Information Management, 34*(6), 770–779. doi:10.1016/j.ijinfomgt.2014.07.003

Ayoko, O. B., Konrad, A. M., & Boyle, M. V. (2012). Online work: Managing conflict and emotions for performance in virtual teams. *European Management Journal, 30*(2), 156–174. doi:10.1016/j.emj.2011.10.001

Blau, I., & Caspi, A. (2009). What Type of Collaboration Helps? Psychological Ownership, Perceived Learning and Outcome Quality of Collaboration Using Google Docs. *Quality*, 48–55. Retrieved from http://telem-pub.openu.ac.il/users/chais/2009/noon/1_1.pdf

Colomo-Palacios, R., Casado-Lumbreras, C., Soto-Acosta, P., García-Peñalvo, F., & Tovar, E. (2014). Project managers in global software development teams: A study of the effects on productivity and performance. *Software Quality Journal, 22*(1), 3–19. doi:10.100711219-012-9191-x

Colomo-Palacios, R., Casado-Lumbreras, C., Soto-Acosta, P., Misra, S., & García-Peñalvo, F. J. (2012). Analyzing Human Resource Management Practices Within the GSD Context. *Journal of Global Information Technology Management, 15*(3), 30–54. doi:10.1080/1097198X.2012.10845617

Colomo-Palacios, R., Soto-Acosta, P., García-Peñalvo, F. J., & García-Crespo, Á. (2012). A Study of the Impact of Global Software Development in Packaged Software Release Planning. *Journal of Universal Computer Science, 18*(19), 2646–2668. doi:10.3217/jucs-018-19-2646

Cummings, J., & Pletcher, C. (2011). Why Project Networks Beat Project Teams. *MIT Sloan Management Review, 52*(3), 75–83.

Dafoulas, G., & Macaulay, L. (2002). Investigating Cultural Differences in Virtual Software Teams. *The Electronic Journal on Information Systems in Developing Countries, 7*(1), 1–14. doi:10.1002/j.1681-4835.2002.tb00040.x

Draghici, A., & Draghici, G. (2013). Lessons Learned for ECQA LLP-LdV Projects' Management. *Procedia Technology, 9*(0), 876–885.

Ebrahim, N. A. (2015). Virtual R&D Teams: A New Model for Product Development. *International Journal of Innovation, 3*(2), 1–27. doi:10.5585/iji.v3i2.43

Eloranta, E., Hameri, A. P., & Lahti, M. (2001). Improved project management through improved document management. *Computers in Industry, 45*(3), 231–243. doi:10.1016/S0166-3615(01)00099-9

EU Commission. (2014a). *Draft General Budget of the European Commission for the financial year 2015*. Retrieved from http://ec.europa.eu/budget/annual/lib/documents/2015/DB/DB2015_WDI_en.pdf

EU Commission. (2014b). *Multiannual financial framework 2014-2020 and EU budget 2014 - Directorate-General for the Budget - EU Bookshop*. doi:10.2761/9592

EU Commission. (2015). *H2020 Calls*. Retrieved 1 October 2015, from https://ec.europa.eu/research/participants/portal/desktop/en/opportunities/h2020/master_calls.html

Gibbs, J. L., Sivunen, A., & Boyraz, M. (2017). Investigating the impacts of team type and design on virtual team processes. *Human Resource Management Review*, *27*(4), 590–603. doi:10.1016/j.hrmr.2016.12.006

Gilson, L. L., Maynard, M. T., Young, N. C. J., Vartiainen, M., & Hakonen, M. (2015). Virtual Teams Research: 10 Years, 10 Themes, and 10 Opportunities. *Journal of Management*, *41*(5), 1313–1337. doi:10.1177/0149206314559946

Guzmán, J. G., Ramos, J. S., Seco, A. A., & Esteban, A. S. (2010). How to get mature global virtual teams: A framework to improve team process management in distributed software teams. *Software Quality Journal*, *18*(4), 409–435. doi:10.100711219-010-9096-5

Harej, K., & Horvat, R. V. (2007). Project Management Principles and Virtual Teams for Information Systems Development: Preliminary Proposal. In *2007 29th International Conference on Information Technology Interfaces* (pp. 483–487). Academic Press. 10.1109/ITI.2007.4283819

Hertel, G., Geister, S., & Konradt, U. (2005). Managing virtual teams: A review of current empirical research. *Human Resource Management Review*, *15*(1), 69–95. doi:10.1016/j.hrmr.2005.01.002

Hoch, J. E., & Kozlowski, S. W. J. (2014). Leading virtual teams: Hierarchical leadership, structural supports, and shared team leadership. *The Journal of Applied Psychology*, *99*(3), 390–403. doi:10.1037/a0030264 PMID:23205494

Horvat, R. V., Harej, K., & Rozman, T. (2006). Skill card and certification system for certified EU project manager. *28th International Conference on Information Technology Interfaces*. 10.1109/ITI.2006.1708518

Huls, C., Piggott, J., & Zwiers, T. (2014). Influence of cultural factors on establishing trust within Global Virtual Teams. *Scifiempire.Net*. Retrieved from http://scifiempire.net/wordpress/wp-content/uploads/2011/12/Influence-of-cultural-factors-on-establishing-trust-within-Global-Virtual-Teams.pdf

Joinson, C. (2002, June). Managing virtual teams. *HRMagazine*, 69–73. doi:10.1002/ert.20205

Katz, R., & Tushman, M. (1979). Communication patterns, project performance, and task characteristics: An empirical evaluation and integration in an R&D setting. *Organizational Behavior and Human Performance*, *23*(2), 139–162. doi:10.1016/0030-5073(79)90053-9

Kimble, C. (2011). Building effective virtual teams: How to overcome the problems of trust and identity in virtual teams. *Global Business & Organizational Excellence*, *30*(2), 6–15. doi:10.1002/joe.20364

Lockwood, J. (2015). Virtual team management: What is causing communication breakdown? *Language and Intercultural Communication*, *15*(1), 125–140. doi:10.1080/14708477.2014.985310

Mansor, A. Z. (2012). Google Docs as a Collaborating Tool for Academicians. *Procedia: Social and Behavioral Sciences*, *59*, 411–419. doi:10.1016/j.sbspro.2012.09.295

Misra, S., & Akman, I. (2014). A cognitive model for meetings in the software development process. *Human Factors and Ergonomics in Manufacturing*, *24*(1), 1–13. doi:10.1002/hfm.20344

Misra, S., Colomo-Palacios, R., Pusatli, T., & Soto-Acosta, P. (2013). A Discussion on the Role of People in Global Software Development. *Tehnicki Vjesnik-Technical Gazette, 20*(3), 525–531.

Nepelski, D., Van Roy, V., & Pesole, A. (2019). The organisational and geographic diversity and innovation potential of EU-funded research networks. *The Journal of Technology Transfer, 44*(2), 359–380. doi:10.100710961-018-9692-2

Nicoletti, B. (2012). Project Management and Cloud Computing. *PM World Today, 14*(1), 1–11. Retrieved from http://search.ebscohost.com/login.aspx?direct=true&db=bth&AN=74028642&site=ehost-live

O'Reilly, T. (2005). *What Is Web 2.0*. O'Reilly Media. Retrieved 24 November 2015, from http://www.oreilly.com/pub/a/web2/archive/what-is-web-20.html?page=1

Olariu, C., & Aldea, C. C. (2014). Managing Processes for Virtual Teams – A BPM Approach. *Procedia: Social and Behavioral Sciences, 109*(0), 380–384. doi:10.1016/j.sbspro.2013.12.476

Riemer, K., & Schellhammer, S. (2019). *Collaboration in the Digital Age: Diverse, Relevant and Challenging*. Cham: Springer. doi:10.1007/978-3-319-94487-6

Rozman, T., Maio, B., & Alexeeva, I. (2019). *How to develop a course (A manual for trainers)* (T. Rozman, Ed.). Maribor: BICERO Ltd. Retrieved from https://succeed.bicero.com/results/io6-manual

Salaheldin, S. I., Sharif, K., & Al Alami, M. (2010). Utilization of Project Management Software in Qatari Government Organizations. *International Journal of Human Capital and Information Technology Professionals, 1*(1), 1–15. doi:10.4018/jhcitp.2010091101

Schwarz, B. B. (2005). Do EU funded projects enable collaboration between scientists? the case of R&D in web-based collaborative learning environments. *Computers & Education, 45*(3), 375–382. doi:10.1016/j.compedu.2005.04.009

Seshadri, V., & Elangovan, N. (2019a). Distances in Geographically Distributed Team: A Review. *Research Review International Journal of Multidisciplinary, 4*(3).

Seshadri, V., & Elangovan, N. (2019b). Role of Manager in Geographically Distributed Team: A Review. *Journal of Management, 6*(1), 122–129. doi:10.34218/JOM.6.1.2019.013

Shea, T. P., Sherer, P. D., Quilling, R. D., & Blewett, C. N. (2011). Managing Global Virtual Teams Across Classrooms, Students and Faculty. *Journal of Teaching in International Business, 22*(4), 300–313. doi:10.1080/08975930.2011.653911

Suwantarathip, O., & Wichadee, S. (2014). The Effects of Collaborative Writing Activity Using Google Docs on Students' Writing Abilities. *Turkish Online Journal of Educational Technology, 13*(2005), 148–156. Retrieved from http://eric.ed.gov/?q=Google+Docs&ff1=dtySince_2010&id=EJ1022935

Tan, X., & Kim, Y. (2015). User acceptance of SaaS-based collaboration tools: A case of Google Docs. *Journal of Enterprise Information Management, 28*(3), 423–442. doi:10.1108/JEIM-04-2014-0039

Watkins, M. (2013). *Making Virtual Teams Work: Ten Basic Principles*. Retrieved 25 November 2015, from https://hbr.org/2013/06/making-virtual-teams-work-ten/

Watson, R. (2006). Extending Google Docs to Collaborate on Research Papers. *Toowoomba Queensland AU The University of Southern Queensland Australia*. Retrieved from http://www.sci.usq.edu.au/staff/dekeyser/googledocs.pdf

Woolley, D. R. (1994). PLATO: The Emergence of Online Community. *Matrix News*. Retrieved from http://www.thinkofit.com/plato/dwplato.htm

Zhou, W., Simpson, E., & Domizi, D. P. (2012). Google Docs in an Out-of-Class Collaborative Writing Activity. *International Journal on Teaching and Learning in Higher Education*, *24*(3), 359–375. Retrieved from http://www.isetl.org/ijtlhe/

Zulch, B. (2014). ScienceDirect Communication: The foundation of project management. *Procedia Technology*, *16*(16), 1000–1009. doi:10.1016/j.protcy.2014.10.054

ENDNOTES

[1]   Logos of Google Drive, Dropbox and Office365 are property of their respective owners.

[2]   http://www.1stwebdesigner.com/project-management-collaboration-tools/

[3]   https://www.linkedin.com/pulse/20141014102142-12084826-why-do-people-resist-to-use-shared-cloud-based-document-management-systems-such-as-google-drive-dropbox-office365?trk=mp-reader-card

[4]   https://www.bicero.com/projects/engaging

[5]   http://www.succeedproject.eu

[6]   http://www.teachsus.eu

[7]   www.ecqa.org

Chapter 22
Human Factors in Distance Learning

Leon J. M. Rothkrantz
Czech Technical University in Prague, Czech Republic

Siska Fitrianie
Delft University of Technology, The Netherlands

ABSTRACT

In this chapter, the authors present a massive open online course (MOOC) on a flooding disaster in the city of Prague. The goal of the MOOC is to increase awareness of citizens of Prague about flooding disasters and to provide a training facility for first responders and the crisis management team of the city. The MOOC is modeled and organized as an IT project. A dedicated didactical model has been designed for distant-learning. To complete a MOOC successfully, three human factors have to be considered: physical ergonomics, cognitive ergonomics, and organizational ergonomics. As an example of interactive learning materials, the authors describe a game-based assignment, where students have to take a role in the virtual crisis management team and to save citizens, properties, and infrastructure as much as possible. This assignment is organized as IT projects, where the human factors play again an important role. The chapter will also discuss educational experiments.

DOI: 10.4018/978-1-7998-1279-1.ch022

INTRODUCTION

Recently we could observe an enormous grow in dedicated distant-learning courses, called MOOCs (Massive Open Online Courses). Much outstanding higher education, such as MIT and Harvard, started a consortium edX to develop MOOCs based on regular courses at those institutes. Many other universities started similar consortia to distribute courses for distant-learning. Students all over the world can enroll in MOOCs. MOOCs are free of charge; usually, they have no entrance requirements and are available 24/7. There have been many MOOCs developed for IT and business-oriented students.

Distant-learning courses have been developed for students who are unable to attend lectures because these students have regular duties, such as jobs, taking care of family members, live in remote locations, or suffer from disabilities. Nowadays, distant-learning material has also developed as supporting materials for regular students. Over the years, many ways of distant-learning have been developed. For example, the distribution of printed or digital books and lecture notes, and regular video lectures that have been recorded and are available online as video lectures. MOOCs differ in many aspects from traditional distant-learning. The learning material is highly interactive and composed of visual presentations such as images, audios, and videos. Gaming and simulations are also often used as learning materials. Others are based on cooperation using different social media tools.

One of the problems of MOOCs is the high dropout rate. Many students stop their course even before these students have been started or shortly after starting the course. Most MOOCs are self-paced courses, students can enroll anonymously and because of the massive character, there is no supervision individually. The challenge of the designers of MOOCs is to reduce the number of dropout students to a minimum. This can be realized by using dedicated didactic models with a focus on human factors. The process of teaching-learning is about transferring and processing information. Usually, the learning content of a course plays a dominant role. However, human factors such as cognitive abilities, motivation, self-paced behavior, and cooperation have their impact on the learning process. We developed a dedicated didactical model for distant-learning that included human factors covering the following three overlapping areas:

1. **Human anatomical, physiological and biomechanical characteristics**. To perform optimally, students should have a good physical and psychological condition. However, in the weeks of exams, students are supposed to study more than 60-70 hours a week, in which most of the time sitting behind a computer screen. This yields more and more students suffering a burn-out syndrome that emerges from bad physical-healthy conditions.
2. **Cognitive social characteristics**. An academic study involves cognitive abilities as perception, memorizing information, information processing, reasoning, task analysis, cooperation and performance evaluation.
3. **Organizational, environmental characteristics**. Study-learning processes should be structured according to an appropriate didactical model. The teaching-learning activities should be modeled and structured by a distant-learning tool, an online learning platform and learning management tool, supporting optimal access to the learning material, supporting learning activities and cooperation between students.

In 2019, we launched a dedicated MOOC on the flooding of Prague[1]. One of the goals of the MOOC was to increase awareness of flooding disasters of civilians of Prague. Another goal was to provide a training platform for the city council and first responders. Visualization, simulation, and gaming were used to activate students and to support the learning process. In this chapter, we present some of the developed distant-learning modules and report about experiments with students playing a crisis game. The role of a teacher in a classical-classroom learning has been analyzed and how the role of a teacher is emulated in the study material and modeled by a dedicated didactical model. In particular, we will highlight and discuss human factors.

The outline of this chapter is as follows. In the next sections, we will discuss the methodology and background material. Next, we will present didactic models designed for a (regular) classroom and distant-learning. We continue to discuss didactic experiments concerning the design, implementation of the current MOOC using Moodle and test of preliminary prototypes.

METHODOLOGY

This research is based on a huge literature survey on the role of human factors in a classical face to face teaching. An initial attempt started in 1953 on causes of success and failure of academic studies at Dutch Universities. A team of eight prominent professors in the Netherlands specialized involved in educational research were involved in this study. Delft University of Technology (TUDelft) was selected as a test case. A cohort of 2.570 first-year students was surveyed by a dedicated questionnaire. In parallel, these students were requested to take part in a psychological assessment procedure. Written tests were used to assess the cognitive and personal characteristics of students. The results showed that the performance of students on their secondary school in exact topics was the best predictors of study-success or failure. Results of psychological testing had no added value. In 1990, this study was repeated for a cohort of 354 students in Mathematics and Physics with similar results.

Prof. Piet Jansen (1960-2000) from the University of Leuven developed and tested a dedicated questionnaire, to research the causes of study-success or -failure. An adapted version of the questionnaire was used to assess students Mathematics and Computer Science at TUDelft. From 1998 to 2000, more than 2000 first-year students yearly were invited by a group of student counselors to discuss the study progress and their wellbeing as first-year students. The progress reports were documented in study progress reports. The results of the assessment studies were used to develop the didactical model displayed in Figure 1.

Since 2014 to present, the authors participating in the research project ETN-FETCH focused on future Education and Training. More than 70 European universities represented by educational researchers were participating in this project. One of the work-packages of the project is on the development of MOOCs and the role of social media in distant-learning. In the first year of the project, all participants were requested to fill in a questionnaire with statements about distant-learning including MOOCs. While some participants in the project developed their own MOOCs using Moodle as a development platform, many other participants were not in favor of MOOCs. The outcomes of the questionnaire were presented at progress meetings of the project and the yearly learning conferences. Furthermore, one of the goals of the ETN-FETCH project was to develop new didactical models for distant-learning. The current model as displayed in Figure 2 was presented at project progress meetings and the yearly conference on e-learning organized in the framework of the educational project. The incremental progress of the didactical model was also presented in progress reports of the project and at the related learning conferences.

The discussed MOOC fits in the framework of the ETN-FETCH project. Defining the goal, design, implementation, choice of implementation platform and test of a MOOC can be considered as a complex IT project. Students and first responders play an important role in the development of the MOOC. In

Figure 1. Didactic model based on the interaction of students with the teaching-learning environment

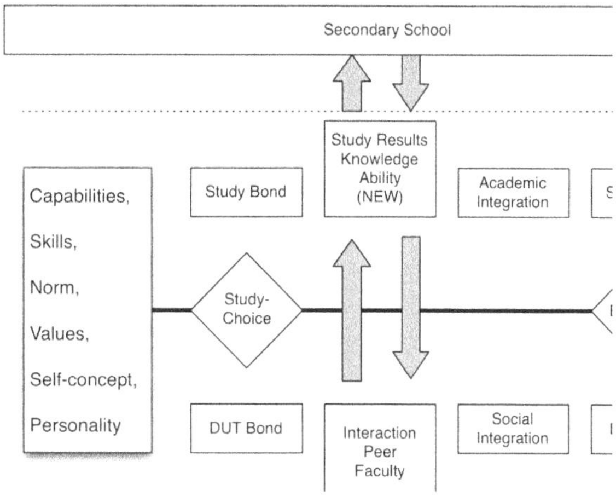

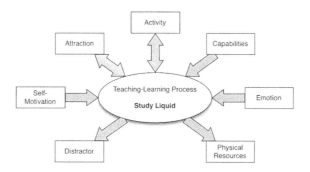

Figure 2. Didactic model describing the momentary interaction student learning material

learning modules, several aspects of a flooding disaster are discussed. One of the innovative educational aspects of MOOCs is interaction and simulation and cooperation and the introduction of a didactic model for distant-learning. As participants playing in the crisis game, they have to face different human factors. Negotiation, cooperation between persons with different characters and responsibilities are one of the aspects for participants in the MOOC. Other aspects that participants have to train are how to handle a shortage of people, time pressure and time management common to all IT projects.

Another motivation for the research is a smart city symposium that is annually organized in Prague since 2013. One of the topics is the security and safety of the city. The developed prototypes of the MOOC on security management of flooding at Prague has been presented at the Symposium and described in papers published in the Symposium Proceedings. Representatives of the Board of the city, first responders and students were participants of the Symposium and target audience of the MOOC. During the Symposium the representatives and designers of the MOOC had many fruitful discussions. The outcome of the discussions resulted in modifications of the design of the MOOC. The design process of the MOOC by developing successive prototypes can be characterized as an incremental approach. However, experiences of MOOC designers from TUDelft and ETN-FETCH partners showed that evaluation of MOOCs by questionnaires is complicated mainly because of the low response rate. Therefore, it was decided to test the prototypes of the MOOCs in small groups under the supervision of designers of the MOOC. Participating students in these sessions were requested to fill in some questionnaires and there were also group wise/individual discussions between the designers of the MOOCs and students.

BACKGROUND

MOOCs, Distant-learning

Haggard et al. (2013) wrote an extensive literature review of Massive Open Online Courses and other forms of online distant-learning. They reviewed more than 100 research papers and came to the following conclusions:

- Conflicting perspectives on MOOCs divide education communities. Reviewing the current literature, it can be concluded that the discussion is still going on. The assumption that MOOCs are free of charge is under discussion. The platform Coursera was one of the first to ask tuition fees from students. As a consequence, the number of students finishing MOOCs increases significantly.
- Learning practitioners disagree about the value of MOOCs. Most learning practitioners agree that MOOCs resulted in big changes in didactic models of distant-learning, design of innovative learning material including game technology, simulations and improved the interaction of students with the learning material. More critical practitioners note that the benefits of MOOCs were already realized in distant-learning and that MOOCs are based on poor didactical theories and pedagogical approaches.
- Reporting of MOOC learner experiences is positive. Well-known researchers of the most outstanding Universities published MOOCs. Underprivileged students all over the world got access to many MOOCs and were enthusiastic about that.
- The MOOC is maturing and engaging with its business and accreditation issues. It can be concluded that most Universities, even the critical ones offer now MOOCs.

Oblinger (2006) edited a book on learning spaces. More than 20 authors published papers about learning in classrooms (learning) and interactions among individuals (informal learning). Especially the ideas on informal learning provide a basis for learning communities using social media in MOOCs. At this moment there is a trend of integrating MOOCs in regular classroom courses. In this way, the basic ideas of MOOCs, interaction with the learning material and social interaction with peers are introduced in regular classroom teaching. Authors of the book stress already the fact that learning can take place anytime, anywhere. This was the basic research topic of the ETC-FETCH project which was the starting point of the MOOC on the flooding of Prague.

The European Union Association (EUA) published an occasional paper in 2013 on MOOCs for discussion in the EUA Council. Gaebel (2014) wrote an update of this paper. The main issues are International MOOCs facilitators and European's reactions. The European based platforms are discussed and the European participation in Coursera and edX.

Mali (2016) presents an overview of MOOCs. The author provides a historical overview of MOOCs and the main publishing platforms. The benefits of MOOCs for underprivileged people were stressed. The authors searched for papers on MOOCs using Google Scholar and ERIC. Between 2013 and 2014, in total 4,590 papers were detected in peer review Journals. In ERIC 131 publications were detected. Of special interest was the challenge of MOOCs such as high dropout rate, ineffective assessment also discussed in the current paper, recognition of exams, and finally hardware and internet facility. The investments of MOOCs platforms Coursera, Audacity, edX are discussed. In India, a new platform has been designed called Swayam (Study Webs of Active-Learning for Young Aspiring Minds). A similar attempt is Moodle in Europe, used as a platform for the current MOOC on the flooding of Prague.

Didactic Models

The didactic Adagio of the famous Dutch mathematician and didactic specialist in mathematics Freudenthal (1973) was, "You can learn mathematics only by doing and discover mathematics in the real world". For him was teaching mathematics an educational task and it should be context-sensitive and application-oriented. Students should be able to design mathematical models and translate real-world problems formulated in natural language in a mathematical language. Gomes et al. (2006) state that it is very important to give students opportunities to reflect on and clarify their thinking about mathematical ideas. They discovered that one of the obstacles students frequently coped with in solving a programming problem lies in transforming a textual solution into mathematical language.

Most of the current didactic models fit in the discovery learning tradition developed around 1960. Piaget, Dewey, Vygotsky and Freire, and many others support constructivist learning (http://edX.org, Wikipedia). Up to then, drill and practice were one of the favorite pedagogical principles in mathematics. Now the focus is on learning based on personal and societal experience. Our developed didactic model FETCH 2.0 is based on similar ideas. The question is of course how to implement this didactic model in the developed MOOC. The oldest, and still the most powerful, teaching tactic for fostering critical thinking is Socratic teaching. In Socratic teaching, the focus is on giving students questions, not answers. The next step is that students themselves learn to generate questions around a learning text.

Human Factors

The Journal of Human Factors and Ergonomics Society publishes peer-reviewed scientific studies in human factors/ergonomics was founded in 1958. The Journal publishes papers not only on theoretical models but also on applications of human factors concerning the relationship between people and technologies, tools, environments, and systems. Published papers present innovative work on human capabilities and their limitations. The focus is on a better understanding of cognitive, physical, behavioral, physiological, social, developmental, affective, and motivational aspects of human performance. Articles encompass a wide range of multidisciplinary approaches. However, in this chapter, some selected articles are reviewed focusing on human factors related to distant-learning and MOOCs on crisis management.

At the Netherlands Defense Academy, there is a strong interest in research in Human Factors (Boer, 2007). Military Defense is involved in the context of high risk. The security of the personal and equipment is of high importance. Military Defense applies complicated technologies with information technology as the main application area. Human factors play a crucial role. In the past, human operators were involved in the interaction with complex technological systems in the area of air defense. Nowadays complex technologies are involved in all areas of the military domain. In this complex context, human factors can cause an incident, accident or even a complete disaster. Risk management is an important topic in the military domain. Research on human factors resulted in more insight into security and developed instruments for risk management. In this chapter risk management in the military domain is linked to success and failure in distant-learning. The developed models around human error will be transferred from the military domain to distant-learning.

Disse et al. (2017) present a MOOC on flooding disasters. The focus of the MOOC is on the prediction of flooding disasters in Europe based on hydrological models. Next measurements are discussed to prevent or reduce the damage of flooding. Flooding disaster models are highly probabilistic models. Via risk assessment models, a flooding disaster will be predicted and human factors assessed which have a great impact on a flooding disaster. There is a focus on didactical models and how to reduce the drop-rate from the course. Human Factors in the overlapping areas of technology, management, and analysis of human behavior are discussed.

Human factors engineering is also known as ergonomics. Lewis (2011) provides an overview of human factors engineering. The focus of human factors engineering is on understanding the potential and limitations of human abilities. The design of human-machine systems uses this knowledge. The discipline of human factors engineering lies between the field of Human-computer interaction and the field of usability engineering. In the paper the following three topics are discussed:

- A definition of human factors engineering/ergonomics
- A short history of human factors engineering
- Fundamentals of human factor engineering
- Human factors engineering and usability testing.

From 1953 to 1957, there was a big research project running at TUDelft on delay in the study progress and dropout of students from their study (Bottema and Bakker, 1959). The first goal of the research was to get insight into the causality of study delay and dropout. The second goal was to research if it was possible to predict study success or delay. The researchers found six factors playing a role in study success or failure: wrong study choice, insufficient capabilities, bad study methods, personal problems, external components, social adaptation. The project at Delft was the start of many research projects on "study success or study failure. The procedure was to find characteristics of students and Universities to provide a basis for prediction of the study success in the future. All students from the first three years got a psychological assessment. Well-known IQ-test, personality assessment, test for verbal and nonverbal abilities were used and typical test for technical abilities. From these students, the results of exams were collected and the results of the exams at secondary school. A group of student counselors interviewed them about personal characteristics, personal situation, and personal problems. The results of exact courses as mathematics, physics, and chemistry at secondary school were the best predictors of study success or study failure at the university. The results of psychological assessment had no added value. A study at a Technical University requires exact abilities and the exams at secondary school are based on some years of study at that school. In 1984 the study at Delft was reproduced at the Faculties of Mathematics, Physics, and Informatics (Rothkrantz, 2016a). However, the results were similar. The psychological assessment resulted in additional characteristics of students but these variables had no added value on the prediction of study success.

Jansen and de Neeve (1988) were involved in research on teaching and learning in higher education. In the whole research, a student with his/her study and exam experience and perception of teaching behavior is the focus of attention. Janssen perceives studying as "deep level learning" and teaching as facilitating studying. Together with Goethem and Lacante, Janssen researched studied experiences of students (Lacante, 1983). They developed a questionnaire of more than 100 items and surveyed first-year students at the University of Leuven. After analyzing the responses of students using factor analysis, they discovered three underlying components: intrinsically motivation, self-confidence, and activity. These components are similar to the Osgood dimensions evaluation, potency, and activity (Osgood, 1957). In 1990 the author performed again similar research at TUDelft.

Tinto (1975) introduced a theoretical longitudinal model showing how student and University characteristics have their impact on the interaction student-university in the course of the time. The model considers three systems: student, university and social system. According to Tinto, a student will enter the university based on certain social backgrounds, personality, and pre-education, which create an attachment with the University and goal of education. The student's motivation and expectation express this bonding. Influenced by two systems, the academic and social and their interaction, this bonding changed and eventually results in the dropout of the student.

A student as an open system as a composition of interacting parts has been described by many researchers. The composing parts are considered as information processing subsystems. They receive information, process information, and broadcast information. To consider human beings as information processing systems is a generally accepted idea. Wilbrink (1997) describes the individual learning process of a student as a sequence of states similar to complex, goal-directed open systems.

Rothkrantz (2015a, 2015b, 2016c, 2016d) introduced a didactical model for distant-learning based on the use of social media. The focus of that model was on communication with and supports by peers in a social network of friends. In the current model, we focus on individual learning, on the interaction of students with the learning material.

The development of the MOOC Flooding management in Prague[1] has been reported as an IntechOpen book chapter (Rothkrantz and Fitrianie, 2018). During the development years, prototypes of the MOOC and the founding ideas with background material have been published as papers in distant-learning conferences and as progress reports of ETC-FETCH project. These progress reports enable discussion with project partners and inspired project partners to perform similar experiments. A special interest was into the experiments using social media and cooperation with peers. A successful matching algorithm was designed to match peers in similar or heterogeneous groups.

Successive didactical models were also presented as papers on e-learning conferences. An interesting idea was to integrate MOOCs learning material in regular courses. Originally at TUDelft, MOOCs were designed for students not registered as regular students to save tuition fees. However, the design of MOOCs has generated a lot of innovative educational materials. A dedicated designed methodology enables the integration of MOOC material in regular courses (Rothkrantz, 2018). A successful didactic innovation was the integration of inquiry-based learning as a new teaching-learning method (Rothkrantz, 2018). On the other hand, Rothkrantz (2016b) discussed experiments to reduce drop-off rates.

The first preliminary evaluation of the online MOOC is also described in a paper presented at (Roth-krantz, 2017a, 2017b, 2017c). A problem with the use of questionnaires in MOOCs evaluation was the low response rate. Experiments were performed analyzing student interaction with their smartphone. Assignments in the current MOOC start always with a simple question to register starting interaction with students.

DIDACTIC MODEL IN DISTANT-LEARNING

A study can be considered as a complex interaction process between students, learning material, in a complex learning and social environment. Human factors play an important role in the high dropout rate of students in the teaching-learning process. To understand the process of success or failure of a study, human factors have to be researched. The impact of human factors on the study process has to be assessed. Human factors can cause failures or disasters in the interaction process of humans with technical systems and their environment. In this chapter, To research the causality, factors, and circumstances resulting in a dropout process uses the general theory of human factors. To understand the teaching-learning process, we develop a general didactic model. The components in this model will be considered as human factors. We also present a survey study to validate the model.

Human factors will be studied not only in the context of the complex study process but also in the study material. A MOOC has been developed on a flooding disaster in Prague. Human factors have been researched in the flooding disaster context. It is important to know which human factors play an important role in the causality, factors, and circumstances contributing to the emergence of disasters. A crisis management team in the city council is responsible for all actions during a crisis, starting from building barriers, rescue people and provide help for the victims. During flooding, disaster operators often have difficulties to interact with available technology, and disaster assessment of context-awareness is a complex process. This is caused by complex processes, failing information or even because of fake information.

Didactic Model for Regular Courses

Many didactic models have been developed for regular courses. In this section, a didactic model is presented developed in 1980 for students Mathematics and Informatics at TUDelft. This model was validated by a set of questionnaires based on the components of the model. This validation study was used to research study success and failure of students at TUDelft. The research of study success and failure has a long history at TUDelft.

All first-year students were requested to fill in questionnaires focussed on study success and failure. Parallel to the survey study, all these students were requested to take part in a psychological assessment procedure. These students were again requested to fill in a psychological test on personality, technical and cognitive abilities, including verbal and nonverbal tests. At the end of the psychological assessment, there was an interview with a psychologist about students' well-being, experiences with the study, study environment, teachers and peers. Students involved in a dropout process, not only could immediately be recognized by reporting their study experiences, but also by nonverbal aspects expressed in their body language. The problem is how to detect the onset of the dropout process and to offer support and help for students getting into problems. A student or teacher tutor and regular meetings could provide help (Rothkrantz, 2015c).

As stated before, as predictors of study success and failure can use the grades for the mathematics and physics courses. These grades were strongly related to grades at secondary school for courses in mathematics and physics. All the results of the psychological assessment did not have an additional predictive value. Probably personality characteristics, cognitive and technical characteristic are also included in the academic performance of mathematical and technical courses. However, assessments using questionnaires were used to obtain knowledge about the study-success or failure on an individual level.

In Figure 1, a didactic model has been displayed used for regular courses at TUDelft. Describing students as open systems implies an ecological attitude concerning causality. Context and evolution have to be considered. The success of a study is not only dependent on student characteristics as capabilities, knowledge, used study methods, but is the result of a complex interaction process. This will be the basic idea underlying the didactic model presented in Figure 1.

Students are driven by a high motivation to complete the study to realize the defined study goals. Furthermore, during the study progress, the interaction student with the teaching-learning process, environment, and context can increase or reduce the motivation. Emotions are known as driving forces of all kinds of behavior including study behavior. A strong negative mood is not a positive stimulus for a successful study process. In some cases, the will to succeed can overrule negative moods and feelings. However, in exit interviews of dropouts that negative feelings about the study, study environment and study community are dominant (Rothkrantz, 2016a).

Applying the theory of human factors, the individual components of the didactic model can be reviewed from the following three main factors:

- **Human, physiologic factor**. This factor is not explicitly defined in the didactic model, only implicit in the skills and capabilities components. Study stress is a regular phenome in an academic study. Students should be able to handle an overdose of stress to control burn-out syndrome's symptoms. There is a strong relation between mind and body. Physical illness often has a mental causality. The model should include explicitly psycho-somatic fitness. Students have to take care of healthy food, enough sleep, and relaxation.
- **Cognitive, social factor**. This factor is represented by many components in the model such as knowledge, abilities, social interaction with peers. An important aspect of the cognitive human factor is emotions. Students should enjoy their study and the interaction with peers and study environment. In the current model, affective aspects are underrepresented.
- **Organization, environmental factors**. This factor is also represented in many individual components in the model such as social interaction environment, integration study environment, binding with study and Faculty. These components describe the interaction of a student with its study environment. The organization of a supporting study environment is another topic.

To validate the didactic model, we performed a survey study in 1983. All students Informatics (*n* = 160) were requested to fill in a questionnaire of 190 items on a 3-point Likert scale. In these items, students were questioned about their opinions, motivations, assessments, experiences concerning the study, study environment and study conditions with a focus on the interactive aspect. We stress the dynamic aspect of the interaction process. The survey measures the situation at a specific time moment. Especially, the items related to the affective component are time-dependent.

The items were distributed over 10 topics: study choice (i1-i25), study motivation (i26-i36), study environment (i37-i58), teaching (i59-i65), counselling (i66-i70), study problems (i71-i85), study methods (i86-i97), preconditions (i98-i101), personal data (i102-i110), study skills (i111-i130), causalities of study delay (i131-i161), study progress (i162-i175), social network (i175-i190). The results showed that 80% of the variables show a significant difference between the groups of students passing, 0, 1, 2, 3 or 4 exams successfully at the first exam session in October. It was possible to use these variables to predict study success or failure.

Didactic Model for Distant-learning Courses

We found that the didactic model as discussed in the preceding section could not be used to study the dropout process in distant-learning. Another model was needed to describe the interaction process between students with their study material and study environment and study peers. There are fundamental differences between regular courses and online courses concerning the dropout problem:

- The dropout of students in regular courses is usually a long-time process. Dropout in distant-learning can happen in a fraction of second if students losing their interest or motivation.
- Regular courses are usually compulsory courses part of a final exam, and students have to pay tuition fees. Distant-learning courses are free of choice. However, the dropout rates of distant-learning course reduce if students have to pay tuition fees.
- Distant-learning courses can be followed anytime, anywhere. This provides enormous freedom for students. Regular courses have many constraints in time and location.
- Regular courses are usually presented in lecture halls. Students are accompanied by peers and study friends and usually, it is only allowed to leave a lecture during the breaks. Distant-learning courses are rather anonymously, and students can log off any time.
- Many distant-learning courses are self-paced courses without a teacher as a course manager. A lot of self-discipline is needed to take part in distant-learning courses. In regular courses, a teacher has the lead and is the manager of the course.
- In regular courses, a teacher can have more feeling with his/her students. If the attention of the audience is dropping down, the teacher can give examples or a summary. In distant-learning courses, there is no direct feedback with students.
- Distant-learning courses are usually asynchronous, remote in place and time. Cooperation between students is more complicated compared to regular courses.

Given all the differences between regular courses and distant-learning courses, there was a need for a new didactic model adapted for distant-learning. In the case of distant-learning courses including MOOCs, the focus should be on direct interaction student-learning material within a short time window of interaction. We stress the fact that the interaction is a dynamic process which can increase or decrease in intensity. In Figure 2, a new didactic model is displayed. This model is concentrated on the teaching-learning process on micro-level.

A key factor in this model is played by affective phenomena. We consider an affect as a pattern of observable behavior to express a subjective feeling or emotion. These emotions can be translated to the learning context. The learning material should have the interest of students. It should attract and surprises them. The interaction with peers should provide pleasure and feeling to be accepted and appreciated by the learning community. Passing the exams gives feelings of proud and high self-respect. A negative impact on the study behavior can cause emotions of panic or heavy stress during an exam, or if students remain indifferent exposed with the learning material. The learning context should give students hope to pass the exam successfully and do not get into panic or feared. In the following, we discuss the components of the interaction model in more detail.

Attraction

An important component in the interaction student learning material is the interest of students. As long as the learning material is interesting, they keep on board. However, as soon the learning material gets boring, they lose their interest and the dropout process has been started. In the case of regular courses, there is a lot of pressure of peers, Institute, teaching schemas to follow lectures the other day. New topics provide opportunities for a new start. Usually, this is missing in the case of MOOCs. By the huge number of students, an individual tutoring is difficult to realize. A dedicated didactic approach is needed. The span of attention or control is very short, only some minutes. A varied way of presentation of learning material is needed by showing movies, video lectures, simulations and interesting applied assignments for students. Positive experiences of the students with the learning material can increase the attraction. For example, after solving assignments, understanding the learning material, or after positive feedback of peers or tutor.

Capabilities

A student assumes at the start he/she has sufficient capabilities to complete the course successfully. However, when he/she interacts with the learning material and it could be that the materials are far beyond his/her capabilities, the dropout process has been started. Regular face to face courses does not allow a student to leave the teaching hall. When many students lose their interest, an experienced teacher starts a summary, a clarifying example to get students back in the teaching-learning process. In regular courses, there is a support of peers during the breaks or after the lectures. In MOOCs social support of peers is wanted but usually less developed. There is a trend to develop MOOCs as self-paced courses for individual students. That makes these students vulnerable to negative interactions.

Activity

Attractive learning material and required capabilities are prerequisites of a positive interaction process of a student with his/her learning material. Next, a student is assumed to play an active role in this process. Many students read the description of the offered courses; they even enroll in the courses. However, the next step is to start the study activity. Most MOOCs are not designed for passive students; a lot of activity is required varying from posing and answering questions, making assignments and involvement in project activities. After positive feedback from the interaction process of students with the learning material, the activity can be increased.

Distraction

Interest and sufficient capabilities are the positive drives of the interaction students with the learning material. However, there are also two negative drives. Distraction is the first negative drive. In the case of MOOCs, students usually study in a stimulus rich environment. The computer used for taking the course offers a lot of alternatives for distraction especially when the study material gets boring or is beyond the capabilities of students.

Physiology

A second negative drive is the physiological state of the students. If a student gets hungry, sleepy he/she can start a break. A lot of discipline is needed for a restart and to keep the length of the break under control. In the case of regular courses, there are social rules, institutional rules regulating breaks.

Self-Motivation

In a classroom setting, a teacher can motivate his/her students and to push them to activities. In distant-learning, this is more complicated and can only be realized by the learning material. A student in distant-learning courses is assumed to motivate himself. In some cases, fellow students can take the role of tutor. A low degree of self-motivation in self-paced courses is the main factor to explain the dropout rates of students in MOOCs (Rothkrantz, 2016).

Emotions

We stressed already that affective components as feelings and emotions have a huge impact on successful study behavior of students. Successive negative emotions can result in a negative mood of students and in that state, they are very sensitive to the dropout.

EVALUATION

The development of the MOOC Flooding Management in Prague has been started in 2014 at TUDelft. Since that time developed preliminary modules, didactic models and results of experiments on distant-learning were presented at the e-learning conferences and on the Smart City Symposium of Prague. Since May 2019 a prototype of the MOOC on the flooding of Prague is online[1]. The MOOC is still under development. Employees of TUDelft developed more than 25 MOOCs successfully have used the course development tool edX. Some of these courses are rather successful and have more than 100.000 students every year. However, only a minority of participants completed the course. Some of the courses are distant-learning versions of regular courses and completed by students before starting their study at TUDelft. Other courses as water management and solar cells are popular for students from developing countries. The current MOOC has been developed to increase the awareness of citizens of Prague and to train first responders how to behave during flooding disasters.

ETN-FETCH Project

This section summarizes all the evaluation studies. The project started with a critical review of the literature on MOOCs. A summary can be found in the section related work of this paper. Next researchers involved in educational research from 67 European universities were requested to comment on the design of the current MOOC and the evaluation studies of the first developed prototypes of the MOOC. Next experiments at two technical universities in Delft and Prague are reported.

The current MOOC-project started in the framework of the ETN-FETCH project. This European Thematic network Program was supported by the European Community and was focused on future training and education. The research question was how to support learning at anytime, anywhere. Researchers from 67 European Universities were involved in the project. Further, at the very beginning in 2013, ENT-FETCH partners were surveyed to assess which partners had experience in the development of MOOCs and the use of social media. Participants were requested to answer some questions with a yes or no. Six examples of these questions are:

Q1: You are interested in MOOCs/distance learning?

Q2: You have (some) experience in the development of MOOCs/distance learning?

Q3: You are interested in the use of social media?

Q4: You have some experience in the use of social media?

Q5: Your institute or university developed some material for MOOCs or distance learning?

Q6: Your institute or university has some experience in the use of social media in education?

The results of the short questionnaire, that are displayed in Table 1, can be concluded that most researchers were informed about MOOCs but not impressed by the educational aspects. Designers of the current MOOC had to take into account the critical comment of ENT-FETCH partners. At the end of the questionnaire, there was a request for general comment. All the 67 respondents provided short/long comment, which can be summarized under the following headings:

Table 1. Frequencies item response all ENT-FETCH partners

Category-Response/Questions	Q1-User Interest MOOCs-DL	Q2-User Experience Development MOOCs-DL	Q3-User Interest Social Media DL	Q4-User Experience Social Media DL	Q5-University Experience in Development MOOCs-DL	Q6-University Experience Use Social Media
Yes	63	37	64	45	42	33
Not	1	20	1	18	19	28
Yes/No	3	10	2	4	6	6

Topic 1 Development of new didactical models around distant-learning

Many researchers stressed that the most appealing characteristic of MOOCs/Distance Learning is that these courses provide an opportunity to link participating students, especially via social media platforms. To be part of a community of students, sharing a common interest and providing information and help in solving the course problems or assignments, will boost the intrinsic motivation of students. However, students need to be accepted and active members of communicating groups of students.

One of the critical comments on MOOCs is that they only provide study material and superficial learning support of students. There is no pressure on students for deep learning. Only students with a strong discipline or intrinsic motivation can profit from MOOCs. It also proves that many foreign students and elderly people take part in MOOCs. In interviews, they state that they like the opportunity to take lectures anytime anywhere from the best universities about interesting topics presented in a discovery channel-way.

At regular courses, students find their peers during social meetings, coffee breaks or are stimulated or forced by lecturers to create teams. Visual appearance and oral communication play an important role. If students are not accepted members of a social network, they will lose their interest in visiting courses. In the case of MOOCs and DL, it is even more important for students to be accepted as a member of the course community. For MOOCs with many participating students' lecturers play a minor facilitating role. Peer groups should emerge from the student community. There should be a virtual meeting place for students and a matching procedure.

Topic 2 Social Media Platforms

Students active on social media platforms, such as Facebook, are used to share their activities and experiences with their "friends". One of the goals of the current MOOC is to find ways that students participating in a MOOC or Distant-learning course create active groups of "study friends" discussing their course experiences via social media. These experiences can range from asking for help, asking for comment on solutions of problems/assignments or sharing new ideas or findings or finding partners in different roles to take part in study projects. Some partners report that they have experience in a regular distant-learning. Social networks (Facebook, LinkedIn) are used to communicate with friends, colleagues and other people and to find out the latest news and information. Social media is also used for information sharing (YouTube, SlideShare or Scribd) and information publishing (e.g. Wikipedias).

Topic 3 MOOCs

Some partners raise critical questions about MOOCs and social media and consider it as hype for some time. The main argument against MOOCs is the high drop-off rate and the fact that teachers are not involved as supervisors. Many students visit MOOCs in the same way as popular news channels or TV broadcasts. Movies attract the attention of students as passive consumers. As soon the explanation part started students zap away.

Topic 4 Educational tools and platforms

Some partners reported that they already use tools to improve the interaction between students and lecturers, including social media. The coming survey about the use of social media in distance learning will provide more detailed information.

Ututi is a start-up at Vilnius University. It is developed as a tool to create private social networks for Universities and Colleges (http://ututi.com). Ututi is a platform for creating academic social networks. It helps engage students and teachers and improve the quality of studies. Here students and teachers can create groups online, use the mailing list for communication and the file storage for sharing information. What is more, here, teachers will create for courses information where students can access, share and comment on study materials.

FeedbackFruits is a start-up at TUDelft developing software to improve the interaction between students and teachers (http://icto.tudelft.nl/tools/feedbackfruits/). FeedbackFruits strives to improve education by providing students and lecturers with the tools that will transform the way they interact and learn. They have created an online study community that encourages students to participate in lectures and share study material to facilitate the core of education. The tools are integrated with BlackBoard, the distance learning tool at TUDelft.

MediaWiki is free server-based software, which is licensed under the GNU General Public License (GPL) (http://MediaWiki.org). Some ENT-FETCH partners used MediaWiki engine to give information for my Laboratory exercises or lectures.

Topic 5: Platforms to develop and distribute educational material

Most partners involved in developing distant-learning material used Moodle (an acronym for Modular Object-Oriented Dynamic Learning Environment) is a free software e-learning platform, also known as a Learning Management System or Virtual Learning Environment (VLE) (http://moodle.com). The designers of the MOOC course also decided to use Moodle. One of the main reasons is that Moodle is free of charge. However, compared to edX, Coursera, and other MOOC platforms, Moodle is not focused on courses developed at Universities. Instead, the focus is on courses developed at secondary schools.

Survey Research

In general, MOOCs are evaluated by questionnaires. Unfortunately, the response rate is rather low. As alternative data analytics methods are used to analyze the interaction of students with learning material. The MOOC on the flooding of Prague has been developed using the dedicated didactic learning models as presented in Figure 2. To evaluate this specific model the following controlled experiments were performed:

- **Experiments with students in Delft**. Every year, on average 500 students start their study Mathematics or Computer Science at TUDelft. A week before the lectures start about 250 students take part in a so-called introduction weekend. During that weekend there are a lot of socializing activities and information round. There are also some courses to familiarize students with academic lectures. In the last three years, learning materials from the MOOC on the flooding of Prague have been selected as one of the topics. The topic is presented to all students as a lecture by the first author of the paper. Next, the students perform one of the management assignments in small discussion groups with a tutor as a discussion leader. Students are supposed to play a role in the crisis management team and list some actions as displayed in figure 4 in order of priority. To conclude, students have to fill in a questionnaire under the supervision of tutor students. The results are displayed in Table 2. In total 685 students took part in this controlled experiment over the last three years.

- **Experiments with students in Prague**. The last three years, the first author presents a summer course for 25-30 Erasmus students at the Czech Technical University of Prague. The learning materials of the MOOC have been used as course material for the summer course. After the course, students have to fill in a questionnaire. Part of the results is displayed in Table 2.
- **Experiment with first responders in Prague**. At regular times during the year, there are training sessions for first responders in the field. These sessions are difficult to organize. For example, flooding is difficult to realize. In a digital version, flooding disasters can be simulated. It is also convenient for first responders to take the training anytime, anywhere without interrupting regular duties. The MOOC provides the facilities and is highly appreciated because of that reason. To test the MOOC sessions, a small group of responders were organized and the MOOC instructional material was used as common classroom teaching (Rothkrantz, 2018)

We validated the model in Figure 2 using exit interviews of students. Drop-off students usually receive a questionnaire to research the causality of a drop-off. However, the response to such a questionnaire is usually very low. In the try-out sessions of the MOOC on the flooding in Prague, a group of 225 students from TUDelft and the Czech Technical University in Prague. Students were selected to participate in the survey and requested to follow the MOOC. In total 183 students participated in the survey. The high number of participants was probably caused by the fact that the survey was not anonymously. The questionnaires were processed confidentially. After completion of the course, the students were requested to fill in a questionnaire with ten statements. Students were requested to give their opinion if they agree or do not agree with the statements using a 5-point Likert scale (1=disagree ... 5=agree). Table 2 shows the results of the questionnaire.

Table 2. Frequencies item response surveys in Delft and Prague

		Option				
	Items	**1**	**2**	**3**	**4**	**5**
I1	I miss the presence of peers during MOOCs	28	42	85	21	7
I2	I regularly switch to other websites during the MOOCs	19	28	58	46	32
I3	I regularly feel sleepy during the MOOCs	18	32	69	41	23
I4	I like the YouTube movies in the MOOC	8	38	54	65	18
I5	As soon mathematical formulas appear in the text, I switch to another topic	15	42	73	39	14
I6	I have problems finding the right time and location to take part in MOOC courses	12	25	98	33	15
I7	The games are very attractive for me	7	43	68	52	13
I8	MOOCs offer interesting self-study courses	8	24	109	35	9

From the table, the following was concluded:

- A majority of students prefers individual, self-paced courses. However, cooperation between students was one of the educational goals. Interaction via Forum or social media is practiced by many students in their daily life.
- As expected, many students prefer visual study material such as movies, simulations. This is also one of the innovative, attractive aspects of MOOCs.
- The internet and social media prevent students from following MOOCs.
- Students easily lose their concentration. The span of control is 10-15 minutes. Taking food, drinks or breaks is one of the attractive aspects of MOOCs but can initiate long breaks or even drop-off.

HUMAN FACTORS IN THE DIDACTIC MODEL FOR DISTANT-LEARNING

In the didactic model as displayed in Figure 2, human factors have a prominent role. This was also confirmed in the validation experiment. Human Factors can correlate with each of the different components in the model as shown in Table 3.

Since the didactical model in Figure 2 is focused on the micro-level of teaching-learning interaction, the processes on the meta and macro level are disregarded. The open-source learning environment distant-learning tool Moodle has been selected for financial reasons. Other more expensive tools as edX offer a better organization and public relation. MOOCs in the framework of edX are no longer free of charge. However, as soon as students have to pay some amount of money to take part in the course, the drop-off rate decreases. However, entrance fees limit the free access of students and exclude some students taking part in the course. On the other hand, in the development of educational material and structure of the lessons, human factors have considered explicitly.

Table 3. Components of the didactical model that correspond with the human factor

	Anatomical, Physiological, Biomechanical characteristics	Cognitive characteristics	Organizational, Environmental characteristics
Attraction			X
Activity	X		
Capabilities		X	
Self-motivation		X	
Emotion		X	
Distractor			X
Physical Resources	X		

FLOODING CRISIS MANAGEMENT GAME

In this game, students take an active part in the simulation of several flooding events. A central role in the game is played by the crisis management team composed of the mayor of the city, the head of fire-brigade, and the police officers, the medical doctors and the technicians (Figure 3). Students have to take one of the roles in the crisis management team. In the crisis game, the management team will be confronted with the daily progress of a crisis. Daily, the crisis team is provided with information of upcoming crisis events such as weather forecast, increasing the height of the water level in the river, breaches of dikes, flooded areas, collapsing bridges and houses and reports about victims and calls for help and information (Figure 4).

The game enables players to handle upcoming simulated crisis events. The events are generated by a predefined crisis event script generator. The script is based on the real-life flooding in Prague which happened in 2002. The city of Prague is situated along the Vltava River. This river is a typical rain river. In the case of heavy rains in the area of East Germany and the Western part of the Czech Republic, the water level in the Vltava River and confluent streams will raise. The water could pass the dikes and flooding has been started. To reduce the damage of flooding to people, building and infrastructure in the city of Prague several actions can be taken such as building dams of sandbags along with the river, opening dams in the water reservoirs, closing metro lines, evacuating people.

Every day the crisis management team is supposed to take some action after deliberation in the team. There are more actions than available days so the management team has to set priorities. In Figure 4 all the possible actions are displayed. It could happen that actions are conflicting with each other. Closing the metro prevents inundation of the metro line but slows down fast evacuation of people. Raising barriers and walls of sandbags along with the river delays inundation of the river quays. However, these walls prevent sightseeing and taking tourist boats from the quay. Therefore, actions have to be taken at the right time to reduce resistance from the habitants of Prague.

The crisis game is highly probabilistic. In a real crisis, people do not know what is happening the next day. Rescue actions can be up-scaled or down-scaled. However, waiting for a long time before taking some action can result in sudden flooding and result in victims and damage to building and infrastructure. It should also be stressed that members of the team have different responsibilities which could result in conflicting actions. Members of the team are supposed to start a negotiation process before taking the next action.

Figure 3. Crisis management team

Figure 4. Possible preventive actions from the crisis management team

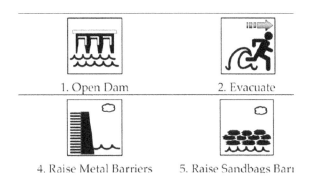

IT Sources

The key players in the crisis management game are the members of the crisis team. The crisis team is composed of the following players: major of the city (chairman of the city Council), head of the police, head of the fire brigade, medical doctor and communication officer. The crisis management game is a sequence of successive days during a virtual flooding crisis. Every day the team will be confronted with the situation on that day, the ongoing events and expected thread. The management team selects after ample deliberation an action from a list of possible actions on that day. There are conflicting actions and there is a heavy time pressure to take the right actions. To take an action the team members have access to the following IT sources:

1. **Weather predictions**. Available is the weather forecast for the next days. As usually weather forecast is highly probabilistic.
2. **Water heights**. The rise of the water of the past days is available. Via statistical tools, it is possible to compute the probable rise of the water in the coming days.
3. **Ongoing events**. Events such as flooded areas, evacuating people, accidents and incidents.
4. **Messages via crisis App**. All people in the crisis area can download a dedicated crisis app on their smartphone. Via this app, they can report in a nonverbal way by pictograms about their observations.
5. **Reports**. Officials can send reports about their observations and findings via their smartphones distributed over the whole crisis area.
6. **Smart cameras**. Across the whole city, there is a network of smart cameras. Via these cameras, it is possible to send video streams to the crisis room.
7. **Crisis information channels**. A dedicated Crisis Newspaper and crisis TV with reports of crisis events, interviews and opinions of the journalists will communicate updates of crisis events.

Human Factors

During the management game the following three human factors play an important role in the crisis team:

1. **Human anatomical, physiological and biomechanical characteristics**. Following a MOOC course for a longer time requires a lot of motivation, self-discipline, and endurance. Different from video conferencing, participants are not visible and can stay anonymously during the session. The greatest

problem is the vigilance of the participants. Fatigue, boredom or losing attention and concentration are great challenges for the successful functioning of the crisis team. Members of the crisis team are supposed to read all the updates from the communication channels and take an active part in the negotiation.

2. **Cognitive social characteristics**. A crisis team has to make decisions based on multiple heterogeneous information sources. Perception of complex situations and reasoning based on extracted features requires many cognitive abilities. However, a successful negotiation process in a team requires also a lot of social abilities of the participants. The participants to realize their goals use different negotiation strategies and dialogue models.

3. **Organizational, environmental characteristics**. Students playing a role in the crisis team are usually remote in place and time. The mayor of the city plays the role of chairman of the crisis team. His/her responsibility is that all members of the team keep involved in the decision-making process. Negotiations in the team usually take place via social media. The tool which is used for the implementation of the MOOC offers the opportunity to communicate via a digital Forum. Participants can place their statements on a blackboard. Others can comment on these statements. In the end, the crisis team has to make a conclusion or decision. The team is composed of five members so by the majority of votes the team comes always to a final decision. The crisis team should be alert to changing situations and conditions in the crisis environment. Working in a crisis team is very context-sensitive.

EVALUATION AND DISCUSSION

The goal of the paper was to research the use of Human Factors in the design, implementation, and execution of distant-learning courses. Design, implementation, and testing of MOOCs are considered as complex IT projects involving many Human Factors. A dedicated MOOC on the flooding of Prague was selected. The design of the MOOC took place in the framework of a European project ITC-FETCH. In total 67 European Universities were involved in the project. Discussion, negotiation, and taking decisions taking care of 67 partners is a complex IT-process with many involving human factors. The first test results of the MOOC make clear that students consider learning via MOOC as a completely different process compared to individually paced learning in regular classroom teaching. Planning and defining study goals, motivation, control of behavior are human factors playing an important role in completing a MOOC successfully.

In this chapter, we present some of the learning material, to give the reader a flavor of learning material involving visualization, interaction, and cooperation of participants. Cooperation between participants using social media supposed to strengthen the membership of participants to a learning community, preventing early drop-off of the MOOC. After reviewing the literature, three clusters of human factors were defined. A new didactic model was introduced, and the components of that model were related to the defined human factors. In this chapter, a MOOC was presented as an example of distant-learning. As an assignment, a management game was described as an example of interaction with student learning materials. In the design, we have considered the three clusters of human factors related to the assignment.

The second goal of this paper was to discuss different ways to reduce the high drop-off rate in distant-learning. From literature, it is known that human factors play an important role during crisis and failure of IT projects. Using a dedicated designed didactic model, we discussed possible human factors playing a role in the success or failure of an academic study. The use of attractive, visual interactive learning material was tested as one of the didactic approaches to increase the presence, involvements, and bonding of students. The first preliminary results of test experiments were promising. The MOOC is now online. It is expected that many students and civilians of the city of Prague will follow the MOOC. First responders and crisis team members are also stimulated to take part in the MOOCs. New assessment methods have been developed including surveys on the use of human factors. Next future it is expected that the validity of the introduced new concepts around human factors will be demonstrated.

REFERENCES

Boer, P., Richardson, R., & Kramer, E. (2007). On the importance of "Human Factors" and security in the organization of military defense. *Military Spectator.*, *176*(3), 121–128.

Bottema, O., & Bakker, H. (1959). *Mislukking en vertraging van de studie. Verslag van een onderzoek verricht aan de Technische Hogeschool te Delft 1953-1957 (Dutch)*. Technische Hogeschool Hogeschool Delft.

Disse, M., Nacken, H., & Mitterer, J. (2017). *Flood Risk Management*. Retrieved from https://classcentral.com › edX.

Freudenthal, H. (1973). *Mathematics as an educational task*. Springer Science & Business Media.

Gaebel. M. (2014). *MOOCs*. EUA Occasional Papers.

Gomes, A., Carmo, L., Bigotte, E., & Mendes, A. (2006). Mathematics and programming problem solving. *Third E-Learning Conference – Computer Science Education*, 1-5.

Haggard, S. (2013) *The maturing of the MOOC*. Department for Business, Innovation and Skills. Bis Research paper 130. Retrieved from http://hdl.voced.edu.au/10707/270884.September2013

Janssen, P., & de Neve, H. (1988). *Studeren en doceren aan het Hoger Onderwijs*. Leuven, Belgium: Uitgeverij Acco.

Lacante, M. (1983). Van intelligentie, persoonlijkheid, studiestrategie en studeergedrag naar studieresultaat. *Pedagogische Studiën*, *60*, 289–299.

Lewis, J. J. (2011). Human Factors Engineering. In *Encyclopedia of Software Engineering* (pp. 383–394). Taylor & Francis.

Mali, A. (2016). *Massive Open Online Courses*. EduInspire.

Oblinger, D. G. (2006) *Learning spaces*. EDUCAUSE. Retrieved from http://educause.edu/learningspaces

Osgood, C. E., Suci, G., & Tannenbaum, P. (1957). *The measurement of meaning*. Urbana, IL: University of Illinois Press.

Rothkrantz, L. J. M. (2009). E-learning in virtual environments. *Communication & Cognition, 42*(1&2), 37–52.

Rothkrantz, L. J. M. (2014) New Didactical Modals in Open and Online Learning based on Social media. *International Conference on e-Learning*, 9-18.

Rothkrantz, L. J. M. (2015a) From e-Learning to m-learning: a MOOC case study. *International Conference on e-Learning*.

Rothkrantz, L. J. M. (2015b). How Social Media Facilitate Learning Communities and Peer Groups around MOOCs. *International Journal of Human Capital and Information Technology Professionals, 6*(1), 1–13. doi:10.4018/ijhcitp.2015010101

Rothkrantz, L. J. M. (2015c). Inquiry based learning as didactic model in distant-learning. *International Journal on Information Technologies & Security, 7*(4).

Rothkrantz, L. J. M. (2016a) Didactic model for e-learning and regular courses. *International Conference on e-Learning, 15*, 156-162.

Rothkrantz, L. J. M. (2016b) Dropout rates of regular courses and MOOCs. *Proceedings of the 8th International Conference on Computer Supported Education (CSEDU)*, 9-18. 10.5220/0006811600010001

Rothkrantz, L. J. M. (2016c) Flood control of the smart city Prague. *Smart Cities Symposium Prague (SCSP)*, 1-7. 10.1109/SCSP.2016.7501043

Rothkrantz, L. J. M. (2016e) On the Use of Social Media in Distance Learning. *Proceedings of the 17th International Conference on Computer Systems and Technologies*, 347-354. 10.1145/2983468.2983514

Rothkrantz, L. J. M. (2017a) An Affective Distant-learning Model Using Avatars as User Stand-in. *Proceedings of the 18th International Conference on Computer Systems and Technologies*, 288-295. 10.1145/3134302.3134314

Rothkrantz, L. J. M. (2017b). Affective didactic models in higher education. *International Journal of Human Capital and Information Technology Professionals, 8*(4), 50–66. doi:10.4018/IJHCITP.2017100105

Rothkrantz, L. J. M. (2017c). New Didactic Models for MOOCs. *CSEDU*, 505-512.

Rothkrantz, L. J. M. (2018). Integration of MOOCs in regular courses. *Proceedings of the 19th International Conference on Computer Systems and Technologies*, 144-151.

Rothkrantz, L. J. M., & Fitrianie, S. (2018). *Public Awareness and Education for Flooding Disasters. In Crisis Management-Theory and Practice*. IntechOpen.

Sawyer, S., & Tapia, A. (2005). The sociotechnical nature of mobile computing work: Evidence from a study of policing in the United States. *International Journal of Technology and Human Interaction, 1*(3), 1–14. doi:10.4018/jthi.2005070101

Tinto, V. (1975). Dropout from Higher Education: A theoretical synthesis of recent research. *Review of Educational Research, 45*(1), 89–125. doi:10.3102/00346543045001089

Wegerif, R. (1998). The social dimension of asynchronous learning networks. *Journal of Asynchronous Learning Networks*, *2*(1), 34–49.

Wikipedia.org. (n.d.). *Inquiry-based learning*. Retrieved from https://en.wikipedia.org/wiki/Inquiry-based_learning

Wilbrink, B. (1997). Assessment in historical perspective. *Studies in Educational Evaluation*, *23*(1), 31–48. doi:10.1016/S0191-491X(97)00003-5

ENDNOTE

[1]   CTU-MOOC Flooding Management in Prague can be accessed at https://insyprojects.ewi.tudelft.nl/moodle/

Chapter 23
Employee Engagement in India:
Organizational Effectiveness, People, and Performance in IT Companies

Jitendra Singh Tomar

ⓘ https://orcid.org/0000-0003-2880-5495

Amity University, India

ABSTRACT

Rise in economy and higher global standards are making Indian organizations to develop employee-centric HR policies for optimal use of workforce. Organizations, operating in global environment, are more sophisticated, have better HR policies, leading to increased productivity through better engagements. A better engaged workforce has improved the bottom lines of these companies significantly. This study explores employee engagement factors by recording perception of 500 employees serving 10 prime business sectors in India and compares the engagement antecedents in these sectors. Thematic analysis is done on identified themes: insightful work, pragmatic management, positive work environment, growth opportunity, and engaging leadership. These significant factors are visualized specifically for IT sector. By resolving the engagement issues raised in this study, it is anticipated that the employers can address overall efficiency of their workforce and improve the employer-employee relationship.

INTRODUCTION

The human asset is a key component of any organization and is core to its competitiveness and success. Organizations are incorporating new HR practices to address the critical matters on job performance, task performance, organizational citizenship behaviour, productivity, discretionary effort, affective commitment, and continuance commitment of its manpower and keep the employees engaged. The investment in people is one key area that lean organizations focuses on (Maskell, Baggaley, and Grasso, 2011).

The high levels of employee engagement translate into retention of talent, foster customer loyalty, and improve organizational performance and stakeholder value (Lockwood, 2007). The effective employee engagements drive increase productivity, profits, and customer satisfaction for the organization

DOI: 10.4018/978-1-7998-1279-1.ch023

(Harter, Schmidt, & Hayes, 2002; Siddhanta & Roy, 2012), it also stems to make employees happier, more satisfied, and more fulfilled, and want to remain with the organisation (Adejoh and Adejoh, 2013).

Organizations are emphasizing on use their employee's talents, knowledge, skills, and vigour (Bodankin and Tziner, 2009). Knowing the engagement level of the workforce within the enterprise can be the foundation for organizational change and on-going success (Havill, 2010). This enables the organizations to pick the competency of their human asset and ensure that the manpower is employed in their precise roles and are cognitively, emotionally and behaviourally invested in their jobs (Dalas, Lam, Weiss, Weich, and Hulin, 2009).

Agile organizations are the outcome of engaged employees. Novel information flows in the organization and engaged workers proactively modify their work environment in order to stay engaged (Baker, 2011). Organizations are realizing that advancements cannot be fruitful without wilful involvement and engagement of employees. Concepts like Organizational Citizenship Behaviour (OCB) have surfaced advocating that efficiency and productivity lie within the employees' ability and commitment.

The organizations are solicitous about their employees and invest considerable resource to improve employee engagement (Xu & Thomas, 2011) and prioritize employee training, involvement, and empowerment (Maskell, Baggaley, and Grasso, 2011). The resources invested are reckoned necessary for development of the organization (Brás and Rodrigues, 2007). The investment is pivotal for business growth as well as for serving competitive advantage (Balfour and Wechsler, 1996). The organizations are automating the HRM modules and are investing in Employee Information Management Systems (EIMS) to effectively manage employee information (Oduh, Misra, Robertas, and Rytis, 2018) for better analysis and pass the benefits to them.

Employee engagement could lead to vital job creation in Asian countries (Gallup, 2013) like India. Employee engagement is higher in double-digit growth companies which are exceeding average industry revenue growth (Markos & Sridevi, 2010). For a developing country like India with good economic growth prospective, the organizations could increase their competitive advantage with affective human asset policies and contribute towards holistic growth of economy (Ellis and Sorensen, 2007).

Definition: Employee Engagement

The concept is contextually defined and there is no single guideline on the subject matter. Employee engagement is more associated with the JD-R (Job Demand – Resource) model which divulges that resource requirements are based on job demands and support available to the employee (Karasek et al., 1998). The contextual paradigm is also supported by the studies carried out by (Freeney & Fellenz, 2013; Kühnel, Sonnentag, & Bledow, 2012; Menguc et al., 2013; Wang et al., 2013). Engagement is considered as emotional, physical and cognitive connexion of employees with their profession. It is the dedication and vigour of the employees towards their work (Schaufeli et al., 2002). Employee engagement is a multidimensional approach that is based on various factors or drivers leading to satisfaction of employees (Saks, 2006).

Employee engagement is "a positive attitude held by the employee towards the organization and its value. An engaged employee is aware of business context, and works with colleagues to improve performance within the job for the benefit of the organization (Jenkins and Delbridge, 2013). The organization must work to develop and nurture engagement, which requires a two-way relationship between employer and employee" (Robinson et al., 2004). It is the level of employee's commitment and involvement with their organization and its values (Sadique, 2014).

Employee engagement is different from employee satisfaction and merely satisfaction does not help in retaining the best and brightest talent (Fernandez, 2007). Engagement refers to passion and willingness of an employee to commit him for the success of the organization which is beyond satisfaction (Macey & Schnieder, 2008). The job engagement vanguards the organizational performance, job satisfaction is a part of it. It is an employee's gist of purpose, personal initiative, effort, and persistence directed towards organizational goals (Soni, 2013). Employee satisfaction and OCB cannot be taken as independent attributes of human resource management and are integral part of employee engagement (Robinson et al, 2004).

Employee Engagement: Benefits

There are multifarious benefits of investing in employee engagement. Engagement is a positive experience (Schaufeli et al., 2006) which impacts employee productivity (Lockwood, 2007). The top performing employees are highly engaged and have long tenures (Levinson, 2007) and this figure is almost 85% (Blessing White, 2008). Engaged employees are determined, proactive, committed and their self-efficacy is an outcome of their engagement (Seijts & Crim, 2006). Higher employee engagement impacts business success since employee engagement, customer satisfaction, productivity, and profit are correlated (Harter et al., 2002). Higher engagement leads to higher productivity, customer satisfaction, and sales (Hewitt Associates, 2004). Engaged employees promote the organization and its product & services, better understand the customer needs (Right Management, 2006), and create loyal customers (Levinson, 2007). Higher customer loyalty is seen in the organizations having better engagement practices (Pont, 2004) and has its proven links to bottom line results.

Feeling valued and involved translates into accrued benefits for the organization by reducing absenteeism (Cohen, 1993; Barber et al., 1999), employee turnover (Cohen, 1991), intention to leave (Balfour and Wechsler, 1996), and intention to search for alternative employers (Cohen, 1993). On the other hand, it leashes upsurge in job performance (Mathieu and Zajac, 1990), job satisfaction (Vandenberg and Lance, 1992), business outcomes such as revenues (Barber et al., 1999), productivity (Harter et al., 2002; Arrowsmith & Parker, 2013), and profit (Harter et al., 2002; Maslach, 2011; Schaufeli et al., 2002; Markos and Sridevi, 2010). It also mutates return to shareholders (Walker Information Inc., 2000) such as customer satisfaction (Harter et al., 2002; Brown and Lam, 2008; Gonring, 2008).

A valued employee exhibits progressive attitude, takes pride, and preaches high about the organization (Ologbo and Saudah, 2011), directly and indirectly promotes his organization and its products within his social groups reflecting his belief in the organization and its services (Mochama, 2013), feels enabled and builds two way rapport (Reissner and Pagan, 2013), behave magnanimously, develops a better camaraderie with fellow beings, and build good teams (Viljevac, Cooper-Thomas, and Saks, 2012), is committed beyond the job description, understand larger requirements on macro level, and is willing to help organization voluntarily (Freeney and Fellenz, 2013).

Employee engagement, good orientation, and citizenship behavior bestows better individual performances and organization's comprehensive well-being (Jose and Mampilly, 2012). An engaged employee is enthusiastic about the work and workplace (Bui, Hodge, Shackelford, and Acsell, 2011), trust the organization (Catteeuw, 2007), serves actively for better organizational transformations (Alfes, Shantz, Truss, and Soane, 2013), exhibit better interpersonal knacks being respectful to associates and assist them in performing better (Arrowsmith and Parker, 2013), can be believed upon (Jenkins and Delbridge, 2013).), goes beyond the requirements of the job (Kühnel, Sonnentag,, and Bledow, 2012), deem organization higher than his personal motives (Townsend, Wilkinson, and Burgess, 2014), relates with the organization (Aladwan, Bhanugopan, and Fish, 2013), update his skill set to latest (Reissner and Pagan, 2013), and avail prospects to augment organizational performance (Francis, Ramdhony, Reddington, and Staines, 2013).

Effective application of drivers of employee engagement induce equal levels of engagement and satisfaction in work and life roles of an employee (Greenhaus, Collins, & Shaw, 2003) establishing a Work Life Balance (WLB). WLB perceives work and life as separate fields fulfilling two different but essential needs of an individual (Clark, 2000). Through application of engagement attributes, organizations make sure that individuals give equivalent amounts of time, get psychologically involved, and attain identical levels of role-related satisfaction in both work and life (Hill et al., 2007). Since substantial investment of resources is needed for implementation of these attributes as part of work-life initiative (Fegley, 2007), the effectiveness of these attributes is of great concern to the organizations (Morris, Heames, & McMillan, 2011; Morris, Storberg-Walker, & McMillan et al., 2009). A successful work-life initiative endures strategic value and results in managing employee absenteeism (Madsen, 2003) and turnover intentions (Batt & Valcour, 2003), enhances employee job satisfaction (Derry, 2008), increase the employee commitment (Harpern, 2005), improves firm productivity (Bloom, Kretschmer, & Van Reenen, 2009), enhances organizational success (Kossek & Friede, 2006; Morris et al., 2009), and results in boosted interests of stakeholders (Konrad & Mangel, 2000; Perry-Smith & Blum, 2000).

A better work-life balance influences creativity and innovation in an organization enabling them to withstand a competitive edge in the market (Debruyne, Moenaert, Griffin, Hart, Hultink, & Robben, 2002; Dewett & Jones, 2001; Greve & Taylor, 2000; Thompson, 2003). The creativity and innovation bring strategic advantage to an organization by playing a vital role in its profitability (Eisenhardt & Tabrizi, 1995; Geroski, Machin, & Van Reenen, 1993). A creative manpower impacts important crucial aspects of organizational functioning such as organization planning (Mumford, Bedell-Avers, & Hunter, 2008), teamwork, collaboration, and organization citizenship behavior (Ayers, Dahlstrom, & Skinner, 1997; McGourty, Tarshis, & Dominick, 1996) increased job satisfaction (Amabile, Schatzel, Moneta, & Kramer, 2004), and effective crisis management (Tushman & O'Reilly, 1996). Creativity is an outcome of satisfied manpower and functions as a determinant to innovative behaviors in organizations (Amabile, Conti, Coon, Lazenby, & Herron, 1996; Mumford, Hester, & Robledo, 2012). Work–life initiatives stimulate employee creativity and assist organizations in laying successful business strategies. As acknowledged by modern organizations, creativity is deemed as a valuable asset contributing to organization's success (McLean, 2005; Shalley & Gilson, 2004). Fulfilment of engagement attributes is foreseen as a key business strategy by organizations to progress in the competitive arena (Bakker, 2011).

Drivers of Employee Engagement

Research shows that committed employees perform better and it is beneficial for the organisations to understand the drivers of engagement. There are plenteous facets of working life that are intensely correlated with engagement levels. Involvement in decision making, freedom to ideate and the appreciation & credence given to their views, opportunities for job enhancement, organization's concern for employees' health and wellbeing, are vital eccentricities that drive the engagement (Robinson, Perryman, and Hayday, 2004).

Most researches advocates the non-financial drivers impacting employee engagement. As social being, human resource is not motivated by money alone (Grawitch, Gottschalk, and Munz, 2006). Employees prefer to work in the organizations in which they find meaning at work. Once basic aspirations are fulfilled, employees look to align value-meaning leading to true connection with the organization (Penna, 2007). The opportunity to feed their views and opinions upwards is one of the most important drivers of people's engagement (CIPD, 2006). Almost two third's (60%) of the employees seek opportunities for advancement in their profession (BlessingWhite, 2006). Opportunity to voice the decision and address of employees' well-being are identified as important factors for engagement (Towers Perrin Talent Report, 2003).

The personal attributes and organizational context plays a key role in employee engagement (Townsend, Wilkinson, and Burges, 2014). A person having knowledge, skills, abilities, temperament, attitudes and personality must be supported by affective HR practices, physical and social setting, and leadership in the organization to yield maximum from an employee (Vance, 2006). The employee engagement is intimately allied to the organizational practices. The employees working in a friendly and amiable environment feel more engaged (Clifton, 2008). Organizations those can align efforts with strategy, empower the employees, build effective teams, enable people to develop, and give recognition to its employees have more congenial setup and have highly engaged workforce (DDI, 2005).

Job satisfaction, family friendliness, co-operation, health and safety, pay and benefits, equal opportunities and fair treatment, communication, performance appraisal, immediate management, and T&D and career are the drivers of engagement from low importance to high importance, refer Figure 1, which makes the employees feel valued and involved (Robinson, Perryman, and Hayday, 2004).

The non-financial drivers also motivate the employees to prefer a workplace that fulfils their aspirations (Penna, 2007). The opportunity to feed their views upwards (CIPD, 2006), advancement in the profession (Blessing White, 2006), opportunity to voice decisions, and well-being (Saks, 2006) are important engagement factors. Similar non-financial engagement drivers are advocated in engagement model by IES (Robinson, et. al., 2004), refer Figure 2.

The positive commitment of employees is based on trust in management, work satisfaction, involvement in decision-making, employee relations, salary, and Job challenge (Kersley at. el., 2006). Feeling engaged is feeling valued, which upsurges the self-belief and involvement of employees and pays astounding dividends (Wintner, 2010). Organizational culture and commitment impacts the important drivers. Say, Stay, and Strive – the 3S are the three engagement predictors (Hewitt, 2004) whereas Connect, Career, Clarity, Convey, Control, Congratulate, Contribute, Collaborate, Credibility & Confidence are 10 quality 'C' engagement factors (Seijit, 2006). Based on the minutiae, engagement drivers are categorized in three dimensions i.e. intellectual engagement, affective engagement, and social engagement (ACAS, 2010).

Figure 1. The drivers of employee engagement, (Source: Robinson et. al., 2004)

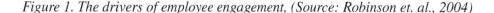
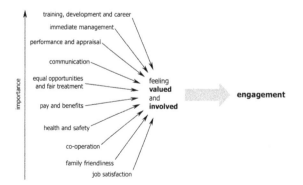

Figure 2. The engagement model, (Source: Robinson et. al. 2004)

Engagement Parameters: Impact on Individual and Organizational Proficiency

Training, Development, and Career - Organizations are focusing on Perceived Investment in Employees' Development (PIED). The investment in human resource is critical for organization's success (Ferris et al., 1999). The employee development brings positivity in their attitude and behavior affecting organizational outcomes (Wintner, 2010; Kular, Gatenby, Rees, Soane, and Truss, 2008). The organizations are keen on employees' training and development as it will not only improves the skill set but also increases loyalty, job satisfaction, and intent to stay longer (Costen and Salazar, 2011). The quality training programs results in higher satisfaction and reduced turnover (Choi and Dickson, 2009). Effective training leads to 0.6% increase in productivity and a 0.3% increase in hourly efficiency (Christian, Garza, and Slaughter, 2011). The commitment of employee is based on his judgement of organizational efforts in providing him the training (Jenkins and Delbridge, 2013). Organizations are inducing AI based trainings for comprehensive development of its employees. The benefits of using AI based training tools are already known in academia (Ikedinachi, Misra, Assibong, Olu-Owolabi, Maskeliunas, & Damasevicius, 2019). The organizations are adopting persuasive technologies and using techniques like gamification to impact people's behaviour, motivate them, engage them, and impact work environment (Herranz et. al., 2015).

Immediate Management - Management and its relationship with employees play a vital role in positively connecting employees to the organization (Barber et al, 1999). A manager is a key to an engaged work force (Harter, Schmidt, and Hayes, 2002). Better commitments are exhibited by employees having improved association with their immediate managers (Green et al., 1996). The healthier relationship contributes to better motivation at work (CIPD, 2001), and is a significant element in fortifying individual performance (Settoon et al, 1996). The immediate management's positive behavior, visage, and higher effectiveness results in better organizational performance (Luthans, Avey, Avolio, Norman, and Combs, 2006). The managers are in continuous dialect with the subordinates which ensure effective planning and support organizational goals (Cano, Fernández-Sanz, and Misra, 2013). Enigmatically, the employee trust higher level management which connects directly to lower strata of employees surpassing mid management (Freeney and Fellenz, 2013).

Performance Appraisal - Performance appraisal is one of the most important and critical HR practice that directly affects the positivity in organization manpower (Gupta and Kumar, 2012). Organizations constitute effective and transparent appraisal system for valuing their employees resulting in improved organizational performance (DeNisi and Pritchard, 2006; Gorning, 2008; Xu & Thomas, 2011). The quality of the performance appraisal process transmutes in organizational commitment, better work satisfaction, and less intent to leave the job (Shantz, Alfes, Truss, and Soane, 2013).

Communication - The interpersonal connect through open communications among the stakeholders leads to engagement in employees [CIPD, 2006). The camaraderie with the higher management and with equals assures less deviance (Christopher and Tanwar, 2012). Employees who are less sceptic about organization's policy matter feel more engaged. They are unlikely to get indulged in negativity due to better dialogue (Perrin, 2003; BlessingWhite, 2008). Organizations that support two way communications and permits employee to voice their suggestions and ideas, gain trust of employees (Ellis and Sorensen, 2007). This enables internal co-operation among various levels, departments, and stakeholders (Dernovsek, 2008). An engaged employee believes in the management's effectiveness and expect open and clear communication with all levels of the organization (Salanova, Agut, and Peiro, 2005).

Equal opportunities and fair treatment – The more people feel that organizations implement policies in a fair way, more they perceive fair promotional opportunities (Schaufeli, Bakker, and Van Rhenen, 2009). There is a visible relationship between performance appraisal fairness and engagement (Gupta and Kumar, 2012). Employee perception of unfair treatment is strengthened during role change, structural changes, and cost-cutting (Kontakos and Stepp, 2007) and organizations need to be transparent during organizational changes (Havill, 2010). If appreciated and fairly treated, employees tend to willingly engage with organizations (Costen and Salazar, 2011). If an organization is viewed as equal opportunity employer, it will comprise of highly engaged workforce (Choi and Dickson, 2009). The successful organizations face less deviances since employees experience fair treatment (Alfes et at., 2013), work in environment which impedes harassment and bullying (Xu and Thomas, 2011), experience no demographical discrimination (Green et al., 1996), have equal opportunities of internal promotions (Pandey & Sharma, 2016), and have equal rights (Kersley et. al, 2006). The equality of opportunity inculcates a positive feeling in an employee resulting in firm's efficacy (Hartog and Belschak, 2012).

Pay and benefits – One of the reasons for an employee's belief on organization is economic safety (WU and Lebreton, 2011). Pay and employment relationship is viewed as variables having mutual dependence (Yıldıza and Alpkan, 2015). A good pay package and periodical appreciation is considered as an essential act by an employee towards appreciating him (Coffman, 2005). The employees commit more, exert better efforts, and perform better when recognized, praised, and rewarded through better pay cheques (Kinsey, 2009). The bottom line in "Hierarchy of engagement" model analogous to Maslow's "Need hierarchy" model which states that pay and benefits are the basic needs (Penna, 2007). Once the basic is met, employee seeks development opportunities such as trainings, promotion, and rise to leadership position (Redman, 2011). There after employee aligns value meaning to his work by feeling connected, intuit purpose in his work, and create a better organization (Markos and Sridevi, 2010).

Health and Safety – Ergonomics plays a vital role in engaging an employee (Jose and Mampilly, 2012). The organizations which emphasize on health and safety, address risk factors and health hazards, maintain high security standards, and comply to regulations and laws are trusted more resulting in highly efficient environment (Wefald, and Downey, 2009). An effective organization addresses safety of its employees and equipment (Nelson, Macik-Frey, and Quick, 2007), lay down its safety policy with definite objective (Cortina, Magley, Williams, and Langhout, 2001), makes employee more secure and confident, raising the efficacy standards (Poyner and Warne, 1988). Employees working in a risk-free and "Zero accident" work environment tend to be more engaged (Havill, 2010). An organization that is considered better by its employees provide better physical working environment, clean working environment, health and safety training, quality of equipment, occupational health services, and security at the workplace (Langelaan, Bakker, Schaufeli, Van Rhenen, and Van Doornen, 2006) and hence experience better employee engagement.

Cooperation - Effective co-operation within the organization is a key to happy employment and better organization (Rotundo and Sackett, 2002). A cohesive cooperation among various departments and between distinct teams results is better camaraderie and employee satisfaction (DeRue and Morgeson, 2007). Employee feel more secured due to ease of dialog between trade unions and management resulting in more effective organization (Gravenkemper, 2007). In addition, employees trust the organizations where management and trade unions work in tandem to address the tribulations through joint staff committee (Ahmad and Omar, 2013). The trust of employee is sturdier due to effective collaboration and support among the departments which results in better cooperation and performance (Barsade, 2002), making the organization more agile and provides satisfaction to the employees (Arrowsmith and Parker, 2013).

Family friendliness – A family friendly policy addresses the work-life balance equation, reduces the workplace stress, and increases the engagement levels (Grawitch et.al., 2006). The affective organizational commitment is justified by availability of family-responsive benefits (Akgunduz, Bardakoglu, and Alkan, 2015). The organizations offering family benefits are rated as highly caring organizations by the employees and understood as providing them social security to an extent (Casademunt, Cabrera, and Molina, 2015). Such benefits, perceived as rewards, increase the commitment and inculcate higher satisfaction levels in employees (Jaggi and Bahl, 2016).

Job Satisfaction – Job satisfaction is a significant constituent of commitment (Biswas and Bhatnagar, 2013). Job satisfaction is positively connected to employee performance (Goel, Gupta, and Rastogi, 2013) and generates positive outcome. Organizations that provide better job satisfaction have better fit policies (Bakker, 2011), make the work environment enjoyable and stimulate better growth of its employees (Kristof-Brown and Guay, 2011). Job satisfaction is a prime cause of performance and organizational commitment (Jose and Mampilly, 2012) and results in improvement in service quality (Snipes et al, 2005). A satisfied employee understands that his job is a versatile task, with lot of variance, and poses him a challenge which he accepts (Sand, Cangemi, and Ingram, 2011). Job satisfaction inculcates a strong feeling of accomplishment in an employee bestowing him with pleasure and feeling of belongingness (Chen et. al, 2016) which benefit the organization.

Economy: A Vital Impact on Employee Engagement

The economy is influential in shaping employee attitudes toward work and the work–life interface. The economic conditions influence employee attitudes such as job satisfaction, employee engagement, and work–life balance. These attitudes influence their responses to managerial actions as well as their decisions to remain invested in an organization (Harrison, Newman and Roth, 2006). A better understanding of employee attitude results in effective management of employee well-being, making well-informed HRM decisions, and managing organizations effectively (Rich, Lepine and Crawford, 2010).

The strength of economy as well as changes in economic indicators influences job satisfaction and work–life balance. Impact of a strong economy on job satisfaction and work life balance are opposite. A strong economy leads to higher job satisfaction and lower work-life balance as employees are more focused on prospective career opportunities resulting in unintended, negative consequences for work–life balance (Gareis, Barnett, Ertel, & Berkman, 2009). In a weak economy, employees might recalibrate their expectations for work–life balance and invest more in personal and work roles (Michel, Kotrba, Mitchelson, Clark, and Baltes, 2010).

Organizations experience that effectiveness of programs designed to enhance employee attitudes could be increased by especially considering macroeconomic conditions (Stephen, 2008). Further, these macro-economic conditions could lead to change in job satisfaction and WLB even without any change in policies. An understanding of economic conditions and its impact on employee attitudes may result in development of appropriate assessment tools for employees as their behaviour is influenced by external environment to that of an organization (Purvi and Schmidt).

India is the 6th fastest growing economy in the world after US, China, Japan, Germany, and UK with a GDP of $2.61 Trillion, is projected to grow at 7.1 per cent in fiscal year 2020, and is expected to be a 5 Trillion economy by 2024 (WESP, 2019). The work culture in India is expected to improve amidst growth of economy but the pace will be slow. The prime reason of this offset is that Indian organizations are majorly MSMEs that employ more than 85% of Indian workforce (Pachouri and Sharma, 2016). These are small sized organizations with a workforce which generally lack in education, competency, and higher incomes (Sudan, 2005). In times of economic downturn, the lack of maturity in small sized organizations may lead to organizational imbalance resulting in dissatisfied employees (Moen, 1999). These economic downturns may be fatal to such organizations as they take higher time to revive out of the crisis during which they also focus less on employee satisfaction attributes (Singh, Garg, Suresh & Deshmukh, 2008).

On the other hand, employees of large organizations tend be more educated and to have higher income than employees of small- and medium sized employers (Rathod, 2007). IT companies in India are majorly big players sourcing with Fortune 500 and Global 2000 corporations from developed economies. Indian IT companies have set up over 1,000 global delivery centres in about 80 countries and are leading sourcing destinations across the world accounting for approximately 55% market share of the USD 185-190 billion global services sourcing business in 2017-18. By 2020, this sector is expected to reach USD 225 billion target (IBEF, 2019). The Indian IT companies inherit the work culture from their international clients and have more organized HR policies. In addition, the Indian IT organizations have skill full and intellectual workforce which is handsomely paid, update their competency, and have better prospects as compared to their counter parts in other Indian Industries (Kummamuru and Murthy, 2016). The Indian multinationals are having identical culture to that of Indian IT organizations where satisfactions levels of employees are higher. In totality, these IT organizations and multinationals are served by less than 15% of the total Indian workforce limiting beneficial HR policies only to this segment of workforce (Thakur, 2012). Majorly the HR policies in Indian organizations are not at par with the world standards resulting in less committed workforce as per the standards given by Gallup (2010).

Employee Engagement Practices in India

On the onset, India is very resilient in implementation of regulations as major businesses in India are unregulated and unorganized (The Joint Committee of Industry and Government, 2013). India had been building its economy since its independence and has seen frequent and drastic changes in its setup due to global changes (Shanumugam and Krishnaveni, 2012). The environmental changes impacts Indian organizations and they rebuild their structures, setups, technology, and people mind set (Mishra, Kapse, and Bavad, 2013). The employee welfare in business organizations has lagged, prime focus being to settle first in ever changing scenario (Kumar and Swetha, 2011). The employee engagement parameters are either not understood or gets neglected in growing organizations (Luthans, Youssef, and Avolio, 2007). Also being culture dynamic country, the meanings and methods of employee engagement are quite varied and get overlooked sometimes (Soni, 2003). The complex culture in India binds investment, markets, organizations, people, technology, and trade (Friedman, 2007). Change in economy is impacting the culture and vice versa, leading to changes in organizations (Cojocaru, 2011). In such unsure environments, where the engagement policies are missing, the self-commitment of employees in Indian organizations is an outcome of inner psychological state (Goel, Gupta, and Rastogi, 2013). In Indian organizations, the Psychological Capital is very strong and is basis for employee commitment and organizational success.

Indian organization having global presence review their employee engagement practices frequently and constitute effective employee centric HR policies, but to an extent (Bhasin, 2010). The employees in India have less clarity on their formal and informal roles, definite work profiles, and job description (Thakur, 2012). This is true with organizations across the sectors in India. Employees in private hospitals in India strongly opine about improper recognition they receive in their organization (Swaminathan and Aramvalarthan, 2013). Private banks in India lack in effective communication to and from employees resulting in less engaged manpower having weak psychological empowerment (Sarangee and Srivastava, 2012; Jose and Mamphilly, 2014). Indian PSUs reflect five engagement factors namely meaningful task, recognition and support, motivation and cooperation, feedback and opportunity, and career development & growth to be addressed (Singh and Sanjeev, 2013).

The Indian organizations have shown significant reduction in level of employee engagement (Balakrishnan and Masthan, 2013). The key driver that is identified for lower engagement levels is the internal communication (Pandey and David, 2013). Employees are cynic about organization and its policy matter, and indulge in negativity due to poor dialogue (Desai, Majumdar, and Prabhu, 2010) hampering the efficacy of the organization (Perrin, 2003; BlessingWhite, 2008). Organization supporting two way communications permitting employee to voice their suggestions and ideas develops trust within organization (Ellis and Sorensen, 2007) but lack of the same is witnessed in Indian organizations which remain closed with dialogue to and from management and employees (Kotni, 2011), thus face less engagement levels. Indian retail sectors reports high productivity due to training and skill enhancements of their frontline workers (Handa and Gulati, 2014). The Indian IT sector reflects on relationship among the fairness in performance appraisal and level of engagement (Thakur, 2014). This dimension is also true with other industries in India revealing significant relationship among employee engagement and performance appraisal (Gupta and Kumar, 2013). IT sector being more organized show better engagement trends compared to other sectors in India. IT, healthcare, Engineering, media, tourism, retail, infrastructure, telecommunication, education, and banking sectors are rated from high to low in order of their engagement practices in India (Tomar, 2017a).

The engagement policies in Indian SMEs sector are much more alarming. Indian SME sector employees more than 85% of working population but their contribution towards growth in economy is very limited (Tomar, 2017b). The prominent reason behind these figures is considered to be employee inefficiency (Jose and Mampilly, 2012). The reason is lack of knowledge and skill, inappropriate skill utilization, and no intent to upgrade the same (Soni, 2013). The SMEs needs to replicate the policies of MNC in best interest of employees, improve two-way communication, do various fit mappings, provide comfortable work environment, provide skill enhancement opportunities to employees, establish reward mechanism, built a working culture, and assign the accountability at all levels to upsurge business performance (Gummadi and Devi, 2013). In addition, these establishments have high central management control which needs decentralization offering more freedom for decision making (Sadique, 2014). The employees with over 10 years of association with these SMEs feel more engaged (Goel, Gupta, and Rastogi, 2013) and survive without skill update, bringing stagnation to self and organization (Bhasin, 2010).

In Indian organization, employee engagement has acted as a mediator variable between Perceived Organizational Support (POS) and Person – Organization fit (P-O fit). POS and P-O fit, as antecedents to organizational commitment and job satisfaction, affect the employee engagement and display higher degree of correlation among organizational commitment and job satisfaction (Biswas &Bhatnagar, 2013).

OBJECTIVE OF THE STUDY

The important articles reviewed in this research have emphasised on various determinants / predictors / antecedents of employee engagement. The reviewed articles were accessed from 'Google Scholar' and 'EBSCO' database. To explore the literature on employee engagement practices in various business sectors, EBSCO database was searched. The search using 'Employee Engagement' keyword ceded 6327 articles. The voluminous number got further reduced with sector specific search extracting 39 articles in Aviation, 102 articles in Banking & Financial Service, 31 articles in IT, 29 articles in Insurance, 52 articles in retail, 36 articles in Tourism, 38 articles in Media and Entertainment, 76 articles in Healthcare, 48 articles in Logistics, 76 articles in Telecommunication Sector.

Even though the engagement practices in various organizations in these sectors had been studied by researchers, literature on how these organizations differ in applying engagement practices was in scarce. The articles rarely compared the engagement practices in various organizations. Even if they did, the comparison was limited to enterprises in the same sector.

This research intends to do a study on employee engagement practices in various companies in distinct but prominent business sectors in India. It aims at:

1. Comparing employee engagement practices in organizations of IT sector vis-à-vis organizations of other sectors in India,
2. Assessment of employee engagement attributes in IT software companies in India.

METHODOLOGY

Sample and Procedure

Keeping in view the current economic scenario in India, 10 sectors namely Aviation, Banking & Financial Service, Information Technology, Insurance, Retail, Tourism, Media and Entertainment, Healthcare, Logistics, and Telecommunication Sector were chosen for the study based on the predicted growth prospects, and their domineering role in growth of Indian Economy (Economictimes, 2019).

Edifying meetings were held with the management of various organizations in these sectors and 05 organizations from each of the 10 sectors were chosen. The IT organizations chosen for the study were mainly into software services. The organizations chosen in Banking and Financial Services were from

Private Sector. Also, 10 employees from each organization participated in the study; hence final sample consisted of 500 employees. Of the respondents, 29.8% (n=149) were female and 70.2% (n=351) were male.

The mean age of respondents was 34.8 years. Also, of the respondents, 38.2% (n=191) had work experience of below 05 years, 29.6% (n=148) had 06-10 years of experience, 19.2% (n=96) had 11-15 years of experience, 8.4% (n=39) had 16-20 years' experience, and 5.2% (n=26) had worked for over 20 years. 71.6% (n=358) respondents were engaged at the decision making levels whereas 28.4% (n=142) were working at non-decision making levels. The employees were chosen with convenience and judgement. In case an employee experienced distress in participating, another employee with similar profile was chosen from same organization.

A questionnaire was administered to the sample employees. The riposte administration consumed ~15 minutes. The questionnaire was sent to the respondents through mail and Google Forms link. The anonymity and confidentiality of the collected information was assured to the sample. The survey was conducted during January 20196 to March 2019.

Instruments

The 'Employee Engagement Survey' scale was developed in discussion with two groups. The first group comprised of HR Managers from 10 organizations i.e. 01organization from each chosen sectors. The second group included 05 HR professors. Deliberations by the group members were made on various engagement drivers swotted in reviewed literature. Grounded theory (Glaser & Strauss, 1967) was used to classify the engagement drivers after developing a consensus among the group members. The classified categories were 'Insightful Work', 'Pragmatic Management', 'Positive Work Environment', 'Growth Opportunity', and 'Engaging Leadership', which both groups considered as prime engagement attributes.

A questionnaire to be administered by sample employees was designed consisting of above mentioned 05 engagement attributes. The Questionnaire comprised of 20 items i.e. 04 items each for 05 classified attributes. The responses of participants were recorded on a 7 point Likert scale with anchors 1-Highly Disagree, 2-Moderately Disagree, 3-Slightly Disagree, 4-Neutral, 5-Slightly Agree, 6-Moderately Agree, and 7-Highly Agree where 1 was the lowest and 7 was the highest score. These items are presented in the Appendix.

A pilot study was conducted with 20 employees working across 10 chosen sectors. The reliability of the questionnaire was measured using Cronbach's alpha which yielded a score of 0.73. The internal consistencies (Cronbach's alphas) for 'Insightful Work', 'Pragmatic Management', 'Positive Work Environment', 'Growth Opportunity', and 'Engaging Leadership' scales were 0.76, 0.85, 0.81, 0.78, and 0.71 respectively. The instrument met the acceptable level of reliability and was considered suitable for use in current study.

Data Aggregation

Aggregated measure of engagement attributes as variables was done using ICC (1) which yielded average value of 0.33 ranging across 0.39 for 'Positive Work Environment' to 0.24 for 'Engaging Leadership.' The other values were 0.38 for 'Insightful Work', 0.38 for 'Pragmatic Management', and 0.29 for 'Growth Opportunity.' All ICC (1) values adhere to the recommended value of 0.12 (James, 1982).

Also, the average ICC (2) value was 0.79 ranging from 0.92 for 'Insightful Work' to 0.71 for 'Engaging Leadership.' All the attributes cohere to the criteria of 0.60 (Glick, 1985). Multivariate analysis of variance was applied to analyse the significant differences in the engagement practices among 10 chosen sectors. All 05 attributes were included in the analysis. Multivariate result F = 3.61, p < 0.001indicated that the sectors differed significantly on these attributes.

ANALYSIS AND RESULT

The participant's views on employee engagement practices in their respective organizations were recorded. The responses were received from 500 employees and reliability was tested by applying Cronbach's Alpha which yielded a score of 0.79 from the instrument. The score was similar to that of pilot study and was within the acceptable reliability range. The internal consistencies (Cronbach's alphas) for 'Insightful Work', 'Pragmatic Management', 'Positive Work Environment', 'Growth Opportunity', and 'Engaging Leadership' were 0.87, 0.80, 0.88, 0.74, and 0.70 respectively and fall in the acceptable range. There were no populations to compare this sample since no other study has done the comparative analysis of engagement practices in organizations of chosen sectors. MANOVA was applied to explore if employees in chosen sectors differ on 05 engagement attributes. The obtained multivariate result of F = 3.17 indicated a non-significant Wilks's Lambda. There was no significant difference among the employees of 10 selected sectors on the engagement attributes.

Table 1 shows mean values, standard deviations, and internal consistencies. The data reflects that engagement dimensions (Attributes) were positively interrelated (r = 0.39).

Comparison of employee engagement practices in IT software organisations vis-à-vis organizations in other prominent growth sectors in India.

The data collected through 20 item instrument from 500 employees across 10 sectors was analysed to weigh employee engagement practices in organizations of these sectors in India. Participants specified their responses on a 7 point Likert scale with anchors 1-Highly Disagree, 2-Moderately Disagree, 3-Slightly Disagree, 4-Neutral, 5-Slightly Agree, 6-Moderately Agree, and 7-Highly Agree where 1 was the lowest and 7 was the highest score. Therefore, the minimum cumulative possible score from a respondent was 20 if all 20 items in the instrument were given the lowest score of 1. Similarly, the maximum cumulative score possible was 140 if a respondent gives highest score of 7 to all 20 items in a questionnaire.

Table 1. Means, standard deviations, and internal consistencies

Variable	M	SD	Alpha	1	2	3	4	5
1. Insightful work	3.59	0.69	0.81	-				
2. Pragmatic Management	3.67	0.62	0.78	0.52****	-			
3. Positive Work Environment	4.08	0.76	0.83	0.55****	0.59****	-		
4. Growth Opportunity	4.99	0.48	0.79	0.23****	0.25***	0.27****	-	
5. Engaging Leadership	4.42	0.89	0.73	0.44****	0.29****	0.39****	0.36****	-
*p < 0.10, **p < 0.05, ***p < 0.01, ***p < 0.001								

Based on the recorded scores from employees, ranging from minimum 20 to highest 140, the employees were grouped into three categories

- Disengaged Employees - having score of 60 & below: who does not feel connected,
- Neutral Employees - having score range of 61 to 80: who sleep walk the day, and
- Engaged Employees - having score of above 80: who feel connected to their organization.

The engagement status of employees from 10 chosen sectors from being highly disengaged to highly engaged, based on the recorded scores, is illustrated in Table 2.

The numbers of engaged / disengaged employees rate the organization as world class, average, or sub-average organization. As per Gallup (2010), an organization shall be rated as:

- World Class Organization – having more than 67% 'engaged' employees, and less than 7% 'highly disengaged' employees,
- Average Organization – with 67% to 33% 'engaged' employees, and 7% to 18% 'highly disengaged' employees, and
- Below Average Organization – having less than 33% 'engaged' employees and more than 18% 'highly disengaged' employees.

As per the data illustrated in Table 2, the organizations in Information Technology, Aviation, and Healthcare sectors in India have world class engagement practices as they have 76.5%, 72.2%, & 67.6% 'engaged' employees and 3.2%, 4.8%, & 6.9.0% 'highly disengaged' employees respectively. The organizations in Retail, Tourism, Telecommunication, and Media & Entertainment show average engagement practices with 59.8%, 59.0%, 47.7%, and 37.9% 'engaged' employees, and 9.9%, 11.6%, 13.8%, and 17.3% 'highly disengaged' employees respectively. Bleak engagement practices were observed in Banking and Financial Services, Insurance, and Logistics sector which recorded disquieting figures of only 29.8%, 28.0%, and 24.7% 'engaged' employees' and 20.6%, 21.9%, and 22.4% of 'highly disengaged' employees respectively. The glum figures show that these organizations fall below the criteria of average organizations and trail far below the IT sector in having quality engagement practices.

IT sector organizations have better engagement practices vis-à-vis other sectors in India. IT sector is followed by Aviation, and Healthcare sectors. Based on the criteria by Gallup (2010), organizations in these three sectors in India are rated as world class organizations. Retail, Tourism, Telecommunication, and Media & Entertainment sectors comprise of organizations having mediocre employee engagement practices. Banking and Financial Services, Insurance, and Logistics sectors in India have trifling engagement practices.

Assessment of Engagement Attributes in IT Software Companies in India

In this study, the responses of 50 employees from IT sector were segregated from the total data. The data of these 50 respondents was then analysed to predict the most prominent engagement attribute among 'Insightful Work', 'Pragmatic Management', 'Positive Work Environment', 'Growth Opportunity', and 'Engaging Leadership'. In the instrument, each engagement attribute had 04 questions measured on a scale of 01 to 07. Thus, the minimum and maximum possible scores for an engagement attribute were 04 and 28 respectively.

Employee Engagement in India

Table 2. Employee engagement status in various sectors

	(1) Highly Disengaged (Score Range: 20)	(2) Moderately Disengaged (Score Range: 21-40)	(3) Slightly Disengaged (Score Range: 41-60)	(4) Neutral (Score Range: 61-80)	(5) Slightly Engaged (Score Range: 81-100)	(6) Moderately Engaged (Score Range: 101-120)	(7) Highly Engaged (Score Range: 121-140)	Total Respondents	Disengaged (%) (Score Range: 60 & below)	Neutral (%) (Score Range: 61-80)	Engaged (%) (Score Range: 81 & above)
	Employee (%)									Employee (%)	
Information Technology	3.3	4.0	7.2	9.1	17.6	27.1	31.7	50	14.6	9.8	75.6
Aviation	4.8	4.9	8.1	10.8	16.6	25.4	30.2	50	14.9	10.1	75.0
Healthcare	6.9	7.8	8.5	9.2	15.6	24.2	27.8	50	23.4	8.2	68.4
Retail	9.9	9.8	11.4	9.1	13.4	20.5	25.9	50	31.9	9.1	59.0
Tourism	11.6	9.1	10.2	10.1	15.0	21.3	22.7	50	32.1	10.1	57.8
Telecommunication	13.8	12.8	14.9	10.8	13.1	16.9	17.7	50	41.3	10.4	48.3
Media and Entertainment	17.3	16.8	16.9	11.1	11.3	12.2	14.4	50	45.7	13.8	40.5
Banking & Financial Service	20.6	18.2	19.1	12.3	11.1	8.6	10.1	50	58.1	12.1	29.8
Insurance	21.9	18.6	20.4	11.1	12.0	7.8	8.2	50	59.1	13.2	27.7
Logistics	22.4	19.6	21.3	12.0	10.4	7.2	7.1	50	59.4	12.7	27.9

The rankings of these attributes were based on number of employees agreeing with the attribute by imparting a score of 17 or higher to that attribute. The percentage of employees valuing the five engagement attributes is given in Table 3 and Table 4.

Table 4 reflects that 23% respondents opined that their organization provides them 'Growth Opportunity' and Growth is the most prominent milieu that IT companies tender to its employees. 'Insightful Work' got second preference with 19% employees giving it the highest score extenuating that the organization gives them autonomy, assign tasks as per their competency, and give them time to rejuvenate. The third and fourth weighed attributes were 'Pragmatic Management' and 'Positive Work Environment' each getting affirmation from 18% employees. The lowest rated attribute was 'Engaging Leadership' getting apt score from only 12% employees indicating apprehensions about leadership. The respondents diatribe that the leadership lacks in transparency, honesty, and don't inspire them.

Thus, the engagement attributes in IT companies in India in order of rankings and preferences by the employees are 'Growth Opportunity', 'Insightful Work', 'Positive Work Environment', 'Pragmatic Management', and 'Engaging Leadership.'

Table 3. Valuation of engagement attributes in it organizations in India

	(1) Highly Disagree (Score Range: 4)	(2) Moderately Disagree (Score Range: 5 - 8)	(3) Slightly Disagree (Score Range: 9 - 12)	(4) Neutral (Score Range: 13 - 16)	(5) Slightly Agree (Score Range: 17 - 20)	(6) Moderately Agree (Score Range: 21 - 24)	(7) Highly Agree (Score Range: 25 - 28)
	Percentage of Employees						
Insightful Work	1	1	1	3	5	5	9
Pragmatic Management	2	1	2	2	4	6	8
Positive Work Environment	1	1	1	4	4	6	8
Growth Opportunity	1	1	2	5	7	6	10
Engaging Leadership	1	1	1	3	3	5	4

Table 4. Cumulative percentage of employees agreeing and disagreeing with engagement attribute

	Disagree (Score Range: 12 & below)	Neutral (Score Range: 13 - 16)	Agree (Score Range: 17 & above)
	Total Percentage of Employees		
Insightful Work	3	3	19
Pragmatic Management	5	2	18
Positive Work Environment	3	4	18
Growth Opportunity	4	5	23
Engaging Leadership	3	3	12

CONCLUSION

The employee engagement directly coerces productivity and efficiency of an organization. The emphasis is laid on connecting with the employees, engaging them with positivity, and helps them associate with the organization. Successful firms incorporate high level of employee engagement and have passionate employees who associate individual goals with the organizational goals and are committed beyond the job description.

To have effective employee engagement certain practices are must for the organization to exemplify their efficiency.

1. Organizations practice insightful working environment by giving autonomy and decision-making power to its employees, do appropriate competency mapping before, and give time to relax and rejuvenate.
2. Role of leadership is of prime importance in engaging people. The talent and interest of the employees should be matched with the organizational objectives. The purpose, mission, and soul of the organization must be aligned with that of the employees. The leadership must be open and transparent in the communication, and invest in their employees for achieving higher proficiency.
3. Growth is an important parameter which keeps the employees engaged. The organization must facilitate talent mobility by giving new assignments in cross functional areas. The employees should be allowed to learn on the job, take developmental assignments, and adopt new methodologies. Organization's high impact learning culture highly influences the employees to work positively and the prospective advancement in career graph upsurges commitment of the employees.
4. It's mandatory to have positive working environment in an organization for employee engagement. Employees are committed to their work in the organizations which appreciate and recognize their efforts. Organizations having diverse work culture, offering flexible and supportive work environment, and running wellness programs for its employees have more engaged employee base.
5. Organizations should have clear and transparent goals, must nurture and develop the future managers, mentor and coach its employees, and have effective appraisal system to recognize the luminous efforts of its employees. The committed employees appreciate these efforts of their company which are crucial for their positive engagement.

The level of employee engagement in Indian organizations is subpar. The analysis discloses high level of employee disengagement across major sectors since the scores on various employee engagement attributes are low and unsatisfactory. The IT sector along with Aviation and Healthcare show appreciable practices for engaging its employees where as other important sectors such as Retail, Tourism, Telecommunication, and Media & Entertainment have to bring lot of amendments in their policies to gain confidence of their employees. The organizations in Banking & Financial Services, Insurance, and Logistics, showed bleak practices to engage their employees and emerged as below par organization. Organizations in these sectors needs to introspect their policies and amend them accordingly to meet the world class standards. They should make their employees feel cared for, take interest in their careers and help them to grow professionally.

Examining the engagement practices in organizations in IT sector, it is inferred that the employees are impressed with the Growth Opportunities which their organization offers them. Other engagement attributes such as Insightful Work, Applied Management, and Good Working Environment are also aptly practiced in these IT organizations. The result also shows that among all 05 attributes, the employees have low confidence in the leadership and believe that the leadership lacks in transparency and fails to inspire them. IT organization needs to improve the confidence of employees on the leadership.

LIMITATIONS

The study probed to infer the employee engagement practices in IT companies vis-à-vis companies in other domains. The study investigated engagement policies and the key drivers for employee engagement in these companies. The study helps in understanding that the quality practices are bleak in Indian organizations. The study was conducted meticulously but was challenged on certain facades.

1. The foremost limitation is that the study is cross sectional and hence raises a concern about common method bias.
2. Also, the engagement attributes used in the study are coherent with the reviewed literature but with change in attributes, the response of employees may diverge. Also, the study may have missed to incorporate some important drivers since information on uniform engagement drivers practiced across heterogeneous organizations was not available.
3. Also, result may vary with different set of organizations under the chosen sectors. Furthermore, the data collection involved a convenient sampling approach rather than a probabilistic approach such as random sampling method. Hence, in generalizing the results to a larger population, caution is required.
4. Only 5 companies in each domain were considered. The larger sample size could have led to more precise inference.
5. The study explores and compares engagement policies of companies in 10 domains. The companies in other domain may have better engagement policies which are not explored in current study.
6. In the present analysis, the employee's responses across organizations in each sector were aggregated. The state of engagement practices in individual organizations in a specific sector may not be in equilibrium with the overall result.
7. The potential limitation of this study is the scope of the review conducted. The databases that were investigated for relevant content denied access to articles in numerous cases due to membership access regulations. Hence, some valuable inferences were not considered in this research.
8. The study lacks a comparison between the success of firms having effective engagement policies, and the firms where these policies are missing.

SCOPE FOR FUTURE STUDY

The study infers state of engagement practices in organizations however it does not explore the impact of employee's individual personality traits on organizational efficacy. A study on intensifying and moderating effect of employee's personality traits like self-efficacy, self-esteem, and exchange ideology on efficiency of the organization may be conducted in future.

A research may be conducted on effect of experimental interventions on employees that will increase their level of engagement. A comparative analysis may be done on how industries differ in practicing various interventions such as job design and career management interventions along with numerous other interventions.

Also, a study may be done on how effective adoption of crucial engagement practices impacts the short-term and long-term outcome of organizations in various sectors. The research could be extended to study the impact of employee engagement policies on cost, time, efficiency, and revenue of IT organizations vis-à-vis organizations in other sectors.

This study does not include the difficulties faced by organizations in adopting new and innovative engagement practices. A study may be carried out on issues and difficulties in implementing employee engagement policies in IT and other organizations.

REFERENCES

ACAS. (2010). *Building employee engagement.* ACAS Policy Discussion Papers. Retrieved January14, 2019, from http://www.acas.org.uk/media/pdf/ s/1/Building_employee_engagement-accessible-version-Jun-2012.pdf

Adejoh, M. A., & Adejoh, L. L. (2013). Handling negative deviant behavior of front-line employees in service organizations. *International Journal of Current Research and Review*, *5*(4), 23–30.

Ahmad, A., & Omar, Z. (2013). Abusive Supervision and Deviant Workplace Behavior: The Mediating Role of Work-Family Conflict. *The Journal of Human Resource and Adult Learning*, *9*(2), 124–130.

Akgunduz, Y., Bardakoglu, O., & Alkan, C. E. (2015). The moderating role of job resourcefulness in the impact of work–family and family–work life conflict on the burnout levels of travel agency employees. *Turizam*, *19*(3), 111–126. doi:10.5937/Turizam1503111A

Aladwan, K., Bhanugopan, R., & Fish, A. (2013). Why do employees jump ship? Examining intent to quit employment in a non-western cultural context. *Employee Relations*, *35*(4), 408–422. doi:10.1108/ER-03-2012-0027

Alfes, K., Shantz, A. D., Truss, C., & Soane, E. C. (2013). The link between perceived human resource management practices, engagement and employee behaviour: A moderated mediation model. *International Journal of Human Resource Management*, *24*(2), 330–351. doi:10.1080/09585192.2012.679950

Amabile, T. M., Conti, R., Coon, H., Lazenby, J., & Herron, M. (1996). Assessing the work environment for creativity. *Academy of Management Journal*, *39*, 1154–1184.

Amabile, T. M., Schatzel, E. A., Moneta, G. B., & Kramer, S. J. (2004). Leader behaviors and the work environment for creativity: Perceived leader support. *The Leadership Quarterly*, *15*(1), 5–32. doi:10.1016/j.leaqua.2003.12.003

Arrowsmith, J., & Parker, J. (2013). The meaning of 'employee engagement' for the values and roles of the HRM function. *International Journal of Human Resource Management*, *24*(14), 2692–2712. doi:10.1080/09585192.2013.763842

Ayers, D., Dahlstrom, R., & Skinner, S. J. (1997). An exploratory investigation of organizational antecedents to new product success. *JMR, Journal of Marketing Research*, *34*(1), 107–116. doi:10.1177/002224379703400109

Baker, J. V. (2011). *The effects of change management on employee engagement: Using lean principles to increase engagement*. California State University.

Bakker, A. B. (2011). An evidence-based model of work engagement. *Current Directions in Psychological Science*, *20*(4), 265–269. doi:10.1177/0963721411414534

Balakrishnan, C., & Masthan, D. (2013). Impact of Internal Communication on Employee Engagement A Study at Delhi International Airport. *International Journal of Scientific and Research Publications*, *3*(8), 1–13.

Balfour, D., & Wechsler, B. (1996). Organizational commitment: Antecedents and outcomes in public organisations. *Public Productivity and Management Review*, *29*(3), 256–277. doi:10.2307/3380574

Barber L, Hayday S, Bevan S (1999). *From people to profits*. IES Report 355.

Barsade, S. (2002). The ripple effect: Emotional contagion and its influence on group behavior. *Administrative Science Quarterly*, *47*(4), 644–677. doi:10.2307/3094912

Batt, R., & Valcour, P. M. (2003). Human resources practices as predictors of work-family outcomes and employee turnover. *Industrial Relations*, *42*(2), 189–220. doi:10.1111/1468-232X.00287

Baumruk, R. (2004). The missing link: The role of employee engagement in business success. *Workspan*, *47*, 48–52.

Bhasin, M. L. (2010). Corporate Governance Disclosure Practices: The Portrait of a Developing Country. *International Journal of Business and Management*, *5*(4), 150–167.

Biswas, S., & Bhatnagar, J. (2013). Mediator analysis of employee engagement: Role of perceived organizational support, P-O Fit, organizational commitment and Job Satisfaction. *Vikalpa*, *38*(1), 27–40. doi:10.1177/0256090920130103

Bloom, N., Kretschmer, T., & Van Reenen, J. (2009). Work-life balance, management practices and productivity. In R. B. Freeman & K. L. Shaw (Eds.), *International differences in the business practices and productivity of firms* (pp. 15–54). Chicago, IL: University of Chicago Press. doi:10.7208/chicago/9780226261959.003.0002

Bodankin, M., & Tziner, A. (2009). Constructive deviance, destructive deviance and personality: How do they interrelate. *Amfiteatru Economic Journal*, *11*(26), 549–564.

Brás, F. A., & Rodrigues, L. L. (2007). Accounting for firms' training programs: An exploratory study. *Journal Human Resource Costing & Accounting*, *11*(3), 229–250. doi:10.1108/14013380710843791

Brown, S. P., & Lam, S. K. (2008). A meta-analysis of relationships linking employee satisfaction to customer responses. *Journal of Retailing*, *84*(3), 243–255. doi:10.1016/j.jretai.2008.06.001

Bui, J., Hodge, A., Shackelford, A., & Acsell, J. (2011). Factors contributing to burnout among perfusionists in the United States. *Perfusion*, *26*(6), 461–466. doi:10.1177/0267659111411521 PMID:21665910

Cano, C., Fernández-Sanz, L., & Misra, S. (2013). Featuring CIO: Roles, Skills and Soft Skills. *International Journal of Human Capital and Information Technology Professionals*, *4*(1), 22–33. doi:10.4018/jhcitp.2013010103

Casademunt, A. M. L., Cabrera, A. M. G., & Molina, D. G. C. (2015). National culture, work-life balance and employee well-being in European tourism firms: The moderating effect of uncertainty avoidance values. *Tourism & Management Studies*, *11*(1), 62–69.

Catteeuw, F. (2007). Employee engagement: Boosting productivity in turbulent times. *Organization Development Journal*, *25*(2), 151–157.

Chen, L. L., Fahb, B. C. Y., & Jin, T. C. (2016). Perceived organizational support and workplace deviance in the voluntary sector. *Procedia Economics and Finance*, *35*, 468–475. doi:10.1016/S2212-5671(16)00058-7

Choi, Y., & Dickson, D. R. (2009). A Case Study into the Benefits of Management Training Programs: Impacts on Hotel Employee Turnover and Satisfaction Level. *Journal of Human Resources in Hospitality & Tourism*, *9*(1), 103–116. doi:10.1080/15332840903336499

Christian, M.S., Garza, A.S., & Slaughter, J.E. (2011). Work Engagement: A Quantitative Review a Test of Its Relations with Task and Contextual Performance. *Personnel Psychology, 64*(1), 89-136. .01203.x doi:10.1111/j.1744-6570.2010

Christopher, D., & Tanwar, A. (2012). Knowledge management in outsourcing environment: People empowering people. *The IUP Journal of Knowledge Management*, *10*(2), 61–86.

CIPD. (2001). *Employers' perceptions of the psychological contract*. CIPD Report 112.

CIPD. (2006). *Reflections on employee Engagement: Change agenda*. CIPD. Retrieved January 04, 2019, from http://www.cipd.co.uk/changeagendas

Clark, S. C. (2000). Work/family border theory: A new theory of work/family balance. *Human Relations*, *53*(6), 747–770. doi:10.1177/0018726700536001

Cohen, A. (1991). Career stage as a moderator of the relationship between organisational commitment and its outcomes: A meta-analysis. *Journal of Occupational Psychology*, *64*(3), 253–268. doi:10.1111/j.2044-8325.1991.tb00558.x

Cohen, A. (1993). Age and tenure in relation to organisational commitment: A meta-analysis. *Basic and Applied Social Psychology*, *14*(2), 143–159. doi:10.120715324834basp1402_2

Cojocaru, M. (2011). Cultural Globalization In The Context Of International Business. *Review of International Comparative Management*, *12*(5), 993–999.

Cortina, L. M., Magley, V. J., Williams, J. H., & Langhout, R. D. (2001). Incivility in the workplace: Incidence and impact. *Journal of Occupational Health Psychology*, *6*(1), 64–80. doi:10.1037/1076-8998.6.1.64 PMID:11199258

Costen, W. M., & Salazar, J. (2011). The Impact of Training and Development on Employee Job Satisfaction, Loyalty, and Intent to Stay in the Lodging Industry. *Journal of Human Resources in Hospitality & Tourism*, *10*(3), 273–284. doi:10.1080/15332845.2011.555734

Dalal, R. S., Lam, H., Weiss, H. M., Weich, E. R., & Hulin, C. L. (2009). A Within-Person Approach to Work Behavior and Performance: Concurrent and Lagged Citizenship-Counter Productivity Association and Dynamic Relationship With Affect and Overall Job Performance. *Academy of Management Journal*, *52*(5), 1061–1068. doi:10.5465/amj.2009.44636148

DDI. (2005). *Predicting Employee Engagement*. DDI International, Inc. Retrieved December 25, 2018, from http://www.ddiworld.com

Debruyne, M., Moenaert, R., Griffin, A., Hart, S., Hultink, E. J., & Robben, H. (2002). The impact of new product launch strategies on competitive reaction in industrial markets. *Journal of Product Innovation Management*, *19*(2), 159–170. doi:10.1016/S0737-6782(01)00135-7

Deery, M. (2008). Talent management, work-life balance and retention strategies. *International Journal of Contemporary Hospitality Management*, *20*(7), 792–806. doi:10.1108/09596110810897619

DeNisi, A. S., & Pritchard, R. D. (2006). Performance Appraisal, Performance Management and Improving Individual Performance: A Motivational Framework. *Management and Organization Review*, *2*(2), 253–277. doi:10.1111/j.1740-8784.2006.00042.x

Dernovsek, D. (2008). *Creating highly engaged and committed employee starts at the top and ends at the bottom line Credit Union Magazine*. Credit Union National Association, Inc.

DeRue, D. S., & Morgeson, F. P. (2007). Stability and change in person-team and person-role fit over time: The effects of growth satisfaction, performance, and general self-efficacy. *The Journal of Applied Psychology*, *92*(5), 1242–1253. doi:10.1037/0021-9010.92.5.1242 PMID:17845083

Desai, M., Majumdar, B., & Prabhu, G. P. (2010). A study on employee engagement in two Indian businesses. *Asian Journal of Management Research*, *1*, 81–97.

Dewett, T., & Jones, G. R. (2001). The role of information technology in the organization: A review, model, and assessment. *Journal of Management*, *27*(3), 313–346. doi:10.1177/014920630102700306

Economictimes. (2019). *Sectors that are likely to outperform in 2019*. Retrieved February 2019 from https://economictimes.indiatimes.com/markets/stocks/news/sectors-that-are-likely-to-outperform-in-2019/articleshow/67326199.cms

Eisenhardt, K. M., & Tabrizi, B. N. (1995). Accelerating adaptive processes: Product innovation in the global computer industry. *Administrative Science Quarterly*, *40*(1), 84–110. doi:10.2307/2393701

Ellis, C. M., & Sorensen, A. (2007). Assessing Employee Engagement: The Key to Improving Productivity. *Perspectives, 15*(1).

Fegley, S. (2007). *2007 benefits: A survey report by the Society for Human Resource Management*. Alexandria, VA: Society for Human Resource Management. Retrieved from http://www.shrm.org/publications/hrmagazine/editorialcontent/documents/2007%20benefits%20survey%20report.pdf

Ferguson, A. (2007). *Employee engagement: Does it exist, and if so, how does it relate to performance, other constructs and individual differences?* Retrieved February 19, 2019, from http://www.lifethatworks. com/Employee-Engagement.prn.pdf

Fernandez, C. P. (2007). Employee engagement. *Journal of Public Health Management and Practice.* Retrieved on January 13, 2016, from http://find.galegroup.com

Ferris, G. R., Hochwarter, W. A., Buckley, M. R., Harrell-Cook, G., & Frink, D. D. (1999). Human Resources Management: Some New Directions. *Journal of Management, 25*(3), 385–415. doi:10.1177/014920639902500306

Francis, H. M., Ramdhony, A., Reddington, M., & Staines, H. (2013). Opening spaces for conversational practice: A conduit for effective engagement strategies and productive working arrangements. *International Journal of Human Resource Management, 24*(14), 2713–2740. doi:10.1080/09585192.2013.781530

Freeney, Y., & Fellenz, M. R. (2013). Work engagement, job design and the role of the social context at work: Exploring antecedents from a relational perspective. *Human Relations, 66*(11), 1427–1445. doi:10.1177/0018726713478245

Friedman, B. A. (2007). Globalization implications for human resource management roles. *Employ Response Rights Journal, 19*(3), 157–171. doi:10.100710672-007-9043-1

Gallup Inc. (2010). *Employee engagement: What's your engagement ratio?* Retrieved February 06, 2019, from http://www.gallup.com/consulting/121535/Employee-Engagement-Overview Brochure.aspx.

Gallup, Inc. (2013). *State of the global workplace.* Employee Engagement Insights for Business Leaders Worldwide. Retrieved February 07, 2019, from http://www.gallup.com/ services/178517/state-global-workplace.aspx

Gareis, K. C., Barnett, R. C., Ertel, K. A., & Berkman, L. F. (2009). Work-family enrichment and conflict: Additive effects, buffering, or balance? *Journal of Marriage and the Family, 71*(3), 696–707. doi:10.1111/j.1741-3737.2009.00627.x

Geroski, P., Machin, S., & Van Reenen, J. (1993). The profitability of innovating firms. *The Rand Journal of Economics, 24*(2), 198–211. doi:10.2307/2555757

Glaser, B., & Strauss, A. (1967). *The discovery of grounded theory: Strategies for qualitative research.* New York: Aldine de Gruyter.

Glick, W. H. (1985). Conceptualizing and measuring organizational and psychological climate: Pitfalls in multilevel research. *Academy of Management Review, 10*(3), 601–616. doi:10.5465/amr.1985.4279045

Goel, A. K., Gupta, N., & Rastogi, R. (2013). Measuring the level of employee engagement: A study from Indian automobile sector. *International Journal of Indian Culture and Business Management, 6*(1), 5–21. doi:10.1504/IJICBM.2013.050710

Gonring, M. P. (2008). Customer loyalty and employee engagement: An alignment for value. *The Journal of Business Strategy, 29*(4), 29–40. doi:10.1108/02756660810887060

Gravenkemper, S. (2007). Building Community in Organizations: Principles of Engagement. *Consulting Psychology Journal: Practice and Research, 59*(3), 203–208. doi:10.1037/1065-9293.59.3.203

Grawitch, M. J., Gottschalk, M., & Munz, D. C. (2006). The path to a healthy workplace: A critical review linking healthy workplace practices, employee well-being, and organizational improvements. *Consulting Psychology Journal: Practice and Research, 58*(3), 129–147. doi:10.1037/1065-9293.58.3.129

Green, S., Anderson, S., & Shivers, S. (1996). Demographics and organisational influences on leader-member exchange and related work attitudes. *Organizational Behavior and Human Decision Processes, 66*(2), 203–214. doi:10.1006/obhd.1996.0049

Greenhaus, J. H., Collins, K. M., & Shaw, J. D. (2003). The relation between work–family balance and quality of life. *Journal of Vocational Behavior, 63*(3), 510–531. doi:10.1016/S0001-8791(02)00042-8

Greve, H. R., & Taylor, A. (2000). Innovations as catalysts for organizational change: Shifts in organizational cognition and search. *Administrative Science Quarterly, 45*(1), 54–80. doi:10.2307/2666979

Gummadi, A., & Devi, A. (2013). An empirical study on the relationship between determinants of employee engagement among the banking professionals of Guntur urban region. *Global Journal of Commerce and Management Perspective, 2*(5), 23–28.

Gupta, V., & Kumar, S. (2012). Impact of performance appraisal justice on employee engagement: A study of Indian professionals. *Employee Relations, 35*(1), 61–78. doi:10.1108/01425451311279410

Handa, M., & Gulati, A. (2014). Employee Engagement Does Individual Personality Matter. *Journal of Management Research, 14*(1), 57–67.

Harrison, D. A., Newman, D. A., & Roth, P. L. (2006). How important are job attitudes? Meta-analytic comparisons of integrative behavioural outcomes and time sequences. *Academy of Management Journal, 49*(2), 305–325. doi:10.5465/amj.2006.20786077

Harter, J. K., Schmidt, F. L., & Hayes, T. L. (2002). Business-unit-level relationship between employee satisfaction, employee engagement, and business outcomes: A meta-analysis. *The Journal of Applied Psychology, 87*(2), 268–279. doi:10.1037/0021-9010.87.2.268 PMID:12002955

Havill, L. (2010). A new type of engagement. *The CPA Journal, 80*(7), 14.

Healthcare Financial Management Association. (2011). Open workspace environment improves employee engagement. *HFM Magazine, 65*(10), 30.

Herranz-Sánchez, E., Colomo-Palacios, R., & de Amescua-Seco, A. (2015). Gamiware: A gamification platform for software process improvement. *Communications in Computer and Information Science, 543*, 127–139. doi:10.1007/978-3-319-24647-5_11

Hewitt Associates LLC. (2004). *Research Brief: employee engagement higher at double digit growth companies.* Retrieved from www.hewitt.com

Hill, E. J., Allen, S., Jacob, J., Bair, A. F., Bikhazi, S. L., Van Langeveld, A., ... Walker, E. (2007). Work family facilitation: Expanding theoretical understanding through qualitative exploration. *Advances in Developing Human Resources, 9*(4), 507–526. doi:10.1177/1523422307305490

IBEF. (2019). *IT & ITeS Industry in India*. Indian Brand Equity Foundation. Accessed from https://www.ibef.org/industry/information-technology-india.aspx

IBEF. (n.d.). *Industry - India Brand Equity Foundation*. Retrieved December 22, 2018, from http://www.ibef.org/industry.aspx

Ikedinachi, A. P., Misra, S., Assibong, P. A., Olu-Owolabi, E. F., Maskeliunas, R., & Damasevicius, R. (2019). Artificial Intelligence, Smart Classrooms and Online Education in the 21st Century: Implications for Human Development. *Journal of Cases on Information Technology*, *21*(3), 66–79. doi:10.4018/JCIT.2019070105

Jaggi, S., & Bahl, S. K. (2016). Exploring the impact of work life balance on the employee and organisational growth. *International Journal of Engineering and Management Research*, *6*(2), 1–5.

James, L. R. (1982). Aggregation bias in estimates of perceptual agreement. *The Journal of Applied Psychology*, *67*(2), 219–229. doi:10.1037/0021-9010.67.2.219

Jenkins, S., & Delbridge, R. (2013). Context matters: Examining 'soft' and 'hard' approaches to employee engagement in two workplaces. *International Journal of Human Resource Management*, *24*(14), 2670–2691. doi:10.1080/09585192.2013.770780

Jose, G., & Mampilly, S. R. (2012). Satisfaction with HR Practices and Employee Engagement: A Social Exchange. *Perspective Journal of Economics and Behavioral Studies*, *4*(7), 423–430.

Kahn, W. A. (1990). Psychological conditions of personal engagement and disengagement at work. *Academy of Management Journal*, *33*(4), 692–724.

Kersley, B., Alpin, C., Forth, J., Bryson, A., Bewley, H., Dix, G., & Oxenbridge, S. (2006). *Inside the Workplace: First finding WERS 2004*. London: Routledge. Retrieved January 12, 2019, from www.routledge.com/textbooks/0415378133/pdf/insideWP.pdf

Kinsey, C. (2009). Using rewards and benefits to motivate and engage. *Strategic HR Review*, *8*(2), 47. doi:10.1108hr.2009.37208bab.005

Konrad, A. M., & Mangel, R. (2000). The impact of work-life programs on firm productivity. *Strategic Management Journal*, *21*(12), 1225–1237. doi:10.1002/1097-0266(200012)21:12<1225::AID-SMJ135>3.0.CO;2-3

Kontakos, A., & Stepp, P. (2007). *Employee engagement and fairness in the workplace*. Ithaca, NY: Center for Advanced Human Resource Studies, Cornell University.

Kossek, E. E., & Friede, A. (2006). The business case: Managerial perspectives on work and the family. In M. Pitt-Catsouphes, E. E. Kossek, & S. Sweet (Eds.), *The work and family handbook: Multi-disciplinary perspectives, methods, and approaches* (pp. 611–626). Mahwah, NJ: Lawrence Erlbaum. Retrieved from http://ellenkossek.lir.msu.edu/documents/businesscase.pdf

Kotni, D. P. (2011). *Dynamics of employee engagement: A case study,* International. *Journal of Management & Business Studies*, *1*(2), 31–35.

Kristof-Brown, A., & Guay, R. P. (2011). Person–environment fit. In APA Handbooks in Psychology. APA. doi:10.1037/12171-001

Kühnel, J., Sonnentag, S., & Bledow, R. (2012). Resources and time pressure as day-level antecedents of work engagement. *Journal of Occupational and Organizational Psychology*, *85*(1), 181–198. doi:10.1111/j.2044-8325.2011.02022.x

Kular, S., Gatenby, M., Rees, C., Soane, E., & Truss, K. (2008). *Employee Engagement: A literature review.* Kingston Business School: Working Paper Series, 19.

Kumar, D. P., & Swetha, G. (2011). *A prognostic examination of employee engagement from its historical roots.* International Journal of Trade. *Economics and Finance*, *2*(3), 232–241.

Kummamuru, S., & Murthy, N.P. (2016). *Exploring the Complex Interface between IT Professional and HR: Building Flexibility Applying Cybernetic Concepts.* doi:10.1007/978-81-322-2380-1_10

Langelaan, S., Bakker, A. B., Schaufeli, W. B., Van Rhenen, W., & Van Doornen, L. J. P. (2006). Do burned-out and work-engaged employees differ in the functioning of the hypothalamic-pituitary-adrenal axis? *Scandinavian Journal of Work, Environment & Health*, *32*(5), 339–348. doi:10.5271jweh.1029 PMID:17091201

Levinson, E. (2007). *Developing High Employee Engagement Makes Good Business Sense.* Retrieved December 19, 2018, from www.interactionassociates.com/ideas/2007 /05/developing_high_ employee_ engagement_makes_good_business_sense.php

Lockwood, N. R. (2007). Leveraging Employee Engagement for Competitive Advantage: HR's strategic role. *SHRM Research Quarterly, 1*, 1-10.

Luthans, F., Avey, J. B., Avolio, B. J., Norman, S. M., & Combs, G. M. (2006). Psychological capital development: Toward a micro-intervention. *Journal of Organizational Behavior*, *27*(3), 387–393. doi:10.1002/job.373

Luthans, F., Youssef, C. M., & Avolio, B. J. (2007). *Psychological capital: developing the human competitive edge*. Oxford, UK: Oxford University Press.

Macey, W.H., & Schneider, B. (2008). The Meaning of Employee Engagement. *Industrial and Organizational Psychology: Perspectives on Science and Practice, 1*(1), 3-30. Doi:10.1111/j.1754-9434.2007.0002.x

Right Management. (2006). *Measuring True Employee Engagement*. Philadelphia: Right Management.

Mani, V. (2011). Analysis of Employee Engagement and its predictors. *International Journal of Human Resource Studies.*, *1*(2), 15–27. doi:10.5296/ijhrs.v1i2.955

Markos, S., & Sridevi, N. S. (2010). Employee Engagement: The Key to Improving Performance. *International Journal of Business and Management*, *5*(12), 89–96.

Maskell, B., Baggaley, B., & Grasso, L. (2011). *Practical Lean Accounting: A Proven System for Measuring and Managing the Lean Enterprise* (2nd ed.). Productivity Press.

Maslach, C. (2011). Engagement research: Some thoughts from a burnout perspective. *European Journal of Work and Organizational Psychology*, *20*(1), 47–52. doi:10.1080/1359432X.2010.537034

Mathieu, J., & Zajac, D. (1990). A review and meta-analysis of the antecedents, correlates, and consequences of organisational commitment. *Psychological Bulletin, 108*(2), 171–194. doi:10.1037/0033-2909.108.2.171

McGourty, J., Tarshis, L. A., & Dominick, P. (1996). Managing innovation: Lessons from world class organizations. *International Journal of Technology Management, 11*, 354–368. doi:10.1504/IJTM.1996.025438

McLean, L. D. (2005). Organizational culture's influence on creativity and innovation: A review of the literature and implications for human resource development. *Advances in Developing Human Resources, 7*(2), 226–246. doi:10.1177/1523422305274528

Michel, J. S., Kotrba, L. M., Mitchelson, J. K., Clark, M. A., & Baltes, B. B. (2010). Antecedents of work-family conflict: A meta-analytic review. *Journal of Organizational Behavior, 32*(5), 689–725. doi:10.1002/job.695

Mishra, D., Kapse, S., & Bavad, D. (2013). Employee engagement at banks in Kutch. *International Journal of Application or Innovation in Engineering & Management, 2*(7), 349–358.

Mochama, V. K. (2013). An assessment of the criteria used in allocating different types of employee benefits at the Kenya pipeline company, Eldoret, Kenya. *Journal of Emerging Trends in Economics and Management Science, 4*(2), 268–273.

Moen, Ø. (1999). The Relationship Between Firm Size, Competitive Advantages and Export Performance Revisited. *International Small Business Journal, 18*(1), 53–72. doi:10.1177/0266242699181003

Morris, M. L., Heames, J. T., & McMillan, H. S. (2011). Human resource executives' perceptions and measurement of the strategic impact of work/life initiatives. *Human Resource Development Quarterly, 22*(3), 265–295. doi:10.1002/hrdq.20082

Morris, M. L., Storberg-Walker, J., & McMillan, H. S. (2009). Developing an OD-intervention metric system with the use of applied theory-building methodology: A work/life-intervention example. *Human Resource Development Quarterly, 20*(4), 419–449. doi:10.1002/hrdq.20026

Mumford, M. D., Bedell-Avers, K. E., & Hunter, S. T. (2008). Planning for innovation: A multi-level perspective. In M. D. Mumford, S. T. Hunter, & K. E. Bedell-Avers (Eds.), *Innovation in organizations: A multi-level perspective* (pp. 107–154). Oxford, UK: Elsevier.

Mumford, M. D., Hester, K. S., & Robledo, I. C. (2012). Creativity in organizations: Importance and approaches. In M. D. Mumford (Ed.), *Handbook of organizational creativity* (pp. 3–16). San Diego, CA: Elsevier. doi:10.1016/B978-0-12-374714-3.00001-X

Nelson, D. L., Macik-Frey, M., & Quick, J. C. (2007). Advances in Occupational Health: From a Stressful Beginning to a Positive Future. *Journal of Management, 33*(6), 809–840. doi:10.1177/0149206307307634

Oduh, I., Misra, S., Robertas, D., & Rytis, M. (2018). *Cloud Based Simple Employee Management Information System: A Model for African Small and Medium Enterprises*. doi:10.1007/978-3-319-73450-7_12

Ologbo, C. A., & Saudah, S. (2011). Engaging People who Drive Execution and Organizational Performance. *American Journal of Economics and Business Administration, 3*(3), 569–575. doi:10.3844/ajebasp.2011.569.575

Pachouri, A., & Sharma, S. (2016). Barriers to Innovation in Indian Small and Medium-Sized Enterprises. Asian Development Bank Institute, 588.

Pandey, S., & David, S. (2013). A study of engagement at work: What drives employee engagement. *European Journal of Commerce and Management Research, 2*(7), 155–161.

Pandey, S., & Sharma, V. (2016). Understanding Work-Related Stress, Job Conditions, Work Culture and Workaholism Phenomenon as Predictors of HR Crisis: An Empirical Study of the Indian IT Sector. *International Journal of Human Capital and Information Technology Professionals, 7*(2), 68–80. doi:10.4018/IJHCITP.2016040105

Penna. (2007). *Meaning at Work Research Report.* Retrieved February 10, 2019, from http:// www.e-penna.com/ newsopinion /research.aspx

Perrin, T. (2003). *Working Today: Understanding What Drives Employee Engagement.* The 2003 Towers Perrin Talent Report U.S Report. Retrieved from http://www.towersperrin.com/tp/getwebcachedoc? Webc = HRS/USA/2003/200309/Talent_2003.pdf

Perry-Smith, J. E., & Blum, T. C. (2000). Work-family human resource bundles and perceived organizational performance. *Academy of Management Journal, 43*, 1107–1117. doi:10.2307/1556339

Pont, J. (2004). Are they really 'On the Job?' *Potentials*, 32-37.

Poyner, C., & Warne, B. (1988). *Preventing violence to staff. London: Health and Safety Executive.* H.M.S.O.

Purvi, S., & Schmidt, L. (2011). *Macroeconomic Conditions and Updating of Expectations by Older Americans.* Working Paper, 259. University of Michigan Retirement Research Center. Accessed at http://www.mrrc.isr.umich.edu/publications/papers/pdf/wp259.pdf

Rathod, C (2007). Contribution of Indian Small Scale entrepreneurs to economic growth in India: Opportunities and Challenges in Global economy. *Prabandh-Journal of Management & Research.*

Redman, J. (2011). A development program to improve leadership capability and employee engagement. *Strategic HR Review, 10*(6), 11–18. doi:10.1108/14754391111172779

Reissner, S., & Pagan, V. (2013). Generating employee engagement in a public–private partnership: Management communication activities and employee experiences. *International Journal of Human Resource Management, 24*(14), 2741–2759. doi:10.1080/09585192.2013.765497

Rich, B. L., Lepine, J. A., & Crawford, E. R. (2010). Job engagement: Antecedents and effects on job performance. *Academy of Management Journal, 53*(3), 617–635. doi:10.5465/amj.2010.51468988

Richman, A. (2006). Everyone wants an engaged workforce how can you create it? *Workspan*, (49), 36-39.

Robinson, D., Perryman, S., & Hayday, S. (2004). *The Drivers of Employee Engagement, Report 408.* Retrieved January 18, 2019, from http://www. employment-studies.co.uk/report-summaries/report-summary-drivers-employee-engagement

Rotundo, M., & Sackett, P. R. (2002). The Relative Importance of Task, Citizenship, and Counterproductive Performance to Global Ratings of Job Performance: A Policy-Capturing Approach. *The Journal of Applied Psychology*, *87*(1), 66–80. doi:10.1037/0021-9010.87.1.66 PMID:11916217

Sadiqe, M. (2014). Employee Engagement in Hospitality Industry in India: An Overview. *Global Journal of Finance and Management.*, *6*(4), 375–378.

Saks, A. M. (2006). Antecedents and consequences of employee engagement. *Journal of Managerial Psychology*, *21*(7), 600–619. doi:10.1108/02683940610690169

Salanova, M., Agut, S., & Peiro, J. M. (2005). Linking organizational resources and work engagement to employee performance and customer loyalty: The mediation of service climate. *The Journal of Applied Psychology*, *90*(6), 1217–1227. doi:10.1037/0021-9010.90.6.1217 PMID:16316275

Sand, T., Cangemi, J., & Ingram, J. (2011). Say again? What do associates really want at work? *Organization Development Journal*, *29*(2), 101–107.

Sarangee, S., & Srivastava, R. K. (2012). Driving Employee Engagement in Nationalized Banks in India. *2012 International Conference on Economics, Business Innovation.*

Schaufeli, W., Martı'nez, I., Marque's-Pinto, A., Salanova, M., & Bakker, A. B. (2002). Burnout and engagement in university students: A cross nation study. *Journal of Cross-Cultural Psychology*, *33*(5), 464–481. doi:10.1177/0022022102033005003

Schaufeli, W. B., Bakker, A. B., & Salanova, M. (2006). The measurement of work engagement with a short questionnaire: A cross-national study. *Educational and Psychological Measurement*, *66*(4), 701–716. doi:10.1177/0013164405282471

Schaufeli, W. B., Bakker, A. B., & Van Rhenen, W. (2009). How changes in job demands and resources predict burnout, work engagement, and sickness absenteeism. *Journal of Organizational Behavior*, *30*(7), 893–917. doi:10.1002/job.595

Seijit, G. M., & Crim, D. (2006). What engages the employees the most or, the ten C's of employee engagement. *Ivey Business Journal Online*.

Shalley, C. E., & Gilson, L. L. (2004). What leaders need to know: A review of social and contextual factors that can foster or hinder creativity. *The Leadership Quarterly*, *15*(1), 33–53. doi:10.1016/j.leaqua.2003.12.004

Shantz, A., Alfes, K., Truss, C., & Soane, E. (2013). The role of employee engagement in the relationship between job design and task performance, citizenship and deviant behaviours. *International Journal of Human Resource Management*, *24*(13), 2608–2627. doi:10.1080/09585192.2012.744334

Shanumugam, P., & Krishnaveni, R. (2012). Employee Engagement: An Introspection Into its Conceptualization. *International Journal of Social Science & Interdisciplinary Research*, *1*(9), 186–194.

Singh, A., & Sanjeev, R. (2013). Employee engagement in a public sector undertaking: An investigation. *International Journal of Management Research & Business Strategy*, *2*(2), 93–100.

Singh, R., Garg, K., & Deshmukh, S. G. (2008). Challenges and strategies for competitiveness of SMEs: A case study in the Indian context. *International Journal of Services and Operations Management*, 4(2), 181–200. doi:10.1504/IJSOM.2008.016610

Soni, B. S. (2013). Employee engagement - A key to organizational success in 21st Century. *Voice of Research.*, 1(4), 51–55.

Stephen, L. (2008). Rethinking risk in the new economy: Age and cohort effects on unemployment and re-employment. *Human Resources*, 61, 1259–1292.

Sudan, F. K. (2005), Challenges in Micro and Small Scale Enterprises Development: Some Policy Issues. *Synergy: I. T. S. Journal of IT and Management*, 3(2), 67-81.

Thakur, P. (2014). A research paper on the effect of employee engagement on job satisfaction in IT sector. *Journal of Business Management & Social Sciences Research*, 3(5), 31–30.

The Joint Committee of Industry and Government. (2013). *White Paper On Stimulation Of Investment Of Private Sector Into Research And Development In India*. Department of Science & Technology, Ministry of Science & Technology, Government of India.

Thompson, L. (2003). Improving the creativity of organizational work groups. *The Academy of Management Executive*, 17(1), 96–111. doi:10.5465/AME.2003.9474814

Tomar, J. S. (2017a). Employee Engagement Practices in IT Sector Vis-à-Vis Other Sectors in India. *International Journal of Human Capital and Information Technology Professionals*, 8(3), 1–14. doi:10.4018/IJHCITP.2017070101

Tomar, J. S. (2017b). Influence of Strategic Priorities of SMEs on Their Decision to Adopt ERP. *International Journal of Scientific Research and Management*, 5(11), 7423–7436.

Townsend, K., Wilkinson, A., & Burgess, J. (2014). Routes to partial success: Collaborative employment relations and employee engagement. *International Journal of Human Resource Management*, 25(6), 915–930. doi:10.1080/09585192.2012.743478

Truss, C., Soane, E., Edwards, C., Wisdom, K., Croll, A., & Burnett, J. (2006). *Working Life: Employee Attitudes and Engagement 2006*. London: CIPD.

Tushman, M. L., & O'Reilly, C. A. III. (1996). Ambidextrous organizations: Managing evolutionary and revolutionary change. *California Management Review*, 38(4), 8–30. doi:10.2307/41165852

Vandenberg, R., & Lance, C. (1992). Satisfaction and organisational commitment. *Journal of Management*, 18, 153–167. doi:10.1177/014920639201800110

Viljevac, A., Cooper-Thomas, H. D., & Saks, A. M. (2012). An investigation into the validity of two measures of work engagement. *International Journal of Human Resource Management*, 23(17), 3692–3709. doi:10.1080/09585192.2011.639542

Walker Information Inc. (2000). *Employee Commitment and the Bottom Line: Ethical Issues in the Employer-Employee Relationship*. Work.

Wefald, A. J., & Downey, R. G. (2009). Construct Dimensionality of Engagement and Its Relation with Satisfaction. *The Journal of Psychology, 143*(1), 91–111. doi:10.3200/JRLP.143.1.91-112 PMID:19157075

WESP – The World Economic Situation and Prospects. (2019). *India Projected to grow at 7.1% in FY'20.* Retrieved from https://economictimes.indiatimes.com/topic/World-Economic-Situation-and-Prospects

White, B. (2006). *Employee Engagement Report 2006.* BlessingWhite, Inc. Retrieved December 21, 2018, from http:// www.blessingwhite.com

White, B. (2008). *The Employee Engagement Equation in India.* BlessingWhite and HR Anexi. Accessed from www.blessingwhite.com

Wintner, S. L. (2010). *10 key financial performance indicators for architecture and engineering firms.* Retrieved March 6, 2012, from http://www.axium.com/blog/?p=2360

Wu, J., & Lebreton, J. M. (2011). Reconsidering the dispositional basis of counterproductive work behavior: The role of aberrant personality. *Personnel Psychology Banner, 64*(3), 593–626. doi:10.1111/j.1744-6570.2011.01220.x

Xu, J., & Thomas, H. C. (2011). How can leaders achieve high employee engagement? *Leadership and Organization Development Journal, 32*(4), 399–416. doi:10.1108/01437731111134661

Yıldıza, B., & Alpkan, L. (2015). A theoretical model on the proposed predictors of destructive deviant workplace behaviors and the mediator role of alienation. *Procedia: Social and Behavioral Sciences, 210*, 330–338. doi:10.1016/j.sbspro.2015.11.373

APPENDIX: SURVEY INSTRUMENT

Employee Engagement Survey

(Employee's Perception of Employee Engagement Practices in their Organization)

Questionnaire

Engagement Attributes and Questions

1. Insightful work
   a. Does your organization give more autonomy, decision-making power, time, and support?
   b. Does your company do the competency mapping of "fit factors" other than GPA and academic scores before assigning a job?
   c. Are the sizes of task specific teams appropriate, and as per the volume of work?
   d. Does your organization offer the employees time to think, create, and rest to rejuvenate?

2. Pragmatic management
   a. Are the goals set by the management simple, clear, transparent, and are frequently revisited?
   b. Is the management actively involved in the role of coach as a friend, philosopher, and guide?
   c. Is the management keen on nurturing leadership and developing future managers & leaders?
   d. Does the performance appraisal methodology evaluate the efforts of an employee effectively?

3. Positive work environment
   a. Does your organization offer you flexible and supportive work environment?
   b. Does your company offer wellness program, and recreational facilities like swimming pool, yoga centres?
   c. Does your organization have culture of appreciation, and continuous recognition program?
   d. Does your organization try to cultivate diversity and include it in the organizational culture?

4. Growth opportunity
   a. Does your company let people learn on the job, take developmental assignments, and give support when they need?
   b. Does your company support internal mobility by giving new assignments in various areas?
   c. Are the employees given the liberty to try and adopt new methodologies in your organization?
   d. Does the experiential learning of the employees in the organization help them climb the professional ladder?

5. Engaging Leadership
   a. Are the purpose, mission, and soul of the organization aligned with that of the employees?
   b. Does your company invest in people, both in their professional and personal lives?
   c. Does your company have a policy of rapid, open, transparent communications?
   d. Does the management inspire the employees through their words, communications, and actions, and engage everyone in the organization?

Chapter 24

Approaches and Methods for Individual Performance Assessment in Information Systems Projects

José Luís Pereira
University of Minho, Portugal

João Varajão
University of Minho, Portugal

Carlos Sousa Pinto
University of Minho, Portugal

António Silva
University of Minho, Portugal

ABSTRACT

Organizations have to manage human resources effectively, as these are fundamental to their success. Indeed, it is widely recognized that human resources have a direct influence in the performance of organizations. Therefore, organizational success is highly dependent on an adequate management of human resources. In this context, the performance assessment of people is crucial, as it is an important process for implementing efficient and effective motivational and rewarding systems. However, in the case of information systems projects, there is not much research work focused on human resources performance evaluation. This chapter aims to contribute to fill this gap by reviewing several approaches and methods for performance assessment, which can be applied to information systems projects. The presented approaches and methods are focused on personality, behaviors, comparison, and outcomes/results.

DOI: 10.4018/978-1-7998-1279-1.ch024

INTRODUCTION

In order to be successful in an increasingly competitive business environment, organizations have to manage their human resources effectively and efficiently (Pereira, Varajão, Sá & Silva, 2019). To be able to deal with the continuous challenges they are subjected to, modern organizations make all the efforts to attract the best people. The fact is, more and more, organizations performance is intimately dependent on the competences, skills, abilities and even psychological traits of their personnel. Therefore, organizations have to assure a proper management of their human resources.

The performance evaluation is an important component of the human resources management activity, bringing together different approaches and methods which contribute to improve the results of organizations. With the evolution of human resources management, it has become clear that human performance not only needs to be planned taking into account organizational objectives, but also needs to be assessed and oriented to achieve those objectives.

The appraisal of human resources performance is thus fundamental in virtually all projects and organizations, and the case of information systems projects is no exception. These projects "have maintained an unfortunate reputation when it comes to success", since most of them exhibit serious problems in terms of meeting the scope, the time or the budget (Varajão, Dominguez, Ribeiro & Paiva, 2014). The success of information systems projects depends on rigorous project management processes, in which aspects such as the involvement of top management and customers, the definition of clear objectives and requirements, an effective management of human resources, among others, are critical (Colomo-Palacios, Gonzalez-Carrasco, Lopez-Cuadrado, Trigo & Varajão, 2014).

Although people recognize performance appraisal to be essential to the management of human resources and a key factor that influences the success of organizations and organizational projects, there is little research focused on the particular case of information systems projects.

Even though the area of performance evaluation is acknowledged as essential in human resources management and fundamental to the success of organizations and projects, there is not much research that focuses on the particular case of information systems projects (Moura, Dominguez & Varajão, 2019; Pereira et al., 2019). The present chapter aims to contribute to fill this gap by reviewing performance appraisal approaches and methods which may be successfully applied in the case of information systems projects.

The study presented in this chapter is an improved version of the article previously published on International Journal of Human Capital and Information Technology Professionals titled "Performance Appraisal Approaches and Methods for IT/IS Projects: A Review" (Silva, Varajão, Pereira & Pinto, 2017), and it is organized as follows: in the following section, the authors discuss the importance of performance evaluation; the third section describes the different types of information systems projects; in the fourth section the authors present several approaches and methods for performance appraisal identified in the literature; finally, some concluding remarks and future work ideas are presented in section five.

BACKGROUND

Performance Assessment

Performance assessment comprises an evaluation, measurement and systematic comparison of individual, group and organizational variables, supported in a formally established set of competences and/ or predefined objectives (Chiavenato, 2003). The performance of an individual originates from her/his competences (knowledge, experience, and attitudes), her/his personality, her/his motivation, her/his interpersonal relations, the working atmosphere and the characteristics of the project and the organization (Sarmento, Rosinha & Silva, 2015; Pereira et al., 2019; Lussier & Hendon, 2016).

In organizations, it is common to implement performance measurement processes to assist, at the organizational level, in administrative decisions (e.g., salaries, promotions, compensations, transfers and dismissals) and, at the individual level, to help people to recognize the assessment made based on their performance (positive or negative), but also to allow the evaluator to give the employee feedback on her/ his performance and how to improve. This evaluation process confirms the quality of the recruitment and selection process of employees, allows one to verify the effectiveness of paid training, and seeks to improve team and the organizational climate (Bernadin, Kane, Ross, Spina & Johnson, 1995; Carrel, Elbert & Hatfield, 2000).

Performance evaluation should be carried out with particular caution, since employees who are dissatisfied with the results of their assessment processes may leave the organization. The turnover of human resources involved in information systems projects may represent a loss of valuable knowledge and organizational experience, accumulated over the years, with direct and immediate implications in projects where such resources are involved. This fact also generates new costs associated with the recruitment and training of replacement personnel, thus delaying project completion (Pee, Kankanhalli, Tan & Tham, 2014). The successful implementation of the evaluation processes requires commitment, involvement and active participation of all stakeholders, through a process of effective communication, openness, and orientation to improvement, so that all stakeholders receive continuous feedback on their performance (Fletcher, 2001).

The performance evaluation is mainly associated with measuring processes. In order to implement a performance evaluation process, it is important to carefully think about the objectives that are to be achieved and the procedure that follows, thus defining who, when and how to participate in the evaluation process (Lussier & Hendon, 2016). The performance appraisal process should be based on the close proximity between the appraiser and the assessed employee: this proximity guarantees a more complete performance appraisal and provides fast and effective feedback to the assessed employee (Sanyal & Biswas, 2014).

Empirical research on high-tech firms (e.g., Thamhain, 2004; Sun, Xu & Shang, 2014) found that (1) personal and team rewards and evaluation (e.g., career opportunities and job security) were strongly associated with team performance; and (2) by rewarding, leadership can improve project teams' performance (Moura et al., 2019). According to Thamhain's (2004) sixth recommendation ("create proper reward systems"), there should be systems that recognize both individual and team performance (Varajão & Moura, 2018). However, performance management and performance appraisal is a process absent or applied inadequately in many organizations (Colomo-Palacios, Casado-Lumbreras, Soto-Acosta, Misra & García-Peñalvo, 2012).

Information Systems Projects

There have been increasing levels of investment in information systems by organizations over the last few years, implying significant changes in the way of doing business (Gonzálvez-Gallego, Molina-Castillo, Soto-Acosta, Varajao & Trigo, 2015; Ogwueleka, Misra, Palacios & Fernandez, 2015; Trigo, Varajão, Figueiredo & Barroso, 2007). It is well accepted and somewhat consensual that information systems are critical for the development of virtually any human organization. Involving people, processes, information technology, and other organizational resources and structure, which facilitate the acquisition, storage, processing and transmission of data, information, and knowledge in an organization (Pearlson, Saunders & Galletta, 2016), information systems require constant attention to fulfil their role adequately and to keep pace with the changes of the information and business moving needs of organizations (Varajão, 2018b).

Information systems projects are complex and creative processes (often requiring a variety of technologies) that are flexible to develop (Sudhakar, Farooq & Patnaik, 2011; Stagnaro & Piotrowski, 2014; Weimar, Nugroho, Visser & Plaat, 2013); they also integrate technology, human resources, processes, and data. These projects have a temporal dimension that usually spans for as short as a few months to as long as a few years (De Leoz, Tripathi, Tahmasbi & Petter, 2013). An information systems project is carried out by a team (which is gathered for this specific purpose), usually, to create an information technology solution that did not exist before (Sudhakar et al., 2011; Moura et al., 2019). Not surprisingly, research on the development of information systems projects (Thamhain, 2004; Collins & Schragle-Law, 2010; Sudhakar et al., 2011; De Leoz et al., 2013) suggests that this development is human centric, reinforcing the importance of performance assessment aiming to implement proper motivational and rewarding systems.

Information systems projects are temporary endeavors that involve the creation of some unique outcome. This outcome can take very different forms, for example: an information technology component (e.g., a software application; the migration of data to a new support; the upgrade of the enterprise' information technology infrastructure); or a change in an enterprise that aims at achieving some mid/long-term benefit resulting from the implantation of a new information technology application (Varajão & Carvalho, 2018).

There are several types of information systems projects intended to satisfy the different needs of organizations (Trigo, Varajão, Barroso, Soto-Acosta, Molina-Castillo & Gonzalvez-Gallego, 2011). Cadle & Yeates (2008) typify information systems projects in eight categories, namely: software development; outsourcing; consultancy and business analysis assignments; system enhancement; disaster recovery; infrastructure implementation; package implementation; and systems migration projects.

Software development arises from the need to build software applications (e.g., Web applications). In this type of project, skills are required to analyze, specify, build, test and implement new software for customers (Misra, Palacios, Pusatli & Acosta, 2013). On the one hand, products can be developed based on an idea or a recognized need in the market, in which the products are developed for prospective clients are unknown until the product is marketed (called Commercial off-the-shelf software development). On the other hand, software can be developed according to the specific needs of each client (custom software development). Software development projects can be performed internally (in-sourcing), externally (outsourcing) using a contractor to provide the software, or by both internal and external teams (selective sourcing) (Varajão, Trigo, Figueiredo, Barroso & Cruz, 2009).

Consultancy and business analysis assignments arise from the need to investigate a business problem or a proposed solution using information systems. This type of project typically involves activities such as the analysis of the technological and/or organizational system (as the object of intervention), and the definition of the As-Is situation, in order to further identify and present possible improvement aspects. In addition, it takes into account the best business practices (Ought-To-Be situation). Finally, the processes are validated by the organization's management team so as to further implement it (To-Be situation).

The system enhancement and disaster recovery projects originated from the need to repair, improve or add new functionalities in order to meet new market requirements, or to comply with new laws and regulations standards, for example. Typically, the team's effort in these types of projects is to maintain and support existing systems. If the team has to improve and develop new features, one of the difficulties that may arise keeping the existing system in operation while adding improvements/features, since there is the risk of damaging existing well-functioning system components.

Infrastructure projects emerge from the need to introduce or replace existing hardware. The entire life-cycle of this type of project is similar to the life-cycle of a software development project.

The package implementation projects arises from the need to implement configurable commercial software products. Today, organizations acquire integrated management systems (commonly known as "Enterprise Resource Planning" - ERP systems), in the form of commercial packages, to support most of their processes (Varajão, Trigo, Figueiredo & Barroso, 2007), to manage their resources (materials, people or equipment) and to integrate existing information systems into a single system. The evolution of technology has changed the way new information systems are developed - from the traditional custom development solutions to the aggregation of off-the-shelf, ready to use components, thus, significantly reducing costs and development time. In this type of project, there are executed activities such as the consulting and analysis of business processes, configuration/parameterization of the systems and the development/adaptation of parts not covered by the software package.

System migration projects are necessary when the current systems are no longer supported (or supportable). In these types of projects, it is necessary to define strategies that can be adopted in the implementation and conversion of data (in case it is needed), training the end-users, and putting the new system into operation (Cadle & Yeates, 2008; Akman, Misra & Altindag, 2011; Akman, Misra & Cafer, 2011).

PERFORMANCE ASSESSMENT APPROACHES AND METHODS

Given the importance of information systems projects, it is essential to implement systematic processes in human resources performance assessment. Poor management of human factors can hinder the success of projects and the use of technologies and information systems (Casado-Lumbreras, Colomo-Palacios, Hernández-López & Soto-Acosta, 2011). In this section, the authors present various approaches and methods for performance appraisal, which can be applied to information systems projects.

In the literature about performance appraisal, it is possible to find several approaches which comprise diverse performance measurement methods (Borman, 1991; Morhman, Resnick-West, & Lawler, 1989; Carrol & Schneier, 1982; Kane & Lawler, 1979). According to Morhman et al. (1989), performance involves the "behavior of a performer in a situation to achieve results". This performer's behavior may manifest itself in a social background which also includes other performers. In this context, one can consider approaches centered on the personality or on the behavior of the performer, in comparison with other performers, and on the results achieved. The measurement instruments are generally organized according to this categorization.

Depending on the element which is taken as a target, different measurement methods are associated. Therefore, for each approach there are more "traditional" performance appraisal methods (past oriented and directed towards attitude and behavior) and more "modern" ones (future-oriented and focused on results). Past oriented methods focus on the performances that have already occurred and which can be measured, making it possible to provide evaluated employees feedback on how to improve their performance and modify their behavior, if necessary. In the future oriented methods, the focus is on employee potential and their future performances, using the setting of future performance objectives and the information obtained from the evaluation process to anticipate possible consequences that may arise for the developer and the project (Aswathappa, 2005).

In Figure 1 the different approaches and associated methods are identified, which are described in the following sections.

Methods Focused on Personality

The methods centered on personality are past oriented and directed to the personality traits of an individual. This is true for character traits and traits acquired during the life-time of an individual. They include the *graphic rating scales method* and the *checklist method*.

Graphic Rating Scales Method

With the graphic rating scales method, initially created by Paterson (1922), the aim is to assign, for each evaluation criterion, one of the scale values that represent the trait and typical behavioral of the evalu-

Figure 1. Performance appraisal approaches and methods

Figure 2. Example of a graphic rating scale

ated. Figure 2 shows an example with an evaluation criteria (autonomy), associated with a scale (from 0 to 3) with predefined levels ("none", "casual", "frequent" and "systematic") which help determine the typical behavioral level of an employee.

This method is one of the most common methods of performance appraisal because it is relatively easy to construct, apply and understand (Latham & Wexley, 1981). It is simple to compare the performances of employees due to the standardization of the evaluation criteria, and the chosen factors (e.g., autonomy) allow the identification of the appreciated (or not appreciated) traits and behaviors in the organization. However, if the trait names, points or anchors are not clearly defined in terms of observable behaviors, it may enhance the subjectivity and *halo/horn* effect, central tendency error, leniency and strictness (Latham, Fay, & Saari, 1979; Rosen et al., 2010).

The halo/horn effect occurs when the classification in one of the criteria (factors or dimensions) is generalized to all others. That is, if the evaluator has an unfavorable opinion of the evaluated employee in a given feature, she/he can assign a score (below average) that she/he believes to be the most adequate to evaluate employee performance, tending to generalize the classification in the item to other evaluated items. This case is referred to as horn effect. Similarly, the halo effect occurs when the evaluator has a favorable opinion in one of the characteristics and generalizes it to the remaining items to be evaluated.

The central tendency error occurs when the evaluator is afraid of making distinctions among employees. This is verified by a trend in the prevalence of quotes around the midpoint of the scale (medium), avoiding extreme quotations (whether positive or negative).

Leniency and strictness, also called gentleness and severity error, occur when the evaluator is very biased when classifying the employee above (leniency) or bellow (strictness) the midpoint of the rating scale. The requirement to justify the assignment of the highest classification of the scale is a way to overcome this error.

Checklist Method

The checklist method identifies traits (using adjectives) or behavioral aspects (using performance descriptions) that evaluators must verify by checking the items that, in their perception, apply to the assessed collaborator. This method has advantages which are similar to the graphic rating scales method (Carrol & Schneier, 1982) and also fits into approaches focusing on behavior as seen in Table 1. However, it does not allow for detailed answers or explanations, unless combined with another method.

Methods Focused on Behaviors

The methods and techniques focused on behaviors gave rise to diverse instruments, but with focus on behavior rather than personality traits. These methods and techniques are also past oriented. They include

Table 1. Examples of the checklist method

Checklist Method focused on personality traits	Checklist Method focused on behaviors
☐ Cooperative	☐ Shows willingness to collaborate with others
☐ Competitive	☐ Shows unwillingness to collaborate with others

the *critical incidents method*, the *forced choice method*, the *behaviorally anchored rating scales method*, the *mixed standard rating scales method* and the *behavioral observation scales method*.

Critical Incidents Method

In the critical incidents method, introduced by Flanagan & Burns (1955), evaluators focus their attention on the exceptional performances of the evaluated collaborators, i.e. they record occurrences representing negative and/or positive performances that are critical to job success. If there is a high number of employees, this method allows managers to remember everything each one of them did well (or not so well), and when (Lussier & Hendon, 2016). Table 2 presents an example of a critical events log.

The positive behaviors that the evaluated collaborator has exhibited should be registered and used later to encourage the pursuit of the expected performance. The negative performances must be registered in order to be changed or eliminated in the future, indicating the appreciated behaviors and clarifying expectations. The use of this method facilitates the interview evaluation because it allows one to clarify and judge concrete behaviors manifested by the evaluated performer and identifies behaviors that should be avoided in the future. Incidents recorded by two or more team members demonstrate and enhance the veracity of the event. But it takes time, control, regular registration and monitoring of the evaluated performer in the development of their work. This may lead to resistance of use or distortion of values by the evaluator and enhance the focus on the negative actions of employees. If the team which will be evaluated is very large, the application of this method may be difficult for evaluators. A comparison of the performance ratings of the employees might also be a limitation as there is no quantification of performance (Lussier & Hendon, 2016).

Forced Choice Method

In the forced choice method, the statements that portray the behavior of the evaluated collaborator are identified. For each block of descriptive phrases, one must place a "+" sign in the statement that best reflects the usual behavior of the evaluated collaborator, or a "-" sign in the statement that less portrays the evaluated employee's usual behavior (Berkshire & Highland, 1953).

This method provides more reliable results that are free of subjective influences, eliminating the hallo effect. However, the adoption of this method is complex, the main difficulty being the preparation of

Table 2. Example of the critical incidents method

Underperformances		Outperformances	
Occurrence Date	**Incident**	**Occurrence Date**	**Incident**
01/11/2019	*C*	*04/11/2019*	*C*
02/11/2019	*A*	*05/11/2019*	*B*
03/11/2019	*B*	*06/11/2019*	*A*
A – Finished the job with minimal effort B – Lost time during the work period C – Did not start the task promptly		A – Finished the job with maximum B – Saved time during the work period C – Started the task immediately	

Table 3. Example of the forced choice method

Identify the statements that, better (+) or worse (-), portray the behavior		
1	Shows willingness to collaborate with others	+
2	Only executes the tasks that are assigned to her/him	-
3	Abstains from team decision making process	-

short phrases that clearly reflect the behavior of the employees, while not omitting relevant behavioral aspects (Berkshire & Highland, 1953).

Behaviorally Anchored Rating Scales Method

The behaviorally anchored rating scales method (BARS), initially created by Smith & Kendall (1963), is similar to the graphic rating scales method, but overcomes the problem of subjectivity by focusing on specific and described behaviors anchored in behavioral skills (Carrol & Schneier, 1982). Being a variant of graphic scales, this method has the same advantages and limitations. As seen in Table 4, for each behavioral skill (e.g., leadership) a rating scale is considered (e.g. 1 to 5) and suitable behaviors to the levels of performance are described (e.g., "unacceptable" "unsatisfactory", "satisfactory", "good" and "excellent").

Mixed Standard Rating Scales Method

The mixed standard rating scales method, proposed by Blanz & Ghiselli (1972), is identical to the behaviorally anchored rating scales method. While in the BARS method each behavioral competence (leadership, efficiency, etc.) is displayed along with the behavioral descriptions of the respective performance levels ("excellent", "good", etc.), in this method the behavioral skills do not appear explicitly and the behavioral anchors of the various skills are presented randomly. Each item can express three different levels of performance: above average [+], average [0] and below average [-]. For example, if an employee has obtained a [-] in a high-performance description, a [-] in a medium performance description and a [+] in a poor performance description, then it means that her/his performance lays between the average and below average level. In Table 5, mixed standard rating scales are presented, where items 1 and 3 show a high performance and items 2 and 4 reflect poor performance.

Table 4. Example of the behaviorally anchored rating scales method

Mark with "X" the statement that better portraits your performance in each competence	
Competence: Leadership	
5 [×] Excellent	Plans, manages, organizes, directs, evaluates and develops the team for continuous improvement
4 [ ] Good	Plans, manages, organizes, directs and evaluates project progress
3 [ ] Satisfactory	Plans and controls the changes and constraints of the plan
2 [ ] Unsatisfactory	Demonstrates little concern in the control of the project plan
1 [ ] Unacceptable	There is no project plan or the plan is too weak

Table 5. Example of the mixed standard rating scales method

Indicate, for each statement, which level portrays the employee performance (above average [+], average [0], or below average [-])	
1 [+]	The project manager assesses and provides feedback to employees in order to continuously improve the team's performance and the project
2 [−]	It may occur that the project manager is not seen as having legitimacy by all team members, regarding decisions
3 [0]	The project manager demonstrates a positive attitude towards employees, is receptive to suggestions and criticism and reveals willingness to help and guide the team
4 [0]	It may occur that the project manager is not receptive to recommendations regarding the predefined plan

Behavioral Observation Scales Method

The behavioral observation scales (BOS) method, initially created by Latham & Wexley (1977), aims to identify the frequency with which the evaluated performer shows the behavior described. The evaluator prepares behavioral descriptions relating to the job performance (or liabilities) in question and must indicate, using a scale (from 1 to 5), the frequency of occurrence of the employee behaviors (see Table 6). The use of this method has advantages similar to those of the BARS method, namely, the ability to provide specific feedback to evaluated employees. However, it is unlikely that this method is based only on observation, excluding inferential judgments.

Methods Focused on Comparison

Given that the work environment of the teams must be created in order to complement and/or to promote the competition, it is possible to evaluate the performance through methods and techniques that allow one to compare individuals with each other. Such methods and techniques include the *forced ranking method*, the *paired comparison method*, the *point rating method* and the *forced distribution method*.

Forced Ranking Method

In the ranking method, the evaluator ranks each element of a group, with the same or an identical position, in a hierarchical list, from the best to the worst, depending on each member's performance, preventing the assignment of the same rating to two or more (see Table 7). This ordering can be done based on the

Table 6. Example of the behavioral observation scales method

Indicate, using the symbol "X", the frequency of the behaviors described, based on the quality competence and specific responsibilities				
1. Reviews the code that the programmer develops				
Always [5]	[4]	[3]	[2]	Never [1]
2. Informs the programmer when there are anomalies in the code				
Always [5]	[4]	[3]	[2]	Never [1]

Table 7. Example of the ranking method

Competence: Efficiency	
1st: *Employee A*	Observation:
2nd: *Employee B*	Observation:
Nth: *Employee C*	Observation:

overall performance or based on pre-defined skills - for example, "Who is the first, the second, the nth more efficient employee?" (Carrel, Elbert & Hatfield, 2000).

Paired Comparison Method

The paired comparison method aims to ensure that each employee is confronted with each other, in order to decide who has the best overall performance (not in a specific competence). It uses the formula N * (N-1) / 2 to determine the total number of pairs to create, assuming that N is equal to the number of employees to evaluate (Carroll & Schneier, 1982).

The evaluator compares two employees, identifying the one she/he considers to have a better overall performance and records the result in a list, allowing hierarchically to classify each employee. Based on Table 8, it is possible to identify, through an example, which employees demonstrate the best and the worst global performance.

This method might become complex and time consuming, depending on the total number of employees to be evaluated, thus enhancing the fatigue error. Also called routine error, this is when the evaluator is not too committed to the evaluation process, especially when she/he has many employees to evaluate and does it continuously without interruption. The assignment of very similar ratings to all employees or ratings in the middle of the table, reflect the error of fatigue or routine.

Point Rating Method

In the point rating method, the evaluator compares, from her/his own perspective, the overall performance of all employees and distributes a fixed amount of points (i.e. 100 points) among them. Table 9 shows an example of use of this method. The assessment can be discretionary and enhances the occurrence of

Table 8. Example of the paired comparison method

	Employee 1 (E1)	Employee 2 (E2)	Employee 3 (E3)	Employee 4 (E4)
E1 *vs.* E2	×			
E3 *vs.* E4				×
E1 *vs.* E3	×			
E2 *vs.* E4	-			×
E4 *vs.* E1	×			
E3 *vs.* E2			×	
Rating	1.º	4.º	3.º	2.º

Table 9. Example of the point rating method

Total score	100 points
Employee 1	*35 points*
Employee 2	*10 points*
Employee 3	*25 points*
Employee 4	*30 points*

the primacy effect, personal biases and/or recency effect, not providing justifications and appropriate feedback to the evaluated employees.

The primacy effect, also known as a first impression error, arises when the first impression of the evaluator about the employee tends to override the employee performance. This error results from the judgment made to the evaluated employee based on her/his looks, the rhythm in which she/he carries out the requests of the leader, the way she/he expresses and relates to colleagues, thus being evaluated subjectively and supported on intangible aspects. The error only occurs a few times, because with the passage of time the first impression will be confirmed or rejected.

The personal biases occurs when the evaluator tends to evaluate an employee based on her/his similarity with himself/herself or with someone she/he knows, in the performance of her/his duties. Note that the error does not occur often because the performance of the evaluated employee will confirm or infer the similarity that the evaluator has perceived.

The recency effect, also referred as contemporary effect, occurs when the evaluator tends to evaluate only the recent actions of the employee, not considering her/his overall performance throughout the development of the project. The emergence of this error is due to the fact that evaluators do not have adequate training to carry out performance reviews.

Forced Distribution Method

The forced distribution method compares each employee with others, joining employees in similar degrees of performance. The evaluator should include a certain percentage of employees in each of the defined degrees. The percentage associated to each degree of performance follows a normal distribution and requires that the highest number of employees be evaluated as average (Carrel et al., 2000). As seen in Table 10, a list of the evaluated employees is formed, with correspondence to each level of performance.

Table 10. Example of the forced distribution method

Rating by overall performance				
Unsatisfactory performance 0% to 10%	Performance to be improved 10% to 20%	Average performance 20% to 40%	Good performance 10% to 20%	Outstanding performance 0% to 10%
Employee 5	Employee 2 Employee 6	Employee 1 Employee 7 Employee 9	Employee 4 Employee 8	Employee 3

The application of this method prevents the occurrence of the *halo/horn* error. However, the assessment can be discretionary and does not provide adequate feedback to the evaluated employee, i.e. the rating of equivalent employees may not correspond to the truth when they are in different degrees of performance.

Methods and Techniques Focused on Results

Regarding these methods and techniques, the evaluation criteria is centered on the results of the activities developed by employees and not on their behavior. Therefore, the evaluation is based on a comparison between the expected results and the actual results of each employee, allowing the identification of her/his strengths and weaknesses, and the corrective actions to adopt. They include the *management by objectives method* and the *performance standards method*.

Management by Objectives Method

The management by objectives (MBO) method, primarily theorized by Drucker (1954), analyzes the results of the employee's performance against predefined goals. The objectives may be previously negotiated between the project leader and the employee, giving rise to a participatory evaluation by objectives, provided that they are aligned with the objectives of the project and the organization's strategic goals. Negotiation allows for a greater involvement of employees, which generates more commitment and, potentially, higher levels of performance.

This method can reduce the degree of subjectivity of evaluation and minimize potential mistakes made by evaluators, if goals are quantified. However, the goals can be difficult to quantify, and if they are not properly defined, they can generate demotivation and can negatively affect the performance of employees. Hence, various projects and organizations use the SMART technique to set their goals, so that they are *Specific*, *Measurable*, *Appropriate* (or *Achievable*), *Relevant* (or *Realistic*) and *Timed* (or *Time-bound*). It is also important that objectives are challenging, motivating, and meet the project's needs, satisfying the expectations of employees (Lussier & Hendon, 2016; Carrell, Elbert & Hatfield, 2000).

As illustrated in Table 11, for each objective and target negotiated and agreed by both the employee and the project leader, the corresponding result that has been obtained is identified by the employee and her/his performance in attaining that goal is characterized by the project leader in a five point scale (from excellent to inadequate).

Performance Standards Method

The performance standards method is frequently used to assess the operational level of work and assumes particular relevance in the scientific organization of labor studies (Taylor, 1911). This method allows for comparisons between pre-defined performance standards and the results of the employee's work, focusing on any deviations and identifying corrective actions to be applied in the future (see Table 12). The comparison of results regarding work factors can be directed to the quantity, speed or quality (Carroll & Schneier, 1982).

Table 11. Example of the Management by Objectives Method

By Employee			By Project Leader				
Agreed Goals & Targets		**Results**	**Excellent**	**Very good**	**Good**	**Adequate**	**Inadequate**
G1:	T1:	R1:					
G2:	T2:	R2:					
G3:	T3:	R3:					
G4:	T4:	R4:					
G5:	T5:	R5:					

Table 12. Example of the Performance Standards Method

Work Factors	**Achieved Level**	**Standard Level**	**Level Deviation**	**Corrective Action**
WF1:				
WF2:				
WFn:				

DISCUSSION AND CONCLUSION

The selection of approaches, methods and techniques to use in performance evaluation is closely related to the context and objectives of organizations or projects. In other words, there is no evaluation technique that can be recommended without considering the context. The evaluation methods and techniques identified in this chapter have both advantages and limitations, and should be implemented taking into consideration the specific objectives of the organization or project.

In order to evaluate the feasibility of using various methods and techniques for performance evaluation in the particular case of information systems, Pereira et al. (2019) carried out a study with a sample of thirteen academic projects. In this study, it was possible to confirm the pertinence of several approaches, methods, and techniques for performance assessment. The evaluation process implemented was bidirectional and proved to be an effective way to assess performance. The evaluation tools (which were the same reported in this chapter) attested to be useful for evaluating team performance, providing justifications for performance, as well as positive and less positive aspects of each team element's behavior. The evaluation process also contributed to equity and collective satisfaction, being a source of motivation for team members to improve their performance and to work effectively together. It was also possible to provide feedback to people, to identify training needs, and to recognize and reward individual performance. Also worth mentioning, the increase in the overall results of projects, as compared to the previous projects, reflecting the improvement in performance that was achieved.

To simplify the selection of the use of evaluation methods or techniques, various criteria can be considered, such as the evaluation objectives (e.g., administrative and development objectives) or the costs of implementation (Ivancevich, 1998; Oberg, 1972): if the main objective is the development and motivation of employees in order to improve their performance, the methods and techniques to consider might be the behaviorally anchored rating scales (BARS), the behavioral observation scales (BOS), the management by objectives (MBO) and/or the critical incidents method; when the aim is to provide information to support administrative decisions (salaries, promotions, transfers and dismissals), one should use different methods and techniques, such as the forced choice, forced distribution and/or graphic rating scales (despite being recommended for promotion decisions, the ranking method and the paired comparison are not recommended in cases of wage increases); in terms of costs, it is recommended to use instruments centered in the comparison with others, namely, the paired comparison, the ranking and the forced distribution methods, as they have low operational costs. Also, the use of graphic rating scales, behaviorally anchored rating scales (BARS), behavioral observation scales (BOS), forced choice and checklists, may have lower costs of application, even though they imply higher costs in their construction.

Intimately related with individual work performance is the motivation of employees. Indeed, practice has shown that highly motivated personnel equals to high performance organizations. While some performance assessment methods might contribute to increase the motivation of employees, it is a fact that a nurturing organizational culture and an adequate workplace environment might be major motivation enablers for the younger generations.

Performance assessment may also be used by organizations to identify recruitment needs. This aspect is particularly true in the case of information systems projects. In the IT area, due to the increasingly higher rhythm of technological evolution, new competences have to be obtained, while present knowledge becomes obsolete and thus, has to be discarded. In this regard, organizations have to undertake new ways of recruiting talent. The old ways of recruiting gifted personnel, using newspaper, radio or television announces (recruitment 1.0) are over. In the present, with the exponential use of the social networks, new approaches to attract talent become the norm (the so-called recruitment 2.0, recruitment 3.0 and so on). Anyway, although modern organizations have innovative ways of recruiting their personnel, the performance assessment of employees continues to be indispensable for an effective human resources management.

In this chapter the authors have discussed several approaches, methods and techniques used in the evaluation of human resources performance, including *approaches focused on personality*, *approaches focused on behaviors*, *approaches focused on comparison* and *approaches focused on results*. All of these seem to be feasibly applied to the case of information systems projects. Unfortunately, there is little research on information systems that has focused on this theme. Aiming to contribute to filling this gap, this chapter discusses the importance of performance evaluation in information systems projects and, thus, reviews the main evaluation approaches, methods and techniques that seem viable to be used in these projects. This study also opens the way for future research, as there are several issues that justify the search for answers, for example, "How often performance evaluation should be done?", "What kind of feedback is more useful to employees?", "Different information systems projects would require the use of different evaluation approaches, methods and techniques?", among many others.

A recent study of Varajão & Carvalho (2018) show that regardless of company size, sector or adopted project management methodology, the evaluation of projects success is currently an informal and rudimentary process mainly focused on the success of project management and not on the success of the projects' deliverables. Given the importance and complexity of the evaluation of projects' success, companies should define and implement systematic processes for success management (Varajão, 2016; Varajão, 2018; Varajão, 2018b) aiming to improve project performance and expected benefits, and individual performance assessment might be an important part of these processes.

The study presented is this chapter is useful, not only for researchers, but also for practitioners, given that it organizes and describes, in a structured way, the different approaches that can be applied in the performance evaluation of information systems projects.

REFERENCES

Akman, I., Misra, S., & Altindag, T. (2011). The Impact of Cognitive and Socio-Demographic Factors on Manager's Simple Thinking Towards Quality Of Meetings In Software Development Projects. *Technical Gazette, 18*(1), 51–56.

Akman, I., Misra, S., & Cafer, F. (2011). The Role of Leadership Cognitive Complexity in Software Development Projects: An Empirical Assessment for Simple Thinking. *Human Factors and Ergonomics in Manufacturing & Service Industries, 21*(5), 516–525. doi:10.1002/hfm.20256

Aswathappa, K. (2005). *Human resource and personnel management: text and cases.* McGraw-Hill.

Berkshire, H., & Highland, R. (1953). Forced-choice performance rating: A methodological study. *Personnel Psychology, 6*(3), 355–378. doi:10.1111/j.1744-6570.1953.tb01503.x

Bernadin, H. J., Kane, J. S., Ross, S., Spina, J., & Johnson, D. L. (1995). Performance Appraisal Design, Development and Implementation. In G. R. Ferris, S. D. Rosen, & D. T. Barnum (Eds.), *Handbook of Human Resource Management.* Cambridge, UK: Wiley-Blackwell.

Blanz, F., & Ghiselli, E. E. (1972). The mixed standard scale: A new rating system. *Personnel Psychology, 25*(2), 185–199. doi:10.1111/j.1744-6570.1972.tb01098.x

Borman, W. (1991). *Job behavior, performance, and effectiveness. Handbook of Industrial and Organizational Psychology.* Palo Alto, CA: Consulting Psychologists Press.

Cadle, J., & Yeates, D. (2008). *Project Management for Information Systems* (5th ed.). Essex, UK: Pearson, Prentice Hall.

Carrell, M. R., Elbert, N. F., & Hatfield, R. D. (2000). *Human Resource Management: Strategies for Managing a Diverse and Global Workforce* (6th ed.). Houghton Mifflin Harcourt.

Carrol, S. J., & Schneier, C. E. (1982). *Performance appraisal and review systems.* Glenview, IL: Scott Foresman.

Casado-Lumbreras, C., Colomo-Palacios, R., Hernández-López, A., & Soto-Acosta, P. (2011). Personnel Performance Appraisal Coverage in ITIL, COBIT and CMMi: A Study from the Perspective of People-CMM. *International Journal of Knowledge Society Research, 2*(2), 59–70. doi:10.4018/jksr.2011040106

Chiavenato, I. (2003). *Recursos Humanos: o capital humano das organizações* (8th ed.). São Paulo: Editora Atlas.

Collins, J. S. & Schragle-Law, S. (2010). IT Project Teams and Their Leaders: Interaction Expectations. *Leadership and Organizational Management, 1.*

Colomo-Palacios, R., Casado-Lumbreras, C., Soto-Acosta, P., Misra, S., & García-Peñalvo, F. J. (2012). Analyzing human resource management practices within the GSD context. *Journal of Global Information Technology Management*, *15*(3), 30–54. doi:10.1080/1097198X.2012.10845617

Colomo-Palacios, R., González-Carrasco, I., López-Cuadrado, J. L., Trigo, A., & Varajão, J. E. (2014). I-Competere: Using applied intelligence in search of competency gaps in software project managers. *Information Systems Frontiers*, *16*(4), 607–625. doi:10.100710796-012-9369-6

De Leoz, G., Tripathi, A., Tahmasbi, N., & Petter, S. (2013), Examining high performance teams in information systems projects. *Proceedings of the 19th Americas Conference on Information Systems.*

Drucker, P. F. (1954). *The practice of management*. New York: Harper.

Flanagan, J. C., & Burns, R. K. (1955). The employee performance record; a new appraisal and development tool. *Harvard Business Review*, *5*, 95–102.

Fletcher, C. (2001). Performance appraisal and management: The developing research agenda. *Journal of Occupational and Organizational Psychology*, *74*(4), 473–487. doi:10.1348/096317901167488

Gonzálvez-Gallego, N., Molina-Castillo, F.-J., Soto-Acosta, P., Varajão, J., & Trigo, A. (2015). Using integrated information systems in supply chain management. *Enterprise Information Systems*, *9*(2), 210–232. doi:10.1080/17517575.2013.879209

Ivancevich, J. (1998). *Human Resource Management* (7th ed.). New York: McGraw-Hill.

Kane, J. S., & Lawler, E. E. (1979). Performance appraisal effectiveness. Its assessment and determinants. *Research in Organizational Behavior*, *1*(1), 425–478.

Latham, G. P., Fay, C. H., & Saari, L. M. (1979). The development of behavioral observation scales for appraising the performance of foremen. *Personnel Psychology*, *32*(2), 299–311. doi:10.1111/j.1744-6570.1979.tb02136.x

Latham, G. P., & Wexley, K. N. (1977). Behavioral observation scales for performance appraisal purposes. *Personnel Psychology*, *30*(2), 255–268. doi:10.1111/j.1744-6570.1977.tb02092.x

Latham, G. P., & Wexley, K. N. (1981). *Increasing productivity through performance appraisal*. Reading, MA: Addison-Wesley.

Lussier, R. N., & Hendon, J. R. (2016). *Human Resource Management: Functions, Applications, and Skill Development* (2nd ed.). Singapore: SAGE Publications, Inc.

Misra, S., Palacios, R. C., Pusatli, T., & Acosta, P. S. (2013). A Discussion On The Role Of People In Global Software Development. *Technical Gazette*, *20*(3), 525–531.

Morhman, A., Resnick-West, S., & Lawler, E. (1989). *Designing Performance Appraisal Systems: aligning appraisals and organizational realities*. San Francisco: Jossey-Bass.

Moura, I., Dominguez, C., & Varajão, J. (2019). Information systems project teams: Factors for high performance, *Team Performance Management. International Journal (Toronto, Ont.)*, *25*(1/2), 69–83.

Oberg, W. (1972). Make performance appraisal relevant. *Harvard Business Review*, *50*(1), 61–67.

Ogwueleka, F., Misra, S., Palacios, R. C., & Fernandez, L. (2015). Neural Network and Classification Approach in Identifying Customer Behavior in The Banking Sector: A Case Study of An International Bank. *Human Factors and Ergonomics in Manufacturing & Service Industries, 25*(1), 28–42.

Paterson, D. G. (1922). The Scott Company graphic rating scale. *Journal of Personnel Research, 1,* 351–376.

Pearlson, K., Saunders, C., & Galletta, D. (2016). Managing and Using Information Systems (6th ed.). Wiley.

Pee, L. G., Kankanhalli, A., Tan, G. W., & Tham, G. Z. (2014). Mitigating the Impact of Member Turnover in Information Systems Development Projects. *IEEE Transactions on Engineering Management, 61*(4), 702–716. doi:10.1109/TEM.2014.2332339

Pereira, J. L., Varajão, J., Sá, J. O., & Silva, A. (2019). Performance Evaluation in IST Projects: A Case Study. In *Information Systems for Industry 4.0 - Proceedings of the 18th Conference of the Portuguese Association for Information Systems* (pp. 13-27). Springer International Publishing. 10.1007/978-3-030-14850-8_2

Rosen, M., Weaver, S., Lazzara, E., Salas, E., Wu, T., Silvestri, S., ... King, H. (2010). Tools for Evaluating Team Performance in Simulation-Based Training. *Journal of Emergencies, Trauma and Shock, 3*(4), 353–359. doi:10.4103/0974-2700.70746 PMID:21063558

Sanyal, M. K., & Biswas, S. B. (2014). Employee Motivation from Performance Appraisal Implications: Test of a Theory in the Software Industry in West Bengal (India). *Procedia Economics and Finance, 11,* 182–196. doi:10.1016/S2212-5671(14)00187-7

Sarmento, M., Rosinha, A., & Silva, J. (2015). *Avaliação do Desempenho*. Lisboa: Escolar Editora.

Silva, A., Varajão, J., Pereira, J. L., & Pinto, C. S. (2017). Performance Appraisal Approaches and Methods for IT/IS Projects: A Review. *International Journal of Human Capital and Information Technology Professionals, 8*(3), 15–28. doi:10.4018/IJHCITP.2017070102

Smith, P. C., & Kendall, L. M. (1963). Retranslations of expectations: An approach to the construction of unambiguous anchors for rating scales. *The Journal of Applied Psychology, 47*(2), 147–155. doi:10.1037/h0047060

Stagnaro, C., & Piotrowski, C. (2014). Shared leadership: A critical component in IT project management. *Journal of Technology Research, 5*(October), 1–21.

Sudhakar, G., Farooq, A., & Patnaik, S. (2011). Soft factors affecting the performance of software development teams. *Team Performance Management, 17*(3/4), 187–205.

Sun, W., Xu, A., & Shang, Y. (2014). Transformational leadership, team climate, and team performance within the NPD team: Evidence from China. *Asia Pacific Journal of Management, 31*(1), 127–147. doi:10.100710490-012-9327-3

Taylor, F. (1911). *The Principles of Scientific Management*. Harper & Brothers.

Thamhain, H. (2004). Linkages of project environment to performance: Lessons for team leadership. *International Journal of Project Management, 22*(2), 533–544. doi:10.1016/j.ijproman.2004.04.005

Trigo, A., Varajão, J., Barroso, J., Soto-Acosta, P., Molina-Castillo, F. J., & Gonzalvez-Gallego, N. (2011). Enterprise Information Systems Adoption in Iberian Large Companies: Motivations and Trends. In M. Tavana (Ed.), *Managing Adaptability, Intervention, and People in Enterprise Information Systems* (pp. 204–228). Information Resources Management Association. doi:10.4018/978-1-60960-529-2.ch010

Trigo, A., Varajão, J., Figueiredo, N., & Barroso, J. (2007). Information Systems and Technology Adoption By the Portuguese Large Companies. *Proceedings of the European and Mediterranean Conference on Information Systems.*

Varajão, J. (2016). Success Management as a PM knowledge area - work-in-progress. *Procedia Computer Science, 100*, 1095–1102. doi:10.1016/j.procs.2016.09.256

Varajão, J. (2018a). A new process for success management - bringing order to a typically ad-hoc area. *Journal of Modern Project Management, 5*(3), 94–99.

Varajão, J. (2018b). The many facets of information systems (+projects) success. *International Journal of Information Systems and Project Management, 6*(4), 5–13.

Varajão, J., & Carvalho, J. Á. (2018). Evaluating the Success of IS/IT Projects: How Are Companies Doing It? *13th Pre-ICIS International Research Workshop on Information Technology Project Management.*

Varajão, J., Dominguez, C., Ribeiro, P., & Paiva, A. (2014). Critical Success Aspects in Project Management: Similarities and Differences Between the Construction and the Software Industry. *Technical Gazette, 21*(2), 583–589.

Varajão, J., & Moura, I. (2018). Leading Information Systems Academic Teams to High Performance. *Proceedings of the 24th Americas Conference on Information Systems.*

Varajao, J., Trigo, A., Figueiredo, N., Barroso, J., & Cruz, J. B. (2009). Information systems services outsourcing reality in large Portuguese organisations. *International Journal of Business Information Systems, 4*(1), 125–142. doi:10.1504/IJBIS.2009.021606

Weimar, E., Nugroho, A., Visser, J., & Plaat, A. (2013). Towards high performance software teamwork. *Proceedings of the 17th International Conference on Evaluation and Assessment in Software Engineering.*

ADDITIONAL READING

Baskerville, R. L. (1999). Investigating information systems with action research. *Communications of AIS, 2*(3), 4.

Burlea, A. S. (2009). Success Factors for an Information Systems Projects Team Creating New Context. In Innovation and Knowledge Management in Twin Track Economies Challenges Solutions, 13, 936–941.

Coens, T., & Jenkins, M. (2000). *Abolishing Performance Appraisals: Why They Backfire and What to Do Instead.* San Francisco, CA: Berrett-Koehler.

Levy, P. E., & Williams, J. R. (2004). The social context of performance appraisal: A review and framework for the future. *Journal of Management, 30*(6), 881–905. doi:10.1016/j.jm.2004.06.005

Mcmurtrey, M. E., Downey, J. P., Zeltmann, S. M., & Friedman, W. H. (2008). Critical Skill Sets of Entry-Level IT Professionals: An Empirical Examination of Perceptions from Field Personnel. *Journal of Information Technology Education, 7*, 101–120. doi:10.28945/181

Pettijohn, C. E., Pettijohn, L. S., & Kent, J. L. (2003). Performance appraisals: Usage, criteria and observations. *Journal of Management Development, 20*(9), 754–771. doi:10.1108/EUM0000000006159

Roberts, G. (2003). Employee performance appraisal system participation: A technique that works. *Public Personnel Management, 32*(2), 333–340.

Smither, J. W. (1998). *Performance appraisal: State of the art in practice*. San Francisco: Jossey-Bass.

Spinks, N., Wells, B., & Meche, M. (1999). Appraising the appraisals: Computerized performance appraisal systems. *Career Development International, 4*(2), 94–100. doi:10.1108/13620439910254713

KEY TERMS AND DEFINITIONS

Assessment: The process of systematically collect data about someone, using a variety of methods and tools, in order to measure and evaluate her/his work qualities.

Human Resources: The people who constitute the workforce of an organization. Also known as employees or personnel, they are responsible for the execution of the work that, ultimately, will allow organizations to achieve their goals.

Human Resources Management: The management of human resources in organizations aims to create the conditions to recruit, develop and preserve the most talented employees. In the end, it is responsible for maintaining the motivation and productivity of the workforce.

Information System: A set of interrelated socio-technical components that work together to collect and store data about organizational operations, and to process and distribute information to support decision making, coordination and control in an organization.

Information Systems Project: A specific kind of project in which an Information System is planned, developed and implemented in an organization.

Performance Appraisal: The evaluation of an employee's work performance and individual contribution to an organization. Organizations make performance appraisals in order to evaluate employee's skills, competences, work achievements and deficiencies. The main purpose is to give feedback to employees regarding improvement needs and future evolution.

Recruitment: The process of hiring the most adequate candidate for a job position in an organization. It includes analyzing the requirements of the job position, attracting and selecting the best candidate, and integrating the new employee in the organization.

Chapter 25

A Critical Assessment and Enhancement of Metrics for the Management of Scarce Human Resources

Olaf Radant

Ginkgo Management Consulting, Germany

Vladimir Stantchev

https://orcid.org/0000-0002-1551-419X

SRH Hochschule-Berlin, Germany

ABSTRACT

The effect of digitalization and its transformative power in all aspects of corporate strategies and organizations are visible everywhere. As leaders try to make sense of the "digital tornado" and prepare, try out, and set courses in new business directions, the authors propose to take a step back and focus on what is still at the core of corporate change – the people of your organization. In this chapter, the authors reflect on the forces and challenges that employees are facing in times of rapid and digitally driven change. They also mirror this, considering structural, sociological, and demographic change in the workforce, especially with regards to younger employees. They provide a set of fundamental metrics that can quantify the human resource strategy of an organization to derive measures which can be controlled via a DMAIC cycle. This contribution is an extended version of and includes an enhanced set of metrics to address challenges of digitalization and agile work environments. Further, approaches to possible solutions and first steps for an implementation in companies are presented.

DOI: 10.4018/978-1-7998-1279-1.ch025

INTRODUCTION

Keywords like agile or fluid organizations are on everyone's mind right now and rightfully so. In a permanently changing business environment, companies and especially their HR strategies and departments must adapt to changes in the market to be more agile and customer oriented than ever before. To succeed, the productivity of employees is the key solution to changing business environments. Therefore, the allocation and retention of these scarce resources in the best possible way is even more important.

One of the main challenges for companies is to improve the enterprise not only on the side of the organizational and process level but to develop new strategies and approaches in human resource management (Painter-Morland, Kirk, Deslandes, & Tansley, 2019). Only a symbiosis of the discipline's information technology, organization, psychology and management will enable relevant and indispensable employees to promote loyalty to the company (Adeinat & Kassim, 2019). Loyal employees are happy employees which ultimately fosters the productivity of employees.

In this fast pace environment, it is simply not enough to just implement organizational changes like building squads, tribes or chapters. There are several other layers to that topic that a company must consider if it wants to be more responsive (Dhir, 2019; Thorgren & Caiman, 2019). The usage of big data, state of the art technology and new ways of working are building a triangle to enable a company to manage and lead their personnel in the best way possible and to derive measures for further development.

Companies need to put their people first. In times of automation, robotics and artificial intelligence, innovations by a company's own employees will be the lifeblood and key to success in the future. A loss of talent should not be tolerated in any circumstances and companies need to take the appropriate measures to counteract such possibly harmful developments (Singh, 2019).

This paper is a critical examination and an enhancement of the results of the research of the authors from 2016 in the area of agile organizations and leadership. Also, findings and experiences of the implementation of this framework from several projects with different companies are included.

DERIVATION OF METRICS FOR A FRAMEWORK TO MANAGE SCARCE RESOURCES – THE RESULTS OF 2016

The results from the initial structured literature review are still as important as they were in 2016. Therefore, we haven´t change the finding that are presented in the following section.

Search Strategy

The research strategy follows the model of the structured literature review. It includes search terms, literature resources and search process, which are detailed one by one as follows:

The search string has to be defined based on the population under study, and the keywords and their synonyms. Therefore, the study population includes the relevant keywords from all five layers of the proposed framework.

With this population the list of keywords and their synonyms, used to generate the search string was:

- employee wages: employee salary
- education of employees: education of personnel, untapped potential in organizations
- psychological development of employees: psychological changes of employees
- workplace environment: workplace optimization, workplace development
- Work life balance

To generate the search string a Boolean language with AND and OR, and quotation marks for exact text were used. The string format is recognized by all sources of information used, as well as many others. So finally the search string used is as follows: ("employee wages" OR "employee salary") AND ("education of employees" OR "education of personnel" OR "untapped potential in organizations") AND ("psychological development of employees" OR "psychological changes of employees ") AND ("workplace environment " OR "workplace optimization" OR "workplace development") AND ("work life balance"). Given the variety of sources to be consulted electronically via the web, five electronic databases of established literature resources were used for the present SLR. This systematic review considers the following list of sources:

- IEEE Digital Library (http://ieeexplore.ieee.org),
- ACM Digital Library (http://portal.acm.org),
- SpringerLink (http://link.springer.com),
- IDEAS Digital Library (http://ideas.repec.org/) and
- ScienceDirect (http://www.sciencedirect.com/)

The SLR was conducted in the following way: at first, the named digital libraries were searched according to the defined search items for relevant publications. Second, the publications found were reviewed by title and abstract in order to estimate their relevance for the topic. After that, a full text review was conducted which leads to a set of primary studies. Fourth, the primary studies were reviewed whether there are references to other publications with other relevant papers to this topic.

Figure 1. Search process metrics

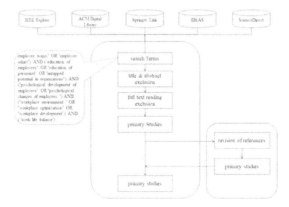

The data extracted from each paper was documented and kept in a reference manager. After identification of the papers, the following data was extracted:

- source (journal or conference),
- title,
- authors,
- publication year,
- classification,
- summary of the research, including which questions were solved.

The goal of this SLR is to identify which preliminary papers and other scientific materials are published about corresponding metrics up to this date (August 2015). For this reason, it is mandatory to develop a set of research questions to search, identify and extract the significant publications. The questions this work proposes are the following:

RQ1: What are metrics for the identified factors for fundamental wages for high skilled employees in IT-departments?

RQ2: What are metrics for the identified factors for measures to optimize and educate the employee pool with reference to untapped potential within an organization?

RQ3: What are metrics for the identified factors for measures to support the psychological healthiness of the employees?

RQ4: What are metrics for the identified factors for measures to optimize the work environment of the employees?

RQ5: What are metrics for the identified factors for measures to support the work-life balance of the employees?

The search strategy, search terms, literature resources and search process will be the same as before. The specific approach can be read in the previous chapter.

The data extracted from each paper was documented and kept in a reference manager. After identification of the papers, the following data was extracted:

- source (journal or conference),
- title,
- authors,
- publication year,
- classification,
- summary of the research, including which questions were solved.

Based on the criteria for classifying papers, all the papers were reviewed, and the corresponding data was extracted. With the information collected in that form, it was possible to obtain qualitative and quantitative information to answer the planned research questions. In particular, the following information was collected:

- metrics for fundamental wages for high skilled employees in IT-departments,

- metrics for measures to optimize and educate the employee pool,
- metrics for measures to support the psychological healthiness,
- metrics for measures to optimize the work environment,
- metrics for measures to support the work-life balance.

For a better understanding and organization of the researched publications, a classification was conducted. For this purpose, the publications were divided into five areas. These areas are defined according to the search terms.

Included and excluded studies are presented in stages following the search process described above. Because of the length of some of the list of references, they have been hosted online and can be downloaded at any time.

Once initial search results were retrieved, an exclusion/inclusion review procedure was applied with the following inclusion and exclusion criteria:

- Inclusion criteria:
  - publications that match one of the search items,
  - publications, that are related to an allocation of resources in scarce resource situations,
  - publications, that are related to Information Technology departments,
  - publications, that are related to more than five EU-Countries,
  - publications, that are related to a highly qualified workforce,
  - publications, that are related to the research questions.
- Exclusion criteria:
  - publications that not match one of the search items,
  - publications that are published before or on the 31.12.2004.

Primary studies obtained in the first phase

The first search was conducted in August 2015, returning 300 papers in total. Irrelevant and duplicate papers were removed and a set of 296 unique papers remained. The result is shown in the following table.

Of the 191 searched papers, 4 were duplicated. Table 2 shows the distribution of the searched papers and its source with reference to the search items.

Of these remaining 296 results, 43 were discarded for being incomplete or not related to the research questions. Of the 253 remaining, 124 were excluded after reading the title and abstract, which left 129 results to be filtered by full-text reading using the inclusion and exclusion criteria. If there was doubt

Table 1. First phase results without filtering

IEE Explore	43
ACM Digital Library	51
ScienceDirect	81
Springer Link	55
IDEAS	69
Total	300
Total (without duplication)	**296**

Table 2. First phase results – distribution without duplication

	IEEE	ACM	Science Direct	Springer Link	IDEAS	Sum
Employee wages	9	4	22	10	13	58
Education of employees	14	23	10	8	12	67
Psychological development of employees	5	5	20	22	16	68
Workplace environment	5	9	9	5	9	37
Work life balance	8	10	20	9	19	66
Sum	41	51	81	54	69	**296**

Table 3. First phase results

Excluded	124
Included	**129**
Total	253

Table 4. Second phase results

Excluded	58
Included	**71**
Total	129

about the relevance of a publication, it was included in the relevant group, leaving the possibility of discarding the paper during the next phase when the full texts of the papers were studied.

Primary studies obtained from the second phase

The reference lists from the primary studies obtained from the first phase were retrieved and the same filters previously used were applied to them. A total of 129 references were obtained by reading the title and abstract. From these references, 71 were finally selected using the criteria of inclusion and exclusion.

Findings

In this section, the final papers will be matched to the research questions. Furthermore, the research questions are tried to answer with the help of these papers. The findings of the SLR are shown in the following chapter in which the five research questions are answered.

RQ1: What are metrics for fundamental wages for high skilled employees in IT-departments?

1.   Earnings per employee /timeframe after tax

This metric represents the earnings of an employee after payment of taxes, social insurance and other indirect labour costs (Eurostat, 2013). Labour Costs are the total expenditure spend by employers for the purpose of employing staff. The following table contains data on average hourly labour costs which are defined as total labour costs divided by the corresponding number of hours worked by the yearly average number of employees, expressed in full-time units. Labour costs cover wages and salaries and non-wage costs, employers social contributions plus taxes less subsidies (Eurostat, 2014a).

Recommended Assessment Method: Labour costs in € per timeframe.

2.   Earnings per employee /timeframe after tax/ incl. incentives

This metric represents the earnings of an employee after payment of taxes, social insurance and other indirect labour costs inclusive possible incentives like bonus or car services (Weiguo & Yanchun, 2010).

Recommended Assessment Method: Earnings per employee per timeframe

3.   Labour costs per unit or price/unit labour cost ratio pre-tax

Given that software development is highly intensive in human capital, the key factor for industry is personnel (Devarakonda, Gupta, & Tang, 2013). Therefore it is important to compare the costs of a produced unit or the provision of a service with the needed labour costs to achieve the result (Diao, Keller, Parekh, & Marinov, 2007; Gabrisch, 2008).

Recommended Assessment Method:

$$Labour\ costs\ per\ unit = \frac{labour\ costs}{price\ per\ unit}$$

4.   Future growth of labour costs pre-taxes

Since labour costs one of the important factors for the competitiveness of an IT-Company it is therefore essential to project the future growth of labour costs. This can be achieved through a consideration of different variables for example the raise of employee compensation in average (including wages, salaries in cash and in kind, employers' social security contributions), vocational training costs, other expenditure such as recruitment costs, spending on working clothes and employment taxes regarded as labour costs minus any subsidies received (Eurostat, 2014a).

Recommended Assessment Method: Projection via statistical extrapolation

5.   Comparison of indirect labour costs in European Union

This metric evaluates the differences of indirect labour costs in different countries and in this case for the EU, but it can easily be extended to other counties or continents.

Recommended Assessment Method: For similar currencies, like in the Euro Area, the statistics of the EU can be used. For countries with different currencies the calculation is the following.

$$Comparison\ of\ labour\ costs\ in\ non\ \ countries = \frac{labour\ costs\ country\ A}{labour\ costs\ country\ B}$$

Country A represents the basis value and country B the reference value of the calculation. Via this calculation, an index is created which allows a company to calculate the value of every spend Euro of labour costs in comparison to other countries.

Gender Pay Gap

The gender pay gap, which represents the imbalances in wages between men and women. It is defined as the difference between the average gross hourly earnings of men and women expressed as a percentage of the average gross hourly earnings of men (Eurostat, 2015). The following table represents the unadjusted gender pay gap in Enterprises employing 10 or more employees which compares the hourly earnings of men and women in general (Peruzzi, 2015).

Due to the high number of variables, the gender pay gap needs to be adjusted. The general aim of adjusting the gender pay gap is to include a range of personal characteristics which may differ, and which may therefore explain some of the difference in average pay between men and women. Reasons for the difference can be the chosen profession, the level of experience, negotiating skills etc. For example, the adjusted gender pay gap in Germany in the year 2010 was 7% (Destatis, 2014).

Recommended Assessment Method: Comparison of the average salary of men to the average salary of women, if necessary, per department.

6. Earnings per IT-employee in average to other departments after tax and earnings per IT-employee in average to other (IT-) companies after tax

Since wages are not the, but one of the important reasons for employees to stay in a company it is necessary for a firm to pay satisfying wages (Institute for opinion survey Allensbach, 2014). Since every employee defines the term satisfying on their own, a company should orientate their wage policy on the average payments of the market.

Recommended Assessment Method: Comparison of the average salary of department one to the average salary of department two.

RQ2: What are metrics for measures to optimize and educate the employee pool with reference to untapped potential within an organization?

1. Real output (gross value added) divided by the total number of persons employed

The essential aim of a company is to produce goods and sell them on the market to make profit. The performance of employees is a substantial factor to achieve this goal. Gross value added (GVA) measures the contribution to an economy of an individual producer, industry, sector or region (Financial Times Lexicon, 2013). It provides a financial value for the amount of goods and services that have been produced, less the cost of all inputs and raw materials that are directly attributable to that production. This metric can serve as an orientation and major benchmark for the success of implemented measures in a company.

Recommended Assessment Method:

$$\text{Gross value added} = \frac{Real\ output\ in\quad per\ timeframe}{Number\ of\ employees}.$$

2. Evaluation of throughput time and lead time

For any company, productivity is one of the major ratios. The evaluation of throughput time and lead time offers a deeper insight in this complex issue. Throughput time is the period required for a material, part, or subassembly to pass through the manufacturing process and lead time is the number of minutes, hours, or days that must be allowed for the completion of an opetion or process, or must elapse before a desired action takes place (van den Bos, Kemper, & de Waal, 2014).

Recommended Assessment Method: Throughput time and lead time in timeframe.

3. Expenditure for education of a company or department

It is assumed, that higher economic value added transmits to higher human capital correlated with higher level of education and thus higher expenditure of education (Verner, 2011). This metric analyses the investments in training of employees and is calculated by dividing the total costs of training and the number of employees of the whole company or a specific department.

Recommended Assessment Method: Sum per timeframe per company or department.

4. Number of employees in training per year

This metric simply states the number of employees in training measures per year. It can easily be extended to gain further information by dividing the number of employees in training per year and the total number of employees in a company and putting these figures in a relation.

Recommended Assessment Method:

$$\frac{Number\ of\ employees\ in\ training}{Total\ number\ of\ employees} \times 100$$

5. Employee requirements analysis

A company has to be aware of the development of their employees and the needed profiles to gain a growth in productivity and revenues in future (Dainty, Raidén, & Neale, 2009). Therefore, an analysis to answer the following questions is needed:

- Which profiles does the company need to fulfil my strategic goals?
- How many employees does the company need to achieve my strategic goals?
- How many new hires does the company have to recruit per year?

This analysis should be a recurrent process every year. Also, the underlying assumptions and goals need to be audited as well to determine necessary changes. A possible qualitative method to gain the needed information could be a survey conducted with the different heads of departments. To conduct a quantitative measurement, basic elements for an employee requirements analysis are needed:

- the current employee capacity,
- estimations for the workload in a timeframe per employee or workstation,
- an evaluation of the proposed changes with a consideration of the impact on the required staffing and
- a plausibility check against references.

After the collection of the data, possible seasonal peaks need to be added to estimate the utilization of the employees over a timeframe of a year.

Recommended Assessment Method: Statistics of current utilization of employees in comparison to needed utilization to fulfil requirements of the market.

6. Employee potential analysis

The identification and development of high potential employees (commonly referred to as talent management) has been pinpointed by both management scholars and practitioners as one of the major challenges faced by the twenty-first century human resource function (Dries, 2012). So as important as the information which profiles, I need in the future is the information what kind of potential and potentials does the company have in their organization. With a tool like an employee survey in connection with employee work appraisals it is possible to derive employees which for example want to work in other departments, want to develop themselves in a certain way or are feasible candidates for executive careers. Further, the identification of those "hidden gems" in an organization is crucial (Pollitt, 2005).

Recommended Assessment Method: Survey with middle management executives to filter possible candidates.

7. Age distribution analysis

The complex of the best age distribution of a company, in contrast to the size distribution, is rarely discussed in the literature (Cirillo, 2010; Coad, 2010). For the conduction of an age distribution analysis, only few data are needed:

- date of birth
- date of entering the company
- department

- organizational status
- contract status (temporary employment, permanent contract)

Recommended Assessment Method: Analysis via age statistics of departments and hierarchical structure of company.

8.   Employee performance management system (goal setting, monitoring and evaluation)

The employee performance management system is an organized assessment process for employees in a company or department of a company. It is used to ensure that employee's activities and outcomes are aligned with the organisation's objectives and strategy (Becker, Antuar, & Everett, 2011). Employees that achieve the organisational goals are rewarded with favourable reviews and bonuses in line with their performance and contribution to the organisation. Tools of an employee performance management system are e.g. goal-setting (planning), monitoring (feedback) and evaluation (appraising) (Decramer, Smolders, & Vanderstraeten, 2013).

Recommended Assessment Method: Existence of employee performance management system and corresponding policies to foster a satisfying usage.

9.   IT vacancies in company

This metric represents the vacant positions of an IT-department. According to BITKOM, the information technology union in Germany, there are 41.000 job vacancies for IT experts in Germany in 2013 (Pfisterer, 2013). Almost three-quarters (71%) of ICT companies are looking for software developers, especially with skills on cloud computing (53%) and big data (44%), followed by knowledge in social media (34%), programming of classical web properties (28%) and mobile websites or apps (26%). Similar numbers can be found in mostly all countries in Europe (Empirica, 2013, 2014).

Recommended Assessment Method: Investigation of current utilization and possible utilization if all market requirements are met.

10.   Female integration and leadership programs

It is necessary to encourage cultural changes to make IT departments more attractive to women. However, there are high hurdles, as expectations diverge greatly from those of men (Ahuja, 2002) and interpersonal skills are a much more important factor (Cappelli, 2000). Female students and employees attach above average importance to a profession that can be arranged well with family and private life, in which they can help other people and promises them a good working environment (Institute for opinion survey Allensbach, 2014).

Recommended Assessment Method: Existence of diversity programs and corresponding policies to foster a satisfying usage. Yearly evaluation of the success of these programs via survey and statistical analysis. The programs should be aligned to actual needs of women, which should be compiled via survey.

Retention Rate

The retention rate is a figure which represents a comparison the number of employees which are employed by the beginning and the end of a year or timeframe. This number is an important indicator for a company because it displays the number of employees which needed to be recruited only compensate the losses of workforce of the year and remain on the same headcount (Allen, Armstrong, Reid, & Riemenschneider, 2009).

Recommended Assessment Method:

$$Retention\ rate = \frac{number\ of\ employees\ t_1}{number\ of\ employees\ t_2}$$

11. Gap analysis between existing and targeted skills of employees

The company's strategy sets the target for the development of the organization and its employees. It defines the necessary skills that are needed to fulfil the goals of the strategy. A gap analysis between existing and targeted skills of employee's reveals missing skills and capabilities of the workforce in comparison to the strategy of the company. If a company conduct this analysis, they will be able to allocate and promote them in the best possible way. Often the actual employment is not equal to the actual skills of the employees (Colomo-Palacios, Casado-Lumbreras, Soto-Acosta, García-Peñalvo, & Tovar-Caro, 2013).

Recommended Assessment Method: Survey with middle management executives and derivation of an action plan to close identified gaps.

12. Educational strategy and lifelong learning programs

Due to a highly changing IT-environment, lifelong learning is a must for every employee and company to stay competitive. Companies that support a culture of lifelong learning will have a competitive edge on the market. These programs are an essential part of the educational strategy of a company and should be audited at least every year to include necessary changes and review the success of the learning measures. As many observers have noted, programmers can easily become obsolete when the programming languages that they know fall out of favour (Cappelli, 2000). A constant development of the knowledge of the employees is thus fundamentally.

Recommended Assessment Method: Existence, development and yearly evaluation of educational strategies and corresponding policies.

13. Knowledge management/ transfer initiative/ system

KM is fundamentally the management of the corporate knowledge and intelligent assets that can improve a range of organizational performance characteristics and add value by enabling an enterprise to act more intelligently (Bose, 2004). In a globalized world, it has become crucial for global organisations to have the ability to convert all precious data to useful knowledge (Hasan & Zhou, 2015). The challenge for companies is the motivation of the employees to share their knowledge with other people, which will be even more important with a scarcity of resources and a reduction of available employees with needed knowledge. Especially for IT-departments it is necessary to implement knowledge management initiatives because often head monopolies are generated due to a needed high degree of specialization (Corbin, Dunbar, & Zhu, 2007).

Recommended Assessment Method: Existence of a knowledge management system and corresponding policies to foster the usage and data quality.

RQ3: What are metrics for measures to support the psychological healthiness of the employees?

1. Company culture

The company culture defines the acting, work ethic and behaviour of employees on nearly every level of a company. According to Ken Favaro, Senior Manager of the consulting company Strategy& the culture often tops the strategy of a company (Favaro, 2014): "Strategy is on paper whereas culture determines how things get done. Anyone can come up with a fancy strategy, but it's much harder to build a winning culture. Moreover, a brilliant strategy without a great culture is 'all hat and no cattle,' while a company with a winning culture can succeed even if its strategy is mediocre. Plus, it's much easier to change strategy than culture." Strategy and culture need to foster themselves and mature together to achieve the desired results (Dickmann, 2006).

Recommended Assessment Method: Figure determined via employee survey aligned with the company's vision, values, norms.

2. Hierarchical structure and organizational permeability

The structure of a company and its permeability is one of the important factors for young graduates (Institute for opinion survey Allensbach, 2014). This generation of possible employees is unlike other generations, a segment of employees which is considered to be in need of focused attention and with unique and challenging expectations like participation in companies decision making (Shatat, El-Baz, & Hariga, 2010). Therefore, a company needs to foster and promote employee participation especially through the middle management of the company. Also, a fair amount of decent career opportunities is necessary, to provide a sufficient permeability of the organization which meet the expectations of younger employees.

Recommended Assessment Method: Degrees of freedom of management level in given timeframe and existence of employee participation programs.

3. Employee expectations

Organizations need to make sure that not only the performance and the learning agility of their employees is high, but also their commitment. In order to achieve high commitment, organizations need to establish an employment relationship with them based on mutual benefit (Dries, 2013). Demands and expectations of employees are based on the job they perform, the possibilities of progress, the ways of controlling their work, as well as compensation. Also, the expectations of highly educated workforce, and their satisfaction with the workplace and the assignments they fulfil is a very important factor of the success of the organisation. (Jaksic & Jaksic, 2013).

Recommended Assessment Method: Expectations gathered with employee survey.

4. Existence of employee wellbeing programs

Employee wellbeing programs are not initiatives to pamper employees, they are helping an organization to reduce illness and therefore a loss of workforce (Dunning, 2015). Organizations health and wellness offerings have expanded beyond traditional programs, which formerly focused on physical health, to integrated well-being programs are now including mental and emotional health, financial health, work life effectiveness, and workplace environment and stress (Spears, 2012).

Recommended Assessment Method: Existence of policies and programs developed with employee representatives or work councils.

5. Psychological induced Sick days of employees

IT employees facing high job demands (Zeng, Zheng, & Shi, 2010). The stress factor with the highest influence on the working people is emotional exhaustion. In consideration of this, it does not surprise that the impact of the demographic change on IT personnel is relatively high compared to other departments. (Zeng et al., 2010). The outcome of this situation is a high rate of mental or physiological illnesses, like boreout and burnout (Christensen & Knardahl, 2012) and a lower level of quality and productiveness of the department and the employees.

Recommended Assessment Method: Psychological induced Sick days of employees in a given timeframe:

$$\frac{psychological\ induced\ sick\ day\ of\ company\ or\ department\ in\ timeframe}{number\ of\ workdays\ in\ timeframe}$$

6. Rate of change in used technology/ timeframe and time of adoption

Additionally, to the factors mentioned above, Lee et al. pointed out that technologically induced stress is a crucial multiplier. This is caused due strong technological transformation of an organization (Lee, Foo, & Cunningham, 1995).

Recommended Assessment Method: The assessment method depends on the type of the organization. The measurements could be releases per year, major patches and updates or the number of new applications or programs which are launched in a given timeframe.

7.   Job complexity

The complexity of a working field is still one of the main reasons for psychological diseases like depression or burnout. Complexity is a term which will define every employee for himself. However, the stress report of the German governmental organization BAUA conducted a survey which researched the main stressors for a complex work environment. These stressors are e.g. different tasks at the same time, pressure from deadlines or interruptions in the workplace (Kliner, Rennert, & Richter, 2015).

Recommended Assessment Method: Variety of working fields per employee and number of waiting tasks. Distractions, interruptions and necessary task-switching in the workplace identified via process analysis or employee survey

8.   IT misuse and security policy breaches in the workplace

With the commonly known positive effects of Information Technology, several downsides came along with this development. Several studies explored the implications of IT-induced technology stress, technology addiction and IT misuse in the workplace. (Monideepa Tarafdar, John D'Arcy, Ofir Turel, & Ashish Gupta, 2014).

Recommended Assessment Method: Number of reported incidents.

9.   Reported incidents of workplace violence, mobbing and bullying

The definition of workplace violence, mobbing and bullying refers to situations where a person repeatedly and over a period of time is exposed to negative acts (i.e. constant abuse, offensive remarks or teasing, ridicule or social exclusion) on the part of co-workers, supervisors, or subordinates (Branch, Ramsay, & Barker, 2013; Einarsen, 1999). These issues have obviously large consequences for individuals, including higher body-mass, chronic diseases and illnesses, certified and uncertified absence which results in unproductive employee behaviour (Boddy, 2014; Devonish, 2013).

Recommended Assessment Method: Number of reported incidents.

10.   Job (in)security: status of used employment contracts in an organization

The definition of job insecurity is regarded as an overall concern about the continuous existence of the workplace in the future (Chambel & Fontinha, 2009). Besides the economic development of a company, research has proven that the contract status of employees has both, positive and negative influence of the well-being of an employee (Bernhard-Oettel, Sverke, & De Witte, 2005; Martin Olsthoorn, 2014).

Recommended Assessment Method:

$$\frac{number\ of\ part\ time\ comtracts}{number\ of\ all\ employee\ contracts}$$

11.   Work environment and office design which supports employee networking determined via employee survey

Human beings need interaction and company in their personal and professional life for their wellbeing in order to perform on a high level and be productive. From a psychological standpoint, an office should have several characteristics to support this issue like social density, view quality and type or light quality (Aries, Veitch, & Newsham, 2010).

Recommended Assessment Method: Existence of an office plan which includes latest scientific research and has not only the best utilization of workstations as its goal.

RQ4: What are metrics for measures to optimize the work environment of the employees?

1.   Implementation of proper security policies like EU directive 89/391, DIN 4543

The objective of Directives like 89/391/EEC or DIN 4543 is to foster and improve the protection of workers through measures regarding the prevention of work-related risks, the protection of safety and health, the elimination of risk and accident factors and also the informing, consultation, balanced participation and physiological training of workers (Niskanen, Naumanen, & Hirvonen, 2012). These directives implemented responsibilities and obligations of employers in form of risk assessments, creation of protection, prevention services and the duties of (Martínez Aires, Rubio Gámez, & Gibb, 2010).

Recommended Assessment Method: Existence of workplace design plans and implemented policies which supports psychological healthiness.

2.   High level of flexibility in the work organization and allocation of employees via job rotation, job enlargement, job enrichment

A flexible organization supports various positive developments for a company and its employees. Besides the mentioned benefits for the knowledge transfer within the organization, learning, development and a higher satisfaction of the employees (Bennett, 2003), different environments and movements support a greater psychological health and reduce ergonomic risks (Otto & Scholl, 2012).

Recommended Assessment Method: Existence of policies that support a high level of flexibility in the organization.

RQ5: What are metrics for measures to support the work-life balance of the employees?

1.   Work-life/ family policies

The goal of work-life or families in companies is to generate greater productivity of employees due to a higher satisfaction. These policies assisting employees to simultaneously fulfil their responsibilities both at work and at home (McDonald, Guthrie, Bradley, & Shakespeare-Finch, 2005). These policies cannot just include regulations and rules for part-time employment or paid leave. They also have to support career opportunities especially for women, because despite women and mothers increased involvement in paid work, little change has taken place in the organization and provision of unpaid domestic and care work (Baxter & Chesters, 2011).

Recommended Assessment Method: Existence of Work-life/ family policies, which are constantly reviewed via employee and management surveys to provide the best balance between

2.   Financial costs/ benefits of company in the context of Work-life Balance

Work-life initiatives are often a reason for discussion within the management of companies because they don't provide instant improvement of productivity or an increase of revenue (Todd & Binns, 2013). Of course, the installed initiatives need to be controlled and questioned if they provide the anticipated results. A controlling of the implemented policies requires an inclusion of different variables and an evaluation via a business case. Obvious variables are the productivity of the individual, the number of sick days due to child illness, annual spending in work-life initiatives or the number of employees which use these opportunities. Also, further variables like turnover intention, retention rate have to take into consideration as well. This case should be a long-term examination of the retrieved figures and statistics.

Recommended Assessment Method: Calculation of a business case which considers the relevant productivity measures of the company or department and the employee. This Business Case should be controlled in certain timeframes.

3.   Innovative working (time) models

There are several different working models which can be offered to employees. The most common models are trust-based working time (Singe & Croucher, 2003), flexible work schedule (Coenen & Kok, 2014), annualised and variable working hours (Corominas & Pastor, 2010), job-sharing (Crampton & Mishra, 2005), part-time employment (Rose, Hewitt, & Baxter, 2013), home office (Răvaş, 2013), tele-work (Coenen & Kok, 2014) and working-time accounts (Lusa & Pastor, 2011).

Recommended Assessment Method: Calculation of a business case which considers the relevant productivity measures of the company or department and the employee. The variables of this business case should be controlled in certain timeframes.

4.   Availability of employees

The common business day for employees has a nine to five schedule and is limited to workdays. In reality, these agreements are shifting to overtime duties and a permanent availability via e-mail or other communication channels (McMenamin, 2007). As described in earlier chapters, permanent availability has negative effects on employees and could result in a decline of productivity. Several companies like BMW, Volkswagen and Mercedes block the devices of their employees after certain working hours to limit communication and allow the employees to recover from the workday (Kaufmann, 2014).

Recommended Assessment Method: Communication (traffic) in leisure time of employees.

5.   Working time per week per timeframe

The working time per employee in a given timeframe has important effects on employees. It defines in the most part its productivity, rates of error or the well-being in of the individual in general. For a society and also a company in a whole it provides advantages regarding social equity through redistribution of working hours and raises voluntary social engagement (Buhl & Acosta, 2015).

Recommended Assessment Method: Evaluation of the working hours of employee or department per
       timeframe.

NOVEL RESEARCH CONTRIBUTIONS SINCE CONDUCTING THE ORIGINAL RESEARCH

The results of 2016 have not lost their actuality but are more important than ever. Since a large number of companies are trying to transfer their rigid hierarchies in agile and fluid organizations, the results of 2016 have to be extended by one area, which is called *organizational conditions and leadership*. Consequently, a sixth research question was built.

RQ6: What are metrics for measures to support organizational change and leadership for agile organi-
       zations?

The answering of this question follows the same presented approach of 2016 supplemented with the search term organisational conditions and leadership. The new search string as Boolean language with AND and OR, and quotation marks for exact text is the following. The search string is used as follows: ("employee wages" OR "employee salary") AND ("education of employees" OR "education of personnel" OR "untapped potential in organizations") AND ("psychological development of employees" OR "psychological changes of employees ") AND ("workplace environment " OR "workplace optimization" OR "workplace development") AND ("work life balance") AND ("organizational conditions" OR "organizational change" OR "leadership"). The following metrics present the enhancement of the framework researched and developed in 2016.

1.   Methodological competence of employees and leadership

The transformation of a hierarchical to an agile organisation is a huge step for companies. The basis for the transformation is a deep understanding of agile frameworks and methods. Starting from the top of the organization, leaders as role models, have to understand the opportunities, challenges and risks that are associated with these changes. Employees on the other hand need the methodological competence to execute the changes on the operational level (Niemi & Laine, 2016). A change like this can only be successful if both parties comply to an agile organization (Poston & PATEL, 2016).

Recommended Assessment Method: Training investments devoted to methodological development of employees

2. Speed of decision making

Due to the high rate of usage of agile methods in projects and organizations, the speed of decision making has to adapt to that circumstance as well (Feng et al., 2018). This is a huge task, especially if companies are in the change from traditional, hierarchical decision-making to shared decision-making (Moe, Aurum, & Dybå, 2012) processes. But, to overcome the challenge of fast changing markets and environments, this is a necessity (Radant, Colomo-Palacios, & Stantchev, 2016b).

Recommended Assessment Method: Needed time for selected decisions in organizations

3. Distribution of responsibilities

As mentioned, companies must adapt to the fast-changing environments of the economic world. One part of this adoption is the right distribution of responsibilities. If the goal of the company is an agile environment, leaders must let traditional views of responsibilities go and trust their employees that they make the right decisions (Malgorzata Ali, 2016). These circumstances have to be formalized in job descriptions of the employees to empower them to make these decisions without having to fear consequences.

Recommended Assessment Method: Content of job specifications and job descriptions

4. Innovative power of an organization

To gain and generate business value, companies must understand and quickly respond to a number of market forces and innovations are the key to success (Paz, 2017). Due to the increasingly rapid pace of change in technology, organizations need to foster innovative thinking within their employees and departments (Chesbrough & Brunswicker, 2013). The basis are processes that support innovations and an environment that allows employees to share and discuss thoughts and ideas.

Recommended Assessment Method: Number of innovations in a timeframe; patent utilization ration, funding of innovation processes; Success rate of projects which are based on innovation; number of innovative ideas by employees in a timeframe

5. Servant leadership

(Front-line) managers are critical to an organization's performance as their ability to motivate and direct staff is fundamental. But several studies have shown that they are often too focused on their operative work (Holtzhausen & de Klerk, 2018; Pathak, Parker, & Holesgrove, 2015). Therefore, they are not able to concentrate on the development and management of their staff. The results are e.g. underperforming employees and less innovation. Furthermore, the actual corporate environments are mostly not helpful to counteract these problems. Because of the short-term focus and the figure-driven orientation of the companies, long-term investments in employees and a change of the way of work are often seen as "lost money". But in the current labour environment with less loyal employees and scarcity of resources, this is a harmful strategy in the long run.

Recommended Assessment Method: Results gathered with employee survey or distribution of working hours of (front) line managers

6.   Agility of the organization

Since the process of the change to an agile organization is tough and time intense, it is reasonable to measure the progress of the transformation regularly. This will allow the employees to see the success on a quantified level and it allows leadership to identify possible weak spots to derive measures for optimization (Horlach, Drews, Schirmer, & Boehmann, 2017).

Recommended Assessment Method: Organizational model; Flexibilization of teams and work

After the inclusion of a sixth area, the distribution of metrics is the following

These metrics provide companies with a toolset to assess themselves and quantify their actual state regarding labour in general and their human resource policies in particular. Especially regarding the expectations of generation Y. The identified metrics answer the question "how" human resources in times of scarcity of talent should be measured. The presented metrics enable organizations and their respective executives to assess their already implemented measures derive potential threats as well as potential new measures to complement the existing strategies.

The presented findings are subject to the usual limitations of a literature review. The results completely rely on previously published research, the availability of these studies using the method outlined in the search methodology and the appropriateness of these studies with the criteria of the selection/exclusion procedure. However, the results provide a strong fundament for further research activities.

Table 5. Distribution of metrics after including a sixth area

Area	Metrics
Employee wages	8
Education of employees and untapped potential in organizations	14
Psychological development of employees	11
Workplace environment	2
Work life balance	5
Organizational conditions and leadership	6
Sum	**46**

APPROACHES TO SOLUTIONS FOR COMPANIES

There are no "silver bullet" solutions and rarely best practices to tackle these kind of personnel related challenges. On the one hand because of the inherent differences in every organization and on the other hand due to the pace of the economic, sociological and technology changes. The best example for the fundamental impact of e.g. a technological change is the introduction of the iPhone eleven years ago and how it changed our ways of working, thinking and living.

Every generation has different perceptions and opinions how something should be done. Statistics show that the generation of the baby-boomers will retire in the next five to seven years (Eurostat, 2014b). This means, that companies have exactly this timeframe to incorporate changes in their organizations to meet the changed expectations of the workforce. These new expectations refer mostly to the management of their respective superiors and the way how a workday is organized. For employees of the generation Y and Z, flexibility is one of the most important factors. The basis for that is the management with goals and objectives.

This mind-set requires to challenge the actual processes and helps to include levels of flexibility in the work environment which will have profound effects on the productivity of the employees. The developments of the fourth industrial revolution are showing a lot of possible methods and tools which would benefit the employees as well as the companies. Apart from that, quantitative surveys showed that the salary is still an important factor for the workforce, but it is far away from being the most important one as it was in earlier years and decades. A study has shown, that 36% of employees would give up $5,000 a year in salary to be happier at work (Rebecca Henderson, 2018). Employee compensation is a short-term solution which satisfies short-term needs, when not raised significantly periodically.

The overall aim of HR departments should be to provide companies with insights to better understand possible long-term needs of the staff and how they can align them with e.g. organizational optimization of the company. With the goal of identifying all pain points and value drivers of their employees, companies need a holistic and transparent view on their employees which allows them to identify threats, derive measures and evaluate their success (Radant, 2014). The first step is a common understanding regarding the way of working, the company culture and the way in which employees should be managed. This leads to an understanding of how the organization should be built. Any discussion about tools and technology should follow this step and incorporate chosen strategic and organizational concepts.

Changes regarding organization, personnel and culture are critical endeavours which should be implemented with caution and enough time(Radant, Colomo-Palacios, & Stantchev, 2014). Initiatives in this area mostly aren't failing because of budget or time constraints but because of the impatience of management. As mentioned earlier, there is no simple pattern for employee management in the future. Nevertheless, every manager can gain loyalty of employees with the following nine steps to improve productivity.

1. Measure employee engagement – Start measuring employees' passion about work and the work environment.
2. Identify what employees like – By gathering praise in addition to concerns, your company can find out if its engagement efforts make a meaningful, lasting contribution to employees.
3. Help employees see the big picture – Employees want to contribute and make a difference. Help them to see the big picture and how they contribute to a functioning whole. This will also empower employees to make decisions, which raises commitment.

4. Use training to increase confidence – Employees need training to do their job confidently and to facilitate career advancement.
5. Promote team building – Encourage team building activities among employee groups to create trust and acceptance. Strong, loyal teams provide acceptance, and teamwork between departments provides positive communication and work atmosphere.
6. Build a supportive environment – Often, dissatisfaction with wages and benefits masks problems that relate back to acceptance by a team or manager. Encourage employees to be outspoken.
7. Don't be afraid to tell the truth – Respect your employees through degrees of transparency. Give your employees information to understand shifts in corporate policy.
8. Recognize employee contributions – Recognition from a supervisor of at least two ranks above an employee makes a meaningful, engaging difference in employee morale.
9. Controlling of measures – Use DMAIC cycles to control the effects and benefits of the implemented measures. Use this method also to assess yourself and your actions.

Besides the daily use of these nine steps, if a company wants to take on this journey, transparency is key and therefore data is key (Joh & White, 2018). Regular employee surveys can be a first step for companies but normally they will deliver the same old results and insights. It is therefore recommended to build small interdisciplinary teams, depending on the size of the organization, that deliver their results and messages anonymously. With this method, management can identify possible weak spots and find room for improvement. The basis for productivity is always leadership that reflects the needs of the employees and a state-of-the-art technology that fits the current and future business needs (Eom, 2015). If that foundation is in place, companies should concentrate their activities on measures that foster productivity, happiness and loyalty. Unfortunately, there are no interchangeable measure that will work in every company and every department, every time.

The leadership of a company has to understand how the way we work is already changing and will change in the upcoming years (Bellou, Xanthopoulou, Gkorezis, Xanthopoulou, & Gkorezis, 2018). To be in the hunt for high profile employees, they must adapt to that circumstance. The following figure is specifying the actual situation and compares the current working culture with the working life of employees in the future.

It is therefore important, that leadership and employees work together to find solutions that benefits the organization and the personnel at the same time with the common goal to achieve higher productivity, more innovation and higher retention (Radant et al., 2016b). An important side effect is that management shows to the employees, that they are taking the needs of the employees seriously and that they are an integral part of the company. If detailed measures are identified, the company should not be hesitant to pilot them in a department or small area in the organization and if they are working, spread them out to other departments.

FIRST STEPS OF AN IMPLEMENTATION IN ORGANIZATIONS

As stated, employees are the most important asset for a company, especially in times of digitalization and scarcity of talent. Therefore, the most important information for management is what kind of employees does the company need in the future. Based on extensive research and different customer engagements in several industries, the authors recommend the following steps to tackle this issue in a sustainable manner.

Besides the already mentioned need for transparency, the first step is to create the awareness that change is required. Key questions are:

1. What is the strategic situation of the company and which employees are needed in the future to achieve the strategic goals?
2. How good is my retention rate in comparison to my competitors and what are the reasons for the results?
3. What is the cultural situation in the organization? Is there a gap between expectations of employees and management and if yes, why is that the case?

The main output from this phase is the case for change, which outlines the necessity for a transformation. This case states the current situation of the company with regards to human resources and the organization as well as actual challenges and emerging threats. These examples could be, for instance, a high retention rate or a high average age of employees. It is important that the management team acknowledges that the organization needs to change, recognizes potential and significant benefits and has engaged employees to conduct further analysis (Radant, Colomo-Palacios, & Stantchev, 2016a). Possible further results are age analyses or demographic outlooks for the company and the market, possible references from other companies currently facing similar problems.

The second step is the combination of the results of the key questions with the company's strategy to identify gaps between the long-term goals of the organization and the current state. The outcomes will lead to a better understanding of the situation and are necessary to derive measures going forward, weather they are cultural, technical or strategy based. To measure the success of the initiative, 46 metrics to quantify the success are presented in this publication.

The journey to put your people first, is a journey that the whole organization has to go together. Organizations are responsible for the development and healthiness of their employees. This was already the case before, but now it is a much more needed prerequisite than ever for a company to be successful. This challenge can't be solved by HR departments alone and is a task for every manager, every day of the week.

REFERENCES

Ahuja, M. K. (2002). Women in the information technology profession: A literature review, synthesis and research agenda. *European Journal of Information Systems*, *11*(1), 20–34. doi:10.1057/palgrave.ejis.3000417

Allen, M. W., Armstrong, D. J., Reid, M. F., & Riemenschneider, C. K. (2009). IT Employee Retention: Employee Expectations and Workplace Environments. *Proceedings of the Special Interest Group on Management Information System's 47th Annual Conference on Computer Personnel Research*, 95–100. 10.1145/1542130.1542148

Aries, M. B. C., Veitch, J. A., & Newsham, G. R. (2010). Windows, view, and office characteristics predict physical and psychological discomfort. *Journal of Environmental Psychology*, *30*(4), 533–541. doi:10.1016/j.jenvp.2009.12.004

Baxter, J., & Chesters, J. (2011). Perceptions of Work-Family Balance: How Effective are Family-Friendly Policies? *Australian Journal of Labour Economics*, *14*(2), 139–151.

Becker, K., Antuar, N., & Everett, C. (2011). Implementing an employee performance management system in a nonprofit organization. *Nonprofit Management & Leadership*, *21*(3), 255–271. doi:10.1002/nml.20024

Bellou, V., Xanthopoulou, D., Gkorezis, P., Xanthopoulou, D., & Gkorezis, P. (2018, April 27). *Organizational change and employee functioning : Investigating boundary conditions*. doi:10.4324/9781315386102-2

Bennett, B. (2003). Job rotation. *Training Strategies for Tomorrow*, *17*(4), 7.

Bernhard-Oettel, C., Sverke, M., & De Witte, H. (2005). Comparing three alternative types of employment with permanent full-time work: How do employment contract and perceived job conditions relate to health complaints? *Work and Stress*, *19*(4), 301–318. doi:10.1080/02678370500408723

Boddy, C. R. (2014). Corporate Psychopaths, Conflict, Employee Affective Well-Being and Counterproductive Work Behaviour. *Journal of Business Ethics*, *121*(1), 107–121. doi:10.100710551-013-1688-0

Bose, R. (2004). Knowledge management metrics. *Industrial Management & Data Systems*, *104*(5/6), 457–468. doi:10.1108/02635570410543771

Branch, S., Ramsay, S., & Barker, M. (2013). Workplace Bullying, Mobbing and General Harassment: A Review. *International Journal of Management Reviews*, *15*(3), 280–299. doi:10.1111/j.1468-2370.2012.00339.x

Buhl, J., & Acosta, J. (2015). Work less, do less? *Sustainability Science*, 1–16. doi:10.100711625-015-0322-8

Cappelli, P. (2000). Is there a shortage of information technology workers. *A Report to McKinsey and Company*. Retrieved from http://knowledge.wharton.upenn.edu/papers/979.pdf

Chambel, M. J., & Fontinha, R. (2009). Contingencies of Contingent Employment: Psychological Contract, Job Insecurity and Employability of Contracted Workers. *Revista de Psicología del Trabajo y de las Organizaciones*, *25*(3), 207–217. doi:10.43211576-59622009000300002

Chesbrough, H., & Brunswicker, S. (2013). *Managing Open Innovation in Large Firms*. Academic Press.

Christensen, J. O., & Knardahl, S. (2012). Work and headache: A prospective study of psychological, social, and mechanical predictors of headache severity. *Pain*, *153*(10), 2119–2132. doi:10.1016/j.pain.2012.07.009 PMID:22906887

Cirillo, P. (2010). An analysis of the size distribution of Italian firms by age. *Physica A*, *389*(3), 459–466. doi:10.1016/j.physa.2009.09.049

Coad, A. (2010). Investigating the Exponential Age Distribution of Firms. *Economics*, *4*(17), 1–30A.

Coenen, M., & Kok, R. A. W. (2014). Workplace flexibility and new product development performance: The role of telework and flexible work schedules. *European Management Journal*, *32*(4), 564–576. doi:10.1016/j.emj.2013.12.003

Colomo-Palacios, R., Casado-Lumbreras, C., Soto-Acosta, P., García-Peñalvo, F. J., & Tovar-Caro, E. (2013). Competence gaps in software personnel: A multi-organizational study. *Computers in Human Behavior, 29*(2), 456–461. doi:10.1016/j.chb.2012.04.021

Corbin, R. D., Dunbar, C. B., & Zhu, Q. (2007). A three-tier knowledge management scheme for software engineering support and innovation. *Journal of Systems and Software, 80*(9), 1494–1505. doi:10.1016/j.jss.2007.01.013

Corominas, A., & Pastor, R. (2010). Replanning working time under annualised working hours. *International Journal of Production Research, 48*(5), 1493–1515. doi:10.1080/00207540802582227

Crampton, S. M., & Mishra, J. M. (2005). Job Sharing: A Viable Work Alternative for the New Millennium. *The Journal of Applied Management and Entrepreneurship, 10*(2), 13–34.

Dainty, A. R. J., Raidén, A. B., & Neale, R. H. (2009). Incorporating employee resourcing requirements into deployment decision making. *Project Management Journal, 40*(2), 7–18. doi:10.1002/pmj.20119

Decramer, A., Smolders, C., & Vanderstraeten, A. (2013). Employee performance management culture and system features in higher education: Relationship with employee performance management satisfaction. *International Journal of Human Resource Management, 24*(2), 352–371. doi:10.1080/09585192.2012.680602

Destatis. (2014). *Pressemitteilungen - Verdienstunterschied zwischen Frauen und Männern in Deutschland weiterhin bei 22% - Statistisches Bundesamt (Destatis).* Retrieved August 29, 2015, from https://www.destatis.de/DE/PresseService/Presse/Pressemitteilungen/2015/03/PD15_099_621.html

Devarakonda, M., Gupta, P., & Tang, C. (2013). Labor Cost Reduction with Cloud: An End-to-End View. *2013 IEEE Sixth International Conference on Cloud Computing (CLOUD)*, 534–540. 10.1109/CLOUD.2013.90

Devonish, D. (2013). Workplace bullying, employee performance and behaviors: The mediating role of psychological well-being. *Employee Relations, 35*(6), 630–647. doi:10.1108/ER-01-2013-0004

Diao, Y., Keller, A., Parekh, S., & Marinov, V. V. (2007). Predicting Labor Cost through IT Management Complexity Metrics. *10th IFIP/IEEE International Symposium on Integrated Network Management, 2007. IM '07*, 274–283. 10.1109/INM.2007.374792

Dickmann, F. J. (2006). Ensuring "Strategy" Isn't On 'Culture's Breakfast Plate. *Credit Union Journal, 10*(45), 4–4.

Dries, N. (2012). *The role of learning agility and career variety in the identification and development of high potential employees.* Retrieved September 6, 2015, from http://www.emeraldinsight.com.strauss.uc3m.es:8080/doi/pdfplus/10.1108/00483481211212977

Dries, N. (2013). Adding value with learning agility: How to identify and develop high-potential employees. *Development and Learning in Organizations, 27*(5), 24–26. doi:10.1108/dlo-07-2013-0043

Dunning, M. (2015). Employers look beyond wellness: Many companies have modified their benefits programs to include incentives aimed at improving their employees' overall well-being. *Business Insurance, 49*(13). Retrieved from http://search.proquest.com.strauss.uc3m.es:8080/docview/1691108317/citation

Einarsen, S. (1999). The nature and causes of bullying at work. *International Journal of Manpower, 20*(1/2), 16–27. doi:10.1108/01437729910268588

Empirica. (2013). *E-Skills for jobs in europe: measuring progress and moving ahead.* Retrieved from Prepared for the European Commission website: http://eskills-monitor2013.eu/fileadmin/monitor2013/documents/MONITOR_Final_Report.pdf

Empirica. (2014). *e-Skills in Europe - Countryreport Spain.* European Commission.

Eom, M. T. (2015). How Can Organization Retain IT Personnel? Impact of IT Manager's Leadership on IT Personnel's Intention to Stay. *Information Systems Management, 32*(4), 316–330. doi:10.1080/10580530.2015.1080001

Eurostat. (2013, January). *Labour costs per hour in euro, whole economy.* Retrieved August 29, 2015, from http://ec.europa.eu/eurostat/statistics-explained/index.php/Earnings_statistics

Eurostat. (2014a). *Hourly labour costs - Statistics Explained.* Retrieved August 29, 2015, from http://ec.europa.eu/eurostat/statistics-explained/index.php/Hourly_labour_costs

Eurostat. (2014b). *Population and population change statistics.* Retrieved from http://epp.eurostat.ec.europa.eu/statistics_explained/index.php/Population_and_population_change_statistics#

Eurostat. (2015, February 1). *Gender pay gap statistics - Statistics Explained.* Retrieved August 29, 2015, from http://ec.europa.eu/eurostat/statistics-explained/index.php/Gender_pay_gap_statistics

Favaro, K. (2014, May 22). *Strategy or Culture: Which Is More Important?* Retrieved October 17, 2015, from strategy+business website: http://www.strategy-business.com/blog/Strategy-or-Culture-Which-Is-More-Important?gko=26c64

Feng, Y., Huang, H., Cheng, G., Chen, C., Huang, J., Liu, Z., & Huang, K. (2018). An Optimization Model to Evaluate Dynamic Assignment Capability of Agile Organization. *2018 4th International Conference on Big Data and Information Analytics (BigDIA)*, 1–6. 10.1109/BigDIA.2018.8632798

Financial Times Lexicon. (2013). *Gross Value Added definition.* Retrieved September 5, 2015, from http://lexicon.ft.com/Term?term=gross%20value%20added%20GVA

Gabrisch, H. (2008). *Institutional deficits in the euro area: the problem of divergent labour costs.* Retrieved August 29, 2015, from http://search.proquest.com.strauss.uc3m.es:8080/docview/209551006?pq-origsite=summon

Hasan, M., & Zhou, S. N. (2015). Knowledge Management in Global Organisations. *International Business Research, 8*(6), 165–173. doi:10.5539/ibr.v8n6p165

Henderson, R. (2018). *2018 Randstad Talent Trends Report.* Retrieved from https://www.randstad.it/hrsolutions/talent-trends-report-2018.pdf

Holtzhausen, N., & de Klerk, J. J. (2018). Servant leadership and the Scrum team's effectiveness. *Leadership and Organization Development Journal, 39*(7), 873–882. doi:10.1108/LODJ-05-2018-0193

Horlach, B., Drews, P., Schirmer, I., & Boehmann, T. (2017, January 4). *Increasing the Agility of IT Delivery: Five Types of Bimodal IT Organization.* doi:10.24251/HICSS.2017.656

Institute for opinion survey Allensbach. (2014). *Study conditions in 2014 - Study finance, foreign travel, and living situation*. Retrieved from http://www.sts-kd.de/reemtsma/Studie-Lang-Allensbach-2014h.pdf

Jaksic, M., & Jaksic, M. (2013). Performance Management and Employee Satisfaction. *Montenegrin Journal of Economics*, *9*(1), 85–92.

Joh, E., & White, W. (2018). How We Can Apply AI, and Deep Learning to our HR Functional Transformation and Core Talent Processes? *Student Works*. Retrieved from https://digitalcommons.ilr.cornell.edu/student/200

Kaufmann, M. (2014, February 17). Erreichbarkeit nach Dienstschluss Deutsche Konzerne kämpfen gegen den Handy-Wahn. *Spiegel Online*. Retrieved from http://www.spiegel.de/karriere/berufsleben/erreichbar-nach-dienstschluss-massnahmen-der-konzerne-a-954029.html

Kliner, K., Rennert, D., & Richter, M. (2015, July). *BKK Gesundheitsatlas*. Retrieved October 17, 2015, from http://www.bkk-dachverband.de/fileadmin/publikationen/gesundheitsatlas/BKK_Gesundheitsatlas_2015.pdf

Lee, T. S., Foo, C. T., & Cunningham, B. (1995). Role of organizational demographics in managing technology-induced stress. *Engineering Management Conference, 1995. Global Engineering Management: Emerging Trends in the Asia Pacific., Proceedings of 1995 IEEE Annual International*, 38–43. 10.1109/IEMC.1995.523906

Lusa, A., & Pastor, R. (2011). Planning working time accounts under demand uncertainty. *Computers & Operations Research*, *38*(2), 517–524. doi:10.1016/j.cor.2010.07.012

Malgorzata Ali, I. (2016). Doing the Organizational Tango: Symbiotic Relationship between Formal and Informal Organizational Structures for an Agile Organization. *Interdisciplinary Journal of Information, Knowledge, and Management, 11*, 55–72. doi:10.28945/3439

Martínez Aires, M. D., Rubio Gámez, M. C., & Gibb, A. (2010). Prevention through design: The effect of European Directives on construction workplace accidents. *Safety Science*, *48*(2), 248–258. doi:10.1016/j.ssci.2009.09.004

McDonald, P., Guthrie, D., Bradley, L., & Shakespeare-Finch, J. (2005). Investigating work-family policy aims and employee experiences. *Employee Relations*, *27*(4/5), 478–494. doi:10.1108/01425450510612013

McMenamin, T. M. (2007). A time to work: Recent trends in shift work and flexible schedules. *Monthly Labor Review*, *130*(12), 3–15.

Moe, N. B., Aurum, A., & Dybå, T. (2012). Challenges of shared decision-making: A multiple case study of agile software development. *Information and Software Technology*, *54*(8), 853–865. doi:10.1016/j.infsof.2011.11.006

Niemi, E., & Laine, S. (2016). Competence Management System Design Principles: Action Design Research. *ICIS 2016 Proceedings*. Retrieved from https://aisel.aisnet.org/icis2016/ISDesign/Presentations/4

Niskanen, T., Naumanen, P., & Hirvonen, M. L. (2012). An evaluation of EU legislation concerning risk assessment and preventive measures in occupational safety and health. *Applied Ergonomics*, *43*(5), 829–842. doi:10.1016/j.apergo.2011.12.003 PMID:22233692

Olsthoorn, M. (2014). Measuring Precarious Employment: A Proposal for Two Indicators of Precarious Employment Based on Set-Theory and Tested with Dutch Labor Market-Data - Springer. *Social Indicators Research*, *119*(1), 421–441. doi:10.100711205-013-0480-y

Otto, A., & Scholl, A. (2012). Reducing ergonomic risks by job rotation scheduling. *OR-Spektrum*, *35*(3), 711–733. doi:10.100700291-012-0291-6

Pathak, R., Parker, D. W., & Holesgrove, M. (2015). Improving productivity with self-organised teams and agile leadership. *International Journal of Productivity and Performance Management*, *64*(1), 112–128. doi:10.1108/IJPPM-10-2013-0178

Peruzzi, M. (2015). Contradictions and misalignments in the EU approach towards the gender pay gap. *Cambridge Journal of Economics*, *39*(2), 441–465. doi:10.1093/cje/bev007

Pfisterer, D. S. (2013, October 29). *39.000 job vacancies for IT experts*. Retrieved October 31, 2014, from http://www.bitkom.org/de/themen/54633_77765.aspx

Pollitt, D. (2005). Leadership succession planning "affects commercial success.". *Human Resource Management International Digest*, *13*(1), 36–38. doi:10.1108/09670730510576419

Poston, R., & Patel, J. (2016). Making Sense of Resistance to Agile Adoption in Waterfall Organizations: Social Intelligence and Leadership. *AMCIS 2016 Proceedings*. Retrieved from https://aisel.aisnet.org/amcis2016/ITProj/Presentations/34

Radant, O. (2014). Demographic Change: The Reasons, Implications and Consequences for IT Departments. *International Journal of Human Capital and Information Technology Professionals*, *5*(1), 41–54. doi:10.4018/ijhcitp.2014010104

Radant, O., Colomo-Palacios, R., & Stantchev, V. (2014). Analysis of Reasons, Implications and Consequences of Demographic Change for IT Departments in Times of Scarcity of Talent: A Systematic Review. *International Journal of Knowledge Management*, *10*(4), 1–15. doi:10.4018/ijkm.2014100101

Radant, O., Colomo-Palacios, R., & Stantchev, V. (2016a). Assessment of Continuing Educational Measures in Software Engineering: A View from the Industry. *Trends in Software Engineering for Engineering Education*, *32*(2), 905–914.

Radant, O., Colomo-Palacios, R., & Stantchev, V. (2016b). Factors for the Management of Scarce Human Resources and Highly Skilled Employees in IT-Departments: A Systematic Review. *Journal of Information Technology Research*, *9*(1), 65–82. doi:10.4018/JITR.2016010105

Radant, O., & Stantchev, V. (2018). Metrics for the Management of IT Personnel: A Systematic Literature Review. *International Journal of Human Capital and Information Technology Professionals*, *9*(2), 32–51. doi:10.4018/IJHCITP.2018040103

Răvaş, O.-C. (2013). Homeworking Contract and Teleworking - Importance and Role in the Economy. *Annals of the University of Petrosani. Economics*, *13*(2), 221–230.

Rose, J., Hewitt, B., & Baxter, J. (2013). Women and part-time employment Easing or squeezing time pressure? *Journal of Sociology (Melbourne, Vic.)*, *49*(1), 41–59. doi:10.1177/1440783311419907

Shatat, A., El-Baz, H., & Hariga, M. (2010). Employee expectations: Perception of Generation-Y engineers in the UAE. *2010 Second International Conference on Engineering Systems Management and Its Applications (ICESMA)*, 1–6.

Singe, I., & Croucher, R. (2003). The management of trust-based working time in Germany. *Personnel Review*, *32*(4), 492–509. doi:10.1108/00483480310477551

Spears, V. P. (2012). Employee Wellness Programs Expand to Well-Being. *Employee Benefit Plan Review*, *66*(11), 30.

Tarafdar, M., D'Arcy, J., Turel, O., & Gupta, A. (2014, December 16). *The Dark Side of Information Technology*. Retrieved September 26, 2015, from MIT Sloan Management Review website: http://sloanreview.mit.edu/article/the-dark-side-of-information-technology/

Todd, P., & Binns, J. (2013). Work-life Balance: Is it Now a Problem for Management? *Gender, Work and Organization*, *20*(3), 219–231. doi:10.1111/j.1468-0432.2011.00564.x

van den Bos, A., Kemper, B., & de Waal, V. (2014). A study on how to improve the throughput time of Lean Six Sigma projects in a construction company. *International Journal of Lean Six Sigma*, *5*(2), 226–212. doi:10.1108/IJLSS-10-2013-0055

Verner, T. (2011). National Competitiveness and Expenditure on Education, Research and Development. *Journal of Competitiveness*, *3*(2). Retrieved from http://search.proquest.com.strauss.uc3m.es:8080/docview/1315218679/abstract

Weiguo, C., & Yanchun, L. (2010). Research on Motivation System of Employees-Analysis of Human Resources Management from a Psychological Perspective. *2010 International Conference on Management and Service Science (MASS)*, 1–4. 10.1109/ICMSS.2010.5578035

Zeng, C., Zheng, S., & Shi, K. (2010). Relationship between job demands-resources and job burnout of IT employees. *2010 IEEE 2nd Symposium on Web Society (SWS)*, 548–553. 10.1109/SWS.2010.5607390

Chapter 26
Human Attitude Towards the Use of IT in Education:
Academy and Social Media

Silvia Gaftandzhieva
University of Plovdiv Paisii Hilendarski, Bulgaria

Rositsa Doneva
University of Plovdiv Paisii Hilendarski, Bulgaria

ABSTRACT

This chapter aims to explore the human attitude towards the use of IT in education, especially teacher attitudes towards the use of social media in teaching practice. The study is based on a survey questionnaire, which aims to investigate to what extent and for what purposes teachers from different countries from all over the world use social networking in their teaching practice. The chapter presents the method (an exploratory survey using questionnaire for data collection), organization of the study, and thorough analyses of the results in accordance with the study objectives. Finally, summarized results of the survey are presented, depending on the continent where the countries of the participants are located. The analysis of the survey results is presented on the basis of valid responses of 19,987 teachers from 75 countries around the world who participated in the survey.

INTRODUCTION

Students in the 21st century (referred to as the digital generation, digital natives) are growing up constantly connected to the world around them through smartphones, tablets, and computers. Marc Prensky (Prensky, 2001) defines the term "digital native" and applies it to a new group of students enrolling in educational establishments referring to the young generation as "native speakers" of the digital language of computers, videos, video games, social media and other sites on the internet. IT are changing the process of teaching and learning during last decade. IT experts have developed a lot of applications which can be used by teachers and students in the learning process.

DOI: 10.4018/978-1-7998-1279-1.ch026

Millennial learning styles require teachers acquire skills to adapt to digital learning. Nowadays, teachers from all over the world use IT to do and provide students with learning resources, video and audio materials that students can access at any time using their computers, notebooks, smartphones, etc. In order to meet the unique learning needs of digital natives, teachers need to move away from traditional teaching methods that are disconnected from the way students learn today (Morgan, 2014). Students from the digital age thrive on creative and engaging activities, varied sources of information, and a more energetic environment. Teachers are faced with the challenge to understand how they communicate and interact with the world in order to meet the needs of today's students and to teach more effectively.

Nowadays social networking is becoming a more and more powerful tool for communication, sharing of information and discussions on various topics. According to a worldwide survey, approximately 2 billion web surfers are using social networks today (Statista, 2018). The characteristics of social platforms, such as shared content and user-generated content, make them a powerful tool that helps to deliver a quality, personalized and student-centered education. Social networking sites have a significant presence in the contemporary higher education instsitutions and more and more teachers are showing an interest in taking advantage of the possibilities they offer for learning (Hortigüela-Alcalá, Sánchez-Santamaría, Pérez-Pueyo & Abella-García, 2019).

The wide academic and research interest in the use of social networking for educational purposes in higher education is the natural result of the constantly growing popularity of social networking.

According to Pearson (Seaman & Tinti-Kane, 2013), a learning company that promotes the effective use of technology, "A majority of faculty now use social media in a professional context (any aspect of their profession outside of teaching). Use of social media for teaching purposes has lagged even more, but like the other patterns of use, it has increased every year. The number of faculty who use social media in the classroom still does not represent a majority, but teaching use continues its steady year-to-year growth. Faculties are sophisticated consumers of social media. In general, they see considerable potential in the application of social media and technology to their teaching, but not without a number of serious barriers".

Likely the most significant and life changing technologies of the 21st century is the adoption of social media as major components of educational activities (Anderson, 2019). In recent years there has been extensive academic and research interest in the use of social networking for educational purposes (Acharya, Patel & Jethava, 2013; Voorn & Kommers, 2013; Wang, Woo, Quek, Yang & Liu, 2011; Kropf, 2013; Arquero, & Romero-Frías, 2013; Alam, 2018; Carapina, Bjelobrk & Duk, 2013; Ghanem, El-Gafy & Abdelrazig, 2014; Rothkrantz, 2015; Doneva & Gaftandzhieva, 2016; Zancanaro & Domingues, 2018; Awidi, Paynter, & Vujosevic, 2019; Saini & Abraham, 2019; Dommett, 2019; Aleksandrova & Parusheva, 2019; Anderson, 2019; Vivakaran, 2018; Zachos, Paraskevopoulou-Kollia, & Anagnostopoulos, 2018) and the presentation of higher education institutions and courses on social networks (Golubić & Lasić-Lazić, 2012; Golubić, 2017; Zancanaro & Domingues, 2018; Kumar & Nanda, 2019). Some educational institutions use social media educational system to support learning and interaction on campus, foster and encourage active learners' participation in the school system (Azeta et al. 2014).

A number of surveys have been conducted worldwide on the use of social networks by teachers and students (Hendee, 2014; Faculty Focus, 2011; Zanamwe, Rupere, & Kufandirimbwa, 2013; Mardikyan & Bozanta, 2017; Moran, Seaman, & Tinti-Kane, 2011; Kolan & Dzandza, 2018; Abu-Shanab, & Al-Tarawneh, 2015; Prestridge, 2019; Luguetti, Goodyear, & André, 2019; Awidi, Paynter, & Vujosevic, 2019; Saini & Abraham, 2019). The results of these surveys show that teachers do not use social networking sites for communication with their students (Ghanem, El-Gafy & Abdelrazig, 2014; Hendee,

2014; Faculty Focus, 2011) and during lessons (Hendee, 2014). Teachers use social networking sites to share information and resources with educators, to create professional learning communities and to connect with peers and colleagues (edWeb, 2009), to improve students' engagement in their course and their educational experience (Hendee, 2014; Mardikyan & Bozanta, 2017; Rutherford, 2010; Rodriguez, 2011; Junco, Elavsky & Heiberger, 2013; Awidi, Paynter, & Vujosevic, 2019; Saini & Abraham, 2019), to expand their own professional learning opportunities on social media platforms (Prestridge, 2019), to support the development of an authentic sport experience (Luguetti, Goodyear, & André, 2019). These surveys are held within a university or country. Therefore, the summarised results of these surveys do not allow us to draw conclusions about the attitude of teachers towards the use of social networks worldwide.

The chapter aims to explore the human attitude toward the use of IT in education, especially the teachers' attitude towards the use of social media in teaching practice. The study is based on a survey questionnaire, which aims to investigate to what extent teachers from different countries from all over the world use social networking sites in their teaching practice for different purposes on the basis of results from filled questionnaires. The attitude towards the use of social networking in higher education in general is examined. The study is intended to seek dependences between the answers related to the above issues and different teachers' characteristics, on the point of view if the teachers are well informed about social networking sites, or whether they participate in interest groups or research related with social networking and higher education. Finally, summarized results of the survey are presented, depending on the continent where the countries of the participants are located.

The chapter presents the method, organization of the study and thorough analyses of the results in accordance with the study objectives. Some general conclusions about the latest trends in the use of social networking in education are derived.

DESIGN OF THE STUDY

This section describes briefly the process for data collection and analysis, in order to contextualise the sections that follow.

The study´s method is based on an empirical approach – an exploratory survey using questionnaire for data collection. The questionnaire, used for data collection, contains 20 questions divided into three sections (see Appendix 1). It has been used to study the attitude towards the use of social networking in Bulgarian higher education (Doneva & Gaftandzhieva, 2017).

The questions in Section 1. Personal Information for participant (see Appendix 1) aim to determine the profile of respondents: gender, age, degree, title, university, country. This section contains also the question of the degree of awareness of participants about social networking to ensure the reliability of conclusions drawn from the analysis of the inquiry results.

In order to examine teachers' attitude towards the use of social networking for educational purposes, the main part of the questionnaire includes two sections - Opinion on the use of social networks in teaching practice (Section 2, see Appendix 1) and Opinion on the use of social networking for educational purposes in general (Section 3, see Appendix 1). Most of the questions are multiple choice. Respondents should state the extent of their agreement with formulated statements on the 5-point Likert-type scale in which 1 = Strongly Disagree (SD), 2 = Disagree (D), 3 = Neutral (N), 4 = Agree (A) and 5 = Strongly Agree (SA). There is an open-ended question for teachers at the end of the second and third part of the questionnaire. Teachers can indicate how they use social networking in their teaching practice, as well as why they consider that the use of social networks in education has a negative effect (if so).

The questionnaire was sent by email to teachers from different countries from all over the world. After collecting the data through the questionnaires, they were analysed using Microsoft Excel.

FINDINGS AND DISCUSSIONS

Respondents' Profile

The analysis of the survey results is presented on the basis of valid responses of 19 987 teachers from 75 countries around the world who participated in the survey. All countries with participants are marked with a certain color depending on the continent where they are located. Figure 1 presents the number of participants from each continent. 121 teachers did not answer the question about the country in which they work.

Out of the total number of teachers 49.75% are male and 55.25% are female. The largest group of teachers (28.34%) is above 55 years old, 26.75% of teachers are 45-54 years old and 24.76% of teachers are 35-44 years old. The smallest groups of teachers are 25-34 years old (17.34%) and below 25 years old (2.81%). Half of the teachers have a Ph.D. degree (50.08%) and D.Sc. degree (3.47%). Table 1 presents a summary profile of respondents based on the gathered demographic and other personal data.

Most surveyed teachers are familiar with social networking – 65.49% answered Yes and 29.94% Yes/ No to the question "Are you well informed about social networking (e.g. Facebook, Twitter, Google+, Bebo, Myspace, LinkedIn, etc.)?". Figure 2 presents the percentage of answers given by their faculty position and age group.

Survey Results

An analysis of the answers given on the statements from Section 2 shows that a significant smaller part of surveyed teachers use the social networking sites to communicate with their students (51.96% answered SD or D, and 18.27% answered N to Statement 8) and participate in online social networking groups for information sharing, discussion and organization of courses (56.80% answered SD or D to

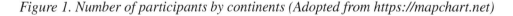

Figure 1. Number of participants by continents (Adopted from https://mapchart.net)

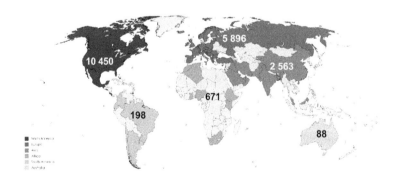

Table 1. Respondents' profile

Respondent's Information	Total		Male		Female	
	Number	Percent	Number	Percent	Number	Percent
Age						
Below 25	561	2.81%	209	1.05%	352	1.76%
25-34	3 465	17.34%	1 518	7.59%	1 947	9.75%
35-44	4 950	24.76%	2 453	12.27%	2 497	12.49%
45-54	5 346	26.75%	2 475	12.39%	2 871	14.36%
Above 55	5 665	28.34%	3 289	16.45%	2 376	11.89%
Degree						
PhD	10 010	50.08%	6 017	30.10%	3 993	19.98%
D.Sc.	693	3.47%	396	1.98%	297	1.49%
Other	9 284	46.45%	3 531	17.67%	5 753	8.78%
Faculty Position						
Assistant	1 210	6.05%	583	2.92%	627	3.13%
Assistant Professor	4 829	24.16%	2 618	13.10%	2 211	11.06%
Associate Professor	3 487	17.45%	1 969	9.86%	1 518	7.59%
Professor	4 697	23.50%	2 585	12.93%	2 112	10.57%
Other	5 764	28.84%	2 189	10.95%	3 575	17.89%

Figure 2. Percentage of the answers to Question 7 according to teachers' faculty position and age group

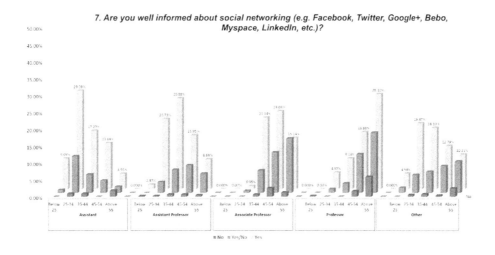

Statement 9, and 60.54% answered SD or D to Statement 10). The percentage of teachers who believe that the use of social networking during the lesson increases the engagement of students is even smaller - only 18.40% (see answers to Statement 11). The number of teachers who participate in online groups interested in the use of social networking for educational purposes is also small - 32.63%. 53.03% of the surveyed teachers have a public profile in a social networking site to share research interests and to connect with like-minded people (Statement 13). Finally, when teachers are asked to agree that the use of social networking has a positive effect on student achievement and increases the involvement and interest of students in the training, 39.62% of teachers stated that they are SD or D with Statement 14 and 41.06% of teachers stated that they are SD or D with Statement 15. Table 2 presents summarized results of Section 2.

The majority of teachers (see. Table 3.) agree that the use of social networking in education can be useful - 24.71% answered SA to Statement 17 and 36.05% answered A. Significantly greater is the number of teachers who agree that the role of social networking in education will increase – 36.12% answered SA and 37.83% answered A to Statement 18. This shows that despite the relatively low rate of the current use of social networking, the majority of teachers are likely to use social networks in the future. The answers given on Statement 19 show that the low rate of use of social networks at the moment is probably due also to the low level of participation of teachers in research on the use of social networking in education – only 5 764 teachers (28.97%) stated participation in such research.

Table 2. Using of social networking sites in teachers' academic practice

Statement	1=SD	2=D	3=N	4=A	5=SA
8. You often use social networking sites for communication and consultation with your students.	6 919 (34.62%)	3 465 (17.34%)	3 652 (18.27%)	3 608 (18.05%)	2 343 (11.72%)
9. You participate in social networking group/groups with your students for information sharing and discussions on the courses.	7 777 (38.91%)	3 575 (17.89%)	3 454 (17.28%)	3 256 (16.29%)	1 925 (9.63%)
10. You participate in social networking group/groups with your students for organization of the courses.	7 777 (42.38%)	3 630 (18.16%)	3 300 (16.51%)	2 948 (14.75%)	1 639 (8.20%)
11. You use social networking sites during the lesson in order to increase students' involvement and to keep track of their reactions.	9 526 (47.85%)	4 004 (20.11%)	2 717 (13.65%)	2 299 (11.55%)	1 364 (6.85%)
12. You participate in online group/groups interested in the use of social networking for educational purposes.	6 963 (34.84%)	3 091 (15.47%)	3 410 (17.06%)	4 092 (20.47%)	2 431 (12.16%)
13. You have a public profile in some of social networking sites to share yours research interests and to connect with a wide range of people with similar preferences.	3 630 (18.17%)	2 365 (11.84%)	3 338 (16.96%)	5 346 (26.76%)	5 247 (26.27%)
14. The use of social networking sites in your teaching practice has a positive effect on the student achievements.	5 489 (27.46%)	2 431 (12.16%)	6 424 (32.14%)	3 630 (18.33%)	1 980 (9.91%)
15. The use of social networking sites in your teaching practice increases the involvement and interest of students in the training.	5 676 (28.40%)	2 530 (12.66%)	5 720 (28.62%)	4 048 (20.25%)	2 013 (10.07%)

Table 3. Using of social networking for educational purposes in general

Statement	1=SD	2=D	3=N	4=A	5=SA
17. Social networking sites are/can be useful in education.	1 210 (6.05%)	1 749 (8.75%)	4 884 (24.44%)	7 205 (36.05%)	4 939 (24.71%)
18. The role of social networking sites will increase.	902 (4.52%)	1 001 (5.01%)	3 300 (16.52%)	7 557 (37.83%)	7 216 (36.12%)
19. You participate in research related to the use of social networking sites in education.	7 150 (35.93%)	3 366 (16.92%)	3 619 (18.19%)	3 399 (17.08%)	2 365 (11.89%)

Overall, the survey results show that teachers have a negative attitude towards the use of social networking in their academic practice (an average grade 2.58 on the eight statements from Section 2 of the questionnaire). Although the surveyed teachers do not use social networking sites in their teaching practice now, they believe that social networking sites can be useful for education in general and have a positive attitude towards the use of social networking for educational purposes (an average grade 3.38 on the three statements from Section 3 of the questionnaire). Figure 3 presents the average grades on statements from Section 2 and Section 3 of the questionnaire given by the teachers.

The survey results do not confirm results of the same survey conducted in Bulgaria (Doneva & Gaftandzhieva, 2017) in a full degree. Unlike their colleagues around the world, teachers in Bulgaria are more active in the use of social networking sites for communication with their students. Also small, but relatively larger than in the world, part of the Bulgarian teachers use social networking sites for information sharing, discussions and course organization. Surveyed teachers within this survey are more active than Bulgarian teachers in the use of social networking during lesson, participation in online groups interesting in the use of social networking for educational purposes. Bulgarian teachers gave significant higher grades on statements that the role of social networking in education will increase and social networking can be useful for education, but they are less involved in research related to the use of social networking in education than their colleagues from other countries.

The most results obtained are in line with the findings of other surveys on the use of social networking in education. For example some surveys conducted among teachers (Ghanem, El-Gafy & Abdelrazig, 2014; Hendee, 2014; Faculty Focus, 2011) show that teachers do not use social networks for communication with their students and prefer to use conventional communication channels (email, phone calls, and text messaging respectively). The conclusion that a small number of teachers use social networking during lessons also confirms the results of another survey (Hendee, 2014). The finding that most teachers use social networking sites to share their research interests and to connect with a wide range of people with similar preferences confirms the results of other surveys (edWeb, 2009; Vivakaran, 2018). These surveys concludes that teachers use social networking to share information and resources with educators, to create professional learning communities and to connect with peers and colleagues. Moreover, the positive attitude of the teachers towards the statements that social networking sites can be useful in education and their role in education will increase, substantiates the teachers' expectation to increase their use of social media in the future (Faculty Focus, 2011). However, some of the findings from the

Figure 3. Average grades on statements from Section 2 and Section 3

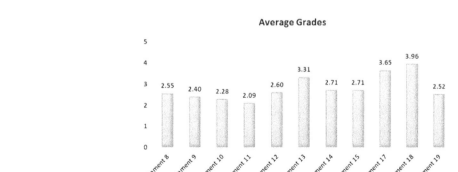

current survey do not correspond to those of other studies. This study's conclusions that the use of social networks doesn't increase students' engagement and interest while studying their course differ from the conclusions of other studies, according to which the use of social networks improve students' engagement in their course and their educational experience, on the one hand (Hendee, 2014; Mardikyan & Bozanta, 2017; Rutherford, 2010; Rodriguez, 2011; Junco, Elavsky & Heiberger, 2013; Saini & Abraham, 2019), and peer interaction and students' interaction with faculty members, on the other (Zanamwe, Rupere, & Kufandirimbwa, 2013; Mardikyan & Bozanta, 2017). The findings do not corroborate the results of another studies (Kolan & Dzandza, 2018; Awidi, Paynter, & Vujosevic, 2019; Hortigüela-Alcalá, Sánchez-Santamaría, Pérez-Pueyo & Abella-García, 2019) conducted among the students, according to which the use of social networking increases their understanding of topics discussed in class and improves their grades (Kolan & Dzandza, 2018), encourage them to learn through their Facebook engagement (Awidi, Paynter, & Vujosevic, 2019) and increase both student motivation and involvement, as well as their degree of achievement (Hortigüela-Alcalá, Sánchez-Santamaría, Pérez-Pueyo& Abella-García, 2019). This persuasion contradicts the opinion of surveyed teachers that the use of social networking sites in their teaching practice does not have a positive effect on student achievements.

Analysis According to the Teachers' Extent of Knowledge About Social Networking

The analysis of the answers to Question 7 shows that not all of the surveyed teachers are well informed about social networking. Therefore, it is natural for teachers who are not familiar with social networking sites to use them less often in their academic practice and not to be positive about their use in education. A detailed analysis of the answers to all questions was made to examine the extent to which the use of social networking in the academic practice of the surveyed teachers and their opinion on the use of social networking for education purposes in general are related to the teachers' extent of knowledge about social networking.

Figure 4 and Figure 5 present detailed results in percentage of the answers to the statements from Section 2 and Section 3 in the questionnaire teachers gave according to their extent of knowledge about social networking. The analysis shows that the most positive attitude towards the use of social networks in teaching practice and in education pertains to teachers (answered SA and A to the statements from Section 2 and Section 3) who are familiar with social networking (answered Yes to the Question 7), followed by teachers who are not fully informed about social networking (answered Yes/No to the Question 7). It is interesting to note that even teachers who answered they are unfamiliar with social networking believe that social networking sites can be useful for education and they are convinced that the role of social networks in education will increase (see Figure 5).

The analysis shows that teachers who are familiar with social networking gave the highest average grades (the average of the given answers ranging from 1 to 5), followed by teachers who are not fully informed about social networking and teachers who are not familiar with social networks at all. Overall, teachers from all groups do not use social networking in their academic practice and gave an average grade below 3 to the statements in Section 2. Although teachers do not use social networking sites now

Figure 4. Percentage of answers to Statements 8-15 according to degree of information about social networking

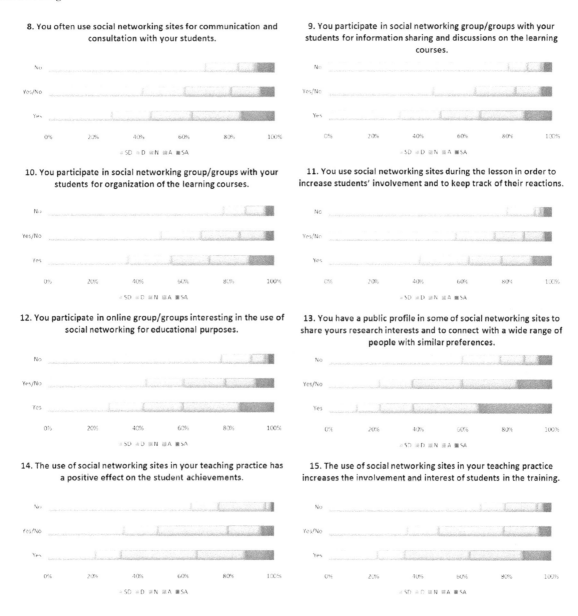

and they do not participate actively in research related to the use of social networking sites in education (an average grade below 3 to Statement 19 by all groups of the surveyed teachers), all teachers are positive about the use of social networking in education, believe that social networking sites can be useful for education and they are convinced that their role in education will increase (an average grade above 3 to Statement 17 and to Statement 18 by all groups of the surveyed teachers), see Figure 6.

Figure 5. Percentage of answers to Statements 17-19 according to degree of information about social networking

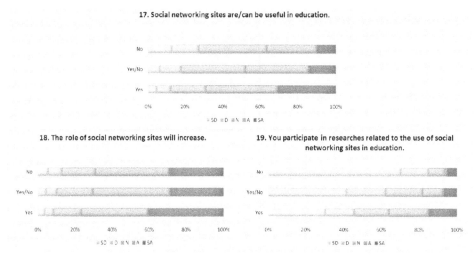

Figure 6. Average grades on statements from Section 2 and Section 3 according to degree of information about social networking

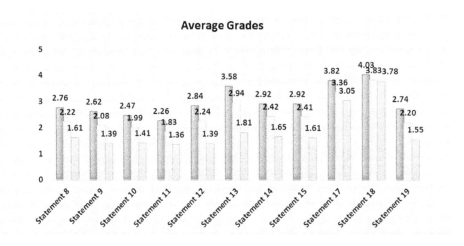

Analysis According to the Teachers' Participation in Groups

A small part of the surveyed teachers participate in groups interested in the use of social networking for educational purposes - only 6 523 (32.64%) of the surveyed teachers answered A or SA to Statement 12. You participate in online group/groups interested in the use of social networking for educational purposes. Significantly higher is the number of teachers who do not participate in groups interested in the use social networks for educational purposes – 10 054 of the surveyed teachers answered SD or D to Statement 12 (50.30%).

Table 4 presents the number of answers given by teachers who do not participate in groups interested in the use of social networking for educational purposes. The results show that teachers who do not participate in such groups rarely use social networking sites in their teaching practice. The analysis of the answers shows that teachers are skeptical towards the use of social networking for communication and consultation with their students, discussions on the studied material and organization of training courses – only 12.03% answered A or SA to Statement 8, 9.73% answered A or SA to Statement 9 and 6.24% answered A or SA to Statement 10. Most teachers are strongly against the use of social networking sites during lessons – only 4.06% of teachers gave answers A or SA to Statement 11. Teachers are skeptical that the use of social networking sites has a positive effect on students' achievements and that it increases their involvement and interest in the training – 9.19% of teachers gave answer A or SA to Statement 14 and 10.06% of teachers gave answer A or SA to Statement 15.

The teachers who participate in groups interested in the use of social networking for educational purposes are more positive and actively use social networks in their academic practice. Table 5 presents the number of responses from teachers participating in such groups. The analysis of the answers shows that most of the surveyed teachers use social networking for communication and consultation with their students, discussions about the studied material and organization of courses – 56.16% answered SA or A to Statement 8, 52.28% answered A or SA to Statement 9 and 49.92% answered A or SA to Statement 10. A significant part of surveyed teachers have a positive attitude towards the use of social networking sites during lessons – 42.37% of teachers answered A or SA to Statement 11. Most teachers believe that the use of social networking sites has a positive effect on students' achievements and that it increases

Table 4. Using of social networking sites in teaching practice according to answers on Statement 12 (SD=1 and D=2)

Statement	SD=1	D=2	N=3	A=4	SA=5
8. You often use social networking sites for communication and consultation with your students.	5 511 (54.81%)	2 134 (21.23%)	1 199 (11.93%)	671 (6.67%)	539 (5.36%)
9. You participate in social networking group/groups with your students for information sharing and discussions on the courses.	6 248 (62.14%)	2 035 (20.24%)	792 (7.88%)	671 (6.67%)	539 (3.06%)
10. You participate in social networking group/ groups with your students for organization of the courses.	6 765 (67.29%)	1 848 (18.38%)	814 (8.10%)	451 (4.49%)	176 (1.75%)
11. You use social networking sites during the lesson in order to increase students' involvement and to keep track of their reactions.	7 271 (72.56%)	1 958 (19.54%)	385 (3.84%)	286 (2.85%)	121 (1.21%)
13. You have a public profile in some of social networking sites to share yours research interests and to connect with a wide range of people with similar preferences.	3 146 (31.29%)	1 518 (15.10%)	1 485 (14.77%)	2 145 (21.33%)	1 760 (17.51%)
14. The use of social networking sites in your teaching practice has a positive effect on the student achievements.	4 796 (47.70%)	1 496 (14.86%)	2 838 (28.23%)	627 (6.24%)	297 (2.95%)
15. The use of social networking sites in your teaching practice increases the involvement and interest of students in the training.	4 807 (47.81%)	1 672 (16.63%)	2 563 (25.49%)	693 (6.89%)	319 (3.17%)

Table 5. Using of social networking sites in teaching practice according to answers on Statement 12 (A=4 and SA=5)

Statement	SD=1	D=2	N=3	A=4	SA=5
8. You often use social networking sites for communication and consultation with your students.	770 (11.80%)	781 (11.97%)	1 309 (20.07%)	2 178 (33.39%)	1 485 (22.77%)
9. You participate in social networking group/groups with your students for information sharing and discussions on the courses.	836 (12.82%)	946 (14.50%)	1 331 (20.40%)	2 024 (31.03%)	1 386 (21.25%)
10. You participate in social networking group/groups with your students for organization of the courses.	946 (14.50%)	1 089 (16.69%)	1 232 (18.89%)	1 958 (30.02%)	1 298 (19.90%)
11. You use social networking sites during the lesson in order to increase students' involvement and to keep track of their reactions.	1 375 (21.19%)	1 221 (18.81%)	1 144 (17.63%)	1 650 (25.42%)	1 100 (16.95%)
13. You have a public profile in some of social networking sites to share yours research interests and to connect with a wide range of people with similar preferences.	253 (3.89%)	396 (6.08%)	836 (12.84%)	2 244 (34.46%)	2 783 (42.74%)
14. The use of social networking sites in your teaching practice has a positive effect on the student achievements.	286 (4.38%)	484 (7.42%)	1 947 (29.85%)	2 343 (35.92%)	1 463 (22.43%)
15. The use of social networking sites in your teaching practice increases the involvement and interest of students in the training.	363 (5.56%)	484 (7.42%)	1 639 (25.13%)	2 629 (40.30%)	1 408 (21.59%)

their involvement and interest in the training – 58.35% of teachers answered A or SA to Statement 14 and 61.89% of teachers answered A or SA to Statement 15.

The analysis of the answers clearly shows (see Figure 7) that teachers who participate in groups interested in the use of social networking sites for educational purposes gave higher average grades of all statements in Section 2. These teachers gave an average grade above 3 to the six statements in Section 2. Although they have a positive attitude towards social networking in general, a small part of them use social networking sites during lessons - an average grade 2.98 on Statement 11.

Figure 7. Average grades on statements from Section 2 according to answers on Statement 12

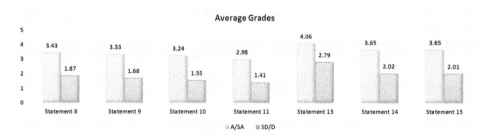

Analysis According to the Teachers' Participation in Research for Social Networking

Analysis of the answers to *Statement 19. You participate in research related to the use of social networking sites in education* shows that a significant small part of the teachers participate in research related to the use of social networking sites in education - only 5 764 (28.97%) of the surveyed teachers answered A or SA. More than half of the surveyed teachers do not participate in such research – 10 516 of the teachers answered SD or D to Statement 19 (52.85%) (see Table 3, Statement 19). In order to establish the extent to which the positive attitude towards the use of social networking in education of the surveyed teachers is related to their scientific interests, a detailed analysis of the answers to all statements in Section 3 according to the teachers' participation in social networking research was made.

Table 6 and Table 7 present the analysis of the answers to the statements in Section 3 of the questionnaire according to teachers' participation in research related to the use of social networking sites in education. The analysis of the answers shows that teachers who do not participate in research related to the use of social networking believe that the use of social networking in education can have a positive effect and their role in education will increase – 47.80% answered A or SA to Statement 17 and 66.49% answered A or SA to Statement 18 (see Table 6). Most of the surveyed teachers that participate in such research have a positive attitude towards the use of social networking sites for educational purposes in general – only 330 (5.73%) teachers stated that social networking sites can't be useful in education and 242 (4.20%) teachers stated that their role will not increase (see Table 7).

The analysis of the answers clearly shows (see Figure 8) that all teachers gave high average grades (above 3) to Statement 17 and Statement 18. Logically teachers who participate in research related to the use of social networking sites in education are more positive to their use and gave higher average grades (above 4).

Table 6. Using of social networking for educational purposes in general according to answers on Statement 19 (SD=1 and D=2)

Statement	SD=1	D=2	N=3	A=4	SA=5
17. Social networking sites are/can be useful in education.	1 034 (9.83%)	1 309 (12.45%)	3 146 (29.92%)	3 256 (30.96%)	1 771 (16.84%)
18. The role of social networking sites will increase.	715 (6.81%)	748 (7.12%)	2 057 (19.58%)	3 839 (36.54%)	3 146 (29.95%)

Table 7. Using of social networking for educational purposes in general according to answers on Statement 19 (A=4 and SA=5)

Statement	SD=1	D=2	N=3	A=4	SA=5
17. Social networking sites are/can be useful in education.	88 (1.53%)	242 (4.20%)	605 (10.50%)	2 519 (43.70%)	2 310 (40.08%)
18. The role of social networking sites will increase.	121 (2.10%)	121 (2.10%)	473 (8.21%)	2 200 (38.17%)	2 849 (49.43%)

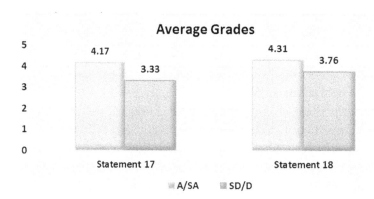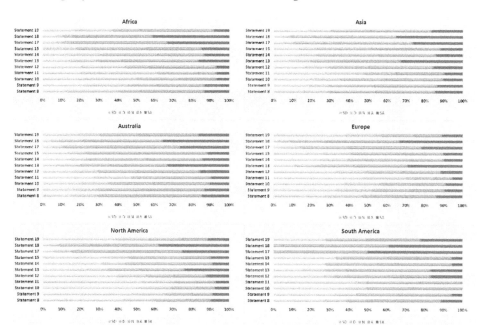

Figure 8. Average grades on statements from Section 3 according to answers on Statement 19

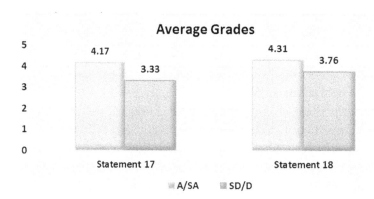

Analysis According to the Continent Where Teachers Work

In order to establish the extent to which the attitude towards the use of social networking in education of the surveyed teachers depends on the continent where they are located, a detailed analysis of the answers to all statements according to the continent was made. Figure 9 presents detailed results in percentage of the answers of the statements from Section 2 and Section 3 of the questionnaire given by the surveyed teachers from sixth continents.

Table 8 presents the average grades given by teachers from the sixth continents. The analysis of the answers shows that the surveyed teachers from all countries do not use social networking sites in their teaching practice as a whole (see average grades on Statement 8-15). Teachers from Asia stated that they use social networking sites for communication, consultation and discussions with students (an average

Figure 9. Percentage of answers to Statement 8-19 according to continent

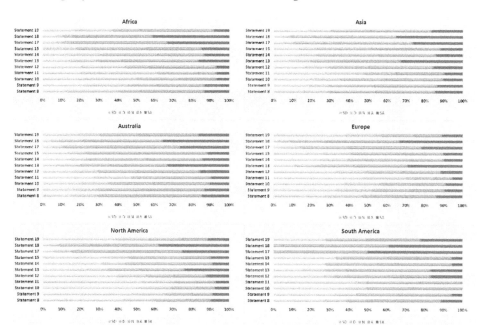

Table 8. Average answers by continents

Statement	Africa	Asia	Australia	Europe	North America	South America
8. You often use social networking sites for communication and consultation with your students.	3.07	3.13	1.88	2.71	2.28	2.94
9. You participate in social networking group/groups with your students for information sharing and discussions on the courses.	2.82	3.12	1.75	2.49	2.15	2.61
10. You participate in social networking group/groups with your students for organization of the courses.	2.59	2.94	1.75	2.40	2.03	2.39
11. You use social networking sites during the lesson in order to increase students' involvement and to keep track of their reactions.	2.39	2.68	1.63	2.00	1.98	2.28
12. You participate in online group/groups interested in the use of social networking for educational purposes.	2.84	3.17	2.00	2.58	2.45	2.94
13. You have a public profile in some of social networking sites to share yours research interests and to connect with a wide range of people with similar preferences.	3.30	3.67	3.25	3.50	3.12	3.33
14. The use of social networking sites in your teaching practice has a positive effect on the student achievements.	3.13	3.22	2.00	2.73	2.55	2.78
15. The use of social networking sites in your teaching practice increases the involvement and interest of students in the training.	3.41	3.22	2.00	2.73	2.55	2.78
17. Social networking sites are/can be useful in education.	3.97	3.82	2.88	3.62	3.60	4.44
18. The role of social networking sites will increase.	4.05	3.99	3.25	3.92	3.98	4.33
19. You participate in research related to the use of social networking sites in education.	3.00	3.14	2.88	2.40	2.39	3.17

grade 3.13 to Statement 8 and 3.12 to Statement 9). Also, they are the most active in groups interested in the use of social networking for educational purposes (an average grade 3.17 to Statements 12), sharing of research interests (the highest average grade to Statement 13). Teachers from Asia have the most positive attitude towards the statement that the use of social networking sites in education has a positive effect on the student achievements (an average grade above 3 to Statements 14). Teachers from Africa have the most positive attitude towards the statement that social networking sites increase the interest and involvement of students in the training, followed by teachers from Asia (an average grade above 3 to Statement 15). Most teachers believe that the use of social networking in education can have a positive effect and their role in education will increase – only teachers from Australia are skeptical about this statement. Teachers from all countries gave average grades above 3 to Statement 18 and Statement 19. Although the answers given and the conviction of teachers for positive effects and the role of social networking, only teachers from Asia, North America and South America participate in research related to the use of social networking for educational purposes (an average grade above 3 to Statement 19).

Figure 10 presents the average grades of all statements in Section 2 and Section 3 given by the surveyed teachers calculated according to the continent where they are located. Average grades are presented in parentheses – the first number is the average grade on statements in Section 2 and the second number is the average grade on statements in Section 3. The map clearly shows that teachers do not use social networking sites in their teaching practice now – only teachers from Asia have a positive attitude towards the use of social networking sites in teaching practice (an average grade 3.14 on Section 2). All teachers think that in general the use of social networking sites can be useful for education and the educational role of the social networks will increase in the coming years (an average grade above 3 on Section 3).

CONCLUSION

Due to the resource constraints the survey does not claim to be representative and has some limitations. The most important limitation is the number of participants. Around 100 000 teachers from all over the world (randomly selected) were asked to participate in the study, but only 19 987 of them filled in the questionnaire. Some of the invited teachers refused to participate because of various reasons - doubts about the reliability of the survey, spam attacks, etc.

The study gives a clear answer to the research questions – what is the extent to which teachers from different countries all over the world use social networking sites in their teaching practice for different purposes and what is their attitude towards the use of social networking in education in general.

The survey results show that teachers do not use social networking for educational purposes in their teaching practice today (an average grade 2.58 on the eight statements from Section 2 of the question-naire). Only about 30% of the surveyed teachers actually use social networking for the following purposes:

- Communication and consultations;
- Holding discussions on the courses, highlighting of some topics, sharing of lecture notes;
- Increase involvement, cooperation and interest of students;
- Encourage creative writing;
- Sending additional materials and sharing information;
- Guidance for doing assignments/projects and manage progress on projects;
- Organization of the learning activities on specific courses or as a whole and keep students up–to-date on class activities, homework, assignments, midterms;

Figure 10. Average grades on statements according to continent (Adopted from https://mapchart.net)

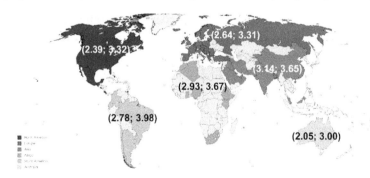

- Sharing research, best practises and communication with colleagues;
- Publication of events, activities and stories of interest to students;
- Announcement and invitation to workshops, conferences and other professional events;
- Course promotion;
- Contact alumni and former students;
- Open up discussion and exchange of ideas/opinions;
- Building networks between students from different programs or years;
- Help students connect to professionals in their field of interest.

It is natural that teachers who participate in groups interested in the use of social networking sites for educational purposes gave higher average grades of all statements in Section 2 (above 3) than teachers who do not participate in such groups. The average grades of all statements in Section 2 and Section 3 given by the surveyed teachers calculated according to the continent where they are located clearly shows that teachers' attitude towards the use of social networking for educational purposes depends on the continent where teachers are located.

Although the most surveyed teachers do not use social networking sites in their teaching practice now, they agree that the educational role of the social networks will increase in the coming years. Teachers from all continents believe that in general social networking sites can be useful for education (an average grade 3.38 on the three statements from Section 3 of the questionnaire). The answers of the open-ended question at the end of Section 3 show that most teachers today have a negative attitude towards the use of social networking for organizational/teaching activities for the following reasons:

- Distraction of the students and incompatibility to data protection regulations;
- Lack of person-to-person natural and intuitive communication and valuable direct interaction;
- Social networking sites are much informal and give to students too much freedom;
- It requires time to manage it - set up a social network channel for a course, update the social media channel, monitor and comment on it;
- It is hard to stay current with all the different social networking apps that students use;
- Danger of superficiality, lack of a reflective approach to learning;
- Sharing mechanisms blur the boundary between private and public/academic public;
- It is not a reflexive research-tool and does not allow for thorough ethical review process;
- Plagiarism, lack of motivation, laziness of thought and analytical skills, severe drop in communication and presentation skills, etc.;
- Some issues connected to privacy, security, archiving, and ethics;
- In terms of knowledge sharing, it dilutes the information and the objective value is subjected to crowd (mis)interpretation;
- It can blur boundaries between students and instructors;
- It is likely that social media will devalue the role of academics and education;
- Too many boundaries and ethical issues that higher education has yet to address.

The negative attitude of teachers today is related to the fact that not all of them are well informed about social networking and a significant small part of them participate in research related to the opportunities for the use of social networking in education. Teachers who have a positive attitude to the use of social networking for educational purposes believe that their use is quite beneficial if the networking site is created for educational purposes only and if the students are properly targeted to the use of the social networks and have clear guidelines. According to them if social networking is used wisely and properly social networking can enhance the learning experience and enhance the ability of the students to collaborate with others. They think that social networks are one of the channels they can use to communicate effectively with students. According to them social networking can be a useful tool for creation of a sense of community and share resources, for organising and motivating students, for research networking and production. Furthermore, teachers stated that social networking can create interaction and increase the knowledge of the students (especially in language teaching). Some teachers think also that opportunities for research, interaction and collaboration online can play a significant impact on students' achievement and learning. Teachers who do not use actively social networking for organizational/teaching activities today think that all this possibly will change in the next years with new students (with new social media behaviour) coming in.

ACKNOWLEDGMENT

This research was supported by the project "Intelligent Data Analysis for Improving the Learning Outcomes" of the Scientific Research Fund at the University of Plovdiv "Paisii Hilendarski" [grant number MU19-FTF-001] and the project "Digitalization of Economy in a big data environment" funded under the procedure "Creation and development of centres of competence" of Operational Programme "Science and education for smart growth" [grant number BG05M2OP001-1.002-0002-C].

REFERENCES

Abu-Shanab, E., & Al-Tarawneh, H. (2015). The Influence of Social Networks on High School Students' Performance. *International Journal of Web-Based Learning and Teaching Technologies*, *10*(2), 49–59. doi:10.4018/IJWLTT.2015040104

Acharya, V., Patel, Ad., & Jethava, S. (2013). A Survey on Social Networking to Enhance the Teaching and Learning Process. *International Journal of Advanced Research in Computer Science and Software Engineering*, *3*(6), 528–531.

Alam, L. (2018). *Teaching with web 2.0 technologies: Twitter, wikis & blogs.* Retrieved from https://tv.unsw.edu.au/files//unswPDF/CS_Web2_LTTO.pdf

Aleksandrova, Y., & Parusheva, S. (2019). Social Media Usage Patterns in Higher Education Institutions – An Empirical Study. *International Journal of Emerging Technologies in Learning*, *14*(5), 108–121. doi:10.3991/ijet.v14i05.9720

Anderson, T. (2019). Challenges and Opportunities for use of Social Media in Higher Education. *Journal of Learning for Development*, *6*(1), 6–19.

Arquero, J. L., & Romero-Frías, E. (2013). Using social network sites in Higher Education: An experience in business studies. *Innovations in Education and Teaching International*, *50*(3), 238–249. doi:10.1080/14703297.2012.760772

Aviles, M., & Eastman, J. K. (2012). Utilizing technology effectively to improve millennials' educational performance. *Journal of International Education in Business*, *5*(2), 96–113. doi:10.1108/18363261211281726

Awidi, I. T., Paynter, M., & Vujosevic, T. (2019). Facebook group in the learning design of a higher education course: An analysis of factors influencing positive learning experience for students. *Computers & Education*, *129*, 106–121. doi:10.1016/j.compedu.2018.10.018

Azeta, A., Omoregbe, N., Ayo, C., Raymond, A., Oroge, A., & Misra, S. (2014). *An anti-cultism social education media system. In Global Summit on Computer & Information Technology* (pp. 1–5). Sousse: GSCIT. doi:10.1109/GSCIT.2014.6970097

Carapina, M., Bjelobrk, D., & Duk, S. (2013). *Web 2.0 tools in Croatian higher education: An overview. In Proceeding of Information & Communication Technology Electronics & Microelectronics (MIPRO 2013)* (Vol. 36, pp. 676–680). Opatija, Croatia: MIPRO.

Dommett, E. (2019). Understanding student use of twitter and online forums in higher education. *Education and Information Technologies*, *24*(1), 325–343. doi:10.100710639-018-9776-5

Doneva, R., & Gaftandzhieva, S. (2017). Social Media in Bulgarian Higher Education: An Exploratory Survey. *International Journal of Human Capital and Information Technology Professionals*, *8*(3), 67–83. doi:10.4018/IJHCITP.2017100106

edWeb. (2009). *A Survey of K-12 Educators on Social Networking and Content-Sharing Tools*. Retrieved from https://www.edweb.net/fimages/op/K12Survey.pdf

Faculty Focus. (2011). *Social Media Usage Trends Among Higher Education Faculty*. Retrieved from https://www.facultyfocus.com/free-reports/social-media-usage-trends-among-higher-education-faculty/

Ghanem, A., El-Gafy, M., & Abdelrazig, Y. (2014). Survey of the Current Use of Social Networking in Construction Education. *Proceedings of the 50th ASC Annual International Conference.*

Golubić, K. (2017). *The Role of Social Networks in the Presentation of Croatian Higher Education Institutions* (Unpublished Doctoral Dissertation). University of Zagreb, Croatia.

Golubić, K., & Lasić-Lazić, J. (2012) Analysis of On-line Survey about Need for Presence of Higher Education Institutions on Social Networks: A Step towards Creation of Communication Strategy. *Journal of Computing and Information Technology*, *20*(3), 189-194.

Hendee, C. (2014). *Teachers have mixed feelings on using social media in classrooms*. Retrieved from https://www.bizjournals.com/denver/news/2014/02/11/teachers-have-mixed-feelings-on-using.html

Hortigüela-Alcalá, D., Sánchez-Santamaría, J., Pérez-Pueyo, Á., & Abella-García, V. (2019). Social networks to promote motivation and learning in higher education from the students' perspective. *Innovations in Education and Teaching International*, *56*(4), 412–422. doi:10.1080/14703297.2019.1579665

Junco, R., Elavsky, C. M., & Heiberger, G. (2013). Putting twitter to the test: Assessing outcomes for student collaboration, engagement and success. *British Journal of Educational Technology*, *44*(2), 273–287. doi:10.1111/j.1467-8535.2012.01284.x

Kolan, B., & Dzandza, P. (2018). Effect of Social Media on Academic Performance of Students in Ghanaian Universities: A Case Study of University of Ghana, Legon. *Library Philosophy and Practice (e-journal)*, 1637.

Kropf, D. (2013). Connectivism: 21st Century's New Learning Theory. *European Journal of Open, Distance and e-Learning*, *16*(2), 13-24.

Kumar, V., & Nanda, P. (2019). Social Media in Higher Education: A Framework for Continuous Engagement. *International Journal of Information and Communication Technology Education*, *15*(1), 97–108. doi:10.4018/IJICTE.2019010107

Luguetti, C., Goodyear, V. A., & André, M. H. (2019). That is like a 24 hours-day tournament: Using social media to further an authentic sport experience within sport education. *Sport Education and Society*, *24*(1), 78–91. doi:10.1080/13573322.2017.1292235

Mardikyan, S., & Bozanta, A. (2017). The effects of social media use on collaborative learning: A case of Turkey. *Turkish Online Journal of Distance Education-TOJDE*, *18*(1), 96–110. doi:10.17718/tojde.285719

Moran, M., Seaman, J., & Tinti-Kane, H. (2011). *Teaching, Learning, and Sharing: How Today's Higher Education Faculty Use Social Media*. Boston, MA: Pearson Learning Solutions. Retrieved from https://files.eric.ed.gov/fulltext/ED535130.pdf

Morgan, H. (2014). Using digital story projects to help students improve in reading and writing. *Reading Improvement*, *51*(1), 20–26.

Prensky, M. (2001). Digital Natives, Digital Immigrants. *On the Horizon*, *9*(5), 1–6. doi:10.1108/10748120110424816

Prestridge, S. (2019). Categorising teachers' use of social media for their professional learning: A self-generating professional learning paradigm. *Computers & Education*, *129*, 143–158. doi:10.1016/j.compedu.2018.11.003

Rodriguez, J. (2011). Social media use in higher education: Key areas to consider for educators. *MERLOT Journal of Online Learning and Teaching*, *7*(4), 539–550.

Rothkrantz, L. (2015). How Social Media Facilitate Learning Communities and Peer Groups around MOOCS. *International Journal of Human Capital and Information Technology Professionals*, *6*(1), 1–13. doi:10.4018/ijhcitp.2015010101

Rutherford, C. (2010). Using online social media to support preservice student engagement. *MERLOT Journal of Online Learning and Teaching*, *6*(4), 703–711.

Saini, C., & Abraham, J. (2019). Implementing Facebook-based instructional approach in pre-service teacher education: An empirical investigation. *Computers & Education*, *128*, 243–255. doi:10.1016/j.compedu.2018.09.025

Seaman, J., & Tinti-Kane, H. (2013). *Social Media for teaching and learning*. Boston, MA: Pearson Learning Solutions. Retrieved from https://www.onlinelearningsurvey.com/reports/social-media-for-teaching-and-learning-2013-report.pdf

Statista. (2018). *Most popular social networks worldwide as of January 2018, ranked by number of active users (in millions)*. Retrieved from https://www.statista.com/statistics/272014/global-social-networks-ranked-by-number-of-users/

Vivakaran, M. (2018). Social Media Technologies and Higher Education: Examing its Usage and Penetration Level as Educational Aids in India. *The Online Journal of Distance Education and e-Learning*, *6*(3), 21-29.

Voorn, R. J., & Kommers, P. (2013). Social media and higher education: Introversion and collaborative learning from the student's perspective. *International Journal of Social Media and Interactive Learning Environments*, *1*(1), 59–71. doi:10.1504/IJSMILE.2013.051650

Wang, Q., Woo, H. L., Quek, C. L., Yang, Y., & Liu, M. (2011). Using the Facebook group as learning management system: An exploratory study. *British Journal of Educational Technology*, *43*(3), 428–438. doi:10.1111/j.1467-8535.2011.01195.x

Zachos, G., Paraskevopoulou-Kollia, E., & Anagnostopoulos, I. (2018). Social Media Use in Higher Education: A Review. *Education in Science*, *8*(4), 194. doi:10.3390/educsci8040194

Zanamwe, N., Rupere, T., & Kufandirimbwa, O. (2013). Use of Social Networking Technologies in Higher Education in Zimbabwe: A learners' perspective. *International Journal of Computer and Information Technology*, *2*(1), 8–18.

Zancanaro, A., & Domingues, M. (2018). Massive open online courses (MOOC) for teaching Portuguese for foreigners. *Turkish Online Journal of Distance Education-TOJDE*, *19*(2), 4–20. doi:10.17718/tojde.415602

KEY TERMS AND DEFINITIONS

Digital Native: An individual who was born after the broad adoption of digital technology and grew up with them.

Professional Learning Community: A group of educators, motivated by a shared learning vision, who collaborate to improve teaching skills and the academic performance of students.

Shareable Content: A content with a potential to be transmitted, or shared, by a third party.

Social Media: A website or a software application designed to allow people to communicate and share content quickly, efficiently and in real time on the Internet using a computer or mobile phone or similar.

Social Networking: The process of creating, building and expanding virtual communities and links between people online, often through social media sites such as Facebook, Twitter, etc.

Social Platform: Web-based technology and solutions behind a social media.

User-Generated Content: Any form of content, such as images, blogs, videos, text and audio, that have been created and posted by consumers or end-users on online platforms and is publicly available to others.

APPENDIX

Section 1. Personal Information for Participant

1. What is your gender?
    ○ male   ○ female
2. How old are you?
    ○ below 25   ○ 25-34   ○ 35-44   ○ 45-54   ○ above 55
3. What is your scientific degree?
    ○ PhD   ○ D.Sc.   ○Other
4. What is your academic position?
    ○Assistant   ○Assistant Professor   ○Associate Professor   ○Professor   ○Other
5. In which university/institute/academy are you working?
6. In which country are you working?
7. Are you well informed about social networking (e.g. Facebook, Twitter, Google+, Bebo, Myspace, LinkedIn, etc.)?
    ○Yes   ○Yes/No   ○No

Please, give your opinion on the statement from Section II and Section III by expressing your agreement / disagreement in the following five-point scale:
1. Strongly disagree;   2. Disagree;   3. Neutral;   4. Agree;   5. Strongly agree.

Section 2. Opinion on the Use of Social Networks in Teaching Practice

8. You often use social networking sites for communication and consultation with your students.
    ○1. Strongly disagree   ○2. Disagree   ○3. Neutral   ○4. Agree   ○5. Strongly agree.
9. You participate in social networking group/groups with your students for information sharing and discussions on the courses.
    ○1. Strongly disagree   ○2. Disagree   ○3. Neutral   ○4. Agree   ○5. Strongly agree.
10. You participate in social networking group/groups with your students for organization of the courses.
    ○1. Strongly disagree   ○2. Disagree   ○3. Neutral   ○4. Agree   ○5. Strongly agree.
11. You use social networking sites during the lesson in order to increase students' involvement and to keep track of their reactions.
    ○1. Strongly disagree   ○2. Disagree   ○3. Neutral   ○4. Agree   ○5. Strongly agree.
12. You participate in online group/groups interested in the use of social networking for educational purposes.
    ○1. Strongly disagree   ○2. Disagree   ○3. Neutral   ○4. Agree   ○5. Strongly agree.
13. You have a public profile in some of social networking sites to share yours research interests and to connect with a wide range of people with similar preferences.
    ○1. Strongly disagree   ○2. Disagree   ○3. Neutral   ○4. Agree   ○5. Strongly agree.
14. The use of social networking sites in your teaching practice has a positive effect on the student achievements.
    ○1. Strongly disagree   ○2. Disagree   ○3. Neutral   ○4. Agree   ○5. Strongly agree.

15. The use of social networking sites in your teaching practice increases the involvement and interest of students in the training.
    ○1. Strongly disagree   ○2. Disagree   ○3. Neutral   ○4. Agree   ○5. Strongly agree.

16. You use social networking sites in your teaching practice in ways other than those stated above – please specify.

Section 3. Opinion on the Use of Social Networking for Educational Purposes in General

17. Social networking sites are/can be useful in education.
    ○1. Strongly disagree   ○2. Disagree   ○3. Neutral   ○4. Agree   ○5. Strongly agree.

18. The role of social networking sites will increase.
    ○1. Strongly disagree   ○2. Disagree   ○3. Neutral   ○4. Agree   ○5. Strongly agree.

19. You participate in researches related to the use of social networking sites in education.
    ○1. Strongly disagree   ○2. Disagree   ○3. Neutral   ○4. Agree   ○5. Strongly agree.

20. You think that the use of social networking sites for educational purposes has a rather negative effect - specify.

Compilation of References

Aamodt, M. G. (2015). Using background checks in the employee selection process. In C. Hanvey & K. Sady (Eds.), *Practitioner's Guide to Legal Issues in Organizations*. New York: Springer. doi:10.1007/978-3-319-11143-8_4

Abawajy, J. (2014). User preference of cyber security awareness delivery methods. *Behaviour & Information Technology*, *33*(3), 237–248. doi:10.1080/0144929X.2012.708787

Abayomi, A. A., Kolawole, C., & Olabode, T. (2013). Domestic Violence and Death: Women as an Endangered Gender in Nigeria. *American Journal of Sociological Research*, *3*(3), 53–60.

Abdellatif, H. J. (2014, September). ERP in higher education: a deeper look on developing countries. In *2014 International Conference on Education Technologies and Computers (ICETC)* (pp. 73-78). IEEE. 10.1109/ICETC.2014.6998905

Abed, J., & Roland, W. H. (2016). Understanding deterrence theory in security compliance behavior: A quantitative meta-analysis approach. *SAIS 2016 Proceedings*. Retrieved from http://aisel.aisnet.org/sais2016/28

Abe, I. (2012). Defining and awareness of sexual harassment among selected University students in Lagos metropolis, Nigeria. *Journal of Emerging Trends in Educational Research and Policy Studies*, *3*(3), 1–3.

Abràmoff, M. D., Garvin, M. K., & Sonka, M. (2010). Retinal imaging and image analysis. *IEEE Reviews in Biomedical Engineering*, *3*, 169–208. doi:10.1109/RBME.2010.2084567 PMID:22275207

Abran, A., Khelifi, A., Suryn, W., & Seffah, A. (2003). Usability Meanings and Interpretations in ISO Standards. *Software Quality Journal*, *11*(4), 325–338. doi:10.1023/A:1025869312943

Abugabah, A., & Sanzogni, L. (2010). Enterprise Resource Planning (ERP) System in Higher Education: A literature Review and Implications. *International Journal of Humanities and Social Science*, *5*(6), 395–399.

Abu-Shanab, E., & Al-Tarawneh, H. (2015). The Influence of Social Networks on High School Students' Performance. *International Journal of Web-Based Learning and Teaching Technologies*, *10*(2), 49–59. doi:10.4018/IJWLTT.2015040104

ACAS. (2010). *Building employee engagement*. ACAS Policy Discussion Papers. Retrieved January 14, 2019, from http://www.acas.org.uk/media/pdf/s/1/Building_employee_engagement-accessible-version-Jun-2012.pdf

Acharya, V., Patel, Ad., & Jethava, S. (2013). A Survey on Social Networking to Enhance the Teaching and Learning Process. *International Journal of Advanced Research in Computer Science and Software Engineering*, *3*(6), 528–531.

Achieving the Sustainable Development Goals through ICT. (2015, December). *United Nations Department of Economic and Social Affairs News*. Retrieved from https://www.un.org/development/desa/en/news/administration/achieving-sustdev-through-icts.html

Adejoh, M. A., & Adejoh, L. L. (2013). Handling negative deviant behavior of front-line employees in service organizations. *International Journal of Current Research and Review*, *5*(4), 23–30.

Adepoju, S. A., Oyefolahan, I. O., Abdullahi, M. B., & Mohammed, A. A. (2018). Integrated Usability Evaluation Framework for University Websites. *I-Manager's Journal of Information Technology, 8*(1), 19–27.

Adepoju, S. A., & Shehu, I. S. (2014). Usability Evaluation of Academic Websites Using Automated Tools. In *3rd International Conference on User Science and Engineering (i-USEr)* (pp. 186–191). Shah Alam, Malaysia: IEEE. 10.1109/IUSER.2014.7002700

Adewumi, A., Omoregbe, N., & Misra, S. (2016). Usability Evaluation of Mobile Access To Institutional Repository. *International Journal of Pharmacy & Technology, 8*(4), 22892–22905.

Adeyinka, A. A., Adebiyi, M. O., Akande, N. O., Ogundokun, R. O., Kayode, A. A., & Oladele, T. O. (2019, July). A Deep Convolutional Encoder-Decoder Architecture for Retinal Blood Vessels Segmentation. In *International Conference on Computational Science and Its Applications* (pp. 180-189). Springer. 10.1007/978-3-030-24308-1_15

Afsarmanesh, H., Sargolzaei, M., & Shadi, M. (2012). A Framework for Automated Service Composition in Collaborative Networks. In L. Camarinha-Matos, L. Xu, & H. Afsarmanesh (Eds.), *Collaborative Networks in the Internet of Services* (Vol. 380, pp. 63–73). Springer Berlin Heidelberg. doi:10.1007/978-3-642-32775-9_7

Agathonos, C. (2016). *Human-Computer Interaction And Security*. Academic Press.

Agbugah, F. (2015). *Poverty is the main cause of violence against women in Nigeria: Noi Polls*. Retrieved 2nd March, 2017 from http://venturesafrica.com/poverty-is-the-main-cause-of-domestic-violence-in-nigeria-noi-polls/

Agievich, V. (2014). *Mathematical model and multi-criteria analysis of designing large-scale enterprise roadmap*. PhD thesis.

Agrawal, S., & Awekar, A. (2018). Deep learning for detecting cyberbullying across multiple social media platforms. Lecture Notes in Computer Science, 10772, 141–153. doi:10.1007/978-3-319-76941-7_11

Aguziendu, C. (2017). *Domestic violence law against women in Eti-Osa LGA* (Unpublished thesis). Department of Political Science & International Relations, Covenant University, Ota, Ogun State, Nigeria.

Ahmad, A., & Omar, Z. (2013). Abusive Supervision and Deviant Workplace Behavior: The Mediating Role of Work-Family Conflict. *The Journal of Human Resource and Adult Learning, 9*(2), 124–130.

Ahmad, S., & Schroeder, R. G. (2003). The impact of human resource management practices on operational performance: Recognising country and industry differences. *Journal of Operations Management, 21*(1), 19–25. doi:10.1016/S0272-6963(02)00056-6

Ahmed, F., Capretz, L. F., & Campbell, P. (2012). Evaluating the demand for soft skills in software development. *IT Professional, 14*(1), 44–49. doi:10.1109/MITP.2012.7 PMID:23397361

Ahn, T., Ryu, S., & Han, I. (2007). The impact of Web quality and playfulness on user acceptance of online retailing. *Information & Management, 44*(3), 263–275. doi:10.1016/j.im.2006.12.008

Ahuja, M. K. (2002). Women in the information technology profession: A literature review, synthesis and research agenda. *European Journal of Information Systems, 11*(1), 20–34. doi:10.1057/palgrave.ejis.3000417

Aihie, O. N. (2009). Prevalence of domestic violence in Nigeria: Implications for counselling. *Edo Journal of Counselling, 2*(1). Retrieved 17th March, 2017 from the website https://www.ajol.info/index.php/afrrev/article/viewFile/69290/57319

Ajayi, I. A., Ekundayo, H. T., & Osalusi, F. M. (2010). Menace of cultism in Nigerian tertiary institutions: The way out. *Anthropologist, 12*(3), 155–160. doi:10.1080/09720073.2010.11891147

Ajayi, P., Omoregbe, N., Adeloye, D., & Misra, S. (2016). Development of a Secured Cloud Based Health Information System for Antenatal and Postnatal Clinic in an African Country. Frontiers in Artificial Intelligence and Applications: Vol. 282. *Advances in Digital Technologies*. Doi:10.3233/978-1-61499-637-8-197

Akgunduz, Y., Bardakoglu, O., & Alkan, C. E. (2015). The moderating role of job resourcefulness in the impact of work–family and family–work life conflict on the burnout levels of travel agency employees. *Turizam*, *19*(3), 111–126. doi:10.5937/Turizam1503111A

Akman, I., Misra, S., & Altindag, T. (2011). The Impact of Cognitive and Socio-Demographic Factors on Manager's Simple Thinking Towards Quality Of Meetings In Software Development Projects. *Technical Gazette*, *18*(1), 51–56.

Akman, I., Misra, S., & Cafer, F. (2011). The Role of Leadership Cognitive Complexity in Software Development Projects: An Empirical Assessment for Simple Thinking. *Human Factors and Ergonomics in Manufacturing & Service Industries*, *21*(5), 516–525. doi:10.1002/hfm.20256

Aladwan, K., Bhanugopan, R., & Fish, A. (2013). Why do employees jump ship? Examining intent to quit employment in a non-western cultural context. *Employee Relations*, *35*(4), 408–422. doi:10.1108/ER-03-2012-0027

Alalwan, A. A. (2018). Investigating the impact of social media advertising features on customer purchase intention. *International Journal of Information Management*, *42*, 65–77. doi:10.1016/j.ijinfomgt.2018.06.001

Alam, L. (2018). *Teaching with web 2.0 technologies: Twitter, wikis & blogs*. Retrieved from https://tv.unsw.edu.au/files//unswPDF/CS_Web2_LTTO.pdf

Alampay, E. A., & Hechanova, R. M. (2010). Monitoring employee use of the internet in Philippine organizations. *The Electronic Journal on Information Systems in Developing Countries*, *40*(5), 1–20. doi:10.1002/j.1681-4835.2010.tb00287.x

Alasem, A. N. (2013). Evaluating the Usability of Saudi Digital Library's Interface (SDL). In *World Congress on Engineering and Computer Science* (*Vol. I*, pp. 178–181). Academic Press.

Alba, E., & Chicano, F. (2007). Software project management with gas. *Information Sciences*, *177*(1), 2380–2401. doi:10.1016/j.ins.2006.12.020

ALdayel, A. I., Aldayel, M. S., & Al-Mudimigh, A. S. (2011). The Critical Success Factors of ERP implementation in Higher Education in Saudi Arabia: A Case Study. *Journal of Information Technology & Economic Development*, *2*(2), 1–16.

Ale Ebrahim, N., Ahmed, S., & Taha, Z. (2009). Virtual Teams: A Literature Review. *Australian Journal of Basic and Applied Sciences*, *3*(3), 2653–2669. doi:10.2139srn.1501443

Aleksandrova, Y., & Parusheva, S. (2019). Social Media Usage Patterns in Higher Education Institutions – An Empirical Study. *International Journal of Emerging Technologies in Learning*, *14*(5), 108–121. doi:10.3991/ijet.v14i05.9720

Al-faries, A., Al-khalifa, H. S., Al-razgan, M. S., & Al-duwais, M. (2013). Evaluating the Accessibility and Usability of Top Saudi E- Government Services. In *7th International Conference on Theory and Practice of Electronic Governance* (pp. 60–63). Seoul: ACM.

Alfes, K., Shantz, A. D., Truss, C., & Soane, E. C. (2013). The link between perceived human resource management practices, engagement and employee behaviour: A moderated mediation model. *International Journal of Human Resource Management*, *24*(2), 330–351. doi:10.1080/09585192.2012.679950

Al-Hadi, M. A., & Al-Shaibany, N. A. (2017). Critical success factors (CSFs) of ERP in higher education institutions. *International Journal (Toronto, Ont.)*, *7*(4), 92–95.

Alhawamdeh, M. (2007). The Role of Knowledge Management in Building E-Business Strategy. *Proceedings of the World Congress on Engineering and Computer Science 2007.*

AliCloud. (2019). *Alibaba Cloud (Aliyun).* Retrieved from https://intl.aliyun.com

Ali, M., & Miller, L. (2017). ERP system implementation in large enterprises–a systematic literature review. *Journal of Enterprise Information Management, 30*(4), 666–692. doi:10.1108/JEIM-07-2014-0071

Al-khalifa, H. S. (2012). A framework for evaluating university mobile websites. *Online Information Review, 2011*(2011). doi:10.1108/OIR-12-2012-0231

Allen, M. W., Armstrong, D. J., Reid, M. F., & Riemenschneider, C. K. (2009). IT Employee Retention: Employee Expectations and Workplace Environments. *Proceedings of the Special Interest Group on Management Information System's 47th Annual Conference on Computer Personnel Research*, 95–100. 10.1145/1542130.1542148

Almeida, M. V., & Soares, A. L. (2014). Knowledge sharing in project-based organizations: Overcoming the informational limbo. *International Journal of Information Management, 34*(6), 770–779. doi:10.1016/j.ijinfomgt.2014.07.003

Almotiri, J., Elleithy, K., & Elleithy, A. (2018). Retinal Vessels Segmentation Techniques and Algorithms: A Survey. *Applied Sciences, 8*(2), 155. doi:10.3390/app8020155

Aloini, D., Dulmin, R., & Mininno, V. (2007). Risk management in ERP project introduction: Review of the literature. *Information & Management, 44*(6), 547–567. doi:10.1016/j.im.2007.05.004

AL-Qudah, M. K. M., Osman, A., Ab Halim, M. S., & Al-Shatanawi, H. A. (2014). The effect of human resources planning and training and development on organizational performance in the government sector in Jordan. *International Journal of Academic Research in Business and Social Sciences, 4*(4).

Althonayan, M., & Althonayan, A. (2017). E-government system evaluation: The case of users' performance using ERP systems in higher education. *Transforming Government: People. Process and Policy, 11*(3), 306–342.

Althunibat, A., Al-mahadeen, B. M., Altarawneh, F., & Al–Qarem, F. A. (2019, April). The Acceptance of using Enterprise Resource Planning (ERP) System in Higher Education: A Case Study of Jordanian Universities. In *2019 IEEE Jordan International Joint Conference on Electrical Engineering and Information Technology (JEEIT)* (pp. 315-318). IEEE. 10.1109/JEEIT.2019.8717451

Alwan, M., Wiley, D., & Nobel, J. (2007). *A program of the American Association of Homes and Services for the Aging (AAHSA).* C. Foundation, Ed.

Amabile, T. M., Conti, R., Coon, H., Lazenby, J., & Herron, M. (1996). Assessing the work environment for creativity. *Academy of Management Journal, 39*, 1154–1184.

Amabile, T. M., Schatzel, E. A., Moneta, G. B., & Kramer, S. J. (2004). Leader behaviors and the work environment for creativity: Perceived leader support. *The Leadership Quarterly, 15*(1), 5–32. doi:10.1016/j.leaqua.2003.12.003

Amarachi, A. A., Okolie, S. O., & Ajaegbu, C. (2013). Information security management system: Emerging issues and prospect. *IOSR Journal of Computer Engineering., 12*(3), 96–102. doi:10.9790/0661-12396102

Amberger, J. S., & Hamosh, A. (2017). Searching Online Mendelian Inheritance in Man (OMIM): A Knowledgebase of Human Genes and Genetic Phenotypes. *Current Protocols in Bioinformatics, 58*(1). PMID:28654725

Amid, A., Moalagh, M., & Ravasan, A. Z. (2012). Identification and classification of ERP critical failure factors in Iranian industries. *Information Systems, 37*(3), 227–237. doi:10.1016/j.is.2011.10.010

Anders, C. (2012, August). Are they learning or cheating? Online teaching's dilemma. *Forbes*, 16.

Anderson, L. W., David, R. K., Peter, W. A., Kathleen, A. C., Meyer, R. E., Pentrich, P. R., . . . Wittrock, M. C. (2013). A Taxonomy for Learning, Teaching & Assessing. Pearson New International Edition.

Anderson, T. (2019). Challenges and Opportunities for use of Social Media in Higher Education. *Journal of Learning for Development*, *6*(1), 6–19.

Andersson, A. (2016). Communication barriers in an interorganizational ERP-project. *International Journal of Managing Projects in Business*, *9*(1), 214–233. doi:10.1108/IJMPB-06-2015-0047

André, M., Baldoquín, M. G., & Acuña, S. T. (2011). Formal model for assigning human resources to teams in software projects. *Information and Software Technology*, *53*(3), 259–275. doi:10.1016/j.infsof.2010.11.011

Andrews, A. (2017). Alexander Peysakhovich's theory on artificial intelligence. *Pacific Standard Magazine*. Retrieved from https://psmag.com/magazine/alexander-peysakhovich-30-under-30

Andrianto, A. (2019, April). Impact of Enterprise Resource Planning (ERP) implementation on user performance: Studies at University of Jember. *Journal of Physics: Conference Series*, *1211*(1), 012040. doi:10.1088/1742-6596/1211/1/012040

Angst, C. M., Block, E. S., D'Arcy, J., & Kelley, K. (2017). When do IT security investments matter? Accounting for the influence of institutional factors in the context of healthcare data breaches. *Management Information Systems Quarterly*, *41*(3), 893–916. doi:10.25300/MISQ/2017/41.3.10

Anusha, & Rama, N. (2016). A Novel Website Quality and Usability Evaluation Framework for Online Shopping Websites. *Indian Journal of Science and Technology, 9*(36). doi:10.17485/ijst/2016/v9i36/93821

APA. (2018). *Definition of Psychology*. Retrieved from http://www.apa.org/support/about-apa.aspx - 20/4/18

Apt, K. R., & Wallace, M. (2007). *Constraint logic programming using eclipse*. New York, NY: Cambridge University Press.

Aries, M. B. C., Veitch, J. A., & Newsham, G. R. (2010). Windows, view, and office characteristics predict physical and psychological discomfort. *Journal of Environmental Psychology*, *30*(4), 533–541. doi:10.1016/j.jenvp.2009.12.004

Arisi, R. O. (2011). Cultural violence and the Nigerian woman. *An International Multidisciplinary Journal, Ethiopia*, *5*(4), 369–381.

Armstrong, S. (2014). Artificial intelligence poses 'extinction risk' to humanity says Oxford University's Stuart Armstrong. *Huffington Post UK*. Retrieved from http://www.huffingtonpost.co.uk/2014/03/12/extinction-artificial-intelligence-oxford-stuart-armstrong_n_4947082.html

Arquero, J. L., & Romero-Frías, E. (2013). Using social network sites in Higher Education: An experience in business studies. *Innovations in Education and Teaching International*, *50*(3), 238–249. doi:10.1080/14703297.2012.760772

Arrowsmith, J., & Parker, J. (2013). The meaning of 'employee engagement' for the values and roles of the HRM function. *International Journal of Human Resource Management*, *24*(14), 2692–2712. doi:10.1080/09585192.2013.763842

Asani, O., Omotosho, A., Omonigho, J., Longe, O. B., & Gbadamosi, B. (2018). A Real Time Gesture Engineered Captcha. *International Journal of Mechanical Engineering and Technology*, *9*(12), 618–629.

Asare-Bediako, K. (2011). *Human resource management in Ghana lacks strategic focus*. Ghana News Agency. Retrieved from http://www.ghananewsagency.org/social/human-resource-management-in-ghana-lacks-strategic-focus—27174

Aswathappa, K. (2005). *Human resource and personnel management: text and cases*. McGraw-Hill.

Au, C. H., & Fung, W. S. (2019). Integrating knowledge management into information security: From audit to practice. *International Journal of Knowledge Management*, *15*(1), 37–52. doi:10.4018/IJKM.2019010103

Aut, D. B. (2019). *AutDB: a Genetic Database for Autism Spectrum Disorders*. Retrieved from http://www.mindspec.org/products/autdb/

Aviles, M., & Eastman, J. K. (2012). Utilizing technology effectively to improve millennials' educational performance. *Journal of International Education in Business*, *5*(2), 96–113. doi:10.1108/18363261211281726

Awidi, I. T., Paynter, M., & Vujosevic, T. (2019). Facebook group in the learning design of a higher education course: An analysis of factors influencing positive learning experience for students. *Computers & Education*, *129*, 106–121. doi:10.1016/j.compedu.2018.10.018

Ayers, D., Dahlstrom, R., & Skinner, S. J. (1997). An exploratory investigation of organizational antecedents to new product success. *JMR, Journal of Marketing Research*, *34*(1), 107–116. doi:10.1177/002224379703400109

Ayoko, O. B., Konrad, A. M., & Boyle, M. V. (2012). Online work: Managing conflict and emotions for performance in virtual teams. *European Management Journal*, *30*(2), 156–174. doi:10.1016/j.emj.2011.10.001

Azeta, A. A., Iboroma, D. A., Ige, O. O., Fawehinmi, O. A., & Ogunde, B. (2018). *A DevOps Software Architecture for Recommender Systems in Digital Library*. In 13th International Conference on eLearning (ICEL), Cape Town, South Africa.

Azeta, A. A., Omoregbe, N. A., Ayo, C. K., Raymond, A., Oroge, A., & Misra, S. (2014). An Anti-Cultism Social Education Media System. Computer & Information Technology (GSCIT), 2014 IEEE Global Summit, 1-5. doi:10.1109/GSCIT.2014.6970097

Azeta, A. A., Omoregbe, N. A., Misra, S., Adewumi, A., & Olokunde, T. O. (2016). Adapted Cloudlet for Mobile Distance Learning: Design, prototype and evaluation. Frontiers in Artificial Intelligence and Applications, 282, 220-228.

Azeta, A. A., Misra, S., Azeta, V. I., & Osamor, V. C. (2019). Determining suitability of speech-enabled examination result management system. *Wireless Networks*, 1–8.

Azuela, J., H., S., Gerhard, R., Jean, S., & Cortés, U. (2005). *Advances in artificial intelligence theory*. Center for Computing Research of IPN.

Baecher, P., Fischlin, M., Gordon, L., Langenberg, R., Lutzow, M., & Schroder, D. (2010). CAPTCHAs: the good, the bad and the ugly. In F. C. Frieling (Ed.), *Sicherheit* (Vol. 170, pp. 353–365). LNI.

Baida, Z., Gordijn, J., & Omelayenko, B. (2004). *A shared service terminology for online service provisioning*. Paper presented at the 6th International Conference on Electronic Commerce, Delft, The Netherlands. 10.1145/1052220.1052222

Bai, Y., Yao, Z., & Dou, Y. F. (2015). Effect of social commerce factors on user purchase behavior: An empirical investigation from renren. com. *International Journal of Information Management*, *35*(5), 538–550. doi:10.1016/j.ijinfomgt.2015.04.011

Bakare, K. A. (2013). Low level of education in Nigeria: Causes and solution. *Information Nigeria*. Retrieved 1ˢᵗ March, 2017 from http://www.informationng.com/2013/02/low-level-of-education-in-nigeria-causes-and-solution.html

Baker, F. B. (1985). *The Basics of Item Response Theory*. Heinemann.

Baker, J. V. (2011). *The effects of change management on employee engagement: Using lean principles to increase engagement*. California State University.

Bakker, A. B. (2011). An evidence-based model of work engagement. *Current Directions in Psychological Science*, *20*(4), 265–269. doi:10.1177/0963721411414534

Balakrishnan, B. K., Dahnil, M. I., & Yi, W. J. (2014). The impact of social media marketing medium toward purchase intention and brand loyalty among generation Y. *Procedia: Social and Behavioral Sciences*, *148*, 177–185. doi:10.1016/j.sbspro.2014.07.032

Balakrishnan, C., & Masthan, D. (2013). Impact of Internal Communication on Employee Engagement A Study at Delhi International Airport. *International Journal of Scientific and Research Publications*, *3*(8), 1–13.

Baldissera, T. A., & Camarinha-Matos, L. M. (2016a). Services Personalization Approach for a Collaborative Care Ecosystem. In H. Afsarmanesh, M. L. Camarinha-Matos, & A. Lucas Soares (Eds.), *Collaboration in a Hyperconnected World: 17th IFIP WG 5.5 Working Conference on Virtual Enterprises, PRO-VE 2016, Porto, Portugal, October 3-5, 2016, Proceedings* (pp. 443-456). Cham: Springer International Publishing. 10.1007/978-3-319-45390-3_38

Baldissera, T. A., & Camarinha-Matos, L. M. (2016b). Towards a Collaborative Business Ecosystem for Elderly Care. In M. L. Camarinha-Matos, A. J. Falcão, N. Vafaei, & S. Najdi (Eds.), *Technological Innovation for Cyber-Physical Systems: 7th IFIP WG 5.5/SOCOLNET Advanced Doctoral Conference on Computing, Electrical and Industrial Systems, DoCEIS 2016, Costa de Caparica, Portugal, April 11-13, 2016, Proceedings* (pp. 24-34). Cham: Springer International Publishing. 10.1007/978-3-319-31165-4_3

Baldissera, T. A., & Camarinha-Matos, L. M. (2018). *Services Evolution in Elderly Care Ecosystems*. Paper presented at the Working Conference on Virtual Enterprises.

Baldissera, T. A., Camarinha Matos, L. M., & DeFaveri, C. (2017a). Designing elderly care ecosystem in collaborative networks environment. *International Conference on Computing, Networking and Informatics*. 10.1109/ICCNI.2017.8123818

Baldissera, T. A., Camarinha-Matos, L. M., & DeFaveri, C. (2017b). Service Personalization Requirements for Elderly Care in a Collaborative Environment. In L. M. Camarinha-Matos, M. Parreira-Rocha, & J. Ramezani (Eds.), *Technological Innovation for Smart Systems, DoCEIS 2017* (pp. 20–28). Springer. doi:10.1007/978-3-319-56077-9_2

Balfour, D., & Wechsler, B. (1996). Organizational commitment: Antecedents and outcomes in public organisations. *Public Productivity and Management Review*, *29*(3), 256–277. doi:10.2307/3380574

Balkin, J. M. (1987). Deconstructive practice and legal theory. *Yale L.J.*, *96*(15).

Balkin, J. M. (1987). Deconstructive practice and legal theory. *Yale L.J.*, *96*.

Balkin, J., M. (1987). Deconstructive practice and legal theory. *Yale L.J.*, *96*(15).

Balozian, P., Leidner, D., & Warkentin, M. (2019). Managers' and employees' differing responses to security approaches. *Journal of Computer Information Systems*, *59*(3), 197–210. doi:10.1080/08874417.2017.1318687

Barber L, Hayday S, Bevan S (1999). *From people to profits*. IES Report 355.

Bari. (2014). Quality Frameworks and Standards in E-Learning Systems. *International Journal of the Computer, the Internet and Management*, *22*(3), 1-7.

Barsade, S. (2002). The ripple effect: Emotional contagion and its influence on group behavior. *Administrative Science Quarterly*, *47*(4), 644–677. doi:10.2307/3094912

Bartell, M. (2003). Internationalization of universities: A university culture-based framework. *Higher Education*, *45*(1), 43–70. doi:10.1023/A:1021225514599

Barua, A., Konana, P., Whinston, A., & Yin, F. (2001). *Managing E-Business Transformation: Opportunities and Value Assessment. Center for Research in Electronic Commerce*. The University of Texas at Austin.

Ba, S., & Pavlou, P. A. (2002). Evidence of the effect of trust building technology in electronic markets: Price premiums and buyer behavior. *Management Information Systems Quarterly*, *26*(3), 243–268. doi:10.2307/4132332

Bashshur, M. R., & Burak, O. C. (2015). When voice matters: A multilevel review of the impact of voice in organizations. *Journal of Management*, *41*(5), 1530–1554. doi:10.1177/0149206314558302

Bassellier, G., & Benbasat, I. (2004). Business competence of information technology professionals: Conceptual development and influence on IT-business partnerships. *Management Information Systems Quarterly*, *28*(4), 673–694. doi:10.2307/25148659

Basu, K. (2013). Faculty groups consider how to respond to MOOCs. *Inside Higher Ed*. Retrieved from https://ipfs.io/ipfs/QmXoypizjW3WknFiJnKLwHCnL72vedxjQkDDP1mXWo6uco/wiki/Massive_open_online_course.html

Bath, T. G., Bozdag, S., Afzal, V., & Crowther, D. (2011). Lims Portal and BonsaiLIMS: Development of a lab information management system for translational medicine. *Source Code for Biology and Medicine*, *6*(1), 9. doi:10.1186/1751-0473-6-9 PMID:21569484

Battaglio, P., Goodman, D., & French, P. E. (2017). Contracting out for municipal human resources: Analyzing the role of human capital in the make or buy decision. *Public Administration Quarterly*, *41*(2), 297–333.

Batt, R., & Valcour, P. M. (2003). Human resources practices as predictors of work-family outcomes and employee turnover. *Industrial Relations*, *42*(2), 189–220. doi:10.1111/1468-232X.00287

Baumruk, R. (2004). The missing link: The role of employee engagement in business success. *Workspan*, *47*, 48–52.

Baur, C., Wiestler, B., Albarqouni, S., & Navab, N. (2019, May). Fusing Unsupervised and Supervised Deep Learning for White Matter Lesion Segmentation. In *International Conference on Medical Imaging with Deep Learning* (pp. 63-72). Academic Press.

Baxter, J., & Chesters, J. (2011). Perceptions of Work-Family Balance: How Effective are Family-Friendly Policies? *Australian Journal of Labour Economics*, *14*(2), 139–151.

Baxter, R. J., Holderness, D. K. Jr, & Wood, D. A. (2016). Applying basic gamification techniques to it compliance training: Evidence from the lab and field. *Journal of Information Systems*, *30*(3), 119–133. doi:10.2308/isys-51341

Becker, K., Antuar, N., & Everett, C. (2011). Implementing an employee performance management system in a nonprofit organization. *Nonprofit Management & Leadership*, *21*(3), 255–271. doi:10.1002/nml.20024

Bellou, V., Xanthopoulou, D., Gkorezis, P., Xanthopoulou, D., & Gkorezis, P. (2018, April 27). *Organizational change and employee functioning : Investigating boundary conditions*. doi:10.4324/9781315386102-2

Benavides, D., Segura, S., & Ruiz-Cortés, A. (2010). Automated analysis of feature models 20 years later: A literature review. *Information Systems*, *35*(6), 615–636. doi:10.1016/j.is.2010.01.001

Bennett, T. M. (2009). A study of the management leadership style preferred by it subordinates. *Journal of Organizational Culture, Communications & Conflict, 13*(2).

Bennett, B. (2003). Job rotation. *Training Strategies for Tomorrow*, *17*(4), 7.

Bennett, S., Skelton, J., & Lunn, K. (2005). *Schaum's Outlines UML* (2nd ed.). McGraw-Hill International.

Berkshire, H., & Highland, R. (1953). Forced-choice performance rating: A methodological study. *Personnel Psychology*, *6*(3), 355–378. doi:10.1111/j.1744-6570.1953.tb01503.x

Berkum, N. L., Erez Lieberman-Aiden, E., Williams, L., Imakaev, M., Gnirke, A., Mirny, L. A., ... Lander, E. S. (2010). Hi-C: A Method to Study the Three-dimensional Architecture of Genomes. *Journal of Visualized Experiments*, (39): 1869. PMID:20461051

Bernadin, H. J., Kane, J. S., Ross, S., Spina, J., & Johnson, D. L. (1995). Performance Appraisal Design, Development and Implementation. In G. R. Ferris, S. D. Rosen, & D. T. Barnum (Eds.), *Handbook of Human Resource Management*. Cambridge, UK: Wiley-Blackwell.

Bernhard-Oettel, C., Sverke, M., & De Witte, H. (2005). Comparing three alternative types of employment with permanent full-time work: How do employment contract and perceived job conditions relate to health complaints? *Work and Stress*, *19*(4), 301–318. doi:10.1080/02678370500408723

Bernik, I., & Prislan, K. (2016). Measuring Information Security Performance with 10 by 10 model for holistic state evaluation. *PLoS One*, *11*(9), 1–33. doi:10.1371/journal.pone.0163050 PMID:27655001

Bettencourt, L., Ostrom, A., Brown, S., & Roundtree, R. (2005). Client Co-production in Knowledge-intensive Business Services. In T. O. U.-S. Publications (Ed.), *Operations management: a strategic approach* (pp. 273–283). London, UK: Academic Press. doi:10.2307/41166145

Bézivin, J. (2005). On the unification power of models. *Software & Systems Modeling*, *4*(2), 171–188. doi:10.100710270-005-0079-0

Bhamangol, B., Nandavadekar, V., & Khilari, S. (2011). Enterprise resource planning (erp) system in higher education, a literature review. *International Journal of Management Research and Development*, *1*(1), 1–7.

Bhasin, M. L. (2010). Corporate Governance Disclosure Practices: The Portrait of a Developing Country. *International Journal of Business and Management*, *5*(4), 150–167.

Bhattacharya, C. B., Sen, S., & Korschun, D. (2012). Using corporate social responsibility to win the war for talent. *MIT Sloan Management Review*, *49*, 37–44.

Bhattacharya, P. (2016). Strategizing and innovating with enterprise systems: The case of a Public University. *Journal of Cases on Information Technology*, *18*(2), 1–15. doi:10.4018/JCIT.2016040101

Bhattacharya, S., Trehan, G., & Kaur, K. (2018). Factors Determining Psychological Contract of IT Employees in India. *International Journal of Human Capital and Information Technology Professionals*, *9*(1), 37–52. doi:10.4018/IJHCITP.2018010103

Bhattacherjee, A. (2002). Individual trust in online firms: Scale development and initial test. *Journal of Management Information Systems*, *19*(1), 211–241. doi:10.1080/07421222.2002.11045715

Bidwell, M., & Briscoe, F. (2010). The dynamics of interorganizational careers. *Organization Science*, *21*(5), 1034–1053. doi:10.1287/orsc.1090.0492

Bienstein, P., & Werner, N. (2018). *Using Machine Learning to Detect Cyberbullying*. Psychische Gesundheit Bei Intellektueller Entwicklungsstörung. doi:10.1109/ICMLA.2011.152

Biswas, S., & Bhatnagar, J. (2013). Mediator analysis of employee engagement: Role of perceived organizational support, P-O Fit, organizational commitment and Job Satisfaction. *Vikalpa*, *38*(1), 27–40. doi:10.1177/0256090920130103

Bititci, U., Garengo, P., Dörfler, V., & Nudurupati, S. (2012). Performance measurement: Challenges for tomorrow. *International Journal of Management Reviews*, *14*(3), 305–327. doi:10.1111/j.1468-2370.2011.00318.x

Blackburn, R., & Rosen, B. (1993). Total quality and human resources management: lessons learned from Baldrige Award-winning companies. *Academy of Management Perspectives, 7*(3).

Blair, D., & Sisakhti, R. (2007). Sales training: what makes it work? *T & D Magazine.* Retrieved from www.astd.org/astd/Publications/TD_Magazine/2007_pdf/August/0708ExecSum.htm

Blanz, F., & Ghiselli, E. E. (1972). The mixed standard scale: A new rating system. *Personnel Psychology, 25*(2), 185–199. doi:10.1111/j.1744-6570.1972.tb01098.x

Blau, I., & Caspi, A. (2009). What Type of Collaboration Helps? Psychological Ownership, Perceived Learning and Outcome Quality of Collaboration Using Google Docs. *Quality,* 48–55. Retrieved from http://telem-pub.openu.ac.il/users/chais/2009/noon/1_1.pdf

Bloom, B. (1956). *Taxonomy of Educational Objectives.* Handbook One.

Bloom, N., Kretschmer, T., & Van Reenen, J. (2009). Work-life balance, management practices and productivity. In R. B. Freeman & K. L. Shaw (Eds.), *International differences in the business practices and productivity of firms* (pp. 15–54). Chicago, IL: University of Chicago Press. doi:10.7208/chicago/9780226261959.003.0002

Bodankin, M., & Tziner, A. (2009). Constructive deviance, destructive deviance and personality: How do they interrelate. *Amfiteatru Economic Journal, 11*(26), 549–564.

Boddy, C. R. (2014). Corporate Psychopaths, Conflict, Employee Affective Well-Being and Counterproductive Work Behaviour. *Journal of Business Ethics, 121*(1), 107–121. doi:10.100710551-013-1688-0

Boer, P., Richardson, R., & Kramer, E. (2007). On the importance of "Human Factors" and security in the organization of military defense. *Military Spectator., 176*(3), 121–128.

Bootstrap. (2019). *Bootstrap.* Retrieved from http://getbootstrap.com/

Borman, W. (1991). *Job behavior, performance, and effectiveness. Handbook of Industrial and Organizational Psychology.* Palo Alto, CA: Consulting Psychologists Press.

Bosc, R. (2004). Knowledge management metrics. *Industrial Management & Data Systems, 104*(5/6), 457–468. doi:10.1108/02635570410543771

Boss, S. R., Galletta, D. F., Lowry, P. B., Moody, G. D., & Polak, P. (2015). What do systems users have to fear? Using fear appeals to engender threats and fear that motivate protective security behaviors. *Management Information Systems Quarterly, 39*(4), 837–864. doi:10.25300/MISQ/2015/39.4.5

Bostik, O., & Klecka, J. (2018). Recognition of CAPTCHA Characters by Supervised Machine Learning Algorithms. *IFAC-PapersOnLine, 51*(6), 208–213. doi:10.1016/j.ifacol.2018.07.155

Botella, P., Burgués, X., Carvallo, J. P., Franch, X., Grau, G., Marco, J., & Quer, C. (2004). ISO / IEC 9126 in practice: what do we need to know? *Software Measurement European Forum.*

Bottema, O., & Bakker, H. (1959). *Mislukking en vertraging van de studie. Verslag van een onderzoek verricht aan de Technische Hogeschool te Delft 1953-1957 (Dutch).* Technische Hogeschool Hogeschool Delft.

Bouchard, M., & Malm, A. (2016). Social network analysis and its contribution to research on crime and criminal justice. *Oxford Handbooks Online.*

Boynton, A. C., & Zmud, R. W. (1984). An assessment of critical success factors. *Sloan Management Review, 25*(4), 17–27.

Boza, B. C., Schiaffino, S., Teyseyre, A., & Godoy, D. (2014). An Approach for Knowledge Discovery in a Web Usability Context. In *Brazilian Symposium on Human Factors in Computing Systems* (*Vol. 13*, pp. 393–396). Foz do Iguaçu, Brazil: Academic Press.

Branch, M. R. (n.d.). *Instructional Design: The ADDIE approach*. Springer Verlag.

Branch, S., Ramsay, S., & Barker, M. (2013). Workplace Bullying, Mobbing and General Harassment: A Review. *International Journal of Management Reviews*, *15*(3), 280–299. doi:10.1111/j.1468-2370.2012.00339.x

Brás, F. A., & Rodrigues, L. L. (2007). Accounting for firms' training programs: An exploratory study. *Journal Human Resource Costing & Accounting*, *11*(3), 229–250. doi:10.1108/14013380710843791

Brodić, D., & Amelio, A. (2017). Analysis of the Human-Computer Interaction on the Example of Image-Based CAPTCHA by Association Rule Mining. In L. Gamberini, A. Spagnolli, G. Jacucci, B. Blankertz, & J. Freeman (Eds.), Lecture Notes in Computer Science: Vol. 9961. *Symbiotic Interaction. Symbiotic 2016*. Cham: Springer. doi:10.1007/978-3-319-57753-1_4

Brody, R. G. (2010). Beyond the basic background check: Hiring the "right" employees. *Management Research Review*, *33*(3), 210–223. doi:10.1108/01409171011030372

Brody, R. G., & Cox, V. L. (2015). Background investigations a comparative analysis of background checks and federal security clearance investigations. *Business Studies Journal*, *7*(1), 84–94.

Brooks, D., & Collins, G. (2012). The campus tsunami. *New York Times*.

Brown, A., Johnston, S., & Kelly, K. (2002). *Using service-oriented architecture and component-based development to build web service applications*. Rational Software Corporation.

Brown, A., & Wallnau, K. (1996). A framework for evaluating software technology. *Software, IEEE*, *13*(5), 39–49. doi:10.1109/52.536457

Brown, S. P., & Lam, S. K. (2008). A meta-analysis of relationships linking employee satisfaction to customer responses. *Journal of Retailing*, *84*(3), 243–255. doi:10.1016/j.jretai.2008.06.001

Bruce, C. (1994). *Supervising literature reviews*. UK. In O. Zuber-Skerritt & Y. Ryan (Eds.), *Quality in postgraduate education*. Kogan Page.

Brucker, P., Drexl, A., Mhring, R., Neumann, K., & Pesch, E. (1999). Resource constrained project scheduling: Notation, classification, models, and methods. *European Journal of Operational Research*, *112*(1), 3–41. doi:10.1016/S0377-2217(98)00204-5

Brunner, J. J., & Miranda, D. (2016). *Educación Superior en Iberoamérica. Report 2016*. Santiago, Chile: CINDA.

Brunner, J. J., & Pedraja Rejas, L. (2017). Challenges to higher education governance in Ibero-America. *Ingeniare. Revista Chilena de Ingeniería*, *25*(1), 2–4. doi:10.4067/S0718-33052017000100002

Bryant, M. (2014). 'Artificial intelligence could kill us all'. Meet the man who takes that risk seriously. *The Next Web (TNW) Online publication*. Retrieved from https://thenextweb.com/insider/2014/03/08/ai-could-kill-all-meet-mantakes-risk- seriously/#.tnw_hVchaHqU

Buckl, S., Buschle, M., Johnson, P., Matthes, F., & Schweda, C. M. (2011). A meta-language for Enterprise Architecture analysis. *Enterprise, Business-Process and Information Systems Modeling*, 511–525.

Buckl, S., Matthes, F., & Schweda, C. M. (2009). Classifying enterprise architecture analysis approaches. *Enterprise Interoperability*, 66–79.

Buhl, J., & Acosta, J. (2015). Work less, do less? *Sustainability Science*, 1–16. doi:10.100711625-015-0322-8

Bui, J., Hodge, A., Shackelford, A., & Acsell, J. (2011). Factors contributing to burnout among perfusionists in the United States. *Perfusion*, *26*(6), 461–466. doi:10.1177/0267659111411521 PMID:21665910

Bullen, C. V., Abraham, T., Gallagher, K., Simon, J. C., & Zwieg, P. (2009). IT workforce trends: Implications for curriculum and hiring. *Communications of the Association for Information Systems*, *24*(1), 9.

Bumgarner, J., & Borg, S. (2007). *US-CCU Cyber-Security Questionnaire*. US-CCU (Cyber Consequences Unit) Cyber-Security Check. Retrieved from www.usccu.us

Burns, A. J., Posey, C., Roberts, T. L., & Lowry, P. B. (2017). Examining the relationship of organisational insiders' psychological capital with information security threat and coping appraisals. *Computers in Human Behavior*, *68*, 190–209. doi:10.1016/j.chb.2016.11.018

Bursztein, E., Bethard, S., Fabry, C., Mitchell, J., & Jurafsky, D. (2010). How good are humans at solving CAPTCHA? *Proceedings of the 2010 IEEE Symposium on Security and Privacy*, 399-413. 10.1109/SP.2010.31

Byrd, T. A., Lewis, B. R., & Turner, D. E. (2004). The impact of IT personnel skills on IS infrastructure and competitive IS. *Information Resources Management Journal*, *17*(2), 38–62. doi:10.4018/irmj.2004040103

Byrne, P. H. (1997). *Analysis and science in Aristotle*. SUNY Press.

Cadle, J., & Yeates, D. (2008). *Project Management for Information Systems* (5th ed.). Essex, UK: Pearson, Prentice Hall.

Calisir, F., Gumussoy, C. A., Bayraktaroglu, A. E., & Saygivar, E. (2011). *Usability and Functionality : A Comparison of Key Project Personnel ' s and Potential users ' Evaluations*. World Academy of Science, Engineering and Technology.

Camarinha-Matos, L. M. (2013). *Collaborative Business Ecosystems and Virtual Enterprises: IFIP TC5 / WG5.5 Third Working Conference on Infrastructures for Virtual Enterprises ... in Information and Communication Technology*. Springer Publishing Company, Incorporated.

Camarinha-Matos, L. M., Afsarmanesh, H., & Ferrada, F. (2010b). *Collaborative networks approach to active ageing*. Paper presented at the 4th International Conference on Pervasive Computing Technologies for Healthcare (PervasiveHealth), Munich, Germany. 10.4108/ICST.PERVASIVEHEALTH2010.8866

Camarinha-Matos, L. M. (2016). Collaborative smart grids–A survey on trends. *Renewable & Sustainable Energy Reviews*, *65*, 283–294. doi:10.1016/j.rser.2016.06.093

Camarinha-Matos, L. M., & Afsarmanesh, H. (2008a). Classes of collaborative networks. In I. S. Reference (Ed.), *Encyclopedia of Networked and Virtual Organizations* (pp. 193–198). Academic Press. doi:10.4018/978-1-59904-885-7.ch026

Camarinha-Matos, L. M., & Afsarmanesh, H. (2008b). *Collaborative Networks: Reference Modeling*. Springer Science & Business Media.

Camarinha-Matos, L. M., Afsarmanesh, H., & Boucher, X. (2010a). The Role of Collaborative Networks in Sustainability. In L. Camarinha-Matos, X. Boucher, & H. Afsarmanesh (Eds.), *Collaborative Networks for a Sustainable World* (Vol. 336, pp. 1–16). Springer Berlin Heidelberg. doi:10.1007/978-3-642-15961-9_1

Camarinha-Matos, L. M., Afsarmanesh, H., Ferrada, F., Oliveira, A. I., & Rosas, J. (2013). A comprehensive research roadmap for ICT and ageing. *Studies in Informatics and Control*, *22*(3), 233–254. doi:10.24846/v22i3y201301

Camarinha-Matos, L. M., Rosas, J., Oliveira, A. I., & Ferrada, F. (2012). A Collaborative Services Ecosystem for Ambient Assisted Living. In L. Camarinha-Matos, L. Xu, & H. Afsarmanesh (Eds.), *Collaborative Networks in the Internet of Services* (Vol. 380, pp. 117–127). Springer Berlin Heidelberg. doi:10.1007/978-3-642-32775-9_12

Camarinha-Matos, L. M., Rosas, J., Oliveira, A. I., & Ferrada, F. (2015). Care services ecosystem for ambient assisted living. *Enterprise Information Systems*, *9*(5-6), 607–633.

Cameron, E., & Green, M. (2015). *Making sense of change management: A complete guide to the models, tools and techniques of organizational change*. Kogan Page Publishers.

Cano, C., Fernández-Sanz, L., & Misra, S. (2013). Featuring CIO: Roles, Skills and Soft Skills. *International Journal of Human Capital and Information Technology Professionals*, *4*(1), 22–33. doi:10.4018/jhcitp.2013010103

Cao, M., & Zhang, Q. (2011). Supply chain collaboration: Impact on collaborative advantage and firm performance. *Journal of Operations Management*, *29*(3), 163–180. doi:10.1016/j.jom.2010.12.008

CapGemini. (2007). *Trends in Business transformation - Survey of European Executives*. CapGemini Consulting and The Economist Intelligence Unit.

CapGemini. (2009). Business transformation: From crisis response to radical changes that will create tomorrow's business. A Capgemini Consulting survey.

Cappelli, P. (2000). Is there a shortage of information technology workers. *A Report to McKinsey and Company*. Retrieved from http://knowledge.wharton.upenn.edu/papers/979.pdf

Carapina, M., Bjelobrk, D., & Duk, S. (2013). *Web 2.0 tools in Croatian higher education: An overview. In Proceeding of Information & Communication Technology Electronics & Microelectronics (MIPRO 2013)* (Vol. 36, pp. 676–680). Opatija, Croatia: MIPRO.

Carlsson, M., & Mildner, P. (2010). *Sicstus Prolog - The First 25 years*. Academic Press.

Carrell, M. R., Elbert, N. F., & Hatfield, R. D. (2000). *Human Resource Management: Strategies for Managing a Diverse and Global Workforce* (6th ed.). Houghton Mifflin Harcourt.

Carretero Gómez, S., Vuorikari, R., & Punie, Y. (2017). *DigComp 2.1: The Digital Competence Framework for Citizens with eight proficiency levels and examples of use*. Publications Office of the European Union.

Carrol, S. J., & Schneier, C. E. (1982). *Performance appraisal and review systems*. Glenview, IL: Scott Foresman.

Casademunt, A. M. L., Cabrera, A. M. G., & Molina, D. G. C. (2015). National culture, work-life balance and employee well-being in European tourism firms: The moderating effect of uncertainty avoidance values. *Tourism & Management Studies*, *11*(1), 62–69.

Casado-Lumbreras, C., Colomo-Palacios, R., Hernández-López, A., & Soto-Acosta, P. (2011). Personnel Performance Appraisal Coverage in ITIL, COBIT and CMMi: A Study from the Perspective of People-CMM. *International Journal of Knowledge Society Research*, *2*(2), 59–70. doi:10.4018/jksr.2011040106

Catteeuw, F. (2007). Employee engagement: Boosting productivity in turbulent times. *Organization Development Journal*, *25*(2), 151–157.

Cearley, D., Walker, M., & Burke, B. (2016). *Top 10 Strategic Technology Trends for 2017*. Academic Press.

CEN. (2018a). *CWA 16458-1:2018. European ICT professionals role profiles, Version 2 – Part 1: The 30 ICT profiles*. CEN.

CEN. (2018b). *EN 16234-1:2016. e-Competence Framework (e-CF) - A common European Framework for ICT Professionals in all industry sectors - Part 1: Framework*. CEN.

Cerny, C. A., & Kaiser, H. F. (1977). A study of a measure of sampling adequacy for factor-analytic correlation matrices. *Multivariate Behavioral Research*, *12*(1), 43–47. doi:10.120715327906mbr1201_3 PMID:26804143

Chamba-Eras, L., Jacome-Galarza, L., Guaman-Quinche, R., Coronel-Romero, E., & Jaramillo, M. L. -. (2017). Analysis of usability of universities Web portals using the Prometheus tool - SIRIUS. In *Fourth International Conference on eDemocracy & eGovernment (ICEDEG)* (pp. 195–199). IEEE. 10.1109/ICEDEG.2017.7962533

Chambel, M. J., & Fontinha, R. (2009). Contingencies of Contingent Employment: Psychological Contract, Job Insecurity and Employability of Contracted Workers. *Revista de Psicología del Trabajo y de las Organizaciones, 25*(3), 207–217. doi:10.43211576-59622009000300002

Chamberlain, S. (2018). Preventing violence isn't partisan: Time to reauthorize violence against women act. *The Hill*. Retrieved on the 25th of October, 2018 from https://thehill.com/blogs/congress-blog/civil-rights/406597-preventing-violence-isnt-partisan-time-to-reauthorize

Chanopas, A., Krairit, D., & Ba Khang, D. (2006). Managing information technology infrastructure: A new flexibility framework. *Management Research News, 29*(10), 632–651. doi:10.1108/01409170610712335

Chapple, K. (2006). Networks to Nerdistan: The Role of Labor Market Intermediaries in the Entry-level IT Labor Market. *International Journal of Urban and Regional Research, 30*(3), 548–563. doi:10.1111/j.1468-2427.2006.00674.x

Charness, N., & Jastrzembki, T. S. (2009). Geronthecnology. In P. Saariluoma & H. Isomaki (Eds.), *In Future Interaction II* (pp. 1–30). London: Springer.

Chatterjee, C. (2016). Measurement of E-Learning Quality. *3rd International Conference on Advanced Computing and Communication Systems*, 38-42.

Chatzakou, D., Kourtellis, N., Blackburn, J., De Cristofaro, E., Stringhini, G., & Vakali, A. (2017). *Mean Birds: Detecting Aggression and Bullying on Twitter*. Academic Press. doi:10.1145/3091478.3091487

Chaudhari, V. V., Dhawale, C., & Misra, S. (2016). *Sentiment analysis classification: A brief review*. Academic Press.

Chaudhary, S., Berki, E., Li, L., & Valtanen, J. (2015). Time Up for Phishing with Effective Anti-Phishing Research Strategies. *International Journal of Human Capital and Information Technology Professionals, 6*(2), 49–64. doi:10.4018/IJHCITP.2015040104

Chaushi, B. A., Chaushi, A., & Ismaili, F. (2018, May). ERP systems in higher education institutions: Review of the information systems and ERP modules. In *2018 41st International Convention on Information and Communication Technology, Electronics and Microelectronics (MIPRO)* (pp. 1487-1494). IEEE.

Chebli, C. M., Kallon, M. P., Harleston, K. K., & Mansaray, A. (2007). The Impact Of Cultism In Tertiary Education Institution Campuses: A Case Study Of Foural Bay College, Milton Margai College Of Education And Technology And Freetown Teachers College. Education Research Network for West and Central African (ERNWACA). Ernwaca Research Grants Programme 2007.

Chen, A., Lu, Y., & Wang, B. (2017). Customers' purchase decision-making process in social commerce: A social learning perspective. *International Journal of Information Management, 37*(6), 627–638. doi:10.1016/j.ijinfomgt.2017.05.001

Chen, C. C., & Chang, Y. C. (2018). What drives purchase intention on Airbnb? Perspectives of consumer reviews, information quality, and media richness. *Telematics and Informatics, 35*(5), 1512–1523. doi:10.1016/j.tele.2018.03.019

Cheng, I. (2015). *Factors Affecting the Usability of Educational Portals and their Influence on the Information Practices of Pre-Collegiate Educators*. Academic Press.

Chen, L. L., Fahb, B. C. Y., & Jin, T. C. (2016). Perceived organizational support and workplace deviance in the voluntary sector. *Procedia Economics and Finance, 35*, 468–475. doi:10.1016/S2212-5671(16)00058-7

Chen, L., Bentley, P., & Rueckert, D. (2017). Fully automatic acute ischemic lesion segmentation in DWI using convolutional neural networks. *NeuroImage. Clinical, 15*, 633–643. doi:10.1016/j.nicl.2017.06.016 PMID:28664034

Chen, Y. H., & Barnes, S. (2007). Initial trust and online buyer behaviour. *Industrial Management & Data Systems, 107*(1), 21–36. doi:10.1108/02635570710719034

Chen, Y., & Xie, J. (2005). Third-party product review and firm marketing strategy. *Marketing Science, 24*(2), 218–240. doi:10.1287/mksc.1040.0089

Cherdantseva, Y., & Hilton, J. (2013). Information security and information assurance. The discussion about the meaning, scope and goals. In F. Almeida & I. Portela (Eds.), *Organisational, Legal, and Technological Dimensions of Information System Administrator*. IGI Global Publishing.

Chesbrough, H., & Brunswicker, S. (2013). *Managing Open Innovation in Large Firms*. Academic Press.

Chevalier, J. A., & Mayzlin, D. (2006). The effect of word of mouth on sales: Online book reviews. *JMR, Journal of Marketing Research, 43*(3), 345–354. doi:10.1509/jmkr.43.3.345

Chiarini, G., Ray, P., Akter, S., Masella, C., & Ganz, A. (2013). mHealth technologies for chronic diseases and elders: A systematic review. *Selected Areas in Communications. IEEE Journal on, 31*(9), 6–18.

Chiavenato, I. (2003). *Recursos Humanos: o capital humano das organizações* (8th ed.). São Paulo: Editora Atlas.

Chijoke, O. J., & Abifarin, O. (2013). *An appraisal of protection against domestic violence law of Lagos state, 2007.* Retrieved 3rd November, from http://abuad.edu.ng/an-appraisal-of-protection-against-domestic-violence-law-of-lagos-state-2007/

Chin, W. W. (1998). The partial least squares approach to structural equation modeling. *Modern Methods for Business Research, 295*(2), 295-336.

Chinnah, P. C., & Amabibi, F. (2019). Cultism And Sustainable National Development In Nigeria. *Economics And Social Sciences. Academic Journal, 1*(2), 2019.

Chinwokwu E. C. (2013). Terrorism and the Dilemmas of Combating the Menace in Nigeria. *International Journal of Humanities and Social Science, 3*(4), 265-272.

Chlebus, G., Schenk, A., Moltz, J. H., van Ginneken, B., Hahn, H. K., & Meine, H. (2018). Automatic liver tumor segmentation in CT with fully convolutional neural networks and object-based postprocessing. *Scientific Reports, 8*(1), 15497. doi:10.103841598-018-33860-7 PMID:30341319

Choco Team. (2010). *Choco: An open source java constraint programming library (Research report No. 10-02-INFO)*. École des Mines de Nantes.

Cho, H., & Fiorito, S. S. (2009). Acceptance of online customization for apparel shopping. *International Journal of Retail & Distribution Management, 37*(5), 389–407. doi:10.1108/09590550910954892

Choi, Y. (2017). Human resource management and security policy compliance. *International Journal of Human Capital and Information Technology Professionals, 8*(3), 14. doi:10.4018/IJHCITP.2017070105

Choi, Y., & Dickson, D. R. (2009). A Case Study into the Benefits of Management Training Programs: Impacts on Hotel Employee Turnover and Satisfaction Level. *Journal of Human Resources in Hospitality & Tourism, 9*(1), 103–116. doi:10.1080/15332840903336499

Chondamrongkul, N. (2018). ERP implementation in university: A case study in Thailand. *International Journal of Business Information Systems, 27*(2), 177–192. doi:10.1504/IJBIS.2018.089109

Christensen, J. O., & Knardahl, S. (2012). Work and headache: A prospective study of psychological, social, and mechanical predictors of headache severity. *Pain*, *153*(10), 2119–2132. doi:10.1016/j.pain.2012.07.009 PMID:22906887

Christian, M.S., Garza, A.S., & Slaughter, J.E. (2011). Work Engagement: A Quantitative Review a Test of Its Relations with Task and Contextual Performance. *Personnel Psychology*, *64*(1), 89-136. .01203.x doi:10.1111/j.1744-6570.2010

Christopher, D., & Tanwar, A. (2012). Knowledge management in outsourcing environment: People empowering people. *The IUP Journal of Knowledge Management*, *10*(2), 61–86.

Chuang, C. (2016, March). The Critical Success Factors for ERP Implementation in Higher Education. In *Proceedings of International Academic Conferences* (No. 3305901). International Institute of Social and Economic Sciences. 10.20472/IAC.2016.021.008

Chun, A.H.W. (2004). The Agile Teaching/Learning Methodology and Its e-Learning Platform. *Lecture Notes in Computer Science, 3143.*

CIPD. (2001). *Employers' perceptions of the psychological contract.* CIPD Report 112.

CIPD. (2006). *Reflections on employee Engagement: Change agenda.* CIPD. Retrieved January 04, 2019, from http://www.cipd.co.uk/changeagendas

Cirillo, P. (2010). An analysis of the size distribution of Italian firms by age. *Physica A*, *389*(3), 459–466. doi:10.1016/j.physa.2009.09.049

Clark, S. C. (2000). Work/family border theory: A new theory of work/family balance. *Human Relations*, *53*(6), 747–770. doi:10.1177/0018726700536001

CLEEN Foundation. (2013). National Crime Victimization Surveys. *National Crime Victimization and Safety Survey.* Retrieved from cleenfoundation.blogspot.com/2013/10/public-presentation-of-findings-of.html

Cliffe, S. (1999). ERP implementation. *Harvard Business Review*, *77*(1), 16–17. PMID:10345391

Coad, A. (2010). Investigating the Exponential Age Distribution of Firms. *Economics*, *4*(17), 1–30A.

Cock, P. J. A., Fields, C. J., Goto, N., Heuer, M. L., & Rice, P. M. (2009). The Sanger FASTQ file format for sequences with quality scores, and the Solexa/Illumina FASTQ variants. *Nucleic Acids Research*, *38*(6), 1767–1771. doi:10.1093/nar/gkp1137 PMID:20015970

Codella, N. C., Gutman, D., Celebi, M. E., Helba, B., Marchetti, M. A., Dusza, S. W., ... Huang, H. K. (2007). Computer-aided diagnosis (CAD) and image-guided decision support. *Computerized Medical Imaging and Graphics*, *4*(31), 195–197.

Coenen, M., & Kok, R. A. W. (2014). Workplace flexibility and new product development performance: The role of telework and flexible work schedules. *European Management Journal*, *32*(4), 564–576. doi:10.1016/j.emj.2013.12.003

Cohen, A. (1991). Career stage as a moderator of the relationship between organisational commitment and its outcomes: A meta-analysis. *Journal of Occupational Psychology*, *64*(3), 253–268. doi:10.1111/j.2044-8325.1991.tb00558.x

Cohen, A. (1993). Age and tenure in relation to organisational commitment: A meta-analysis. *Basic and Applied Social Psychology*, *14*(2), 143–159. doi:10.120715324834basp1402_2

Cohen, J., Cohen, P., West, S. G., & Aiken, L. S. (2003). *Applied Multiple Regression/Correlation Analysis for the Behavioral Sciences* (3rd ed.). Mahwah, NJ: Lawrence Erlbaum Associates, Publishers.

Cohen, L., Manion, L., & Morison, K. (2000). *Research methods in education.* London: Routledge Falmer.

Cojocaru, M. (2011). Cultural Globalization In The Context Of International Business. *Review of International Comparative Management, 12*(5), 993–999.

Collins, J. S. & Schragle-Law, S. (2010). IT Project Teams and Their Leaders: Interaction Expectations. *Leadership and Organizational Management, 1.*

Colomo-Palacios, R., Casado-Lumbreras, C., Soto-Acosta, P., García-Peñalvo, F. J., & Tovar-Caro, E. (2013). Competence gaps in software personnel: A multi-organizational study. *Computers in Human Behavior, 29*(2), 456–461. doi:10.1016/j.chb.2012.04.021

Colomo-Palacios, R., Casado-Lumbreras, C., Soto-Acosta, P., García-Peñalvo, F., & Tovar, E. (2014). Project managers in global software development teams: A study of the effects on productivity and performance. *Software Quality Journal, 22*(1), 3–19. doi:10.100711219-012-9191-x

Colomo-Palacios, R., Casado-Lumbreras, C., Soto-Acosta, P., Misra, S., & García-Peñalvo, F. J. (2012). Analyzing Human Resource Management Practices Within the GSD Context. *Journal of Global Information Technology Management, 15*(3), 30–54. doi:10.1080/1097198X.2012.10845617

Colomo-Palacios, R., González-Carrasco, I., López-Cuadrado, J. L., Trigo, A., & Varajão, J. E. (2014). I-Competere: Using applied intelligence in search of competency gaps in software project managers. *Information Systems Frontiers, 16*(4), 607–625. doi:10.100710796-012-9369-6

Colomo-Palacios, R., Soto-Acosta, P., García-Peñalvo, F. J., & García-Crespo, Á. (2012). A Study of the Impact of Global Software Development in Packaged Software Release Planning. *Journal of Universal Computer Science, 18*(19), 2646–2668. doi:10.3217/jucs-018-19-2646

Corbin, R. D., Dunbar, C. B., & Zhu, Q. (2007). A three-tier knowledge management scheme for software engineering support and innovation. *Journal of Systems and Software, 80*(9), 1494–1505. doi:10.1016/j.jss.2007.01.013

Corominas, A., & Pastor, R. (2010). Replanning working time under annualised working hours. *International Journal of Production Research, 48*(5), 1493–1515. doi:10.1080/00207540802582227

Correia, A., Gonçalves, A., & Misra, S. (2019). Integrating the Scrum Framework and Lean Six Sigma. *Lecture Notes in Computer Science, 11623.*

Cortina, L. M., Magley, V. J., Williams, J. H., & Langhout, R. D. (2001). Incivility in the workplace: Incidence and impact. *Journal of Occupational Health Psychology, 6*(1), 64–80. doi:10.1037/1076-8998.6.1.64 PMID:11199258

Costen, W. M., & Salazar, J. (2011). The Impact of Training and Development on Employee Job Satisfaction, Loyalty, and Intent to Stay in the Lodging Industry. *Journal of Human Resources in Hospitality & Tourism, 10*(3), 273–284. doi:10.1080/15332845.2011.555734

Council of the European Union. (2017). *Council Recommendation on the European Qualifications Framework for lifelong learning and repealing the Recommendation of the European Parliament and of the Council of 23 April 2008 on the establishment of the European Qualifications Framework for lifelong learning.* author.

Cox, J. (1998). An introduction to Marx's theory of Alienation. *International Socialism: Quarterly Journal of the Socialist Workers Party, 79*(5).

Cox. J. (1998). An introduction to Marx's theory of alienation. *International Socialism: Quarterly Journal of the Socialist Workers Party, 5*(79).

Crampton, S. M., & Mishra, J. M. (2005). Job Sharing: A Viable Work Alternative for the New Millennium. *The Journal of Applied Management and Entrepreneurship, 10*(2), 13–34.

Cram, W. A., D'Arcy, J., & Proudfoot, J. G. (2019). Seeing the Forest and the Trees: AMeta-Analysis of the Antecedents to Information Security Policy Compliance. *Management Information Systems Quarterly*, *43*(2), 1–24. doi:10.25300/MISQ/2019/15117

Creswell, J. W. (2003). *Research design: Qualitative and quantitative approaches*. Thousand Oaks, CA: SAGE.

Crevier, D. (1993). *A.I, The tumultuous search for artificial intelligence*. New York, NY: Basic Books.

Crispim, J. A., & de Sousa, J. P. (2010). Partner selection in virtual enterprises. *International Journal of Production Research*, *48*(3), 683–707. doi:10.1080/00207540802425369

Cua, F., & Reames, S. (2013). Theory versus application: A study to determine the right choice in deploying an enterprise resource planning (ERP) system. *International Journal of Information Systems in the Service Sector*, *5*(4), 47–62. doi:10.4018/ijisss.2013100104

Cummings, J., & Pletcher, C. (2011). Why Project Networks Beat Project Teams. *MIT Sloan Management Review*, *52*(3), 75–83.

Cybercrime Unit. (2016). *Government will fight Cyber Crime*. Retrieved from http://cybercrime.gov.gh/?p=313

Cybermetrics. (2019). *Ranking of web of universities*. Retrieved from https://www.webometrics.info/en/africa/nigeria

Czaja, S. J., & Lee, C. C. (2009). Information Technology and Older Adults. In A. Sears & J. A. Jacko (Eds.), *Human-Computer Interaction: Designing for Diverse Users and Domains* (pp. 18–30). CRC Press. doi:10.1201/9781420088885.ch2

D'Arcy, J., & Greene, G. (2014). Security culture and the employment relationship as drivers of employees' security compliance. *Information Management & Computer Security*, *22*(5), 474–489. doi:10.1108/IMCS-08-2013-0057

D'Souza, M. J., & Rodrigues, P. (2015). Extreme Pedagogy: An Agile Teaching-Learning Methodology for Engineering Education. *Indian Journal of Science and Technology*, *8*(9), 828–833. doi:10.17485/ijst/2015/v8i9/53274

Da Veiga, A. (2016). Comparing the information security culture of employees who had read the information security policy and those who had not: Illustrated through an empirical study. *Information & Computer Security*, *24*(2), 139–151. doi:10.1108/ICS-12-2015-0048

Daellenbach, H., McNickle, D., & Dye, S. (2012). *Management Science - Decision-making through systems thinking* (2nd ed.). Palgrave Macmillan.

Dafoulas, G., & Macaulay, L. (2002). Investigating Cultural Differences in Virtual Software Teams. *The Electronic Journal on Information Systems in Developing Countries*, *7*(1), 1–14. doi:10.1002/j.1681-4835.2002.tb00040.x

Daher, L., & Elkabani, I. (2012). Usability Evaluation of Some Lebanese Universities Web Portals. In *International Arab Conference on Information Technology* (pp. 10–13). Academic Press.

Dahnil, M. I., Marzuki, K. M., Langgat, J., & Fabeil, N. F. (2014). Factors influencing SMEs adoption of social media marketing. *Procedia: Social and Behavioral Sciences*, *148*, 119–126. doi:10.1016/j.sbspro.2014.07.025

Dainty, A. R. J., Raidén, A. B., & Neale, R. H. (2009). Incorporating employee resourcing requirements into deployment decision making. *Project Management Journal*, *40*(2), 7–18. doi:10.1002/pmj.20119

Dalal, R. S., Lam, H., Weiss, H. M., Weich, E. R., & Hulin, C. L. (2009). A Within-Person Approach to Work Behavior and Performance: Concurrent and Lagged Citizenship-Counter Productivity Association and Dynamic Relationship With Affect and Overall Job Performance. *Academy of Management Journal*, *52*(5), 1061–1068. doi:10.5465/amj.2009.44636148

Dani, H., Li, J., & Liu, H. (2017). Sentiment Informed Cyberbullying Detection in Social Media. Lecture Notes in Computer Science, 10534, 52–67. doi:10.1007/978-3-319-71249-9_4

Dash, S. K., Patro, S., & Behera, B. K. (2013). Teaching Methods and its Efficacy: An Evaluation by Students. *Journal of Indian Acad Forensic Med, 35*(4), 321–324.

Das, T., & Patil, S. R. (2014). A Review of Current Trends in Usability Evaluation Methods. *International Journal of Engineering Research & Technology, 3*(9), 837–840.

Data Mining Techniques, Information Technology for People-Centered Development. (2011). Nigeria Computer Society (NCS).

Davey, T. (2017). Artificial Intelligence and the Future of Work: An Interview With Moshe Vardi. *Future of Life*. Retrieved from https://futureoflife.org/2017/06/14/artificial-

David, M., & Colleen, A. (2013). *Effectiveness of active learning in the arts and science*. Humanities Department Faculty Publications & Research paper 45.

Davis, F. D., Bagozzi, R. P., & Warshaw, P. R. J. M. s. (1989). *User acceptance of computer technology: a comparison of two theoretical models*. Academic Press.

Davis, F. D., Jr. (1986). *A technology acceptance model for empirically testing new end-user information systems: Theory and results* (Doctoral dissertation). Massachusetts Institute of Technology.

Davis, F. D. (1989). Perceived usefulness, perceived ease of use, and user acceptance of information technology. *Management Information Systems Quarterly, 13*(3), 319–340. doi:10.2307/249008

DDI. (2005). *Predicting Employee Engagement*. DDI International, Inc. Retrieved December 25, 2018, from http://www.ddiworld.com

De la Barra, C.L., Crawford, B., Soto, R., Misra, S., & Monfroy, E. (2013). Agile Software Development: It Is about Knowledge Management and Creativity. *Lecture Notes in Computer Science, 7973.*

De Leoz, G., Tripathi, A., Tahmasbi, N., & Petter, S. (2013), Examining high performance teams in information systems projects. *Proceedings of the 19th Americas Conference on Information Systems.*

Debruyne, M., Moenaert, R., Griffin, A., Hart, S., Hultink, E. J., & Robben, H. (2002). The impact of new product launch strategies on competitive reaction in industrial markets. *Journal of Product Innovation Management, 19*(2), 159–170. doi:10.1016/S0737-6782(01)00135-7

Decramer, A., Smolders, C., & Vanderstraeten, A. (2013). Employee performance management culture and system features in higher education: Relationship with employee performance management satisfaction. *International Journal of Human Resource Management, 24*(2), 352–371. doi:10.1080/09585192.2012.680602

Deedam, F. B., Thomas, E., & Taylor, O. E. (2018). *Accessibility and Usability Evaluation of State-Owned Universities Website in Nigeria*. Academic Press.

Deery, M. (2008). Talent management, work-life balance and retention strategies. *International Journal of Contemporary Hospitality Management, 20*(7), 792–806. doi:10.1108/09596110810897619

DeNisi, A. S., & Pritchard, R. D. (2006). Performance Appraisal, Performance Management and Improving Individual Performance: A Motivational Framework. *Management and Organization Review, 2*(2), 253–277. doi:10.1111/j.1740-8784.2006.00042.x

Dernovsek, D. (2008). *Creating highly engaged and committed employee starts at the top and ends at the bottom line Credit Union Magazine*. Credit Union National Association, Inc.

Derrida, J. (1992). *Force of law: Deconstruction*. Academic Press.

Derrida, J. (1976). *Of Grammatology*. Baltimore, MD: Johns Hopkins University Press.

DeRue, D. S., & Morgeson, F. P. (2007). Stability and change in person-team and person-role fit over time: The effects of growth satisfaction, performance, and general self-efficacy. *The Journal of Applied Psychology*, *92*(5), 1242–1253. doi:10.1037/0021-9010.92.5.1242 PMID:17845083

Desai, M., Majumdar, B., & Prabhu, G. P. (2010). A study on employee engagement in two Indian businesses. *Asian Journal of Management Research*, *1*, 81–97.

Desmond, C. (2013). Management of change. *IEEE Engineering Management Review 41*(3).

Destatis. (2014). *Pressemitteilungen - Verdienstunterschied zwischen Frauen und Männern in Deutschland weiterhin bei 22% - Statistisches Bundesamt (Destatis)*. Retrieved August 29, 2015, from https://www.destatis.de/DE/PresseService/Presse/Pressemitteilungen/2015/03/PD15_099_621.html

Devarakonda, M., Gupta, P., & Tang, C. (2013). Labor Cost Reduction with Cloud: An End-to-End View. *2013 IEEE Sixth International Conference on Cloud Computing (CLOUD)*, 534–540. 10.1109/CLOUD.2013.90

Devonish, D. (2013). Workplace bullying, employee performance and behaviors: The mediating role of psychological well-being. *Employee Relations*, *35*(6), 630–647. doi:10.1108/ER-01-2013-0004

Dewett, T., & Jones, G. R. (2001). The role of information technology in the organization: A review, model, and assessment. *Journal of Management*, *27*(3), 313–346. doi:10.1177/014920630102700306

Dezdar, S., & Ainin, S. (2011). Examining ERP implementation success from a project environment perspective. *Business Process Management Journal*, *17*(6), 919–939. doi:10.1108/14637151111182693

Diao, Y., Keller, A., Parekh, S., & Marinov, V. V. (2007). Predicting Labor Cost through IT Management Complexity Metrics. *10th IFIP/IEEE International Symposium on Integrated Network Management, 2007. IM '07*, 274–283. 10.1109/INM.2007.374792

Dickmann, F. J. (2006). Ensuring "Strategy" Isn't On 'Culture's Breakfast Plate. *Credit Union Journal*, *10*(45), 4–4.

Dictionary of Philosophy. (1984). Alienation. In The Dictionary of Philosophy (2nd ed.). Academic Press.

Diderot, D. (1993). Conversation of a father with his children (P. N. Furbank, Trans.). In FurbankP. N. (Ed.), *This is not a story and other stories* (pp. 126–159). Oxford, UK: Oxford University Press.

Dinakar, K., Picard, R., & Lieberman, H. (2015). Common sense reasoning for detection, prevention, and mitigation of cyberbullying. *International Joint Conference on Artificial Intelligence*, (3), 4168–4172. 10.1145/2362394.2362400

Dincbas, M., Van Hentenryck, P., Simonis, H., Aggoun, A., & Herold, A. (1988). The Chip system: Constraint handling in Prolog. In E. Lusk & R. Overbeek (Eds.), *9th international conference on automated deduction* (Vol. 310, p. 774-775). Springer Berlin Heidelberg.

Disse, M., Nacken, H., & Mitterer, J. (2017). *Flood Risk Management*. Retrieved from https://classcentral.com › edX.

Dixson, D. D., & Worrell, F. C. (2016). Formative and Summative Assessment in the Classroom. *Journal of Theory into Practice*, *55*(2), 153–159. doi:10.1080/00405841.2016.1148989

Docker. (2019). *Docker*. Retrieved from www.docker.com

Dominic, P. D., Jati, H., & Hanim, S. (2013). University Website Quality Comparison by Using Non-parametric Statistical Test: A case study from Malaysia. *International Journal Operational Research, 16*(3), 349–374.

Dommett, E. (2019). Understanding student use of twitter and online forums in higher education. *Education and Information Technologies, 24*(1), 325–343. doi:10.100710639-018-9776-5

Doneva, R., & Gaftandzhieva, S. (2017). Social Media in Bulgarian Higher Education: An Exploratory Survey. *International Journal of Human Capital and Information Technology Professionals, 8*(3), 67–83. doi:10.4018/IJHCITP.2017100106

Draft, S. (2013). *Computer Science Curricula 2013*. Academic Press.

Draghici, A., & Draghici, G. (2013). Lessons Learned for ECQA LLP-LdV Projects' Management. *Procedia Technology, 9*(0), 876–885.

Dries, N. (2012). *The role of learning agility and career variety in the identification and development of high potential employees*. Retrieved September 6, 2015, from http://www.emeraldinsight.com.strauss.uc3m.es:8080/doi/pdf-plus/10.1108/00483481211212977

Dries, N. (2013). Adding value with learning agility: How to identify and develop high-potential employees. *Development and Learning in Organizations, 27*(5), 24–26. doi:10.1108/dlo-07-2013-0043

Driscoll, C., & McKee, M. (2007). Restorying a culture of ethical and spiritual values: A role for leader storytelling. *Journal of Business Ethics, 73*(2), 205–217. doi:10.100710551-006-9191-5

Drucker, P. F. (1954). *The practice of management*. New York: Harper.

D'Souza, D., Polina, P., & Yampolskiy, R. (2012). Avatar CAPTCHA: Telling computers and humans apart via face classification. *Proceedings of Electro/Information Technology (EIT)*. Doi:10.1109/EIT.2012.6220734

Dumisani, X., Chux, G. I., Andre, S., & Joyce, N. (2014). The Impact of Employer-Employee Relationships on Business Growth. *Journal of Economics, 5*(3), 313–324. doi:10.1080/09765239.2014.11885007

Dunk, A. S. (2004). Product life cycle cost analysis: The impact of customer profiling, competitive advantage, and quality of IS information. *Management Accounting Research, 15*(4), 401–414. doi:10.1016/j.mar.2004.04.001

Dunning, M. (2015). Employers look beyond wellness: Many companies have modified their benefits programs to include incentives aimed at improving their employees' overall well-being. *Business Insurance, 49*(13). Retrieved from http://search.proquest.com.strauss.uc3m.es:8080/docview/1691108317/citation

Durall Gazulla, E., Gros Salvat, B., Maina, M. F., Johnson, L., & Adams, S. (2012). *Perspectivas tecnológicas: educación superior en Iberoamérica 2012-2017*. Academic Press.

Durden, O. (2019). *The advantages of monitoring employees*. Retrieved from https://smallbusiness.chron.com/advantages-monitoring-employees-18428.html

Dylan, W. (2013). Assessment: The Bridge between Teaching and Learning. *Voices from the Middle, 21*(2), 15–22.

Eagly, A. H., & Chaiken, S. (1993). *The psychology of attitudes*. Harcourt Brace Jovanovich College Publishers.

Ebrahim, N. A. (2015). Virtual R&D Teams: A New Model for Product Development. *International Journal of Innovation, 3*(2), 1–27. doi:10.5585/iji.v3i2.43

ECharts. (2019). *ECharts*. Retrieved from https://ecomfe.github.io/echarts- doc/public/en/index.html

Economictimes. (2019). *Sectors that are likely to outperform in 2019*. Retrieved February 2019 from https://economictimes.indiatimes.com/markets/stocks/news/sectors-that-are-likely-to-outperform-in-2019/articleshow/67326199.cms

ECS. (2019). *Alibaba Cloud Elastic Compute Service (ECS)*. Retrieved from https://intl.aliyun.com/product/ecs

edWeb. (2009). *A Survey of K-12 Educators on Social Networking and Content-Sharing Tools*. Retrieved from https://www.edweb.net/fimages/op/K12Survey.pdf

EEOC vrs Freeman (2013). *Court Slams EEOC on Background Check Lawsuit No. 09-CV-2573*. Retrieved from https://www.employmentlawspotlight.com/2013/08/court-slams-eeoc-on-background-check-lawsuit/

Egoeze, F., Misra, S., Akman, I., & Colomo-palacios, R. (2014). An Evaluation of ICT Infrastructure and Application in Nigeria Universities. *Acta Polytechnica Hungarica*, *11*(9), 115–129. Retrieved from http://www.uni-obuda.hu/journal/Egoeze_Misra_Akman_Colomo-Palacios_55.pdf

Ehie, I. C., & Madsen, M. (2005). Identifying critical issues in enterprise resource planning (ERP) implementation. *Computers in Industry*, *56*(6), 545–557. doi:10.1016/j.compind.2005.02.006

Einarsen, S. (1999). The nature and causes of bullying at work. *International Journal of Manpower*, *20*(1/2), 16–27. doi:10.1108/01437729910268588

Eisenhardt, K. M., & Tabrizi, B. N. (1995). Accelerating adaptive processes: Product innovation in the global computer industry. *Administrative Science Quarterly*, *40*(1), 84–110. doi:10.2307/2393701

Ekeanyanwu, N. T., & Igbinoba, A. (2007). The Media And Cultism In Nigerian Higher Institutions Of Learning: A Study Of Coverage, Treatment And Relevance. *International Journal of Communication*, (6).

El–Agamy, R., & Tsuda, K. (2013). Development of vision for IT engineers' required skills by analysis of ITSS applying text mining. *International Journal of Computer Applications in Technology*, *48*(2), 162–172. doi:10.1504/IJCAT.2013.056021

Elliott, M. A. (2007). *Stigmergic collaboration: A theoretical framework for mass collaboration* (PhD). University of Melbourne. Retrieved from http://hdl.handle.net/11343/39359

Ellis, C. M., & Sorensen, A. (2007). Assessing Employee Engagement: The Key to Improving Productivity. *Perspectives, 15*(1).

Eloranta, E., Hameri, A. P., & Lahti, M. (2001). Improved project management through improved document management. *Computers in Industry*, *45*(3), 231–243. doi:10.1016/S0166-3615(01)00099-9

El-Sabaa, S. (2001). The skills and career path of an effective project manager. *International Journal of Project Management*, *19*(1), 1–7. doi:10.1016/S0263-7863(99)00034-4

Empirica. (2013). *E-Skills for jobs in europe: measuring progress and moving ahead*. Retrieved from Prepared for the European Commission website: http://eskills-monitor2013.eu/fileadmin/monitor2013/documents/MONITOR_Final_Report.pdf

Empirica. (2014). *e-Skills in Europe - Countryreport Spain*. European Commission.

Eom, M. T. (2015). How Can Organization Retain IT Personnel? Impact of IT Manager's Leadership on IT Personnel's Intention to Stay. *Information Systems Management*, *32*(4), 316–330. doi:10.1080/10580530.2015.1080001

Ernst & Young LLP. (2016). *On Future of Digital Content Consumption in India*. Author.

Esfijani, A. (2018). Measuring Quality in Online Education: A Meta-synthesis. *American Journal of Distance Education*, *32*(1), 57–73. doi:10.1080/08923647.2018.1417658

Esmeria, G. J., & Seva, R. R. (2017). Web Usability : A Literature Review. In *De La Salle University Research Congress*. Retrieved from www.dlsu.edu.ph/conferences/dlsu-research-congress-proceedings/.../SEE-I-013.pdf

EU Commission. (2014a). *Draft General Budget of the European Commission for the financial year 2015*. Retrieved from http://ec.europa.eu/budget/annual/lib/documents/2015/DB/DB2015_WDI_en.pdf

EU Commission. (2014b). *Multiannual financial framework 2014-2020 and EU budget 2014 - Directorate-General for the Budget - EU Bookshop*. doi:10.2761/9592

EU Commission. (2015). *H2020 Calls*. Retrieved 1 October 2015, from https://ec.europa.eu/research/participants/portal/desktop/en/opportunities/h2020/master_calls.html

European Commission. (2015). *e-Skills for ICT Professionalism. Creating a European Foundational ICT Body of Knowledge. European Commission*. ESCO: European Classification of Skills/Competences, Qualifications and Occupations. Retrieved July 2017, from https://www.ec.europa.eu/esco/portal/document/en/8e9cf30d-9799-4f95-ae29-e05c725b24c7

European e-Competence Framework. (n.d.). *e-CF 3.0 Profiling tool on-line*. Retrieved July 2017, from http://www.ecompetences.eu/e-cf-3-0-and-ict-profiles-on-line-tool

Eurostat. (2013, January). *Labour costs per hour in euro, whole economy*. Retrieved August 29, 2015, from http://ec.europa.eu/eurostat/statistics-explained/index.php/Earnings_statistics

Eurostat. (2014a). *Hourly labour costs - Statistics Explained*. Retrieved August 29, 2015, from http://ec.europa.eu/eurostat/statistics-explained/index.php/Hourly_labour_costs

Eurostat. (2014b). *Population and population change statistics*. Retrieved from http://epp.eurostat.ec.europa.eu/statistics_explained/index.php/Population_and_population_change_statistics#

Eurostat. (2015, February 1). *Gender pay gap statistics - Statistics Explained*. Retrieved August 29, 2015, from http://ec.europa.eu/eurostat/statistics-explained/index.php/Gender_pay_gap_statistics

Evaluation Briefs. (2008). *Data collection method for program evaluation questions*. Retrieved 7th February, 2017 from https://www.cdc.gov/healthyyouth/evaluation/pdf/briefly.pdf

Evenson, S., & Dubberly, H. (2010). Designing for service: Creating an experience advantage. In G. Salvendy & W. Karwowski (Eds.), *Introduction to Service Engineering* (pp. 403–413). John Wiley & Sons.

Eze, U. L. (2017). *The violence against person's prohibition act, 2015*. Retrieved 8th March, 2017 from https://donlaz.wordpress.com/20

Eze-Anaba, I. (2010). Domestic violence and legal reforms in Nigeria: Prospects and challenges. *Cardozo Journal of Law and Gender*, *14*(21), 15–18.

Ezema, V. S., Ota, M. S., & Abah, G. O. (2017). Activities of Cultist and Measures for Eradicating Cultism among Secondary School Students in Nigeria: Implication for Child Development and Counselling. *European Journal of Social Sciences*, *55*(3), 254-261.

Faculty Focus. (2011). *Social Media Usage Trends Among Higher Education Faculty*. Retrieved from https://www.facultyfocus.com/free-reports/social-media-usage-trends-among-higher-education-faculty/

Fadelelmoula, A. A. (2018). The effects of the critical success factors for ERP implementation on the comprehensive achievement of the crucial roles of information systems in the higher education sector. *Interdisciplinary Journal of Information, Knowledge, and Management*, *13*, 21–44. doi:10.28945/3942

Faily, S., & Fléchais, I. (2010). Analysing and Visualising Security and Usability in IRIS. *2010 International Conference on Availability, Reliability and Security*. 10.1109/ARES.2010.28

Falana, F. (2013). A law to provide protection against domestic violence and for connected purposes. Lagos: Women Empowerment and Legal Aid (WELA).

Farrakhan, I. (2012). *The true meaning of education.* FCN Publishing. Retrieved from http://www.finalcall.com/artman/publish/Minister_Loui s_Farrakhan_9/article_8731.shtml

Faryadi, Q. (2011). Cyber bullying and academic performance. *International Journal Of Computational Engineering Research, 1*(1), 23–30.

Favaro, K. (2014, May 22). *Strategy or Culture: Which Is More Important?* Retrieved October 17, 2015, from strategy+business website: http://www.strategy-business.com/blog/Strategy-or-Culture-Which-Is-More-Important?gko=26c64

Fayoku, K. O. (2011). Campus Cultism in Nigeria's Higher Education Institutions: Origins, Development and Suggestions for Control. *Makerere Journal of Higher Education, 3*(1).

Fegley, S. (2007). *2007 benefits: A survey report by the Society for Human Resource Management.* Alexandria, VA: Society for Human Resource Management. Retrieved from http://www.shrm.org/publications/hrmagazine/editorialcontent/documents/2007%20benefits%20survey%20report.pdf

Felfel, H., Ayadi, O., & Masmoudi, F. (2017). Pareto Optimal Solution Selection for a Multi-Site Supply Chain Planning Problem Using the VIKOR and TOPSIS Methods. *International Journal of Service Science, Management, Engineering, and Technology.* Doi:10.4018/IJSSMET.2017070102

Feng, Y., Huang, H., Cheng, G., Chen, C., Huang, J., Liu, Z., & Huang, K. (2018). An Optimization Model to Evaluate Dynamic Assignment Capability of Agile Organization. *2018 4th International Conference on Big Data and Information Analytics (BigDIA)*, 1–6. 10.1109/BigDIA.2018.8632798

Fengler, W. (2014). *The End of the Population Pyramid.* Retrieved from http://www.economist.com/blogs/graphicdetail/2014/11/daily-chart-10

Ferguson, A. (2007). *Employee engagement: Does it exist, and if so, how does it relate to performance, other constructs and individual differences?* Retrieved February 19, 2019, from http://www.lifethatworks.com/Employee-Engagement.prn.pdf

Fernández Sanz, L., Gómez Pérez, J., & Castillo Martínez, A. (2017). e-Skills Match: A framework for mapping and integrating the main skills, knowledge and competence standards and models for ICT occupations. *Computer Standards & Interfaces, 51*, 30–42. doi:10.1016/j.csi.2016.11.004

Fernandez, C. P. (2007). Employee engagement. *Journal of Public Health Management and Practice.* Retrieved on January 13, 2016, from http://find.galegroup.com

Fernández, A., & Hill, P. (2000). A comparative study of eight Constraint Programming Languages over the boolean and finite domains. *Constraints, 5*(3), 275–301. doi:10.1023/A:1009816801567

Ferrario, R., & Guarino, N. (2009). Towards an Ontological Foundation for Services Science. In D. John, F. Dieter, & T. Paolo (Eds.), *Future Internet --- FIS 2008* (pp. 152–169). Springer-Verlag. doi:10.1007/978-3-642-00985-3_13

Ferris, G. R., Hochwarter, W. A., Buckley, M. R., Harrell-Cook, G., & Frink, D. D. (1999). Human Resources Management: Some New Directions. *Journal of Management, 25*(3), 385–415. doi:10.1177/014920639902500306

Fielding, R. T. (2000). *Architectural Styles and the Design of Network-based Software Architectures.* PhD Dissertation.

Fiet, J. O., Norton, W. I. Jr, & Clouse, V. G. (2007). Systematic search as a source of technical innovation: An empirical test. *Journal of Engineering and Technology Management, 24*(4), 329–346. doi:10.1016/j.jengtecman.2007.09.001

Financial Times Lexicon. (2013). *Gross Value Added definition*. Retrieved September 5, 2015, from http://lexicon.ft.com/Term?term=gross%20value%20added%20GVA

Fink, L., & Neumann, S. (2009). Exploring the perceived business value of the flexibility enabled by information technology infrastructure. *Information & Management*, *46*(2), 90–99. doi:10.1016/j.im.2008.11.007

Flanagan, J. C., & Burns, R. K. (1955). The employee performance record; a new appraisal and development tool. *Harvard Business Review*, *5*, 95–102.

Fletcher, C. (2001). Performance appraisal and management: The developing research agenda. *Journal of Occupational and Organizational Psychology*, *74*(4), 473–487. doi:10.1348/096317901167488

Florez, H., Sanchez, M., & Villalobos, J. (2014c). Supporting drafts for enterprise modeling. *2014 IEEE 9th Computing Colombian Conference (9CCC)*, 200–206.

Florez, H., Sanchez, M., Villalobos, J., & Vega, G. (2012). Coevolution Assistance for Enterprise Architecture Models. *Models And Evolution (ME 2012) Workshop at The ACM/IEEE 15th International Conference on Model Driven Engineering Languages And Systems (MoDELS 2012)*.

Florez, H., & Leon, M. (2018). Model Driven Engineering Approach to Configure Software Reusable Components. *International Conference on Applied Informatics*, 352–363. 10.1007/978-3-030-01535-0_26

Florez, H., Sánchez, M., & Villalobos, J. (2013). Embracing Imperfection in Enterprise Architecture Models. *CEUR Workshop Proceedings*, *1023*, 8–17.

Florez, H., Sanchez, M., & Villalobos, J. (2014a). Extensible Model-based Approach for Supporting Automatic Enterprise Analysis. *18th IEEE International Enterprise Distributed Object Computing Conference (EDOC)*, 32–41. 10.1109/EDOC.2014.15

Florez, H., Sanchez, M., & Villalobos, J. (2014b). iArchiMate: A Tool for Managing Imperfection in Enterprise Models. *18th IEEE International Enterprise Distributed Object Computing Conference Workshops and Demonstrations (EDOCW)*, 201–210. 10.1109/EDOCW.2014.38

Florez, H., Sanchez, M., & Villalobos, J. (2016). A catalog of automated analysis methods for enterprise models. *SpringerPlus*, *5*(406), 1–24. PMID:27047732

Florez, H., Sánchez, M., & Villalobos, J. (2016). Analysis of Imprecise Enterprise Models. *International Workshop on Business Process Modeling, Development and Support*, 349–364.

FORAGRO. (2010). *Agriculture and rural prosperity from the perspective of technological research and innovation in LAC: FORAGRO Position 2010*. Retrieved from http://www.fao.org/docs/eims/upload/276851/foragro_presentation_english_f_1a.pdf

Ford, J., Willey, L., White, B. J., & Domagalski, T. (2015). New concerns in electronic employee monitoring: Have you checked your policies lately? *Journal of Legal, Ethical & Regulatory Issues*, *18*(1), 51–70.

Fornell, C., & Larcker, D.F. (1981). Evaluating structural equation models with unobservable variables and measurement error. *Journal of Marketing Research, 18*(1), 39-50.

Foster, S., & Dyer, C. (2010). *Ending violence against women and human trafficking: A Guide to new strategies*. Retrieved from http://www.ncdsv.org/images/GlobePartnerendVAW_EndVAWTraffickingToolikit_3-2010.pdf

Francis, H. M., Ramdhony, A., Reddington, M., & Staines, H. (2013). Opening spaces for conversational practice: A conduit for effective engagement strategies and productive working arrangements. *International Journal of Human Resource Management*, *24*(14), 2713–2740. doi:10.1080/09585192.2013.781530

Frank, U. (2014a). Enterprise modelling: The next steps. *Enterprise Modelling and Information Systems Architectures*, *9*(1), 22–37. doi:10.100740786-014-0003-6

Frank, U. (2014b). Multi-perspective enterprise modeling: Foundational concepts, prospects and future research challenges. *Software & Systems Modeling*, *13*(3), 941–962. doi:10.100710270-012-0273-9

Freedom Of Expression. (2018). The Human Rights Problem With Social Media Monitoring. *Accessnow*. Retrieved 11 August 2019 From Https://Www.Accessnow.Org/13503-2/

Freeney, Y., & Fellenz, M. R. (2013). Work engagement, job design and the role of the social context at work: Exploring antecedents from a relational perspective. *Human Relations*, *66*(11), 1427–1445. doi:10.1177/0018726713478245

Freidman, A. (2011). *Freshness Update + Social Media = Happy Users*. Retrieved from http://searchengineland.com/freshnessupdate-social-media-happy-users-102880

Freudenthal, H. (1973). *Mathematics as an educational task*. Springer Science & Business Media.

Friedman, L. T. (2013). Revolution hits the Universities. *New York Times*.

Friedman, B. A. (2007). Globalization implications for human resource management roles. *Employ Response Rights Journal*, *19*(3), 157–171. doi:10.100710672-007-9043-1

Frühwirth, T., & Abdennadher, S. (2005). *Principles of constraint systems and constraint solvers*. Academic Press.

Frühwirth, T. (1998). Theory and practice of constraint handling rules. *The Journal of Logic Programming*, *37*(1-3), 95–138. doi:10.1016/S0743-1066(98)10005-5

Frühwirth, T., & Raiser, F. (Eds.). (2011). *Constraint handling rules: Compilation, execution, and analysis. Academic Press.*

Fu, W., Breininger, K., Würfl, T., Ravikumar, N., Schaffert, R., & Maier, A. (2017). *Frangi-Net: A Neural Network Approach to Vessel Segmentation*. arXiv preprint arXiv:1711.03345

Fuentes, D., & Fiore, N. (2014). The LifeWatch approach to the exploration of distributed species information. *ZooKeys*, *463*, 133–148. doi:10.3897/zookeys.463.8397 PMID:25589865

Furnell, S., & Thomson, K. L. (2009). From culture to disobedience: Recognizing the varying user acceptance of IT security. *Computer Fraud & Security*, *2*(2), 5–10. doi:10.1016/S1361-3723(09)70019-3

Gabrisch, H. (2008). *Institutional deficits in the euro area: the problem of divergent labour costs*. Retrieved August 29, 2015, from http://search.proquest.com.strauss.uc3m.es:8080/docview/209551006?pq-origsite=summon

Gaebel. M. (2014). *MOOCs*. EUA Occasional Papers.

Gais, H. (2014). Is the developing world "MOOC'd out"? *Al Jazeera*. Retrieved from http://america.aljazeera.com/opinions/2014/7/mooc-education-

Gallagher, K. P., Kaiser, K. M., Simon, J. C., Beath, C. M., & Goles, T. (2010). The requisite variety of skills for IT professionals. *Communications of the ACM*, *53*(6), 144–148. doi:10.1145/1743546.1743584

Gallagher, K. P., Worrell, J. L. J., & Mason, R. M. (2012). The negotiation and selection of horizontal mechanisms to support post-implementation ERP organizations. *Information Technology & People*, *25*(1), 4–30. doi:10.1108/09593841211204326

Gallup Inc. (2010). *Employee engagement: What's your engagement ratio?* Retrieved February 06, 2019, from http://www.gallup.com/consulting/121535/Employee-Engagement-Overview Brochure.aspx.

Gallup, Inc. (2013). *State of the global workplace.* Employee Engagement Insights for Business Leaders Worldwide. Retrieved February 07, 2019, from http://www.gallup.com/ services/178517/state-global-workplace.aspx

Ganayaupfu, E. M. (2013). Teaching Methods and Students Academic Performances. *International Journal of Humanities & Social Sciences Inversion, 12*(9), 29–35.

Ganguly, B., Dash, S. B., Cyr, D., & Head, M. (2010). The effects of website design on purchase intention in online shopping: The mediating role of trust and the moderating role of culture. *International Journal of Electronic Business, 8*(4-5), 302–330. doi:10.1504/IJEB.2010.035289

Gardner, H. (1999). *Intelligence Reframed: Multiple Intelligences for the 21st Century.* New York: Basic Books.

Gareis, K. C., Barnett, R. C., Ertel, K. A., & Berkman, L. F. (2009). Work-family enrichment and conflict: Additive effects, buffering, or balance? *Journal of Marriage and the Family, 71*(3), 696–707. doi:10.1111/j.1741-3737.2009.00627.x

Garfinkel, S. L., & Lipford, H. R. (2014). Usable Security: History, Themes, and Challenges. Usable Security: History. Themes, and Challenges. Academic Press.

Gartner, I. (2018). *Gartner's 2018 Hype Cycle for Emerging Technologies Identifies Three Key Trends That Organizations Must Track to Gain Competitive Advantage.* Retrieved from http://www.gartner.com/doc/2847417?refval=&pcp=mpe#a-1321928256

Gartner. (2005). *External Service Providers' SOA Frameworks and Offerings: Capgemini.* Gartner.

Gartner. (2013). *Scenario Toolkit: Using EA to Support Business Transformation.* Gartner Inc.

GATK. (2019). *Genome Analysis Toolkit (GATK).* Retrieved from https://software.broadinstitute.org/gatk

Gecode Team. (2006). *Gecode: Generic constraint development environment.* Available from http://www.gecode.org

Gedik, R., Kalathia, D., Egilmez, G., & Kirac, E. (2018). A constraint programming approach for solving unrelated parallel machine scheduling problem. *Computers & Industrial Engineering, 121,* 139–149. doi:10.1016/j.cie.2018.05.014

Gefen, D., & Ridings, C. M. (2003). IT acceptance: Managing user—IT group boundaries. *ACM SIGMIS Database: the DATABASE for Advances in Information Systems, 34*(3), 25–40. doi:10.1145/937742.937746

Gefen, D., & Straub, D. W. (2004). Consumer trust in B2C e-Commerce and the importance of social presence: Experiments in e-Products and e-Services. *Omega, 32*(6), 407–424. doi:10.1016/j.omega.2004.01.006

Geisser, S. (1974). A Predictive Approach to the Random Effects Model. *Biometrika, 61*(1), 101–107. doi:10.1093/biomet/61.1.101

GeneSifter. (2019). *GeneSifter Lab Edition.* Retrieved from http://www.cambridgesoft.com/services/ SupportNews/details/?SupportNews=124

Gent, I. P., Jefferson, C., & Miguel, I. (2006). Minion: A fast scalable constraint solver. In *Proceedings of ECAI 2006, riva del garda* (pp. 98 - 102). IOS Press.

Geroski, P., Machin, S., & Van Reenen, J. (1993). The profitability of innovating firms. *The Rand Journal of Economics, 24*(2), 198–211. doi:10.2307/2555757

Ghafourifar, A. (2017). 14 ways AI will impact the education sector. *Entefy.* Retrieved from https://venturebeat.com/2017/07/23/14-ways-ai-will-impact-the-education-sector/

Ghanem, A., El-Gafy, M., & Abdelrazig, Y. (2014). Survey of the Current Use of Social Networking in Construction Education. *Proceedings of the 50th ASC Annual International Conference.*

Gibbs, J. L., Sivunen, A., & Boyraz, M. (2017). Investigating the impacts of team type and design on virtual team processes. *Human Resource Management Review, 27*(4), 590–603. doi:10.1016/j.hrmr.2016.12.006

Gillenson, M. L., & Sherrell, D. L. (2002). Enticing online consumers: An extended technology acceptance perspective. *Information & Management, 39*(8), 705–719. doi:10.1016/S0378-7206(01)00127-6

Gilson, L. L., Maynard, M. T., Young, N. C. J., Vartiainen, M., & Hakonen, M. (2015). Virtual Teams Research: 10 Years, 10 Themes, and 10 Opportunities. *Journal of Management, 41*(5), 1313–1337. doi:10.1177/0149206314559946

Ginsberg, C. (1994). Killing a Chinese Mandarin: The moral implications of distance. *Critical Inquiry, 21*(Autumn), 46–60. doi:10.1086/448740

Glaser, B., & Strauss, A. (1967). *The discovery of grounded theory: Strategies for qualitative research.* New York: Aldine de Gruyter.

Glick, L. (2005). *Criminology.* Retrieved 19th February, 2017 from http://catalogue.pearsoned.co.uk/samplechapter/020540278X.pdf

Glick, W. H. (1985). Conceptualizing and measuring organizational and psychological climate: Pitfalls in multilevel research. *Academy of Management Review, 10*(3), 601–616. doi:10.5465/amr.1985.4279045

Go, A., Bhayani, R., & Huang, L. (2007). Twitter Sentiment Classification using Distant Supervision. *Sedimentary Geology, 195*(1–2), 75–90. doi:10.1016/j.sedgeo.2006.07.004

Goel, A. K., Gupta, N., & Rastogi, R. (2013). Measuring the level of employee engagement: A study from Indian automobile sector. *International Journal of Indian Culture and Business Management, 6*(1), 5–21. doi:10.1504/IJICBM.2013.050710

Golubić, K. (2017). *The Role of Social Networks in the Presentation of Croatian Higher Education Institutions* (Unpublished Doctoral Dissertation). University of Zagreb, Croatia.

Golubić, K., & Lasić-Lazić, J. (2012) Analysis of On-line Survey about Need for Presence of Higher Education Institutions on Social Networks: A Step towards Creation of Communication Strategy. *Journal of Computing and Information Technology, 20*(3), 189-194.

Gomes, A., Carmo, L., Bigotte, E., & Mendes, A. (2006). Mathematics and programming problem solving. *Third E-Learning Conference – Computer Science Education*, 1-5.

Gómez, P., Sánchez, M., Florez, H., & Villalobos, J. (2014). An approach to the co-creation of models and metamodels in Enterprise Architecture Projects. *Journal of Object Technology, 13*(3), 2:1. doi:10.5381/jot.2014.13.3.a2

Gonring, M. P. (2008). Customer loyalty and employee engagement: An alignment for value. *The Journal of Business Strategy, 29*(4), 29–40. doi:10.1108/02756660810887060

González, M. P., Lorés, J., & Granollers, A. (2008). Enhancing usability testing through datamining techniques: A novel approach to detecting usability problem patterns for a context of use. *Information and Software Technology, 50*(6), 547–568. doi:10.1016/j.infsof.2007.06.001

Gonzalez, P. A., Ashworth, L., & McKeen, J. (2019). The CIO stereotype: Content, bias, and impact. *The Journal of Strategic Information Systems, 28*(1), 83–99. doi:10.1016/j.jsis.2018.09.002

González-Pérez, L. I., Ramírez-Montoya, M., & García-Peñalvo, F. J. (2018). User Experience in Institutional Repositories: A Systematic Literature Review. *International Journal of Human Capital and Information Technology Professionals*, *9*(1), 70–86. doi:10.4018/IJHCITP.2018010105

Gonzálvez-Gallego, N., Molina-Castillo, F.-J., Soto-Acosta, P., Varajão, J., & Trigo, A. (2015). Using integrated information systems in supply chain management. *Enterprise Information Systems*, *9*(2), 210–232. doi:10.1080/17517575.2013.879209

Goodman, D., French, P. E., & Battaglio, R. P. Jr. (2015). Determinants of local government workforce planning. *American Review of Public Administration*, *45*(2), 135–152. doi:10.1177/0275074013486179

Goodmark, L. (2018). *The violence against women act is unlikely to deter domestic violence — here's why*. The conversation .com Flipboarad.

Gordon, K. T. (2007). *Looking for ways to get people talking about your products? The new social shopping trend can help you build buzz*. Academic Press.

Gouldner, A. W. (1984). *The two Marxisms*. New York: Oxford University Press.

Gouldner, A. W. (1984). *The two Maxims*. New York: Oxford University Press.

Graça, P., & Camarinha-Matos, L. (2015). The Need of Performance Indicators for Collaborative Business Ecosystems. In L. M. Camarinha-Matos, T. A. Baldissera, G. Di Orio, & F. Marques (Eds.), *Technological Innovation for Cloud-Based Engineering Systems* (Vol. 450, pp. 22–30). Springer International Publishing. doi:10.1007/978-3-319-16766-4_3

Gravenkemper, S. (2007). Building Community in Organizations: Principles of Engagement. *Consulting Psychology Journal: Practice and Research*, *59*(3), 203–208. doi:10.1037/1065-9293.59.3.203

Grawitch, M. J., Gottschalk, M., & Munz, D. C. (2006). The path to a healthy workplace: A critical review linking healthy workplace practices, employee well-being, and organizational improvements. *Consulting Psychology Journal: Practice and Research*, *58*(3), 129–147. doi:10.1037/1065-9293.58.3.129

Greene, G. (1974). The third man. In G. Greene (Ed.), *The third man and the fallen idol* (pp. 3–148). London: Heinemann.

Greenhaus, J. H., Collins, K. M., & Shaw, J. D. (2003). The relation between work–family balance and quality of life. *Journal of Vocational Behavior*, *63*(3), 510–531. doi:10.1016/S0001-8791(02)00042-8

Green, S., Anderson, S., & Shivers, S. (1996). Demographics and organisational influences on leader-member exchange and related work attitudes. *Organizational Behavior and Human Decision Processes*, *66*(2), 203–214. doi:10.1006/obhd.1996.0049

Greve, H. R., & Taylor, A. (2000). Innovations as catalysts for organizational change: Shifts in organizational cognition and search. *Administrative Science Quarterly*, *45*(1), 54–80. doi:10.2307/2666979

Grimes, S. M., & Ji, H. P. (2014). MendeLIMS: A web-based laboratory information management system for clinical genome sequencing. *BMC Bioinformatics*, *15*(1), 290. doi:10.1186/1471-2105-15-290 PMID:25159034

Gruzd, A., Wellman, B., & Takhteyev, Y. (2011). Imagining Twitter as an Imagined Community. *The American Behavioral Scientist*, *55*(10), 1294–1318. doi:10.1177/0002764211409378

GSA. (2019). *Infinium Global Screening Array-24 Kit*. Retrieved from https://www.illumina.com/products/by-type/microarray-kits/infinium-global-screening.html

Guajardo, P. H., Mato, D., Grimaldo, H., Gacel-Ávila, J., Lemaitre, M. J., Guarga, R., & Ramírez, R. (2018). *Tendencias de la educación superior en América Latina y el Caribe 2018*. Academic Press.

Gulati, R. (1995). Does familiarity breed trust? The implications of repeated ties for contractual choice in alliances. *Academy of Management Journal, 38*(1), 85–112.

Gummadi, A., & Devi, A. (2013). An empirical study on the relationship between determinants of employee engagement among the banking professionals of Guntur urban region. *Global Journal of Commerce and Management Perspective, 2*(5), 23–28.

Gunasekare, U. (2015). *Mixed Research Method as the Third Research Paradigm: A Literature Review.* University of Kelaniya.

Gunawan, D. D., & Huarng, K. H. (2015). Viral effects of social network and media on consumers' purchase intention. *Journal of Business Research, 68*(11), 2237–2241. doi:10.1016/j.jbusres.2015.06.004

Gupta, V., & Kumar, S. (2012). Impact of performance appraisal justice on employee engagement: A study of Indian professionals. *Employee Relations, 35*(1), 61–78. doi:10.1108/01425451311279410

Gustin, S. (2011). IBM Watson Super Computer Wins Practice Jeopardy Round. *Wired Business Online publication.* Retrieved from https://www.wired.com/2011/01/ibm- watson-jeopardy/

Guttman, L. (1954). Some necessary conditions for common-factor analysis. *Psychometrika, 19*(2), 149–161. doi:10.1007/BF02289162

Guzmán, J. G., Ramos, J. S., Seco, A. A., & Esteban, A. S. (2010). How to get mature global virtual teams: A framework to improve team process management in distributed software teams. *Software Quality Journal, 18*(4), 409–435. doi:10.100711219-010-9096-5

Haan, D. W. (2008). *Violence as an essential contested concept: Violence in Europe.* New York: Springer New York.

Haggard, S. (2013) *The maturing of the MOOC.* Department for Business, Innovation and Skills. Bis Research paper 130. Retrieved from http://hdl.voced.edu.au/10707/270884.September2013

Hair, J. F., Hult, G. T. M., Ringle, C. M., & Sarstedt, M. (2014). *A primer on partial least squares structural equation modeling (PLS-SEM).* Thousand Oaks, CA: Sage.

Hair, J. F., Ringle, C. M., & Sarstedt, M. (2011). PLS-SEM: Indeed a silver bullet. *Journal of Marketing Theory and Practice, 19*(2), 139–151. doi:10.2753/MTP1069-6679190202

Hair, J. F., Sarstedt, M., Ringle, C., & Mena, J. A. (2012). An assessment of the use of partial least squares structural equation modeling in marketing research. *Journal of the Academy of Marketing Science, 40*(3), 414–433. doi:10.100711747-011-0261-6

Hajli, N. (2015). Social commerce constructs and consumer's intention to buy. *International Journal of Information Management, 35*(2), 183–191. doi:10.1016/j.ijinfomgt.2014.12.005

Halpern, A. (2018, April). Skin lesion analysis toward melanoma detection: A challenge at the 2017 international symposium on biomedical imaging (isbi), hosted by the international skin imaging collaboration (isic). In *2018 IEEE 15th International Symposium on Biomedical Imaging (ISBI 2018)* (pp. 168-172). IEEE.

Handa, M., & Gulati, A. (2014). Employee Engagement Does Individual Personality Matter. *Journal of Management Research, 14*(1), 57–67.

Harakalova, M., Nijman, I. J., Medic, J., Mokry, M., Renkens, I., Blankensteijn, J. D., ... Cuppen, E. (2011). Genomic DNA Pooling Strategy for Next-Generation Sequencing-Based Rare Variant Discovery in Abdominal Aortic Aneurysm Regions of Interest - Challenges and Limitations. *Journal of Cardiovascular Translational Research*, *4*(3), 271–280. doi:10.100712265-011-9263-5 PMID:21360310

Harej, K., & Horvat, R. V. (2007). Project Management Principles and Virtual Teams for Information Systems Development: Preliminary Proposal. In *2007 29th International Conference on Information Technology Interfaces* (pp. 483–487). Academic Press. 10.1109/ITI.2007.4283819

Harrison, D. A., Newman, D. A., & Roth, P. L. (2006). How important are job attitudes? Meta-analytic comparisons of integrative behavioural outcomes and time sequences. *Academy of Management Journal*, *49*(2), 305–325. doi:10.5465/amj.2006.20786077

Hart, B. (2015). *A shame of Nigeria: Statistics of violence against women*. Retrieved 3rd November, 2016 from www.naija.com/430683-every-fourth-nigerian-woman-suufers-domestic-violence https://www.unicef.org/nigeria/.../Nigeria-demographic-and-health-survey- 2013.pdf

Harter, J. K., Schmidt, F. L., & Hayes, T. L. (2002). Business-unit-level relationship between employee satisfaction, employee engagement, and business outcomes: A meta-analysis. *The Journal of Applied Psychology*, *87*(2), 268–279. doi:10.1037/0021-9010.87.2.268 PMID:12002955

Hasan, L. (2013). Heuristic Evaluation of Three Jordanian University Websites. *Informatics in Education*, *12*(2), 231–251.

Hasan, M., & Zhou, S. N. (2015). Knowledge Management in Global Organisations. *International Business Research*, *8*(6), 165–173. doi:10.5539/ibr.v8n6p165

Hasibuan, Z. A., & Dantes, G. R. (2012). Priority of key success factors (KSFS) on enterprise resource planning (ERP) system implementation life cycle. *Journal of Enterprise Resource Planning Studies*, *2*, 1–15. doi:10.5171/2011.122627

Hassan, W. K. A. (2016). A Survey of Current Research on Captcha. *International Journal of Computer Science and Engineering Survey*, *7*(3), 141–157.

Havill, L. (2010). A new type of engagement. *The CPA Journal*, *80*(7), 14.

Hawking, S., Tegmark, M., Russell, S., & Wilczek, F. (2014). Transcending complacency on Super-intelligent machines. *Hoffpost*. Online publication. http://www.huffingtonpost.com/stephen-hawking/artificial-intelligenceb5174265.html

Hawk, S., Kaiser, K. M., Goles, T., Bullen, C. V., Simon, J. C., Beath, C. M., ... Frampton, K. (2012). The information technology workforce: A comparison of critical skills of clients and service providers. *Information Systems Management*, *29*(1), 2–12. doi:10.1080/10580530.2012.634292

Healthcare Financial Management Association. (2011). Open workspace environment improves employee engagement. *HFM Magazine*, *65*(10), 30.

Hebrard, E., & Siala, M. (2007). *Mistral 2.0. LAAS-CNRS*. Universite de Toulouse, CNRS.

Heidary Dahooie, J., Beheshti Jazan Abadi, E., Vanaki, A. S., & Firoozfar, H. R. (2018). Competency-based IT personnel selection using a hybrid SWARA and ARAS-G methodology. *Human Factors and Ergonomics in Manufacturing & Service Industries*, *28*(1), 5–16. doi:10.1002/hfm.20713

Help Age International. (2018). *Global AgeWatch Index 2018*. Retrieved from http://www.helpage.org/global-agewatch/

Hendee, C. (2014). *Teachers have mixed feelings on using social media in classrooms*. Retrieved from https://www.bizjournals.com/denver/news/2014/02/11/teachers-have-mixed-feelings-on-using.html

Henderson, R. (2018). *2018 Randstad Talent Trends Report*. Retrieved from https://www.randstad.it/hrsolutions/talent-trends-report-2018.pdf

Hendon, M., Powell, L., & Wimmer, H. (2017). Emotional intelligence and communication levels in information technology professionals. *Computers in Human Behavior, 71*, 165–171. doi:10.1016/j.chb.2017.01.048

Hendry, E. R. (2014). What happens when artificial intelligence turns on us? *Smithsonian.com*. Retrieved from http://www.smithsonianmag.com/innovation/what-happens-when- artificial-intelligence-turns-us-180949415/

Hennig-Thurau, T., Gwinner, K., Walsh, G., & Gremler, D. (2004). Electronic Word-of-Mouth Via Consumer Opinion Platforms: What Motivates Consumers to Articulate Themselves on the Internet? *Journal of Interactive Marketing, 18*(1), 38–52. doi:10.1002/dir.10073

Henseler, J., Ringle, C. M., & Sinkovics, R. R. (2009). The use of partial least squares path modeling in international marketing. *Advances in International Marketing, 20*, 277-319.

Hentenryck, M. (2005). The comet programming language and system. *Principles and Practice of Constraint Programming - CP 2005, 11th International Conference*, 881-881.

Hentenryck, M., Saraswat, V., & Deville, Y. (1998). Design, implementation, and evaluation of the constraint language cc(FD). *The Journal of Logic Programming, 37*(1-3), 139–164. doi:10.1016/S0743-1066(98)10006-7

Herath, T., & Rao, H. R. (2009). Protection motivation and deterrence: A framework for security policy compliance in organisations. *European Journal of Information Systems, 18*(2), 106–125. doi:10.1057/ejis.2009.6

Herranz-Sánchez, E., Colomo-Palacios, R., & de Amescua-Seco, A. (2015). Gamiware: A gamification platform for software process improvement. *Communications in Computer and Information Science, 543*, 127–139. doi:10.1007/978-3-319-24647-5_11

Hertel, G., Geister, S., & Konradt, U. (2005). Managing virtual teams: A review of current empirical research. *Human Resource Management Review, 15*(1), 69–95. doi:10.1016/j.hrmr.2005.01.002

Hewitt Associates LLC. (2004). *Research Brief: employee engagement higher at double digit growth companies*. Retrieved from www.hewitt.com

Hidalgo, J. G., & Alvarez, G. (2011). CAPTCHAs: An Artificial Intelligence Application to Web Security. Advances in Computers, 83, 109–181.

Hill, E. J., Allen, S., Jacob, J., Bair, A. F., Bikhazi, S. L., Van Langeveld, A., ... Walker, E. (2007). Work family facilitation: Expanding theoretical understanding through qualitative exploration. *Advances in Developing Human Resources, 9*(4), 507–526. doi:10.1177/1523422307305490

Hill, T. P. (1977). On goods and services. *Review of Income and Wealth, 23*(4), 315–338. doi:10.1111/j.1475-4991.1977.tb00021.x

Hinduja, S., & Patchin, J. W. (2010). Bullying, cyberbullying, and suicide. *Archives of Suicide Research, 14*(3), 206–221. doi:10.1080/13811118.2010.494133 PMID:20658375

Hirshfield, L., Bobko, P., Barelka, A. J., Costa, M. R., Funke, G. J., Mancuso, V. F., & Knott, B. A. (2019). The role of human operators' suspicion in the detection of cyber attacks. Cyber Law, Privacy, and Security: Concepts, Methodologies, Tools, and Applications, 1482-1499.

Ho, S. Y., & Frampton, K. (2010). A competency model for the information technology workforce: Implications for training and selection. CAIS, 27, 5.

Hoch, J. E., & Kozlowski, S. W. J. (2014). Leading virtual teams: Hierarchical leadership, structural supports, and shared team leadership. *The Journal of Applied Psychology*, *99*(3), 390–403. doi:10.1037/a0030264 PMID:23205494

Hochreiter, S., & Schmidhuber, J. (1997). Long Short-Term Memory. *Neural Computation*, *9*(8), 1–32. PMID:9377276

Holsapple, C., Sena, M., & Wagner, W. (2019). The perceived success of ERP systems for decision support. *Information Technology Management*, *20*(1), 1–7. doi:10.100710799-017-0285-9

Holt, M., Lang, B., & Sutton, S. G. (2017). Potential employees' ethical perceptions of active monitoring: The dark side of data analytics. *Journal of Information Systems*, *31*(2), 107–124. doi:10.2308/isys-51580

Holton, D. (2013). *The spectrum of opinion about MOOCs.* Centre for Teaching and Learning Excellence. Embry-Riddle Aeronautical University.

Holtzhausen, N., & de Klerk, J. J. (2018). Servant leadership and the Scrum team's effectiveness. *Leadership and Organization Development Journal*, *39*(7), 873–882. doi:10.1108/LODJ-05-2018-0193

Hong, J., Lee, W., Ha Kim, J., Kim, J., Park, I., & Har, D. (2014). Smart water grid: desalination water management platform. In *Desalination and Water Treatment*. Taylor & Francis.

Hong, I. B., & Cha, H. S. (2013). The mediating role of consumer trust in an online merchant in predicting purchase intention. *International Journal of Information Management*, *33*(6), 927–939. doi:10.1016/j.ijinfomgt.2013.08.007

Hong, J., Suh, E.-H., Kim, J., & Kim, S. (2009). Context-aware system for proactive personalized service based on context history. *Expert Systems with Applications*, *36*(4), 7448–7457. doi:10.1016/j.eswa.2008.09.002

Hon, L. C., & Varathan, K. D. (2015). Cyberbullying Detection System on Twitter. *International Journal of Information Systems and Engineering*, *1*(1), 1–11. doi:10.24924/ijise/2015.11/v3.iss1/36.47

Horlach, B., Drews, P., Schirmer, I., & Boehmann, T. (2017, January 4). *Increasing the Agility of IT Delivery: Five Types of Bimodal IT Organization*. doi:10.24251/HICSS.2017.656

Hortigüela-Alcalá, D., Sánchez-Santamaría, J., Pérez-Pueyo, Á., & Abella-García, V. (2019). Social networks to promote motivation and learning in higher education from the students' perspective. *Innovations in Education and Teaching International*, *56*(4), 412–422. doi:10.1080/14703297.2019.1579665

Horvat, R. V., Harej, K., & Rozman, T. (2006). Skill card and certification system for certified EU project manager. *28th International Conference on Information Technology Interfaces*. 10.1109/ITI.2006.1708518

Hsiao, K. L., Chuan-Chuan Lin, J., Wang, X. Y., Lu, H. P., & Yu, H. (2010). Antecedents and consequences of trust in online product recommendations: An empirical study in social shopping. *Online Information Review*, *34*(6), 935–953. doi:10.1108/14684521011099414

Huang, Q., Inkpen, D., Zhang, J., & Van Bruwaene, D. (2018). Cyberbullying Intervention Based on Convolutional Neural Networks. *Proceedings of the First Workshop on Trolling, Aggression and Cyberbullying (TRAC-2018)*, 61–70. Retrieved from http://aclweb.org/anthology/W18-44%0A700

Hughes, S., Keller, E. W., & Hertz, G. T. (2010). Homeland security initiatives and background checks in higher education. *New Directions for Institutional Research*, *2010*(146), 51–62. doi:10.1002/ir.342

Hulland, J. (1999). Use of partial least squares (PLS) in strategic management research: A review of four recent studies. *Strategic Management Journal*, *20*(2), 195–204. doi:10.1002/(SICI)1097-0266(199902)20:2<195::AID-SMJ13>3.0.CO;2-7

Huls, C., Piggott, J., & Zwiers, T. (2014). Influence of cultural factors on establishing trust within Global Virtual Teams. *Scifiempire.Net*. Retrieved from http://scifiempire.net/wordpress/wp-content/uploads/2011/12/Influence-of-cultural-factors-on-establishing-trust-within-Global-Virtual-Teams.pdf

Human factors. (2011). Healthcare comes home: Chapter 3. In *What is human factors*. The National Academies Press.

Hu, Q., Dinev, T., Hart, P., & Cooke, D. (2012). Managing employee compliance with information security policies: The critical role of top management and organisational culture. *Decision Sciences Journal*, *43*(4), 615–659. doi:10.1111/j.1540-5915.2012.00361.x

Hu, Q., West, R., & Smarandescu, L. (2015). The Role of Self-Control in Information Security Violations: Insights from a Cognitive Neuroscience Perspective. *Journal of Management Information Systems*, *31*(4), 6–48. doi:10.1080/07421 222.2014.1001255

Hüsing, T., Korte, W. B., & Dashja, E. (2015). *e-Skills in Europe Trends and Forecasts for the European ICT Professional and Digital Leadership Labour Markets (2015-2020)*. Empirica Working Paper.

Hussain, O., Dillon, Th., Chang, E., & Hussain, F. (2010). Transactional risk-based decision making system in e-business interactions. *International Journal of ComputSystSci & Eng*, *1*, 15–28.

Hwang, I., Kim, D., Kim, T., & Kim, S. (2017). Why not comply with information security? An empirical approach for the causes of non-compliance. *Online Information Review*, *41*(1), 2–18. doi:10.1108/OIR-11-2015-0358

Iacob, M.-E., & Jonkers, H. (2006). Quantitative analysis of enterprise architectures. *Interoperability of Enterprise Software and Applications*.

IBEF. (2019). *IT & ITeS Industry in India*. Indian Brand Equity Foundation. Accessed from https://www.ibef.org/industry/information-technology-india.aspx

IBEF. (n.d.). *Industry - India Brand Equity Foundation*. Retrieved December 22, 2018, from http://www.ibef.org/industry.aspx

IBM Company. (2006). *IBM ILOG CP*. Author.

Idris, H., Adaja, J., Audu, S., & Aye, G. A. (2016). Analysis of the causes and the effects of sexual harassment on the performance of female employees in some selected organizations in Kogi state, Nigeria. *International Journal of Democratic and Development Studies*, *2*(2), 31–34.

IEEE. Computer Society. (2014). Guide to the Software Engineering Body of Knowledge (SWEBOK(R)): Version 3.0. IEEE Computer Society Press.

Ifinedo, P., & Olsen, D. H. (2015). An Empirical Research on the Impacts of organisational decisions' locus, tasks structure rules, knowledge, and IT function's value on ERP system success. *International Journal of Production Research*, *53*(8), 2554–2568. doi:10.1080/00207543.2014.991047

Ikedinachi, A. P., Misra, S., Assibong, P. A., Olu-Owolabi, E. F., Maskeliunas, R., & Damasevicius, R. (2019). Artificial Intelligence, Smart Classrooms and Online Education in the 21st Century: Implications for Human Development. *Journal of Cases on Information Technology*, *21*(3), 66–79. doi:10.4018/JCIT.2019070105

Ikenwe, I. J., Igbinovia, O. M., & Elogie, A. A. (2016). Information Security in the Digital Age: The Case of Developing Countries. *Chinese Librarianship*, *42*, 16–24.

Illumina, L. I. M. S. (2019). *Illumina LIMS*. Retrieved from https://support.illumina.com.cn/array/array_software/illumina_lims.html

ILO. (2008). Skills for Improved Productivity, Employment Growth and Development. In *International Labour Conference Proceeding* (97th Session). Geneva: ILO.

Independent News. (2015). Retrieved from http://www.independent.co.uk/life-style/gadgets-and-tech/news/stephen-hawking-artificial-intelligence-could-wipe-out-humanity-when-it-gets-too-clever-as-humans-a6686496.html

Institute for opinion survey Allensbach. (2014). *Study conditions in 2014 - Study finance, foreign travel, and living situation*. Retrieved from http://www.sts-kd.de/reemtsma/Studie-Lang-Allensbach-2014h.pdf

International Labour Organization. (n.d.). *International Standard Classification of Occupations*. Retrieved July 2017, from http://www.ilo.org/public/english/bureau/stat/isco/

ISO 9241-11. (1998). *Ergonomic requirements for office work with visual display terminals (vdts) part 11: Guidance on usability. International.*

ISO. (2018). *Ergonomics of human-system interaction -- Part 11: Usability: Definitions and concepts*. ISO. Retrieved from https://www.iso.org/standard/63500.html

Ivancevich, J. (1998). *Human Resource Management* (7th ed.). New York: McGraw-Hill.

Jabar, M. A., Usman, U. A., & Awal, A. (2013). Assessing The Usability Of University Websites From Users ' Perspective. *Australian Journal of Basic and Applied Sciences*, *7*(10), 98–111.

Jackson, N. (2011). *Infographic: Using Social Media to Build Brand Loyalty*. Retrieved from: http://www.theatlantic.com/technology/archive/2011/07/infographic-using-social-media-to- uild-brand-loyalty/241701/

Jacobson, S., Shepherd, J., D'Aquila, M., & Carter, K. (2007). The ERP market sizing report, 2006–2011. *AMR Research*, 29.

Jaffar, J., Michaylov, S., Stuckey, P. J., & Yap, R. H. C. (1992, May). The CLP(r) language and system. *ACM Transactions on Programming Languages and Systems*, *14*(3), 339–395. doi:10.1145/129393.129398

Jagero, P. N., Nhendo, C., Sithole, N., Takaingenhamo, C., & Guvava, N. (2014). An Assessment of the Usability of the Africa University Digital Library, Mutare, Zimbabwe. Academic Press.

Jaggi, S., & Bahl, S. K. (2016). Exploring the impact of work life balance on the employee and organisational growth. *International Journal of Engineering and Management Research*, *6*(2), 1–5.

Jain, S., & Sivaselvan, B. (2012). Usability Aspects of HCI in the Design of CAPTCHAs. *Proceedings of IEEE International Conference on Computational Intelligence and Computing Research 2012*. 10.1109/ICCIC.2012.6510223

Jaksic, M., & Jaksic, M. (2013). Performance Management and Employee Satisfaction. *Montenegrin Journal of Economics*, *9*(1), 85–92.

Jambhekar, N. D., Misra, S., & Dhawale, C. A. (2016). Mobile computing security threats and solution. *International Journal of Pharmacy and Technology*, *8*(4), 23075–23086.

James, L. R. (1982). Aggregation bias in estimates of perceptual agreement. *The Journal of Applied Psychology*, *67*(2), 219–229. doi:10.1037/0021-9010.67.2.219

Janssen, P., & de Neve, H. (1988). *Studeren en doceren aan het Hoger Onderwijs*. Leuven, Belgium: Uitgeverij Acco.

Jaschik, S. (2013). Feminist Anti-MOOC. *Inside Higher Ed*. Available: http://www.insidehighered.com/news/2013/08/19/feminist-professors-create-alternative-moocs

Jasinski, J. L. (2001). Theoretical explanations for violence against women. In *Sourcebook on violence against women.* New Delhi: SAGE Publications. Retrieved 3rd March, 2017 from https://books.google.com.ng/books?hl=en&lr=&id=v 7n5zP3uKn8C&oi=fnd&pg=PA5&dq=how+subculture+of+violence+theory+explain+domestic+violence+against+ women&ots=DHMEdnggP3&sig=9Ngztb0RSYSrjH0diXZBo1-Pzi8&redir_esc=y#v=onepage&q&f=false

Jaska, P. V., & Hogan, P. T. (2006). Effective management of the information technology function. *Management Research News*, *29*(8), 464–470. doi:10.1108/01409170610692789

Javad, A., & Weistroffer, H. R. (2016). Understanding Deterrence Theory in Security Compliance Behavior: A Quantitative Meta-Analysis Approach. *SAIS 2016 Proceedings.* Retrieved from http://aisel.aisnet.org/sais2016/28

Javelin Strategy & Research. (2018). *2018 Identity Fraud: Fraud Enters a New Era of Complexity.* Available online https://www.javelinstrategy.com/coverage-area/2018-identity-fraud-fraud-enters-new-era-complexity

Jayathunga, D. P., Jayawardana, J. M. D. R., Wimaladharma, S. T. C. I., & Herath, H. M. U. M. (2017). Usability Recommendations for an Academic Website : A Case Study. *International Journal of Scientific and Research Publications*, *7*(4), 145–152.

Jenkins, S., & Delbridge, R. (2013). Context matters: Examining 'soft' and 'hard' approaches to employee engagement in two workplaces. *International Journal of Human Resource Management*, *24*(14), 2670–2691. doi:10.1080/0958519 2.2013.770780

Joh, E., & White, W. (2018). How We Can Apply AI, and Deep Learning to our HR Functional Transformation and Core Talent Processes? *Student Works.* Retrieved from https://digitalcommons.ilr.cornell.edu/student/200

Johnson, P., Ullberg, J., Buschle, M., Franke, U., & Shahzad, K. (2013). P 2 AMF: predictive, probabilistic architecture modeling framework. *International IFIP Working Conference on Enterprise Interoperability*, 104–117.

Johnson, P., Johansson, E., Sommestad, T., & Ullberg, J. (2007). A Tool for Enterprise Architecture Analysis. *11th IEEE International Enterprise Distributed Object Computing Conference*, 142–142.

Johnson, P., Lagerström, R., Närman, P., & Simonsson, M. (2007). Enterprise architecture analysis with extended influence diagrams. *Information Systems Frontiers*, *9*(2–3), 163–180. doi:10.100710796-007-9030-y

Johnson, R., & Onwuegbuzie, A. (2004). *Mixed Methods Research: A Research Paradigm Whose Time Has Come.* Sage Journals.

Joinson, C. (2002, June). Managing virtual teams. *HRMagazine*, 69–73. doi:10.1002/ert.20205

Jones, K. R. (2017). *Law Enforcement Use of Social Media as a Crime Fighting Tool. Use Of Social Media As A Crime Fighting Tool* (Master's thesis). University of Oregon.

Jonkers, H., Band, I., & Quartel, D. (2012). *The ArchiSurance Case Study.* The Open Group Case Study (Document Number Y121).

Jonkers, H., Band, I., & Quartel, D. (2012a). *ArchiSurance Case Study.* The Open Group.

Jonkers, H., Lankhorst, M., Van Buuren, R., Hoppenbrouwers, S., Bonsangue, M., & Van Der Torre, L. (2004). Concepts for modeling enterprise architectures. *International Journal of Cooperative Information Systems*, *13*(03), 257–287. doi:10.1142/S0218843004000985

Jorgenson, D. W., & Vu, K. (2005). Information technology and the world economy. *The Scandinavian Journal of Economics*, *107*(4), 631–650. doi:10.1111/j.1467-9442.2005.00430.x

Jose, G., & Mampilly, S. R. (2012). Satisfaction with HR Practices and Employee Engagement: A Social Exchange. *Perspective Journal of Economics and Behavioral Studies*, *4*(7), 423–430.

Joseph, D., Ang, S., Chang, R. H., & Slaughter, S. A. (2010). Practical intelligence in IT: Assessing soft skills of IT professionals. *Communications of the ACM*, *53*(2), 149–154. doi:10.1145/1646353.1646391

JQuery. (2019). *JQuery*. Retrieved from http://jquery.com/

JSON. (2019). *Working with JSON*. Retrieved from https://developer.mozilla.org/en-US/docs/Learn/JavaScript/Objects/JSON

Jula, A., Sundararajan, E., & Othman, Z. (2014). Cloud computing service composition: A systematic literature review. *Expert Systems with Applications*, *41*(8), 3809–3824. doi:10.1016/j.eswa.2013.12.017

Junaini, S. N. (2002). Navigation Design and Usability Evaluation of the Malysian Public University Websites. In *Second National Conference on Cognitive Science* (pp. 181–189). Kuching.

Junco, R., Elavsky, C. M., & Heiberger, G. (2013). Putting twitter to the test: Assessing outcomes for student collaboration, engagement and success. *British Journal of Educational Technology*, *44*(2), 273–287. doi:10.1111/j.1467-8535.2012.01284.x

Kahn, W. A. (1990). Psychological conditions of personal engagement and disengagement at work. *Academy of Management Journal*, *33*(4), 692–724.

Kainda, R., Flechais, I., & Roscoe, A. W. (2010). Security and Usability: Analysis and Evaluation. *2010 International Conference on Availability, Reliability and Security*, 275-282. 10.1109/ARES.2010.77

Kaiser, H. F. (1960). The application of electronic computers to factor analysis. *Educational and Psychological Measurement*, *20*(1), 141–151. doi:10.1177/001316446002000116

Kamoun, F., & Halaweh, M. (2012). User Interface Design and E-Commerce Security Perception: An Empirical Study. *International Journal of E-Business Research*, *8*(2), 15–32. doi:10.4018/jebr.2012040102

Kanakaris, V., Lampropoulos, G., & Siakas, K. (2019). A Survey and a Case-Study Regarding Social Media Security and Privacy on Greek Future IT Professionals. *International Journal of Human Capital and Information Technology Professionals*, *10*(1), 22–37. doi:10.4018/IJHCITP.2019010102

Kanayo, O. (2014). Poverty incidence and reduction strategies in Nigeria: Challenges of meeting 2015 MDG targets. *Journal of Economics*, *5*(2), 201–217. doi:10.1080/09765239.2014.11884997

Kane, J. S., & Lawler, E. E. (1979). Performance appraisal effectiveness. Its assessment and determinants. *Research in Organizational Behavior*, *1*(1), 425–478.

Kapitsaki, G., Kateros, D. A., Foukarakis, I. E., Prezerakos, G. N., Kaklamani, D. I., & Venieris, I. S. (2007). *Service Composition: State of the art and future challenges*. Paper presented at the 2007 16th IST Mobile and Wireless Communications Summit. doi:10.1109/ISTMWC.2007.4299297

Kaplan, A. M., & Haenlein, M. (2010). Users of the world, unite! The challenges and opportunities of Social Media. *Business Horizons*, *53*(1), 59–68. doi:10.1016/j.bushor.2009.09.003

Kappelman, L. A., Jones, M. C., Johnson, V., McLean, E. R., & Boonme, K. (2016). Skills for success at different stages of an IT professional's career. *Communications of the ACM*, *59*(8), 64–70. doi:10.1145/2888391

Karande, S. H., Jain, V. K., & Ghatule, A. P. (2012). ERP implementation: Critical success factors for Indian Universities and higher educational institutions. *Pragyaan Journal of Information Technology*, *10*(2), 24–29.

Karlsson, F., Åström, J., & Karlsson, M. (2015). Information security culture – state-of-the-art review between 2000 and 2013. *Information & Computer Security*, *23*(3), 246–285. doi:10.1108/ICS-05-2014-0033

Kasparove, G. (1996). The day I sensed a new kind of intelligence. *Time Magazine*. Retrieved from http://content.time.com/time/subscriber/article/0,33009,984305-1,00.html

Kaspersky, E., & Furnell, S. (2014). A security education Q&A. *Information Management & Computer Security*, *22*(2), 130–133. doi:10.1108/IMCS-01-2014-0006

Katuo, A., & Budhwar, P. (2006). Human resource management systems andorganizational performance: A test of a mediating model in the Greek manufacturing context. *International Journal of Human Resource Management*, *17*(7), 1223–1253. doi:10.1080/09585190600756525

Katz, R., & Tushman, M. (1979). Communication patterns, project performance, and task characteristics: An empirical evaluation and integration in an R&D setting. *Organizational Behavior and Human Performance*, *23*(2), 139–162. doi:10.1016/0030-5073(79)90053-9

Kaufmann, M. (2014, February 17). Erreichbarkeit nach Dienstschluss Deutsche Konzerne kämpfen gegen den Handy-Wahn. *Spiegel Online*. Retrieved from http://www.spiegel.de/karriere/berufsleben/erreichbar-nach-dienstschluss-massnahmen-der-konzerne-a-954029.html

Kaur, K., & Behal, S. (2014). Captcha and Its Techniques: A Review. *International Journal of Computer Science and Information Technologies*, *5*(5), 6341–6344.

Kaur, K., & Behal, S. (2014). CAPTCHA and its techniques: A review. *International Journal of Computer Science and Information Technologies*, *5*(5), 6341–6344.

Kaur, R., & Garg, S. (2008). Addressing domestic violence against women: An unfinished agenda. *Indian Journal of Community Medicine*, *33*(2), 73–76. doi:10.4103/0970-0218.40871 PMID:19967027

Kaur, S., Kaur, K., & Parminder, K. (2016). Analysis of website usability evaluation methods. In *Computing for Sustainable Global Development (INDIACom), 2016 3rd International Conference on* (pp. 1043–1046). IEEE. Retrieved from http://ieeexplore.ieee.org/abstract/document/7724420/

Kearney, A. T. (2013). Understanding the Needs and Consequences of the Ageing Consumer. *The Consumer Goods Forum*. Retrieved from https://www.atkearney.com/documents/10192/682603/Understanding+the+Needs+and+Consequences+of+the+Aging+Consumer.pdf/6c25ffa3-0999-4b5c-8ff1-afdca0744fdc

Kersley, B., Alpin, C., Forth, J., Bryson, A., Bewley, H., Dix, G., & Oxenbridge, S. (2006). *Inside the Workplace: First finding WERS 2004*. London: Routledge. Retrieved January 12, 2019, from www.routledge.com/textbooks/0415378133/pdf/insideWP.pdf

Khalil, I., Zahoor, K., & Amber, S. (2018). Human Computer Interaction and Security (HCI-Sec). *International Journal of Scientific & Engineering Research.*, *9*(4), 1549–1553. doi:10.14299/ijser.2018.04.04

Khan, B. H., & Joshi, V. (2006). E-Learning Who, What & How? *Journal of Creative Communications*, *1*(1), 61–75. doi:10.1177/097325860500100104

Khan, H. U., & AlShare, K. A. (2019). Violators versus non-violators of information security measures in organizations - A study of distinguishing factors. *Journal of Organizational Computing and Electronic Commerce*, *29*(1), 4–23. doi:10.1080/10919392.2019.1552743

Khan, M. A. (2010). Effects of human resource management practices on organizational performance - An empirical study of oil and gas industry in Pakistan. European Journal of Economics. *Finance and Administrative Sciences*, *24*, 157–175.

Khao, B., Harris, P., & Hartman, S. (2010). Information security governance of enterprise information systems: An approach to legislative compliant. *International Journal of Management and Information Systems*, *14*(3), 49–55.

Kim Lau, S., Yang Ang, A., & Winley, G. (1999). Alignment of technology and information systems tasks: A Singapore perspective. *Industrial Management & Data Systems*, *99*(6), 235–246. doi:10.1108/02635579910253788

Kim Mariott, P. S. (1998). *Programming with Constraints, An introduction*. MIT Press.

Kimble, C. (2011). Building effective virtual teams: How to overcome the problems of trust and identity in virtual teams. *Global Business & Organizational Excellence*, *30*(2), 6–15. doi:10.1002/joe.20364

Kim, D. J., Ferrin, D. L., & Rao, H. R. (2008). A trust-based consumer decision-making model in electronic commerce: The role of trust, perceived risk, and their antecedents. *Decision Support Systems*, *44*(2), 544–564. doi:10.1016/j.dss.2007.07.001

Kim, E. B. (2014). Recommendations for information security awareness training for college students. *Information Management & Computer Security*, *22*(1), 115–126. doi:10.1108/IMCS-01-2013-0005

Kim, G., Shin, B., Kim, K. K., & Lee, H. G. (2011). IT capabilities, process-oriented dynamic capabilities, and firm financial performance. *Journal of the Association for Information Systems*, *12*(7), 487–517. doi:10.17705/1jais.00270

Kim, J., Kang, S., & Lee, K. H. (2018). How social capital impacts the purchase intention of sustainable fashion products. *Journal of Business Research*. doi:10.1016/j.jbusres.2018.10.010

Kim, J., & Lennon, Sh. (2017). *Descriptive Content Analysis on E-Service Research. International Journal of Service Science, Management, Engineering, and Technology*. doi:10.4018/IJSSMET.2017010102

Kim, Y., & Srivastava, J. (2007, August). Impact of social influence in e-commerce decision making. In *Proceedings of the ninth international conference on Electronic commerce* (pp. 293-302). ACM. 10.1145/1282100.1282157

King, R. C., Xia, W., Campbell Quick, J., & Sethi, V. (2005). Socialization and organizational outcomes of information technology professionals. *Career Development International*, *10*(1), 26–51. doi:10.1108/13620430510577619

Kinsey, C. (2009). Using rewards and benefits to motivate and engage. *Strategic HR Review*, *8*(2), 47. doi:10.1108hr.2009.37208bab.005

Kish, L. (1965). *Survey sampling*. New York: John Wiley and Sons Inc.

Kitto, S., & Higgins, V. (2010). Working around ERPs in technological universities. *Science, Technology & Human Values*, *35*(1), 29–54. doi:10.1177/0162243908329535

Kiyea, C., & Yusuf, A. B. (2014). Usability Evaluation of Some Selected Nigerian Universities' Websites. *International Journal of Computers and Applications*, *104*(3), 6–11. doi:10.5120/18180-9071

Klaas, B. S., Olson-Buchanan, J. B., & Anna-Katherine, W. (2012). The determinants of alternative forms of workplace voice: An integrative perspective. *Journal of Management*, *38*(1), 314–345. doi:10.1177/0149206311423823

Kliner, K., Rennert, D., & Richter, M. (2015, July). *BKK Gesundheitsatlas*. Retrieved October 17, 2015, from http://www.bkk-dachverband.de/fileadmin/publikationen/gesundheitsatlas/BKK_Gesundheitsatlas_2015.pdf

Kluever, K. A., & Zanibbi, R. (2009). Balancing usability and security in a video CAPTCHA. *Proceedings of the 5th Symposium on Usable Privacy and Security 2009*. 10.1145/1572532.1572551

Koch, H., Gonzalez, E., & Leidner, D. (2012). Bridging the work/social divide: The emotional response to organizational social networking sites. *European Journal of Information Systems*, *21*(6), 699–717. doi:10.1057/ejis.2012.18

Ko, D. G., Kirsch, L. J., & King, W. R. (2005). Antecedents of knowledge transfer from consultants to clients in enterprise system implementations. *Management Information Systems Quarterly*, *29*(1), 59–85. doi:10.2307/25148668

Koh, R. J. (2018). The Influence of human resource management practices on employee performance in the manufacturing sector in Malaysia. *International Journal of Human Resource Studies, 8*(2).

Kohlborn, T., Korthaus, A., Taizan, C., & Rosemann, M. (2009). Identification and Analysis of Business and Software Services—A Consolidated Approach. *Services Computing. IEEE Transactions on, 2*(1), 50–64. doi:10.1109/TSC.2009.6

Kohlhammer, J., May, T., & Hoffmann, M. (2009). Visual analytics for the strategic decision making process. In *Geo-Spatial Visual Analytics* (pp. 299–310). Springer. doi:10.1007/978-90-481-2899-0_23

Kolan, B., & Dzandza, P. (2018). Effect of Social Media on Academic Performance of Students in Ghanaian Universities: A Case Study of University of Ghana, Legon. *Library Philosophy and Practice (e-journal)*, 1637.

Koller, D., Ng, A., Do, C., & Chen, Z. (2013). Retention and Intention in Massive Open Online Courses. *EDUCAUSE Review Online*. Retrieved from https://er.educause.edu/articles/2013/6/retention-and-intention-in-massive-open-online-courses-in-depth

Kolowich, S. (2013). An open letter to Professor Micheal Sandel from the Philosophy Department at San Jose State University. *Chronicles of Higher Education*. Retrieved from http://chronicle.com/article/TheDocument-Open-Letter-From/138937/

Komatsu, A., Takagi, D., & Takemura, T. (2013). Human aspects of information security: An empirical study of intentional versus actual behavior. *Information Management & Computer Security*, *21*(1), 5–15. doi:10.1108/09685221311314383

Kong, E., Chadee, D., & Raman, R. (2013). Managing Indian IT professionals for global competitiveness: The role of human resource practices in developing knowledge and learning capabilities for innovation. *Knowledge Management Research and Practice*, *11*(4), 334–345. doi:10.1057/kmrp.2012.21

Konnikova, M. (2014). Will MOOCs be flukes? *The New Yorker Online publication*. Retrieved from https://www.newyorker.com/science/maria-konnikova/moocs-failure-solutions

Konrad, A. M., & Mangel, R. (2000). The impact of work-life programs on firm productivity. *Strategic Management Journal*, *21*(12), 1225–1237. doi:10.1002/1097-0266(200012)21:12<1225::AID-SMJ135>3.0.CO;2-3

Kontakos, A., & Stepp, P. (2007). *Employee engagement and fairness in the workplace*. Ithaca, NY: Center for Advanced Human Resource Studies, Cornell University.

Kossek, E. E., & Friede, A. (2006). The business case: Managerial perspectives on work and the family. In M. Pitt-Catsouphes, E. E. Kossek, & S. Sweet (Eds.), *The work and family handbook: Multi-disciplinary perspectives, methods, and approaches* (pp. 611–626). Mahwah, NJ: Lawrence Erlbaum. Retrieved from http://ellenkossek.lir.msu.edu/documents/businesscase.pdf

Kotni, D. P. (2011). *Dynamics of employee engagement: A case study,* International. *Journal of Management & Business Studies, 1*(2), 31–35.

KPMG. (2014). *Over 90 Percent Of U.S. Companies Are Changing Existing Business Models: KPMG Survey*. Retrieved from http://www.kpmg.com/us/en/issuesandinsights/articlespublications/press-releases/pages/over-90-percent-of-us-companies-are-changing-existing-business-models-kpmg-survey.aspx

Krantz, G., & Garcia-Moreno, C. (2005). Violence against women. *Journal of Epidemiology and Community Health*, *59*(10), 818–821. doi:10.1136/jech.2004.022756 PMID:16166351

Krigsman, M. (2008). *Business change failures: 9 success tips*. Retrieved from http://www.zdnet.com/blog/transformationfailures/business-change-failures-9-success-tips/1080

Kristof-Brown, A., & Guay, R. P. (2011). Person–environment fit. In APA Handbooks in Psychology. APA. doi:10.1037/12171-001

Kropf, D. (2013). Connectivism: 21st Century's New Learning Theory. *European Journal of Open, Distance and e-Learning, 16*(2), 13-24.

Krug, E. G., Dahlberg, L. L., Mercy, J. A., Zwi, A. B., & Lozano, R. (Eds.). (2002). World report on violence and health. Geneva, Switzerland: World Health Organization.

Kuchcinski, K., & Szymanek, R. (2010). *Jacop library user's guide*. Available from http://jacopguide.osolpro.com/guideJaCoP.html

Kuchcinski, K. (2019). Constraint Programming in embedded systems design: Considered helpful. *Microprocessors and Microsystems, 69*, 24–34. doi:10.1016/j.micpro.2019.05.012

Kühnel, J., Sonnentag, S., & Bledow, R. (2012). Resources and time pressure as day-level antecedents of work engagement. *Journal of Occupational and Organizational Psychology, 85*(1), 181–198. doi:10.1111/j.2044-8325.2011.02022.x

Kular, S., Gatenby, M., Rees, C., Soane, E., & Truss, K. (2008). *Employee Engagement: A literature review*. Kingston Business School: Working Paper Series, 19.

Kulluru, P. K., Shaikh, T., Bidwai, S., Mannarwar, A., & Shamlani, K. (2016). A Survey on Different Types of CAPTCHA. *IJCA Proceedings on National Conference on Advances in Computing, Communication and Networking ACCNET 2016*.

Kulwicki, A. D. (2002). The practice of honor crimes: A glimpse of domestic violence in the Arab world. *Issues in Mental Health Nursing, 23*(1), 136–138. doi:10.1080/01612840252825491 PMID:11887612

Kumar, D. P., & Swetha, G. (2011). *A prognostic examination of employee engagement from its historical roots*. International Journal of Trade. *Economics and Finance, 2*(3), 232–241.

Kumar, V., & Nanda, P. (2019). Social Media in Higher Education: A Framework for Continuous Engagement. *International Journal of Information and Communication Technology Education, 15*(1), 97–108. doi:10.4018/IJICTE.2019010107

Kummamuru, S., & Murthy, N.P. (2016). *Exploring the Complex Interface between IT Professional and HR: Building Flexibility Applying Cybernetic Concepts*. doi:10.1007/978-81-322-2380-1_10

Kurpjuweit, S., & Winter, R. (2007). Viewpoint-based Meta Model Engineering. *Proceedings of the 2nd International Workshop on Enterprise Modelling and Information Systems Architectures*, 143–161.

Kvavik, R. B. R., Katz, R. N., Beecher, K., Caruso, J., & King, P. (2002). The Promise and Performance of Enterprise Systems for Higher Education. *EDUCAUSE Center for Applied Research, 4*, 1–7.

Kwak, H., Chew, M., Rodriguez, P., Moon, S., & Ahn, Y. Y. (2007). I Tube, You Tube, Everybody Tubes: Analyzing the World's Largest User Generated Content Video System. In *Proc. IMC 2007*. ACM Press.

Kwortnik, R. J. Jr, Lynn, W. M., & Ross, W. T. Jr. (2009). Buyer monitoring: A means to insure personalized service. *JMR, Journal of Marketing Research, 46*(5), 573–583. doi:10.1509/jmkr.46.5.573

Laalaoui, Y., & Bouguila, N. (2014). Pre-run-time scheduling in real-time systems: Current researches and artificial intelligence perspectives. *Expert Systems with Applications, 41*(5), 2196–2210. doi:10.1016/j.eswa.2013.09.018

Lacante, M. (1983). Van intelligentie, persoonlijkheid, studiestrategie en studeergedrag naar studieresultaat. *Pedagogische Studiën*, *60*, 289–299.

Lacey, D. (2010). Understanding and transforming organisational security culture. *Information Management & Computer Security*, *18*(1), 4–13. doi:10.1108/09685221011035223

Lampson, B. W. (2009). Privacy and security - Usable security: How to get it. *Communications of the ACM*, *52*(11), 25–27. doi:10.1145/1592761.1592773

Langelaan, S., Bakker, A. B., Schaufeli, W. B., Van Rhenen, W., & Van Doornen, L. J. P. (2006). Do burned-out and work-engaged employees differ in the functioning of the hypothalamic-pituitary-adrenal axis? *Scandinavian Journal of Work, Environment & Health*, *32*(5), 339–348. doi:10.5271jweh.1029 PMID:17091201

Lang, L., & Pirani, J. A. (2014). *Adapting the Established SIS to Meet Higher Education's Increasingly Dynamic Needs. CDS Spotlight Report. ECAR Research Bulletin.* EDUCAUSE.

Lankhorst, M. (2013). *Enterprise architecture at work: Modelling, communication and analysis.* Springer. doi:10.1007/978-3-642-29651-2

Lanubile, F., Ebert, C., Prikladnicki, R., & Vizcaíno, A. (2010). Collaboration Tools for Global Software Engineering. *IEEE Journals & Magazines*, *27*(2).

Lapiedra, R., Alegre, J., & Chiva, R. (2011). The importance of management innovation and consultant services on ERP implementation success. *Service Industries Journal*, *31*(12), 1907–1919. doi:10.1080/02642069.2011.556189

Laqueur, W. (2003). *No End to War: Terrorism in the Twenty-First Century.* New York: Continuum.

Larrocha, E. R., Minguet, J. M., Díaz, G., Castro, M., Vara, A., Martín, S., & Cristobal, E. S. (2011). Proposals for Postgraduate Students to Reinforce Information Security Management Inside ITIL®. *International Journal of Human Capital and Information Technology Professionals*, *2*(2), 16–25. doi:10.4018/jhcitp.2011040102

Lárusdóttir, M., Cajander, Å., & Gulliksen, J. (2014). Informal feedback rather than performance measurements–user-centred evaluation in Scrum projects. *Behaviour & Information Technology*, *33*(11), 1118–1135. doi:10.1080/014492 9X.2013.857430

Latham, G. P., Fay, C. H., & Saari, L. M. (1979). The development of behavioral observation scales for appraising the performance of foremen. *Personnel Psychology*, *32*(2), 299–311. doi:10.1111/j.1744-6570.1979.tb02136.x

Latham, G. P., & Wexley, K. N. (1977). Behavioral observation scales for performance appraisal purposes. *Personnel Psychology*, *30*(2), 255–268. doi:10.1111/j.1744-6570.1977.tb02092.x

Latham, G. P., & Wexley, K. N. (1981). *Increasing productivity through performance appraisal.* Reading, MA: Addison-Wesley.

Laudon, K. C., & Traver, C. (2016). E-Commerce 2016: Business, Technology, Society. Pearson Higher Ed.

Laudon, K., & Laudon, J. (2011). *Management Information Systems* (11th ed.). Prentice Hall.

Lau, S. K., Winley, G. K., Lau, S. Y., & Tan, K. S. (2013). An exploratory study on the adoption and use of ICT in Myanmar. *The Electronic Journal on Information Systems in Developing Countries*, *59*(1), 1–31. doi:10.1002/j.1681-4835.2013.tb00417.x

Lau, S. K., Winley, G. K., Leung, N. K., Tsang, N., & Lau, S. Y. (2016). An exploratory study of expectation in IT skills in a developing nation: Vietnam. *Journal of Global Information Management*, *24*(1), 1–13. doi:10.4018/JGIM.2016010101

Lawhead, F. W. (2003). A case for artificial intelligence. In Philosophical Journey: An interactive approach (2nd ed.). McGraw Hill.

LawPavalion. (2014). *The violence against persons' prohibition act, of 2015*. Retrieved from Lawpavilion.com on the 11th December, 2018. https://lawpavilion.com/blog/the-violence-against-persons-prohibition-act-2015/

Lazaar, N., Gotlieb, A., & Lebbah, Y. (2012). A CP framework for testing CP. *Constraints, 17*(2), 123–147. doi:10.100710601-012-9116-0

LeadingAge. (2017). *A Look into the Future: Evaluating Business Models for Technology-Enabled Long-Term Services and Supports*. Retrieved from http://www.leadingage.org/uploadedFiles/Content/About/CAST/CAST_Scenario_Planning.pdf

Lecoutre, C., & Tabary, S. (2006). *Abscon 109 a generic CSP Solver*. Academic Press.

Lecoutre, C., Roussel, O., & van Dongen, M. (2010). Promoting robust black-box solvers through competitions. *Constraints, 15*(3), 317–326. doi:10.100710601-010-9092-1

Lee, H. H., Fiore, A. M., & Kim, J. (2006). The role of the technology acceptance model in explaining effects of image interactivity technology on consumer responses. *International Journal of Retail & Distribution Management, 34*(8), 621–644. doi:10.1108/09590550610675949

Lee, T. S., Foo, C. T., & Cunningham, B. (1995). Role of organizational demographics in managing technology-induced stress. *Engineering Management Conference, 1995. Global Engineering Management: Emerging Trends in the Asia Pacific., Proceedings of 1995 IEEE Annual International*, 38–43. 10.1109/IEMC.1995.523906

Lee, W.-P. (2007). Deploying personalized mobile services in an agent-based environment. *Expert Systems with Applications, 32*(4), 1194–1207. doi:10.1016/j.eswa.2006.02.009

Lee, Y. L., & Hsu, C. H. (2011). Usability study of text-based CAPTCHAs. *Displays, 32*(2), 81–86. doi:10.1016/j.displa.2010.12.004

Leggatt, H. (2010). *Rebuild Brand Loyalty with Social Media*. Retrieved from: http://www.bizreport.com/2010/08/price-sensitiveshoppers-still-seeking-out-deals.html

Leidner, S., & Smith, S. M. (2013). Keeping potential job-hoppers' feet on the ground. *Human Resource Management International Digest, 21*(1), 31–33. doi:10.1108/09670731311296492

Lenhart, A., Purcell, K., Smith, A., & Zickuhr, K. (2010). *Social Media & Mobile Internet Use among Teens and Young Adults. Millennials*. Pew Internet & American Life Project.

Lent, B., & Pinkowska, M. (2007). *Human Factor–The key success factor of ICT project management*. Information Systems Architecture and Technology.

Levinson, E. (2007). *Developing High Employee Engagement Makes Good Business Sense*. Retrieved December 19, 2018, from www.interactionassociates.com/ideas/2007/05/developing_high_employee_engagement_makes_good_business_sense.php

Lewis, J. J. (2011). Human Factors Engineering. In *Encyclopedia of Software Engineering* (pp. 383–394). Taylor & Francis.

Leyh, C., Gebhardt, A., & Berton, P. (2017, September). Implementing ERP systems in higher education institutes critical success factors revisited. In *2017 Federated Conference on Computer Science and Information Systems (FedCSIS)* (pp. 913-917). IEEE. 10.15439/2017F364

Li, C. Y. (2017). How social commerce constructs influence customers' social shopping intention? An empirical study of a social commerce website. *Technological Forecasting and Social Change*.

Li, M., Ma, Z., Liu, C., Zhang, G., & Han, Z. (2017). Robust retinal blood vessel segmentation based on reinforcement local descriptions. *BioMed Research International*. PMID:28194407

Lin, K. Y., & Lu, H. P. (2011). Why people use social networking sites: An empirical study integrating network externalities and motivation theory. *Computers in Human Behavior*, *27*(3), 1152–1161. doi:10.1016/j.chb.2010.12.009

Lin, R., van de Ven, N., & Utz, S. (2018). What triggers envy on Social Network Sites? A comparison between shared experiential and material purchases. *Computers in Human Behavior*, *85*, 271–281. doi:10.1016/j.chb.2018.03.049 PMID:30078937

Li, Q. (2006). Cyberbullying in schools: A research of gender differences. *School Psychology International*, *27*(2), 157–170. doi:10.1177/0143034306064547

LISTedTECH. (2017). *Student Information System Software By Total Enrollment*. Retrieved from https://www.listedtech.com/blog/student-information-system-software-total-enrollement

Lockwood, N. R. (2007). Leveraging Employee Engagement for Competitive Advantage: HR's strategic role. *SHRM Research Quarterly, 1*, 1-10.

Lockwood, J. (2015). Virtual team management: What is causing communication breakdown? *Language and Intercultural Communication*, *15*(1), 125–140. doi:10.1080/14708477.2014.985310

Lorenzi, D., Vaidya, J., Uzun, E., Sural, S., & Atluri, V. (2012, December). Attacking image based captchas using image recognition techniques. In *International Conference on Information Systems Security* (pp. 327-342). Springer. 10.1007/978-3-642-35130-3_23

Lowry, P. B., & Wilson, D. (2016). Creating agile organizations through IT: The influence of internal IT service perceptions on IT service quality and IT agility. *The Journal of Strategic Information Systems*, *25*(3), 211–226. doi:10.1016/j.jsis.2016.05.002

Luguetti, C., Goodyear, V. A., & André, M. H. (2019). That is like a 24 hours-day tournament: Using social media to further an authentic sport experience within sport education. *Sport Education and Society*, *24*(1), 78–91. doi:10.1080/13573322.2017.1292235

Lu, H. P., & Hsiao, K. L. (2010). The influence of extro/introversion on the intention to pay for social networking sites. *Information & Management*, *47*(3), 150–157. doi:10.1016/j.im.2010.01.003

Luker, J. M., & Curchack, B. C. (2017). International Perceptions of Cyberbullying Within Higher Education. *Adult Learning*, *28*(4), 144–156. doi:10.1177/1045159517719337

Lumsden, J., & MacKay, L. (2006, August). How does personality affect trust in B2C e-commerce? In *Proceedings of the 8th international conference on Electronic commerce: The new e-commerce: innovations for conquering current barriers, obstacles and limitations to conducting successful business on the internet* (pp. 471-481). ACM. 10.1145/1151454.1151526

Lusa, A., & Pastor, R. (2011). Planning working time accounts under demand uncertainty. *Computers & Operations Research*, *38*(2), 517–524. doi:10.1016/j.cor.2010.07.012

Lussier, R. N., & Hendon, J. R. (2016). *Human Resource Management: Functions, Applications, and Skill Development* (2nd ed.). Singapore: SAGE Publications, Inc.

Luthans, F., Avey, J. B., Avolio, B. J., Norman, S. M., & Combs, G. M. (2006). Psychological capital development: Toward a micro-intervention. *Journal of Organizational Behavior*, *27*(3), 387–393. doi:10.1002/job.373

Luthans, F., Youssef, C. M., & Avolio, B. J. (2007). *Psychological capital: developing the human competitive edge.* Oxford, UK: Oxford University Press.

Macey, W.H., & Schneider, B. (2008). The Meaning of Employee Engagement. *Industrial and Organizational Psychology: Perspectives on Science and Practice, 1*(1), 3-30. Doi:10.1111/j.1754-9434.2007.0002.x

Mahatanankoon, P. (2007). Exploring the impact of essential IT skills on career satisfaction and organisational commitment of information systems professionals. *International Journal of Information Systems and Change Management, 2*(1), 50–68. doi:10.1504/IJISCM.2007.013881

Makama, G. A. (2013). Patriarchy and gender inequality in Nigeria: The way forward. *European Scientific Journal, 9*(17), 140-145.

Makanjuola, O. A. (1999). *A Parent and A University Teacher Takes a Look at Cultism in Nigerian Tertiary Institutions.* NAS Annual Converge.

Maldonado, M., & Sierra, V. (2013). User satisfaction as the foundation of the success following an ERP adoption: An empirical study from Latin America. *International Journal of Enterprise Information Systems, 9*(3), 77–99. doi:10.4018/jeis.2013070104

Malgorzata Ali, I. (2016). Doing the Organizational Tango: Symbiotic Relationship between Formal and Informal Organizational Structures for an Agile Organization. *Interdisciplinary Journal of Information, Knowledge, and Management, 11*, 55–72. doi:10.28945/3439

Malhotra, N. K. (2004). *Marketing research: An applied orientation.* Prentice-Hill.

Mali, A. (2016). *Massive Open Online Courses.* EduInspire.

Mandara, M. U. (2004). Female genital mutilation in Nigeria. *International Journal of Gynaecology and Obstetrics: the Official Organ of the International Federation of Gynaecology and Obstetrics, 84*(3), 291–298. doi:10.1016/j.ijgo.2003.06.001 PMID:15001386

Manfreda, A., & Indihar Štemberger, M. (2018). Establishing a partnership between top and IT managers: A necessity in an era of digital transformation. *Information Technology & People,* ITP-01-2017-0001. doi:10.1108/ITP-01-2017-0001

Manian, A., Yurtchi, B. S., & Shadmehri, N. (2014). Identifying & Prioritizing the Factors Influencing on Website Evaluation, A Content Analysis of Literature. *Management Researches in Iran, 18*(1).

Mani, V. (2011). Analysis of Employee Engagement and its predictors. *International Journal of Human Resource Studies., 1*(2), 15–27. doi:10.5296/ijhrs.v1i2.955

Manoharan, R., Ganesan, R., & Sabarinathan, K. (2015). Impac of Hosted Speech Technology for Health Care Service Providers through Call Centers. *Scholarly Research Journal for Interdisciplinary Studies, III*, 2712–2724.

Mansor, A. Z. (2012). Google Docs as a Collaborating Tool for Academicians. *Procedia: Social and Behavioral Sciences, 59*, 411–419. doi:10.1016/j.sbspro.2012.09.295

Manzoor, M., & Hussain, W. (2012). A Web Usability Evaluation Model for Higher Education Providing Universities of Asia. *Science, Technology and Development, 31*(2), 183–192. Retrieved from https://opus.lib.uts.edu.au/bitstream/10453/118304/1/183-192.pdf

Marcos-Pablos, S., & García-Peñalvo, F. J. J. S. (2019). *Technological Ecosystems in Care and Assistance: A Systematic Literature Review.* Academic Press.

Marcus, G. (2013). Why we should think about the threat of Artificial Intelligence. *The New Yorker*. Retrieved from http://www.newyorker.com/tech/elements/why-we-should-think-about-the-threat-of-artificial-intelligence

Marcuse, H. (1998). Some social implications of modern technology. In D. Kellner (Ed.), *Technology, War and Fascism - Collected Papers of Herbert Marcuse* (Vol. 1, pp. 41–65). London: Routledge.

Mardikyan, S., & Bozanta, A. (2017). The effects of social media use on collaborative learning: A case of Turkey. *Turkish Online Journal of Distance Education-TOJDE, 18*(1), 96–110. doi:10.17718/tojde.285719

Marilyn, K. (2013). *Ex-post facto research: Dissertation and scholarly research, Recipes for success*. Seattle, WA: Dissertation Success LLC. Retrieved from http://www.dissertationrecipes.com/wp-content/uploads/2011/04/Ex-Post-Facto- research.pdf

Markides, C. (2011, March). Crossing the Chasm: How to Convert Relevant Research Into Managerially Useful Research. *The Journal of Applied Behavioral Science, 47*(1), 121–134. doi:10.1177/0021886310388162

Markos, S., & Sridevi, N. S. (2010). Employee Engagement: The Key to Improving Performance. *International Journal of Business and Management, 5*(12), 89–96.

Marquart, S. (2017). Aligning super intelligence with human interests. *Future of Life*. Retrieved from https://futureoflife.org/2017/07/18/aligning-superintelligence-with- human-interests/

Martínez Aires, M. D., Rubio Gámez, M. C., & Gibb, A. (2010). Prevention through design: The effect of European Directives on construction workplace accidents. *Safety Science, 48*(2), 248–258. doi:10.1016/j.ssci.2009.09.004

Maskell, B., Baggaley, B., & Grasso, L. (2011). *Practical Lean Accounting: A Proven System for Measuring and Managing the Lean Enterprise* (2nd ed.). Productivity Press.

Maslach, C. (2011). Engagement research: Some thoughts from a burnout perspective. *European Journal of Work and Organizational Psychology, 20*(1), 47–52. doi:10.1080/1359432X.2010.537034

Maslow, A. H. (1943). A theory of human motivation. *Psychological Review, 50*(4), 370–396. doi:10.1037/h0054346

Mathias, B., Oludayo, O., & Ray, M. (2014). Identifying Critical Success Factors: The case of ERP Systems in Higher Education. *The African Journal of Information Systems, 6*(3), 1.

Mathieu, J., & Zajac, D. (1990). A review and meta-analysis of the antecedents, correlates, and consequences of organisational commitment. *Psychological Bulletin, 108*(2), 171–194. doi:10.1037/0033-2909.108.2.171

Mathrani, S., & Mathrani, A. (2013). Understanding the Transformation Process Success Factors in Enterprise System Implementations: An IT Professional's Perspective. *International Journal of Human Capital and Information Technology Professionals, 4*(1), 9–21. doi:10.4018/jhcitp.2013010102

Mayell, H. (2002). Thousands of women killed for family "honor". *National Geographic News*. Retrieved January 25, 2015 from http://news.nationalgeographic.com/news/2002/02/

Mayer, R. C., Davis, J. H., & Schoorman, F. D. (1995). An integrative model of organizational trust. *Academy of Management Review, 20*(3), 709–734. doi:10.5465/amr.1995.9508080335

McCarthy, A. (2010). Third Generation DNA Sequencing: Pacific Biosciences' Single Molecule Real Time Technology. *Chemistry & Biology, 17*(7), 675–676. doi:10.1016/j.chembiol.2010.07.004 PMID:20659677

McCorduck, P. (2004). 'Machines who think': 25th Anniversary Edition. *RAQ Online*. Retrieved from http://www.pamelamc.com/html/machines_who_think.html

McCrohan, K. F., Engel, K., & Harvey, J. W. (2010). Influence of awareness and training on cyber security. *Journal of Internet Commerce*, *9*(1), 23–41. doi:10.1080/15332861.2010.487415

McDonald, P., Guthrie, D., Bradley, L., & Shakespeare-Finch, J. (2005). Investigating work-family policy aims and employee experiences. *Employee Relations*, *27*(4/5), 478–494. doi:10.1108/01425450510612013

McGourty, J., Tarshis, L. A., & Dominick, P. (1996). Managing innovation: Lessons from world class organizations. *International Journal of Technology Management*, *11*, 354–368. doi:10.1504/IJTM.1996.025438

McKnight, D. H., Choudhury, V., & Kacmar, C. (2002). The impact of initial consumer trust on intentions to transact with a web site: A trust building model. *The Journal of Strategic Information Systems*, *11*(3-4), 297–323. doi:10.1016/S0963-8687(02)00020-3

McLean, L. D. (2005). Organizational culture's influence on creativity and innovation: A review of the literature and implications for human resource development. *Advances in Developing Human Resources*, *7*(2), 226–246. doi:10.1177/1523422305274528

McLeod, J., Hare, C., & Johare, R. (2004). Education and training for records management in the electronic environment-the (re) search for an appropriate model. *Information Research*, *9*(3), 179.

McMenamin, T. M. (2007). A time to work: Recent trends in shift work and flexible schedules. *Monthly Labor Review*, *130*(12), 3–15.

McNurlin, B. (2009). *Information Systems Management in Practice* (8th ed.). Prentice Hall.

Mehrotra, D., Pradesh, U., & Pradesh, U. (2017). *Identification of Criteria Affecting the Usability of Academic Institutes Websites*. Academic Press. doi:10.4018/IJTD.2017070102

Melinščak, M., Prentašić, P., & Lončarić, S. (2015, January). Retinal vessel segmentation using deep neural networks. *10th International Conference on Computer Vision Theory and Applications (VISAPP 2015)*. 10.5220/0005313005770582

Metzger, M. J. (2004). Privacy, trust, and disclosure: Exploring barriers to electronic commerce. *Journal of Computer-Mediated Communication, 9*(4).

Metzker, M. L. (2010). Sequencing technologies - the next generation. *Nature Reviews. Genetics, 11*(1), 31–46. doi:10.1038/nrg2626 PMID:19997069

Meyr, H. (2009). Supply chain planning in the German automotive industry. In *Supply Chain Planning* (pp. 1–23). Springer Berlin Heidelberg. doi:10.1007/978-3-540-93775-3_13

Michel, J. S., Kotrba, L. M., Mitchelson, J. K., Clark, M. A., & Baltes, B. B. (2010). Antecedents of work-family conflict: A meta-analytic review. *Journal of Organizational Behavior*, *32*(5), 689–725. doi:10.1002/job.695

Mich, L., French, M., & Cilone, G. (2003). The 2QCV3Q Quality model for the analysis of web site requirements. *Journal of Web Engineering*, *2*, 105–127.

Mikolov, T., Corrado, G., Chen, K., & Dean, J. (2013). Efficient Estimation of Word Representations in Vector Space. *Sciencejournal.Withgoogle*, 1–12.

Millar, S. L., Chambers, M., & Giles, M. J. H. E. (2016). *Service user involvement in mental health care: an evolutionary concept analysis*. Academic Press.

Miller, D. (2017). *Importance of School Monitoring And Evaluation Systems*. Retrieved from http://leansystemssociety.org/importance-of-school-monitoring-and-evaluation-systems/

Mishra, D., Kapse, S., & Bavad, D. (2013). Employee engagement at banks in Kutch. *International Journal of Application or Innovation in Engineering & Management*, *2*(7), 349–358.

Misra, S., Banubakode, S. M., & Dhawale, C. A. (2014). *Novel user interface for text entry on touch screen mobile device for visually impaired users*. Academic Press. doi:10.1109/GSCIT.2014.6970122

Misra, R. K., & Khurana, K. (2018). Analysis of Employability Skill Gap in Information Technology Professionals. *International Journal of Human Capital and Information Technology Professionals*, *9*(3), 53–69. doi:10.4018/IJHCITP.2018070104

Misra, S., & Adewumi, A. (2015). An Analysis of the Suitability of Cloud Computing Services in the Nigerian Education Landscape. *Proceeding of IEEE International Conference on Computing, Communication and Security*, 1-4. 10.1109/CCCS.2015.7374203

Misra, S., & Akman, I. (2014). A cognitive model for meetings in the software development process. *Human Factors and Ergonomics in Manufacturing*, *24*(1), 1–13. doi:10.1002/hfm.20344

Misra, S., Colomo-Palacios, R., Pusatli, T., & Soto-Acosta, P. (2013). A Discussion on the Role of People in Global Software Development. *Tehnicki Vjesnik-Technical Gazette*, *20*(3), 525–531.

Misra, S., Palacios, R. C., Pusatli, T., & Acosta, P. S. (2013). A Discussion On The Role Of People In Global Software Development. *Technical Gazette*, *20*(3), 525–531.

Mochama, V. K. (2013). An assessment of the criteria used in allocating different types of employee benefits at the Kenya pipeline company, Eldoret, Kenya. *Journal of Emerging Trends in Economics and Management Science*, *4*(2), 268–273.

Moe, N. B., Aurum, A., & Dybå, T. (2012). Challenges of shared decision-making: A multiple case study of agile software development. *Information and Software Technology*, *54*(8), 853–865. doi:10.1016/j.infsof.2011.11.006

Moen, Ø. (1999). The Relationship Between Firm Size, Competitive Advantages and Export Performance Revisited. *International Small Business Journal*, *18*(1), 53–72. doi:10.1177/0266242699181003

Mongo, D. B. (2019). *MongoDB*. Retrieved from https://www.mongodb.com/

Moon, J. W., & Kim, Y. G. (2001). Extending the TAM for a World-Wide-Web context. *Information & Management*, *38*(4), 217–230. doi:10.1016/S0378-7206(00)00061-6

Moran, M., Seaman, J., & Tinti-Kane, H. (2011). *Teaching, Learning, and Sharing: How Today's Higher Education Faculty Use Social Media*. Boston, MA: Pearson Learning Solutions. Retrieved from https://files.eric.ed.gov/fulltext/ED535130.pdf

Morello, D. (2005). *The IT Professional Outlook: Where Will We Go From Here?* Gartner, Inc. Retrieved from http://www.gartner.com/id=485489

Morgan, H. (2014). Using digital story projects to help students improve in reading and writing. *Reading Improvement*, *51*(1), 20–26.

Morhman, A., Resnick-West, S., & Lawler, E. (1989). *Designing Performance Appraisal Systems: aligning appraisals and organizational realities*. San Francisco: Jossey-Bass.

Mori, G., & Malik, J. (2003). Recognizing Objects in Adversarial Clutter: Breaking a Visual CAPTCHA. *IEEE Computer Society Conference on Computer Vision and Pattern Recognition*. 10.1109/CVPR.2003.1211347

Morris, M. L., Heames, J. T., & McMillan, H. S. (2011). Human resource executives' perceptions and measurement of the strategic impact of work/life initiatives. *Human Resource Development Quarterly*, *22*(3), 265–295. doi:10.1002/hrdq.20082

Morris, M. L., Storberg-Walker, J., & McMillan, H. S. (2009). Developing an OD-intervention metric system with the use of applied theory-building methodology: A work/life-intervention example. *Human Resource Development Quarterly*, *20*(4), 419–449. doi:10.1002/hrdq.20026

Moura, I., Dominguez, C., & Varajão, J. (2019). Information systems project teams: Factors for high performance, *Team Performance Management*. *International Journal (Toronto, Ont.)*, *25*(1/2), 69–83.

Mudra, A., & Misra, S. (2013) Practical Scrum-Scrum Team: Way to Produce Successful and Quality Software. *IEEE Proceedings on 2013 13th International Conference on Computational Science and its Applications*, 119-123.

Muehlhauser, L., Koch, C., & Russell. (2014). *On machine super- intelligence. Machine Intelligence Research Institute (MIRI)*. Online publication of MIRI: https://intelligence.org/2014/05/13/christof-koch-stuart-russell- machine- super-intelligence/

Mueller, J., Hutter, K., Fueller, J., & Matzler, K. (2011). Virtual worlds as knowledge management platform–a practice-perspective. *Information Systems Journal*, *21*(6), 479–501. doi:10.1111/j.1365-2575.2010.00366.x

Mukhopadhyay, S. C., & Suryadevara, N. K. (2014). Internet of Things: Challenges and Opportunities. In S. C. Mukho-padhyay (Ed.), *Internet of Things* (Vol. 9, pp. 1–17). Springer International Publishing. doi:10.1007/978-3-319-04223-7_1

Mumford, M. D., Bedell-Avers, K. E., & Hunter, S. T. (2008). Planning for innovation: A multi-level perspective. In M. D. Mumford, S. T. Hunter, & K. E. Bedell-Avers (Eds.), *Innovation in organizations: A multi-level perspective* (pp. 107–154). Oxford, UK: Elsevier.

Mumford, M. D., Hester, K. S., & Robledo, I. C. (2012). Creativity in organizations: Importance and approaches. In M. D. Mumford (Ed.), *Handbook of organizational creativity* (pp. 3–16). San Diego, CA: Elsevier. doi:10.1016/B978-0-12-374714-3.00001-X

Munnell, A. H. (2011). *What is the Average Retirement Age?* Retrieved from http://crr.bc.edu/wp-content/uploads/2011/08/IB_11-11-508.pdf

Mustafa, S. H., & Al-Zoua'bi, L. F. (2008). Usability of the Academic Websites of Jordan's Universities An Evaluation Study. In *Proceedings of the 9th International Arab Conference for Information Technology* (pp. 31–40). Academic Press. Retrieved from https://faculty.psau.edu.sa/filedownload/doc-1-pdf-556f391937dfd4398cbac35e050a2177-original.pdf

MyBatis. (2019). *MyBatis*. Retrieved from http://blog.mybatis.org/

NACE. (n.d.). *Eurostat Statistics Explained*. Retrieved July 2017, from http://www.ec.europa.eu/eurostat/statistics-explained/index.php/Main_Page

NAFSA. (2010). *The changing landscape of global higher education*. Washington, DC: Association of International Educators.

Nagle, D. F., Ganger, G. R., Butler, J., Goodson, G., & Sabol, C. (1999). Network Support for Network-Attached Storage. In *Proceedings of Hot Interconnects*. Stanford, CA: Stanford University.

Nagpal, R., Mehrotra, D., & Bhatia, P. (2017). The State of Art in Website Usability Evaluation Methods. In S. Saeed, Y. A. Bamarouf, T. Ramayah, & S. Z. Iqbal (Eds.), *Design Solutions for User-Centric Information Systems* (Vol. 1, pp. 275–296). IGI Global. doi:10.4018/978-1-5225-1944-7.ch015

Nagpal, R., Mehrotra, D., Bhatia, P., & Sharma, A. (2015). FAHP Approach to Rank Educational Websites on Usability. *International Journal of Computing and Digital Systems*, *4*(4), 251–260. doi:10.12785/ijcds/040404

Nahapiet, J., & Ghoshal, S. (1998). Social capital, intellectual capital, and the organizational advantage. *Academy of Management Review*, *23*(2), 242–266. doi:10.5465/amr.1998.533225

Nahar, V., Unankard, S., Li, X., & Pang, C. (2012). Sentiment analysis for effective detection of cyber bullying. Lecture Notes in Computer Science, 7235, 767–774. doi:10.1007/978-3-642-29253-8_75

Naijasky. (2014). *History of Eti-Osa Local Government Area.* Retrieved 1ˢᵗ March, 2017 from http://naijasky.com/eti-osa/137/history-of-eti-osa-local-government-area/3273/

Närman, P., Johnson, P., & Nordstrom, L. (2007). Enterprise Architecture: A Framework Supporting System Quality Analysis. *11th IEEE International Enterprise Distributed Object Computing Conference (EDOC 2007)*, 130–130. 10.1109/EDOC.2007.39

National Population Commission (NPC) [Nigeria] and ICF International. (2014). *Nigeria Demographic and Health Survey 2013.* Abuja, Nigeria: NPC and ICF International.

Naylor, R. W., Lamberton, C. P., & West, P. M. (2012). Beyond the "like" button: The impact of mere virtual presence on brand evaluations and purchase intentions in social media settings. *Journal of Marketing*, *76*(6), 105–120. doi:10.1509/jm.11.0105

Naz, F., Aftab, J., & Awais, M. (2016). Impact of Human Resource Management Practices (HRM) on Performance of SMEs in Multan, Pakistan. *International Journal of Management. Accounting & Economics*, *3*(11), 699–708.

NDHS. (2013). *This report summarizes the findings of the 2013 Nigeria Demographic and Health Survey (NDHS), implemented by the National Population Commission.* NPC.

Nelson, D. L., Macik-Frey, M., & Quick, J. C. (2007). Advances in Occupational Health: From a Stressful Beginning to a Positive Future. *Journal of Management*, *33*(6), 809–840. doi:10.1177/0149206307307634

Nepelski, D., Van Roy, V., & Pesole, A. (2019). The organisational and geographic diversity and innovation potential of EU-funded research networks. *The Journal of Technology Transfer*, *44*(2), 359–380. doi:10.100710961-018-9692-2

Neumann, G. (2002). Programming Languages in Artificial Intelligence. In Encyclopaedia of Information Systems. Academic Press.

Neumann, S., & Fink, L. (2007). Gaining agility through IT personnel capabilities: The mediating role of IT infrastructure capabilities. *Journal of the Association for Information Systems*, *8*(8), 25.

Neumeier, M. (2009). *Innovation Workshop: Brand Strategy + Design Thinking = Transformation.* Pearson.

Newman, N. (2009). *The rise of social media and its impact on mainstream journalism.* Working paper. Reuters Institute for the Study of Journalism.

Ng, C. S. P. (2013). Intention to purchase on social commerce websites across cultures: A cross-regional study. *Information & Management*, *50*(8), 609–620. doi:10.1016/j.im.2013.08.002

Nicoletti, B. (2012). Project Management and Cloud Computing. *PM World Today, 14*(1), 1–11. Retrieved from http://search.ebscohost.com/login.aspx?direct=true&db=bth&AN=74028642&site=ehost-live

Niederlínski, A. (2014). *A gentle guide to Constraint Logic Programming via eclipse* [ksiazka]. Jacek Skalmierski Computer Studio.

Nielsen, J. (1994). Usability inspection methods. *Conference Companion on Human Factors in Computing Systems - CHI '94*, 413–414. doi:10.1145/259963.260531

Nielsen, J. (2012). *Usability 101: Introduction to usability.* Nielsen Norman Group.

Nielsen, J., & Molich, R. (1989, August). Teaching user interface design based on usability engineering. *SIGCHI Bull,* *21*(1), 45–48. doi:10.1145/67880.67885

Nielsen, J., & Molich, R. (1990). Heuristic evaluation of user interfaces. In *Proceedings of the sigchi conference on human factors in computing systems* (pp. 249-256). New York, NY: ACM.

Niemi, E., & Laine, S. (2016). Competence Management System Design Principles: Action Design Research. *ICIS 2016 Proceedings.* Retrieved from https://aisel.aisnet.org/icis2016/ISDesign/Presentations/4

Niskanen, T., Naumanen, P., & Hirvonen, M. L. (2012). An evaluation of EU legislation concerning risk assessment and preventive measures in occupational safety and health. *Applied Ergonomics,* *43*(5), 829–842. doi:10.1016/j.apergo.2011.12.003 PMID:22233692

Nizamani, S., Khoumbati, K., Ismaili, I. A., Nizamani, S., Nizamani, S., & Basir, N. (2017). Testing and validating the ERP success evaluation model for higher education institutes of Pakistan. *International Journal of Business Information Systems,* *25*(2), 165–191. doi:10.1504/IJBIS.2017.083682

NUC. (2019, October). List of Approved Universities In Nigeria Federal. *National Universities Commission.* Retrieved from http://nuc.edu.ng/20th-october-2017-bulletin/

Nunnally, J. C. (1978). *Psychometric theory* (2nd ed.). New York, NY: McGraw-Hill.

NW3C. (2013). *Criminal Use of Social Media.* National White Collar Crime Center.

O'Grady, M. J., Muldoon, C., Dragone, M., Tynan, R., & O'Hare, G. M. (2010). Towards evolutionary ambient assisted living systems. *Journal of Ambient Intelligence and Humanized Computing,* *1*(1), 15–29. doi:10.100712652-009-0003-5

O'mahony, E., Hebrard, E., Holland, A., & Nugent, C. (2008). Using case-based reasoning in an algorithm portfolio for Constraint Solving. *Iris Conference on Artificial Intelligence and Cognitive Science.*

O'Reilly, T. (2005). *What Is Web 2.0.* O'Reilly Media. Retrieved 24 November 2015, from http://www.oreilly.com/pub/a/web2/archive/what-is-web-20.html?page=1

OASIS. (2006). The Framework for eBusiness. An OASIS White Paper. *The OASIS ebXML Joint Committee For OASIS.* Retrieved from www.oasis-open.org

OASIS. (2014). *ISO/IEC and OASIS Collaborate on E-Business Standards-Standards Groups Increase Cross-Participation to Enhance Interoperability.* Retrieved from https://www.oasis-open.org/news/pr/isoiec-and-oasis-collaborate-on-e-business-standards

Oberg, W. (1972). Make performance appraisal relevant. *Harvard Business Review,* *50*(1), 61–67.

Oblinger, D. G. (2006) *Learning spaces.* EDUCAUSE. Retrieved from http://educause.edu/learningspaces

Oduh, I. U., Misra, S., Damaševičius, R., & Maskeliūnas, R. (2018). Cloud Based Simple Employee Management Information System: A Model for African Small and Medium Enterprises. *Advances in Intelligent Systems and Computing,* *721.* 10.1007/978-3-319-73450-7_12

Odukoya, J. A. (2014). *Comparative Analysis of Cambridge O-Levels and WAEC O-Levels examination questions.* Unpublished Paper.

Odukoya, J. A. (2015). *Development Oriented Teaching Testing Model.* Unpublished Paper.

Odun-Ayo, I., Misra, S., Omoregbe, N., Onibere, E., Bulama, Y., & Damasevičius, R. (2017). *Cloud-Based Security Driven Human Resource Management System. In Frontiers in Artificial Intelligence and Applications* (Vol. 295, pp. 96–106). Advances in Digital Technologies.

Ogunjuyigbe, O. P., Akinlo, A., & Ebigbola, A. J. (2005). Violence against Women: An examination of men's attitudes and perceptions about wife beating and contraceptive use. *Journal of African and Asian Studies, 40*(3), 219–229. doi:10.1177/0021909605055070

Oguntuase, B. (1999a). *Open Letter to Nigerian Students on Campus Banditry*. Academic Press.

Oguntuase, B. (1999b). *Violence and Cultism in Tertiary Institutions: The Way Out*. NAS Annual Converge.

Oguntuase, B. (1999c). Cultism and Violence in Higher Institutions of Learning in Nigeria. NAS Capone, University of Lagos.

Ogwueleka, F., Misra, S., Palacios, R. C., & Fernandez, L. (2015). Neural Network and Classification Approach in Identifying Customer Behavior in The Banking Sector: A Case Study of An International Bank. *Human Factors and Ergonomics in Manufacturing & Service Industries, 25*(1), 28–42.

Ojijo, N., Jakinda, D., & Annor-Frempong, I. (2013). *Tropical Agriculture Platform (TAP)*. Retrieved from http://www.tropagplatform.org/

Ojo, A. O., Raman, M., & Downe, A. (2019). Toward green computing practices: A Malaysian study of green belief and attitude among Information Technology professionals. *Journal of Cleaner Production, 224*, 246–255. doi:10.1016/j.jclepro.2019.03.237

Okeke, T. C., Anyaehie, U. S. B., & Ezenyeaku, C. C. K. (2012). An overview of female genital mutilation in Nigeria. *Annals of Medical and Health Sciences Research, 2*(1), 70–73. doi:10.4103/2141-9248.96942 PMID:23209995

Okewu, E., Misra, S., Sanz, L. F., Maskeliūnas, R., & Damaševičius, R. (2018). An e-Environment System for Socio-economic Sustainability and National Security. *Problemy Ekorozwoju, 13*(1), 121–132.

Okland, J. S. (1990). *Total Quality Management- Text with Cases*. Oxford, UK: Butterworth-Heinemann.

Okonkwo, R. O., & Enem, F. O. (2011). *Combating crime and terrorism using data mining techniques*. Nigeria Computer Society (NCS). Available online: http://www.ncs.org.ng/wp-content/uploads/2011/08/ITePED2011-Paper10.pdf

Oladipo, J. A., & Abdulkadir, D. S. (2011). Strategic human resource management and organizational performance in the Nigerian manufacturing sector: An empirical investigation. *International Journal of Business and Management, 6*(9), 46–56.

Olariu, C., & Aldea, C. C. (2014). Managing Processes for Virtual Teams – A BPM Approach. *Procedia: Social and Behavioral Sciences, 109*(0), 380–384. doi:10.1016/j.sbspro.2013.12.476

Olayiwola, O. O. (2013). Education Scenarios in Nigeria. *ABHINAV-International Monthly Journal of Research in Management and Technology, 2*.

Oliver, G. R. (2012). *Foundations of the Assumed Business Operations and Strategy Body of Knowledge (BOSBOK): an Outline of Shareable Knowledge*. Sydney: Darlington Press.

Ollman, B. (1976). *Alienation: Marx's conception of man in capitalist society*. Retrieved from http:www.alienation-theory.com/

Ologbo, C. A., & Saudah, S. (2011). Engaging People who Drive Execution and Organizational Performance. *American Journal of Economics and Business Administration, 3*(3), 569–575. doi:10.3844/ajebasp.2011.569.575

Olsthoorn, M. (2014). Measuring Precarious Employment: A Proposal for Two Indicators of Precarious Employment Based on Set-Theory and Tested with Dutch Labor Market-Data - Springer. *Social Indicators Research, 119*(1), 421–441. doi:10.100711205-013-0480-y

Oluwasanmi, B. V., Akande, O. L., & Taiwo, O. E. (2016). Social Vices And The Effect Of Cultism Activities Among University Undergraduates Of Ekiti State University, Ado-Ekiti, Nigeria. *American Journal of Innovative Research and Applied Sciences.*

OMIM. (2019). *OMIM: An Online Catalog of Human Genes and Genetic Disorders.* Retrieved from https: //omim.org/

Omotosho, A., Asani, E. O., Fiddi, P., & Akande, N. (2019). Image and Password Multifactor Authentication Scheme for e-Voting. *Journal of Engineering and Applied Sciences (Asian Research Publishing Network), 14*(11), 3732–3740. doi:10.3923/jeasci.2019.3732.3740

Onyemelukwe, C. (2015). *Overview of the violence against persons (prohibition) act, 2015.* Centre for Health, Ethics, Law and Development. Retrieved 9th March, 2017 from http://domesticviolence.com.ng/wp-content/uploads/2015/12/OVERVIEW-OF-THE-Violence-Against-Persons-Prohibition-ACT-2015.pdf

Onyemelukwe, C., & Okekeogbu, I. (2017). *The violence against persons (prohibition) act: A CHELD Brief.* CHELD. Retrieved on the 9th March, 2017 from http://cheld.org/wp-content/uploads/2012/04/Violence-Against-Persons-Prohibition-Act-2015-A-CHELD-Brief.pdf

OptaPlanner Team. (2014). *OptaPlanner.* Available from http://www.optaplanner.org/

Oracle. (2019). *Oracle Sales Cloud.* Retrieved from https://cloud.oracle.com/sales-cloud

OscaR Team. (2012). *OscaR: Scala in OR.* Available from https://bitbucket.org/oscarlib/oscar

Osgood, C. E., Suci, G., & Tannenbaum, P. (1957). *The measurement of meaning.* Urbana, IL: University of Illinois Press.

Osho, O., Mohammed, U. L., Nimzing, N. N., Uduimoh, A. A., & Misra, S. (2019). Forensic Analysis of Mobile Banking Apps. In Lecture Notes in Computer Science: Vol. 11623. *Computational Science and Its Applications – ICCSA 2019. ICCSA 2019.* Cham: Springer. doi:10.1007/978-3-030-24308-1_49

Osório, A. L., Afsarmanesh, H., & Camarinha-Matos, L. M. (2010). Towards a Reference Architecture for a Collaborative Intelligent Transport System Infrastructure. In L. Camarinha-Matos, X. Boucher, & H. Afsarmanesh (Eds.), *Collaborative Networks for a Sustainable World* (Vol. 336, pp. 469–477). Springer Berlin Heidelberg. doi:10.1007/978-3-642-15961-9_56

OSS. (2019). *Alibaba Cloud Object Storage Service (OSS).* Retrieved from https://intl.aliyun.com/product/oss

Ossege, C. (2012). Accountability – are we better off without it? *Public Management Review, 14*(5), 585–607. doi:10.1080/14719037.2011.642567

Otto, A., & Scholl, A. (2012). Reducing ergonomic risks by job rotation scheduling. *OR-Spektrum, 35*(3), 711–733. doi:10.100700291-012-0291-6

Overseas Security Advisory Council (OSAC). (2012). *Ghana 2012 OSAC crime and safety report.* Retrieved from https://www.osac.gov

Owen, M., & Raj, J. (2003). *BPMN and business process management.* Introduction to the New Business Process Modeling Standard.

Oyediran, A. K., & Abanihe-Isiugo, C. U. (2005). Perceptions of Nigerian women on domestic violence: Evidence from 2003 Nigeria Demographic and Health Survey. *African Journal of Reproductive Health, 9*(3), 39–41. PMID:16485585

Pachouri, A., & Sharma, S. (2016). Barriers to Innovation in Indian Small and Medium-Sized Enterprises. *Asian Development Bank Institute, 588.*

Palmer, M. T. (1995). Interpersonal communication and virtual reality: Mediating interpersonal relationships. In F. Biocca & M. R. Levy (Eds.), *Communication in the age of virtual reality* (p. 277-299). Hillside, NJ: Lawrence Erlbaum.

Panda, S., & Rath, S. K. (2017). The effect of human IT capability on organizational agility: An empirical analysis. *Management Research Review, 40*(7), 800–820. doi:10.1108/MRR-07-2016-0172

Panda, S., & Rath, S. K. (2018). Information technology capability, knowledge management capability, and organizational agility: The role of environmental factors. *Journal of Management & Organization,* 1–27. doi:10.1017/jmo.2018.9

Pandey, S., & David, S. (2013). A study of engagement at work: What drives employee engagement. *European Journal of Commerce and Management Research, 2*(7), 155–161.

Pandey, S., & Sharma, V. (2016). Understanding Work-Related Stress, Job Conditions, Work Culture and Workaholism Phenomenon as Predictors of HR Crisis: An Empirical Study of the Indian IT Sector. *International Journal of Human Capital and Information Technology Professionals, 7*(2), 68–80. doi:10.4018/IJHCITP.2016040105

Park, D. C., & Reuter-Lorenz, P. (2009). The adaptive brain: Aging and neurocognitive scaffolding. *Annual Review of Psychology, 60*(1), 173–196. doi:10.1146/annurev.psych.59.103006.093656 PMID:19035823

Parker, D. B. (2008). Security accountability in job performance. *Information Systems Security, 3*(4), 16–20. doi:10.1080/10658989509342474

Park, J. Y., Im, K. S., & Kim, J. S. (2011). The role of IT human capability in the knowledge transfer process in IT outsourcing context. *Information & Management, 48*(1), 53–61. doi:10.1016/j.im.2011.01.001

Paterson, D. G. (1922). The Scott Company graphic rating scale. *Journal of Personnel Research, 1,* 351–376.

Pathak, R., Parker, D. W., & Holesgrove, M. (2015). Improving productivity with self-organised teams and agile leadership. *International Journal of Productivity and Performance Management, 64*(1), 112–128. doi:10.1108/IJPPM-10-2013-0178

Patrakosol, B., & Lee, S. M. (2009). IT capabilities, interfirm performance, and the state of economic development. *Industrial Management & Data Systems, 109*(9), 1231–1247. doi:10.1108/02635570911002298

Patrick, H. A. (2012). Commitment of information technology employees in relation to perceived organisational justice. *IUP Journal of Organisational Behavior, 11*(3), 23–40.

Pavlou, P. A. (2003). Consumer acceptance of electronic commerce: Integrating trust and risk with the technology acceptance model. *International Journal of Electronic Commerce, 7*(3), 101–134. doi:10.1080/10864415.2003.11044275

Pearlson, K., Saunders, C., & Galletta, D. (2016). *Managing and Using Information Systems* (6th ed.). Wiley.

Pee, L. G., Kankanhalli, A., & Kim, H. W. (2010). Knowledge sharing in information systems development: A social interdependence perspective. *Journal of the Association for Information Systems, 11*(10), 1. doi:10.17705/1jais.00238

Pee, L. G., Kankanhalli, A., Tan, G. W., & Tham, G. Z. (2014). Mitigating the Impact of Member Turnover in Information Systems Development Projects. *IEEE Transactions on Engineering Management, 61*(4), 702–716. doi:10.1109/TEM.2014.2332339

Penna. (2007). *Meaning at Work Research Report.* Retrieved February 10, 2019, from http:// www.e-penna.com/ newsopinion /research.aspx

Pereira, J. L., Varajão, J., Sá, J. O., & Silva, A. (2019). Performance Evaluation in IST Projects: A Case Study. In *Information Systems for Industry 4.0 - Proceedings of the 18th Conference of the Portuguese Association for Information Systems* (pp. 13-27). Springer International Publishing. 10.1007/978-3-030-14850-8_2

Perrin, T. (2003). *Working Today: Understanding What Drives Employee Engagement.* The 2003 Towers Perrin Talent Report U.S Report. Retrieved from http://www.towersperrin.com/tp/getwebcachedoc?Webc = HRS/USA/2003/200309/Talent_2003.pdf

Perry-Smith, J. E., & Blum, T. C. (2000). Work-family human resource bundles and perceived organizational performance. *Academy of Management Journal, 43,* 1107–1117. doi:10.2307/1556339

Peruzzi, M. (2015). Contradictions and misalignments in the EU approach towards the gender pay gap. *Cambridge Journal of Economics, 39*(2), 441–465. doi:10.1093/cje/bev007

Peters & Pedrycz. (2012). *Software Engineering: An Engineering Approach.* Wiley India.

Peterson, S. (2011). *Why it Worked: Critical Success Factors of a Financial Reform eProjects in Africa. Faculty Research Working Paper Series.* Harvard Kennedy School.

Pfisterer, D. S. (2013, October 29). *39.000 job vacancies for IT experts.* Retrieved October 31, 2014, from http://www.bitkom.org/de/themen/54633_77765.aspx

Pham, Q. T., Misra, S., Huynh, L. N. H., & Ahuja, R. (2019). Investigating Enterprise Resource Planning (ERP) Effect on Work Environment. In Lecture Notes in Computer Science: Vol. 11623. *Computational Science and Its Applications – ICCSA 2019. ICCSA 2019.* Cham: Springer. doi:10.1007/978-3-030-24308-1_50

Pinero, J., Queralt-Rosinach, N., Bravo, A., Deu-Pons, J., Bauer-Mehren, A., Baron, M., ... Furlong, L. (2015). DisGeNET: A discovery platform for the dynamical exploration of human diseases and their genes. *Database (Oxford), 2015*(0), bav028. doi:10.1093/database/bav028 PMID:25877637

Pipan, M., Arch, T., Srdjevic, Z., Srdjevic, B., & Balaban, I. (2014). Group Assessment of Learning Management Systems. *33rd International Conference on Organizational Science Development,* 564-570.

Plaza, I., Martí, N. L., Martin, S., & Medrano, C. (2011). Mobile applications in an aging society: Status and trends. *Journal of Systems and Software, 84*(11), 1977–1988. doi:10.1016/j.jss.2011.05.035

Pollitt, D. (2005). Leadership succession planning "affects commercial success.". *Human Resource Management International Digest, 13*(1), 36–38. doi:10.1108/09670730510576419

Pollock, N., & Cornford, J. (2004). ERP Systems and the university as a "unique" organization. *Information Technology & People, 17*(1), 31–52. doi:10.1108/09593840410522161

Pont, J. (2004). Are they really 'On the Job?' *Potentials,* 32-37.

Poole, D., Mackworth, A., & Goebel, R. (1998). *Computational intelligence: A logical approach.* Oxford University Press.

Porter, M. E. (2008). *Competitive advantage: Creating and sustaining superior performance.* Simon and Schuster.

Posey, C., Roberts, T. L., & Lowry, P. B. (2015). The impact of organisational commitment on insiders' motivation to protect organisational information assets. *Journal of Management Information Systems, 32*(4), 179–214. doi:10.1080/07421222.2015.1138374

Poston, R., & Patel, J. (2016). Making Sense of Resistance to Agile Adoption in Waterfall Organizations: Social Intelligence and Leadership. *AMCIS 2016 Proceedings.* Retrieved from https://aisel.aisnet.org/amcis2016/ITProj/Presentations/34

Powel, W. A., & Barry, J. (2005). An ERP Post-Implementation Review: Planning for the Future by Looking Back. *EDUCAUSE Quarterly*, *28*(3), 40–46.

Power, D. J. (2008). Understanding data-driven decision support systems. *Information Systems Management*, *25*(2), 149–154. doi:10.1080/10580530801941124

Poyner, C., & Warne, B. (1988). *Preventing violence to staff. London: Health and Safety Executive*. H.M.S.O.

Prensky, M. (2001). Digital Natives, Digital Immigrants. *On the Horizon*, *9*(5), 1–6. doi:10.1108/10748120110424816

Prestridge, S. (2019). Categorising teachers' use of social media for their professional learning: A self-generating professional learning paradigm. *Computers & Education*, *129*, 143–158. doi:10.1016/j.compedu.2018.11.003

Price, H., & Tallinn, J. (2012). Artificial intelligence- Can we keep it in the Box? *The Conversation: Academic rigour, journalistic flair*. Retrieved from http://theconversation.com/artificial-intelligence-can-we-keep-it-in-the-box-8541

Pries-Heje, L. (2008). Time, attitude, and user participation: How prior events determine user attitudes in ERP implementation. *International Journal of Enterprise Information Systems*, *4*(3), 48–65. doi:10.4018/jeis.2008070104

Prince, M. (2004). Does Active Learning Works? A Review of the Research. *Journal of Engineering Education*, *93*(3), 223–231. doi:10.1002/j.2168-9830.2004.tb00809.x

ProgenyL. I. M. S. (2019). *Progeny LIMS*. Retrieved from http://www.progenygenetics.com/lims/

PromethION. (2019). *Oxford Nanopore PromethION*. Retrieved from https://nanoporetech.com/products/promethion

Purvi, S., & Schmidt, L. (2011). *Macroeconomic Conditions and Updating of Expectations by Older Americans*. Working Paper, 259. University of Michigan Retirement Research Center. Accessed at http://www.mrrc.isr.umich.edu/publications/papers/pdf/wp259.pdf

Putri, N., & Yusof, S. M. (2009). Critical success factors for implementing quality engineering tools and techniques in malaysian's and indonesian's automotive industries: An Exploratory Study. *Journal Proceedings of the International MultiConference of Engineers and Computer Scientists.*, *2*, 18–20.

Qian, L., Schmidt, E. K., & Scott, R. L. (2015, December). ERP pre-implementation framework for Higher Education Institution: A case study in Purdue University. In *2015 IEEE International Conference on Industrial Engineering and Engineering Management (IEEM)* (pp. 1546-1550). IEEE. 10.1109/IEEM.2015.7385906

Rabaa'i, A. A. (2009). Identifying critical success factors of ERP Systems at the higher education sector. *Third International Symposium on Innovation in Information & Communication Technology*.

Rabaa'i, A. A., Bandara, W., & Gable, G. G. (2009). ERP Systems in the Higher Education Sector: A Descriptive Case Study. *Proceedings of the 20th Australasian Conference on Information Systems*.

Radant, O. (2014). Demographic Change: The Reasons, Implications and Consequences for IT Departments. *International Journal of Human Capital and Information Technology Professionals*, *5*(1), 41–54. doi:10.4018/ijhcitp.2014010104

Radant, O., Colomo-Palacios, R., & Stantchev, V. (2014). Analysis of Reasons, Implications and Consequences of Demographic Change for IT Departments in Times of Scarcity of Talent: A Systematic Review. *International Journal of Knowledge Management*, *10*(4), 1–15. doi:10.4018/ijkm.2014100101

Radant, O., Colomo-Palacios, R., & Stantchev, V. (2016a). Assessment of Continuing Educational Measures in Software Engineering: A View from the Industry. *Trends in Software Engineering for Engineering Education*, *32*(2), 905–914.

Radant, O., Colomo-Palacios, R., & Stantchev, V. (2016b). Factors for the Management of Scarce Human Resources and Highly Skilled Employees in IT-Departments: A Systematic Review. *Journal of Information Technology Research, 9*(1), 65–82. doi:10.4018/JITR.2016010105

Radant, O., & Stantchev, V. (2018). Metrics for the Management of IT Personnel: A Systematic Literature Review. *International Journal of Human Capital and Information Technology Professionals, 9*(2), 32–51. doi:10.4018/IJHCITP.2018040103

Radhakrishna, A., & Raju, S. R. (2015). A study on the effect of human resource development on employment relations. *IUP Journal of Management Research, 14*(3), 28–42.

Radke, K., Boyd, C., Brereton, M., & Nieto, J. G. (2010). How HCI design influences web security decisions. *Proceedings of the 22nd Conference of the Computer-Human Interaction Special Interest Group of Australia on Computer-Human Interaction - OZCHI '10.* 10.1145/1952222.1952276

Radujković, M., & Sjekavica, M. (2017). Project Management Success Factors. *Procedia Engineering, 196,* 607–615. doi:10.1016/j.proeng.2017.08.048

Rahman & Hamed. (2017). E-Learning Service Quality. *International Conference on Research and Innovation in Information Systems,* 1-6.

Rahmanniyay, F., & Junfang Yu, A. (2018). A multi-objective stochastic programming model for project-oriented human-resource management optimization. *International Journal of Management Science and Engineering Management,* 1-9.

Raj, A., Jain, A., Pahwa, T., & Jain, A. (2010). Picture captchas with sequencing: Their types and analysis. *International Journal of Digital Society, 1*(3), 208–220. doi:10.20533/ijds.2040.2570.2010.0026

Ramakrishna, A., & Figueroa, N. (2017). Is seeing believing? Training users on information security: Evidence from Java Applets. *Journal of Information Systems Education, 28*(2), 115–122.

Ram, J., & Corkindale, D. (2014). How "critical" are the critical success factors (CSFs)?: Examining the role of CSFs for ERP. *Business Process Management Journal, 20*(1), 151–174. doi:10.1108/BPMJ-11-2012-0127

Rani, S. (2016). A Review of ERP Implementation in Higher Education Institutions. *International Journal of Advanced Research in Computer Science and Software Engineering, 6*(6), 542–545.

Rantos, K., Fysarakis, K., & Manifavas, C. (2012). How effective is your security awareness program? An evaluation methodology. *Information Security Journal: A Global Perspective, 21*(6), 328-345.

Rathod, C (2007). Contribution of Indian Small Scale entrepreneurs to economic growth in India: Opportunities and Challenges in Global economy. *Prabandh-Journal of Management & Research.*

Rauf, I., Troubitsyna, E., & Porres, I. (2019). A systematic mapping study of API usability evaluation methods. *Computer Science Review, 33,* 49–68. doi:10.1016/j.cosrev.2019.05.001

Răvaş, O.-C. (2013). Homeworking Contract and Teleworking - Importance and Role in the Economy. *Annals of the University of Petrosani. Economics, 13*(2), 221–230.

Razavi, M., Shams Aliee, F., & Badie, K. (2010). An AHP-based approach toward enterprise architecture analysis based on enterprise architecture quality attributes. *Knowledge and Information Systems, 28*(2), 449–472. doi:10.100710115-010-0312-1

RDS. (2019). Alibaba Cloud ApsaraDB for RDS (Relational Database System). Retrieved from https://intl.aliyun.com/product/apsaradb-for-rds

Read, J. (2005). *Using Emoticons to reduce Dependency in Machine Learning Techniques for Sentiment Classification.* Department of Informatics, University of Sussex United Kingdom.

Redman, J. (2011). A development program to improve leadership capability and employee engagement. *Strategic HR Review, 10*(6), 11–18. doi:10.1108/14754391111172779

Reich, B. H., & Kaarst-Brown, M. L. (2003). Creating social and intellectual capital through IT career transitions. *The Journal of Strategic Information Systems, 12*(2), 91–109. doi:10.1016/S0963-8687(03)00017-9

Reissner, S., & Pagan, V. (2013). Generating employee engagement in a public–private partnership: Management communication activities and employee experiences. *International Journal of Human Resource Management, 24*(14), 2741–2759. doi:10.1080/09585192.2013.765497

Reitan, E. (2001). Rape as an essentially contested concept. *Hypatia, 6*(2), 43–66. doi:10.1111/j.1527-2001.2001.tb01058.x

Rhoads, A., & Au, K. F. (2015). PacBio Sequencing and Its Applications. *Genomics, Proteomics & Bioinformatics, 13*(5), 278–289. doi:10.1016/j.gpb.2015.08.002 PMID:26542840

Rich, B. L., Lepine, J. A., & Crawford, E. R. (2010). Job engagement: Antecedents and effects on job performance. *Academy of Management Journal, 53*(3), 617–635. doi:10.5465/amj.2010.51468988

Richman, A. (2006). Everyone wants an engaged workforce how can you create it? *Workspan*, (49), 36-39.

Richter. (2014). Do MOOCS need a special instructional design? *Proceeding of EDULEARN14.*

Ridings, C. M., & Gefen, D. (2004). Virtual community attraction: Why people hang out online. *Journal of Computer-Mediated Communication, 10*(1), 00. doi:10.1111/j.1083-6101.2004.tb00229.x

Riemer, K., & Schellhammer, S. (2019). *Collaboration in the Digital Age: Diverse, Relevant and Challenging.* Cham: Springer. doi:10.1007/978-3-319-94487-6

Right Management. (2006). *Measuring True Employee Engagement.* Philadelphia: Right Management.

Rigon, E. A., Westphall, C. M., dos Santos, D. R., & Westphall, C. B. (2014). A cyclical evaluation model of information security maturity. *Information Management & Computer Security, 22*(3), 265–278. doi:10.1108/IMCS-04-2013-0025

RileyMar, T. (2017). *Artificial intelligence goes deep to beat humans at poker.* Retrieved from http://www.sciencemag.org/news/2017/03/artificial-intelligence-goes-deep-beat-humans-poker

Ringle, C. M., Sarstedt, M., & Mooi, E. A. (2010). Response-based segmentation using finite mixture partial least squares. In Data Mining (pp. 19-49). Springer. doi:10.1007/978-1-4419-1280-0_2

Ringle, C. M., & Sarstedt, M. (2016). Gain more insight from your PLS-SEM results: The importance-performance map analysis. *Industrial Management & Data Systems, 116*(9), 1865–1886. doi:10.1108/IMDS-10-2015-0449

Ritchie, J. (1991). *The Secret World of Cults Angus & Robertson.* Academic Press.

Rivard, R. (2013). EdX Rejected. *Inside Higher Education.* Available at: http//www.insidehighered.com/news/2013/04/19/despite-courtship-amherst-decides-shy-away-star-mooc-provider

Robinson, D., Perryman, S., & Hayday, S. (2004). *The Drivers of Employee Engagement, Report 408.* Retrieved January 18, 2019, from http://www.employment-studies.co.uk/report-summaries/report-summary-drivers-employee-engagement

Robson, J. (1966). *The College Fraternity and Its Modern Role. Menasha.* Banta.

Rodriguez, J. (2011). Social media use in higher education: Key areas to consider for educators. *MERLOT Journal of Online Learning and Teaching*, *7*(4), 539–550.

Romano, M., & Kapelan, Z. (2014). Adaptive water demand forecasting for near real-time management of smart water distribution systems. *Environmental Modelling & Software*, *60*, 265–276. doi:10.1016/j.envsoft.2014.06.016

Rong, G., & Grover, V. (2009). Keeping up-to-date with information technology: Testing a model of technological knowledge renewal effectiveness for IT professionals. *Information & Management*, *46*(7), 376–387. doi:10.1016/j.im.2009.07.002

Rose, J., Hewitt, B., & Baxter, J. (2013). Women and part-time employment Easing or squeezing time pressure? *Journal of Sociology (Melbourne, Vic.)*, *49*(1), 41–59. doi:10.1177/1440783311419907

Rosen, M., Weaver, S., Lazzara, E., Salas, E., Wu, T., Silvestri, S., ... King, H. (2010). Tools for Evaluating Team Performance in Simulation-Based Training. *Journal of Emergencies, Trauma and Shock*, *3*(4), 353–359. doi:10.4103/0974-2700.70746 PMID:21063558

Rossi, F., van Beek, P., & Walsh, T. (2006). *Handbook of Constraint Programming*. Elsevier.

Rossi, R., & Mustaro, P. N. (2014). Process Management for e-learning Quality. *International Journal of Information and Education Technology (IJIET)*, *4*(4), 302–307. doi:10.7763/IJIET.2014.V4.418

Rothkrantz, L. J. M. (2017c). New Didactic Models for MOOCs. *CSEDU*, 505-512.

Rothkrantz, L. J. M. (2009). E-learning in virtual environments. *Communication & Cognition*, *42*(1&2), 37–52.

Rothkrantz, L. J. M. (2014) New Didactical Modals in Open and Online Learning based on Social media. *International Conference on e-Learning*, 9-18.

Rothkrantz, L. J. M. (2015a) From e-Learning to m-learning: a MOOC case study. *International Conference on e-Learning*.

Rothkrantz, L. J. M. (2015b). How Social Media Facilitate Learning Communities and Peer Groups around MOOCs. *International Journal of Human Capital and Information Technology Professionals*, *6*(1), 1–13. doi:10.4018/ijhcitp.2015010101

Rothkrantz, L. J. M. (2015c). Inquiry based learning as didactic model in distant-learning. *International Journal on Information Technologies & Security*, *7*(4).

Rothkrantz, L. J. M. (2016a) Didactic model for e-learning and regular courses. *International Conference on e-Learning*, *15*, 156-162.

Rothkrantz, L. J. M. (2016b) Dropout rates of regular courses and MOOCs. *Proceedings of the 8th International Conference on Computer Supported Education (CSEDU)*, 9-18. 10.5220/0006811600010001

Rothkrantz, L. J. M. (2016c) Flood control of the smart city Prague. *Smart Cities Symposium Prague (SCSP)*, 1-7. 10.1109/SCSP.2016.7501043

Rothkrantz, L. J. M. (2016e) On the Use of Social Media in Distance Learning. *Proceedings of the 17th International Conference on Computer Systems and Technologies*, 347-354. 10.1145/2983468.2983514

Rothkrantz, L. J. M. (2017a) An Affective Distant-learning Model Using Avatars as User Stand-in. *Proceedings of the 18th International Conference on Computer Systems and Technologies*, 288-295. 10.1145/3134302.3134314

Rothkrantz, L. J. M. (2017b). Affective didactic models in higher education. *International Journal of Human Capital and Information Technology Professionals*, *8*(4), 50–66. doi:10.4018/IJHCITP.2017100105

Rothkrantz, L. J. M. (2018). Integration of MOOCs in regular courses. *Proceedings of the 19th International Conference on Computer Systems and Technologies*, 144-151.

Rothkrantz, L. J. M., & Fitrianie, S. (2018). *Public Awareness and Education for Flooding Disasters. In Crisis Management-Theory and Practice*. IntechOpen.

Rotundo, M., & Sackett, P. R. (2002). The Relative Importance of Task, Citizenship, and Counterproductive Performance to Global Ratings of Job Performance: A Policy-Capturing Approach. *The Journal of Applied Psychology*, *87*(1), 66–80. doi:10.1037/0021-9010.87.1.66 PMID:11916217

Rozanski, N., & Woods, E. (2011). *Software systems architecture: working with stakeholders using viewpoints and perspectives*. Addison-Wesley.

Rozman, T., Maio, B., & Alexeeva, I. (2019). *How to develop a course (A manual for trainers)* (T. Rozman, Ed.). Maribor: BICERO Ltd. Retrieved from https://succeed.bicero.com/results/io6-manual

Rubel, S. (2005). *Trends to watch. Part II: social commerce–micro persuasion*. Academic Press.

Rubin, R. (1988). Moral distancing and the use of information technologies: The seven temptations. In J. M. Kizza (Ed.), *Social and ethical effects of the computer revolution* (pp. 124–125). Jefferson: McFarland and Company.

Russell, G. (2004). *The distancing dilemma in distance education*. Retrieved from Monash University: http://www.itdl.org/journal/feb_04/article03.htm

Russell, S. (2015). This artificial intelligence pioneer has a few concerns. *Quanta Magazine*. Retrieved from https://www.wired.com/2015/05/artificial-intelligence-pioneer-concerns/

Russell, S., & Norvig, P. (2003). Artificial Intelligence: A modern approach (3rd ed.). Prentice Hall.

Rutherford, C. (2010). Using online social media to support preservice student engagement. *MERLOT Journal of Online Learning and Teaching*, *6*(4), 703–711.

Saarnio, L., Boström, A.-M., Hedman, R., Gustavsson, P., & Öhlén, J. (2017). Enabling at-homeness for residents living in a nursing home: Reflected experience of nursing home staff. *Journal of Aging Studies*, *43*, 40–45. doi:10.1016/j.jaging.2017.10.001 PMID:29173513

Sabau, G., Munten, M., Bologa, A.-R., Bologa, R., & Surcel, T. (2009). An evaluation framework for higher education ERP systems. *WSEAS Transactions on Computers*, *8*(11), 1790–1799.

Sadiqe, M. (2014). Employee Engagement in Hospitality Industry in India: An Overview. *Global Journal of Finance and Management.*, *6*(4), 375–378.

Safa, N. S., Maple, C., Watson, T., & Von Solms, R. (2018). Motivation and opportunity based model to reduce information security insider threats in organisations. *Journal of Information Security and Applications, 40*, 247-257.

Safa, N. S., Maple, C., Furnell, S., Azad, M. A., Perera, C., Dabbagh, M., & Sookhak, M. (2019). Deterrence and prevention-based model to mitigate information security insider threats in organisations. *Future Generation Computer Systems*, *97*, 587–597. doi:10.1016/j.future.2019.03.024

Saifalislam, K. M., Osman, A., & AlQudah, M. K. (2014). Human resource management practices: Influence of recruitment and selection, and training and development on the organizational performance of the Jordanian Public University. *Journal of Business and Management, 16*(5), 43-46.

Saini, C., & Abraham, J. (2019). Implementing Facebook-based instructional approach in pre-service teacher education: An empirical investigation. *Computers & Education*, *128*, 243–255. doi:10.1016/j.compedu.2018.09.025

Saks, A. M. (2006). Antecedents and consequences of employee engagement. *Journal of Managerial Psychology*, *21*(7), 600–619. doi:10.1108/02683940610690169

Salaheldin, S. I., Sharif, K., & Al Alami, M. (2010). Utilization of Project Management Software in Qatari Government Organizations. *International Journal of Human Capital and Information Technology Professionals*, *1*(1), 1–15. doi:10.4018/jhcitp.2010091101

Salanova, M., Agut, S., & Peiro, J. M. (2005). Linking organizational resources and work engagement to employee performance and customer loyalty: The mediation of service climate. *The Journal of Applied Psychology*, *90*(6), 1217–1227. doi:10.1037/0021-9010.90.6.1217 PMID:16316275

Salawu, S., He, Y., & Lumsden, J. (2017). Approaches to Automated Detection of Cyberbullying: A Survey. *IEEE Transactions on Affective Computing*, *3045*(c), 1–20. doi:10.1109/TAFFC.2017.2761757

Salesforce. (2019). *Salesforce*. Retrieved from https://www.salesforce.com

Sánchez, A. M., & Pérez, M. P. (2005). Supply chain flexibility and firm performance. *International Journal of Operations & Production Management*, *25*(7), 681–700. doi:10.1108/01443570510605090

Sanchez, D., & Florez, H. (2018). Model driven engineering approach to manage peripherals in mobile devices. *International Conference on Computational Science and Its Applications*, 353–364. 10.1007/978-3-319-95171-3_28

Sand, T., Cangemi, J., & Ingram, J. (2011). Say again? What do associates really want at work? *Organization Development Journal*, *29*(2), 101–107.

Santhanam, R., Seligman, L., & Kang, D. (2007). Post implementation knowledge transfers to users and information technology professionals. *Journal of Management Information Systems*, *24*(1), 171–199. doi:10.2753/MIS0742-1222240105

Sanyal, M. K., & Biswas, S. B. (2014). Employee Motivation from Performance Appraisal Implications: Test of a Theory in the Software Industry in West Bengal (India). *Procedia Economics and Finance*, *11*, 182–196. doi:10.1016/S2212-5671(14)00187-7

Sanz, J., Nayak, N., & Becker, V. (2006). Business services as a modeling approach for smart business networks. *IBM Research Devision Almaden Research Center RJ10381 (A0606-001)*, 1-16.

SAP. (2012a). *Business Process Management Business Transformation Academy*. SAP.

SAP. (2013a). GBTP: Global Business Transformation Manager Master Certification (SAP Internal). Business Transformation Academy.

SAP. (2019). *SAP Hybris Sales Cloud*. Retrieved from https://www.sap.com/products/crm-commerce/sales.html

Sarangee, S., & Srivastava, R. K. (2012). Driving Employee Engagement in Nationalized Banks in India. *2012 International Conference on Economics, Business Innovation*.

Sarmento, M., Rosinha, A., & Silva, J. (2015). *Avaliação do Desempenho*. Lisboa: Escolar Editora.

Sarode, A. P., & Deore, S. S. (2017). Role of third party employee verification and background checks in HR management: An overview. *Journal of Commerce & Management Thought*, *8*(1), 86–96. doi:10.5958/0976-478X.2017.00005.2

Satchell, C., & Dourish, P. (2009). Beyond the user: use and non-use in HCI. In *OZCHI 2009: Proceedings of the 21st Annual Conference of the Australian Computer-Human Interaction Special Interest Group (CHISIG) of the Human Factors and Ergonomics Society of Australia (HFESA)*. The University of Melbourne. 10.1145/1738826.1738829

Sattar, T., Ahmad, K., & Hassan, S. M. (2015). The role of human resource practices in employee performance and job satisfaction with mediating effect of employee engagement. *Pakistan Economic and Social Review*, *53*(1), 81–96.

Sawyer, S., & Tapia, A. (2005). The sociotechnical nature of mobile computing work: Evidence from a study of policing in the United States. *International Journal of Technology and Human Interaction, 1*(3), 1–14. doi:10.4018/jthi.2005070101

Saygili, E. E., Ozturkoglu, Y., & Kocakulah, M. C. (2017). End Users' Perceptions of Critical Success Factors in ERP Applications. *International Journal of Enterprise Information Systems, 13*(4), 58–75. doi:10.4018/IJEIS.2017100104

Scagnoli. (2014). How to design an MOOC. *Proceeding of EDULEARN14.*

Schaufeli, W. B., Bakker, A. B., & Salanova, M. (2006). The measurement of work engagement with a short questionnaire: A cross-national study. *Educational and Psychological Measurement, 66*(4), 701–716. doi:10.1177/0013164405282471

Schaufeli, W. B., Bakker, A. B., & Van Rhenen, W. (2009). How changes in job demands and resources predict burnout, work engagement, and sickness absenteeism. *Journal of Organizational Behavior, 30*(7), 893–917. doi:10.1002/job.595

Schaufeli, W., Martı'nez, I., Marque's-Pinto, A., Salanova, M., & Bakker, A. B. (2002). Burnout and engagement in university students: A cross nation study. *Journal of Cross-Cultural Psychology, 33*(5), 464–481. doi:10.1177/0022022102033005003

Schawber, K., & Beedle, M. (2001). *Agile Software Development with Scrum.* Englewood Cliffs, NJ: Prentice Hall.

Schindel, K. (2018). *An analysis of implementing an ERP system in a higher education institution.* Academic Press.

Schlosser, F., Beimborn, D., Weitzel, T., & Wagner, H. T. (2015). Achieving social alignment between business and IT–an empirical evaluation of the efficacy of IT governance mechanisms. *Journal of Information Technology, 30*(2), 119–135. doi:10.1057/jit.2015.2

Schwarz, B. B. (2005). Do EU funded projects enable collaboration between scientists? the case of R&D in web-based collaborative learning environments. *Computers & Education, 45*(3), 375–382. doi:10.1016/j.compedu.2005.04.009

Seaman, J., & Tinti-Kane, H. (2013). *Social Media for teaching and learning.* Boston, MA: Pearson Learning Solutions. Retrieved from https://www.onlinelearningsurvey.com/reports/social-media-for-teaching-and-learning-2013-report.pdf

Seddon, P. B., Calvert, C., & Yang, S. (2010). A multi-project model of key factors affecting organizational benefits from enterprise systems. *Management Information Systems Quarterly, 34*(2), 305–328. doi:10.2307/20721429

See-To, E. W., & Ho, K. K. (2014). Value co-creation and purchase intention in social network sites: The role of electronic Word-of-Mouth and trust–A theoretical analysis. *Computers in Human Behavior, 31,* 182–189. doi:10.1016/j.chb.2013.10.013

Seffah, A., Donyaee, M., Kline, R. B., & Padda, H. K. (2006). Usability measurement and metrics : A consolidated model. *Software Quality Journal, 14*(2), 159–178. doi:10.100711219-006-7600-8

Segrera, F. L. (2010). *Trends and Innovations in Higher Education Reform: Worldwide, Latin America and the Caribbean.* Berkeley, CA: Center for Studies in Higher Education.

Seidewitz, E. (2003). What models mean. *Software, IEEE, 20*(5), 26–32. doi:10.1109/MS.2003.1231147

Seijit, G. M., & Crim, D. (2006). What engages the employees the most or, the ten C's of employee engagement. *Ivey Business Journal Online.*

Sekaran, U., & Bougie, R. J. (2016). *Research methods for business: A skill building approach.* John Wiley & Sons.

Selden, S. C. (2009). *Human capital: Tools and strategies for the public sector.* Washington, DC: CQ Press. doi:10.4135/9781483330754

Selic, B. (2003). The pragmatics of model-driven development. *IEEE Software, 20*(5), 19–25. doi:10.1109/MS.2003.1231146

Serdar, A. M. (2010). Performance management and key performance indicators for higher education institutions in Serbia. *Perspectives of Innovations, Economics and Business, 6*(3), 120–124.

Seshadri, V., & Elangovan, N. (2019a). Distances in Geographically Distributed Team: A Review. *Research Review International Journal of Multidisciplinary, 4*(3).

Seshadri, V., & Elangovan, N. (2019b). Role of Manager in Geographically Distributed Team: A Review. *Journal of Management, 6*(1), 122–129. doi:10.34218/JOM.6.1.2019.013

Shakkah, M. S., Alaqeel, K., Alfageeh, A., & Budiarto, R. (2016). An investigation study on optimizing enterprise resource planning (ERP) implementation in emerging public university: Al Baha university case study. *Iranian Journal of Electrical and Computer Engineering, 6*(4), 1920–1928.

Shalley, C. E., & Gilson, L. L. (2004). What leaders need to know: A review of social and contextual factors that can foster or hinder creativity. *The Leadership Quarterly, 15*(1), 33–53. doi:10.1016/j.leaqua.2003.12.004

Shantz, A., Alfes, K., Truss, C., & Soane, E. (2013). The role of employee engagement in the relationship between job design and task performance, citizenship and deviant behaviours. *International Journal of Human Resource Management, 24*(13), 2608–2627. doi:10.1080/09585192.2012.744334

Shanumugam, P., & Krishnaveni, R. (2012). Employee Engagement: An Introspection Into its Conceptualization. *International Journal of Social Science & Interdisciplinary Research, 1*(9), 186–194.

Sharma, A., & Rani, S. (2016, April). An automatic segmentation & detection of blood vessels and optic disc in retinal images. In *2016 International Conference on Communication and Signal Processing (ICCSP)* (pp. 1674-1678). IEEE. 10.1109/ICCSP.2016.7754449

Sharma, K. (2016). Understanding the concept of honor killing within the social paradigm: A theoretical perspective. *ISOR Journal of Humanities and Social Science, 21*(9), 125–127.

Sharp, J. H., & Lang, G. (2018). Agile in Teaching and Learning: Conceptual Framework and Research Agenda. *Journal of Information Systems Education, 29*(2), 45–52.

Shatat, A. S. (2019). The Impact of ERP System on Academic Performance: A Case Study Approach. *Journal of Information & Knowledge Management*, 1950018.

Shatat, A., El-Baz, H., & Hariga, M. (2010). Employee expectations: Perception of Generation-Y engineers in the UAE. *2010 Second International Conference on Engineering Systems Management and Its Applications (ICESMA)*, 1–6.

Shawgi, E., & Noureldien, N. A. (2015). Usability Measurement Model (UMM): A New Model for Measuring Websites Usability. *International Journal of Information Science, 5*(1), 5–13. doi:10.5923/j.ijis.20150501.02

Shea, T. P., Sherer, P. D., Quilling, R. D., & Blewett, C. N. (2011). Managing Global Virtual Teams Across Classrooms, Students and Faculty. *Journal of Teaching in International Business, 22*(4), 300–313. doi:10.1080/08975930.2011.653911

Shin, B., & Kim, G. (2011). Investigating the reliability of second-order formative measurement in information systems research. *European Journal of Information Systems, 20*(5), 608–623. doi:10.1057/ejis.2011.7

Shoham, S., & Perry, M. (2009). Knowledge management as a mechanism for technological and organizational change management in Israeli universities. *Higher Education, 57*(2), 227–246. doi:10.100710734-008-9148-y

Sicilia, M. A., Cuadrado, J. J., García, E., Rodríguez, D., & Hilera, J. R. (2005). The evaluation of ontological representation of the SWEBOK as a revision tool. *Proceedings of the 9th Annual International Computer Software and Application Conference (COMPSAC)*, 26-28.

Siemens, G. (2012). MOOCs are really a platform [Web Log Post]. Retrieved December 05, 2013, from http://www.elearnspace.org/blog/2012/07/25/ moocs-are-really-a-platform/

Silva, A., Varajão, J., Pereira, J. L., & Pinto, C. S. (2017). Performance Appraisal Approaches and Methods for IT/IS Projects: A Review. *International Journal of Human Capital and Information Technology Professionals*, *8*(3), 15–28. doi:10.4018/IJHCITP.2017070102

Silva, F. O. D. (2018). *Service selection and ranking in Cross-organizational Business Process collaboration (PhD)*. Eindhoven: University of Technology of Eindhoven.

Singe, I., & Croucher, R. (2003). The management of trust-based working time in Germany. *Personnel Review*, *32*(4), 492–509. doi:10.1108/004834480310477551

Singh, A., & Sanjeev, R. (2013). Employee engagement in a public sector undertaking: An investigation. *International Journal of Management Research & Business Strategy*, *2*(2), 93–100.

Singh, R., Garg, K., & Deshmukh, S. G. (2008). Challenges and strategies for competitiveness of SMEs: A case study in the Indian context. *International Journal of Services and Operations Management*, *4*(2), 181–200. doi:10.1504/IJSOM.2008.016610

Sin, S. S., Nor, K. M., & Al-Agaga, A. M. (2012). Factors Affecting Malaysian young consumers' online purchase intention in social media websites. *Procedia: Social and Behavioral Sciences*, *40*, 326–333. doi:10.1016/j.sbspro.2012.03.195

Skapinker, M. (2013). Open web courses are massively overhyped. *Financial Times*. Retrieved 5 April 2013. https://ipfs.io/ipfs/QmXoypizjW3WknFiJnKLwHCnL72vedxjQkDDP1mXWo6uco/wiki/Massive_open_online_course.html

SLB. (2019). *Alibaba Cloud Server Load Balancer (SLB)*. Retrieved from https://intl.aliyun.com/

Smah, S. O. (2001). *Perception and Control of Secret Cult and Gang-induced Difficulties for Quality Living and Learning in Nigerian Universities: The Case study of Universities in the Middle Belt Zone*. Centre for Development Studies University of Jos.

Smith, P. C., & Kendall, L. M. (1963). Retranslations of expectations: An approach to the construction of unambiguous anchors for rating scales. *The Journal of Applied Psychology*, *47*(2), 147–155. doi:10.1037/h0047060

Smith, S. W. (2003). Humans in the loop: Human-computer interaction and security. *IEEE Security & Privacy Magazine*, *1*(3), 75–79. doi:10.1109/MSECP.2003.1203228

Smolka, G. (2004). The development of Oz and mozart. In *Multiparadigm Programming in Mozart/Oz, second international conference, MOZ 2004, charleroi, Belgium, October 7-8, 2004, revised selected and invited papers* (p. 1). Academic Press.

Sokolova, K., & Kefi, H. (2019). Instagram and YouTube bloggers promote it, why should I buy? How credibility and parasocial interaction influence purchase intentions. *Journal of Retailing and Consumer Services*. doi:10.1016/j.jretconser.2019.01.011

Soliman, M., & Karia, N. (2017). Antecedents for the Success of the Adoption of Organizational ERP Among Higher Education Institutions and Competitive Advantage in Egypt. *Technology & Applied Science Research*, *7*(3), 1719–1724.

Sommerville. (2011). *Software Engineering* (9th ed.). Addison-Wesley.

Soni, B. S. (2013). Employee engagement - A key to organizational success in 21st Century. *Voice of Research.*, *1*(4), 51–55.

Soto, R., Crawford, B., Olivares, R., Galleguillos, C., Castro, C., Johnson, F., ... Norero, E. (2016). Using Autonomous Search for Solving Constraint Satisfaction Problems via new modern approaches. *Swarm and Evolutionary Computation*, *30*, 64–77. doi:10.1016/j.swevo.2016.04.003

Soto, R., Crawford, B., Palma, W., Galleguillos, K., Castro, C., Monfroy, E., ... Paredes, F. (2015). Boosting Autonomous Search for CSPs via Skylines. *Inf. Science*, *308*, 38–48. doi:10.1016/j.ins.2015.01.035

Spears, V. P. (2012). Employee Wellness Programs Expand to Well-Being. *Employee Benefit Plan Review*, *66*(11), 30.

Speckert, T., Rychkova, I., Zdravkovic, J., & Nurcan, S. (2013). On the Changing Role of Enterprise Architecture in Decentralized Environments: State of the Art. *Enterprise Distributed Object Computing Conference Workshops (EDOCW), 2013 17th IEEE International*, 310–318.

Speicher, M. (2015). *What is Usability? A Characterization based on ISO 9241-11 and ISO/IEC 25010*. Retrieved from http://arxiv.org/abs/1502.06792

Spicker, P. (1999). *Definitions of poverty: Twelve clusters of meaning*. Retrieved 23rd February, 2017, from http://dds.cepal.org/infancia/guide-to-estimating-child-poverty/bibliografia/capitulo-I/Spicker%20Paul%20(1999)%20Definitions%20of%20poverty%20eleven%20clusters%20of%20meaning.pdf

Spring. (2019). *Spring Framework*. Retrieved from https://spring.io/

Sreejith, S. S., & Mathirajan, M. (2016). Identifying Criteria for Continuous Evaluation of Software Engineers for Reward and Recognition: An Exploratory Research. *International Journal of Human Capital and Information Technology Professionals*, *7*(4), 61–78. doi:10.4018/IJHCITP.2016100105

Staal, J., Abràmoff, M. D., Niemeijer, M., Viergever, M. A., & Van Ginneken, B. (2004). Ridge-based vessel segmentation in color images of the retina. *IEEE Transactions on Medical Imaging*, *23*(4), 501–509. doi:10.1109/TMI.2004.825627 PMID:15084075

Stagnaro, C., & Piotrowski, C. (2014). Shared leadership: A critical component in IT project management. *Journal of Technology Research*, *5*(October), 1–21.

Statista. (2018). *Most popular social networks worldwide as of January 2018, ranked by number of active users (in millions)*. Retrieved from https://www.statista.com/statistics/272014/global-social-networks-ranked-by-number-of-users/

Stephen, L. (2008). Rethinking risk in the new economy: Age and cohort effects on unemployment and re-employment. *Human Resources*, *61*, 1259–1292.

Stewart, J. M., Tittel, E., & Chapple, M. (2005). *Certified Information Systems Security Professional (Study Guide)* (3rd ed.). San Francisco: Sybex.

Stone, M. (1974). Cross-Validatory Choice and Assessment of Statistical Predictions. *Journal of the Royal Statistical Society. Series A (General)*, *36*(2), 111–147.

Straus, M. A. (1990). Measuring intra-family conflict and violence: The conflict tactics (CT) scales. Academic Press.

Styles, M., & Tryfonas, T. (2009). Using penetration testing feedback to cultivate proactive security amongst end-users. *Information Management & Computer Security*, *17*(1), 44–52. doi:10.1108/09685220910944759

Subramaniam, C., Shamsudin, F. M., & Ibrahim, H. (2011). Linking human resource practices and organisational performance: Evidence from small and medium organizations in Malaysia. *Journal Pengurusan*, *32*, 27–37. doi:10.17576/pengurusan-2011-32-04

Subramanyam, M., & Priya, V. (2015). A Study of Captcha Techniques and Development of SUPER Captcha for Secured Web Transactions. *International Journal of Applied Engineering Research, 10*(21).

Sudan, F. K. (2005), Challenges in Micro and Small Scale Enterprises Development: Some Policy Issues. *Synergy: I. T. S. Journal of IT and Management, 3*(2), 67-81.

Sudhakar, G., Farooq, A., & Patnaik, S. (2011). Soft factors affecting the performance of software development teams. *Team Performance Management*, *17*(3/4), 187–205.

Sun, W., Xu, A., & Shang, Y. (2014). Transformational leadership, team climate, and team performance within the NPD team: Evidence from China. *Asia Pacific Journal of Management*, *31*(1), 127–147. doi:10.100710490-012-9327-3

Suo, S. (2013). *Cloud implementation in organizations: Critical success factors, challenges, and impacts on the IT function* (Doctoral dissertation).

Süß, S., & Becker, J. (2013). Competences as the foundation of employability: A qualitative study of German freelancers. *Personnel Review*, *42*(2), 223–240. doi:10.1108/00483481311309393

Suwantarathip, O., & Wichadee, S. (2014). The Effects of Collaborative Writing Activity Using Google Docs on Students' Writing Abilities. *Turkish Online Journal of Educational Technology, 13*(2005), 148–156. Retrieved from http://eric.ed.gov/?q=Google+Docs&ff1=dtySince_2010&id=EJ1022935

Swamynathan, G., Wilson, C., Boe, B., Almeroth, K., & Zhao, B. Y. (2008, August). Do social networks improve e-commerce?: a study on social marketplaces. In *Proceedings of the first workshop on Online social networks* (pp. 1-6). ACM. 10.1145/1397735.1397737

Swartz, D., & Orgill, K. (2001). Higher Education ERP: Lessons Learned. *EDUCAUSE Quarterly*, *24*(2), 20–27.

Syamala, D. B., & Dasaraju, S. R. (2014). *A suggested conceptual framework for employee background Check*. ICBPEM, Knowledge Partner.

Taleb, M., & Cherkaoui, O. (2012, January). Pattern-Oriented Approach for Enterprise Architecture: TOGAF Framework. *Journal of Software Engineering & Applications*, *5*(1), 45–50. doi:10.4236/jsea.2012.51008

Tam, J., Simsa, J., Hyde, S., & Ahn, L. V. (2010). Breaking Audio CAPTCHAs. Advances in Neural Information Processing Systems, 1625-1632.

Tan, X., & Kim, Y. (2015). User acceptance of SaaS-based collaboration tools: A case of Google Docs. *Journal of Enterprise Information Management*, *28*(3), 423–442. doi:10.1108/JEIM-04-2014-0039

Tarafdar, M., D'Arcy, J., Turel, O., & Gupta, A. (2014, December 16). *The Dark Side of Information Technology*. Retrieved September 26, 2015, from MIT Sloan Management Review website: http://sloanreview.mit.edu/article/the-dark-side-of-information-technology/

Tassabehji, R. (2005). Information security threats: From evolution to prominence. In *Evcyclopedia of Multimedia Technology and Networking (Margherita Pagani)*. Idea Group Inc. doi:10.4018/978-1-59140-561-0.ch058

Taylor, F. (1911). *The Principles of Scientific Management*. Harper & Brothers.

Tayouri, D. (2015). The human factor in the social media security –combining education and technology to reduce social engineering risks and damages. In *6th International Conference on Applied Human Factors and Ergonomics (AHFE 2015) and the Affiliated Conferences, AHFE 2015*. Elsevier. 10.1016/j.promfg.2015.07.181

Technopidia. (2017). *Artificial Intelligence Definition*. Retrieved from https://www.techopedia.com/definition/190/artificial-intelligence-ai

Tegmark, M. (2016). Benefits and risks of artificial intelligence. *Future of Life*. Retrieved from https://futureoflife.org/background/benefits- risks-of-artificial- intelligence/

Tenenhaus, M., Vinzi, V. E., Chatelin, Y. M., & Lauro, C. (2005). PLS path modeling. *Computational Statistics & Data Analysis*, *48*(1), 159–205. doi:10.1016/j.csda.2004.03.005

Thakur, M., Blazer, D., & Steffens, D. (2013). *Clinical Manual of Geriatric Psychiatry* (Vol. 1). USA: American Psychiatric Publishing.

Thakur, P. (2014). A research paper on the effect of employee engagement on job satisfaction in IT sector. *Journal of Business Management & Social Sciences Research*, *3*(5), 31–30.

Thamhain, H. (2004). Linkages of project environment to performance: Lessons for team leadership. *International Journal of Project Management*, *22*(2), 533–544. doi:10.1016/j.ijproman.2004.04.005

The Economist. (2000). A survey of E-management-How to be an e-manager. *The Economist*.

The Economist. (2000). Inside the machine. A survey of E-management. *The Economist*.

The Economist. (2016). *Re-educating Rita. A Special Report on Education and Policy*. Retrieved from https://www.economist.com/news/special-report/21700760-artificial-intelligence-will-have-implications-policymakers-education-welfare-and

The Future of Jobs Report. (2018). *The World Economic Forum*. Retrieved from http://www3.weforum.org/docs/WEF_Future_of_Jobs_2018.pdf

The Joint Committee of Industry and Government. (2013). *White Paper On Stimulation Of Investment Of Private Sector Into Research And Development In India*. Department of Science & Technology, Ministry of Science & Technology, Government of India.

The Millennium Development Goals Report. (2015). *United Nations*. Retrieved from United Nations Millennium Development Goals website: https://www.un.org/millenniumgoals/2015_MDG_Report/pdf/MDG%202015%20rev%20(July%201).pdf

The Open Group. (2011a). *Architecture Development Method*. The Open Group. Retrieved from http://pubs.opengroup.org/architecture/togaf9-doc/arch/chap05.html

The Open Group. (2011b). *TOGAF 9.1*. The Open Group. Retrieved from http://www.opengroup.org/subjectareas/enterprise/togaf

The Open Group. (2011c). *Enterprise Architecture Standards*. Retrieved from http://www.opengroup.org/standards/ea

The World Economic Forum. (n.d.). *Global IT report 2015*. Retrieved from http://www3.weforum.org/docs/WEF_Global_IT_Report_2015.pdf

Thomas, A. (2015). *Innovation Insight for Microservices*. Retrieved from https://www.gartner.com/doc/3157319/innovation-insight-microservices

Thompson, L. (2003). Improving the creativity of organizational work groups. *The Academy of Management Executive*, *17*(1), 96–111. doi:10.5465/AME.2003.9474814

Thomson, K., & van Niekerk, J. (2012). Combating information security apathy by encouraging prosocial organisational behaviour. *Information Management & Computer Security*, *20*(1), 39–46. doi:10.1108/09685221211219191

Tidd, J. (2006). *From Knowledge Management to Strategic Competence* (2nd ed.). London, UK: Imperial College. doi:10.1142/p439

Tidd, J., & Bessant, J. (2009). *Managing Innovation, Integrating Technological, Market and Organizational Change* (4th ed.). Wiley.

Tidd, J., & Bessant, J. (2018). *Managing Innovation: Integrating Technological, Market and Organizational Change* (6th ed.). New York: Wiley.

Tiles, L. (2017). *15 Pros and 6 Cons of Artificial Intelligence in the classroom.* Retrieved from https://blogs.technet. com/b/nzedu/archive/2013/01/07/collaboration-and-the-role-of-technology-in-the-21st-century-classroom.aspx

Tinto, V. (1975). Dropout from Higher Education: A theoretical synthesis of recent research. *Review of Educational Research, 45*(1), 89–125. doi:10.3102/00346543045001089

Todd, P., & Binns, J. (2013). Work-life Balance: Is it Now a Problem for Management? *Gender, Work and Organization, 20*(3), 219–231. doi:10.1111/j.1468-0432.2011.00564.x

Tomar, J. S. (2017a). Employee Engagement Practices in IT Sector Vis-à-Vis Other Sectors in India. *International Journal of Human Capital and Information Technology Professionals, 8*(3), 1–14. doi:10.4018/IJHCITP.2017070101

Tomar, J. S. (2017b). Influence of Strategic Priorities of SMEs on Their Decision to Adopt ERP. *International Journal of Scientific Research and Management, 5*(11), 7423–7436.

Townsend, K., Wilkinson, A., & Burgess, J. (2014). Routes to partial success: Collaborative employment relations and employee engagement. *International Journal of Human Resource Management, 25*(6), 915–930. doi:10.1080/095851 92.2012.743478

Trad, A. (2011a). *The Selection and Training Framework* (Thesis). GEM, Grenoble, France.

Trad, A. (2018c). The Transformation Framework's Resources Library. IBISTM.

Trad, A., & Kalpić, D. (2015c). Transformation Framework Proposal for Managers in Business Innovation and Business Transformation eProjects-Intelligent atomic building block architecture. Centeris-Elsevier.

Trad, A., Kalpić, D., & Fertalj, K. (2002). Proactive monitoring of the information system risk and quality. *Information Technology Interfaces, 2002. ITI 2002. Proceedings of the 24th International Conference.*

Trad, A. (2013). *COSC 3750 - DSS, Decision Support Systems – Labs results.* Geneva, Switzerland: Webster University.

Trad, A. (2018a). *The Business Transformation Framework's Resources Library. Internal project.* IBISTM.

Trad, A. (2018b). *The Transformation Framework Proof of Concept. Internal project and paper.* IBISTM.

Trad, A. (2018d). *The Transformation Framework Proof of Concept.* IBISTM.

Trad, A., & Kalpic, D. (2001). *Building an extensible markup language (XML) based Object Mapping System (OMS).* IEEE.

Trad, A., & Kalpić, D. (2011a). The "Selection, Training, Follow and Evaluation (STF), for Manager's in Business Innovation Transformation Projects - The Human Factor". *Conference on Information Technology Interfaces.*

Trad, A., & Kalpić, D. (2013a). *The Selection and Training Framework (STF) for Managers in Business Innovation and Transformation eProjects - The Design and Implementation of the Research Model. 3rd position Award.* IMRA.

Trad, A., & Kalpić, D. (2013b). *The Selection, and Training framework (STF) for Managers in Business Innovation Transformation eProjects - The Literature Review. IEEE 2013.* Centeris.

Trad, A., & Kalpić, D. (2013c). The Selection, and Training Framework (STF) for Managers in Business Innovation Transformation eProjects -The Skills set. *Conference on Information Technology Interfaces.*

Trad, A., & Kalpić, D. (2014a). *The "Selection and Training Framework" (STF) for Manager's in Business Innovation Transformation eProjects" / The mathematical model.* EUROPMENT, Conference.

Trad, A., & Kalpić, D. (2014b). *The Selection and Training Framework (STF) for Managers in (e)Business Innovation Transformation eProjects - Managerial Recommendations*. Centeris, Portugal: IEEE.

Trad, A., & Kalpić, D. (2014c). The Selection, and Training Framework (STF) for Manager's in Business Innovation Transformation eProjects. *Mathematical Modelling*.

Trad, A., & Kalpić, D. (2014d). *The Selection and Training Framework (STF) for Managers in Business Innovation and Transformation eProjects - The Skills set of a Business Transformation Manager*. IMRA.

Trad, A., & Kalpić, D. (2014e). *The Selection and Training Framework (STF) for Managers in Business Innovation and Transformation Projects – The TOGAF recommendations*. Venice, Italy: EUROPMENT.

Trad, A., & Kalpić, D. (2014g). *The Selection and Training Framework (STF) for Managers in Business Innovation and Transformation Projects – The educational recommendations*. Zagreb, Croatia: EDEN.

Trad, A., & Kalpić, D. (2015a). *The Selection, Control, Decision making and Training Framework for Managers in Business Innovation and Transformation eProjects-Decision making model*. EUROPMENT Conference.

Trad, A., & Kalpić, D. (2015b). *The Selection, Control, Decision making and Training Framework for Managers in Business Innovation and Transformation eProjects- Managerial Recommendations for enterprise architecture*. EUROPMENT Conference.

Trad, A., & Kalpić, D. (2016a). *The (e)Business Transformation Framework for (e)Commerce Architecture-Modelling Projects. In Encyclopaedia of E-Commerce Development, Implementation, and Management*. IGI-Global.

Trad, A., & Kalpić, D. (2016b). *A Transformation Framework Proposal for Managers in Business Innovation and Business Transformation Projects-A heuristics decision module's background*. Oxford, UK: ABMR.

Trad, A., & Kalpić, D. (2017a). *An Intelligent Neural Networks Micro Artefact Patterns' Based Enterprise Architecture Model*. IGI-Global.

Trad, A., & Kalpić, D. (2017b). *A Neural Networks Portable and Agnostic Implementation TKM&F for Business Transformation eProjects. The Basic Structure*. Annecy, France: IEEE.

Trad, A., & Kalpić, D. (2017c). *A Neural Networks Portable and Agnostic Implementation TKM&F for Business Transformation eProjects. The Framework*. Annecy, France: IEEE.

Trad, A., & Kalpić, D. (2017d). A Neural Networks Portable and Agnostic Implementation *TKM&F* for Business Transformation eProjects- The Basic Structure. *IEEE Conference on Computational Intelligence*.

Trad, A., & Kalpić, D. (2017e). *The Business Transformation and Enterprise Architecture Framework / The London Inter Bank Offered Rate Crisis - The Model*. Cambridge, UK: ABMR.

Trad, A., & Kalpić, D. (2018a). *The Business Transformation Framework and Enterprise Architecture Framework for Managers in Business Innovation-Knowledge and Intelligence Driven Development (KIDD). Encyclopaedia*. IGI-Global.

Trad, A., & Kalpić, D. (2018b). *The Business Transformation Framework and Enterprise Architecture Framework for Managers in Business Innovation- Knowledge Management in Global Software Engineering (HKMS). In Encyclopaedia of E-Commerce Development, Implementation, and Management*. IGI-Global.

Trad, A., & Kalpić, D. (2018c). *The Business Transformation An applied mathematical model for business transformation-The applied case study. Encyclopaedia*. IGI-Global.

Trad, A., & Kalpić, D. (2018d). *The Business Transformation An applied mathematical model for business transformation- The Research Development eProjects Concept (RDPC). Encyclopaedia*. IGI-Global.

Trad, A., & Kalpić, D. (2018e). *The Business Transformation An applied mathematical model for business transformation-Introduction and basics. Encyclopaedia.* IGI-Global.

Trad, A., & Kalpić, D. (2018f). *An applied mathematical model for business transformation-The Holistic Critical Success Factors Management System (HCSFMS). In Encyclopaedia of E-Commerce Development, Implementation, and Management.* IGI-Global.

Trad, A., & Kalpić, D. (2019a). *The Trad-Kalpić Methodology and Framework. Total lead in business transformation and enterprise architecture projects-A google scholar analysis.* IBISTM.

Trigo, A., Varajão, J., Barroso, J., Soto-Acosta, P., Molina-Castillo, F. J., & Gonzalvez-Gallego, N. (2011). Enterprise Information Systems Adoption in Iberian Large Companies: Motivations and Trends. In M. Tavana (Ed.), *Managing Adaptability, Intervention, and People in Enterprise Information Systems* (pp. 204–228). Information Resources Management Association. doi:10.4018/978-1-60960-529-2.ch010

Trigo, A., Varajão, J., Figueiredo, N., & Barroso, J. (2007). Information Systems and Technology Adoption By the Portuguese Large Companies. *Proceedings of the European and Mediterranean Conference on Information Systems.*

Truss, C., Soane, E., Edwards, C., Wisdom, K., Croll, A., & Burnett, J. (2006). *Working Life: Employee Attitudes and Engagement 2006.* London: CIPD.

Tukool. (2018). *All you need to know about Eti-Osa LGA, Lagos State.* Retrieved from: https://tukool.com/know-nigeria/know-about-lagos/know-about-eti-osa/#The_Government_Of_Eti-Osa

Tulácek, M. (2009). *Constraint Solvers* (Bachelor thesis). Charles University in Prague.

Turban, E., King, D., & Lang, J. (2009). *Introduction to electronic commerce.* Upper Saddle River, NJ: Pearson Education, Inc.

Tushman, M. L., & O'Reilly, C. A. III. (1996). Ambidextrous organizations: Managing evolutionary and revolutionary change. *California Management Review*, *38*(4), 8–30. doi:10.2307/41165852

U.S. Office of Personnel Management. (n.d.). Retrieved from https://www.opm.gov

Ucha, C. (2010). Poverty in Nigeria: Some dimensions and contributing factors. *Global Majority E-Journal*, *1*(1), 46–48.

UCLES, . (2013). *Cambridge International General Secondary Certificate Examination.* London: Cambridge Examination Board.

Udoh, V. C., & Ikezu, U. J. M. (2014). Causes, Effects and Strategies for Eradicating Cultism among Students in Tertiary Institutions in Nigeria a Case Study of Nnamdi Azikiwe University Awka Anambra State, Nigeria. *Quest Journals Journal of Research in Humanities and Social Science, 2*(7), 12-20.

Uhl, L., & Gollenia. (2012). *A Handbook of Business Transformation Management Methodology.* Gower.

Uhuegbu, C., Ukpokolo, I., & Wogu, I. A. (2011). Advances in the History and Philosophy of Science. Lulu Enterprise, Inc.

Ullah, Z., Al-Mudimigh, A. S., Al-Ghamdi, A. A. L.-M., & Saleem, F. (2013). Critical success factors of ERP implementation at higher education institutes: A brief case study. *Information (Japan)*, *16*(10), 7369–7378.

Ulusu, Y., Durmus, E. S., & Yurtkoru, D. (2011). Personality, privacy and trust issues in virtual society. New perspective of contemporary marketing, Athens.

UN. (2019). United Nations Secretariat Guidelines For The Personal Use Of. *Social Medicine (Social Medicine Publication Group).*

UNSKP. (2015). *United Nations – Sustainable Development knowledge platform.* UNSKP.

Uppal, M. A., Ali, S., & Gulliver, S. R. (2018). Factors determining e-learning service quality. *British Journal of Educational Technology, 49*(3), 412–426. doi:10.1111/bjet.12552

Uppal, M., & Rahman, T. (2013). *Business Transformation Made Straight-Forward.* QR Systems Inc.

USMLE. (2019). *United States Medical Licensing Examination – Sample Questions.* Retrieved online: https://www.usmle.org/step-1/

Uzun, E., Chung, S. P., Essa, I., & Lee, W. (2018). rtCaptcha: A Real-Time CAPTCHA Based Liveness Detection System. *Network and Distributed Systems Security (NDSS) Symposium 2018.* 10.14722/ndss.2018.23253

Valentine, R. L. (2014). *Human Resource Management. Stanford, CA: Cengage Learning. SHRM.*

van den Bos, A., Kemper, B., & de Waal, V. (2014). A study on how to improve the throughput time of Lean Six Sigma projects in a construction company. *International Journal of Lean Six Sigma, 5*(2), 226–212. doi:10.1108/IJLSS-10-2013-0055

Van Hee, C., Jacobs, G., Emmery, C., Desmet, B., Lefever, E., & Verhoeven, B. (2018). Automatic Detection of Cyberbullying in Social Media Text. Academic Press. doi:10.1371/journal.pone.0203794

Vance, A., Lowry, P. B., & Eggett, D. (2013). Using accountability to reduce access policy violations in information systems. *Journal of Management Information Systems, 29*(4), 263–290. doi:10.2753/MIS0742-1222290410

Vandenberg, R., & Lance, C. (1992). Satisfaction and organisational commitment. *Journal of Management, 18*, 153–167. doi:10.1177/014920639201800110

Varajão, J. (2016). Success Management as a PM knowledge area - work-in-progress. *Procedia Computer Science, 100*, 1095–1102. doi:10.1016/j.procs.2016.09.256

Varajão, J. (2018a). A new process for success management - bringing order to a typically ad-hoc area. *Journal of Modern Project Management, 5*(3), 94–99.

Varajão, J. (2018b). The many facets of information systems (+projects) success. *International Journal of Information Systems and Project Management, 6*(4), 5–13.

Varajão, J., & Carvalho, J. Á. (2018). Evaluating the Success of IS/IT Projects: How Are Companies Doing It? *13th Pre-ICIS International Research Workshop on Information Technology Project Management.*

Varajão, J., Dominguez, C., Ribeiro, P., & Paiva, A. (2014). Critical Success Aspects in Project Management: Similarities and Differences Between the Construction and the Software Industry. *Technical Gazette, 21*(2), 583–589.

Varajão, J., & Moura, I. (2018). Leading Information Systems Academic Teams to High Performance. *Proceedings of the 24th Americas Conference on Information Systems.*

Varajao, J., Trigo, A., Figueiredo, N., Barroso, J., & Cruz, J. B. (2009). Information systems services outsourcing reality in large Portuguese organisations. *International Journal of Business Information Systems, 4*(1), 125–142. doi:10.1504/IJBIS.2009.021606

Vardi, M. Y. (2012). Will MOOCs destroy academia? *Communications of the ACM, 55*(11), 5. doi:10.1145/2366316.2366317

Vathanophas, V., & Stuart, L. (2009). Enterprise resource planning: Technology acceptance in Thai universities. *Enterprise Information Systems, 3*(2), 133–158. doi:10.1080/17517570802653800

Vega-Velázquez, M., García-Nájera, A., & Cervantes, H. (2018). A Survey on the Software Project Scheduling Problem. *International Journal of Production Economics, 202*, 145–161. doi:10.1016/j.ijpe.2018.04.020

Venkatesh, V., & Bala, H. (2008). Technology acceptance model 3 and a research agenda on interventions. *Decision Sciences*, *39*(2), 273–315. doi:10.1111/j.1540-5915.2008.00192.x

Venkatesh, V., & Davis, F. D. (2000). A theoretical extension of the technology acceptance model: Four longitudinal field studies. *Management Science*, *46*(2), 186–204. doi:10.1287/mnsc.46.2.186.11926

Verner, T. (2011). National Competitiveness and Expenditure on Education, Research and Development. *Journal of Competitiveness*, *3*(2). Retrieved from http://search.proquest.com.strauss.uc3m.es:8080/docview/1315218679/abstract

Verville, J., Bernadas, C., & Halingten, A. (2005). So you're thinking of buying an ERP? Ten critical factors for successful acquisitions. *Journal of Enterprise Information Management*, *18*(6), 665–677. doi:10.1108/17410390510628373

Vesal, S., Ravikumar, N., & Maier, A. (2018). *SkinNet: A Deep Learning Framework for Skin Lesion Segmentation.* arXiv preprint arXiv:1806.09522

Vianna, S. S. (2019). The Set Covering Problem applied to optimization of gas detectors in chemical process plants. *Computers & Chemical Engineering*, *121*, 388–395. doi:10.1016/j.compchemeng.2018.11.008

Vidgen, R., Shaw, S., & Grant, D. B. (2017). Management challenges in creating value from business analytics. *European Journal of Operational Research*, *261*(2), 626–639. doi:10.1016/j.ejor.2017.02.023

Viljevac, A., Cooper-Thomas, H. D., & Saks, A. M. (2012). An investigation into the validity of two measures of work engagement. *International Journal of Human Resource Management*, *23*(17), 3692–3709. doi:10.1080/09585192.2011.639542

Viola, P., & Jones, M. (2001). *Rapid object detection was using a boosted cascade of simple features. Proc. of CVPR.*

Vivakaran, M. (2018). Social Media Technologies and Higher Education: Examing its Usage and Penetration Level as Educational Aids in India. *The Online Journal of Distance Education and e-Learning*, *6*(3), 21-29.

Volpentesta, A. P., & Ammirato, S. (2013). Alternative agrifood networks in a regional area: A case study. *International Journal of Computer Integrated Manufacturing*, *26*(1-2), 55–66. doi:10.1080/0951192X.2012.681911

Von Ahn, L., Blum, M., & Langford, J. (2004). Telling humans and computers apart automatically. *Communications of the ACM*, *47*(2), 56–60. doi:10.1145/966389.966390

von Hellens, L., Nielsen, S., & Beekhuyzen, J. (Eds.). (2005). *Qualitative case studies on implementation of enterprise wide systems*. IGI Global. doi:10.4018/978-1-59140-447-7

von Rosing, M., White, S., Cummins, F., & de Man, H. (2015). *Business Process Model and Notation-BPMN*. Academic Press.

Voorn, R. J., & Kommers, P. (2013). Social media and higher education: Introversion and collaborative learning from the student's perspective. *International Journal of Social Media and Interactive Learning Environments*, *1*(1), 59–71. doi:10.1504/IJSMILE.2013.051650

Vorontsov, E., Cerny, M., Régnier, P., Di Jorio, L., Pal, C. J., Lapointe, R., ... Tang, A. (2019). Deep Learning for Automated Segmentation of Liver Lesions at CT in Patients with Colorectal Cancer Liver Metastases. Radiology. *Artificial Intelligence*, *1*(2), 180014.

Vue. (2019). Retrieved from https://vuejs.org/

Vukadinovic, S., Macuzic, I., Djapan, M., & Milosevic, M. (2018). Early management of human factors in lean industrial systems. *Safety Science*. doi:10.1016/j.ssci.2018.10.008

Wagner, R. K., & Sternberg, R. J. (1985). Practical intelligence in real-world pursuits: The role of tacit knowledge. *Journal of Personality and Social Psychology, 49*(2), 436–458. doi:10.1037/0022-3514.49.2.436

Walker Information Inc. (2000). *Employee Commitment and the Bottom Line: Ethical Issues in the Employer-Employee Relationship*. Work.

Wallace, M., Schimpf, J., Shen, K., & Harvey, W. (2004). On benchmarking Constraint Logic Programming platforms. Response to Fernandez and Hill's "A comparative study of eight constraint programming languages over the boolean and finite domains". *Constraints, 9*(1), 5–34. doi:10.1023/B:CONS.0000006181.40558.37

Wang, S., Higashino, W. A., Hayes, M., & Capretz, M. A. M. (2014). *Service Evolution Patterns*. Paper presented at the 2014 IEEE International Conference on Web Services. doi:10.1109/ICWS.2014.39

Wang, X. P., & An, Y. F. (2010). Building Flexible SOA-Based Enterprise Process Using Decision Services. Paper presented at the e-Business Engineering (ICEBE), 2010 IEEE 7th International Conference.

Wang, Q., Woo, H. L., Quek, C. L., Yang, Y., & Liu, M. (2011). Using the Facebook group as learning management system: An exploratory study. *British Journal of Educational Technology, 43*(3), 428–438. doi:10.1111/j.1467-8535.2011.01195.x

Wang, Y., Chen, Y., & Benitez-Amado, J. (2015). How information technology influences environmental performance: Empirical evidence from China. *International Journal of Information Management, 35*(2), 160–170. doi:10.1016/j.ijinfomgt.2014.11.005

Wanko, C. E. T., Kamdjoug, J. R. K., & Wamba, S. F. (2019, April). Study of a Successful ERP Implementation Using an Extended Information Systems Success Model in Cameroon Universities: Case of CUCA. In *World Conference on Information Systems and Technologies* (pp. 727-737). Springer. 10.1007/978-3-030-16181-1_68

Wardoyo, R., & Wahyuningrum, T. (2018). University Website Quality Ranking using Logarithmic Fuzzy Preference Programming. *Nternational Journal of Electrical and Computer Engineering, 8*(5), 3349–3358. doi:10.11591/ijece.v8i5.pp3349-3358

Waring, T., & Skoumpopoulou, D. (2012). An enterprise resource planning system innovation and its influence on organisational culture: A case study in higher education. *Prometheus (United Kingdom), 30*(4), 427–447.

Warner, C. (2018). *10 Social Media Usage Statistics You Should Know (and What They Mean for Your Marketing Strategy)*. Retrieved from https://www.skyword.com/contentstandard/marketing/10-social-media-usage-statistics-you-should-know-and-what-they-mean-for-your-marketing-strategy/

Waseem, Z., & Hovy, D. (2016). Hateful Symbols or Hateful People? Predictive Features for Hate Speech Detection on Twitter. *Proceedings of the NAACL Student Research Workshop*, 88–93. 10.18653/v1/N16-2013

Washburn, K. (2018). *Violence against women act at risk of lapsing*. Open secret.org. Center for responsive policies. Retrieved from on October, 25th https://www.opensecrets.org/news/2018/10/vawa-at-risk-of-lapsing/

Wasko, M. M., & Faraj, S. (2005). Why should I share? Examining social capital and knowledge contribution in electronic networks of practice. *Management Information Systems Quarterly, 29*(1), 35–57. doi:10.2307/25148667

Watkins, M. (2013). *Making Virtual Teams Work: Ten Basic Principles*. Retrieved 25 November 2015, from https://hbr.org/2013/06/making-virtual-teams-work-ten/

Watson, R. (2006). Extending Google Docs to Collaborate on Research Papers. *Toowoomba Queensland AU The University of Southern Queensland Australia*. Retrieved from http://www.sci.usq.edu.au/staff/dekeyser/googledocs.pdf

Wefald, A. J., & Downey, R. G. (2009). Construct Dimensionality of Engagement and Its Relation with Satisfaction. *The Journal of Psychology*, *143*(1), 91–111. doi:10.3200/JRLP.143.1.91-112 PMID:19157075

Wegerif, R. (1998). The social dimension of asynchronous learning networks. *Journal of Asynchronous Learning Networks*, *2*(1), 34–49.

Weicht, B. (2013). The making of 'the elderly': Constructing the subject of care. *Journal of Aging Studies*, *27*(2), 188–197. doi:10.1016/j.jaging.2013.03.001

Weiguo, C., & Yanchun, L. (2010). Research on Motivation System of Employees-Analysis of Human Resources Management from a Psychological Perspective. *2010 International Conference on Management and Service Science (MASS)*, 1–4. 10.1109/ICMSS.2010.5578035

Weimar, E., Nugroho, A., Visser, J., & Plaat, A. (2013). Towards high performance software teamwork. *Proceedings of the 17th International Conference on Evaluation and Assessment in Software Engineering*.

Weir, C. S., Douglas, G., Richardson, T., & Jack, M. A. (2010). Usable security: User preferences for authentication methods in eBanking and the effects of experience. *Interacting with Computers*, *22*(3), 153–164. doi:10.1016/j.intcom.2009.10.001

Weisberg, J., Te'eni, D., & Arman, L. (2011). Past purchase and intention to purchase in e-commerce: The mediation of social presence and trust. *Internet Research*, *21*(1), 82–96. doi:10.1108/10662241111104893

WESP – The World Economic Situation and Prospects. (2019). *India Projected to grow at 7.1% in FY'20*. Retrieved from https://economictimes.indiatimes.com/topic/World-Economic-Situation-and-Prospects

Wetzels, M., Odekerken-Schröder, G., & Van Oppen, C. (2009). Using PLS path modeling for assessing hierarchical construct models: Guidelines and empirical illustration. *Management Information Systems Quarterly*, *33*(1), 177–195. doi:10.2307/20650284

White, B. (2006). *Employee Engagement Report 2006*. BlessingWhite, Inc. Retrieved December 21, 2018, from http://www.blessingwhite.com

White, B. (2008). *The Employee Engagement Equation in India*. BlessingWhite and HR Anexi. Accessed from www.blessingwhite.com

White, S. A. (2004). Introduction to BPMN. *IBM Cooperation, 2*(0), 0.

White, G. L., Hewitt, B., & Kruck, S. E. (2013). Incorporating global information security and assurance in I.S. education. *Journal of Information Systems Education*, *24*(1), 11–16.

Wikipedia.org. (n.d.). *Inquiry-based learning*. Retrieved from https://en.wikipedia.org/wiki/Inquiry-based_learning

Wilbrink, B. (1997). Assessment in historical perspective. *Studies in Educational Evaluation*, *23*(1), 31–48. doi:10.1016/S0191-491X(97)00003-5

Wilcox, K., & Stephen, A. T. (2013). Are close friends the enemy? Online social networks, self-esteem, and self-control. *The Journal of Consumer Research*, *40*(1), 90–103. doi:10.1086/668794

William Dow, P. M. P., & Taylor, B. (2010). *Project management communications bible* (Vol. 574). John Wiley & Sons.

Wintner, S. L. (2010). *10 key financial performance indicators for architecture and engineering firms*. Retrieved March 6, 2012, from http://www.axium.com/blog/?p=2360

Wixom, B. H., & Todd, P. A. (2005). A theoretical integration of user satisfaction and technology acceptance. *Information Systems Research*, *16*(1), 85–102. doi:10.1287/isre.1050.0042

Wixom, B. H., & Watson, H. J. (2001). An empirical investigation of the factors affecting data warehousing success. *Management Information Systems Quarterly*, *25*(1), 17–41. doi:10.2307/3250957

Wognum, P. M., Krabbendam, J. J., Buhl, H., Ma, X., & Kenett, R. (2004). Improving enterprise system support—A case-based approach. *Advanced Engineering Informatics*, *18*(4), 241–253. doi:10.1016/j.aei.2005.01.007

Wogu, I. A. P., Atayero, A. A. A., Olu-Owolabu, F. E., Sholarin, M. A., Ogbuehi, U. K., Akoleowo, O., & Ubogu, P. C. (2016). *The changing face of education and the dilemma of Massive Open Online Courses (MOOCS) in Nigeria's tertiary institutions: Implications for development*. Paper delivered at the 3rd International Conference on African Development Issues (CU-ICADI2016). Retrieved from https://scholar.google.com/citations?user=J5h7gSwAAAAJ&hl=en

Wogu, I. A. P., Misra, S., Assibong, P. A., Ogiri, S. O., Maskeliunas, R., & Damasevicius, R. (2018). Super-Intelligent machine operations in 21st century manufacturing industries: A boost or doom to political and human development? In *Towards Extensible and Adaptable Methods in Computing*. Springer Nature Singapore Plc. Ltd. Retrieved from https://link.springer.com/chapter/10.1007/978-981-13-2348-5_16

Wogu, I. A. P., Misra, S., Assibong, P. A., Olu-Owolabi, E. F., Maskeliunas, R., & Damasevicius, R. (2019). Artificial Intelligence, Smart Classrooms and Online Education in the 21st Century: Implications for Human Development. *Journal of Case on Information Technology, 21*(3). Retrieved from https://www.igi-global.com/article/artificial-intelligence-smart-classrooms-and-online-education-in-21st-century/227679?camid=4v1

Wogu, I. A. P., Misra, S., Olu-Owolabi, F. E., Assibong, P. A., & Oluwakemi, D. (2018). Artificial intelligence, artificial teachers and the fate of learners in the 21st century education sector: Implications for theory and practice. *International Journal of Pure and Applied Mathematics*, *119*(16), 2245-2259. Retrieved from https://acadpubl.eu/hub/2018-119-16/issue16b.html https://acadpubl.eu/hub/2018-119-16/2/232.pdf

Wogu, I. A. P., Misra, S., Olu-Owolabi, F. E., Assibong, P. A., & Oluwakemi, D. (2018). Artificial Intelligence, Artificial Teachers and the Fate of Learners in the 21st Century Education Sector: Implications for Theory and Practice. *International Journal of Pure and Applied Mathematics*, *119*(16), 2245-2259. Retrieved from https://acadpubl.eu/hub/2018-119-16/issue16b.html https://acadpubl.eu/hub/2018-119-16/2/232.pdf

Wogu, I. A. P., Olu-Owolabi, F. E., Assibong, P. A., Apeh, H. A., Agoha, B. C., Sholarin, M. A., . . . Igbokwe, D. (2017). Artificial Intelligence, Alienation and Ontological Problems of Other Minds: A Critical Investigation into the Future of Man and Machines. *Proceedings of the IEEE International Conference on Computing, Networking and Informatics (ICCNI 2017)*. DOI:10.1109/ICCNI.2017.8123792

Wogu, I. A. P., Olu-Owolabi, F. E., Assibong, P. A., Apeh, H. A., Agoha, B. C., Sholarin, M. A., . . . Igbokwe, D. (2017). *Artificial intelligence, alienation and ontological problems of other minds: A critical investigation into the future of man and machines*. Retrieved from https://www.scopus.com/record/display.uri?eid=2-s2.0-85047079881&origin=resultslist&sort=plf-f&src=s&st1=ICCNI+&nlo=&nlr=&nls=&sid=02fcb90c5e2fe9f02e52574629f67b0d&sot=b&sdt=b&sl=12&s=CONF%28ICCNI+%29&relpos=51&citeCnt=0&searchTerm=

Wogu, I. A. P., Sanjay Misra, J., Assibong, P. A., Adewumi, A., Maskeliunas, R., & Damasevicius, R. (2018). A critical review of the politics of artificial intelligent machines, alienation and the existential risk threat to America's labour force. *Lecture Notes in Computer Science, 10963*, 217-232. Retrieved from https://link.springer.com/chapter/10.1007/978-3-319-95171-3_18

Wogu, I. A. (2010). Ancient Greek Philosophers and their Philosophy. In I. A. Wogu (Ed.), *A Preface to Logic, Philosophy and Human Existence* (pp. 14–62). Lagos, Nigeria: *Pumack Educational Publishers*.

Wogu, I. A. P. (2011). *Problems in mind: A new approach to age long problems and questions in philosophy and the cognitive science of human development*. Pumack Nigeria Limited Education Publishers.

Wogu, I. A. P. (2011). *Problems in Mind: A new approach to age long problems and questions in philosophy and the cognitive science of human development*. Pumack Nigeria Limited Education Publishers.

Wolfgang, M. E., & Ferracuti, F. (1976). *The subculture of violence: towards an integrated theory in criminology*. London: Tavistock. Retrieved from https://lib.ugent.be/en/catalog/rug01:000505954

Woolley, D. R. (1994). PLATO: The Emergence of Online Community. *Matrix News*. Retrieved from http://www.thinkofit.com/plato/dwplato.htm

World Health Organization. (2002). *World report on violence and health: Summary*. Geneva: World Health Organization. Retrieved 15th February, 2017 from, http://www.who.int/violence_injury_prevention/violence/world_report/en/summary_en.pdf?ua=1

Wouter, D. C., Arne, D. R., Tim, D. P., Svenn, D., Peter, D. R., Mojca, S., ... Christine, V. B. (2018). Structural variants identified by Oxford Nanopore PromethION sequencing of the human genome. *bioRxiv, 434118*. doi:10.1101/434118

Wu, J., & Lebreton, J. M. (2011). Reconsidering the dispositional basis of counterproductive work behavior: The role of aberrant personality. *Personnel Psychology Banner, 64*(3), 593–626. doi:10.1111/j.1744-6570.2011.01220.x

Xiancheng, W., Wei, L., Bingyi, M., He, J., Jiang, Z., Xu, W., . . . Zhaomeng, S. (2018). Retina blood vessel segmentation using a U-net based Convolutional neural network. *Procedia Computer Science*.

Xu, L. X. X., Yu, W. F., Lim, R., & Hock, L. E. (2010, July). A methodology for successful implementation of ERP in smaller companies. In *Service Operations and Logistics and Informatics (SOLI), 2010 IEEE International Conference on* (pp. 380-385). IEEE.

Xu, J., & Thomas, H. C. (2011). How can leaders achieve high employee engagement? *Leadership and Organization Development Journal, 32*(4), 399–416. doi:10.1108/01437731111134661

Xu, X., & Wang, Z. (2011). State of the art: Business service and its impacts on manufacturing. *Journal of Intelligent Manufacturing, 22*(5), 653–662. doi:10.100710845-009-0325-3

Yadav, S. S. K., & Bandyopadhayay, A. (2017). Communicating sustainability across the hierarchy of the organisation: A framework for the Indian ITeS sector. *International Journal of Management Practice, 10*(1), 17–29. doi:10.1504/IJMP.2017.080647

Yalman, Y., & Yesilyurt, M. (2013). Information Security Threats and Information Assurance. *TEM Journal, 2*(3), 247–252.

Yang, D. (2013). *Are We MOOC'd Out? Huffington Post*.

Yang, J. (2018). Business Management System for Genomics. In *Proceedings of the 9th IEEE International Conference on Information, Intelligence, Systems and Applications*. Zakynthos, Greece: IEEE.

Yang, J. (2018). Smart Laboratory Information System Accelerates Genomics Research. In *Proceedings of the 9th IEEE International Conference on Information, Intelligence, Systems and Applications*. Zakynthos, Greece: IEEE. 10.1109/IISA.2018.8633685

Yaokumah, W. (2016). The influence of students' characteristics on mobile device security measures. *International Journal of Information Systems and Social Change, 7*(3), 44–66. doi:10.4018/IJISSC.2016070104

Yerlikaya, Z., & Durdu, O. (2017). Evaluation of Accessibility of University Websites : A Case from Turkey. In *International Conference on Human-Computer Interaction (Vol. 4*, pp. 663–668). Academic Press. 10.1007/978-3-319-58753-0_94

Yıldıza, B., & Alpkan, L. (2015). A theoretical model on the proposed predictors of destructive deviant workplace behaviors and the mediator role of alienation. *Procedia: Social and Behavioral Sciences, 210*, 330–338. doi:10.1016/j.sbspro.2015.11.373

Yu, E. S., & Mylopoulos, J. (1995). From ER To "aR"—Modelling Strategic Actor Relationships for Business Process Reengineering. University of Toronto.

Yu, H., Miao, C., Leung, C., & White, T. J. (2017). Towards AI-powered personalization in MOOC learning. *Science of Learning, Nature Partner Journals, 2*(15). doi:10.103841539-017-0016-3

Zachos, G., Paraskevopoulou-Kollia, E., & Anagnostopoulos, I. (2018). Social Media Use in Higher Education: A Review. *Education in Science, 8*(4), 194. doi:10.3390/educsci8040194

Zaman, U., & Saif, M. I. (2016). Perceived accountability and conflict management styles as predictors of job performance of public officials in Pakistan. *Gomal University Journal of Research, 32*(2), 24–35.

Zamudio, L., Aguilar, J. A., Tripp, C., & Misra, S. (2017, July). A Requirements Engineering Techniques Review in Agile Software Development Methods. *Lecture Notes in Computer Science, 1408*, 683-698.

Zanamwe, N., Rupere, T., & Kufandirimbwa, O. (2013). Use of Social Networking Technologies in Higher Education in Zimbabwe: A learners' perspective. *International Journal of Computer and Information Technology, 2*(1), 8–18.

Zancanaro, A., & Domingues, M. (2018). Massive open online courses (MOOC) for teaching Portuguese for foreigners. *Turkish Online Journal of Distance Education-TOJDE, 19*(2), 4–20. doi:10.17718/tojde.415602

Zarei, B., & Naeli, M. (2013). Critical Success Factors in Enterprise Resource Planning Implementation: A Case-Study Approach. In M. Haab & S. Cramer (Eds.), *Enterprise Resource Planning Systems in Higher Education* (pp. 10–21). IGI Global. doi:10.4018/978-1-4666-4153-2.ch002

Zeiler, M. D., Taylor, G. W., & Fergus, R. (2011). Adaptive deconvolutional networks for mid and high level feature learning. *2011 International Conference on Computer Vision, ICCV 2011*, 2018-2025. 10.1109/ICCV.2011.6126474

Zeng, C., Zheng, S., & Shi, K. (2010). Relationship between job demands-resources and job burnout of IT employees. *2010 IEEE 2nd Symposium on Web Society (SWS)*, 548–553. 10.1109/SWS.2010.5607390

Zhang, J., Li, H., & Ziegelmayer, J. L. (2009). Resource or capability? A dissection of SMEs' IT infrastructure flexibility and its relationship with IT responsiveness. *Journal of Computer Information Systems, 50*(1), 46–53.

Zhang, L., & McDowell, W. C. (2009). Am I really at risk? Determinants of online users' intentions to use strong passwords. *Journal of Internet Commerce, 8*(3–4), 180–197. doi:10.1080/15332860903467508

Zhao, X., Xue, L., & Whinston, A. B. (2013). Managing interdependent information security risks: Cyberinsurance, managed security services, and risk pooling arrangements. *Journal of Management Information Systems, 30*(1), 123–152. doi:10.2753/MIS0742-1222300104

Zhou, N. (2012, January). The Language features and architecture of B-prolog. *Theory and Practice of Logic Programming, 12*(1-2), 189–218. doi:10.1017/S1471068411000445

Zhou, W., Simpson, E., & Domizi, D. P. (2012). Google Docs in an Out-of-Class Collaborative Writing Activity. *International Journal on Teaching and Learning in Higher Education, 24*(3), 359–375. Retrieved from http://www.isetl.org/ijtlhe/

Zhu, Q., Sarkis, J., & Lai, K. (2007). Green supply chain management: Pressures, practices and performance within the Chinese automobile industry. *Journal of Cleaner Production, 15*(11–12), 1041–1052. doi:10.1016/j.jclepro.2006.05.021

Zhu, Z., Wang, J., Wang, X., & Wan, X. (2016). Exploring factors of user's peer-influence behavior in social media on purchase intention: Evidence from QQ. *Computers in Human Behavior*, *63*, 980–987. doi:10.1016/j.chb.2016.05.037

Ziemba, E., & Oblak, I. (2013). Critical success factors for ERP systems implementation in public administration. In *Proceedings of the Informing Science and Information Technology Education Conference* (pp. 1-19). Informing Science Institute. 10.28945/1785

Zinnikus, I., Bogdanovich, A., & Schäfer, R. (2017). *An Ontology Based Recommendation System for Elderly and Disabled Persons*. Academic Press.

Zulch, B. (2014). ScienceDirect Communication: The foundation of project management. *Procedia Technology*, *16*(16), 1000–1009. doi:10.1016/j.protcy.2014.10.054

About the Contributors

Sanjay Misra is full Professor of Computer Engineering at Covenant University, Ota, Nigeria. He has 25 years of wide experience in academic administration and researches in various universities in Asia, Europe, and Africa. He is Ph.d. in Information and Know. Engg (Software Engineering) from the University of Alcala, Spain, and M.Tech.(Software Engineering) from Motilal Nehru National Institute of Technology, India. As per SciVal (SCOPUS- Elsevier) analysis- He is most productive researcher (no. 1-) in whole Nigeria during 2012-2017 & 2013-2018(in all subjects), in computer science no 1 in whole country and no 5 in whole continent(Africa) and also in Covenant University (600-800 ranked University by THE) since 2013. Total more than 300 articles with 200 coauthors around the world (the majority of them in Web of science-90 in JCR/SCIE Journals) in the core & application area of Software Engg (SQA, SPI, SPM), Web engg, Health Informatics, Intelligent systems etc. He has delivered more than 80 keynote speeches/invited talks/public lectures in reputed conferences and institutes around the world (traveled around 60 countries). He got several awards for outstanding publications (2014 IET Software Premium Award(UK)), and from TUBITAK-Turkish Higher Education, and Atilim University). He edited (with colleagues) 42 LNCS & 6 IEEE proceedings, editor in chief of book series IT Personnel and Project Management, International Journal of Human Capital and Information Technology Professionals(IJHCITP)-IGI Global, and of 3 journals(IJ) and editor in various SCIE journals.

* * *

Muhammad B. Abdullahi is a trained Mathematician and Computer Scientist. He received his Doctor of Philosophy (PhD) degree in Computer Science and Technology from Central South University, Changsha, Hunan, P. R. China in 2012. He is presently in Computer Science department, Federal University of Technology Minna. His research interests are majorly in the areas of Trust, Security and Privacy issues in Wireless Sensor and Ad-Hoc Networks, Internet of Things (IoTs), Peer-to-Peer Networking, Cloud Computing, Big Data Analytics, Machine Learning, Data Mining, Ambient Intelligence and Computer Science Education. His research results are published in refereed journals and conference proceedings. He is a chartered Information Technology practitioner and a member of the Computer Professionals Registration Council of Nigeria (CPN) and also a full member of Nigeria Computer Society (NCS). He is currently the Vice Chairman of Nigeria Computer Society, Niger State Chapter.

Marion Olubunmi Adebiyi is a Lecturer in the Department of Computer Science, Landmark University, Omu Aran. Her area of research is Bioinformatics. She is a member of Computer Professionals (Registration Council of Nigeria) (CPN), Nigeria Computer Society (NCS) and many others. She is married.

Adekanmi Adeyinka Adegun is a Lecturer in the Department of Computer Science, Landmark University, Omu Aran. He is a member of Computer Professionals (Registration Council of Nigeria) (CPN). He is married.

Emmanuel Adeniyi is a Staff in the Department of Computer Science, College of Pure and Applied Sciences, Landmark University, Omu-Aran, Nigeria. He received Postgraduate Diploma in Computer Science from University of Ilorin, Ilorin, Nigeria. His area of research includes Computer Security, Data Mining.

Solomon Adepoju holds B. Tech (Mathematics /Computer Science) and M.Sc. (Computer Science) from the Federal University of Technology, Minna and University of Ibadan respectively. Presently, he is in Department of Computer Science, Federal University of Technology, Minna. He has co-authored papers which have appeared in some national and international journals He is a member Computer Professional Registration Council of Nigeria (CPN), International Association of Computer Science and Information Technology (IACST), SIGCHI, and International Society on Multi Criteria Decision Making(MCDM) among others. His areas of interest include Human Computer Interaction (website usability/accessibility), ICT4D and MCDM.

Chidiebere Aguziendu was an undergraduate student at Covenant University, from the Department of Political Science and International Relations. She is currently pursuing a Masters Degree.

Suchitra Ajgaonkar is a research scholar at Symbiosis International University. She has a master's degree in Psychology and currently pursuing Ph.D. in Organizational Behavior at Symbiosis International University, Pune, India. She has 8 years of corporate experience and currently works as Assistant Professor of Organizational Behavior at ISB&M, a business school in Pune India. Her research interests are career management, Information Technology human capital, employee engagement, team dynamics, and learning and teaching methodology.

Hosea Apeh is a senior faculty member of the University of Abuja. He has special interests in the area of Education Psychology, and the Theory of Education from where hc has published a couple of articles in both local and international journals. He Presently teaches and conducts research in Educational psychology and in related areas at the University of Abuja.

Emmanuel Asani is a faculty member of the Department of Computer Science, Landmark University, Omuaran, Nigeria. He holds a Bachelor of Science degree in Computer Science from the University of Ilorin and Master's degree in Information Science from the University of Ibadan. Asani has had a bright and progressive academic and professional career demonstrating great aptitude and attendant success in research and development. He is seasoned in conceiving management information systems theories (evidenced by scholastic publications), and initiatives in ICT diffusion and uptake. His research interest in information security has two components vis social and machine learning. The social component seeks to understand the social and organizational context of human behavioral trend as it related to cybercrime. The machine learning component bothers on modelling of mathematical and statistical theories using soft computing tools to solve cybersecurity problems. He has attended and presented papers in both local and international journal with his research efforts appearing in local and international peer reviewed journals. In August 2015, he was honoured at the iSTEAM MINTT conference held at the University of Benin for his contributions to scientific research. He is a motivator, teacher and leader, well loved by his students and mentees. Asani is goal oriented and student to great leaders, who believe in God and are committed to selfless service, integrity and hard work as an important hallmark of success.

Thais Andrea Baldissera is a full professor at Instituto Federal Farroupilha in Brazil. She is PhD (2019) at the New University of Lisbon and member of Collaborative Networks and Distributed Industrial Systems research group at the UNINOVA institute. She has more than 15 years of teaching and from more than 5 years, she had a business career as software engineering, and later as director and administrator, in educations companies. Her main areas of interest include collaborative networks, information system, decision support analysis, ICT and ageing, and collaborative business services.

Luis M. Camarinha-Matos is full professor and head of Robotics and Manufacturing at the New University of Lisbon. He is also the leader of the Collaborative Networks and Distributed Industrial Systems research group at the UNINOVA institute. He has participated in many international and national projects, both as a researcher and as a project coordinator. He is a founding member of the PRO-VE series of conferences and the president of SOCOLNET – Society of Collaborative Networks. His main areas of interest include collaborative enterprise networks, intelligent manufacturing, cyber-physical systems, and ICT and ageing. He has more than 400 publications in refereed Journals and conferences proceedings. He has acted as an evaluator of proposals submitted to several international funding organizations. In 2009 he also got the Doctor Honoris Causa by University "Politehnica" of Bucharest, Romania.

Ana Castillo-Martínez has a BSc (2010), MSc (2012) and PhD (2016) in Computer Science from the University of Alcala, where she is now a Ph.D Assistant Professor in the Computer Science Department,where she has participated in several research projects. Her research interests include mobile devices and energy management. Currently, she has relevant publications on ICT field with publications on international and journals of high impact. Previously, she was working in Iberia (an IAG company) in the Department of Financial Management.

Charles Chukwuedo is a Doctoral Candidate of Philosophy, who currently teaches philosophy related courses at the Federal College of Education Technology, Asaba, Nigeria. He has interests and conducts research in the areas of Political Philosophy, History of Philosophy and Contemporary and Applied Philosophy, where he has also published a couple of articles.

Broderick Crawford is a Full Professor of the Computer Science Department at the Pontifical Catholic University of Valparaíso, Chile. He received his PhD degree in Computer Science from the Universidad Técnica Federico Santa María of Valparaíso, Chile, in 2011. His areas of research interest include mainly

Combinatorial Optimization, Metaheuristics, Global Optimization, and Autonomous Search. In this context, He has published about +300 scientific papers in different international conferences and journals, some of them top ranked in Computer Science, Operational Research, and Artificial Intelligence. Most of these papers are based on the resolution of benchmark and real-world optimization problems.

Manuel de Buenaga is senior researcher at Dept. of Computer Science of University of Alcalá (UAH). His research interests include Intelligent Systems, Natural Language Processing, Big Data and Open Knowledge Applications. He received a Ph.D. in Physics from Universidad Complutense de Madrid in 1996 and he has hold several positions at Universidad Complutense de Madrid, Universidad Europea de Madrid and University of Alcala. He has taken part in more than 20 national and international ICT research projects, heading some of them, with a special focus on web applications and the health domain with academic and industrial partners. He is co-author of more than 100 conferences, book chapters and journal papers in these areas.

Cristiano De Faveri is PhD Student at the New University of Lisbon, where he is a member of the advanced software engineering team, developing his work in the area of cyber deception modeling. He has more than 20 years working in the industry with a focus on software development management, design, implementation, project leadership, and training. His expertise includes critical software solutions for enterprise and telco applications, such as fraud detection, network traffic analysis and control, and DoS mitigation. He also worked as a consultant in startup companies, developing business collaborative networks and user behavior analysis prediction. His main areas of interest include collaborative networks, decision support analysis, security, domain-¬specific languages, and deception-based defense.

Rositsa Doneva is a Professor at the University of Plovdiv "Paisii Hilendarski", Faculty of Physics and Engineering Technologies. Dr. Doneva gained her Ph.D. at October, 1995. She has led/taken part in more than 50 national and international projects in the area of computer science, electronic and distance learning, applications of IT in education, etc. The areas of her academic interest are Intelligent Systems, Conceptual Modelling, Software Engineering, Quality Assurance and Evaluation (of Higher Education, e-Learning, Software, Projects, etc.), Object-oriented Programming, Systems and Technologies for distance and mobile learning. Prof. Doneva is the author of over 110 scientific publications and 40 textbooks and learning materials with over 300 citations.

Morris Edogiawere is a faculty of Igbenigiong University, Okada. His areas of research interests include Political Ideas, Constitutional development, History of Political thought, Issues in Political Philosophy and Principles of international law. He has published a couple of articles in both local and international journals of high reputation.

Ayotunde O. Elegbeleye is a Clinical Psychologist in the Department of Psychology, Covenant University. She had her tertiary education at the University of Ado Ekiti (BSc), University of Lagos (MSc) and Covenant University (PhD.) respectively. She has published a couple of articles in reputable local and international journal outlets.

Maria Angeles Fernandez de Sevilla is an assistant professor at the University of Alcala, Madrid, Spain. Her research interests are probabilistic analysis, computational electromagnetics, expert systems, and optimization techniques.

Luis Fernández-Sanz is an associate professor at Dept. of Computer Science of Universidad de Alcala (UAH). He earned a degree in Computing in 1989 at Universidad Politecnica de Madrid (UPM) and his Ph.D. in Computing with a special award at University of the Basque Country in 1997. With more than 20 years of research and teaching experience (at UPM, Universidad Europea de Madrid and UAH), he is also engaged in the management of the main Spanish Computing Professionals association (ATI: www.ati.es) as vice president and he is chairman of ATI Software Quality group. He has been vice president of CEPIS (Council of European Professional Informatics Societies: www.cepis.org) from 2011 to 2013. With a large number of contributions in refereed impact international journals, conferences and book chapters, his main research interests include technical fields like software quality and engineering and testing and non-technical fields like computing education, especially in multinational settings, IT profession and requirements and skills for IT jobs.

Siska Fitrianie obtained her master degree at Technical Informatics, Delft University of Technology, the Netherlands, in 2002. After doing her two years post-graduate programme at Eindhoven University of Technology, she involved a PhD project with a topic related to adaptive mobile user interface for crisis management and received her doctorate degree from Delft University of Technology in 2010. Currently, she is a researcher at Interactive Intelligence group, Delft University of Technology.

Hector Florez has a Ph.D. in Engineering, M.Sc. in Information and Communication Sciences, M.Sc. in Management, and is a Specialist in Management, Electronics Engineer, Computing Engineer and Mathematician.

Silvia Gaftandzhieva is an Assistant Professor at PU "Paisii Hilendarski". Her research areas include e-learning and distance learning, automated evaluation of quality in higher education, distance learning. She is an author of 45 scientific publications in the field of quality assurance (of HE, e-Learning, Projects, etc.), e-Learning, m-Learning, etc. with over 100 citations.

Gabriela Gerón-Piñón has over 20 years of experience in higher education. She holds a Ph.D. in Business Administration with a focus on IT Management in Higher Education Institutions from Universidad de Cantabria, Spain. Her Master of Science in Quality Systems and Bachelor of Industrial Engineer and Systems are from Tec de Monterrey, Mexico. Her research is focused in how technology supports the international competitiveness of higher education institutions and helps their students succeed obtaining a Summa Cum Laude distinction in her dissertation for her contribution to Latin America internationalization and her Thesis granted the 2018 Innovation, Technology and Industry Award by the Ilustre Colegio Oficial de Titulados Mercantiles y Empresariales de Cantabria. She was part of the Women in Education Leadership Program at Harvard University Graduate School of Education, cohort 2017 and participated as part of the group of visionary leaders for digital transformation at UNESCO in Paris, May 2017. Dr. Geron is the founder of Connecting Iberoamerica, a company that conducts research and provides strategic consultancy to international organizations, companies and universities that want to increase their international competitiveness in the region. Previously, she served as the Engagement

Strategy Director, Operations Manager and Solutions Consultant working with more than 50 universities in Latin America at Ellucian, a global higher education technology company. Dr. Geron has served as Consultant of Universidad de Monterrey and Planning Director of Tec de Monterrey in Mexico. She was faculty member of institutions in Mexico such as Universidad de Monterrey and Instituto Culinario de Mexico. She was a Mentor at the Virtual Incubator (Entrepreneurship Program) at Tec de Monterrey. She is an individual contributor of the International Council for Open and Distance Education (ICDE), Associate Researcher of Universidad de Monterrey (UDEM), reviewer of international journals and collaborate with universities, international organizations and initiatives to connect with universities in Ibero-America. Her areas of expertise include: international higher education, strategic planning, go to market strategy, project management, operations, client engagement, solutions consulting, technology evangelist and research. Her specialties are in: technology trends, institutional accreditation, international rankings, quality systems, online learning, institutional effectiveness and higher education technology management. Dr. Gerón is speaker at international conferences, author of academic papers, chapter books and blogs.

Nkechi Jacinta Ifeanyi-Reuben has a doctorate degree in Computer Science from the University of Port-Harcourt Nigeria. She obtained her M.Sc. and B.Sc. in Computer Science from the University of Ibadan Nigeria and University of Calabar Nigeria respectively. She teaches and conducts research in the Department of Computer Science at Rhema University Nigeria, Aba. She is a member of Computer Professionals (Registration Council) of Nigeria (CPN), Nigeria Computer Society (NCS) and Nigeria Women in Information Technology (NIWIIT). Her research interests include Database, Text mining, Natural Language Processing and Artificial Intelligence.

Jesse Katende is a lecturer with a history of working in the higher education institution. Skilled in Analytical Skills, Microsoft Word, excel, power point, information technology, IT Project Management, Lecturing, and Python. Strong professional with a B.Sc in Information Systems from University Of Botswana, M.Tech in Information Technology from Eastern Mediterranean University, Cyprus and PhD focused in Management Information Systems from Covenant University Ota (active PhD student).

Peace Kumah is currently a doctoral student at the SMC University, Switzerland pursuing Business Administration with specialization in Human Resource Management. She holds MBA (Human Resource Management) degree from Wisconsin International University College, Accra, Ghana. She has several years of teaching experience and occupies leadership positions in various educational institutions. Her research interest includes strategic human resource management, organizational leadership and motivation, change management, employment relations and information technology.

Anil Kumar is serving as an Assistant Professor in the field of Management at Faculty of Management, VNS Group of Institutions Bhopal India. He has completed his PhD from Maulana Azad National Institute of Technology (an institute of national importance) Bhopal India. He has done his MBA from Motial Nehru National Institute of Technology (an institute of national importance) Allahabad India. He has done M.Sc. in Computer Science. He has also qualified UGC-NET (a test to determine eligibility for college and university level lectureship for Indian nationals) in Management. Dr. Kumar has more than 10 years of teaching experience. He has published many articles in reputed international journals that are indexed in UGC, ESCI & SCOPUS. His research area is in Marketing, Green Marketing, Entrepreneurship, Supply Chain Management, Retail and Social Media etc. He has hands on experience in statistical software such as SPSS, AMOS, Smart-PLS and EXCEL. Dr. Kumar is also serving as member of review board and editorial board for various reputed international journals.

Olumide Babatope Longe has a PhD, MACM, MAIS, MIEE, MCPN, MIAENG, MNCS, FASI Chair – Information Systems Programme, American University of Nigeria, Yola Associate Director, Multidisciplinary Research - International Centre for IT & Development Southern University, Baton Rouge, LA, USA Distinguished Fulbright Fellow, McArthur Scholar & MIT Scholar Fellow of the African Scientific Institute Heildelberg Nobel Laureate Forum Fellow ICT University Foundation Endowed Professor of Information Security.

Adamu A. Mohammed bagged his first degree at Usman Danfodio University Sokoto in March 2000 and obtained B.Sc, Mathematics (First Class Honours). In October 2004 and February 2012 respectively, he was awarded M.Tech and Ph.D., Applied Mathematics from the Federal University of Technology, Minna, Niger State. He is an Associate Professor in the department of Mathematics and Applied Science, Federal University of Technology Minna. He is currently the acting Director, Information Technology Services (ITS). He is a Zend Certified PHP Engineer (2014). He is a member of Mathematical Association of Nigerian (MAN), Science Teachers Association of Nigeria (STAN) and Nigerian Mathematical Society (NMS).

Salman Moiz is working as an Associate Professor in the School of Computer and Information Sciences, University of Hyderabad. Earlier he worked as Research Scientist at Centre for Development of Advanced Computing, Bangalore. He also worked as Professor in GITAM University and MVSR Engineering College. He also worked as an Associate Professor in Muffakham Jah College of Engineering and Technology. He did his Ph.D. (CSE) from Osmania University, M.Tech and MCA from Osmania University and M.Phil(CS) from Osmania University. His research interest includes Software Refactoring, Reusability, E-Learning technologies and distributed computing.

Ibiyo Motunrayo graduated with First class (Hons) degree in Computer Science from the Federal University of Technology Minna, Nigeria. She is an information Technology enthusiast with a craving desire to affect human life especially with technological innovations that have the ability to make life more comfortable. She has passion for programming, data mining and Human Computer Interaction because she is of the opinion that a product that is not human friendly needs to be reviewed because the mind of the user is of optimum value.

Netra Neelam has more than 17 years of full-time Teaching, Research, and Administration experience at Graduate and Postgraduate Level.She is currently serving as Professor & Deputy Director at SCMHRD (Symbiosis Centre for Management and Human Resource Development) under Symbiosis International University. She has done her PhD, M.Phil, M.Com and PGDHRM. Psychometric Testing being one of her passions, she is a Certified MBTI® (Myers-Briggs Type Indicator), FIRO® (Fundamental Interpersonal Relations Orientation) and SII® (Strong Interest Inventory) practitioner and actively involved in consulting and counselling assignments. She also conducts training sessions for the professionals giving insights on Understanding Self, Team Building, Conflict Resolution, Personality Development etc. Her research interests are in the area of performance appraisal, decision making styles, culture, commitment, consumer behaviour, team dynamics etc. She is also a Ph.D. guide at Symbiosis International University.

Jonathan Odukoya obtained his doctoral degree in Psychometrics from the Department of Guidance and Counseling, University of Ibadan in 1991. He lectured briefly in the Department of Psychology, Obafemi Awolowo University, Ile-Ife, Nigeria, before joining the Research Division of the West African Examinations Council (WAEC) in Lagos and subsequently in Accra, Ghana where he served for eleven years. Dr. Odukoya is a Senior Lecturer in the Department of Psychology at Covenant University. He is also the National Coordinator of the Educational Research Network for West and Central Africa (ERNWACA) in Nigeria.

Roseline Ogundokun is a Lecturer in the Department of Computer Science, Landmark University, Omu Aran. Her area of research includes Information Security, Human-Computer Interaction, Data Mining, Information Science and Bioinformatics. She holds a Bachelor of Science in Management Information System from Covenant University, Ota; Master of Science in Computer Science from the University of Ilorin, Ilorin; Post Graduate Diploma in Education (PGDE) from the National Teachers' Institute (NTI), Kaduna and; currently a Ph.D. student in the Department of Computer Science, University of Ilorin, Ilorin. She is a member of Nigeria Computer Society (NCS); Computer Professionals (Registration Council of Nigeria) (CPN) and Graduate Member of Nigeria Institute of Management (NIM). She is married.

Ishaq Oyefolahan is currently an Associate Professor at the Department of Information and Media Technology (Information Technology option), Federal University of Technology, Minna, Nigeria. Prior to joining Federal University of Technology Minna, he was an Assistant Professor at the Department of Information Systems, International Islamic University Malaysia. His current area of interests includes; Applied Information Systems, Computer Security, Ontology and Knowledge Engineering. He has published several technical papers in national and international journals and conferences.

José Luís Pereira holds a PhD in Information Systems and Technology and an MSc in Information Systems Management from the University of Minho (UMinho). Currently, he is an Assistant Professor in the Information Systems Department, of UMinho Engineering School, where he has been teaching, among other subjects, courses in Databases, Business Intelligence and Simulation, to graduate and undergraduate students in several IT/IS and engineering degrees. Formerly, he has been Adjunct-Director of undergraduate studies in Business Informatics and Information Systems and Technology, and Director of the Master in Information Systems Engineering and Management. As a researcher, he is a member of the ISTTOS group of the IST line in the ALGORITMI Research Centre, working in the Simulation, Business Process Management (BPM) and Big Data fields, with specific interests in Organizational Decision Support, Business Process Improvement and Big Data solutions. He has been serving in the Program Committees of several conferences, national and international. He is part of the Editorial Review Board of the International Journal of Web Portals (IJWP) and the Editorial Advisory Board of the Journal of Information Systems Engineering & Management. He is a co-organizer of the workshop

"Emerging Trends and Challenges in Business Process Management (ETCBPM)" which is associated with the World Conference on Information Systems and Technology (WorldCIST). He has published several papers in international conferences and journals.

Daniel Perez-Gonzalez is an Associated Professor of Information Systems and Information Technology in the Department of Business Administration at University of Cantabria. He attended Postgraduate Courses in Management at Kiel University (Germany) and received his PhD in MIS from University of Cantabria. Actually He is Chair of the Application of Information Technology for Competitiveness and Innovation Research Group at Cantabria University. He is also member of The European Academy of Management and Business Economics and member of several international committees. He has participated in research projects of the European Commission and the Spanish Interministerial Commission of Science and Technology and published numerous papers in prestigious journals such as Future Generation Computer Systems, International Journal of Information Management, Service business, Electronics Markets, and Journal of Universal Computer Science among others.

Vera Pospelova earned her BSc (2015) in Computer Engineering from the University of Alcala, where she works as researcher in several research projects on skills frameworks and models for labor market and IT profession. Her research interests include medical data processing and non-cognitive skills analysis for the labour market.

Olaf Radant received his graduate degree in business administration (2009) from the University of Applied Sciences in Berlin, Germany and holds a Ph.D. from the Universidad Carlos III de Madrid, Spain (2017) for his research on the strategic and cultural development of companies, especially with consideration of demographic-/ sociologic change and digitalization of organizations. His work at Ginkgo Management Consulting is mainly focused on the areas of strategy-, organizational development and business transformation.

Comfort Roland-Otaru is a research driven scholar. She has been on the faculty of Covenant University between 2009-2012 before she moved on to complete her Doctorate degree in International Law and Diplomacy. She is the Managing Partner at Otaru Otaru & Co. Legal Practitioners where she gives her research endeavors expression in client engagement.

Leon Rothkrantz got a MSc in Mathematics from the Univerity of Utrecht in the Netherlands and a PhD in Mathematics from the University of Amsterdam. He got a MSc in Psychology from the University of Leiden in the Netherlands. He was appointed as Professsssor at the Netherlands Defense Academy and as a visiting Professor at the Czech Technical University in Prague.

Tomislav Rozman is a founder and a manager of the company BICERO Ltd. since 2009. He is also cooperating with DOBA Faculty of Applied Business and Social studies as the Assoc. prof. since 2011 as a developer of the courses related to information technologies, management and smart cities. His background is information systems and computer science. He has been participating in numerous EU-funded projects as a coordinator or partner. His research items can be found: https://www.researchgate.net/profile/Tomislav_Rozman His professional profile can be found: https://www.linkedin.com/in/tomislavrozman/.

Nagendra Sharma is an Assistant Professor of Management at Graphic Era University, Dehradun, India. He received his PhD (Full-time) degree in the area of "Green Marketing" from National Institute of Technology (NIT-Bhopal, India) in the year 2018. He has been awarded with the most prestigious award in for research i.e. Junior Research Fellow from University Grant Commission (UGC), India in the year 2012. Dr. Sharma has 9 years of experience that includes industry, teaching and research. He has published many articles in reputed international journals that are indexed in SCI, ESCI & SCOPUS. His research area is in Green Marketing, Sustainable entrepreneurship, Green Supply Chain Management, Sustainable Business and applied ecological business management. He works on regression analysis, structure equation modelling and others. He is competent with several research software such as SPSS, AMOS, Smart-PLS and LISREL. Dr. Sharma is also serving as member of review board for various reputed international journals. More information about his research can be found on Google scholar, Research gate and LinkedIn.

Pedro Solana-González has a degree in Computer Science from the Polytechnic University of Catalonia (UPC), holds a Master in Applied Mathematics and Computer Science and a PhD in Industrial Engineering from the University of Cantabria (UC). Associated Professor of Business Administration in the Faculty of Business and Economics at UC. Member of the R&D Group of Application of Information Technology for Competitiveness and Innovation, develops my activity in teaching and research in the fields of information systems, knowledge management, project management and information security improving business management. In last years I have participated and directed, being the responsible investigator, over 20 research projects financed both by public bodies - ECO Project (CIP, European Commision), Interministerial Commission for Science and Technology (CICYT), Ministry of Industry Tourism and Sport of the Government of Cantabria - and private industrial companies - Santander Shipyards, Nuclenor, CIC Consulting, Solvay Chemicals - accumulating more than 15 years of experience in project management. Author and speaker in numerous congresses: EMoocs 2017, In-Red 2016, InterTIC, IBIMA, EMCIS, ICAI, ACEDE, AEDEM, SOCOTE; member of scientific committees of several international conferences; and reviewer in journals like Future Generation Computer Systems or Total Quality Management & Business Excellence; I have published several book chapters - IGI Global and InTech Open Science - and articles in national and international journals: IC, EM, IJHCITP, IJTM, EPI, JKDE, BEE - on IT and Management. His research lines are: information systems, knowledge Management, higher education technology management, project management, information security, process management and workflow.

Vladimir Stantchev is the executive director of the Institute of Information Systems at SRH University Berlin where he is a research professor. He is also an affiliated senior researcher with the Networking Group at the International Computer Science Institute (ICSI) in Berkeley, California, USA. Vladimir Stantchev studied law at Sofia University (Sofia, Bulgaria) and also earned his master's degree in computer science from the Humboldt-University in Berlin, Germany. He received his PhD (Dr. rer. nat.) in the area of system architectures from the EECS department of the Berlin Institute of Technology (TU Berlin). His major research interests are in the areas of IT-Governance, Cloud Computing architectures, IT strategy, as well as methods for service and software engineering.

Jitendra Tomar is a Mathematics Graduate and received his MCA degree in 2001. He is a Microsoft Certified Systems Engineer since 2002 and is working as an IS Consultant and an Academician for 18 years now. He has worked as developer and network security expert in the industry. As a trainer and academician, he has conducted numerous MDPs and training programs for the professionals and has been an active associate in academic development. He had been working on funded project and has published 44 research papers in journals of repute.

Antoine Trad is a holder of a PhD in computer sciences degree and a DBA in business administration. Actually I am a lecturer and a researcher at IBISTM in France. Their research field's title is: The Trad-Kalpić, Framework and Methodology" (TKM&F). The TKM&F can be used for Enterprise Architecture, Decision Making Systems, Artificial Intelligence, Audit/Controlling and Training Framework for Managers in Business Innovation and Transformation Projects; where they published more than 100 articles on the related subjects. In this research project they work on inspecting the reasons of failure in business transformation projects; parallel to that they work as a consultant in enterprise architecture projects.

Sara Trigueros-Preciado has more than 10 years of experience in Management of information systems (integrated systems including quality systems, environment and labour risks), Technological Watch, R&D. Emphasising she has worked as an R&D engineer in a multinational for 5 years, with participation in patents. She has experience as a researcher in projects of innovation management, technology watch and ICT. In addition she has teaching experience from: participation in courses as an external teacher, and as an assistant professor currently, in Management of Innovation, Information Systems, Management of Information with ICT, at the Cantabria University from 2011 to now. She also works in an associated centre of the Education Ministry of Spain as an expert instructor of Professional Training in Enterprise & Entrepreneurship. She holds: the degree of Doctor, a Master's degree in Information Technologies and Business, a Master's degree in Prevention of Labour Risks, and a Master's Degree in Education. Also the title of Industrial Technical Engineer. In her research activity is highlighted: The publication of several articles in JCR and in Scopus journals, participation in books and congresses.

Kalu Uche Uwaoma obtained a BA (Hons.) Degree in Media Arts, a Master's of Arts (MA) Degree in Media Arts and Administration and a Doctorate Degree (PhD) from the University of Calabar in 2006, in the area of Broadcast Management). He has special interests in the areas of Media Arts, Broadcasting, and Communication Technology where he has written and presented papers at both local and international conferences. He also has a couple of publications (Books, Books Chapter and Journal Publications) in various reputable local and international journals. he has directed and produced documentaries which have been Aired in state television broadcast stations in Nigeria.

M. Teresa Villalba de Benito holds a PhD in Computer Sciences with special mention to the best dissertation from Universidad de Alcalá, Madrid, a degree in Mathematics and a master' degree in Computer Science from the Universidad Complutense de Madrid, Spain. She is an associate professor in Languages and Computer systems and in charge of a multidisciplinary research group in Educational Technology working in Universidad Europea since 2002. She has led 4 European funded projects and has participated and led other more than 25 national and international research projects. She has published more than 60 research papers, conference papers and books. She has obtained different awards:

the best thesis of her promotion, the best research in ICT Security in Spain in 2011 (Red Seguridad), the best professor (2011-12), and the quality award for the definition of the online model of Personal University. Lately, she has received the David A. Wilson Award for Excellence for Research in Teaching and Learning in Higher Education (2018) which recognizes the trajectory of faculty members in the field of excellence and innovation in higher education teaching and learning.

Ikedinachi Ayodele Power Wogu is an Existentialist Political Philosopher and a researcher in the Department of Political Science & Administration, College of Management and social science, Rhema University. His postgraduate research at the M.Phil and Ph.D. levels was in the areas (Political Philosophy) which focused on addressing and finding solutions to the problems of Leadership Crisis in Nigeria since Independence. He has attended and presented papers on the problem of leadership at International and at local conferences. He has also published core academic textbooks in the areas of Philosophy, the Cognitive Science of Human Development and the History & Philosophy of Science. He also has a couple of journal articles published in reputable international and local journals to his credit. Other areas of research interests for Wogu Power include Contemporary Ethics, Ontology, African Metaphysics and The History and Philosophy of Science, Political Science and logic. He currently teaches Political Philosophy, Logic and Political Science related courses at Rhema University Nigeria in Aba, Abia State Nigeria.

Jitao Yang received his Ph.D. degree in computer science from the Université Paris-Sud (Paris XI), France. He is an associate professor of computer science in the School of Information Science at Beijing Language and Culture University, Beijing, China. His research interests include big data analysis, data mining, information systems, and semantic web.

Index

O

ontological hazards 205
Optical Character Recognition 149, 152-153
Other Minds 205, 209-210

P

participants 110, 124, 173, 179-180, 230, 234-235, 265, 352, 356, 369, 376-381, 384-387, 398-399, 408-409, 412, 416, 431-432, 501, 503-504, 516
patriarchal lines 222
perceived usefulness 260-263, 267, 269-271, 372
performance appraisal 278, 424-426, 429, 453-454, 456-458, 471
Professional Learning Community 521
project management 28-29, 33, 35, 43, 69-71, 81, 85-87, 90-92, 94, 96, 99-101, 133-135, 137-145, 186, 243, 252, 257, 324-325, 342, 344-345, 369-378, 386-387, 389, 391, 453, 466
psychological assessment 28-29, 35, 398, 402-405
purchase intention 260-267, 269-272

R

recruitment 99-100, 278-279, 283, 344, 454, 466, 471, 478
Responsibility and Accountability 278, 283, 290

S

SCARCE RESOURCES 473
segmentation 153, 164-166, 168-169, 171
service composition 108, 113-114, 116, 119, 121, 125
service evolution 114, 116, 121, 125
service personalization 106, 113-114, 119, 124
service recommendation 106, 108
Shareable Content 521
skill development 38, 40, 44, 51
skills set 99, 304-305, 309-310, 314, 319, 322-326, 328, 331-332, 334
social commerce 260-263, 267, 271-272

social media 1-4, 8, 11, 57, 59-61, 66, 260-263, 265, 271, 369, 397-398, 400, 403, 409-411, 416, 482, 501-503, 507, 518, 521
social networking 2, 43, 60, 263, 501-518, 521, 523
Social Platform 521
Software as a Service (SaaS) 341, 365
speed 20, 141, 143, 173, 175, 177, 180-182, 217, 341, 464, 490
super-intelligent machines 205, 210-211, 216
system architecture 51, 142
SYSTEM INTEGRATION 142

T

teaching practice 501, 503-504, 507-508, 511, 514, 516-517, 522
testing 29, 34, 37, 80, 154, 169, 175, 179, 244, 269, 288, 398, 416
training and development 278-279, 281, 294, 425
trivial tasks 149-150, 152-153

U

usability 49, 69-71, 75-81, 90, 150-151, 153, 160, 173-177, 179-182, 192, 369, 402
user-generated content 262, 502, 521

V

VAPPA laws 221, 223-224, 227-229, 236, 238
violence against women 221-222, 224-226, 228-230, 236
virtual learning 243-244, 246, 249, 251, 253-254, 257, 411
virtual teams 43, 369-372, 374, 376, 387

W

Word2Vec 1-2, 7-8, 11
worldwide survey 502

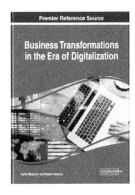

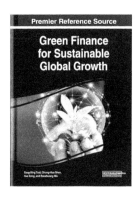

Ensure Quality Research is Introduced to the Academic Community

Become an IGI Global Reviewer for Authored Book Projects

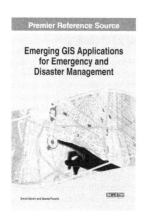 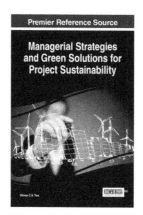  

The overall success of an authored book project is dependent on quality and timely reviews.

In this competitive age of scholarly publishing, constructive and timely feedback significantly expedites the turnaround time of manuscripts from submission to acceptance, allowing the publication and discovery of forward-thinking research at a much more expeditious rate. Several IGI Global authored book projects are currently seeking highly-qualified experts in the field to fill vacancies on their respective editorial review boards:

Applications and Inquiries may be sent to:
development@igi-global.com

Applicants must have a doctorate (or an equivalent degree) as well as publishing and reviewing experience. Reviewers are asked to complete the open-ended evaluation questions with as much detail as possible in a timely, collegial, and constructive manner. All reviewers' tenures run for one-year terms on the editorial review boards and are expected to complete at least three reviews per term. Upon successful completion of this term, reviewers can be considered for an additional term.

If you have a colleague that may be interested in this opportunity,
we encourage you to share this information with them.

IGI Global Proudly Partners With eContent Pro International

Receive a 25% Discount on all Editorial Services

Editorial Services

IGI Global expects all final manuscripts submitted for publication to be in their final form. This means they must be reviewed, revised, and professionally copy edited prior to their final submission. Not only does this support with accelerating the publication process, but it also ensures that the highest quality scholarly work can be disseminated.

English Language Copy Editing

Let eContent Pro International's expert copy editors perform edits on your manuscript to resolve spelling, punctuaion, grammar, syntax, flow, formatting issues and more.

Scientific and Scholarly Editing

Allow colleagues in your research area to examine the content of your manuscript and provide you with valuable feedback and suggestions before submission.

Figure, Table, Chart & Equation Conversions

Do you have poor quality figures? Do you need visual elements in your manuscript created or converted? A design expert can help!

Translation

Need your documjent translated into English? eContent Pro International's expert translators are fluent in English and more than 40 different languages.

Hear What Your Colleagues are Saying About Editorial Services Supported by IGI Global

"The service was very fast, very thorough, and very helpful in ensuring our chapter meets the criteria and requirements of the book's editors. I was quite impressed and happy with your service."

– Prof. Tom Brinthaupt,
Middle Tennessee State University, USA

"I found the work actually spectacular. The editing, formatting, and other checks were very thorough. The turnaround time was great as well. I will definitely use eContent Pro in the future."

– Nickanor Amwata, Lecturer,
University of Kurdistan Hawler, Iraq

"I was impressed that it was done timely, and wherever the content was not clear for the reader, the paper was improved with better readability for the audience."

– Prof. James Chilembwe,
Mzuzu University, Malawi

Email: customerservice@econtentpro.com   **www.igi-global.com/editorial-service-partners**

www.igi-global.com

IGI Global's Transformative Open Access (OA) Model:
How to Turn Your University Library's Database Acquisitions Into a Source of OA Funding

In response to the OA movement and well in advance of Plan S, IGI Global, early last year, unveiled their OA Fee Waiver (Offset Model) Initiative.

Under this initiative, librarians who invest in IGI Global's InfoSci-Books (5,300+ reference books) and/or InfoSci-Journals (185+ scholarly journals) databases will be able to subsidize their patron's OA article processing charges (APC) when their work is submitted and accepted (after the peer review process) into an IGI Global journal.*

How Does it Work?

1. When a library subscribes or perpetually purchases IGI Global's InfoSci-Databases including InfoSci-Books (5,300+ e-books), InfoSci-Journals (185+ e-journals), and/or their discipline/subject-focused subsets, IGI Global will match the library's investment with a fund of equal value to go toward subsidizing the OA article processing charges (APCs) for their patrons.

   Researchers: Be sure to recommend the InfoSci-Books and InfoSci-Journals to take advantage of this initiative.

2. When a student, faculty, or staff member submits a paper and it is accepted (following the peer review) into one of IGI Global's 185+ scholarly journals, the author will have the option to have their paper published under a traditional publishing model or as OA.

3. When the author chooses to have their paper published under OA, IGI Global will notify them of the OA Fee Waiver (Offset Model) Initiative. If the author decides they would like to take advantage of this initiative, IGI Global will deduct the US$ 1,500 APC from the created fund.

4. This fund will be offered on an annual basis and will renew as the subscription is renewed for each year thereafter. IGI Global will manage the fund and award the APC waivers unless the librarian has a preference as to how the funds should be managed.

Hear From the Experts on This Initiative:

"I'm very happy to have been able to make one of my recent research contributions, 'Visualizing the Social Media Conversations of a National Information Technology Professional Association' featured in the *International Journal of Human Capital and Information Technology Professionals*, freely available along with having access to the valuable resources found within IGI Global's InfoSci-Journals database."

– **Prof. Stuart Palmer**,
Deakin University, Australia

For More Information, Visit: www.igi-global.com/publish/contributor-resources/open-access or contact IGI Global's Database Team at eresources@igi-global.com.

CPSIA information can be obtained
at www.ICGtesting.com
Printed in the USA
BVHW020201270123
657284BV00003B/61